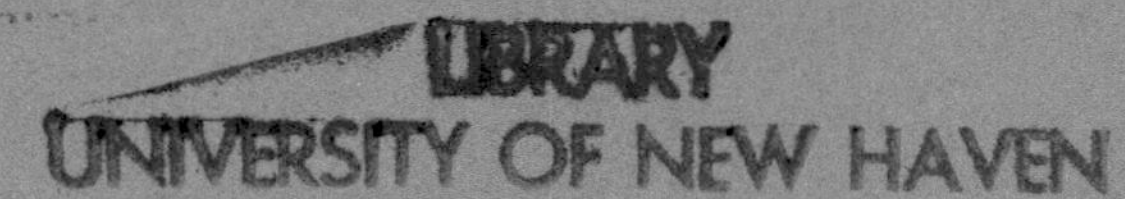

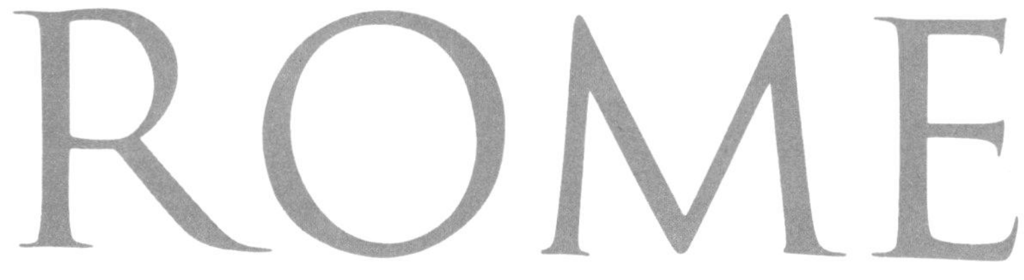

ROME

Profile of a City, 312-1308

by Richard Krautheimer

PRINCETON UNIVERSITY PRESS, NEW JERSEY
1980

Published by Princeton University Press, Princeton, New Jersey
In the United Kingdom: Princeton University Press, Guildford, Surrey

Library of Congress Cataloging in Publication Data will be
found on the last printed page of this book

This book has been composed in VIP Bembo
Designed by Bruce Campbell
Clothbound editions of Princeton University Press books
are printed on acid-free paper, and binding materials are
chosen for strength and durability

Printed in the United States of America by
Meriden Gravure Company, Meriden, Connecticut
Composed by Princeton University Press, Princeton, New Jersey

IN MEMORIAM

MILTON J. LEWINE

Contents

List of Illustrations

Abbreviations

AFMV	Archivo Fotografico Musei Vaticani	GFN	Gabinetto Fotografico Nazionale, Rome
Arch. Phot., Paris	Archives Photographiques, Paris	Lazio	Soprintendenza ai Monumenti del Lazio, Rome
BH	Biblioteca Hertziana, Rome	Savio	Oscar Savio, Photographer, Rome
Bibl. Apost. Vat.	Biblioteca Apostolica Vaticana	Leonard von Matt	Leonard von Matt, Photographer, Buochs, Switzerland
FU	Fototeca Unione, American Academy Rome		

Chapter One

CHAPTER TWO

CHAPTER THREE

CHAPTER EIGHT

CHAPTER NINE

CHAPTER TEN

Chapter Eleven

Chapter Twelve

Chapter Thirteen

Chapter Fourteen

Preface

I have tried in this book to sketch a profile of Rome as a living organism from the time of Constantine in the early fourth century to the removal of the papacy to Avignon, a thousand years later: how the ancient city, still *caput mundi* under Constantine, became the see of the papacy and gradually the spiritual and political focus of the West; how in size and well-being at the same time she shrank to a seemingly insignificant country town; how from the time of Charlemagne and through the High Middle Ages she recovered and grew physically as well as politically, both as a pawn and as a power; what her streets and churches, her houses and mansions, the inhabited vaults of the Colosseum, the fortified monasteries and life on the river, looked like; how the memories of her ancient glories, pagan and Christian, kindled by tradition and by the ever-present monuments of her past, remained alive, even at the lowest points of her fortunes; how, together with the ever-growing might of the Church, spiritual, political, and material, these memories became a potent factor in shaping Rome's dominant place in the medieval world; how that heritage, revived time and again, molded the minds of visitors, patrons, and artists and exerted its impact on church planning, painting, and sculpture and on the way the city grew; and how Rome's buildings and her art want to be seen both as tied to and as reflecting the changing and conflicting political realities and conceits of popes, foreign emperors, and Romans.

In short, I have striven to outline a history of Rome during a thousand years *through*, rather than *of*, her monuments, and of changes in the map of the city. To make such an attempt, even in the form of a profile, may have been foolhardy. The material is vast; and still, after fifty years of one's having known Rome, or believed to, many a house, church, or fresco have escaped attention. Worse, one is forced to trespass time and again in fields others have tilled. Even in areas close to one's own where one knows the monuments and has kept up with scholarly discussion—mosaic or mural painting in my case—one cannot be as footsure as those at home on that ground. Things get worse where one's knowledge is by necessity but general: Church and political history or social and economic conditions. Reading what has been written, looking again and talking to friends working in fields beyond one's ken, helps. But then, there are areas and periods not yet sufficiently explored or indeed unexplored: the art of the tenth and early eleventh centuries, or the population figures of Rome in the Middle Ages, for instance. By and large, therefore, I thought it best to fall back wherever possible on the facts I believe I know: the buildings, whether churches, houses, or fortifications; the changing map of the city and its streets; and the rich documentation pertaining thereto, published or unpublished. They form the framework to hold together this profile of Rome. For me, it was fun to find out so much I did not know after a lifetime and to sum it up: first, for myself; then for my students at the Institute of Fine Arts at New York University in a course repeated once or twice; and now on these pages. I can only hope the reader has some fun too and will forgive the inevitable shortcomings.

My warm thanks go to friends, colleagues, and former students who have helped me along in endless discussions: to Wolfgang Lotz, a mine of information on Rome as on so many other subjects and an encouraging and cautioning friend; to Hans Belting, Caecilie Davis-Weyer, and Judson Emerick, who have allowed me to share their knowledge of and thoughts on Carolingian mosaics and political programs; to Robert Brentano and Arnold Esch and Gerard

E. Caspary, whose counsel on the present state of thinking on the medieval history of Rome has been invaluable.

A very special word of thanks goes to Joan Barclay Lloyd, who from the inception of this book has been my faithful assistant. More than once she has unearthed materials that had escaped me and many an idea or formulation in these pages goes back to hour-long discussions with her. Beyond this intellectual help through constant interchange, she bore the main burden of "housekeeping chores": keeping the files in order, typing the drafts of the manuscript (and there were many!) to the final version; finally, drawing the beautiful maps which illustrate the book. I cannot thank her enough.

Likewise, my warmest thanks go to two more young friends: Deborah Kellogg, who did part of the typing and who shared with me patiently and painstakingly the reading of both galley and page proof; and Charles McClendon, who provided some of the beautiful photographs for this book.

Mrs. Louise McDermott was good enough to prepare the index. Robert E. Brown forebearingly undertook the task of editing the manuscript and seeing it through the Press.

The staffs of the many libraries and photographic archives that I have used in preparing this book have without exception been immensely helpful and generous in giving me their time. Foremost, I want to thank the Bibliotheca Hertziana. The wealth of its collections of both books and photographs is equalled only by the helpfulness of its staffs, and I am particularly obliged to Dr. Hildegarde Giess, Dr. Eva Stahn, and Mrs. Gabriele Fichers, who time and again have provided me with photographs and valuable hints. Likewise I am most grateful to Mrs. Karen Einaudi, in charge of the Fototeca of the American Academy in Rome, for her generosity in providing me with photographs not easily obtainable. I'm equally grateful to the staff of the Vatican Library, in particular to Msgr. José Ruysschaert; and to the staffs of the Firestone Library at Princeton University, and the libraries of the Princeton Theological Seminary and the Institute for Advanced Study, all in Princeton, N.J. Among the photographic archives, thanks are due to the directors and personnel of those of the Vatican Museums, the Commune di Roma, both at the Capitoline Museum and at the Museo di Roma with its splendid collection of old photographs, and to the staff of the Gabinetto Fotografico Nazionale and that of the Sopraintendenza ai Monumenti del Lazio.

Finally, my warm thanks go to the Kress Foundation, which through its vice-president, Mary M. Davis, provided, as generous as ever, a grant that enabled me to spend a term at the Institute for Advanced Study at Princeton during the time the manuscript of this book was edited. My thanks also go to that Institute for its hospitality, and particularly to my friend Professor Irving Lavin, who arranged for it.

Rome, 1979

Part I

Image and Reality

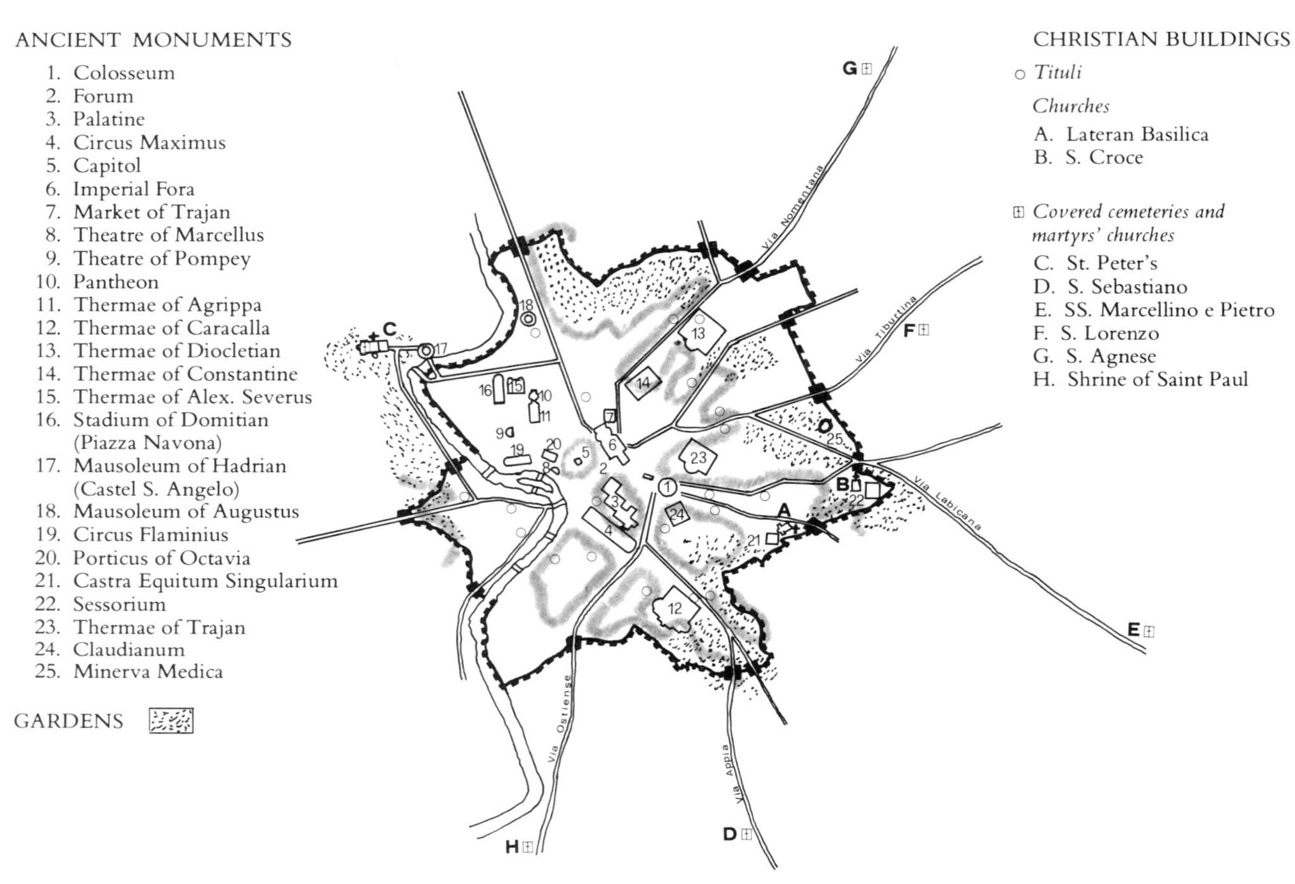

1. Map of the ancient city, as of ca. 330

CHAPTER ONE

Rome and Constantine

By the early fourth century, Rome had grown in the course of a thousand years from a few hill villages into a sprawling metropolis. Christianity had been taking root in the city ever since about A.D. 60, when Peter had preached and Paul had addressed his letter to the Romans. By the end of the second or the middle of the third century, a Christian community, well endowed and established, flourished in Rome. But, properly speaking, the history of Christian Rome starts on October 28, A.D. 312, when Constantine wrested the city from his co-emperor Maxentius, and with it the rule over the entire western half of the Roman Empire. A cavalry battle that started at a defile on the Cassian Road at *saxa rubra* and continued downhill to the Tiber and across the Milvian Bridge—whence its conventional name—ended with the conquest of the capital. Constantine attributed his victory to the Christian God, who in a vision had shown him the Cross. Christianity became Constantine's lodestar; the Christian Church found in him a powerful protector, ever more zealous as, after the conquest of the East in 324, he united the empire. Baptized on his deathbed in 337, he died a member of the church in full standing.

The Rome Constantine entered was larger in area but smaller in population than it had been a hundred years before (fig. 1). The network of highways leading from the city to all parts of the empire, far and near, had been maintained: the Appia to Naples and Brindisi and to the shipping lanes to the East; the Flaminia across Umbria to the northern shores of the Adriatic Sea and beyond to the Danube countries; the Salaria through the Sabine mountains to Ancona and the east coast. Other roads linked up with the countryside and the hill towns close by: with Nomentum (now Mentana); with Praeneste (now Palestrina); with Lavinium; with the seaports of Ostia and Porto. Across the Tiber, the Cassia led into Lombardy by way of Arezzo and Florence, the Aurelia along the west coast to Genova, Provence, Gaul, and Spain. Bridges, some in use today, supported this network of roads. Crossing the Tiber two miles north of town, the Ponte Milvio took care of the Flaminia; to the northeast across the Aniene, the Ponte Salario served the Salaria. From the Cassia two bridges led into the city: the Aelian Bridge at the Mausoleum of Hadrian (now Castel S. Angelo), renamed Ponte S. Angelo, was rebuilt in the 1890s on the old site with original elements; the Neronian Bridge further downstream no longer exists. Via Aurelia, entering the city through Trastevere, was linked to the east bank by four bridges: the Aurelian Bridge, replaced in the fifteenth century by Ponte Sisto; the two bridges crossing the Tiber Island—the Pons Cestius and Pons Fabricius, the latter well preserved (fig. 2); and a hundred meters to the south, not far from S. Maria in Cosmedin, the Aemilian Bridge—its remains, the *Ponte Rotto* (Broken Bridge), still rising high above the river. Across highways and bridges travelers and provisions reached the city as they do today. But the bulk of supplies was shipped from overseas: oil, wine, grain, and heavy timber from North Africa, South Italy, Sicily, Provence, and Spain; luxuries, wines, and marbles from Greece and points east. Unloaded at Ostia or Porto, the Hoboken and Tilbury of ancient Rome, they were reshipped in lighter bottoms upstream to the river wharves at the foot of the Aventine. Parts of the quay for unloading marbles, the *marmorata*, are still seen; so are remains of warehouses—*horrea* in Latin—for storing grain and other goods. Some five hundred meters long, this main wharf seems to have extended as far as the *Ponte Rotto*, where Piranesi later drew it. Opposite and east of Castel S. Angelo, a sec-

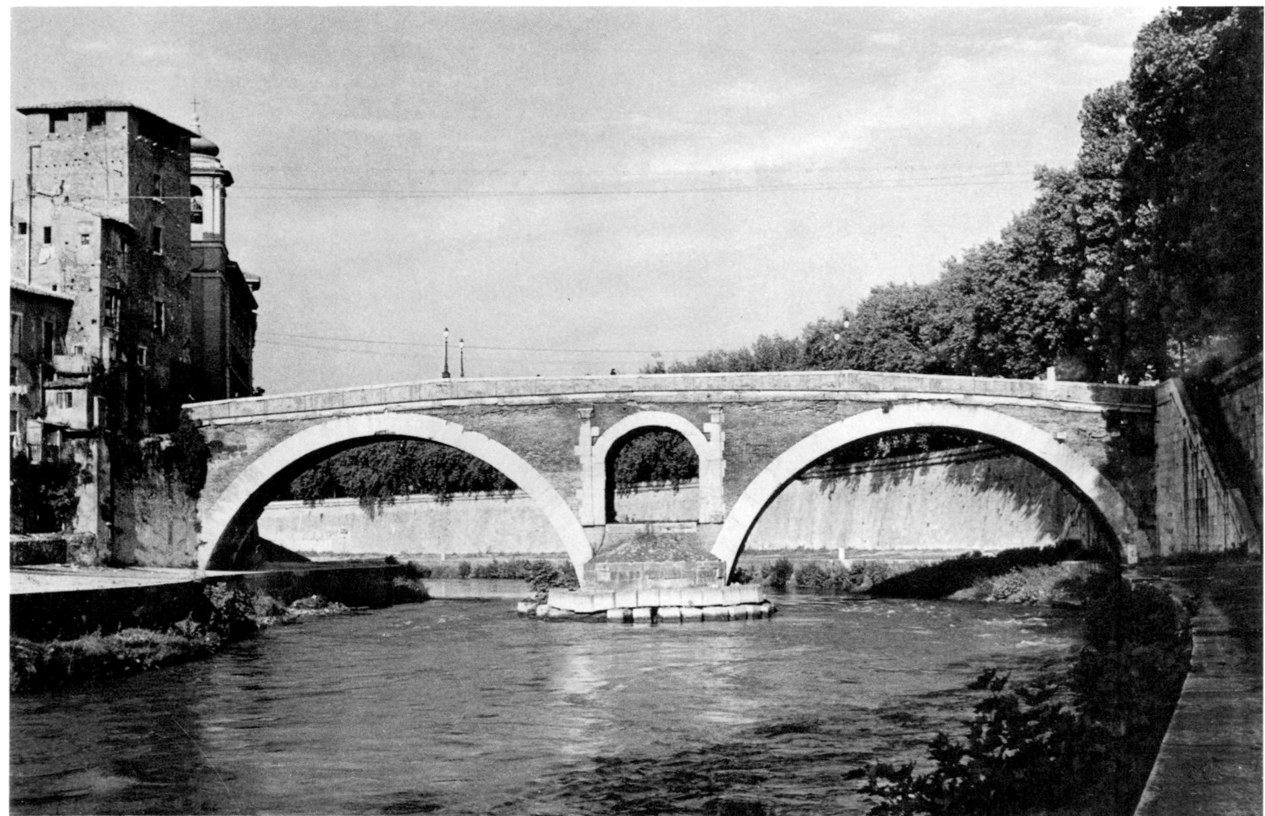

2. The Bridge of Fabricius

ond smaller dockside received goods shipped downstream from northern Latium and Umbria. Rome's water supply was plentiful, flowing into the city over eleven (or, counting branches, nineteen) aqueducts, built from Republican times onward and always kept in good repair. Even now their long rows of arches lace the countryside all around Rome and continue inside the city, as witness those spanning the valley from S. Gregorio Magno to the Palatine and the long arcade of the Claudian Aqueduct from Porta Maggiore all along the crest of the Celian Hill, or the Aqua Julia near the railway station (fig. 3).

In Constantine's day, the population of the city, once perhaps as much as a million or a million and a half, and largely dependent on welfare, had been decreasing ever since provisioning had dwindled during the turbulent years A.D. 230-270. But it still may have stood at around 800,000. Rome had also waned in political significance. As part of the administrative reform devised by Diocletian (285-305), new imperial residences had been built for the four co-emperors of the tetrarchy, to be used as needed: in the east at Nicomedia on the Sea of Marmara, at Antioch, and at Thessalonica; in the Balkans at Sirmium; in the north at Milan, Trier, and York. No emperor now resided in Rome for any length of time. Large sectors of the higher civil and military services had moved to new administrative centers or they had become attached to the mobile courts of the tetrarchy. To be sure, the Senate remained in Rome; but in practice its role as a body was confined to honorific and ceremonial functions and to advisory participation in the city administration. Even the actual government of the city rested with a hierarchy of officials appointed by the emperor. Headed by the city prefect, the *praefectus urbi*, they comprised: the *praefectus annonae*, in charge of provisioning; the police prefect; the supervisor of aqueducts; that of the riverbed and the sewers; officials in charge of the harbors, of public buildings, of street maintenance, of public statues, and more.

Rome, then, was no longer an effective center of power. Nonetheless, in the eyes of the world she remained the true capital of the commonwealth. Her age-old glories were reflected in her literature, from Livy and Virgil to Cassius Dio and the *Historia Augusta*; they were manifest in her monuments, buildings, statues, triumphal arches, and columns; and they were carried by the senatorial class and embodied in the Senate. Individually, some senators and their families still wielded considerable influence through their enormous wealth, social standing, and connections, and through the offices they traditionally held as *praefecti urbi* and consuls in Rome and as governors in the provinces. And although the Senate corporate was in fact powerless, its ceremonial functions were not without significance: it legitimized, albeit *pro forma*, the emperor's election; it approved legislation *pro forma*; and within limits it acted as check and balance for the power of the imperial court. Most important, it represented Rome's history, through both its members and corporality, and its presence made the city the only legitimate seat of government, regardless of the location of actual power at the emperor's court. In the minds of Romans—commoners and aristocrats alike—and of provincials and foreigners—from the Hebrides and the Berber mountains to the courts of the Sassanians and of India—Rome was still THE capital, Mistress of the Empire and hub of the civilized world.

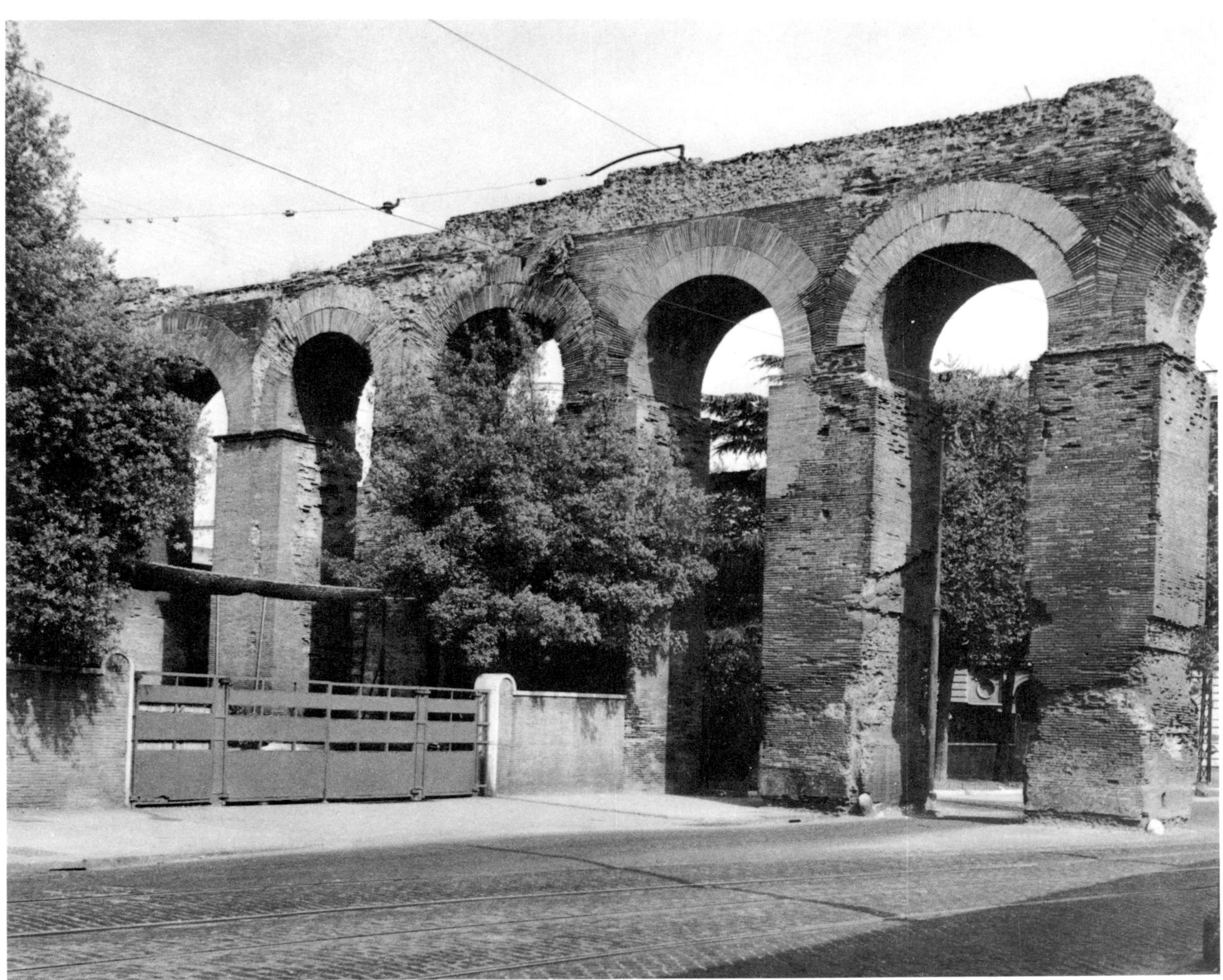

3. Julian Aqueduct (Aqua Julia), near Lateran

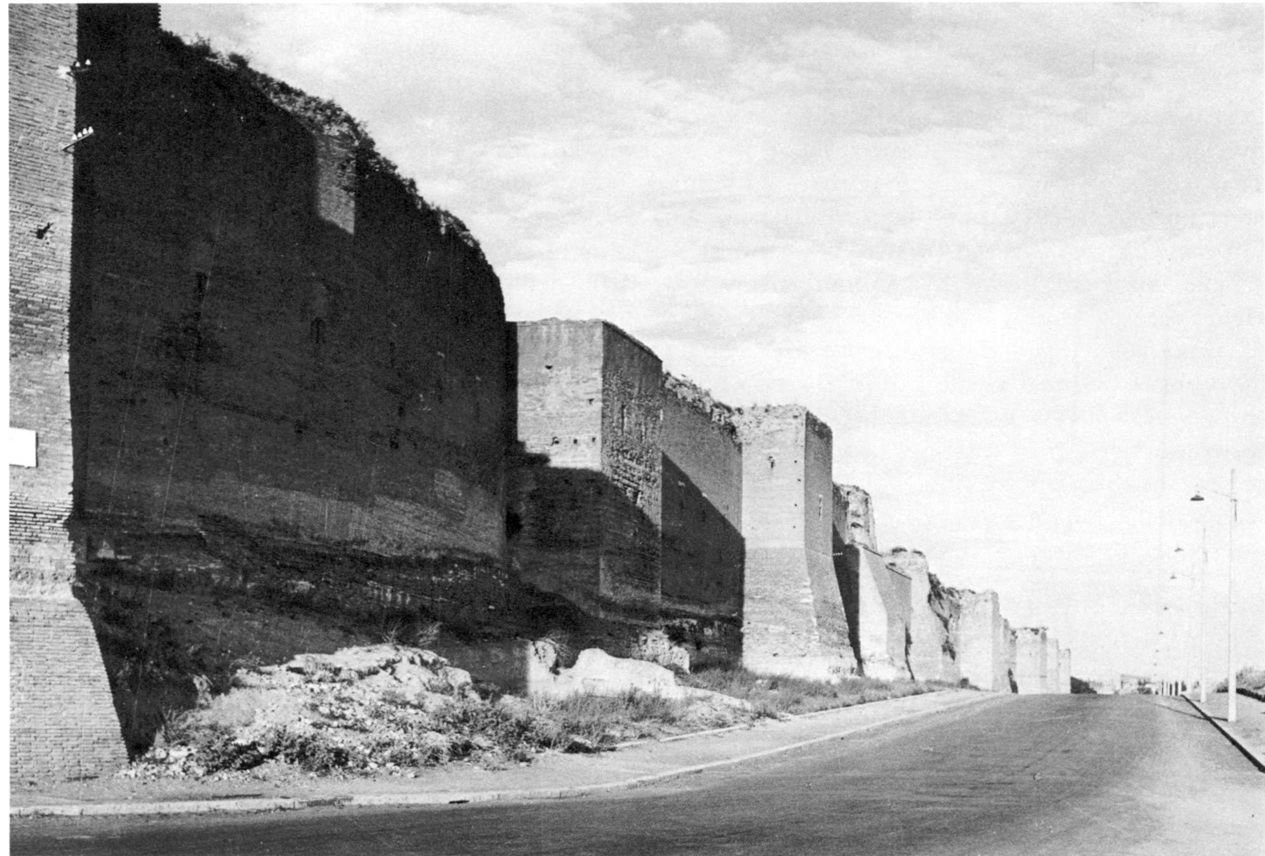

4. Aurelian Walls

Materially, the city had rather improved, if anything, during the forty years preceding Constantine's conquest. The city wall of Republican Rome—wrongly termed the *Servian Wall*—had been swallowed up ever since the first century B.C. by the city's vast expansion; parts of it survive, such as a large tract near the railroad station. To create a modern fortification, the emperors Aurelian and Probus enclosed this expanded Rome in new defensive walls between 272 and 279. Though often repaired, these Aurelian Walls survive to nearly their full length of twelve miles, or eighteen kilometers (fig. 4). Starting upstream on the Tiber, they form a rough square on the left, the eastern bank of the river, enclosing some seven square miles. On the western bank, they form a triangle, protecting the quarter *trans Tiberim*, Trastevere; its apex stands on the crest of the Gianicolo. Fourteen gates supplemented by postern gates open on the highways entering the city, most named after the roads they serve: to the north, Porta Flaminia, now called Porta del Popolo; to the east, toward Tivoli (Tibur), Porta Tiburtina, now Porta S. Lorenzo; to the southeast, Porta Labicana, now Porta Maggiore; to the south, Porta Appia, now Porta S. Sebastiano, and Porta Ostiensis, now Porta S. Paolo; up on the Gianicolo, Porta Aurelia, the present Porta S. Pancrazio—to name only the most important. The Aurelian Walls were raised in 309-312, and again in 402/403. They reached their present impressive height of over fifteen meters in the second building campaign: only then were the half-round or square twin-towers flanking the main gates strengthened or newly built and the gates provided with defensive forecourts. Square towers, originally numbering over 380, project from the walls, always two arrowshots apart at crossfire angles; an arcaded gallery inside links the towers and the gates; crenelations topped the wall and towers. In the same building campaign, the walls were extended along the unprotected east bank of the Tiber, from opposite Trastevere to west of Porta Flaminia—a stretch built over but still visible until the Tiber embankments were laid out some eighty years ago. All the original construction and alterations were built of the materials customary in Roman Imperial times and after: a rubble concrete, strong and resilient, faced with brick curtains. Having survived through the centuries, the city walls and their gates are to this day the greatest monument of late-antique Rome. They formed an impressive defense perimeter, although they could never have been effectively manned; but neither could they be battered down or easily scaled. In any event, they were of unparalleled grandeur, designed to deter by sheer appearance any would-be attacker and to impress on the minds of both Romans and barbarians an image of eternal strength.

The building of the Aurelian Walls had marked the revival in Rome of construction on a large scale after half a century of stagnation; concomitant with the spirit of renewal pervading the policy of the tetrarchy, this revival was aimed at practical ends, such as fortification and sanitation, at political propaganda, and at improving the looks of the capital—ideally still THE capital of the civilized world. It also served to create employment on a scale hardly known for centuries among Rome's welfare population. It entailed training anew building crews, masters and master masons, brick layers and carpenters, sculptors and decorators, glaziers and house painters. It meant pilfering bricks from structures presumably in poor repair and, in short, reorganizing the entire building trade and related trades. The thirty years preceding Constantine's conquest of Rome saw the culmination and the results of this reorganization. The Baths of Diocletian were built on the Esquiline, vaster even than the huge Baths of Caracalla, the last big enterprise preceding the fifty-year slump of the third century. On the Forum Romanum—the Forum proper—after a fire in 283, the new Senate House was erected, as it stands to this day, the Curia Senatus (fig. 5). Opposite, the Basilica Julia, damaged by the same fire, was rebuilt almost entirely. The *rostra* (the speaker's tribune in front of the *curia*) was repaired, backed up by five honorific columns as a monument to Diocletian and his imperial colleagues.

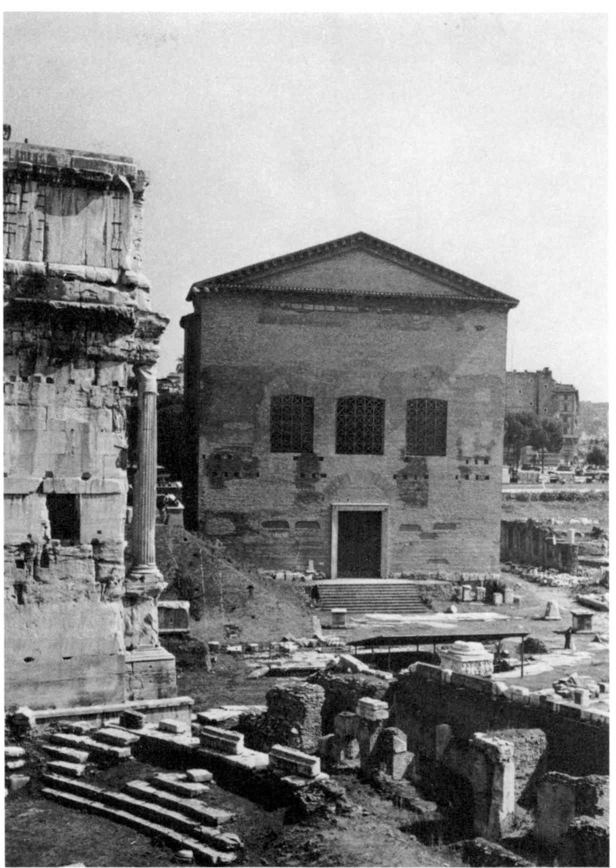

5. Curia Senatus

The enterprises of Maxentius during his short six-year reign, A.D. 306-312, are even more amazing, both in number and grandeur. At the eastern end of the Forum he remodeled from its very foundations Hadrian's Temple of Venus and Roma, facing the Colosseum. Adjoining it and likewise facing the Colosseum, he built within three years, 309-312, the Basilica Nova: a colossal hall, its nave groin-vaulted and flanked on either side by three huge, barrel-vaulted niches—even now the most impressive ruin of the Forum (fig. 6). Finished and slightly altered by Constantine, it bore in popular parlance of the time his name, *Basilica Constantini*. Nearby, an older building, presently housing the church of SS. Cosma e Damiano, was thoroughly remodeled; divided in two by an apsed wall, its front half was revetted with marble incrustation; facing the Forum, a domed rotunda, now erroneously called the *Templum Divi Romuli*, was added and provided with a curved, colonnaded façade (fig. 7). Completed by Constantine—the revetment and the curved façade may well be his—the structure was possibly the audience hall of the city prefect, as has been suggested by Alfred Frazer. On the edge of the city, also along the Aurelian Walls, new buildings were set up. To the east, on the site of the Licinian Gardens, still stands today the ruin of a ten-sided domed garden hall, called the Minerva Medica. To the southeast, in the vast complex of a third-century palace—the Sessorium—rose an apsed hall, later known as the Temple of Venus and Cupid. Built in the early fourth century either by Maxentius or by Constantine, its tall ruin stands just left of today's church of S. Croce in Gerusalemme. Not far off, to the west of the present church of the Lateran, a huge mansion was remodeled and, under Constantine, redecorated with murals, one showing presumably the mythical ancestors of the Constantinian dynasty. On the Via Appia, a villa including a huge circus was laid out and dedicated in 310 to the memory of young Romulus, Maxentius' son; a mausoleum was also built, possibly intended for the Maxentian dynasty. But, the largest and most extensive enterprise undertaken by Maxentius was, of course, the raising of the Aurelian Walls to almost twice their original height. All told, it was an amazing achievement within a six-year reign.

These, then, were the most recent large-scale constructions crowning the imperial splendor of Constantine's new capital. Inside the ring of the walls stretched the city of Rome, as she had

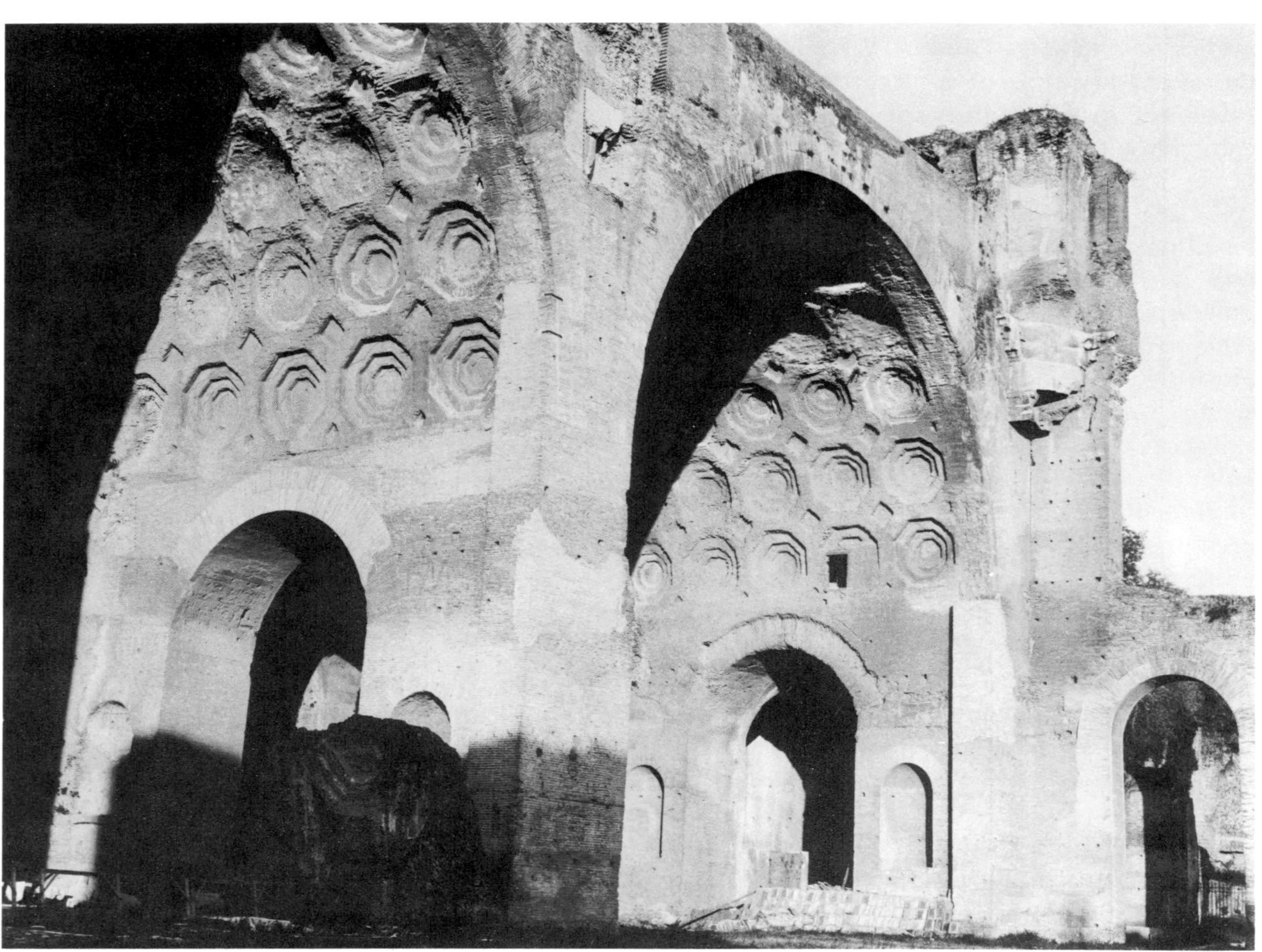

6. Basilica Nova

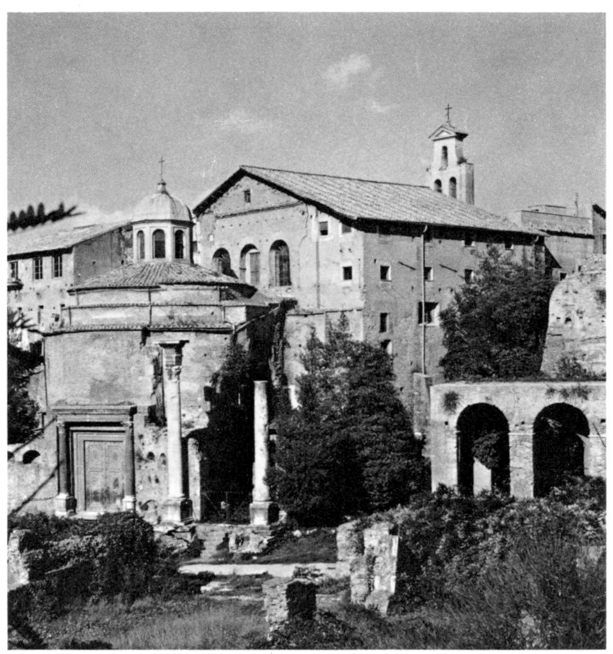

7. Templum Urbis and Vestibule ("Templum Divi Romuli")

grown over the centuries. Starting from the gates, the main arteries brought the cross-country highways toward the city's core. *Via Lata*—"Broadway" literally—now the Corso, led from Porta del Popolo to the foot of the Capitoline Hill. Starting from the Nomentana Gate, along the ridge of the Quirinal and its southwest slope, another road, the Alta Semita, now Via XX Settembre and Via IV Novembre, ended in the same general neighborhood. Splitting off from it and descending into the valley south of the Quirinal, the *vicus longus*, the "long alley," merged with the *vicus patricius*, coming from the Viminal Gate; the former corresponds roughly to the present Via Nazionale, the latter to Via Urbana. Jointly they met a third street, crossing the Esquiline from Porta S. Lorenzo, and continued toward the Forum. From the gates in the southeast quarter, Porta Maggiore and Porta S. Giovanni, two major streets, one supplanted by today's Via Labicana, the other by Via S. Giovanni in Laterano, terminated at the Colosseum. Merging inside the city a ten-minute walk from Porta S. Sebastiano, the Appia and Latina ran through the present *passegiata archeologica* to the southeast corner of the Palatine and continued on, like today's Via dei Cerchi between its south cliff and the Circus Maximus, to Piazza Bocca della Verità and the river. At the corner of the Palatine, the street from the Ostia Gate, now Porta S. Paolo, cut across what are today's Viale Aventino and Via di S. Gregorio, leading again to the Colosseum. Similar streets descended from the Aurelian Gate into Trastevere and from the Vatican to Hadrian's Tomb; across the bridges spanning the Tiber, they joined with the system of main arteries on the east bank. Mostly, these main streets were straight, as if drawn with a ruler, and had steep gradings. They were paved with huge flagstones, but were quite narrow. Even the Corso—considered quite wide, as the Latin name *via lata* suggests—was never more than its present width of roughly ten meters; it was further narrowed by two triumphal arches, one near today's S. Lorenzo in Lucina, the other near S. Maria in Via Lata. Side streets were naturally narrower still, often mere alleys, winding or breaking in sharp angles and rarely paved.

The great streets, then, all ended in the same general area, marked by the Capitoline Hill, Forum, Palatine, and Colosseum. Over the centuries this area had grown into a grand display of state architecture. There, Romans, provincials, and foreigners gawked at temples, palaces, administrative buildings, basilicas, theatres, porticos: heaps of marble, or marble imitation, gilded capitals, triumphal arches, honorific statues—the whole impression not too different, one fears, from that produced by the Monumento Nazionale on Piazza Venezia (fig. 8). To a fourth-century visitor, all this was the grand show that reflected the glory of Rome and her empire. There he saw the great amphitheatre, the Colosseum, where fifty thousand spectators would watch the games (fig. 9). He would see sprawling westward the buildings of the Forum Romanum (fig. 10): the Temple of Venus and Roma; Maxentius' Basilica Nova, completed by Constantine raising its colossal vaults; the Arch of Titus; the presumed audience hall of the city prefect, now SS. Cosma e Damiano, and its circular vestibule; the Temple of Antoninus and Faustina; further down the Basilica Aemilia and the Basilica Julia, the Curia Senatus; the temples of Concord and of Saturn, the Arch of Sep-

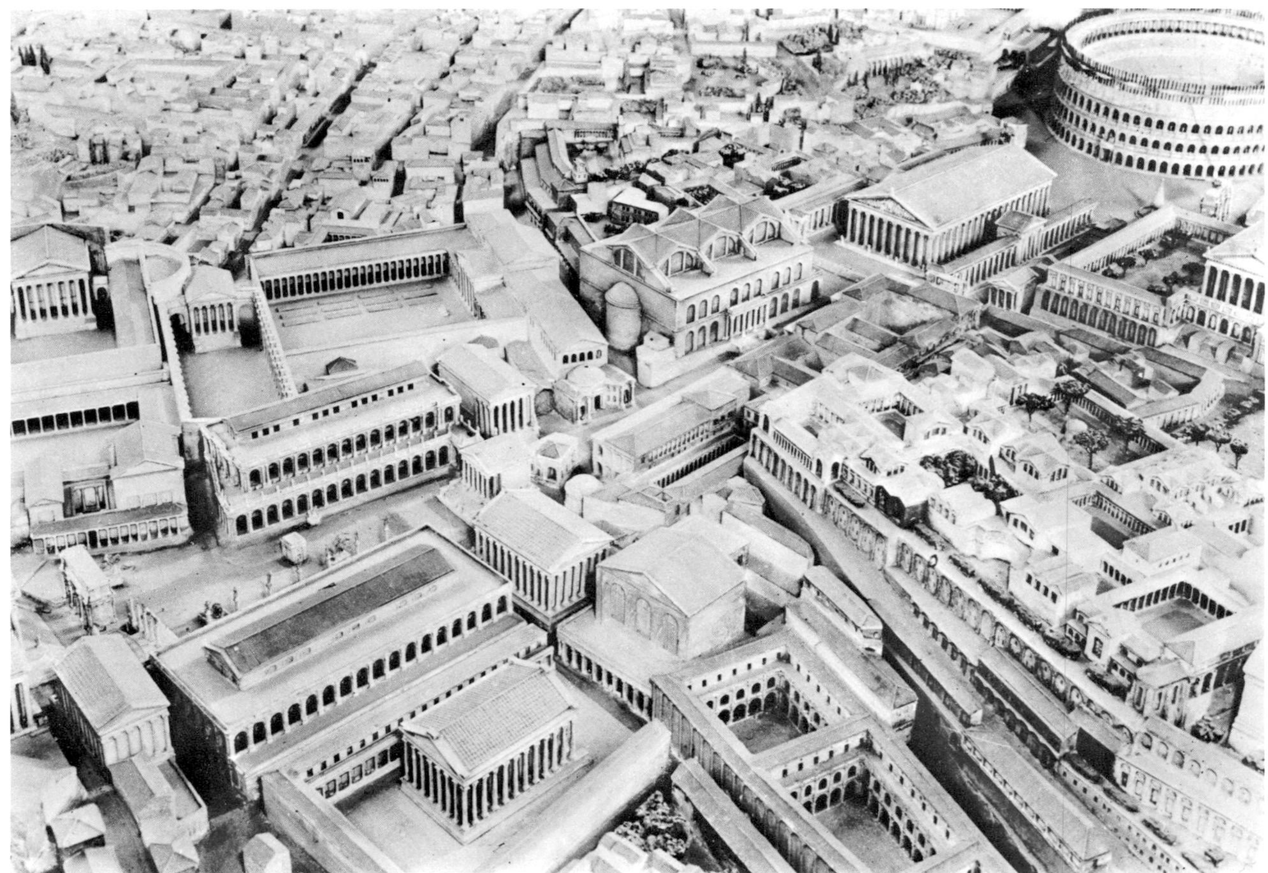

8. Model of Forum, Fora of Vespasian, Nerva and Augustus, and Palatine, Museo della Civiltà Romana, Rome

timius Severus, not to mention dozens of smaller shrines, monuments, and honorific statues; and as a grand backdrop, the Capitoline Hill with its temples, its east cliff marked by the bare base wall, and the arcaded tier of the State Archives, the Tabularium. North of and parallel to the Roman Forum, the row of Imperial Fora had grown for the past three centuries. Their remains today are lined up along or buried under Via dei Fori Imperiali: Vespasian's Forum Pacis, laid out after the end of the Jewish War in A.D. 70; the Forum of Nerva—the colonnade and frieze of its east wall was known through the Middle Ages as the *Colonacce*—completed in A.D. 97; the Forum of Augustus, backed by its soaring rear wall, and the Temple of Mars the Avenger; opposite, adjoining the Roman Forum, the Forum of Caesar with the Temple of Venus, the legendary ancestress of his clan. The largest and the most splendid of all was the Forum of Trajan, consecrated in A.D. 113 after cutting away the southwest spur of the Quirinal Hill. Expanding in vast hemicycles, it sheltered the Basilica Ulpia, the largest basilica in the empire; Trajan's column, soaring high to this day and proclaiming his victories over the Dacians; and two monuments, now lost, the Temple of Trajan Deified, and a statue of himself on horseback. Above the well-preserved eastern hemicycle towered the market of Trajan, a covered souk, housing rows of shops on three and four levels (fig. 11). South of the Roman Forum, the Imperial Palaces rose on the Palantine, as they had grown and spread since the first century A.D.: the most recent part, and still the most impressive in its ruins, was that of Septimius Severus at the southeastern corner, overlooking the valleys to the east and south—the latter all but filled by the Great Circus, the *Circus Maximus*. At the western extremity of the Roman Forum, the

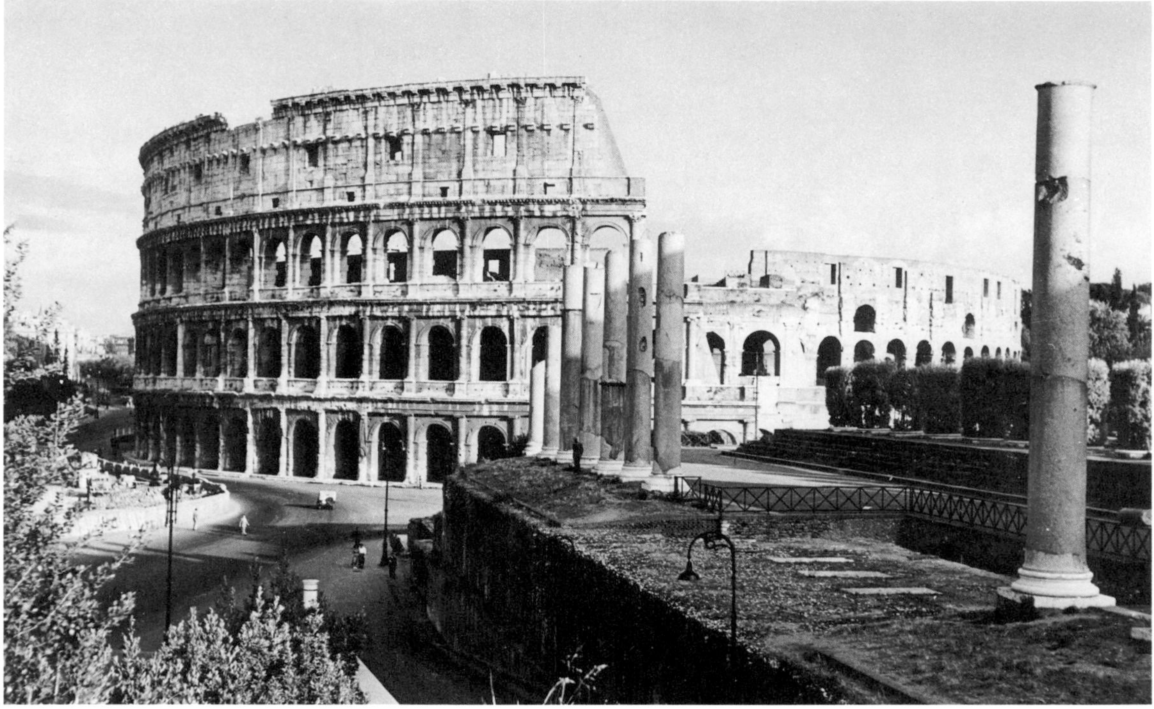

9. Colosseum and (foreground) Temple of Venus and Rome

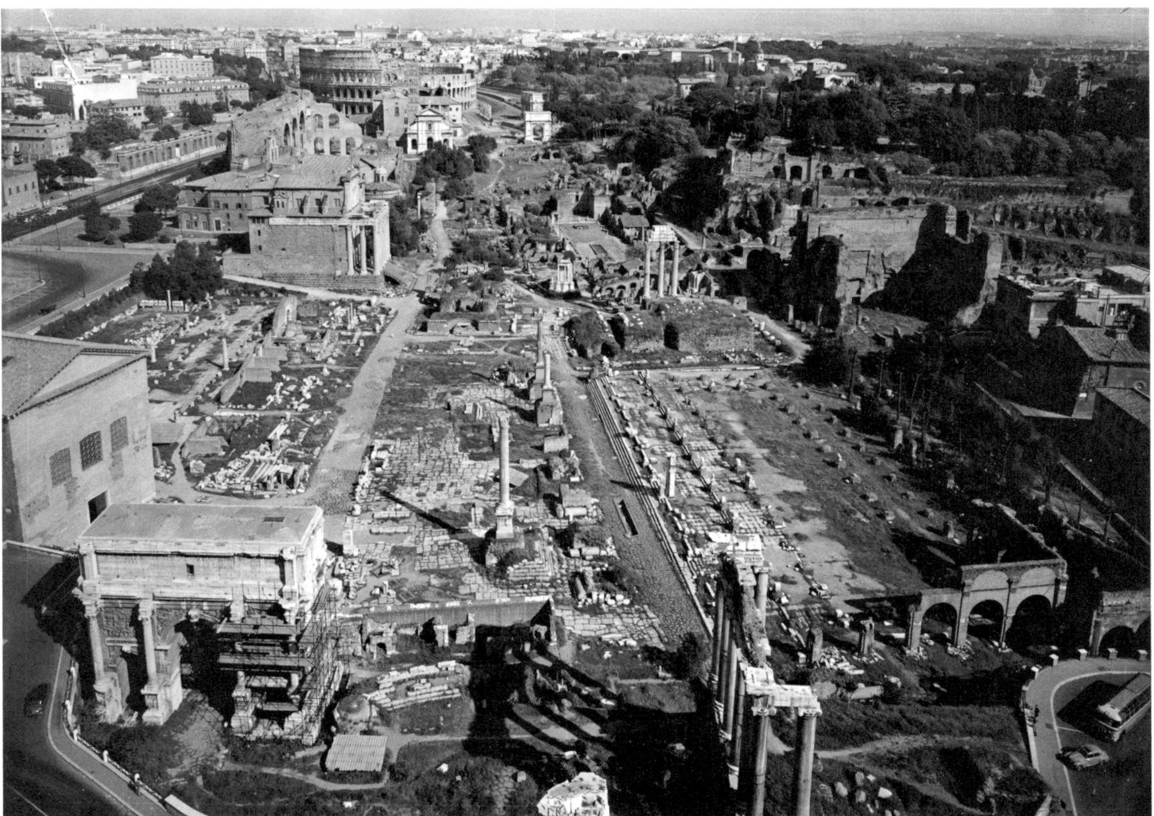

10. Forum, looking east toward Colosseum

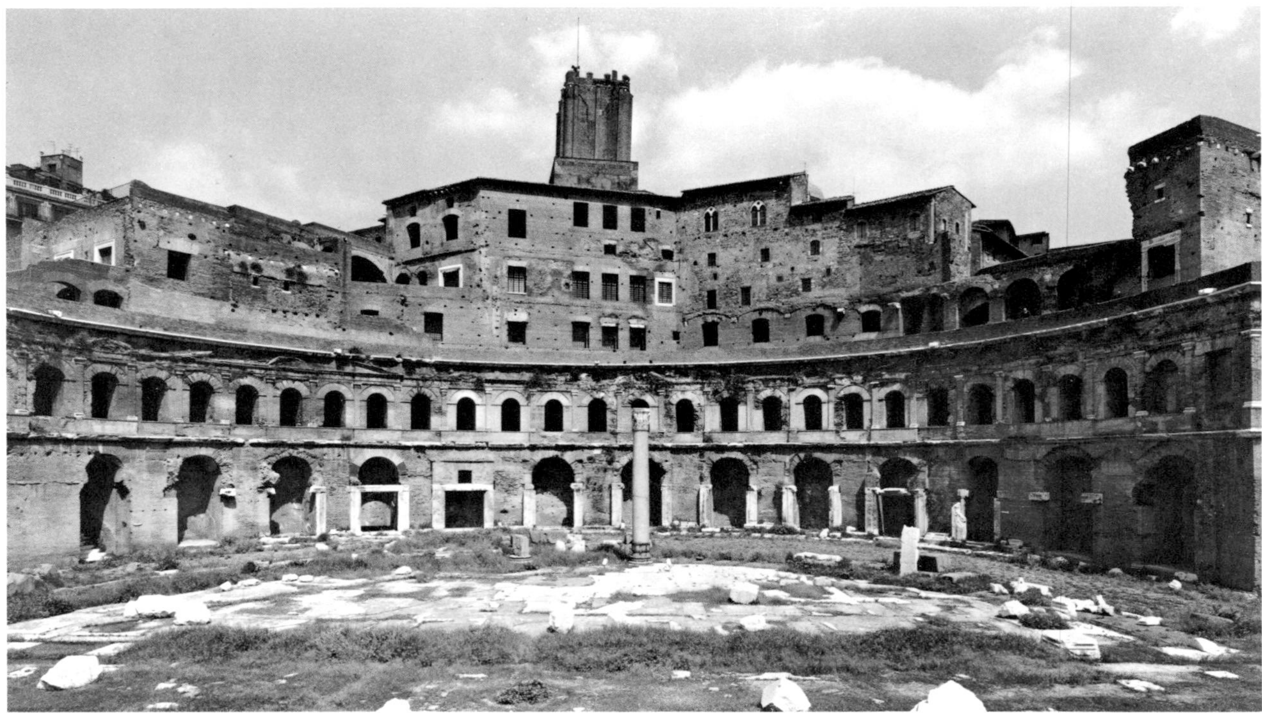

11. Forum and market of Trajan

Capitoline Hill was covered with temples roofed with gilded bronze tiles. There stood the Great Temple of Jupiter, whose foundations now lie buried below the museum wing attached to the Palazzo dei Conservatori.

This huge show area at the very heart of Rome sent its offshoots south, northeast, and west. South of the Capitol and the Palatine lay two smaller market and temple areas: the oil market (the *forum holitorium*), now marked by S. Nicola in Carcere; and the cattle market (the *forum boarium*) at S. Giorgio in Velabro and Piazza Bocca della Verita. Northwest of the Colosseum on the Oppian Hill rose the Golden House of Nero, the Baths of Titus, and the far larger Baths of Trajan—their ruins lofty even now. West of the Capitoline Hill the show continued in even greater magnificence: to the southwest stood the Theatre of Marcellus, dating from the time of Augustus, preserved today excepting its top part and the stage. Of the nearby Portico of Octavia, built in the early first century and rebuilt two hundred years later, a remnant survives in the Ghetto at S. Angelo in Pescheria: a vast rectangular colonnade, it originally enclosed a pair of temples. From there the *Campus Martius*, the Field of Mars, extended west into the bend of the Tiber, opposite what is now Castel S. Angelo, and north to near the Flaminian Gate. On it rose the Theatre of Pompey, now engulfed by medieval and later houses; the Stadium of Domitian, now Piazza Navona; the Baths of Nero, enlarged in the third century by Alexander Severus and extending from the present Piazza Navona to near the Pantheon; the Baths of Agrippa from the time of Augustus, enlarged and rebuilt from the late first to the fourth centuries; and the Pantheon, built by Hadrian to replace a sanctuary founded by Agrippa: the colossal rotunda, preceded by its colonnaded porch and domed, a symbol perhaps of Heaven and towering high over the surroundings then as it does today (fig. 12). Nearer the Corso rose the Temple of Hadrian Deified, now the stock exchange on Piazza di Pietra; on Piazza Colonna, the Column of Marcus Aurelius; to the north, the Mausoleum of Augustus and nearby the obelisk, erected by him as the gnomon of a huge sundial. At the western end of the Campus Martius, Hadrian's Aelian Bridge spanned the Tiber to give access to his mausoleum, Castel S. Angelo, its huge cylindrical shape covered originally with marble plaques and its upper parts decorated with colonnades sheltering statuary—another grand showpiece (fig. 13). Indeed, although outside the city walls, the entire area across the river as far as the Vatican Hill simply continued the wonders of the Campus Martius. Among its monuments, a tomb pyramid, misnamed the *meta Romuli*, survived into the sixteenth century. An obelisk, known in the Middle Ages as the *Terebinth*, rose nearby. Still another stood at the southeast slope of the Vatican Hill, in front of a large round mausoleum of the second century: the mausoleum, known in medieval times as S. Maria della Febbre, appears time and again in drawings, paintings, and engravings until the eighteenth century; the obelisk, the *guglia*, now stands on Bernini's Piazza S. Pietro. North of the mausoleum and now buried underneath the nave of St. Peter's extended a cemetery composed of rows of expensive tomb structures. But the Christian community held fast to a poor, small area in the cemetery, where a niche surmounting the grave commemorated the Apostle Peter's martyrdom. To the south, at the foot of the Vatican Hill, lay the Gardens of Nero and his circus, an earthen racecourse; only recently have its outlines been accurately traced. Another great showpiece along the Tiber, the Naumachia, built for mock sea battles, extended north of the Mausoleum of Hadrian; but all traces seem lost.

The whole show area was enveloped and penetrated by the residential quarters of the metropolis. The *regionaria*, or gazetteers of fourth-century Rome, survey both its public and private buildings. City quarter by city quarter, they list: 28 libraries, 6 obelisks, 8 bridges, 11 fora, 10 basilicas, 11 public baths, 18 aqueducts,

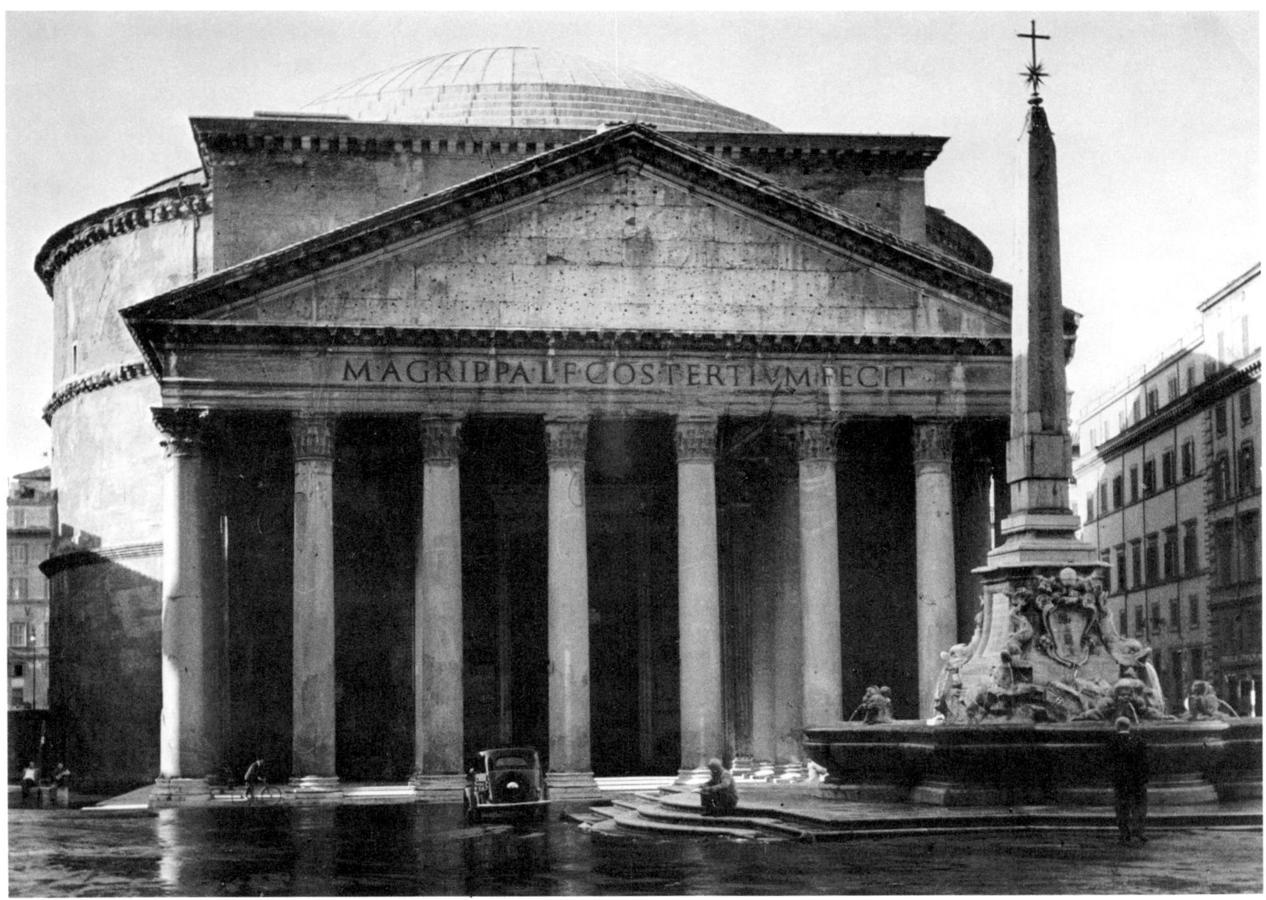

12. Pantheon, exterior

9 circuses and theatres (including a couple for staging mock naval battles); 2 triumphal columns, 15 huge fountains, 22 equestrian statues plus 80 golden and 74 ivory statues, and 36 triumphal arches; in addition there were the barracks of the army, the police, and the fire brigades. Besides this, the gazetteers list 290 granaries and warehouses, 856 private baths, 254 bakeries, and 46 brothels. Finally, they enumerate the buildings where the poor and where the rich lived: over 44,000 *insulae*, presumably multiple dwellings (some think just apartments, but that is unlikely) customary for housing the lower and middle classes; and 1,790 *domus*, private residences and mansions. The types of these latter are well known: low, sprawling structures, their rooms opening into one or more inner courtyards and presumably gardens, as they are found by the hundreds in Pompeii, Herculaneum, and Ostia. The insulae apparently varied a great deal in size, appearance, and material. Only some among the larger ones have survived in Rome, often through having been incorporated into later structures: one is at the foot of the Capitoline Hill (fig. 14); the remains of three lie underneath the church of SS. Giovanni e Paolo on the slope of the Celian Hill, and their façades show in the church's left flank; another was incorporated into the church of S. Anastasia at the southwestern foot of the Palatine, one forms part of the walls of the lower church of S. Clemente; substantial remains of yet others survive on the Esquiline, adjoining the church of S. Martino ai Monti and near S. Prassede; and a large complex of insulae lies buried below the Galleria Colonna in the heart of the city. All follow a standard plan, well known at Ostia also: the ground floor and mezzanine, often protected by arcades, balconies, or overhangs, were given over to shops-cum-storerooms and backroom apartments; the upper floors were divided into apartments of varying sizes, numbering some-

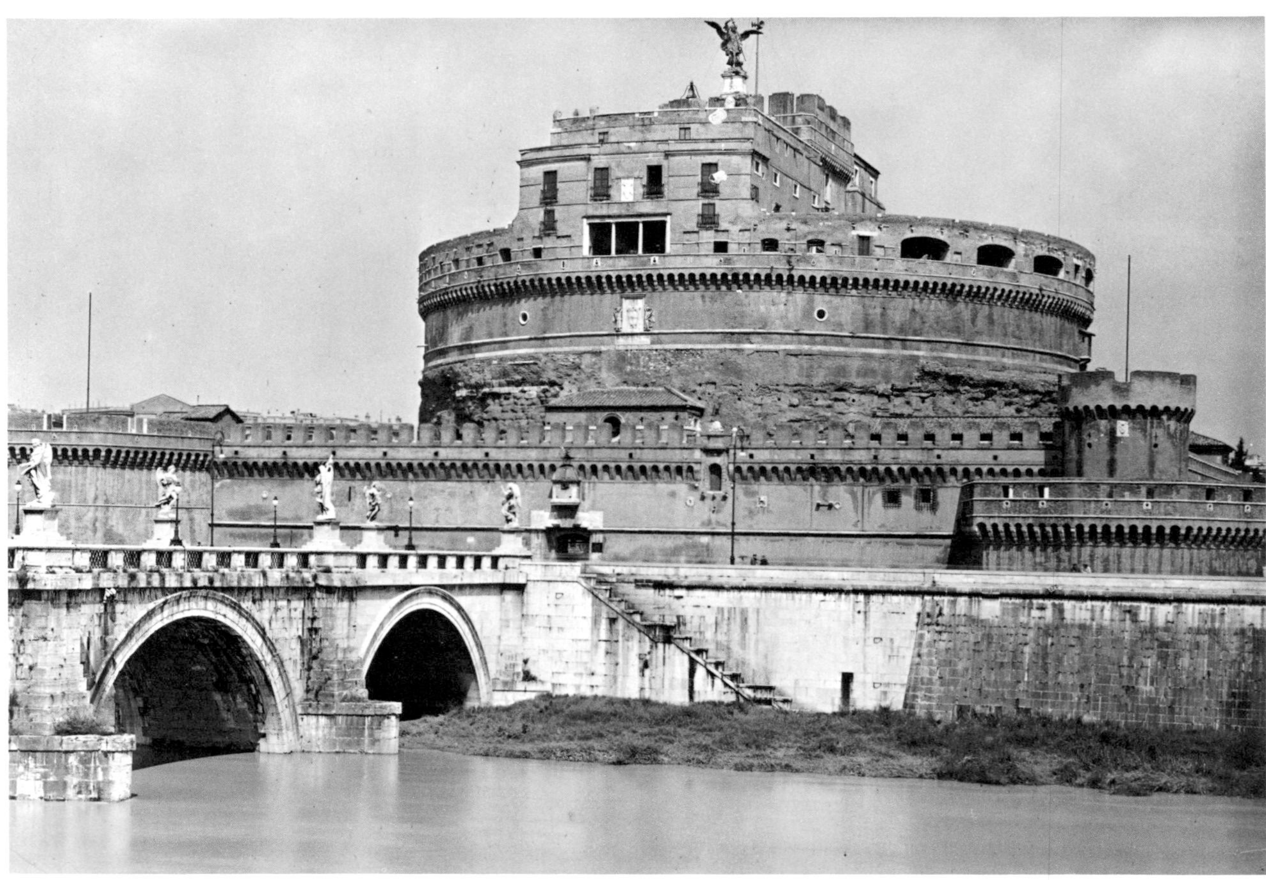

13. Mausoleum of Hadrian and Aelian Bridge (Castel and Ponte S. Angelo)

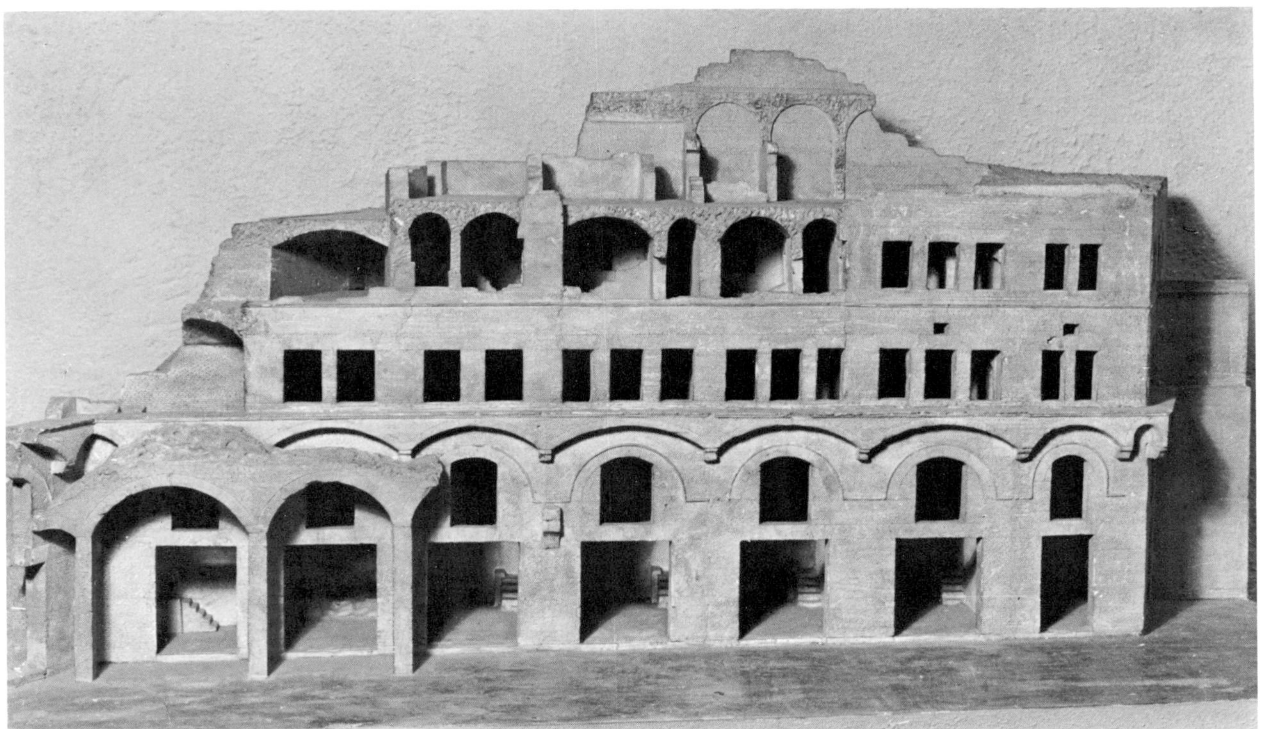

14. Roman tenement house at foot of Capitoline Hill, model

times twenty or more in one building. The length and height of the structures likewise varied: six- and eight-bays long was quite normal, and four or five floors in height was not unusual; indeed, some insulae were geniune skyscrapers. The materials of construction, too, were standard—concrete, faced with brick. All the same, alongside such large apartment houses and tenements there presumably stood innumerable smaller multiple dwellings, two-bays wide or less and possibly with only one or, at most, two upper floors, jerry-built of poor brick, half-timbering, and wood, regular slum buildings. A great marble plan of Rome dated to the early third century and now preserved in fragments, conveys an idea of the blocks of large insulae and the rows of smaller apartment houses. It also shows the streets that these buildings lined: a few, like the Via Biberatica in the market complex of Trajan, were wide for the convenience of shoppers (fig. 15); most were narrow, dark, crowded, and often spanned by diaphragm arches, as may be seen today on the Clivus Scauri on the west slope of the Celian Hill flanking SS. Giovanni e Paolo; all were not unlike those that now crisscross Trastevere—even by the first century B.C. the most densely populated quarter, where immigrants from the East crowded together.

But the tenement houses and show buildings were in no way confined to separate quarters of Imperial Rome. The only parts of town given over exclusively to monumental structures were the Palatine, the Roman Forum, and the Imperial Fora, the latter segregated from the mundane world outside by huge walls. Elsewhere, the tenement houses pushed their way in between the great showpieces wherever there was space. They crowded around the fora and the Capitol, where one of the best-preserved rises as a ruin; they were at the foot of the Palatine facing the Circus Maximus, and opposite the Column of Marcus Aurelius. They invaded the Campus Martius near the Mausoleum of Augustus and in the area between the temples on Largo Argentina and the Pantheon; and they rose among wealthy mansions on the Celian and elsewhere. True, parts of town consisted almost

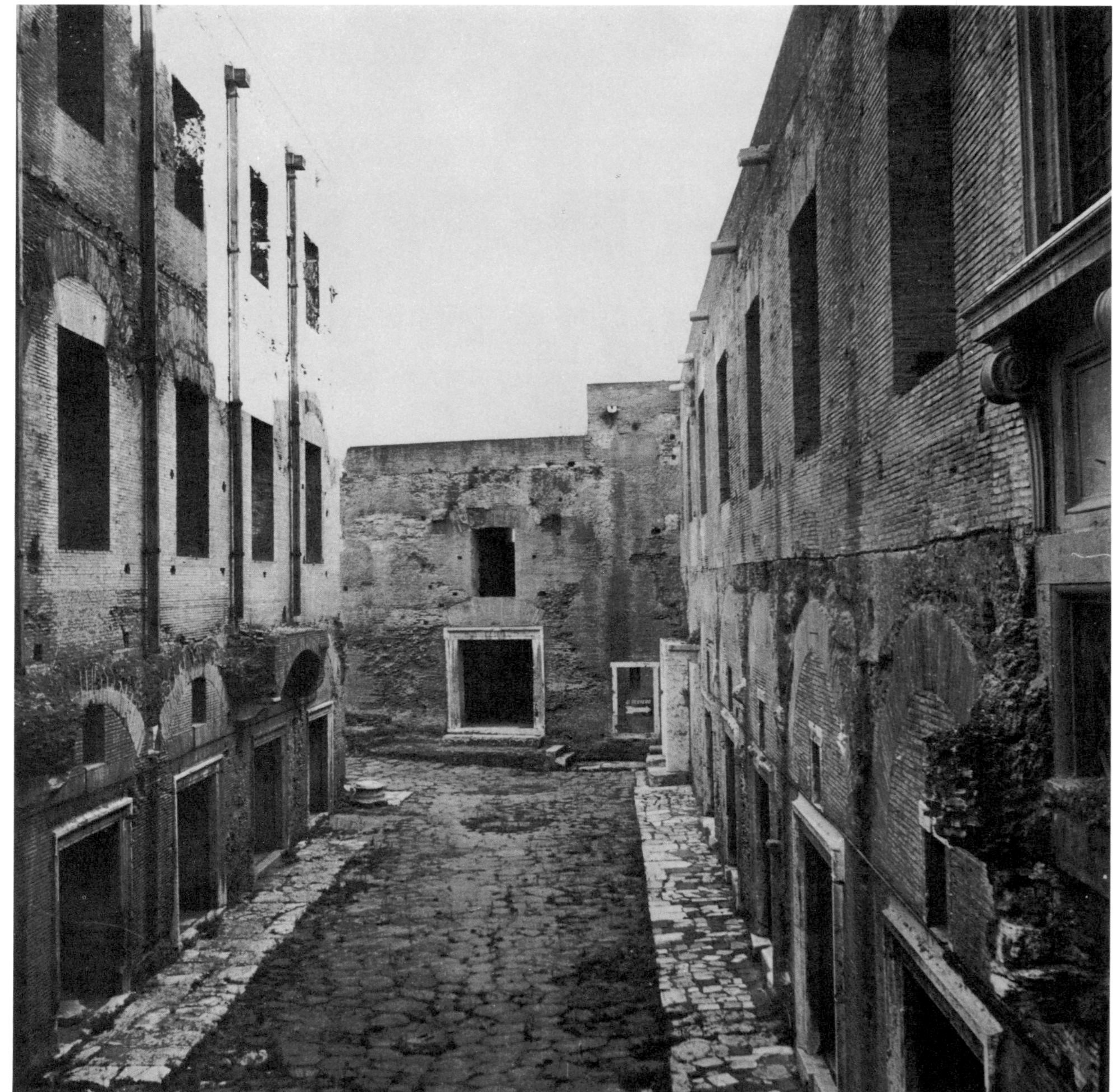

15. Roman street in market of Trajan, Via Biberatica

wholly of tenement houses, primarily in the valleys between the hills, on the slopes, on the Tiber Island and the riverbanks, always threatened by floods. But by and large, tenements, mansions, and public monumental buildings were inextricably intermingled. Ground was expensive and then, as now in the old parts of Rome, public splendor, private wealth, and squalid poverty lived close together.

Only the very rich could afford large sites on which to set up their mansions, surrounded like public buildings by walls to secure the luxury of privacy. Only they could move away to the estates, the mansions and large gardens, which embraced the densely built-up area of imperial Rome in a crescent. In this outer greenbelt extending beyond the Aurelian Walls and occupying the crest of the hills, were the old villa of

Lucullus on the western height of the Pincio, near S. Trinità dei Monti; the Gardens of Sallustius near Via Vittorio Veneto; on the Esquiline, the Villa of Maecenas and the Licinian Gardens, the latter an imperial property; adjoining the city walls on the Celian, two more imperial estates: the Sessorian Palace, enclosing what is now the church of S. Croce in Gerusalemme, and the private amphitheatre nearby, the *amphitheatrum Castrense*; and behind the Lateran Basilica, a large group of mansions, which by the early fourth century were partly or wholly imperial property. In the greenbelt, too, rose the largest and the most lavish of the public baths, those of Caracalla and of Diocletian. This is understandable, given the neighborhood of imperial estates and military barracks: the Castra Praetoria, though no longer used by the Praetorian Guards, at the northeast corner of the Aurelian Walls; the new barracks of the Horse Guards on the site now occupied by S. Giovanni in Laterano; the police barracks underneath Sto. Stefano Rotondo and extending beyond.

We have become used to differentiating sharply between the areas inside and outside the walls, *entro* and *fuori le mura*. But such a distinction, still very real sixty and seventy years ago, dates no earlier than the sixth and seventh centuries. Prior to that, the contrast was anything but clearly marked. When built, the Aurelian Walls cut through the great estates on the rim of the city, and the greenbelt inside the walls continued unchanged outside. The grounds of the Sessorian Palace remained half within and half without the walls, and the villas of the rich extended for many miles along the highways across country: on the Appian Way that of Maxentius, opposite S. Sebastiano, and that of the Quintili further out; on the Tiburtine Road the estate formerly of the Emperor Lucius Verus, now the municipal cemetery, Campo Verano; on the road to Praeneste, the villa of the Gordian emperors, Tor de' Schiavi; others along the Nomentana Road; on the Via Labicana, the villa *duos Lauros*, and the Gardens of Nero at the foot of the Vatican Hill—both imperial property. On the estates and in between rose the mausolea: those of the wealthy—the tombs of Caecilia Metella, of Maxentius' son Romulus, of the Gordians at Tor de' Schiavi are but a few examples; those owned jointly by funerary associations—*columbaria*—their walls set with niches for ash urns; rows of mausolea, like those on the Vatican Hill below St. Peter's; and simple cemeteries for the poor. All were out of town. Roman law forbade burial within the city—the graves found there, including the Mausoleum of Augustus, all antedate the Aurelian Walls; and Hadrian's Mausoleum remained outside.

As outlined, the map of Rome reflects the political, social, and economic situation in A.D. 312. Although real political power had moved away, attached as it was to the new residences and the migratory courts of the tetrarchy, the old ruling families continued to reside in Rome. Their wealth was immense, based primarily on landholdings, vast estates in Italy, North Africa, Gaul, and Spain; their political power focused on the Senate and on the government posts held by their members. The administrative buildings along the fora, the law courts in the basilicas, the buildings of the Senate and of the city prefecture, reflected their standing and power. So did the public buildings erected by their ancestors—the theatres of Marcellus and Pompey; so did the temples of the gods, kept in repair by these families' efforts, whether from private or public funds. No less did their mansions in the greenbelt and the countryside mirror their wealth and power, as did, finally, their mausolea along the roads leading out of Rome. Yet, the map equally and abruptly reflects the seamy side of Rome as well. Occupying a good half of the city was the show area in the center—fora, Capitol, and Campus Martius; the Imperial Palaces on the Palatine and Nero's Golden House; the estates in the greenbelt and the military barracks. The tenements, sheltering the mass of the population, were compressed into narrow strips that enveloped and invaded the center area. Overcrowding, narrow streets, and unsanitary conditions largely made these quarters into slums, where artisans and shopkeepers, small employers and minor officials, freedmen and slaves, who were set up in business by and for their masters, crowded together with the legions of the half-employed and jobless. In fact, Rome's urban masses had been underemployed for centuries, subsisting largely on doles of money, grain, pork, and oil. Yet the public image of Rome was determined by its resplendent show area, its temples, the Imperial Palaces, and the mansions of the rich. Rome was still the head of the civilized world, the *caput mundi*. Eternal Rome, *Roma aeterna*, guaranteed under her rule the eternity of civilization, of prosperity and peace, as foretold by Virgil:

Tu regere imperio populos, Romane,
  memento
Hae tibi erunt artes pacique imponere morem
Parcere subjectis et debellare superbos . . .

Christianity had grown within this milieu, and by 312 as much as a third of Rome's population may have belonged to the Church or sympathized with it. Like the adherents of other foreign gods—Mithras, Isis, the Great Mother, the Syrian gods, the Jewish Jehovah—the Christian congregations owned their places of worship. These were not small sanctuaries like those of the other religions, and obviously not temples like those of the old gods, maintained by the state and its functionaries. Rather, their meeting places were "Houses of the Church," community centers in modern parlance. Identified by the name of the original holder of title to the building—as *titulus Clementis, Anastasiae, Caeciliae, Chrysogoni*—they were ordinary apartment houses, insulae, or smaller mansions, rented, purchased by, or donated to the Church. By the fourth century, twenty-five such tituli are known to have existed in Rome—and given the discrepancy between that number and the size of the Christian community, many of the faithful must have met in additional prayer rooms in private houses, even in Constantine's time. Remodeled as necessary, each community center served a variety of functions: worship, baptism, instruction, welfare, administration, living quarters for the clergy. The meeting places of small sects in modern Harlem or Whitechapel give an idea of what the situation was like in third-century Rome. Occasionally, in the years of religious tolerance just prior to 312, a congregation in Rome may have built a plain, barnlike hall, set aside for worship only: witness the first church of S. Crisogono—its walls now lie buried alongside the medieval church in Trastevere at Ponte Garibaldi. Remains of what may have been community centers survive, incorporated into the walls or foundations of newer churches that were built on their sites—insula-types at S. Giovanni e Paolo and S. Anastasia, a mansion at S. Cecilia. In many cases the names of such tituli survive: prefixed by "Saint"—S. Clemente, Sta. Sabina, S. Crisogono—at present they designate the titular churches assigned to the cardinals of the Church of Rome. Whether remodeled from apartment houses, mansions, or newly built barnlike halls, these "Houses of the Church" were utterly unpretentious. They blended with the hundreds of tenements, old-fashioned mansions, warehouses, and workshops in the popular quarters; and in number—only twenty-five even in the fourth century—they were lost among the forty-four thousand insulae of contemporary Rome. Notwithstanding the large numbers of adherents, then, Christianity had left no visible trace in pre-Constantinian Rome. This was no wonder: the believers came by and large from the middle and lower classes, with but an occasional well-to-do freedman, a lawyer, a civil servant, or an aristocratic lady. Even by the third century, when the new faith had found more adherents among the upper middle class, things did not change essentially. The believers in times of peace—and persecutions were rare, if violent—shunned the public sphere in their policy and in their buildings.

In the countryside, too, beyond the Aurelian Walls, Christian structures were widespread. Burial grounds and cult centers of the congregations were located as a rule on the big estates, the ground being purchased from or donated by the "lord of the manor" to his Christian freedmen and slaves. But like the meeting houses in the city, Christian burial grounds and cult centers were, at a cursory glance, indistinguishable from those serving other sects or, indeed, worshipers of the old gods. Burials took place in cemeteries under the open sky; or else, perhaps according to specifically Christian and Jewish custom, in catacombs: networks of many-storied galleries and tomb chambers underground, designed—for economy's sake—to exploit in

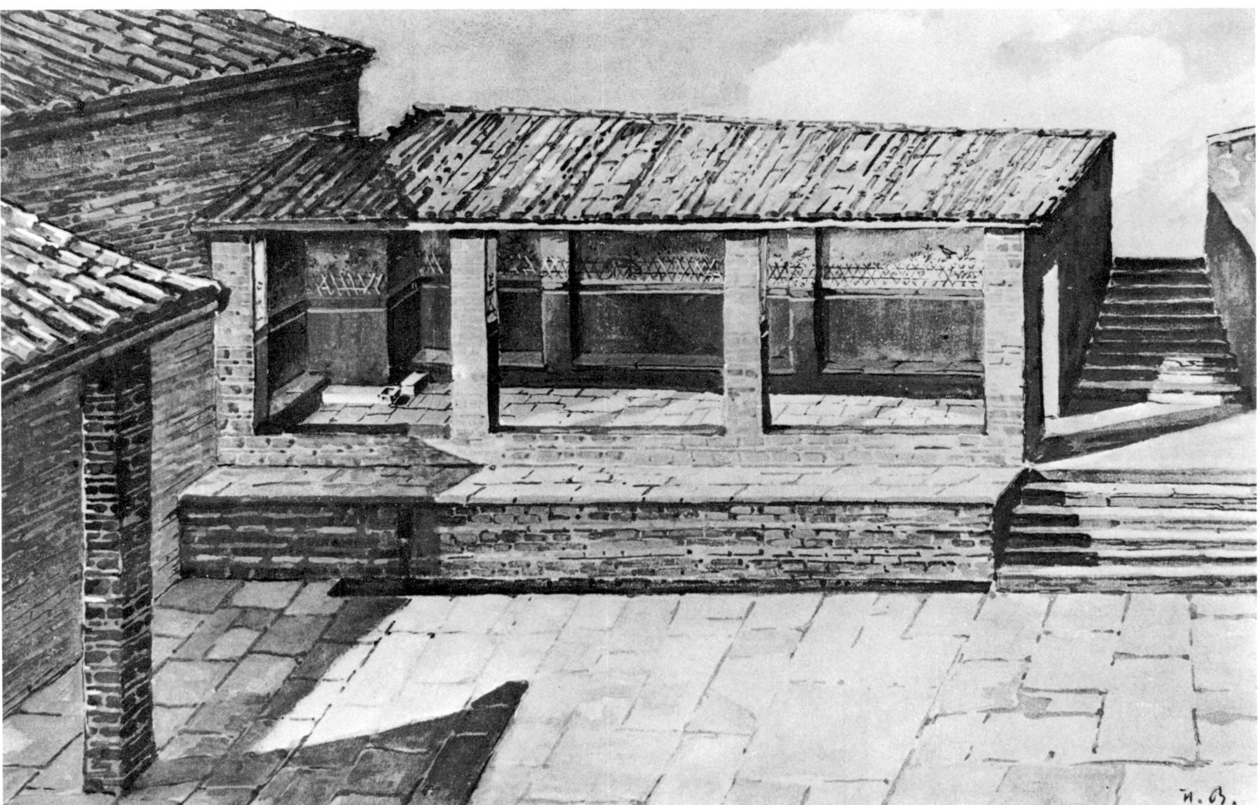

16. S. Sebastiano, reconstruction of memorial courtyard and loggia

depth the expensive available land. That the catacombs served as hiding places or secret meeting halls for the Christian community of Rome is pure legend, quite untrue. Small groups occasionally met in the catacomb chambers for a funeral meal on the anniversary of the deceased, but that is all. Small areas or halls for such funerary banquets were provided in the cemeteries above ground and even in the mausolea intended for wealthy believers, just like those of non-Christians nearby. Equally unpretentious and indistinguishable from their pagan neighbors were the cult centers laid out around Rome at the graves of Christian martyrs. Underneath S. Sebastiano on the Via Appia, one such center served for the veneration of Peter and Paul, the Princes of the Apostles, whose feast or whose relics may have been moved to this spot in A.D. 258 (fig. 16). A small courtyard was terminated by a niche, probably a repository for offerings; a shed opened into the courtyard, its painted rear wall covered by pious visitors with hundreds of graffiti (one dated A.D. 260) recording funerary banquets in honor of the Apostles; a smaller banquet hall, possibly a private and later one, rose nearby; and a long flight of stairs descended to a deep spring; the whole was like any tavern on the green. Commonplace and inconspicuous, too, was the cult center of Saint Peter on the Vatican Hill, uncovered below the church over thirty years ago. Within a cemetery composed mainly of lavish mausolea, many owned by adherents of oriental cults from the nearby oriental quarter in Trastevere, a small plot with a few poor graves was stubbornly retained by a Christian congregation. Between A.D. 160 and 180 it was closed off on one side by a wall, arching over one of the graves; and the grave was marked by a small *aedicula*, or niche, gabled and flanked by columns; a projecting slab served to deposit offerings (fig. 17). Known around A.D. 200 as the "trophy" of Saint Peter, the sign of his victory over death, the monument is further identified by third-century graffiti appealing to

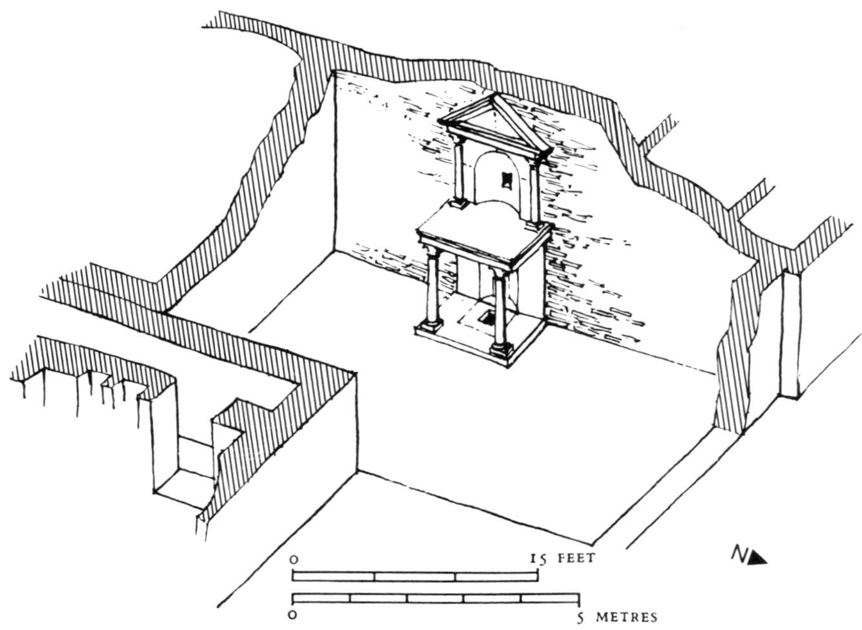

17. St. Peter's, second-century shrine, reconstruction

the Apostle. By the late second century, then, the grave apparently was believed to be his, and it is likely so. Again, the cult center is plain and commonplace. Aediculae just like this marked hundreds of graves around Rome and elsewhere. Nowhere had Christianity made a dent into the physical aspect of the city by 312, within or without the walls. Ordinary visitors to Rome would see the temples of the old gods, the administrative buildings, the palaces, the theatres, the great mansions; they might see the middle-class quarters and, reluctantly, the slums; but they would not notice the Christian community houses or the "trophy" of Saint Peter on the Vatican Hill, unless they were Christians themselves.

To Constantine this state of affairs must have seemed intolerable. He entered Rome, a sympathizer with Christianity if not formally a convert. Soon he evolved a policy largely aimed at securing within his dominions the triumph of Christ, who had granted him victory, and of His Church. In his later years Constantine apparently intended to turn the Roman Empire into a Christian Empire. This ultimate aim evolved slowly, but as early as 313, Christians, both clergy and laymen, stood high among his advisers, and the Church, raised from obscurity, turned into a major political force. Bishops ranked in the court calendar with high government officials; the hierarchy of the Church hardened; in the West the foremost bishop in fact, if not by law, was that of Rome—the term *pope* is late. Concomitantly, the Church acquired, through imperial and private donations, large landholdings and quickly became a powerful economic force. The estates and their income, given by Constantine to maintain his Roman church foundations and their clergy, are precisely known from original lists, later incorporated into the *Liber Pontificalis*, the official chronicle of the papacy. In the beginning of his rule, these gifts included property in Rome and Italy, somewhat later in Sicily, Sardinia, North Africa, and Greece; after his conquest of the East in 324, they included holdings in Egypt, Syria, Cilicia; and the yearly revenues from these lands amounted to 3,700 gold solidi, or roughly $25 million in today's money, for St. Peter's alone. The total income of the Church of Rome under Constantine amounted to 25,000 gold solidi; a very considerable sum, but little compared to the income and wealth of the great families, which at times was tenfold that of the Church.

Within this program of Constantine's, the domestic and private character stressed by the Christian meeting places in houses scattered through town must have been intolerable. The meeting houses in existence could not well be done away with. The congregations in possession would have objected, and it was politically inadvisable to set up Christian buildings in or near the center of Rome with its temples and administrative buildings dominated by the pagan Senate. Where his hands were not bound, for instance regarding imperial property, the emperor turned emphatically to a different category of building—public architecture. Within this category, one building type offered itself naturally: the basilica. Essentially a timber-roofed large hall, it had evolved for centuries ever-new variants of plan and design: with or without clerestory windows, with or without apses, along a transverse or longitudinal axis or both; by the fourth century A.D. it seems the well-lit longitudinal types were preferred. In function, too, basilicas had always served all kinds of needs: as law courts, bazaars, drill halls, sanctuaries, reception halls, and throne rooms—in short, public meeting rooms for scores of functions exercised by the government, the army, municipalities, religious sects, the ruling classes, and the emperor. For the newly arising function as meeting hall for a Christian congregation, the overall *genus* basilica was given as the easily adaptable traditional framework. Within this framework, obviously in collaboration with local church leaders, Constantine's architects evolved all through the empire new variants of the old *genus* for regular churches, martyrs' churches, and covered cemeteries. The most prestigious ones—in Rome, the Holy Land, imperial capitals such as Trier and, later, Constantinople—designed at the command of the emperor, likely received his approval. What interested him, though, was hardly the plan and its details. One supposes he would insist on large size, on resplendent decoration, on showy furnishings, and on simple plans and an uncomplicated building technique to allow rapid construction. Church leaders concerned with the functional requirements of planning would be only too glad to comply with the emperor's insistence on speed and to accept his bounty.

Both for the emperor and the Christian leaders, building and endowing large, resplendent churches as quickly as possible was a major means to demonstrate visibly to Christians and pagans alike the power of the New God and thus to propagate the new faith, promoted by the emperor. This Constantine set out to do following his victory over Maxentius, and as his rule spread over the empire, including the Eastern provinces after 324, churches rose all over, founded by the emperor and the pious ladies of his family. Nonetheless, it must be kept in mind that this policy of Christianization, both in general terms and more specifically in building activity, had its limitations, in Rome more than elsewhere.

Constantine's initial intention may well have been to leave his mark on Rome and to make this, his capital, into a Christian city. Possibly as early as the winter of 312/313 he decided to build at the Lateran a cathedral for the Roman bishop. The *domus Faustae*, a nearby mansion, perhaps imperial property, served as early as the fall of 313 for the meetings of a church council held under the auspices of the emperor. Adjoining it, the barracks of the imperial horseguards were razed—the corps had apparently fought for Maxentius—and in their place the new church was built. Remains survive in the foundations and walls of S. Giovanni in Laterano, remodeled and added to though it was through the centuries: in the Middle Ages; most thoroughly by Borromini in the seventeenth century; and again in the late nineteenth century. A mural at S. Martino ai Monti in Rome shows what Borromini's contemporaries or he himself thought Constantine's church looked like (fig. 18). But all kinds of evidence give a more precise, if less lively, picture (fig. 19). It was a basilica, a large longitudinal hall with a timber roof; the nave, terminated by an apse, was flanked by double aisles on either side, the inner ones higher than the outer ones; sacristies projected on each side near the end of the aisles. Nave and aisles were supported by columns, the former trabeated, the latter arcaded, and lit by large windows. Marble revetment covered the aisle arcades and possibly the aisle walls inside; small columns of precious green-speckled marble carried the aisle arcades —the mural at S. Martino ai Monti shows them, and twenty-four have been reused in Borromini's remodeling flanking the niches in the nave;

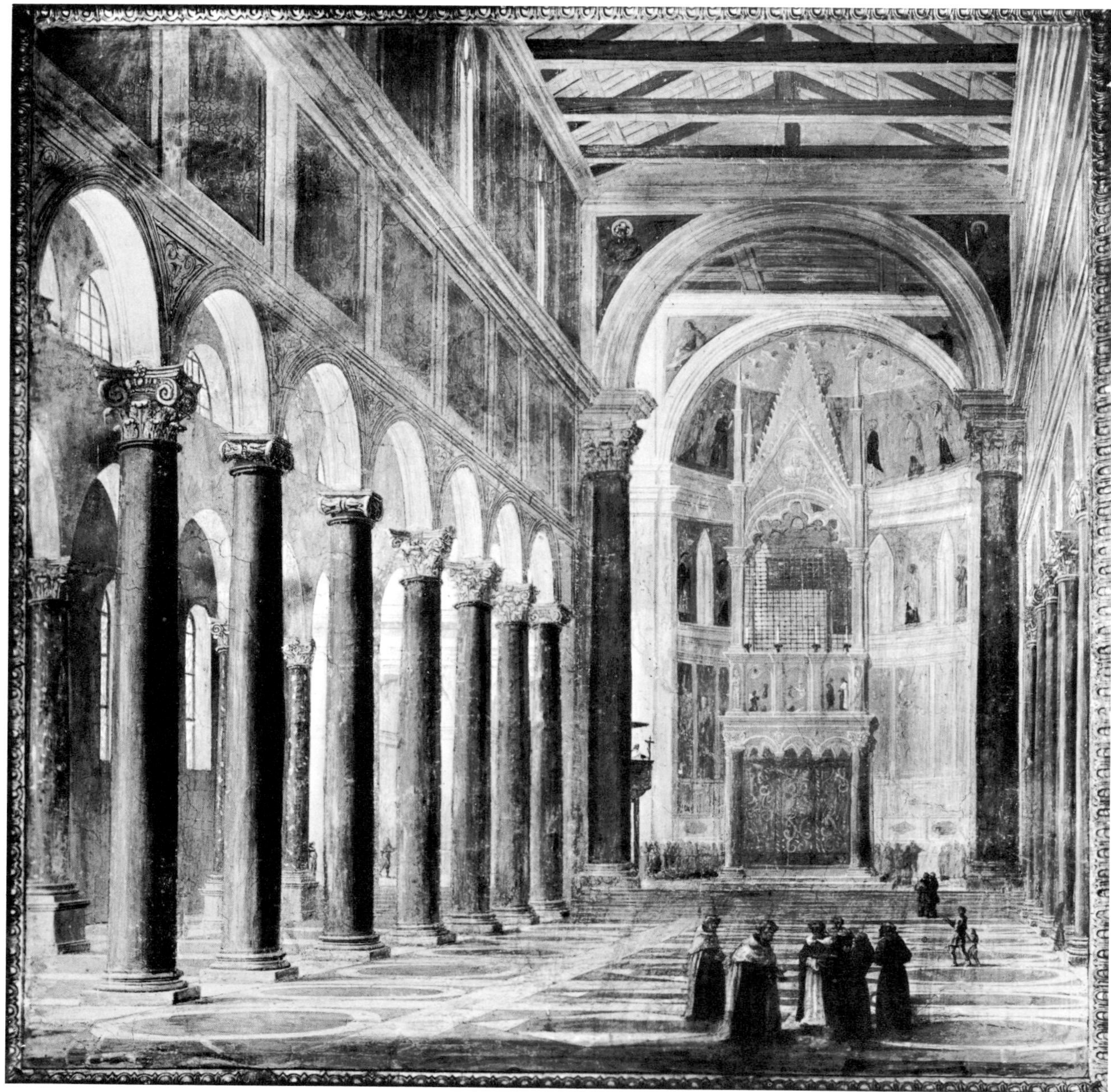

18. Lateran Basilica, reconstruction attempt as of 1650, Gagliardi, fresco, S. Martino ai Monti, Rome

the apse vault of Constantine's church shimmered in gold; gold and silver lighting fixtures and seven silver tables—one presumably the altar, the other to hold offerings—filled nave and chancel; on the chord of the apse, a colonnaded, gabled screen, or a canopy, sheathed in silver, sheltered or carried statues of Christ, the Apostles, and angels. Behind the church, built over part of an older mansion, the baptistery still rises, dating presumably about 315; its inside was remodeled a century later. Clearly, Constantine viewed the Lateran cathedral, his first Church foundation, as a bold new venture in Christian building, a clean break with the unobtrusive, emphatically private, and modest design of the traditional community centers; a variant on one of the foremost types of public monumental buildings; a *basilica*, an audience hall of Christ the King, as it were, competing with the most magnificent public structures in decoration, fur-

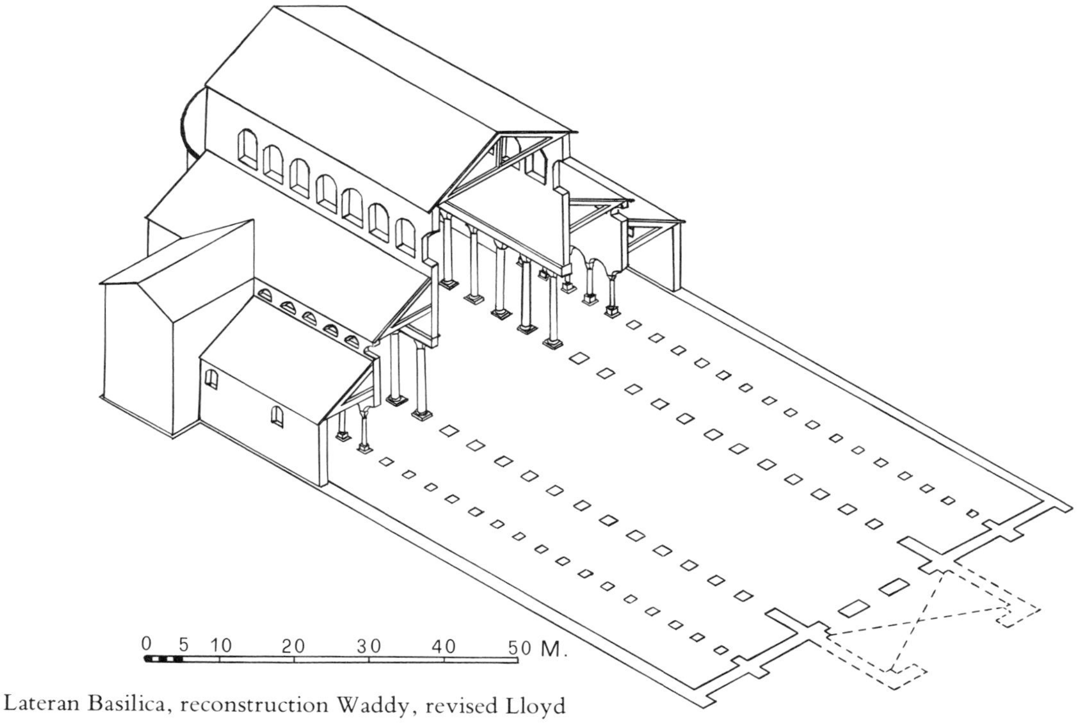

19. Lateran Basilica, reconstruction Waddy, revised Lloyd

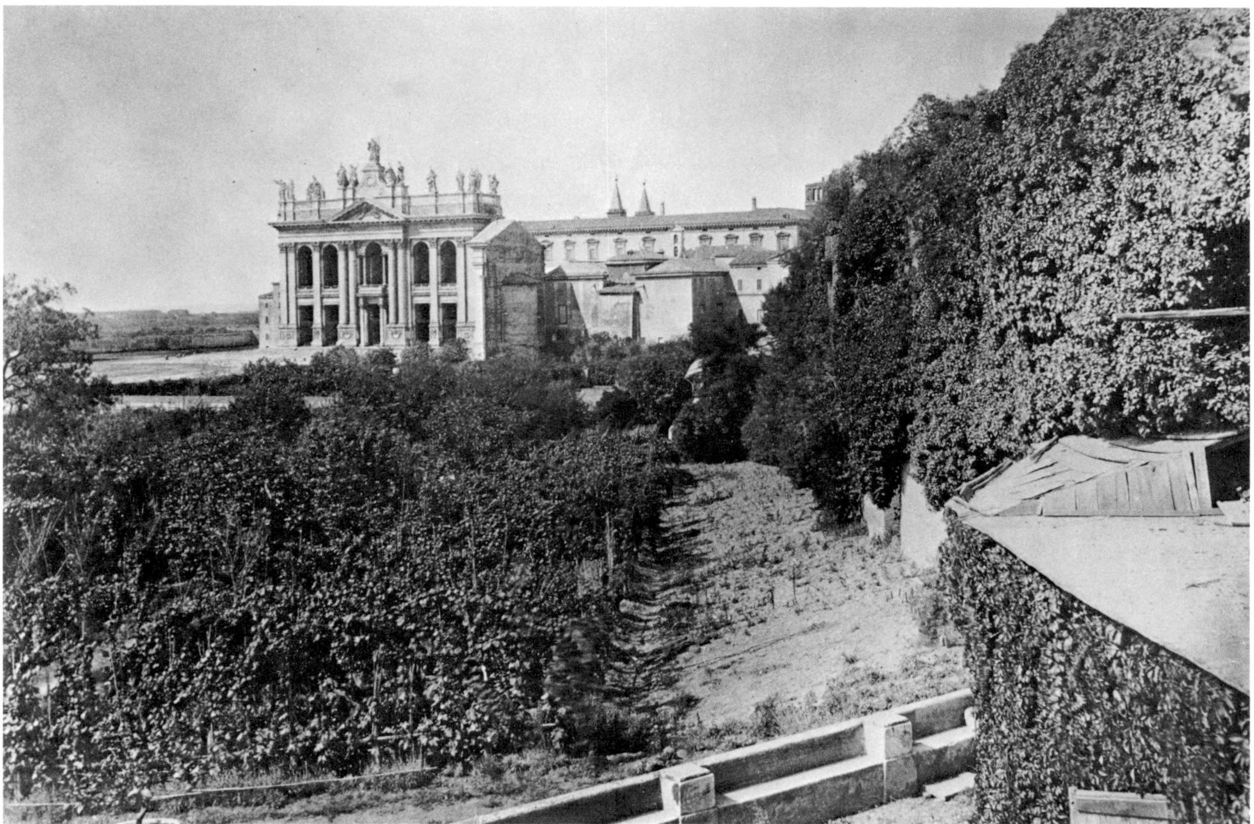

20. Lateran, as of ca. 1870, private collection, Rome

nishings and size—over 98 meters ($333\frac{1}{3}$ Roman feet) long and over 56 meters (190 Roman feet) wide; an imperial foundation in every respect.

Though purported to be public buildings, neither the cathedral nor the baptistery at the Lateran were such in the proper sense. They rose on ground that was at the emperor's free disposal, among mansions and gardens, all or mostly imperial property, tucked away at the edge of the city: not so different, one would like to think, from what the present church looked like a century ago when it rose amidst villas, fields, and vineyards (fig. 20). Even more than the Lateran cathedral, the palace church of the Empress Dowager Helena blended into the buildings of the Sessorian Palace. Founded probably as late as 326-328, and endowed with a relic of the True Cross brought from Jerusalem—hence its name, S. Croce in Gerusalemme—it was installed in a palace hall of early third century date; the old walls are still visible from the outside, and the interior and the splendid façade date from the eighteenth century, overlaying a twelfth-century remodeling. The imperial architect simply added an apse to the old hall and divided the space into three bays by two triple arches thrown across; it would well serve the needs of a palace chapel where their majesties and suite, separated from the servants, would face the clergy around the altar. The private character of the structure could not be brought out more strongly. Seen from the outside at least, it was just another building within the palace complex.

The Lateran Basilica, its baptistery, and S. Croce in Gerusalemme were the only structures built inside the walls of Rome by Constantine and his family for the Church. Located as they were on imperial property and at the very edge of the city, they contributed nothing to transform Rome into a Christian capital. Beyond the walls, the countryside with its great estates was more visibly Christianized with the help of the Constantinian House. Near catacombs and venerated cult centers, mostly on imperial property, structures were built for the Church's use: huge, well-appointed basilicas, visible from afar. In the course of time, those surviving were turned into regular churches; but when built, they were utilized as covered cemeteries. Adjoining catacombs, sheltering the graves of venerated martyrs, or built over old cult centers, they served as burial grounds for the faithful and for funeral banquets honoring them or the martyrs. Mass was celebrated only on a martyr's anniversary, and no permanent clergy was attached to these cemetery structures. One such

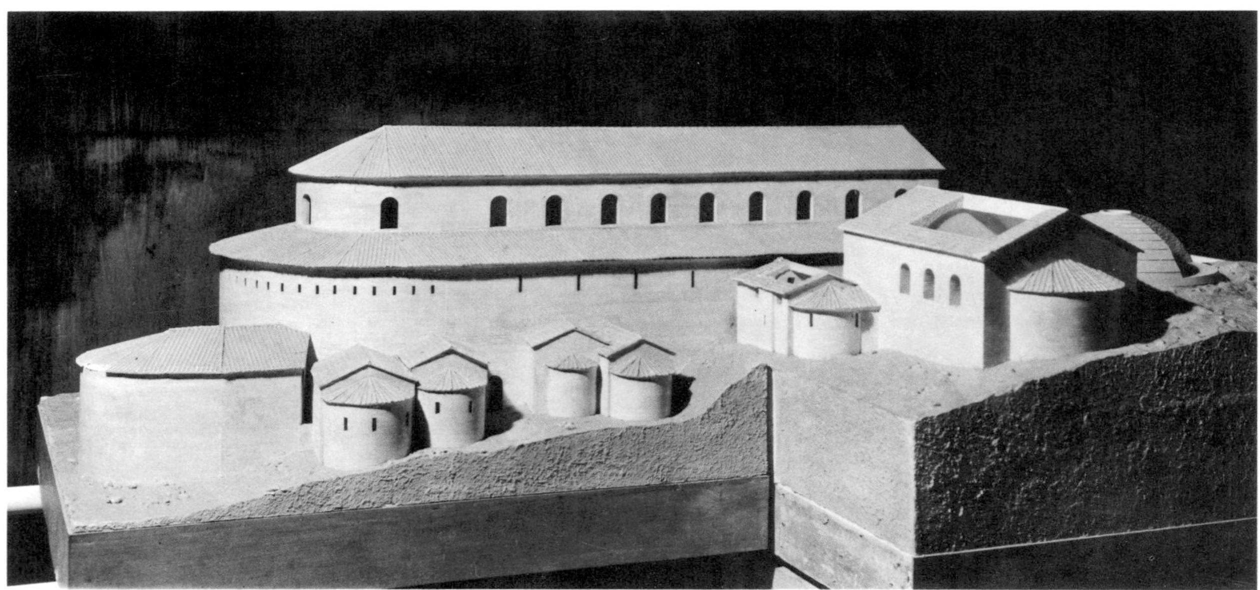

21. S. Sebastiano and attached mausolea, model Pacini

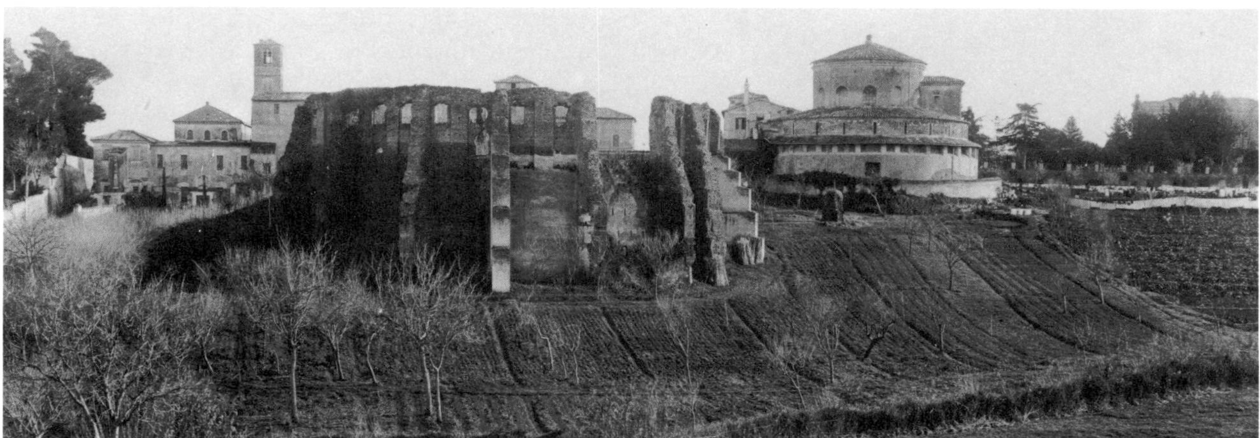

22. Covered Cemetery of S.Agnese and Mausoleum of S. Costanza, as of ca. 1900

covered cemetery, or funeral hall, survives, and though remodeled, its original appearance is easily envisaged: S. Sebastiano, constructed over the third-century cult center of the Apostles on the Appian Way (fig. 21). The present church fills only the nave of the old one, whose grand size again gives an idea of the ambitions either of Constantine or of the local church leaders. Indeed, construction was possibly started on the initiative of the Roman congregation, before Constantine entered the city; no imperial endowment is recorded, but Constantine certainly took over and completed the structure. The nave and aisles communicated through an arcade on piers; and the aisles, linked across the façade through an inner narthex, envelop the apse, U-shaped, in an ambulatory. The floor was entirely carpeted with graves; others were stacked along the walls, shelflike, both above and below floor level; and mausolea of various sizes and plans crowded the building outside. Another funerary basilica of nearly the same plan, though even larger at 98 meters long as against 75 meters, stood by the Tiburtine Road at the foot of the cliff where the grave chamber of Saint Lawrence, richly decorated by Constantine, was long venerated inside a catacomb. U-shaped like that of the basilica on the Appian Way, the ambulatory, rather than the façade, faced the highway and was accessible through five large openings; a portico, still preserved in the eighth century, ran all the way to the city gate, protecting the faithful from sun and rain. The land where the basilica rose, adjoining the present church of S. Lorenzo, had been imperial property ever since the second century. A third funerary basilica of the same plan has been traced on the grounds of the imperial villa *ad duos lauros* on the Via Labicana, adjoining the catacomb and tomb chamber of the martyrs Marcellinus and Peter. Attached to its front portico rose a huge mausoleum, still preserved, which sheltered the sarcophagus of the Empress Dowager Helena; it seems Constantine had originally intended both the sarcophagus and the mausoleum for himself. A fourth hall of this type, an imposing feat of engineering, was built perhaps after Constantine's death by his daughter, Constantina/Constantia, on her estate near the grave of the martyr Agnes on the Via Nomentana. Large parts of the outer walls and their substructures survive to their full height (fig. 22). Against the flank of the covered graveyard whose floor was carpeted with tombs, the imperial princess placed her mausoleum, S. Costanza: large, a full 22.50 meters in diameter; the center domed and resting on twelve pairs of splendid columns and capitals, all spoils from older buildings; the circular aisle barrel-vaulted—a colonnaded outer ambulatory has been lost; the walls inside originally sheathed in marble decoration, the vaults covered with mosaic—only those on the aisle vault remain, but the rest are known from old drawings; and the whole immensely impressive even deprived of such splendor (fig. 23). Jointly, the covered graveyard and the mausoleum con-

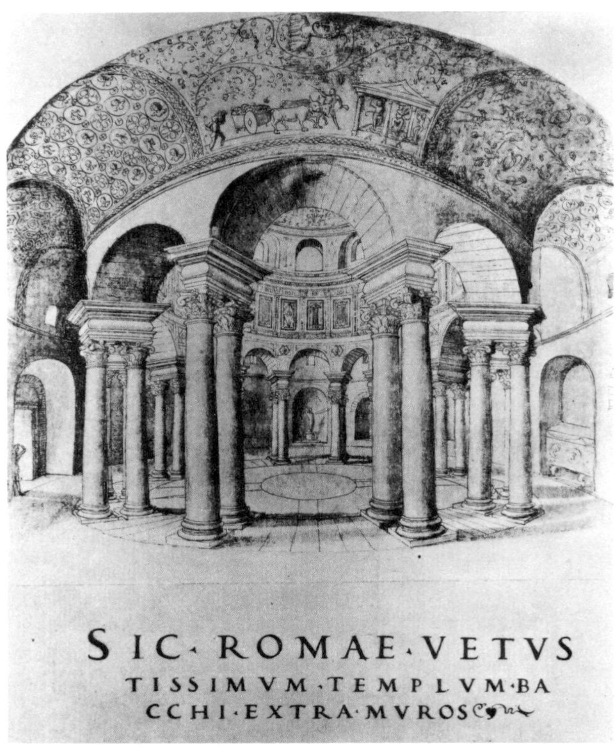

vey the leading features of Constantinian church building: hugeness, a simple plan and exterior, and a gorgeous interior.

St. Peter's, too, although different in plan, was founded by Constantine primarily as a covered cemetery and funerary hall, serving mainly for burials, commemorative banquets, and the veneration of a martyr, the Apostle Saint Peter. Its floor was covered with graves; funerary banquets were customary—Saint Augustine tells of them as late as about A.D. 400; mausolea crowded around its walls, one—S. Maria della Febbre—older than the church and surviving until the eighteenth century. St. Peter's was on an imperial estate out of town: on the shoulder of the Vatican Hill where it sloped down toward the Gardens of Nero. And there is a good chance that, like the Lateran cathedral or the funerary halls at S. Lorenzo or S. Agnese, it stood amidst trees and vineyards. Contrary to other funerary

23. S. Costanza, interior, as of 1538/39, Francisco D'Ollanda, Escurial

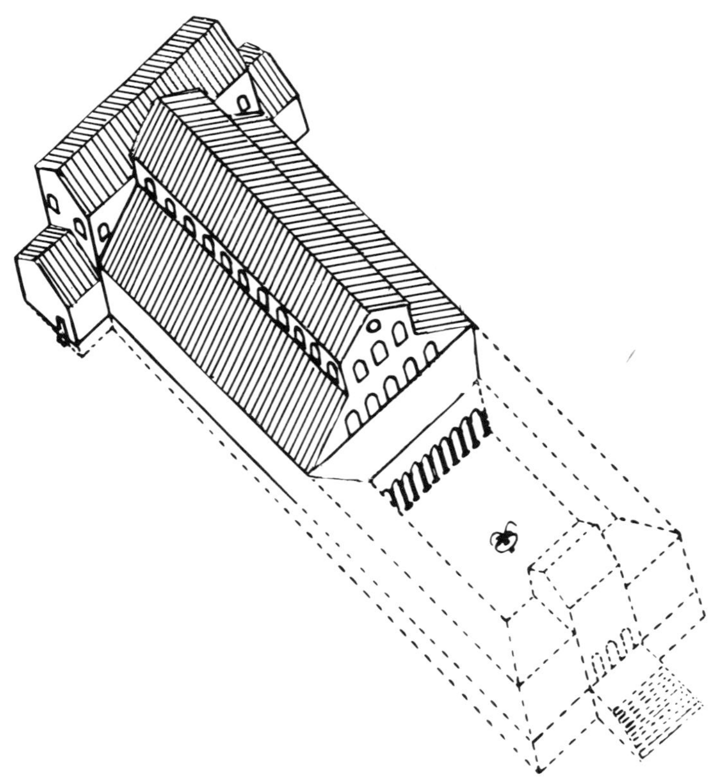

24. St. Peter's, reconstruction, as of ca. 330

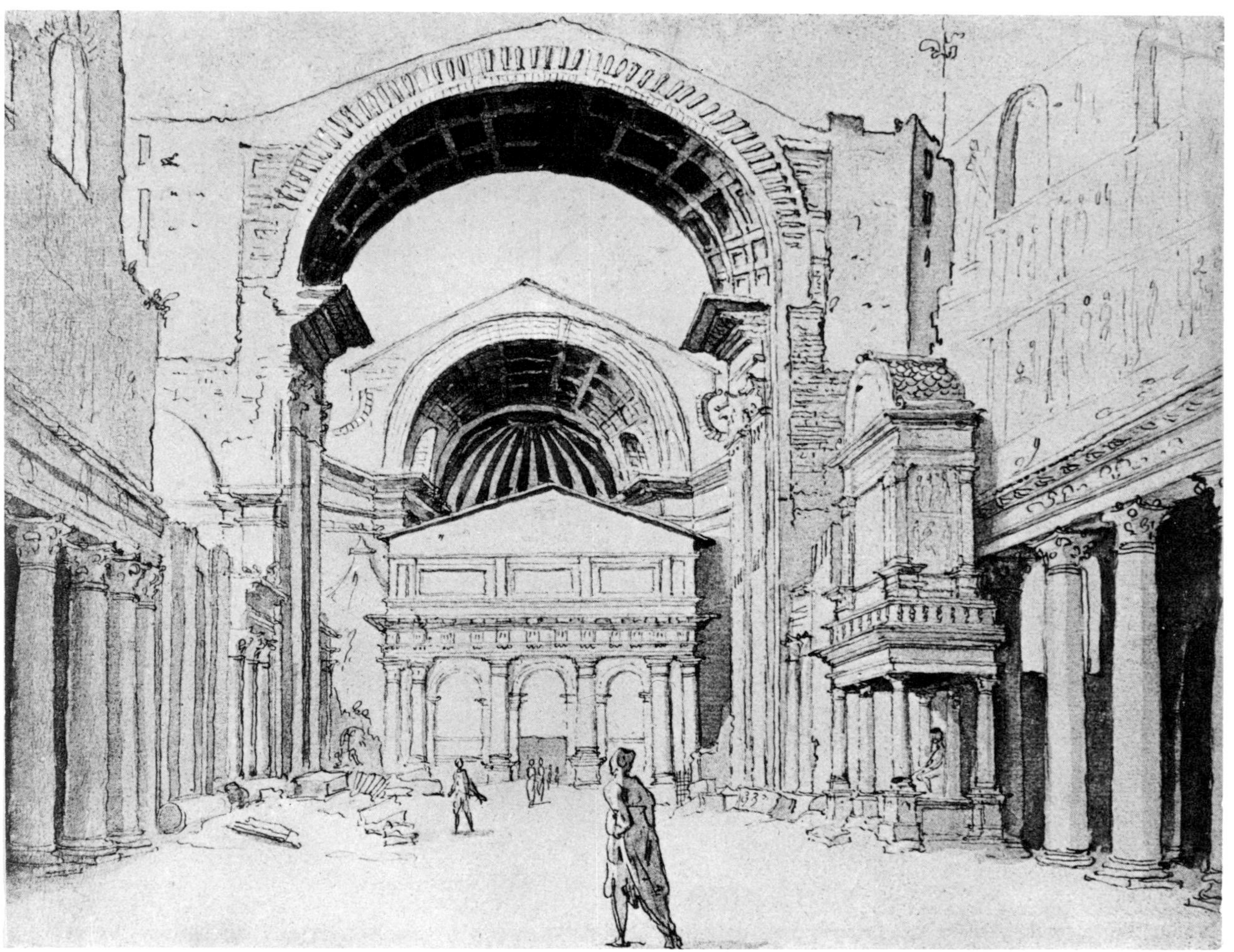

25. St. Peter's, interior, during sixteenth-century rebuilding as of 1534-1536, drawing Marten van Heemskerck, Berlin, Kupferstichkabinett, 79 D2A, fol. 52r

halls, however, the shrine of Saint Peter did not rise outside, in a catacomb, as did the shrines of Saint Lawrence or Saint Agnes. Instead it was made the very focus of the basilica and hence forced a new plan on the emperor's architects. Begun between 319 and 322, and completed by 329, it was placed on a large terrace created by filling in the pagan necropolis and the small Christian cult center therein (fig. 24); only the upper part of the niche, Saint Peter's memorial, remained above the floor level of Constantine's basilica. This, of course, has long since given way to the present great church, New St. Peter's. But Constantine's structure is known in nearly every detail from the remains excavated and from descriptions, paintings, and drawings done before and during its destruction. A drawing by Heemskerck (fig. 25), done while large parts of the basilica had given way already to New St. Peter's, provides at least a faint idea of the colossal size of the structure. Like the Lateran cathedral, St. Peter's was laid out with a nave and doubled aisles, all resting on columns pilfered from older buildings. But unlike the plan of the Lateran church, a transept was interposed between the apse and nave. A long, tall structure, though lower than the nave, it sheltered on the borderline of the apse the shrine of the Apostle, surmounted by a baldacchino flanked by openings, the whole on twisted marble columns with vine scrolls donated by the emperor; some survive, reused in the present church, where guides still point them out, wrongly of course, as having come from Solomon's Temple. An atrium extended in front, and in it stood the *pigna*, a huge pine cone of bronze under a canopy, all parts pilfered from older structures. Towering over the atrium, the façade of the church, slightly altered in the thirteenth century, and its nave walls with their many large windows, presented again the simple planes of the exterior as contrasted with the grandeur of the interior that mark Constantinian church building. The vast size of the structure, larger than any of the other funerary halls and quite a bit larger than the cathedral at the Lateran, shows that large crowds of local Christians and pilgrims were counted on to fill the huge space. As at S. Lorenzo, in order to shelter the pilgrims, a portico of Constantinian date or slightly later ran all the way to the nearest access from the city, the Aelian Bridge near the Mausoleum of Hadrian. To Constantine, it seems, St. Peter's was the most important pilgrimage church, and next to the Lateran cathedral, the outstanding Christian building among those in and near Rome. The furnishings in gold and silver and the endowment donated by him to St. Peter's easily compete with those provided for the cathedral at the Lateran.

Compressed into twenty or twenty-five years, this building activity is impressive enough as a sheer feat of labor organization, providing materials from near and far—bricks, timber, marble—and pushing the work to completion. Its true significance, however, resides in the consistency of the underlying program. The first Christian emperor and his family intended to erect in the capital the buildings needed by the Christian community of the town and the court, and to provide them lavishly with resplendent furnishings and the means for their maintenance: a cathedral with its baptistery and the bishop's residence and offices; a palace church for the empress dowager and the resident court; five or six covered cemeteries located on different roads out of town, all linked to venerated spots: the cult center of the Apostles on the Appian Way, and the graves of the great martyrs, Saint Peter, Saint Lawrence, Saint Agnes, and the deacons Marcellinus and Peter; finally, imperial mausolea linked to two of these structures—one designed, in all likelihood, for Constantine himself, and later ceded to his mother, Helena; the other, S. Costanza, for the princess Constantina.

One all too readily thinks of Constantine as a builder primarily of churches. But a Roman emperor had other obligations as well. He was expected by tradition to place his stamp on public architecture, temples, basilicas, baths, and other civic buildings set up primarily in his capital. Naturally, Constantine shunned temples. But otherwise he did not evade his obligations as a builder of public monumental structures. Though fewer than his churches, his secular buildings in Rome were impressive enough. On the Roman Forum he took over and completed the structures begun by Maxentius, imparting to them his name. In the Basilica Nova, whose walls and vaults were probably in place when Constantine marched into Rome, he finished the decoration and placed his colossal statue into the apse at the short, eastern end. Likewise, he changed the plan by adding on the long sides an apse to the north and an entrance porch to the south; the shift of axis made the flank facing the Forum and the imperial palaces on the Palatine Hill into the main façade; obviously the structure then became the *Basilica Constantini*. Nearby, he completed and dedicated in his name the audience hall and offices of the city prefect, now the church of SS. Cosma e Damiano. An equestrian statue was set up in his honor somewhere on the Forum; it has long since disappeared, but was still known to eighth-century visitors. On the southern slope of the Quirinal, nowadays covered by the Rospigliosi Palace, he built the baths that bore his name, the largest in Rome next to those of Caracalla and Diocletian; their towering ruins were still seen in the sixteenth century. On the Forum Boarium, the old cattle market near the Tiber, at least one monument appears to date from his reign: the *Janus Quadrifrons*, a huge four-sided arch, of massive brickmasonry covered with marble plaques, its ninety-six niches designed to hold statues (fig. 26). The best-known monument of Constantine's day in Rome is the triumphal arch in his name near the Colosseum and across the Ostian Way (fig. 27). Dedicated by the Senate in 315 and decorated with reliefs pilfered for the most part from the Arches of Trajan and Hadrian, it

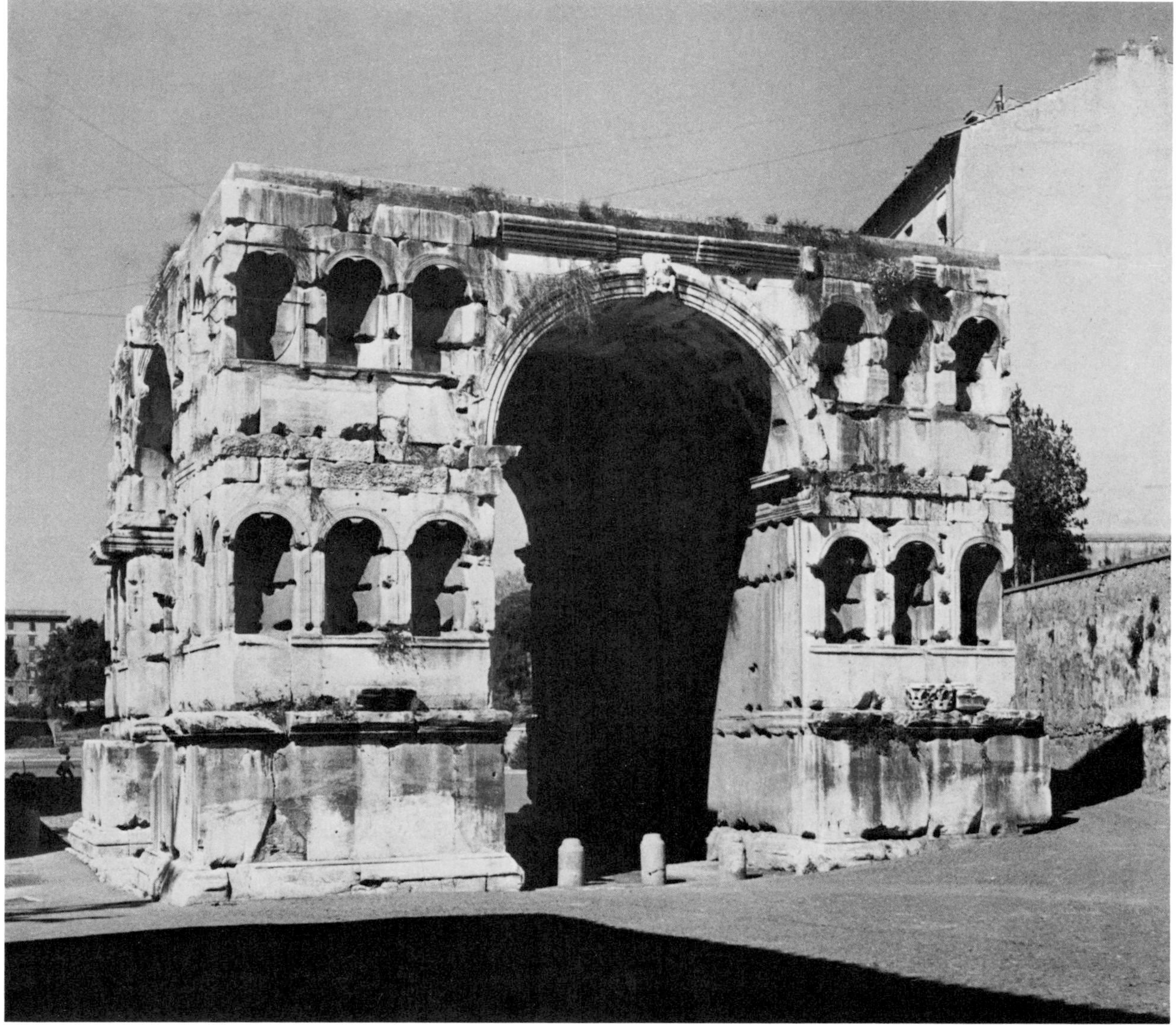

26. Janus Quadrifrons

proclaims Constantine as having won the empire by the guidance of the Godhead, *instinctu divinitatis*.

The intentional vagueness of the inscription reflects the uneasy interplay of the political, social, and religious forces in Constantine's Rome. It was evidently designed to show due deference to the Christian leanings of the emperor and to the new factor within the body politic, the Church and the large Christian congregation in Rome, and at the same time to save the conscience of the pagan element. The great Roman families that dominated the Senate were after all overwhelmingly pagan. They prevailed in the municipal administration and were prominent in the civil service. They were the defenders of the Roman tradition, of the city's glorious past, of her culture, of her old gods. If the emperor adhered to the new Christian God, that was his private affair. It was bad enough that he promoted the Church, that he gave preference to Christians at court. In Rome and beyond, as far as it was in their power, the old families in the Senate were going to place a limit on the spread of the new religion. This is the situation reflected in Constantine's church-building policy

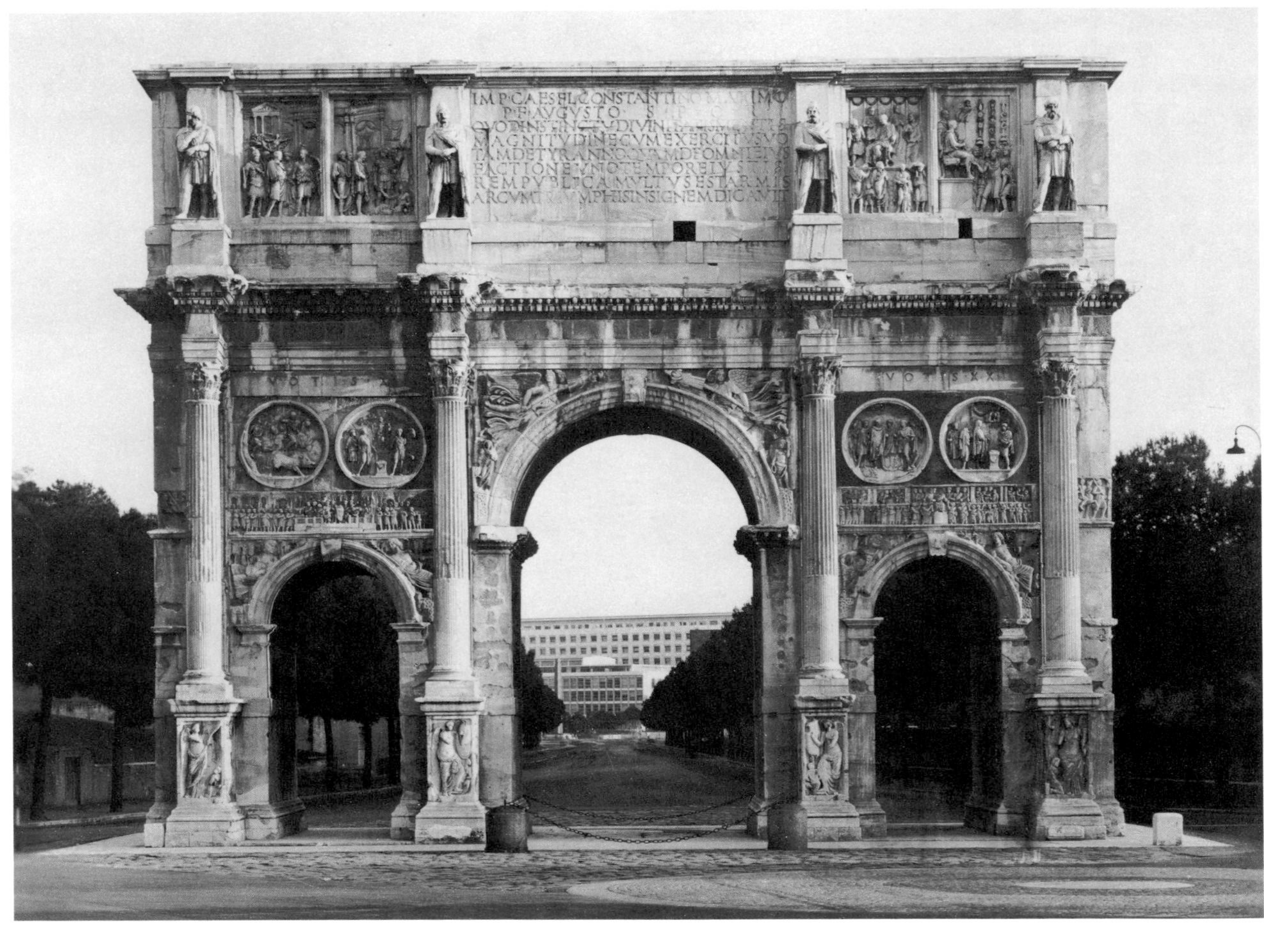

27. Arch of Constantine, from southwest

and in the limitations set upon his program of visibly Christianizing Rome. Just as the Senate appears to have respected the emperor's religious preferences, though without making any real concessions, so Constantine seems to have been intent on sparing pagan feelings while promoting the new faith. With that double aim in mind, he made the churches founded in Rome as large and splendid as possible, lavishly furnished and richly endowed so as to present a new image of Christianity. However, all the shimmering brilliance of marble revetment and marble floors, gilded vaults, lighting fixtures, and altar vessels were reserved for the eyes of the faithful and sympathizers assembled inside—the congregation, the leaders of the Church, the Christian members of the imperial family. Seen from outside, these churches were remarkably plain. Moreover, all were built on imperial estates on the edge of the city in the greenbelt, far from the populated quarters whence the bulk of the congregation would come. Clearly there were practical reasons for choosing such sites: it was imperial land; space was available; and building was less costly than it would have been in the residential quarters. But political expediency counted as well. Close to the city walls and hidden among other palace buildings, the new churches were hardly visible to Rome's casual visitor. They might more easily have noted the covered cemeteries rising on imperial estates in the countryside around the city: that of SS. Marcellino e Pietro on the estate of Helena on the Via Labicana; that of S. Lorenzo, rising in the villa formerly of Lucius Verus, the Verano; that on the estate of Constantina on the Nomentana, where the martyr Agnes rested; that in Nero's Gardens across the Tiber, where Saint

Peter was venerated. Though intended to glorify the faith by their monumental design, all were private donations of Their Majesties, built on private imperial initiative: obviously open to public worship, yet not public buildings of the same standing as a curia, a basilica on the Forum, or a temple of the old gods. In founding them, the emperor acted not so much as head of state, but as an individual of large means, a powerful Friend of the Church. The sites within and around Rome where his church buildings rose were outside the jurisdiction of the civil service, the Senate, and the municipal administration under the control of the senatorial families.

The ambiguous character of Constantine's church buildings in and around Rome is unmistakable. Large, magnificent, and rich, they were claimed to be public buildings, but they were relegated to the edge of the city and they rose on private imperial property. Constantine kept Christianity away from the center of the city, away from the *pomerium*, the legal pagan religious boundary within which were crowded the temples of the old gods and the administrative buildings, both largely maintained by the old aristocracy. There he placed only his civic buildings: the Basilica Nova on the Forum; the triumphal arch at the Colosseum; the Janus Quadrifrons on the cattle market; the baths on the Quirinal. The ambiguity of his building program was determined by the ambiguity of his political aims and the limitations forced on him by the reality of politics in Rome. He shunned the latent conflict with pagan forces, still powerful in Rome, if anywhere. Only once had he disregarded this rule. During the first year of his reign, possibly in the winter of 312–13, he had conspicuously set up in the center of Rome, presumably in the Basilica Nova, his statue carrying the *labarum*, the ensign marked by the X-cross. The challenge was understood as such by his Christian biographer, Eusebius, even a quarter of a century later. Is it too much to suspect that it was equally understood and resented by the pagan contemporaries at the time of the event, and that their reaction taught Constantine caution, as reflected in the location of his church buildings?

When entering Rome in 312, Constantine very possibly thought of turning the city into the Christian capital of a Christian Empire. As time went on, the empire under his guidance became, indeed, more and more Christian. Yet, led by the senatorial aristocracy, Rome resisted. The grand church buildings, Constantine's monuments to the new faith, never reached the core of the city. To the man who had set out to make his dominions Christian, this must have meant failure. An open break with the Senate in 326 caused him never to return to Rome. He went in search of a new capital, and in 330 he set it up in the East: Constantinople. The reasons for the transfer were many—political, strategic, administrative. But alongside such practical considerations, there remains the fact that Rome had failed him. Notwithstanding all his efforts, she had remained essentially pagan. The New Rome on the Bosphorus became what Old Rome was not yet ready to be—a Christian capital of a Christian Empire.

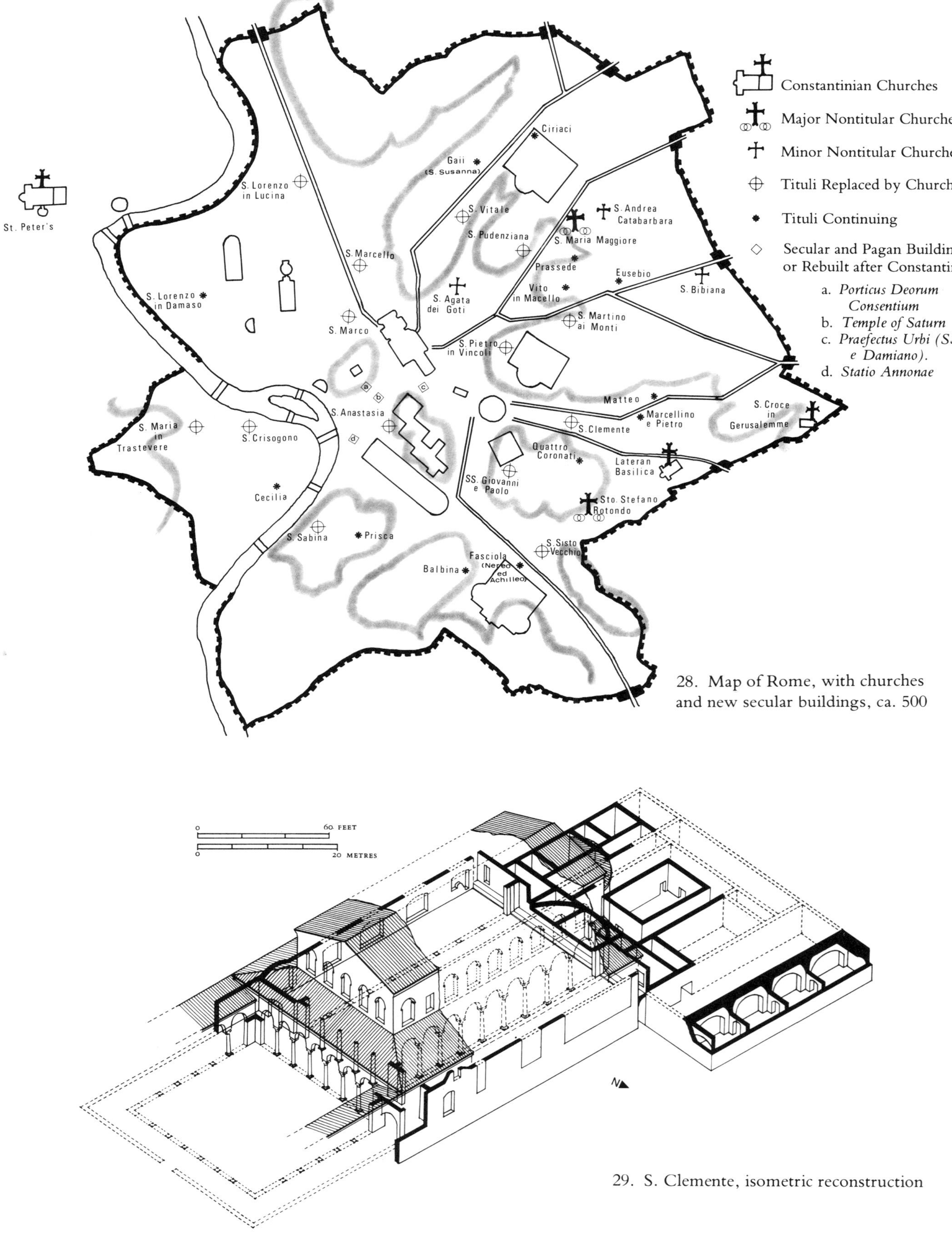

28. Map of Rome, with churches and new secular buildings, ca. 500

29. S. Clemente, isometric reconstruction

CHAPTER TWO

The Christianization of Rome and the Romanization of Christianity

Constantine's departure left Rome in a power vacuum: she was no longer an active capital. The administrative focus of the empire was at the emperor's headquarters, which was quickly stabilized at Constantinople. No emperor ever returned to Rome to take up permanent residence there, but fragments of the administration remained and Rome continued to cling to her claim of being the legitimate capital of the empire and the center of civilized mankind. Equally ambiguous was the Christian identity of Rome. Constantine had failed to turn her from a pagan city into the Christian capital of a Christian Empire. That role was given to Constantinople, the New Rome and the new imperial residence. Inevitably, the transfer damaged the prestige of the Roman-Christian community. To the end of the century, Rome remained a stronghold of paganism, supported by a powerful group of local aristocrats. The Church, though backed by the imperial court and by the urban masses inside the city, had a hard time asserting her position. The struggle, at times bitter, ended early in the fifth century with the triumph of the Church, no longer contested. Only from then on does the map of Rome increasingly reflect the city's Christian character, and this remains so until 1870.

Constantine's church buildings had been confined to sites mostly on imperial estates and always on the edge of the city or outside the walls. Starting in the last year of his life and continuing through the following hundred years, the Church made her presence known by setting up on her own initiative large, monumental places of worship in the residential quarters and often close to the center of Rome, with its temples and public civic structures (fig. 28).

The inconspicuous community centers, the tituli of old, by no means disappeared. Many survived for another five hundred years; some may even have been established in the course of the fourth century. But quite a few were replaced during these same years by lavish new churches. Since they occupied sites long in the hands of the congregations, they were obviously the congregations' property—parish property, as it were; and their construction was financed from the private means of wealthy donors, whether laymen or clergy, among the parishes' membership, or by the bishops of Rome, the popes. Financing the construction of a church may well have been considered an obligation of bishops or presbyters attendant upon the occupation of office, as traditional in the Roman high civil service; an obligation in which wealthy parishioners may have assisted popes and clergy financially less favored. Toward 410, the senator Pammachius, a friend of Saint Jerome and Paulinus of Nola, provided funds for replacing two apartment houses of perhaps an old titulus by a large basilica, SS. Giovanni e Paolo; the house façades, three stories high, were incorporated in the walls of the new church. At the same time, the widow Vestina left a bequest to build the church of S. Vitale. Pope Mark (336) built the first church of S. Marco, incorporating parts of a mansion possibly belonging to his family. His successor, Julius I (337-352) laid out a church on the site of S. Maria in Trastevere. Pope Damasus I (366-384), or perhaps his father—himself a wealthy church dignitary—turned their family mansion into a titulus. Whether the mansion, on the site of the Palazzo della Cancelleria, was only remodeled or replaced by a church of standard type remains in doubt. Nor is it certain whether the new foundation, be it mansion or new church, included among its dependencies the archives of the Roman Church, as an inscription seemed to suggest. In the last decade of the fourth century, the presbyter Leopardus apparently financed the remodeling and decoration of S. Pudenziana, as well as the redecoration of the covered cemetery of S. Lorenzo fuori le mura, first built by Constantine. Between 420 and 430, a priest from Dalmatia named Peter provided the funds for building S. Sabina on the Aventine. But in these last-named buildings, witness the dedicatory inscriptions, the ruling pontiff figures as the fictitious founder alongside the actual donor: it is even possible that he exercised some supervision through a building committee. By the second third of the fifth century, in any event, church building in Rome became both the exclusive prerogative and the responsibility of the papacy alone.

All over, these new churches penetrated toward the interior of the city—patrician suburbs, middle-class quarters, the great show area. Already the first church of S. Marco rose but a stone's throw from the western slope of the Capitoline Hill adjoining Palazzo Venezia; its remains (and those of a sixth-century successor) survive below the pavement of today's basilica, itself a ninth-century structure, remodeled in the fifteenth and again in the eighteenth centuries. Pope Damasus' titulus of S. Lorenzo stood in the midst of the Campus Martius with its theatres and circuses; S. Anastasia, another church founded by him, replaced a shop apartment house, at the foot of the Palatine Hill with its Imperial Palaces. S. Sabina replaced a lavish mansion and a neighboring house in the patrician suburb on the Aventine. S. Pietro in Vincoli, first built around 400, took the place of an equally lavish mansion in the greenbelt on the western spur of the Esquiline. On the other hand, the church of Pope Julius, presumably buried underneath the twelfth-century basilica of S. Maria in Trastevere, rose in a densely populated residential quarter. So did S. Vitale on the popular street running east and west between the Quirinal and Viminal, the *vicus longus*, more or less on the line of Via Nazionale. The basilica of S. Clemente, on the edge of the show area and near the Colosseum and the gladiators' barracks, incorporated in the late fourth century the walls of what may have been a factory building, probably turned into a community center in the third or early fourth century; while the apse of the new basilica arched over a comfortable if small mansion, converted, perhaps shortly after A.D. 200 into a sanctuary of Mithras (fig. 29). SS. Giovanni e Paolo on the west slope of the Celian Hill occupies the site and absorbs the ground floor and upper floors of two apartment houses, transformed into community centers skirting a populous narrow street. Even as late as the pontificate of Sixtus III (432-440), S. Lorenzo in Lucina was built to replace an old community center in the northern Campus Martius near the mausoleum of Augustus and his obelisk.

In their majority the new structures were basilicas of a standard type characteristic of Rome: a nave, long and high, was flanked by aisles and terminated by a semicircular apse; an atrium, a courtyard enveloped by four porticoes, or a narthex, a simple porch, preceded the building; the façades either were opened in arcades as at S. Vitale (fig. 30)—at any rate prior to 420—or were pierced by doors. Inside, the nave and aisles, covered by a timber roof, were separated by arcades on columns as at S. Vitale, but rarely on piers as at S. Lorenzo in Lucina. A chancel, projecting from the apse and segregated by screens, sheltered the altar and the space reserved for the clergy; it was reached over a covered, enclosed pathway (*solea*) extending nearly the full length of the nave. The decoration of the earlier among the basilicas is unknown except for an occasional fragment of marble pavement; figural representations, mosaics, or murals, although long customary in catacombs, were apparently taboo till the late fourth century on the walls or in the apses of Roman churches. Columns, capitals, and bases, as a rule pilfered from classical buildings, were often unequal in size, material, and type. If newly made, the capitals reduced the classical forms to crude simplicity, as at S. Vitale. For the better part of the fourth century, elegance was not the principal preoccupation of the Roman congregations and their leaders. However, the new basilicas differed fundamentally from any older or, indeed, contemporary community center. Whether tenements or mansions, these centers were meant to be inconspicuous, to disappear among the buildings of the neighborhood. On the con-

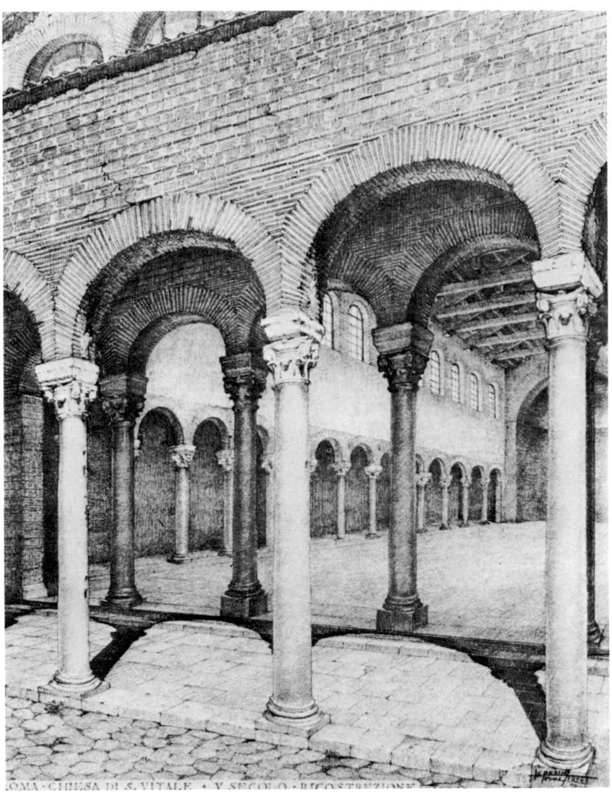

30. S. Vitale, reconstruction of narthex and interior

trary, the new basilicas loudly proclaimed the new standing of the Established Church. They claimed the status of monumental public architecture, of government buildings and palatial reception halls. They were large; they were conspicuous, and they rose high above their surroundings (fig. 31). By the fifth century, the skyline of Rome must have been thoroughly altered by the new Christian structures: structures that were meant to compete with palaces and public buildings and the temples of the gods, from the greenbelt into the very center of the city.

Nonetheless, to the very end of the fourth century, Christian building activity by no means held a monopoly in Rome. Large numbers of non-Christian monuments were repaired, remodeled, newly built, or redecorated: public buildings, great mansions, fora, streets, aqueducts, even temples and sanctuaries. On the Esquiline, the *macellum Liviae*, a market of first-century date enclosed by shops and porticoes, was restored in 367 and again in 378; it stood near the present Piazza Vittorio Emmanuele, where market is held to this day. Near the Tiber bank on what is now Piazza Bocca della Verità, an arcaded and colonnaded loggia has survived, incorporated in the forepart of S. Maria in Cosmedin; built in about A.D. 400, it was presumably the *statio annonae*, where the official in charge of provisioning sat in state. Pagan shrines, likewise, were rebuilt and restored. The pagan element's strength in the senatorial circles of Rome apparently thwarted the imperial policy of suppressing pagan worship and temples in the old capital. The Roman Forum in particular seems to have remained a pagan preserve. Between 337 and 341, a row of statues was set up along the Via Sacra, including pagan divinities. Below the cliff of the Capitoline Hill stands the *porticus deorum consentium*, an elegant little structure sacred to the twelve deities protecting Rome and rebuilt by the city prefect in 367. Nearby, in the Temple of Saturn, around A.D. 400, the powerful columns were reset and provided with Ionic capitals of a crude design, yet of a type unused in Rome for three hundred years (fig. 32). At the opposite end of the Forum, at the foot of the Via Sacra, the Temple of Vesta was restored as late as 394. The great private mansions likewise clung to classical and often pagan traditions. After 331, still in Constantine's reign, a large hall with a single nave and an apse was erected on the Esquiline (fig. 33). Transformed into the church of S. Andrea in Catabarbara, this Basilica of Junius Bassus survived into the seventeenth century; drawings and a few surviving fragments testify to its splendid wall decoration of marble inlay, wholly pagan in character. Similar reception halls of fourth-century date survive elsewhere in Rome though deprived of their decoration: in the church of S. Balbina; in the core of S. Susanna, a hall provided with aisles and galleries; in the Quattro Coronati, where the apse has been incorporated into the present church. A number of similar rich mansions of late-fourth-century date at Ostia likewise attest to the pagan character of their owners, as witness the subjects represented in their wall and pavement decoration.

Indeed, through the fourth century, Rome remained to visitors, unless they came to pray at

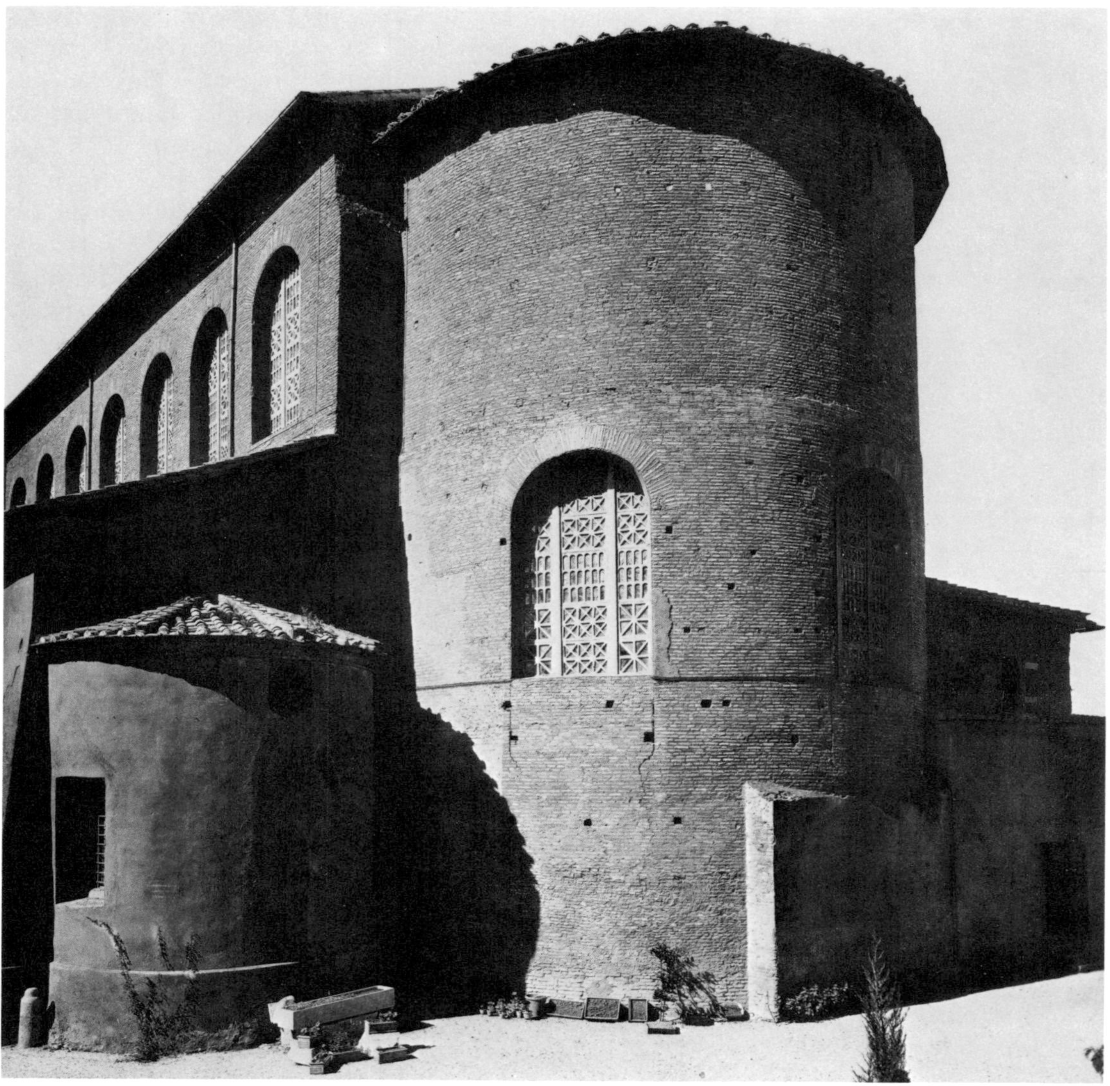

31. S. Sabina, exterior from north

the Christian sanctuaries, an essentially classical, secular, and pagan city. The guided tour given to the Emperor Constantius II in 357 included the Roman Forum, "dazzling by the array of marvels"; the Capitol and the Temple of Jupiter; the Colosseum; the Pantheon, "like a circular city quarter"; the triumphal columns of Trajan and Marcus Aurelius; the Temple of Venus and Roma; Vespasian's Forum Pacis, still crowded in the sixth century with precious statues; the Theatre of Pompey and the Stadium of Domitian; the great circus where he presided over the games and set up the obelisk shipped from Egypt by his father. On the Forum of Trajan, the climax, in front of Trajan's equestrian statue, he was told by a Persian prince in his suite to build "a stable that grand if he, too, wanted that grand a horse."

To be sure, through the fourth century imperial decrees aimed progressively at suppressing pagan cults and sanctuaries: public pagan worship was prohibited in 346; ten years later, the temples were closed; their revenues were confiscated in 364; finally, in 408 a decree provided that all temples were to be put to new, presumably secular use. At the same time, these very decrees and others, ever repeated, enjoined the authorities to protect the temples as public

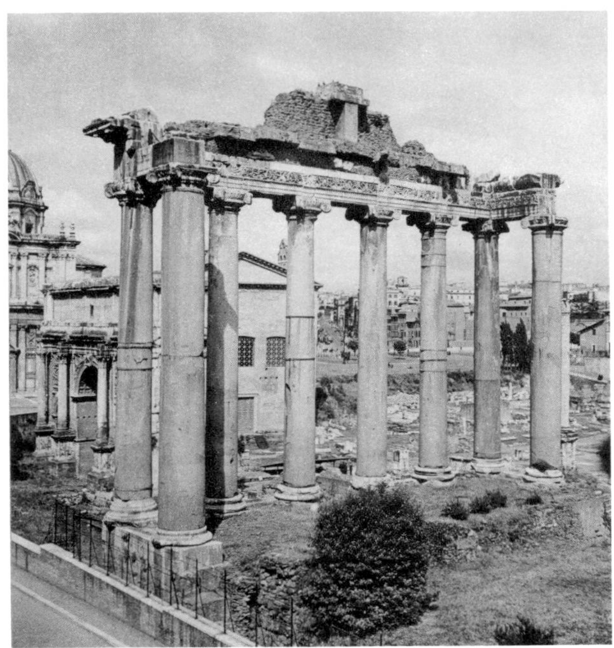

32. Temple of Saturn

monuments and—this the decisive point—as fiscal property. Paganism had been eliminated; but its monuments remained as witnesses of a great past, ever-present testimonies to the might of the city and the empire she once ruled. Even around A.D. 500, Cassiodorus, Roman chancellor of the king of the Goths, Theodoric, admired in awe the Theatre of Pompey with its "caves vaulted with hanging stones, so cleverly joined into beautiful shapes that they resemble more the grottoes of a huge mountain than anything wrought by human hand"; the aqueducts; the sewers as well—for, "what other city can equal Rome above ground, since even her structures below ground are so incomparable"; the "huge crowd of statues, that mighty herd of horses that adorn our city." Some thirty years later, while Rome was besieged by the Goths, Procopius still saw her filled with statues: the shrine of Janus and his bronze statue, seven-and-a-half-feet high, on the Forum Romanum; on the Forum of Vespasian a fountain and a bronze bull, attributed by the connoisseurs of the time—there still were some—to either Phidias or Lysippus; nearby, a bronze calf wrought by Myron and another statue given by an inscription to Phidias. There were more; for, to use his own words, "in that quarter," meaning the Roman Forum and the Fora of the Emperors adjoining it, he saw "many statues attributed to Phidias or Lysippus." The names matter little; but clearly the show center of ancient Rome had yet many statues; the equestrian statue of Constantine may have risen on the Roman Forum as late as the eighth century. Greek that he was, Procopius attributed this wealth of artworks in Rome to the systematic looting of Greece by the Roman victors. But he also admired an artifact that was clearly Roman—a canoe wrought of a single tree trunk, supposedly the boat of Aeneas, kept in a kind of museum on the bank of the Tiber; and while he stressed the care taken by Roman citizens to conserve "the buildings of the city and most of its adornments such as

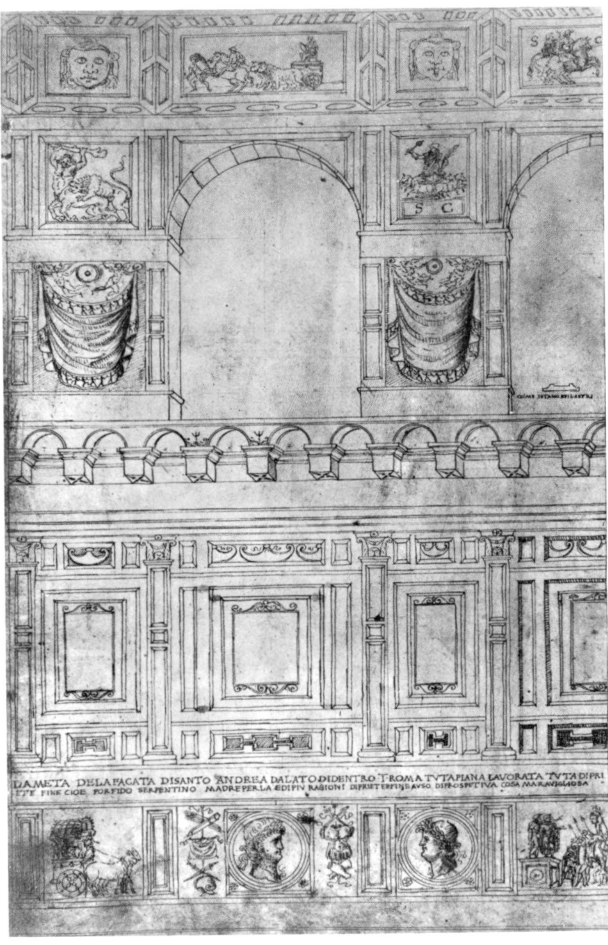

33. Basilica of Junius Bassus, revetment, Giuliano da Sangallo, Barb. lat. 4424, fol. 33v

could through the excellence of their workmanship withstand so long a lapse of time and such neglect," he noted, too, their bad state of preservation.

Visitors, then, such as Procopius, and Romans who cared were well aware of the decay of the city and her monuments. They were ever conscious of seeing but a shadow of the glory that was Rome. Their writings breathe nostalgia—a nostalgia that goes back as a literary *topos* to the fourth century and further. But the image of Rome's greatness persisted. The temples, theatres, and circuses, the thermae, the hundreds of statues in bronze and marble, crumbling or not, testify to that greatness. More powerful than reality, the nostalgic concept of Rome's glory and grandeur remained alive. But, irrational as men are in their outlook on the past and the present, such romantic longing for a greatness lost forever did not interfere with the conviction among the educated and the common people alike that Rome remained the hub of the civilized world and the queen of cities. She was still, as she had been called for centuries, the "one fatherland of divers peoples," the *communis patria* of Cassiodorus, the common homestead of mankind. Visitors came to see, and natives looked for, the grand image, and because they sought it, they found it, embodied in the monuments.

The pagan connotations, inextricably interwoven with ancient Rome, played, it seems, no part in the thinking of a Cassiodorus or a Procopius. To them, paganism no longer represented a danger. The world in which they lived had become Christian. Not so in the late fourth century, when Rome was being Christianized. Then, a dilemma was deeply felt by educated men all over the ancient world in the face of Christianity's triumphant progress. Christian or not, their common aim was to preserve as much as possible of the classical legacy that had shaped their language, culture, and thinking. In the cities and provinces of the East, as at the imperial court, whether in Constantinople or at Milan, among laymen and clergy alike, this aim seemed entirely compatible with the Christian faith. On the contrary, in fourth-century Rome the classical tradition was more often than not bound up with strong pagan convictions. Certainly, by the last third of that century pagans were vastly outnumbered by the Christian masses, in Rome as well as all over the empire: Christians, too, were preponderant in the civil service and at the imperial court. But among the Roman families that held the reins of power in the Senate and in administrative offices, paganism remained strong: an enlightened paganism, drawn from gnostic, neoplatonic, and neopythagorean philosophies and from oriental mystery cults. The worship of the Roman gods was an integral component of a pagan citizen's duties, on national if not on religious grounds: their cult would guarantee the continued greatness of the Empire and of its only legitimate capital, Rome; Christianity, in contrast, would undermine it. Political factors, too, entered into the pagan resistance movement in Rome: resentment of the emperors who had betrayed Old Rome both by their conversion and by their removal to Constantinople; hostility against the ever-increasing number of Christians at court and in the services, formerly the preserve of the great Roman pagan families; and an aversion to

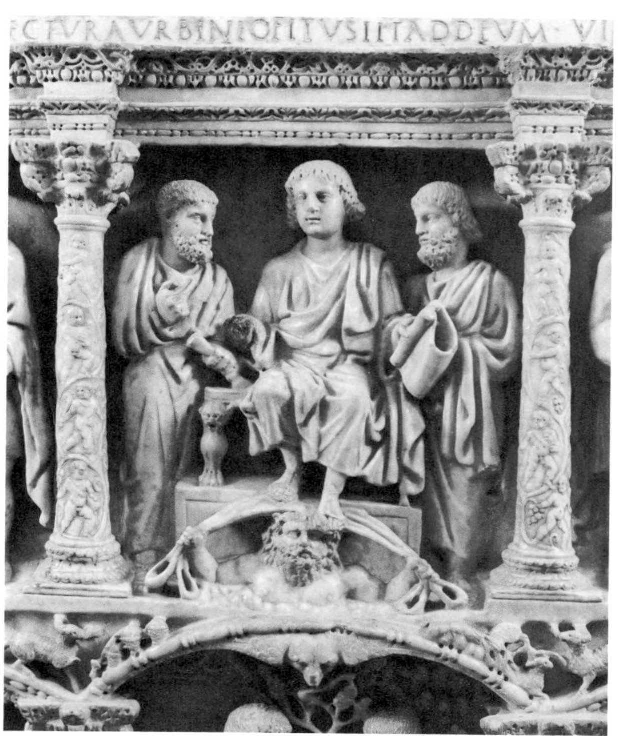

34. Sarcophagus of Junius Bassus, detail, Traditio legis

the culture bound to Christianity. In their aristocratic and tradition-bound eyes the only culture worth its name was the classical Golden Age of antiquity. Hence the works of art they commissioned for themselves strove to revive the art, dead these four hundred years, of Augustan times. The ivory diptych produced around 380 for the Nicomachi and Symmachi, two leading Roman families of the pagan resistance, is prominent as an example of the subtle elegance of the ultimate classical revival. To their circle the new Christian mass culture was bound to appear low-brow in thought, language, and art; and plebeian in origin, as indeed it was. After all, indifference to the classical traditions of antiquity had been inherent in the Church ever since its beginnings; and though this attitude disappeared in the eastern provinces of the Empire, as from the third century members of the intelligentsia replaced the simpler and more fanatical leaders of earlier times, it remained strong in the West. In Rome, till after the middle of the fourth century, clergy and congregations appear to have largely remained indifferent to classical thought, language, and art—aclassical, if not anticlassical. The great pagan families must have been shocked by the crude sarcophagi and gold glasses produced for Christians in fourth-century Rome. They must have been equally shocked by and contemptuous of the great mass of Christian building as they saw it sprouting all over the city: simple in plan, disregarding the classical orders, and filled with columns, capitals, and entablatures, all pilfered from other buildings, and hence often heterogeneous. This is the context in which to view pagan public and private art in these later years, striving to preserve in sacred Rome a classical, national, and pagan note.

Paganism in Rome was finally suppressed in 395. The last pagans from the great Roman families were forced to convert; some probably remained cryptopagans. At the same time, however, from the last third of the century an essential element had changed in the struggle between Christianity and paganism. As Rome turned ever more Christian, the Church turned Roman. It took an affirmative stand regarding the Roman past and the classical tradition, bound though both were to pagan elements. The reasons for the change are many. For one, the Church had become rich: its economic interests were now wed to those of the great land-holding families. In the course of the fourth century, Roman patricians, turned Christian, formed a Christian civil service aristocracy and carried with them the classical heritage that was theirs. The sarcophagus of the younger Junius Bassus (fig. 34)—his father had built the pagan basilica on the Esquiline, but the son, after a term as city prefect, died a Christian in 359—is as sophisticated and classical in design as that of any of his pagan fellow-aristocrats; and his is but one of a group of sarcophagi and metalwork produced in Rome during the last third of the fourth century for upper-class Christians. The same artists worked for pagan and Christian patrons; and a young Christian couple felt no qualms about accepting as a wedding present a silver toilet set decorated in a classical style with pagan divinities—symbols to them void of religious meaning, it seems: witness the Projecta treasure found on the Esquiline, now in the British Museum and dated between 379 and 382 (fig. 35). However, the taste of a small group of patricians changed but little the conservatism of the Christian middle class where crude, aclassical sarcophagi were still being produced. And altogether it would have had little effect, had not the hierarchy of the Church itself, all over the West and in Rome, been penetrated at the same time by educated patricians and by intellectuals linked to their circles: high civil servants, such as Ambrose, turned bishop of Milan and the most powerful political figure of his time; writers, such as Jerome, for twenty years a fashionable spiritual director of well-born Christian ladies in Rome until his retirement to the Holy Land in 385, where he ended his days in 419 at Bethlehem as a hermit of sorts, surrounded by a pious community, male and female; professors of rhetoric, such as Augustine, converted after a deep spiritual crisis, bishop of Hippo in Africa, and the greatest luminary of Early Christian theology; Paulinus, a patrician of immense wealth from Gaul, later bishop of Nola near Naples. In Rome, the new trend in church leadership is best represented by Damasus, elected

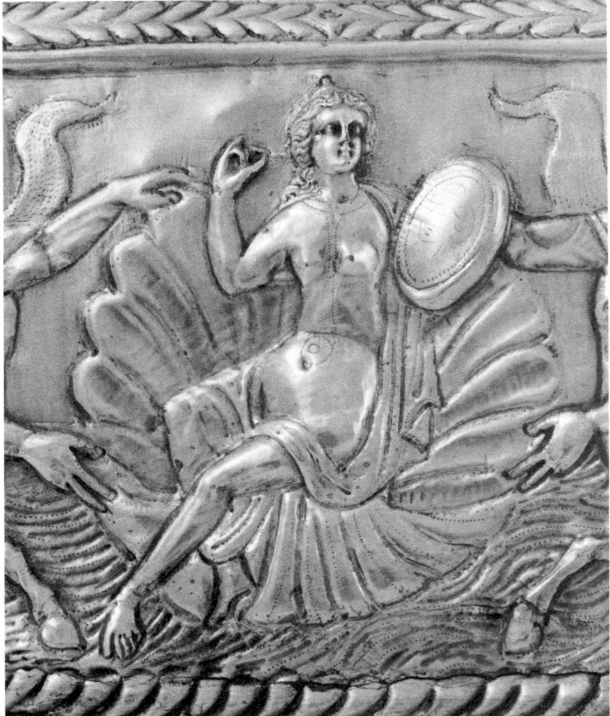

35. Casket from the Bridal Treasure of Projecta, detail, Venus, London, British Museum

Pope in 366 against bloody opposition: son of a high church dignitary; wealthy, ambitious, and eager for the good life; skillful at gaining the ear and the purse strings of rich ladies—malicious tongues called him the earspoon of matrons; a good politician and a Roman nationalist. To defend the standing of Rome and her Church against the claims of the East, supported by the emperors, became the principal aim of his policy. Time and again he stressed the primacy of the Apostolic See of Rome. Far less profound than his great contemporaries, he aimed at wedding the Church to the classical past. Starting with his pontificate, a circle of patrician clerics dominated the Church of Rome, a senate, as Jerome called them, supported by the lay leaders of the great Christian families. From their midst they elected popes—popes who were diplomats and jurists, often the sons of church dignitaries, nearly always Roman born, and always Roman in training. The works of Cicero, Plato, Horace, Virgil, and Ulpian were part and parcel of the thinking and speech of such Christian leaders. To them a world without the classics was as unthinkable as one without Shakespeare would be to the English-speaking cultures; and Eternal Rome, where they had been trained, was still the center of this world.

This created a conflict. The classical past and paganism were, after all, inextricably linked. By absorbing the former, was one not then in danger of falling in with the latter? Jerome, in the 380s was quite sure of it; in a dream, he saw himself condemned to Hell for being a Ciceronian rather than a Christian. "What has Horace to do with the Psalter, Virgil with the Gospels, Cicero with Paul?" he says, echoing the words of Tertullian three hundred years earlier—"What is Athens against Jerusalem?" His escape from the dilemma was to withdraw to the desert of Judaea and, in his later years, to cultivate a new popular Latin, a powerful plain language understandable to all, the *sermo humilis*, which pervades his revision of the Latin Bible, the Vulgate.

But Jerome's was not everybody's way. Ambrose and Augustine accepted the classical heritage without feeling their souls imperiled. Rome, too, even before Damasus' pontificate, had moved toward infusing the art of the Church with a classical, and specifically a Roman, note. In a calendar written as early as 354 and surviving in a sixteenth-century copy, a Roman scribe, Philocalus, had created a neoclassical script, trying to revive in a new version the lettering of Augustus' time; such was the script employed through the last third of the century in the many inscriptions that Damasus placed at the graves of martyrs. Early in the fifth century the new classical current came to the fore in the realm of church decoration; in about 390 a large thermae hall was turned into the church of S. Pudenziana and was redecorated in the subsequent fifteen years. Its apse vault, rather than being sheathed with unadorned gold ground as was that of Constantine's Lateran Basilica, was filled with the earliest figural representation to survive in, and presumably one of the first to be designed for, a Roman church: (fig. 36) Christ sits enthroned, clad in shimmering gold; he is flanked by the Apostles wearing the toga of Roman senators; two female figures stand for the Church of the Jews and that of the Heathen, the

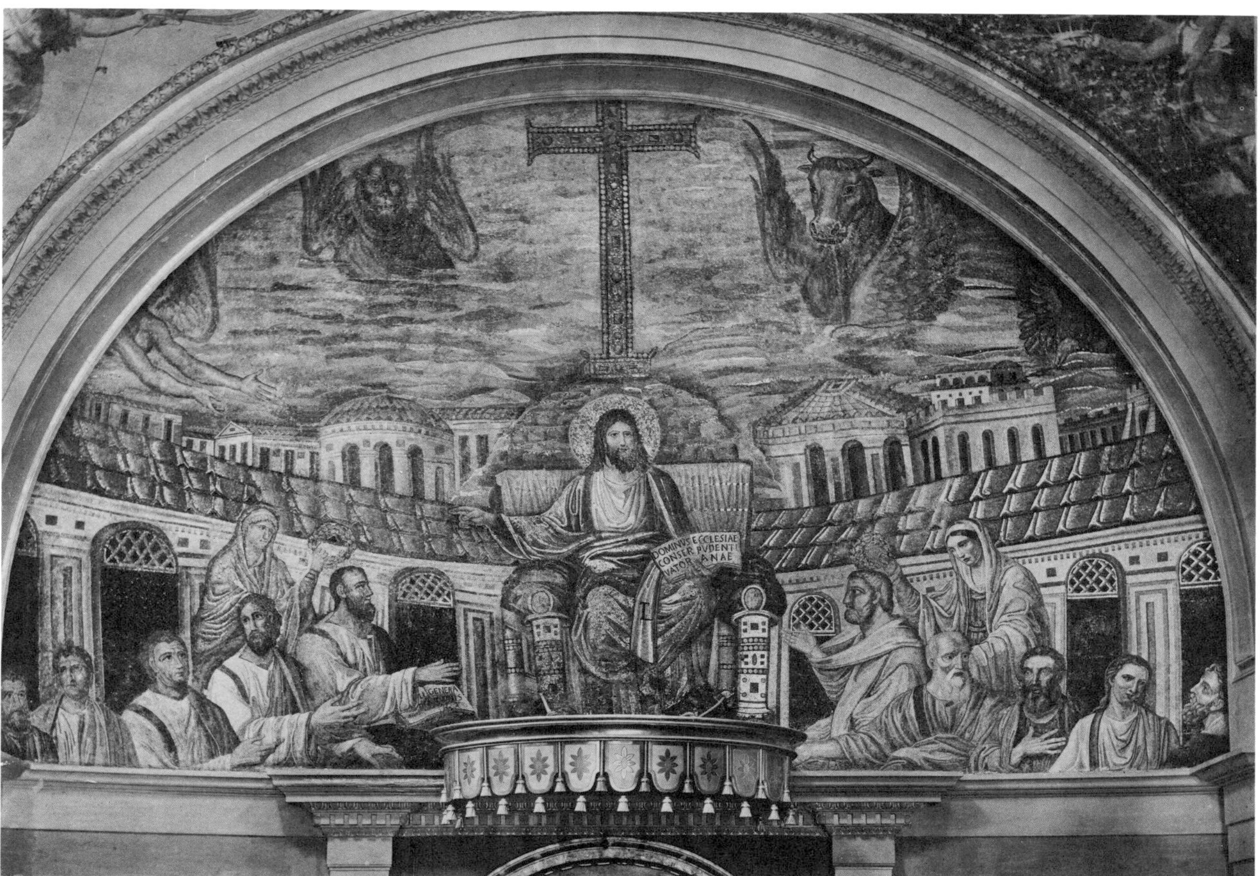

36. S. Pudenziana, apse mosaic

ecclesia ex circumcisione and the *ecclesia ex gentibus*, the former befittingly behind Saint Peter, the latter behind Saint Paul, teacher of the Heathen, the *doctor gentium*; a huge architectural backdrop, palatial in character, closes the scene; and the symbols of the Evangelists, man, lion, ox, and eagle, float in the sky on either side of a jeweled cross. Although overly restored, faces, bodies, gestures, and space, fully credible and converted to Christian use, aim to evoke the art of Rome at its most classical, monumental, and conservative.

Indeed, since the pontificate of Damasus, the Church in Rome had striven to play down its foreign Eastern roots and to present herself as Roman in origin and spirit. As late as the third century, after all, her official language and her leadership had been Greek rather than Latin and Roman; and this, her alien past, was to be cancelled. The poems composed by Damasus work this very theme time and again; Saint Hermes, so he says, was sent to Rome from Greece, and by shedding his blood in Rome for the faith, he became a Roman citizen; Saint Saturninus from Carthage through his martyrdom had become a Roman; Peter and Paul, coming from the East, were, through their deaths for Christ in Rome, now Roman citizens by right. The martyrs whose graves encircle Rome replaced the heroes of pagan antiquity as her patrons Peter and Paul, the Princes of the Apostles, replaced Romulus and Remus as the new founders of the city, a Christian Rome; and their double portraits appeared on gold glasses, like those of the emperors, the two *augusti* on coins; the concord of the Apostles replaced that of the emperors. Through it they guaranteed the rebirth of Rome, the *renovatio urbis*. The idea of Rome's rebirth as the head of the civilized world, the *caput orbis*, had been reflected in the legends of coins since Augustan times. In the later fourth century it became a key term in pagan circles, aimed at a rebirth of the world wrought by revitalizing the glorious past of Rome. At the same time, however, and with a different meaning, it was taken up by the Roman Church. Constantine's theologians had already viewed the Roman Empire as being renewed by him in the name of Christ as a kingdom of God on earth. Toward the end of the century, Ambrose saw the Christian Empire as the fulfilment of Augustus' Pax Romana. At the same time, the hymns of Prudentius reflect the concept of a *renovatio urbis* under the sign of Christianity: "All mankind," he says, and I paraphrase, "came under the rule of the city of Rome, to see the entire world linked by a common bond in the name of Christ. Grant then, Christ, to your Romans a Christian city, a capital Christian like the rest of the world. Peter and Paul shall drive out Jupiter." Rome, Christianized and hallowed through the blood and graves of Peter and Paul and other martyrs, was to renew the world in the name of Christ.

Within this context the most important and conspicuous church building of the late fourth century in Rome finds its place: the basilica of S. Paolo fuori le mura, on the road to Ostia about a twenty-minute walk beyond the city walls. Until 384—notwithstanding the contrary account of a rich Constantinian foundation later inserted in the *Liber Pontificalis*—only a small structure sheltered what appears to be the grave of Saint Paul. The contrast with the huge basilica dedicated by Constantine to Saint Peter is striking—the more so since popular belief had long coupled the Princes of the Apostles as equals; witness their joint memorial on the Appian Way below S. Sebastiano. Even so, in the official view of the Roman Church in Constantine's time, Peter apparently far outranked Paul. This is understandable: the Roman bishop, raised to political prominence by Constantine's policy, claimed precedence in the West of the empire; and Peter, the first bishop of Rome, was the fountainhead of the apostolic succession, the rock on which the Roman Church was founded. In the later fourth century, in light of the new concepts come to the fore—possibly a revival of the popular view—Paul could no longer be relegated to second place; only two hundred years later was Saint Paul definitely moved into the background and Saint Peter again became, as he had been in Constantine's days, the leading saint in Rome and throughout the West. In the late fourth century, the concord of the Apostles predominated and it implied the equal status of Peter and Paul as the common protectors of Rome. Assigning Paul an inferior position was a view clearly untenable in a Church penetrated and led by the Christian intellectuals of the late fourth century. Paul was the philosopher, the intellectual among the Disciples, and hence the model for the new Christian intelligentsia. He was also the Teacher of the Heathen, *doctor gentium*, and thus by implication the champion in the fight against the pagans lingering among the Roman aristocracy.

Hence in 384 it appeared only natural to replace the inconspicuous Constantinian shrine with a basilica emulating St. Peter's. The initiative seems to have come from Damasus—a fitting climax to his efforts to place the Princes of the Apostles on an equal footing. Presumably on his request the ruling emperors—Valentinian II, Theodosius, and Arcadius—financed the construction. The imperial rescript authorizing the start of work reflects the complexities of the political situation in Rome. The city prefect having submitted his report on the site, Their Majesties declare their eagerness to honor the sacred shrine venerated of old with a new building capable of holding the large influx of the faithful. Consequently, the prefect is to consult the ecclesiastical and civil authorities and to obtain from the Senate and the People of Rome permission to build across a country road, thus gaining sufficient space: a respect for local susceptibilities understandable in a situation, sensitive as the last years of the century were to the tensions between the Church, supported by the emperors and the local Christian nobility on the one hand, and the remaining pagan senatorial families on the other. Despite the building's scale, construction was completed in only six or eight years; decoration may have taken a few years longer.

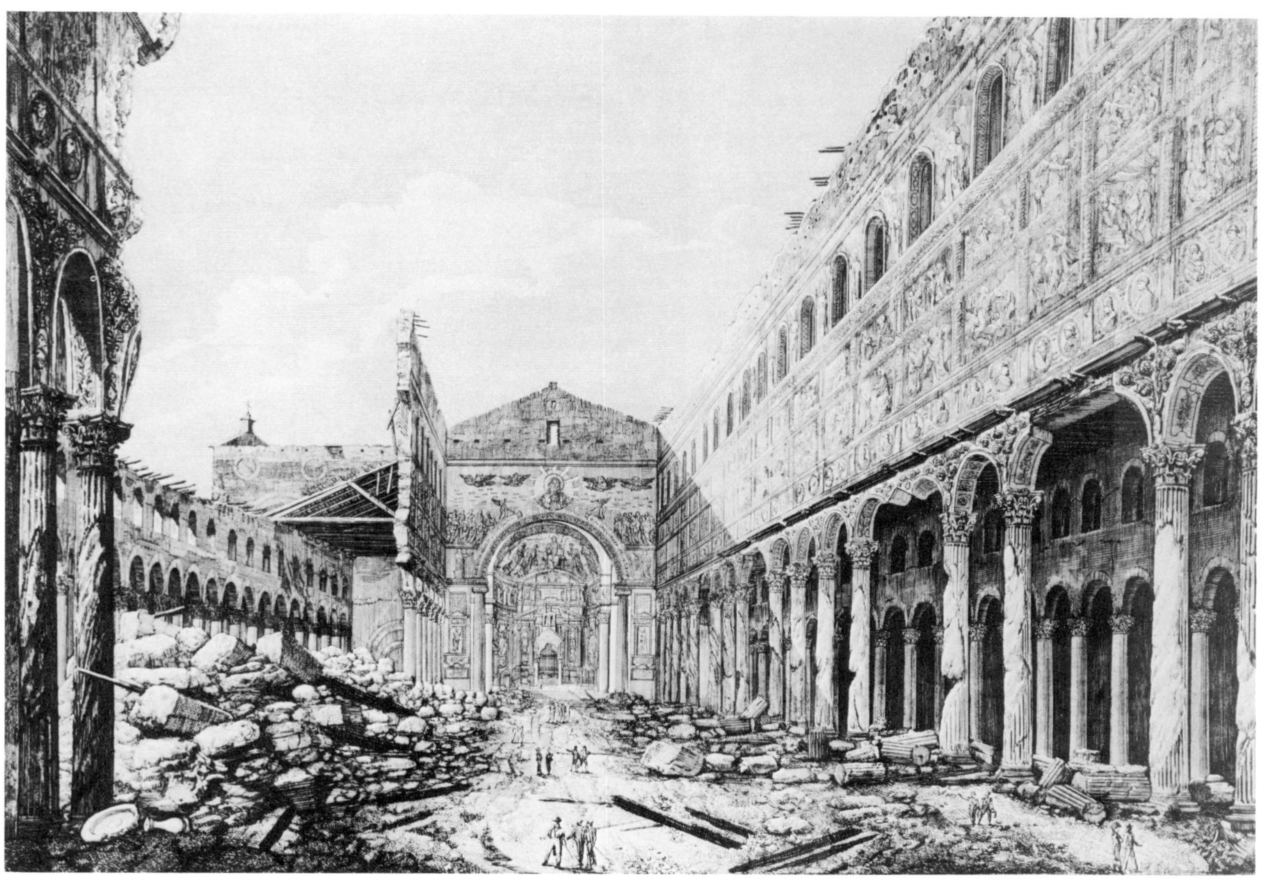

37. S. Paolo fuori le mura, interior after fire of 1823, facing transept and apse, engraving L. Rossini

In grandeur, plan, and size the new basilica was meant to compete with St. Peter's. Today's structure, of course, is a mere replacement for the church that stood until 1823, when it was destroyed by fire. But the building, as it stood then, was the late-fourth-century basilica. A second campaign, made necessary by a fire or earthquake in 441, was limited to repairs and redecoration, and thus to this day the plan, the proportions, and large parts of the fourth-century basilica walls survive. Engravings and drawings done before and after the fire in 1823 convey a fairly accurate idea of the building as it then appeared (fig. 37): a tall and wide nave suffused with light from forty-two windows—compared with twenty-two at St. Peter's; double aisles on either side; an atrium, enveloped by porticoes; an apsed transept, as at St. Peter's, but deeper and higher, to shelter the grave of the Apostle. The forty columns, rather than being pilfered at random, seem to have been carefully chosen, as were the capitals in the nave; those in the aisles were made specifically for the new church in a simplified Corinthian form. A gilded, coffered ceiling spanned the fourth-century nave; and mosaics, possibly ornamental rather than figural, covered its triumphal arch. The fifth-century repairs were marked by equal care and lavishness: to replace twenty-four columns lost in 441, splendid shafts of purplish *pavonazzetto* marble and beautiful Corinthian capitals were chosen; stucco ornament covered the arcades and spandrels; the walls of the nave were frescoed with Biblical scenes; and on the triumphal arch a mosaic showed the Four and Twenty Elders offering their wreaths to Christ.

In both the original and the fifth-century building campaign at S. Paolo fuori le mura, such stress on matching beautiful details, on lavish decoration, and on balanced proportions

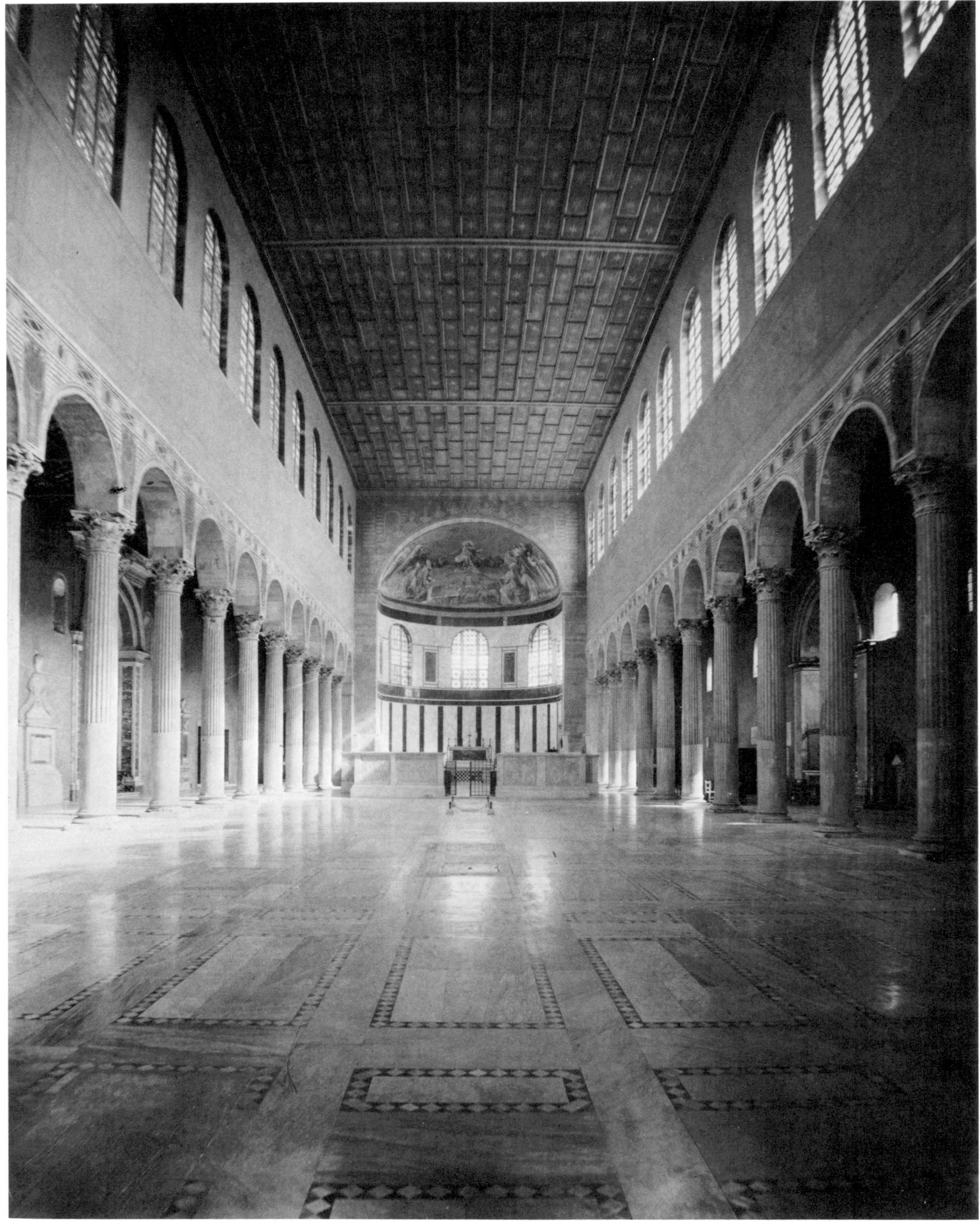

38. S. Sabina, interior

highlights a new classical emphasis in Roman church design. It reaches a climax at S. Sabina on the Aventine (fig. 38). Built around 425, though completed only after 432, that basilica remains the most graceful and splendid Early Christian church to survive in Rome. The noticeably tall nave is supported by a set of superbly carved columns and capitals, purloined from some second-century structure; the windows, extraordinarily large, admit a rich yet subdued light; marble revetment of delicate design covers the spandrels of the arcades—panels with chalices, patens, and shields, set against a ground imitating masonry. The walls from the arcades to the window zone carried mosaics, as did the apse and its arch; the latter known from old engravings bore the busts of Christ and his Apostles in roundels. Of all these mosaics, only the large panel on the inner façade survives; it bears in beautiful lettering *all'antica* the dedicatory inscription of the founder, Peter the Illyrian, flanked by the figures of the Church of the Jews and that of the Pagans—Roman matrons, dignified and solid against the gold ground (fig. 39). Design and lettering of the inscription breathe the same spirit of classical revival as the careful selection of capitals and columns and the splendid proportions of the whole structure.

This fusion into Christian building of a classical and Roman note had started in the last decade of the fourth century; but it reached its peak, strangely enough, only after a major disaster, the first to hit Rome in over a thousand years. In August 410, a raiding party of Visigoths led by Alaric broke into the city and sacked it for three days. There was no resistance. To be sure, the Aurelian Walls had been raised against just that kind of raid only seven years before, and their gates had been provided with towers; but there was no garrison to man the new fortifications. The emperor of the West, Honorius—the empire had been divided into an Eastern and a Western half since 395—sat helplessly in Ravenna, protected by the fleet; the emperor of the East was far away in Constantinople. Thus, the city was open. A number of mansions went up in flames: at the southern tip of the Aventine and around the site of S. Sabina; on the Quirinal, the palace in the Gardens of Sallustius; on the Caelian, the mansion of the Valerii, south of Sto. Stefano Rotondo. On the Forum Romanum, the Basilica Aemilia and the nearby secretarium of the Senate were damaged. Looting was widespread: even the Lateran Basilica was robbed of some of the silver furnishings donated by Constantine; some of the treasure, brought by Vespasian and Titus from Jerusalem was purportedly carried off; and, obviously, there was violence from individual looters. Yet, by and large, the damage was limited. There was no massacre and no organized arson; warning was given to the population and asylum set aside in St. Peter's and St. Paul's; the treasures of both these churches were spared; those of other churches were brought to St. Peter's; and a good deal of private treasure was apparently hidden before looting started—some, like the bridal trousseau of Projecta now in the British Museum, to be recovered only in the seventeenth and eighteenth centuries.

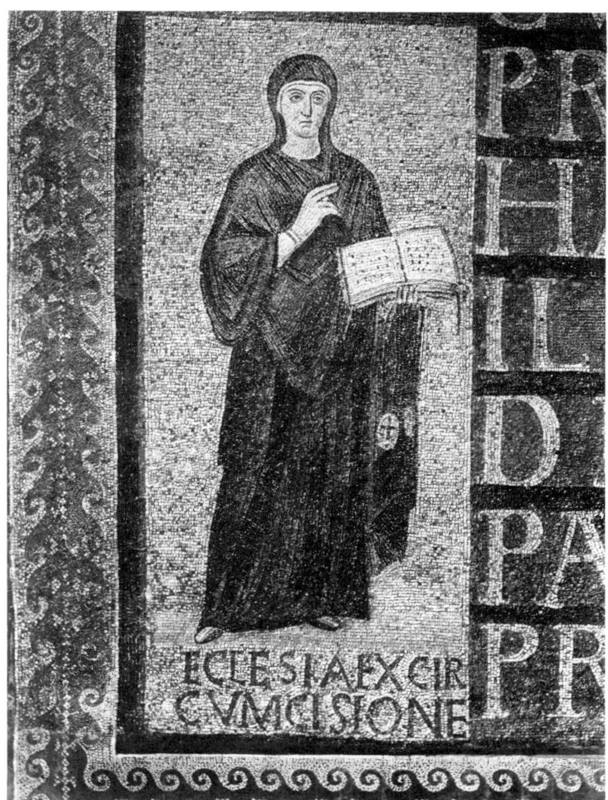

39. S. Sabina, mosaic, detail, *Ecclesia ex Circumcisione*

But the shock caused by the sack of Rome

among both Christian and pagan contemporaries was deep. For more than a thousand years Rome had been—and she still was—the head of the civilized world and its cultural capital. Now she had fallen to a horde of illiterate barbarians from the back of beyond. "It's the end of the world," wrote Jerome; "words fail me, my sobs break in; I cannot dictate. The city to which the whole world once fell, has fallen—*capta est urbs quae totum cepit orbem*"—the play on *urbs* and *orbis* is untranslatable. Pagans and Christians responded differently to the shock. Pagans and cryptopagans saw its cause in the city's and the emperors' having forsaken the old gods; and official policy, regardless of denomination, was simply to cancel the fall of Rome from memory. To Rutilius Namatianus, a high official from Gaul and still openly pagan in 416, it was but a passing setback. Rome was eternal; and Emperor Honorius, the year after the sack, was received with a panegyric worthy of victorious Trajan. This manifests a dichotomy that was to persist over the next thousand years: the city deteriorated and was prey to every enemy; but the image of Rome in all her grandeur lived on or was revived. On the contrary, to austere Christians outside the official sphere, the sack of 410 was a just punishment for the lingering remains of paganism and for their own sins. Augustine saw the remedy in turning away from all worldly government and its inherent evil; mankind was to repent and to strive toward a kingdom not of this world, the *City of God*.

The view of the greatest theologian of his time, though, could not be that of the political leaders at the head of the Church of Rome: Popes Innocent I, Celestine, Sixtus III, Leo I, the Great—the last as archdeacon possibly already responsible for the policies of Celestine and Sixtus. To them, too, old Rome and paganism were dead; but a new, Christian Rome, equally great if different, was to take over. The Church was just as wealthy, papal gifts of silver vessels to churches looted by the Goths were just as rich as before the sack; the city had quickly recovered its economic equilibrium. This Christian Rome, little shaken economically and powerful in faith if not in arms, was to maintain and strengthen her leadership in the West against the claims of the Church of Constantinople; to defend her independence against the emperors; and to evolve a policy both Christian and Roman. Paganism was no longer dangerous; the bond between pagan thought and Rome was cut, as was that between paganism and classical antiquity. But Rome was not to die. The emperor had been unable to safeguard the city. Its safety now rested with its Christian heroes, Peter and Paul, with its bishops, the successors to Saint Peter. They were the only effective power left. Rome was the papacy and the papacy was Rome. Hence, the papacy had to carry on both the political and the classical tradition of Rome, inseparable as they were. The identification of the papacy with Saint Peter and of the Church with Rome and her classical tradition, begun under Damasus, became basic elements of papal policy under Celestine and Sixtus III. A new Rome, Christian and classical, the capital of the pope as spiritual leader of the West and as Peter's successor, took the place of ancient Rome. This view of Rome and of the papacy culminates in the figure of Leo I, the Great, who occupied the Papal See from 440 to 461. "Rome has become the Head of the World through the Holy See of Saint Peter"—these are his words. The term *caput orbis*, handed down from classical antiquity, is filled with new meaning: not her arms, her laws, or her might have made Rome the hub of the world, but the see of Saint Peter, the rock of the Church and fountainhead of her rulers. Leo saw himself as the vicar of Peter; through him the Apostle spoke; he was the undisputed head of the Church in the West; her defender against encroachments of the Eastern Churches; the ruler of the West, if spiritual rather than temporal, in the old Roman tradition.

Roman church building and decoration of the fifth century needs to be seen in this context. To this day it is best represented by S. Maria Maggiore. Rising on the crest of the Esquiline, the church was begun, it seems, in the twenties and completed by Sixtus III (432-440). Though larger in scale, it was built to the plan that by then had become standard in Rome: a tall and wide nave; an aisle on either side; and a semicircular apse at the end of the nave—the transept and its polygonal apse were added in the thir-

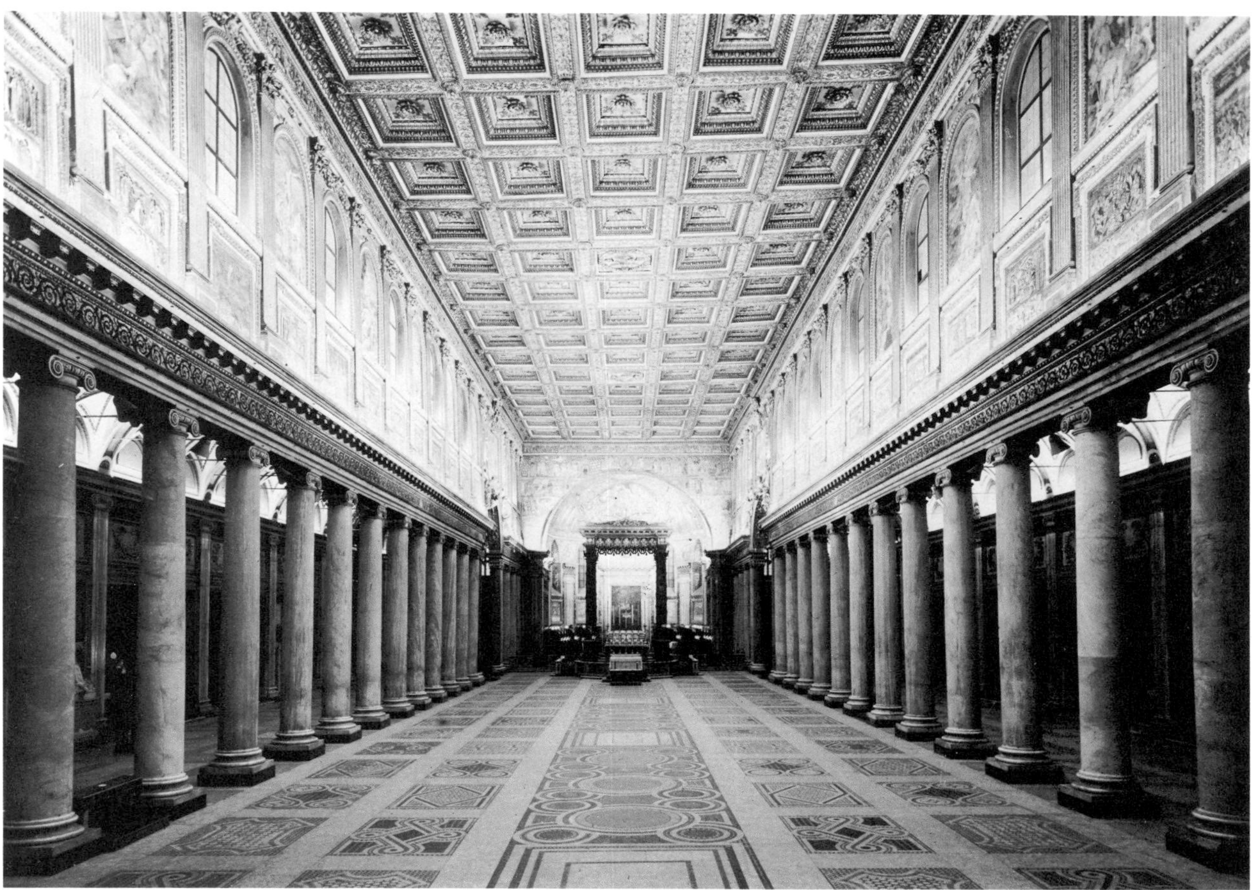

40. S. Maria Maggiore, nave

teenth century and enclosed in a baroque envelope in the seventeenth (fig. 40). But the elevation of the nave, still recognizable despite the alterations of sixteenth- and eighteenth-century date, and known from older drawings, was extraordinary. The two rows of twenty columns, well matched in size and material, were from the outset crowned by Ionic capitals, a type rare in Rome since the second century. They carry the entablature of a classical order, as customary in antiquity, but used before in Roman church building only in Constantine's churches: at the Lateran, at St. Peter's, and in the covered cemetery near S. Lorenzo. Afterwards the type had disappeared from Rome; but it did survive—and that is significant—in the imperial city of Constantinople. At S. Maria Maggiore, moreover, the upper walls of the nave are articulated by a classical order of tall pilasters, terminated originally by an equally classical stucco tendril frieze. The pilasters flank a series of Old Testament scenes in mosaic, each sheltered, prior to 1600, by an aedicula in stucco work, colonnaded and surmounted by alternating triangular and segmented pediments (fig. 41). Above the aediculae, the windows of the clerestory, one to each intercolumniation, were originally framed by a double order of twisted colonettes and an arch, likewise of stucco. A ceiling covered the nave, perhaps coffered like the present fifteenth-century one. Mosaics illustrating Christ's first coming and his youth cover the triumphal arch—originally the apse arch; the apse vault may have borne a mosaic of the Virgin accompanied by five martyrs.

The mosaics, both in the nave and on the apse arch, are among the great manifestations of Christian antiquity (figs. 42, 43). Moses strikes the waters of the Red Sea in a heroic gesture, his toga in light and dark grays and blues, but lined

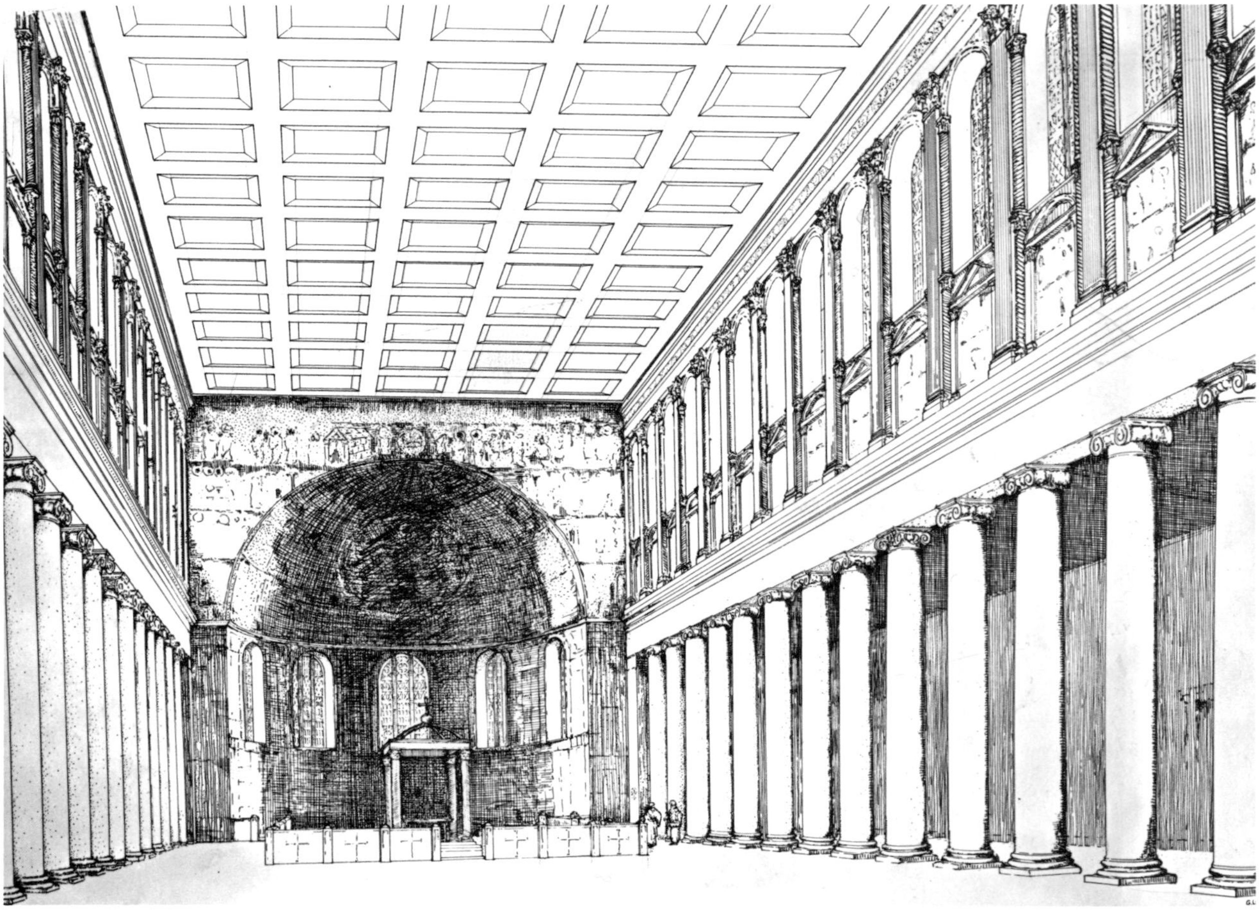

41. S. Maria Maggiore, interior, reconstruction

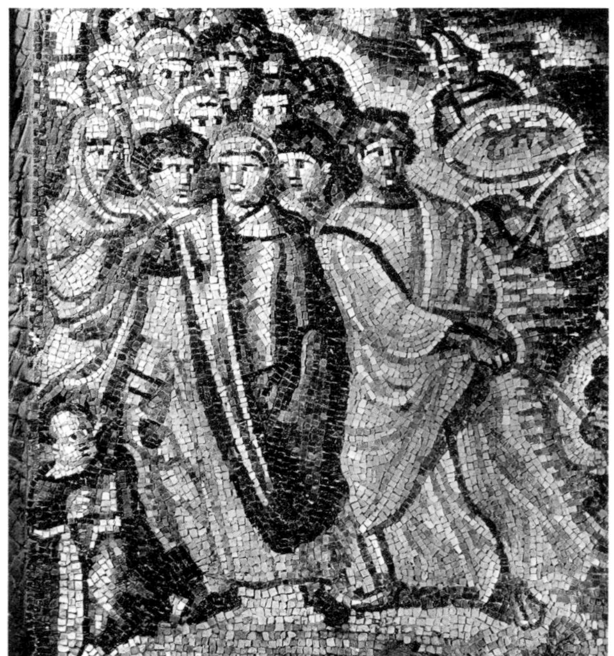

42. S. Maria Maggiore, nave mosaics, *Moses Striking the Waters of the Red Sea*

43. S. Maria Maggiore, nave mosaics, *Egyptians Drowning in the Red Sea*

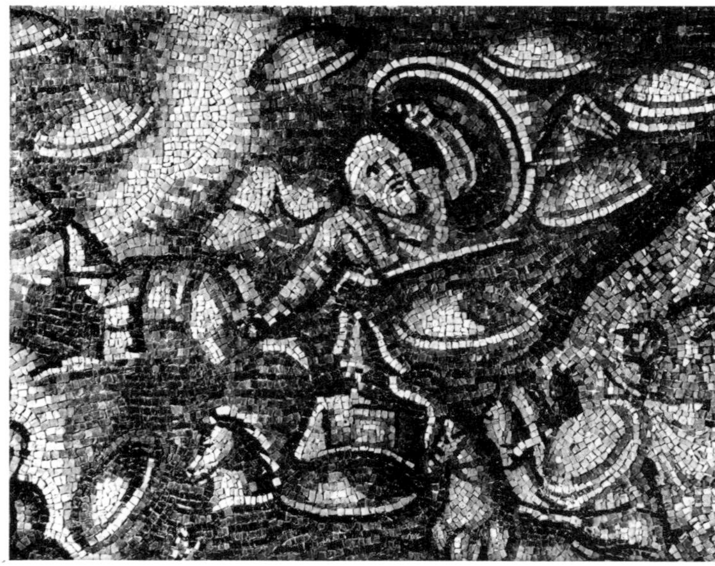

in black, the folds white lines, the tunic underneath light blue; the man next to him wears a deep blue toga over a gray and white tunic. The crowd behind presses endlessly into depth. The Egyptians, clad in blue armor with gold bands and scarlet cloaks wildly flying, drown in the greenish-blue waters; the horses, white or light brown shaded with darker browns, are highlighted in white, the accoutrements a bright red. Composition, figures, gestures and poses, colors, and the impressionistic technique are rooted in a tradition of late-antique mosaics, frescoes, and manuscript painting, which survives in dozens of pavement mosaics in African, Syrian, and Sicilian villas—Piazza Armerina comes to mind—in a few murals, and in a handful of illuminated manuscripts. On the apse arch Christ is enthroned, a young emperor attended by four chamberlains, angels of course (fig. 44). All is presented in a mode of classical gravity and imperial splendor and in the technique as it had formed through late antiquity in Rome: glass cubes, loosely set in diverging colors. The Virgin, in a yet unexplained scene to the right of the apse opening, shows to perfection the impressionistic character of the mosaics (fig. 45): the face in lighter and darker flesh tones with a few dark pink spots; lips, chin, nose marked in deep red; the outlines of red, brown, and black cubes in one and the same curve; jewelry and dress, gold and red. She is an empress graciously walking behind her divine Son and attended by a suite of angels and Joseph to meet the reception committee come to greet her.

The building and its decoration strike one as a manifesto. Classical antiquity is to be reborn—the Ionic order, the pilasters and aediculae were last seen in architecture in the Forum of Trajan; and it is to be reborn in the Christian spirit apparent in the mosaics—the first large-scale cycle of Biblical scenes extant in Rome. The dedicatory inscription on the triumphal arch—"*Sixtus episcopus plebi Dei*," "Sixtus the bishop to the people of God"—has a flavor both Biblical and classical.

S. Maria Maggiore does not stand alone. The signs of a classical renascence also characterize the Lateran Baptistery as remodeled under Sixtus III (fig. 46). The outer walls of Constantine's

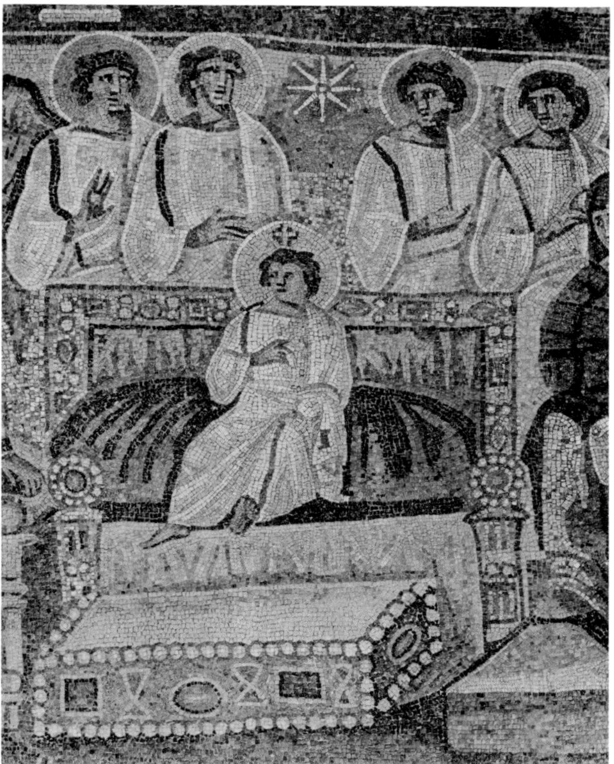

44. S. Maria Maggiore, triumphal arch mosaic, *Christ Enthroned with Four Angels*

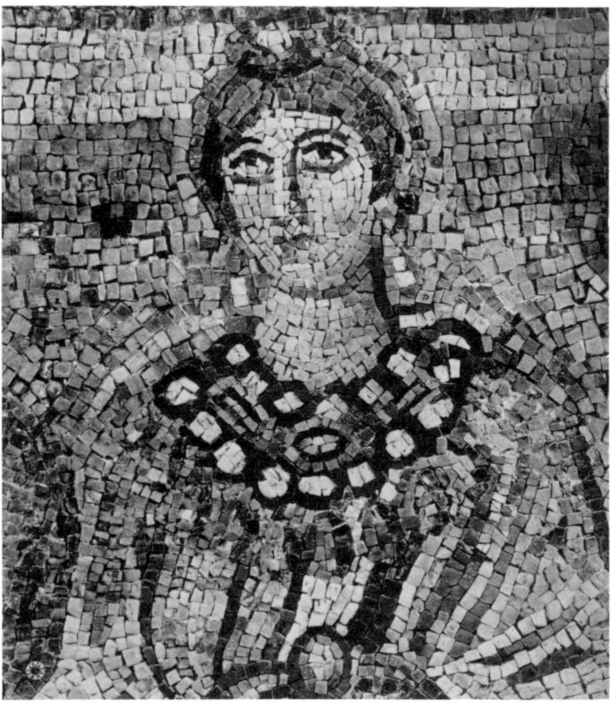

45. S. Maria Maggiore, triumphal arch mosaic, detail, head of Virgin

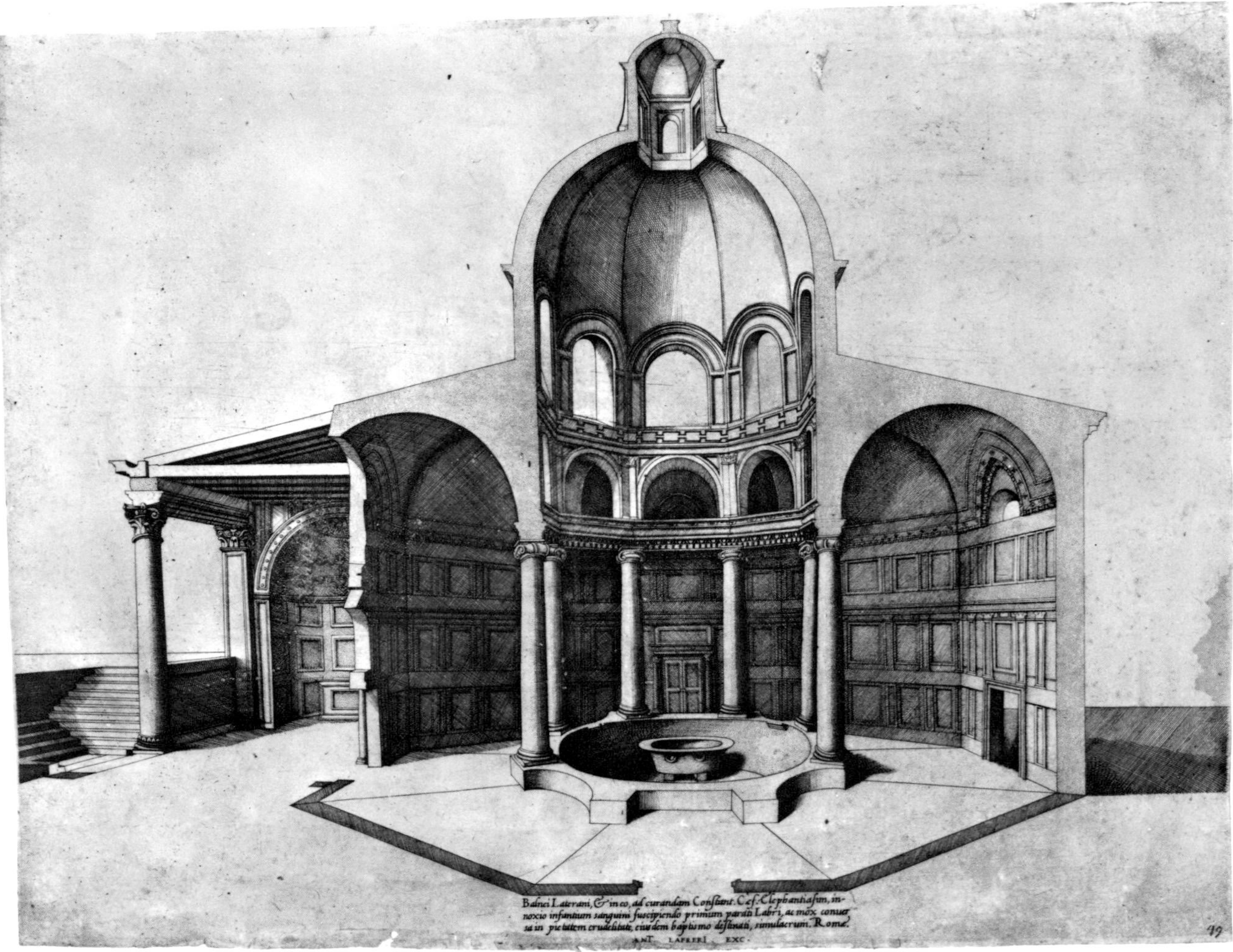

46. Lateran Baptistery, reconstruction ca. 1560, engraving A. Lafréry

octagon were retained; but the new interior—in large part it survives, though overlaid by seventeenth-century decoration—recalls nothing so much as late-antique buildings, such as S. Costanza on the Via Nomentana, the mausoleum of Constantine's daughter. Like that latter, the Lateran Baptistery is divided into a tall central space, encircled by a lower ambulatory; a barrel vault over the ambulatory was decorated with mosaics, preserved till the sixteenth century; the walls were sheathed by colorful marble plaques, articulated by pilasters; there was a dome in the center, melon-shaped it seems, and constructed possibly of wood or cane; eight wide windows opened in the clerestory; the narthex is apsed at either end, its entrance supported by two beautiful columns taken from some classical building; and in the right-hand apse the original mosaic remains, luscious tendrils, gold and green on a deep blue ground. In the opposite apse the corresponding mosaic, long lost, was enlivened by figures of shepherds along the rim—purloined from classical prototypes. Throughout, the revival of antiquity catches the eye. Even a generation after Sixtus III, Pope Hilarus (461-68), in the same spirit, converted into a shrine for a relic of the True Cross what seems to have been a second- or third-century structure near the Lateran Baptistery—the Chapel of the Holy Cross, S. Croce. Although demolished in 1588, it is known well from old engravings and drawings (fig. 47); cross-shaped with domed octagonal corner rooms, all walls sheathed in marble. In the center vault in mosaic were four figures—sixteenth-century archaeologists called them angels; but half-naked as they were, they might as well have been pagan genii. They carried on raised arms a roundel enclosing a cross, perhaps the only feature added by Pope Hilarus. Whether the figures at S. Croce were pagan or celestial, from the sixth century on, four angels in a circle supporting the Cross, the Lamb, or a bust of Christ became a favorite motif in vault mosaics in Ravenna and Rome. In front of the Chapel of the Holy Cross, the three porticoes of a small courtyard rested, as the pope's biographer reports, on columns of wonderful size; and three fountains, apparently made from strigilate sarcophagi, spewed water, that in the center of porphyry and sheltered by porphyry columns, trabeated and gabled, and by bronze grills, the whole decorated with mosaics and columns of colored marble. Nothing survives but drawings and engravings of the chapel, and the description, which reflects the overwhelming impression made on the contemporaries by all that ostentation. Large parts, including most likely the entire Chapel of the Holy Cross, were taken over from antiquity; but whether simply converted for Christian use or newly designed, they reflect the rebirth of a classical art, if late, in this the last phase of Christian antiquity.

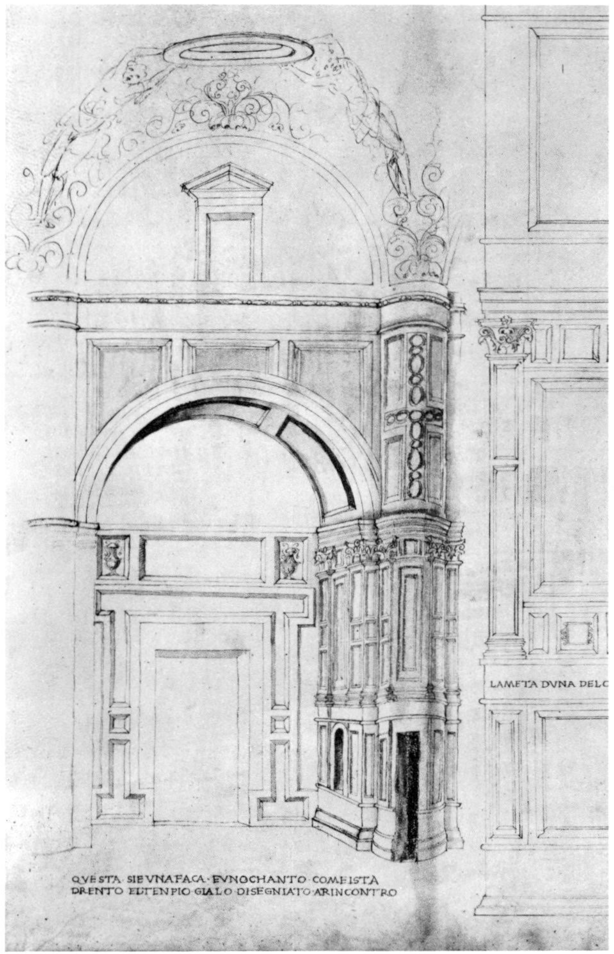

47. Lateran, Oratory of S. Croce, as of ca. 1500, drawing Giuliano da Sangallo, Vatican Library, Barb. lat. 4424, fol. 33ʳ

Attempts to absorb a classical vocabulary in the official art of the Church in Rome reach a high point during the decades between 430 and 460. The sources of the new style go further back: to elegant "classical" sarcophagi commissioned by Christian aristocrats; to S. Paolo, as first built by the three emperors; to the apse mosaic of S. Pudenziana; to S. Sabina on the Aventine, the first church building in Rome fully designed in the new spirit. Indeed, the classical and retrospective flavor of a true renaissance in Roman church building does not truly unfold before the late 420s; it reaches its climax from 432 to 461 in the pontificates of Sixtus III and Leo the Great, and it does not last much beyond the latter date. Leo, great teacher that he was, was keen on instructing his flock both by word and by visual means. As early as the time of Sixtus, he may have drawn up the program for the mosaic cycles in the nave and on the triumphal arch of S. Maria Maggiore. Once he had ascended the See of Saint Peter, he was, it seems, responsible for having the nave walls of the three great fourth-century churches painted with Biblical cycles: one at St. Peter's; another at S. Paolo fuori le mura, where the collapse of part of the fourth-century nave in 441 led to its rebuilding and redecoration; a third, presumably, in Constantine's Lateran Basilica. All are lost and only the first two, repainted in the Middle Ages, are reflected in late copies. But the splendid repairs of the nave colonnades and the framework of the murals at S. Paolo survived until 1823 and still showed the classical note that prevailed at S. Maria Maggiore: classical tendrils crept over the arcade zone and a double order of colonnettes, twisted clockwise and counter-clockwise, framed the double tiers of murals on either wall: murals in large part repainted or, indeed, newly painted in the thirteenth century and moreover known only through clumsy watercolors done in the seventeenth century. Nonetheless, among these copies, some clearly show the hallmarks of late-antique painting: poses, details, and wide airy landscapes.

For the last time, this classical-Christian vocabulary seems to come to the fore, though with diminished strength, at Sto. Stefano Rotondo. Built by Pope Simplicius (468-483) on the Celian Hill, the structure survives in nearly its entirety, save for the decoration of the interior. A circular center space (fig. 48), a full 22 meters wide and equally tall, rises on a circle of Ionic columns carrying an entablature; a dome, presumably built of cane, was to surmount the eleven windows of the clerestory. An ambulatory envelops the center space; from it four tall chapels projected crosswise, and the areas between the chapels were filled by courtyards, presumably containing pools or fountains with entrance corridors along the perimeter and arcaded toward the ambulatory (fig. 49). It is a complex plan possibly linked to Eastern, and

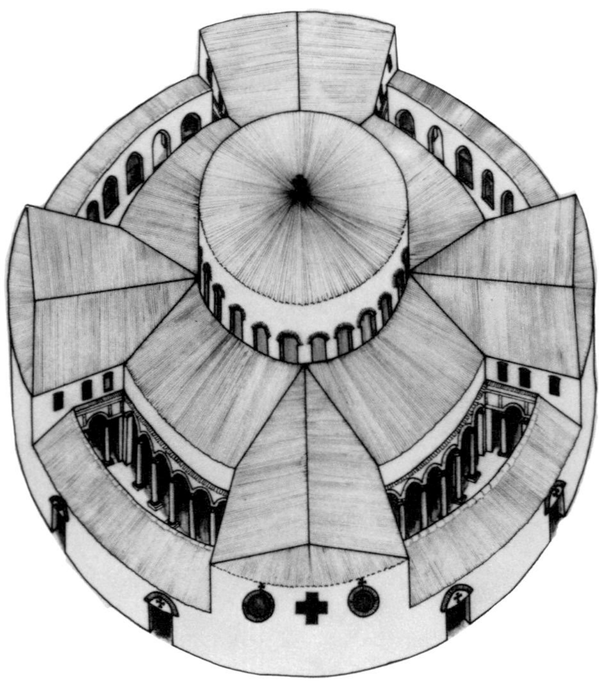

48. Sto. Stefano Rotondo, exterior, reconstruction Spencer Corbett

certainly to earlier imperial, models. The interweaving of dark and well-lit, of open and closed, of high and low spaces (fig. 50) at Sto. Stefano recalls the grouping of pavilions, courtyards, and pools in Hadrian's Villa at Tivoli and in other mansions of late antiquity as they likewise studded the Celian Hill from the Lateran to Sto. Stefano and beyond. At the same time, the vocabulary at Sto. Stefano, while crude in design and execution, stems from the traditions as formed at S. Maria Maggiore: the high pedestals supporting the columns; the Ionic capitals, awkward though they are; the entablature; the decoration surviving in traces sufficient to suggest the original splendor—marble revetment on the walls of the nave and of the chapels, surmounted by painted plaster; marble revetment in the courtyards; marble and mosaic pavements alternating in different areas; elegant stucco profiles on the archivolts between ambulatory and courtyards. Closely linked to both late-antique villa plans and their pavilion architecture and to the classical revival in fifteenth-century church building, Sto. Stefano reflects the complex cultural picture of Rome shortly before A.D. 500.

Church building from the pontificate of Sixtus III through that of Simplicius reflects the papacy's role as the bearer of the classical tradition reborn in fifth-century Rome. It also testifies to the new strength of the Roman bishop, the pope, in ruling his Roman flock. Church building was no longer planned and financed by the parish congregations or by wealthy individuals. With Sixtus III, if not before, the papacy took building activity into its own hands and developed a papal building program. Popes Sixtus III and Hilarus rebuilt the Lateran Baptistery and added the oratories within the compound of the papal palace. It was Pope Leo who commanded that the walls of Rome's great basilicas be decorated with Biblical cycles. The buildings, once founded by emperors, had become the pope's responsibility. With equal clarity the new church buildings of the fifth century reflect their standing as papal foundations. Where at the beginning of the century Pammachius had given the new basilica of SS. Giovanni e Paolo to the congregation of the parish, by the latter part of

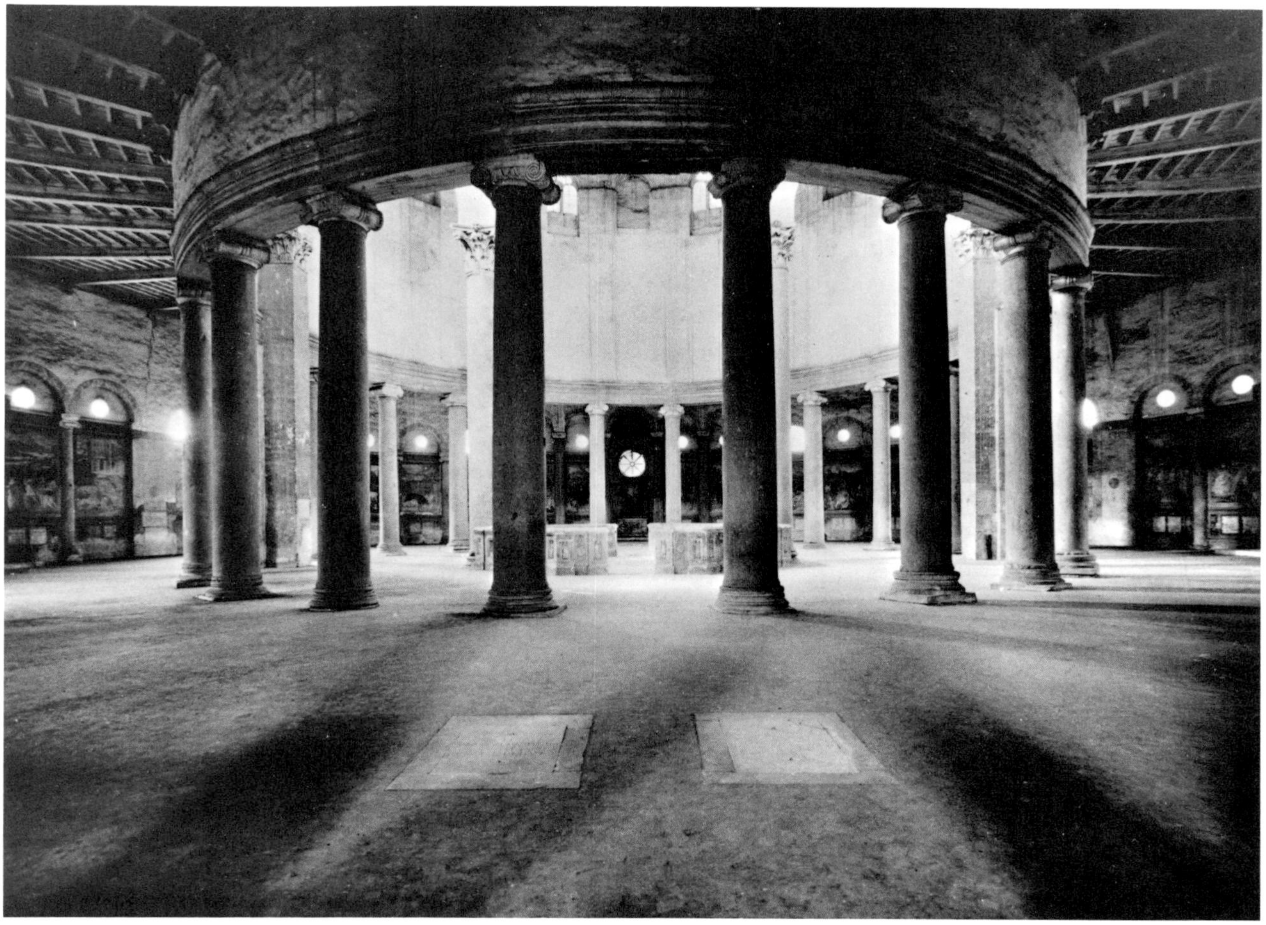

49. Sto. Stefano Rotondo, interior

the century the pope and his clergy, allied to the great Roman families, embodied the Church in Rome. The individual congregations lost the independence they had retained through the fourth century.

The impact the papacy exerted on church building is apparent both in the city and outside the walls, around the sanctuaries of the martyrs. Romans and foreigners alike through the fourth and fifth centuries remained strongly attracted to the martyrs' graves and the prospect of burial in that vicinity. Pope Damasus had his poems inscribed over the tombs of martyrs, and in the early fifth century, three popes sought burial in the catacomb near the tomb chamber of Saint Lawrence; with Leo I, St. Peter's, by then the most highly venerated cemetery church, became the customary burial ground for the popes, remaining so for centuries. Above the catacombs,

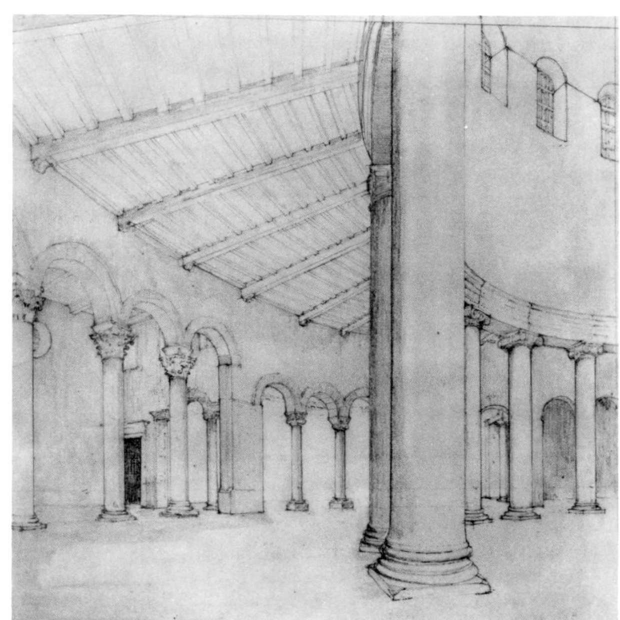

50. Sto. Stefano Rotondo, interior, reconstruction Spencer Corbett

papal building activity was evident all over (fig. 51). Alongside the great covered cemeteries rose smaller but still sizable basilicas, built in the fourth and fifth centuries as shrines of minor martyrs: the scanty remains of S. Valentino on the Flaminian Road, built by Pope Julius I (337–352) and later remodeled, are still to be seen halfway between Porta del Popolo and the Milvian Bridge. Under Leo I, Sto. Stefano on the Via Latina was laid out inside a vast villa complex over the mausoleum of a member of the Anicii family, not far from a group of second-century mausolea, the Tombe Latine. Mausolea, monasteries, hostels, from the fourth into the sixth centuries, crowded around the shrines of the three great martyr saints of Rome—Peter, Paul, and Lawrence. From what has survived in part around S. Sebastiano to this day, and from old records, it is easy to visualize the clusters of buildings around St. Peter's: mausolea, two of them huge rotundas, one antedating the basilica by over a century, the other added around A.D. 400 by the Imperial House; the family vault of the Anicii, a small basilica jutting out behind the apse; dozens of other vaults nearby; and monasteries, the first founded by Leo I, to be followed later by three more. Inside the basilica, Pope Damasus had already installed a baptistery. Around 500, Pope Symmachus built two papal reception halls adjoining the atrium and provided "housing for the poor," pilgrims' hostels rather than almshouses; and, on the Piazza facing the church and obviously for pilgrims, he set up a fountain and a lavatory. At S. Lorenzo fuori le mura Pope Hilarus installed a baptistery and laid out a country house provided with a bath, an open air swimming pool, and two libraries, Greek and Latin. Nearby, he set up a monastery dedicated to Saint Stephen. His successor, Simplicius, built a church for that monastery. The next pope, Felix III, erected a shrine close by in honor of Saint Agapitus; a few years later, Pope Symmachus built "habitations for the poor." Naturally, near the great shrines tradesmen and artisans would settle to care for the needs of, and draw a livelihood from, the pious visitors; so would beggars, as they did until a few decades ago. By the early sixth century, it appears, suburbs had grown up around the three great sanctuaries: on the Tiburtine Road, on the Ostian Way, and at the foot of the Vatican Hill, the latter the *burgus*, the *borgo*. Linked to the city gates by long porticoes, these suburbs were real offshoots of the city, extending into the Campagna. Smaller settlements grew up around other martyrs' graves on the roads to the city. Each had its church—over forty in all—and monasteries, giving the impression by the early sixth century of an area dotted with villas and farms and thoroughly Christianized—an ecclesiastical suburbia. Christian Rome spread far beyond the Aurelian Walls; the countryside was an integral part, and its incorporation into the metropolitan area was largely the work of the papacy in the later fourth and fifth centuries.

At the same time, the map of Rome within the city walls had begun to change. With the pontificate of Sixtus III, the papacy built fewer churches and these, replacing old community centers, were widely scattered over the city. In the urban area proper, papal activity in the fifth century was concentrated primarily on one quarter—the Lateran and its neighborhood. In the Lateran compound, the cathedral was being refurbished: with a figural mosaic in 429 to replace the goldfoil of the apse vault; with a new silver *fastigium*, donated by the emperor in the thirties on the insistence of Sixtus III; in the forties or fifties with Biblical murals on the nave walls. Constantine's Baptistery, remodeled and redecorated by Sixtus III, was expanded thirty years later by attached and adjoining oratories and by a courtyard and a fountain. By roughly that time, it would seem, the Lateran Palace had also been vastly extended to the south and east of the church, possibly in groups of detached pavilions; a last remnant, presumably part of the library and sheltering a seventh-century (?) mural called *Saint Augustine Writing*, survives in the substructure of the Scala Santa. This concentration of building activity on the dependencies of the cathedral—the bishop's church—and on his palace can be appreciated as occurring at a time when the bishop of Rome emerges as the ruler of the city, in fact if not by law.

However, other reasons as well may underlie the concentration of the fifth-century papacy on the Lateran. Ever since Constantine's time,

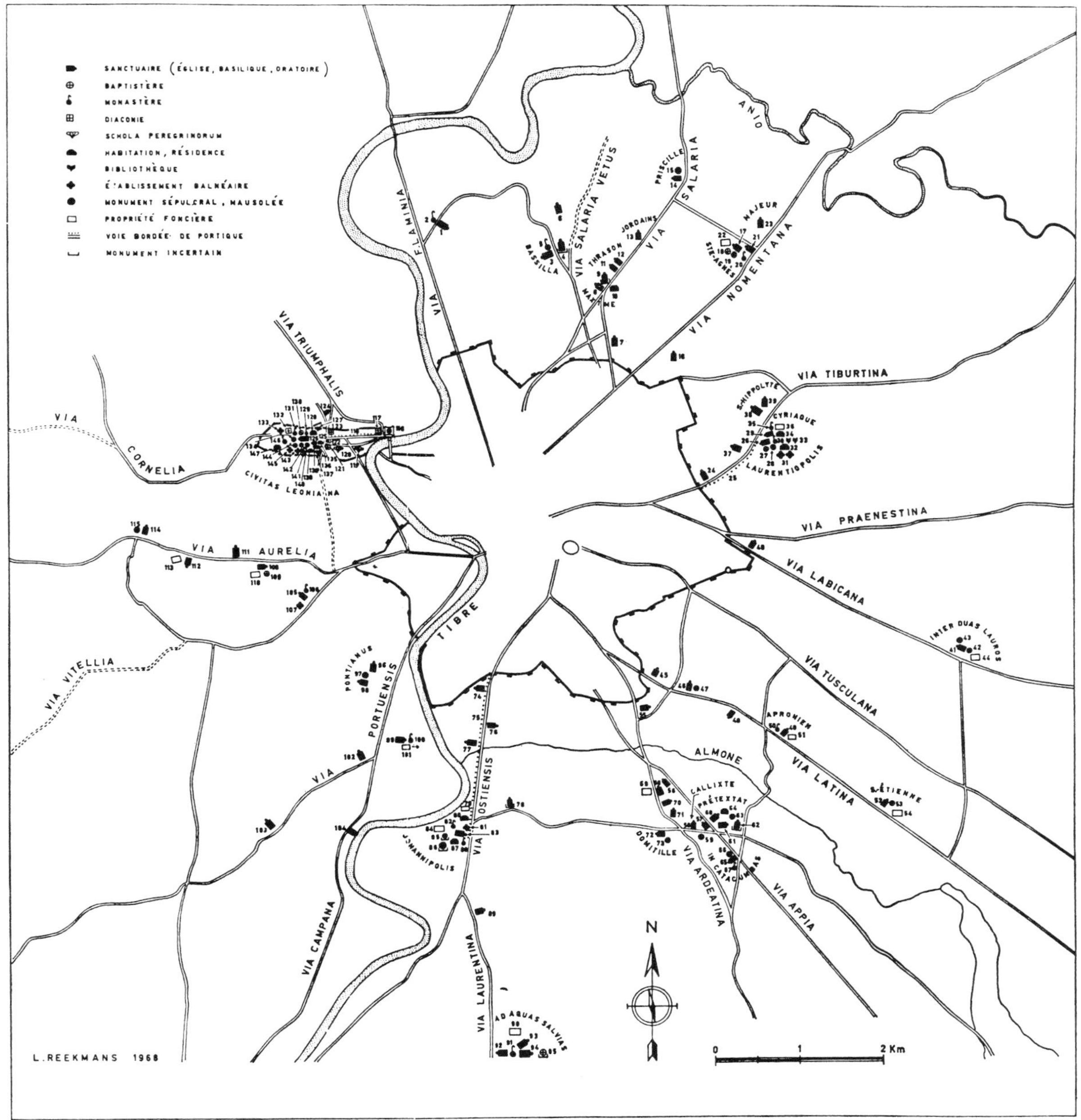

51. Map of sanctuaries outside the walls

the map of Christian Rome presented a dilemma. Constantine had established the Lateran by imperial fiat as the political, religious, and administrative center of Christianity in the city. But this location for the pope's cathedral, its baptistery, and his residence was artificially chosen to suit the political situation as it existed under Constantine and only then. The Christian people of Rome had never before, and never would, attach themselves to the Lateran; it remained the official center of the congregation in the city and only that. They, and likewise the pilgrims from outside Rome, had come long before Constantine to pray and to be buried at the shrines of the martyrs, and they continued to do so long after his reign. Forced by this popular trend, popes and emperors set up, endowed, lavishly decorated and furnished huge basilicas —S. Paolo fuori le mura is an example—at the greatest shrines, those of Lawrence, Paul, Peter; forced by the wish of the faithful to receive baptism, which was believed to be more efficacious near the saints, they installed baptisteries at the shrines—outside town and thus deviating from the episcopal prerogative of conferring baptism. The grave and sanctuary of Saint Peter soon overtook all the others in riches and importance. Romans and visitors in ever larger numbers flocked there to offer prayers and gifts and to beg for salvation. But St. Peter's was miles from the Lateran Cathedral and the papal palace. Indeed, it rose across the Tiber and outside the walls, as befitting a martyr's shrine. Thus it formed a popular focus, clearly competing with the official focus of Christian Rome at the Lateran. The conflict between the two centers, initiated in the early fourth century, continued to dominate the religious history of the city and its map for centuries to come. Throughout the Middle Ages, the claim for primacy between St. Peter's and the Lateran never ends. The dichotomy built into the city map was solved only with the very gradual inclusion of St. Peter's and its surroundings in the city and, in the fifteenth and sixteenth centuries, with the papacy's definitive move across the river and the coterminal rebuilding of the church and the construction of the Vatican Palace. However, from the late fourth century on, the conflict must have been evident, as the building activities near St. Peter's testify, in particular those aimed during the fifth century at serving the needs of the faithful crowds and at accommodating the pope and his suite on the occasional required visits to the shrine.

Given the situation, a reaffirmation of the official center of Christian Rome at the Lateran, where the pope's cathedral, baptistery, and residence were located, would have seemed more than necessary by the middle of the fifth century, to counter the half-legitimate popular center at the Vatican. The Lateran was and remained the political and administrative focus of Rome's Christian community. But, located on the margin of the city near the walls, it was more isolated than ever. Indeed, the map of Rome had begun to change. Quarters, formerly well settled, were gradually abandoned by the inhabitants, while parts of the show zone of Imperial Rome were turned into populous inhabited areas. In the *città bassa*, the population started to move westward into the Campus Martius and the Tiber bend, and their theatres, porticoes, and temples were engulfed by what was to become the densely built-up and populated core of medieval Rome. True, the quarters north of the fora and in the valley between the Quirinal and Viminal, near S. Vitale, were still well settled in the fifth century, and by 470 an Arian community had built their church, S. Agata dei Goti, on the west slope of the Viminal, where it stands to this day. The Esquiline, too, remained well settled, with mansions and popular quarters: the *domus magna* of Junius Bassus near S. Maria Maggiore had become the property, before 470, of a nouveau riche Goth, the mercenary general Vavila; and, to satisfy the needs of the ordinary citizens, the market of Livia was repaired in the fourth century, and continued to function beyond the fifth. But, on the Celian Hill, always thinly settled to the east, west, and north of the Lateran, many of the mansions had been abandoned by their former owners, and a half-empty crescent was formed around the papal palace and the Cathedral of Rome. Their remote location far from the center had been dictated by expedience; and what had been a short-term political advantage in the climate of Constantinian Rome, by the fifth century had turned into a long-range liability. Custom required that baptism be imparted at Easter by the bishop in person; it required the entire Christian community of Rome, by then the whole population, to assemble on major feast days in the cathedral around its bishop; it required the spiritual and political leader of the city to reside close to his people, on both practical and ideological grounds. A site as far distant as the Lateran for the pope's cathedral and residence was decidedly undesirable.

On the other hand, to move himself and his cathedral elsewhere in the city where he had to reside—St. Peter's being outside—was inconceivable. The Lateran Basilica had been established by Constantine, who had turned the known world Christian; it was the signal monument to the triumph of the new faith in the old capital of the world. The palace had served the bishop and his administration for a century and more; it had been enlarged and beautified. Tradition favored retaining the old site and buildings. The papal bureaucracy, comfortably installed and with the inertia inherent in all bureaucracies, was reluctant, one assumes, to move to new quarters. In terms of sheer convenience, the site was not bad: in the greenbelt, airy, with plenty of water from the nearby aqueducts which still functioned well, and easily provisioned from gardens inside and nearby fields outside the walls. Moving was out of the question; other ways had to be found to counter the drawbacks of the Lateran's location.

The crowds of the faithful, who were obliged and eager to attend services celebrated by the pope in person, and of catechumens demanding to be baptized at Easter, were distributed more evenly both in time and space. Baptism at times other than Easter came into use; and from the latter part of the fourth century, baptisteries were installed to supplement the baptistery at the Lateran, both outside and inside the city. Those outside the walls were, one imagines, primarily to serve pilgrims, come to visit the tombs of the martyrs and still unbaptized; but many Romans, too, may well have preferred to receive baptism there believing it to be more effective. Inside the city, baptismal facilities were provided for in nearly all churches newly built in the fifth century: at S. Vitale, S. Lorenzo in Lucina, S. Sabina, S. Marcello al Corso, S. Maria Mag-

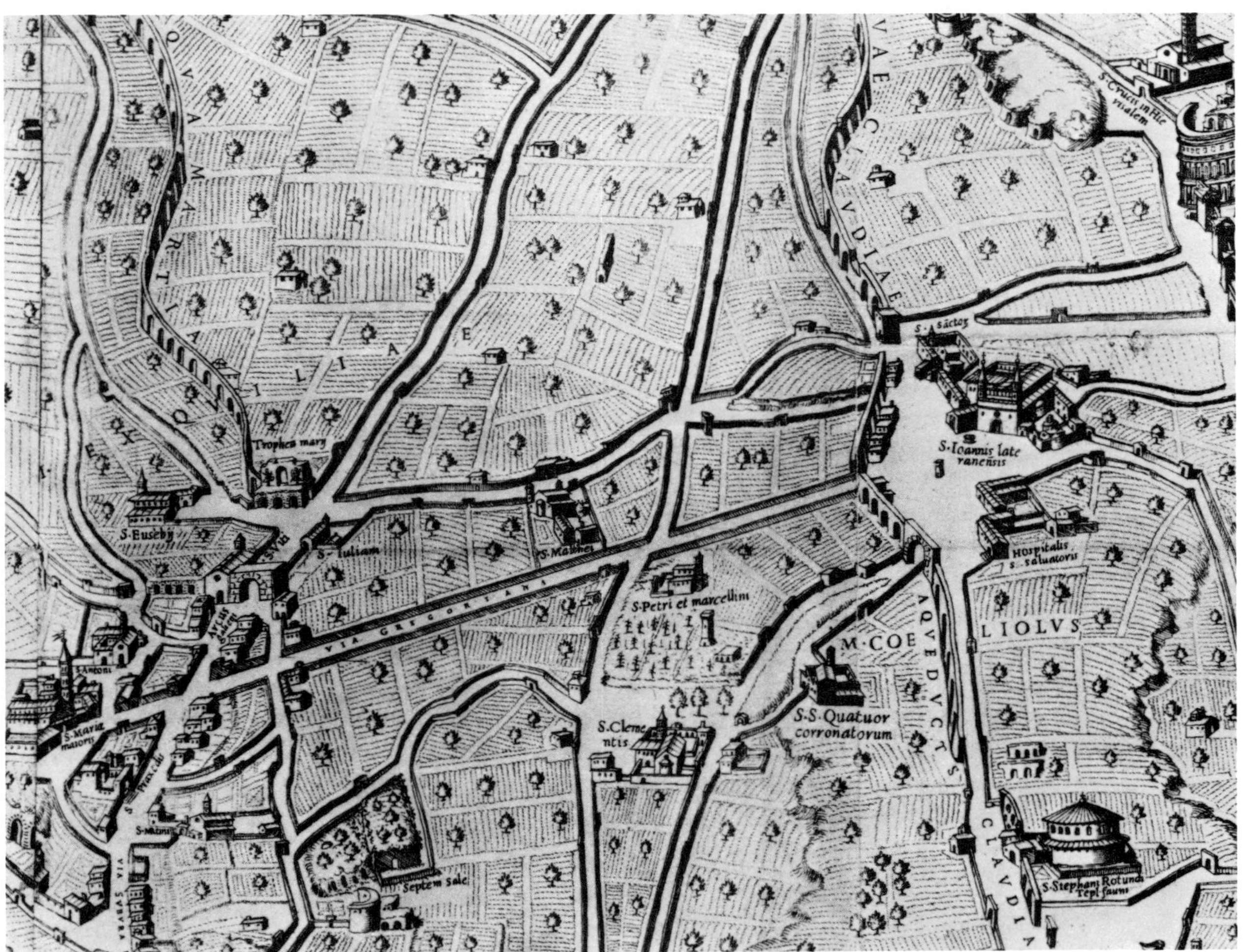

52. Map of Rome, 1577, M. Cartaro ("Large Cartaro Map"), detail showing churches of fifth-century papal quarter

giore. But older churches, too, were newly supplied with baptisteries, like the one attached to the fourth-century church of S. Crisogono in Trastevere. Baptism, then, was apparently imparted all over town by parish priests delegated by the pope.

At the same time, to lessen the crowds that gathered on feast days at the Lateran, Station Services were introduced: services held in churches other than his cathedral by the pope, who would arrive there in solemn procession accompanied by the entire clergy of the Lateran and by the high palace dignitaries, laymen and clerics. The development of these services and the gradual increase in their number—there were ninety-eight by the twelfth century—is far from clear. But they were an accepted liturgical custom in the fifth century, and those of the great feast days took place, aside from the Lateran Cathedral, at S. Croce in Gerusalemme (Good Friday), S. Maria Maggiore (Christmas first Mass), and Sto. Stefano Rotondo (St. Stephen's Day, the day after Christmas). These three churches, one notes, are located on the perimeter of a crescent that enveloped the Lateran, a mile or less distant, easily accessible to the pope and, at least in the case of the latter two, closer to the populated area of the city (fig. 52). All three stand out among Roman churches. None had a clergy or a congregation of its own; apparently they were serviced from the Lateran and designed to serve the entire Roman community. In fact, both S. Maria Maggiore and Sto. Stefano, newly built in the fifth century, are roughly twice as large as any contemporary parish church, be it S. Sabina or S. Pietro in Vincoli; they were laid out, it is clear, to hold huge congregations, *tutta Roma* as it were, the dedication to the People of God (*plebi dei*) perhaps revealing this intention; and they were lavishly decorated as befits churches designed for papal use. They are best understood as extensions of the pope's cathedral, subsidiaries to the Lateran.

They also hint at a conscious attempt of the fifth-century papacy to change the map of Rome. Distant from the old center, S. Croce, Sto. Stefano Rotondo, and S. Maria Maggiore outline in the southeastern sector of the city an ecclesiastical quarter focused on the Lateran; sixteenth-century maps still reflect the situation. Smaller churches, in the last third of the fifth century, rose along and inside the perimeter. Near S. Maria Maggiore, the Basilica of Junius Bassus became around 480 S. Andrea in Catabarbara. Further east and at the same time, the church of S. Bibiana was built. Replaced by a medieval structure that was in turn remodeled by Bernini in 1624, the original basilica in plan and size is unknown. Southwest of S. Maria Maggiore, a church dedicated to Saint Martin around 500 replaced an old titulus to give way in the ninth century to the present structure of S. Martino ai Monti. Some of the mansions abandoned by their former owners may have been occupied, as was that of one of Jerome's devout lady friends on the Aventine, by groups of pious gentlemen and ladies living a communal life; these were forerunners of regular convents. Around the Lateran Palace the dependents of the papal court would naturally settle—high clergy, diplomats, administrative personnel and their households. Nearby and around S. Maria Maggiore smaller folk would crowd, drawing their livelihood and expecting protection from the papal court and the great gentlemen in the area. The southeastern sector of the city was about to become the new hub of Rome, centered on the Lateran and extending in a vast triangle westward, northward, and eastward. Around the pope's cathedral, its annexes, and his palace, a papal quarter was to form, a fifth-century *borgo*, as it were. But the project came to nought. History took a different course.

CHAPTER THREE

The Times of Gregory the Great

Gregory the Great, Saint Gregory, was the first pope of the Middle Ages. He was the founder of medieval Rome, the one to assign her the place she was to hold in the Western world for centuries to come. But he was also the last pope of Christian antiquity, a product of ancient Rome, Christianized; and both facets of his personality need to be taken equally into account.

Born about 540 into the old, wealthy clan of the Anicii, and a great-grandson of Pope Felix III, he grew up on one of the family estates, possibly that on the slopes of the Celian Hill. Adjoining the last great library set up in Rome around 535 by Pope Agapitus, this family mansion stood on the site of the present church and monastery of S. Gregorio Magno. Gregory was trained in the classics and the works of the Christian Fathers, and he entered the civil service at an early age. After a term as city prefect of Rome, he withdrew to a monastic community that he established in the family mansion on the west slope of the Celian. The library, which still stands in large part, was apparently soon incorporated in the monastery. Little remains today of the convent or the mansion, but the majority of the monastic buildings on the estate installed under Gregory or shortly after were listed by his ninth-century biographer: the chapels of St. Barbara and St. Mary; the cells, stables, and cellar; the atrium, whether a courtyard or hall, showing portraits of Gregory's parents on its walls; and, in a small apse behind the cellar, a tondo with Gregory's effigy. Only two of a group of three chapels that rise between the present church and the remains of Agapitus' library incorporate late-Roman, fifth-century, and medieval construction; they may have belonged to the buildings on Gregory's estate. As it stands, this triad of chapels was built or remodeled from older structures in 1602 by the great church historian and reformer, Cardinal Cesare Baronio (fig. 53). The chapel of S. Silvia, on the right, was built from the foundations in 1602, its apse adorned by Guido Reni's angel concert. The chapel of S. Andrea is in the center of the triad; although thoroughly altered at that time—the delightful colonnaded entrance porch replaced an earlier apse—and embellished with frescoes by Reni and Domenichino, it still carries remains of an early-eleventh-century mural high on its rear wall, originally the entrance wall built in fifth-century masonry. Finally, on the left stands the chapel of St. Barbara. It is also called the triclinium, and legend tells of an angel's appearance there among the poor invited to dinner by the saint. Like S. Andrea, this chapel is built over the lower floors of a Roman tenement house. The chapel itself, before being redesigned in 1602, opened wide in a quadruple window and a double entrance, as one would expect in a late-antique summer dining room; is it then possibly the one listed by Gregory's biographer among the monastic structures? Be that as it may, the group of three chapels, as it has risen among the cypress trees since the early seventeenth century, is one of the most attractive, if romantic, highlights of the picturesque Roman scene.

Gregory, after spending three years in the new monastery, took Orders and went as legate to the imperial court at Constantinople. On his return, he became secretary to Pope Pelagius II—prime minister would be a more appropriate term—and in February 590 became his successor. His administrative genius, his diplomatic ability, his political acumen, and his common sense combined to make the fourteen years of his pontificate a turning point in the history of Rome and of Europe.

The immediate tasks confronting Gregory were formidable, both on an administrative and

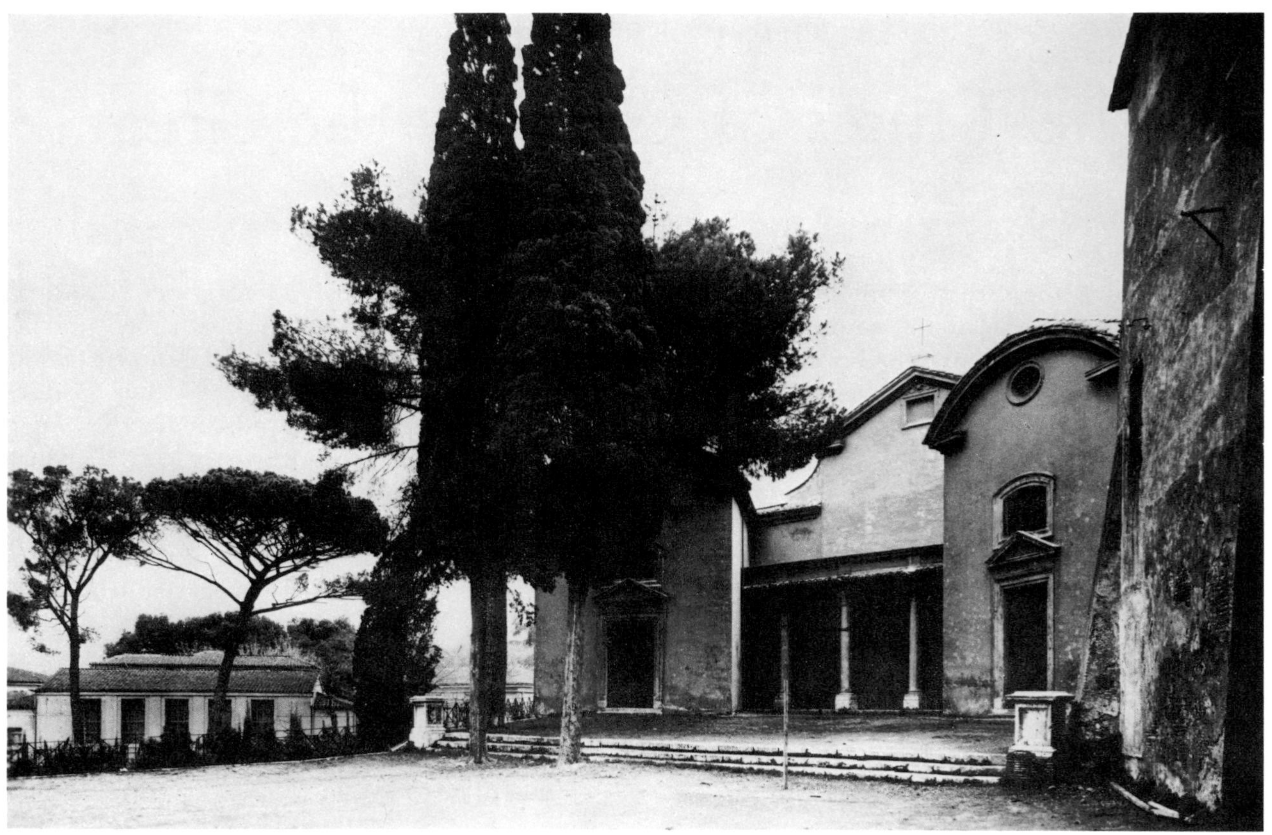

53. Chapels of S. Gregorio Magno

on a diplomatic level. Rome and the possessions of the Church in Italy, the Lands of St. Peter, had to be secured. In the city, provisioning was reorganized, public services and the welfare system maintained, reestablished, and improved. The papal administration had to be tightened: a legal section was built up, staffed by lay lawyers, *defensores*, and headed by a chancellor, the *primicerius*. Thus, a civil service drawn from the laity stood alongside the diplomatic, financial, administrative, and welfare services staffed by clerics, headed by the seven deacons. (During Gregory's pontificate, this organization was supplemented and at times, one gathers, cut across by a "kitchen cabinet," the pope's personal advisers drawn from among his monastic friends.) The administration of the vast landholdings of the Church in Italy, Sardinia, and Sicily was brought to a high efficiency and centrally controlled. Such organizational improvements were closely intertwined with Gregory's diplomatic policies. As things stood, he had to navigate between the claims of Byzantium, since 552 in legitimate occupation of Italy, and the imminent presence of the Longobard invaders, from 568 in possession of ever larger parts of the peninsula. Thus, Rome remained legally a Byzantine city and the pope a more or less loyal subject of the emperor: in fact throughout Gregory's pontificate and far into the seventh century; de jure for another hundred years after that. The Senate and the Roman clergy, assembled in one of the Lateran's halls, acclaimed the portraits of Their Majesties upon their accession to the throne. Relations with the court of Constantinople, where a legate permanently represented the Roman Church, were carefully cultivated. In Rome, Byzantine officials were in evidence, a powerless and inefficient, if at times rapacious, nuisance. Occasionally, the exarch from Ravenna would put in an appearance, if only to loot the papal treasury. The Longobard threat to the possessions of the Church and to Rome itself, on the other hand, was perhaps more acute. Through negotiations naturally not welcomed by the Byzantines, Gregory achieved a truce with the Longobards, annually renewed; Rome and the Lands of Saint Peter were temporarily safe and, indeed, remained so for another century and a half.

Gregory's greater aims and achievements were more far-reaching than such short-term arrangements. To come close to the Christian masses, he faced up to the basic dilemma of his time. The tradition of classical antiquity, as it had been absorbed into the framework of Christianity two hundred years before, remained the only vehicle to convey rational thought, religious or secular. But it was interspersed with pagan images and concepts; besides, it was highbrow in its language and philosophy and thus accessible only to an educated class. It no longer meant anything in Gregory's world to the common man. Among the masses a new culture had grown in its place; Christian, but no longer bound by the philosophical or theological concepts of the early Fathers of the Church and no longer permeated by the pagan elements inherited from classical times. Its language was Latin, but no longer Cicero's or Augustine's. Rooted in age-old popular beliefs, it stressed new forms of religiosity shot through with irrational and magical elements. Only through the medium of this new culture could Gregory hope to reach the people of his day. Only through it could he hope to bridge the chasm dividing the educated from the lower classes. Hence he preached sermon after sermon in the ordinary language of daily life, and on an intellectual and spiritual level easily understood, that of the humble style. Contrary to past custom, too, these sermons were addressed to intellectuals and illiterates alike. Miracles and spirits, good and evil, he treated as full reality, sincerely believing in them as spiritual forces. Where two centuries earlier educated Christians had remained skeptical, Gregory and his contemporaries accepted all this; to work miracles was simply in the nature of the sainted and their relics. To placate the wrath of heaven, he instituted processions and litanies, which were attended by all the clergy and people of Rome. To deal with the spiritual needs of the masses, a new Christianity was to evolve, indifferent or even opposed to the classical tradition and focused instead on a Christian faith rooted in popular and magical beliefs. To lead the people, the clergy from now on would center its attention not on intellectual achievement, much as this might attract its members, but on simple faith and practical tasks.

The alloy of Christianity and the classical tradition that was achieved for a short time in fifth-century Rome, was of no use to this end. Still, Gregory and his times could not do without it. They might reject classical poetry and literature and their pagan images and implications. But they remained bound to the intellectual habits of antiquity, its basic concepts, and its language. Wed to Christian thought, such fundamentals were needed in training leaders among clergy and laity; they underlay the curriculum at the school at the Lateran, the *schola cantorum*, Gregory's foundation according to tradition. With these concepts, moreover, the intellectuals of Gregory's age took over and handed on to later generations the historical tradition of antiquity, with its belief in Rome as the hub of the world. They also took over Rome's clarity of reasoning, its administrative genius, its practical sense of doing first things first: all concepts, eminently Roman and at the same time closely linked to the ideals of the men whom, from about 540, Saint Benedict had welded into a community that later became the Benedictine Order. Rational and practical, their monasticism was based on both prayer and work. Intimately integrated with the life of the rural population and strictly organized, their monasteries became powerful and efficient landholders. By the late eighth century, the Benedictine Order was the only one left in Europe, and for four hundred years it remained the fulcrum of the Roman Church.

Gregory had been close to Benedictine ideals and practice long before his election; his own monastery followed a rule similar to that of Saint Benedict, though probably modified, given its urban location. During his pontificate, the Benedictine congregation throughout the possessions of the Church became a natural ally in guiding his people. At the same time, it became a powerful tool in Gregory's most far-reaching undertaking: the Roman mission to the semibarbarian tribes in Lombardy, Spain, and England, soon to spread to the Low Countries and Germany. Previously, the Franks in Gaul, converted since the end of the fifth century, had been the only tribe in the north to adhere to the Church of Rome; most Germanic tribes, as far as they were Christian, long ago had chosen Arianism. Gregory initiated the conversion of the Arian Longobards through their Catholic queen; he completed the conversion to the Roman Church of the Arian Visigoths in Spain; and a Benedictine mission dispatched by him won over pagan England. Over the next eighty years, British clerics and monks defended Rome's theological and political position against the dissident Irish, until, in the eighth century, Benedictines could carry Roman Christianity to refractory Ireland and to pagan Germany and replace Irish monasticism in France, north Italy, and Switzerland. Whether Gregory initiated the English mission after seeing some Anglo-Saxon slave boys—the play on "Angles" and "Angels" is just too pat—matters little. But it was through him that Rome became the missionary center of Western and Central Europe, the organizational pivot of the Western Church, the spiritual guide of the converted Germanic tribes, and thus both the capital of Western Christianity and an increasingly powerful influence in Western politics throughout the Middle Ages.

These broader issues interlock with Gregory's activities in Rome and their impact on the future history of the city. Based in part on a sermon of the pope's, in part on an eye-witness report, Gregory's biographer paints black on black the state of Rome at the beginning of his pontificate in 590: the Longobards looting and burning all through the countryside; the city flooded by the Tiber; the granaries on its banks destroyed together with old temples; the river sweeping along big water-snakes—dragons he says—and dead cattle; people by the hundreds starving and dying from epidemics; buildings tumbling, the inhabitants in flight, the population decimated; the economy in shambles, only one private banker left in the city. The impression is that everything had collapsed. The natural catastrophe is depicted as the worst ever to hit the city and the breakdown of services and the physical deterioration of Rome as having taken place over the preceding fifty-odd years, caused by the succession of wars and invasions during that time. From this, the conclusion has often been drawn that Gregory's efforts alone remedied the situation. This is true only in part. In a sermon calling for repentance and contrition, Gregory would present only the blackest side of the picture. Natural catastrophes had hit before and would do so for many centuries. The breakdown of services and the physical deterioration of the city had gone on for a long time; warfare over the last two thirds of the sixth century had simply hastened the process. On the other hand, the collapse was far from complete; a skeleton remained both of the essential services and of the urban fabric. They were the foundation on which Gregory built to restore the damage and give Rome a new raison d'être.

By Gregory's time, to be sure, Rome was in bad shape. She was impoverished; her population had shrunk to an estimated 90,000; politically she was merely a town in one of the outer provinces of the East Roman, or Byzantine, Empire, ruled from Ravenna by a Byzantine viceroy. Taken over a century before with the rest of Italy by the Goths, she had lived through a peaceful, if inglorious, forty years under their king, Theodoric, and his chancellor Cassiodorus, Roman of Romans. Then, in 534, Justinian set out to reconquer the West for the East Roman Empire and the true Faith, wresting it from what to him were barbarian and heretical, since Arian, usurpers. Two years later Rome was taken by Belisarius, Justinian's general, then lost again, retaken, lost a second time, and finally captured for good in 552 by Narses, Belisarius' successor—Procopius and after him Robert Graves have given lively accounts of the events. Warfare and sieges devastated the countryside; the economy collapsed in the city and the population shrank to a minimum. But recovery, at least superficially, seems to have been quick under a tight military administration established by the Byzantines. Local masons and

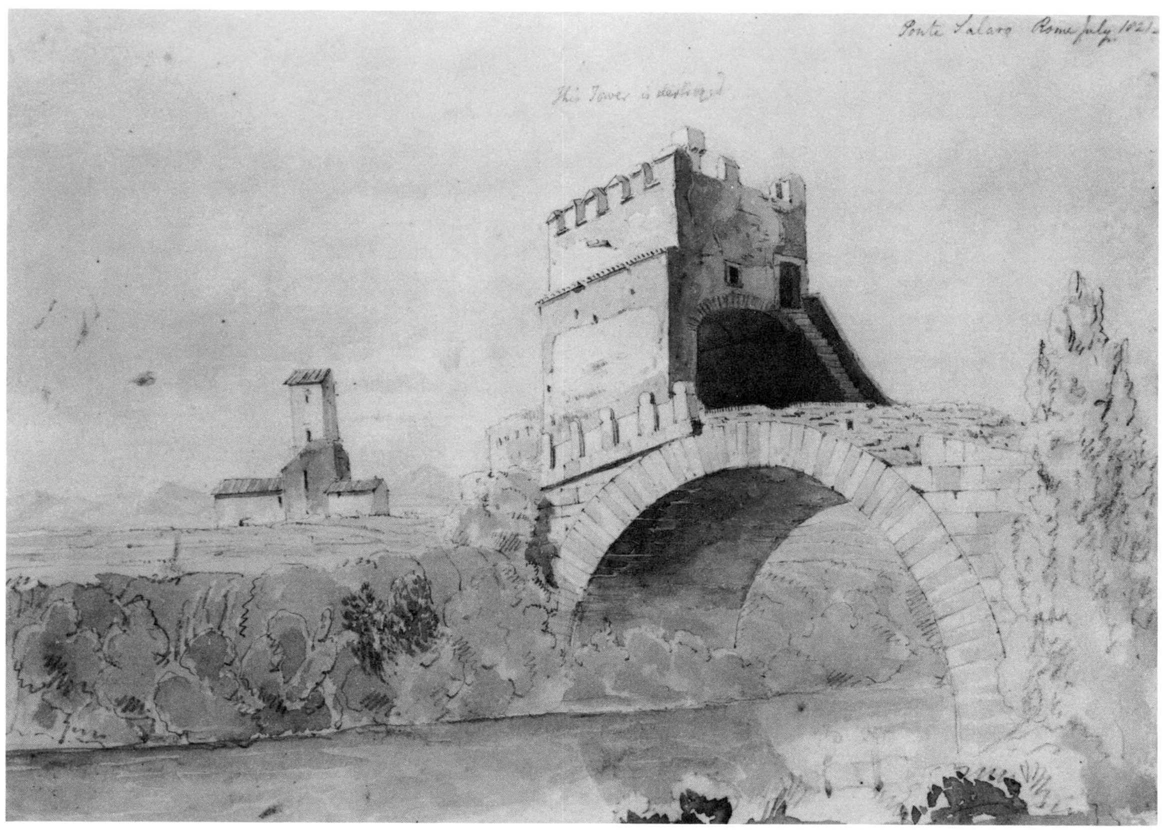

54. Ponte Salario, as in 1821, watercolor, anonymous English, Metropolitan Museum, New York

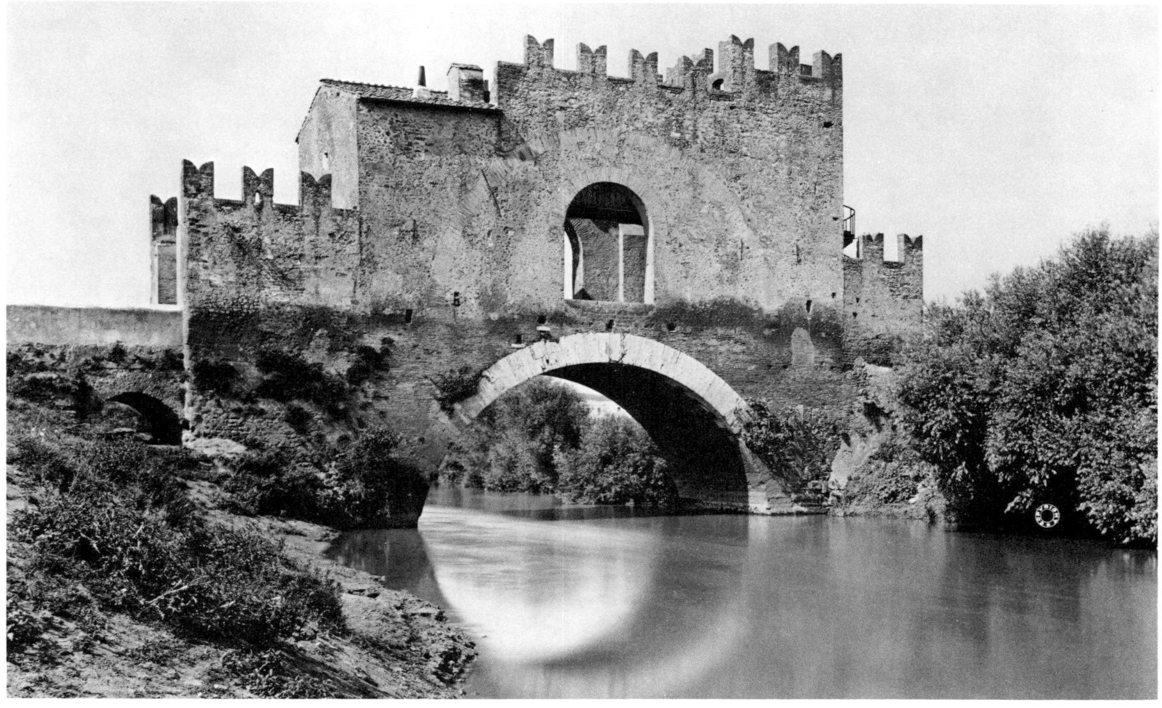

55. Ponte Nomentano, as of ca. 1860

army engineers repaired the Aurelian Walls. The aqueducts were mended and functioned reasonably well for another two hundred years. The country roads were restored and their bridges rebuilt. Two survive: Ponte Salario, rebuilt in 565, but reconstructed again after being blown up in 1867 and stripped of Narses' dedicatory inscription (fig. 54); and Ponte Nomentano, dated 552 and until 1829 surmounted by a crenelated fifteenth-century tower—both favorite *vedute* painted and drawn time and again from the sixteenth through the nineteenth centuries (fig. 55). However, peace and comparative prosperity, as reestablished by the Byzantines, were disrupted again, when starting in 568 the Longobards swept over and occupied large parts of northern and central Italy. When Gregory ascended the See of Saint Peter, they were laying waste to the countryside around Rome. Country bishoprics had to be abandoned and moved to defensible hill towns. The lands of the Church and of the Byzantine government were taken over or threatened by the invaders; the farm population, the rural clergy and monastic congregations fled, many crowding into Rome and swelling the population, ill-provisioned as it was. Three thousand refugee nuns alone had to be fed and clad during Gregory's pontificate.

Catastrophic though they were, these fifty years of warfare only accelerated a process of deterioration that for centuries had worn down the city of Rome. The grand image she had presented in the fifth century, both truly Christian and truly Roman, even then stood against the somber background of worsening economic disorder, fading political power, and slow material decline. Economic deterioration all over the West had long led to the dwindling of food supplies for the urban masses. The estates outside the walls of Rome, long unprofitable, were neglected from the third century and gradually abandoned; the fields, no longer drained, had turned into swamps by 500; malaria made the Campagna di Roma into the unsalutary plain it remained until fifty years ago. Provisioning from overseas was disturbed as early as the third century by peasants' revolts, the increasing need of local centers, and the growing inefficiency of a latifundia agriculture in the face of a shrinking slave economy. It practically came to an end with the occupation of Africa by the Vandals, of Gaul by Burgundians and Franks, and of Spain by Visigoths, all in the course of the fifth century. Only Sicily and South Italy remained as sources of supply, and they were threatened, the one by Vandal pirates, the other by the Gothic Wars and the Longobard invasions. The progressive cutback in supplies aggravated the ever unhealthy conditions in Rome: permanent underemployment, increasing poverty, the abandonment of estates within and near the city that had provided work and subsistence. As early as 396, Paulinus of Nola spoke of "the poor in Rome in need of full support . . . , the pious hordes of miserable people." By the end of the fifth century, famines became a fact of life in Rome, as did epidemics of malaria, cholera, and bubonic plague. Floods like that described by Gregory had been common events from time immemorial, three or four times every century, and remained so till the building of the Tiber embankments around 1900. The *Liber Pontificalis* records four such floods—in 716, 791, 856, and 860—in nearly the same, apparently typical words: the Corso under more than two meters of water; churches and houses flooded from the Porta del Popolo to the foot of the Capitoline Hill and beyond, south as far as Bocca della Verità, west to what is now Ponte Sisto; the pope and his clergy in boats bringing food; the fields on the west bank of the river from St. Peter's to the Milvian Bridge—the meadows, the *Prati*—inundated and the harvest gone. Markers four and five meters up on buildings in the inner city to this day recall similar floods from the fifteenth to the nineteenth centuries. A view of the Pantheon (fig. 184), flooded a hundred and fifty years ago, conveys a faint idea of such ever-repeated disasters; and even today the river can be fearful. Groundwater, too, caused local flooding in the low parts of town; a drawing by Claude Lorrain (or maybe a follower) shows the Forum inundated, probably from groundwater (fig. 56). Under the weight of the economic calamities and the warfare of the fifth and sixth centuries, the social fabric of the city, too, was bound to rend. Except for a few hardy clans, like the Anicii, patrician families moved to the

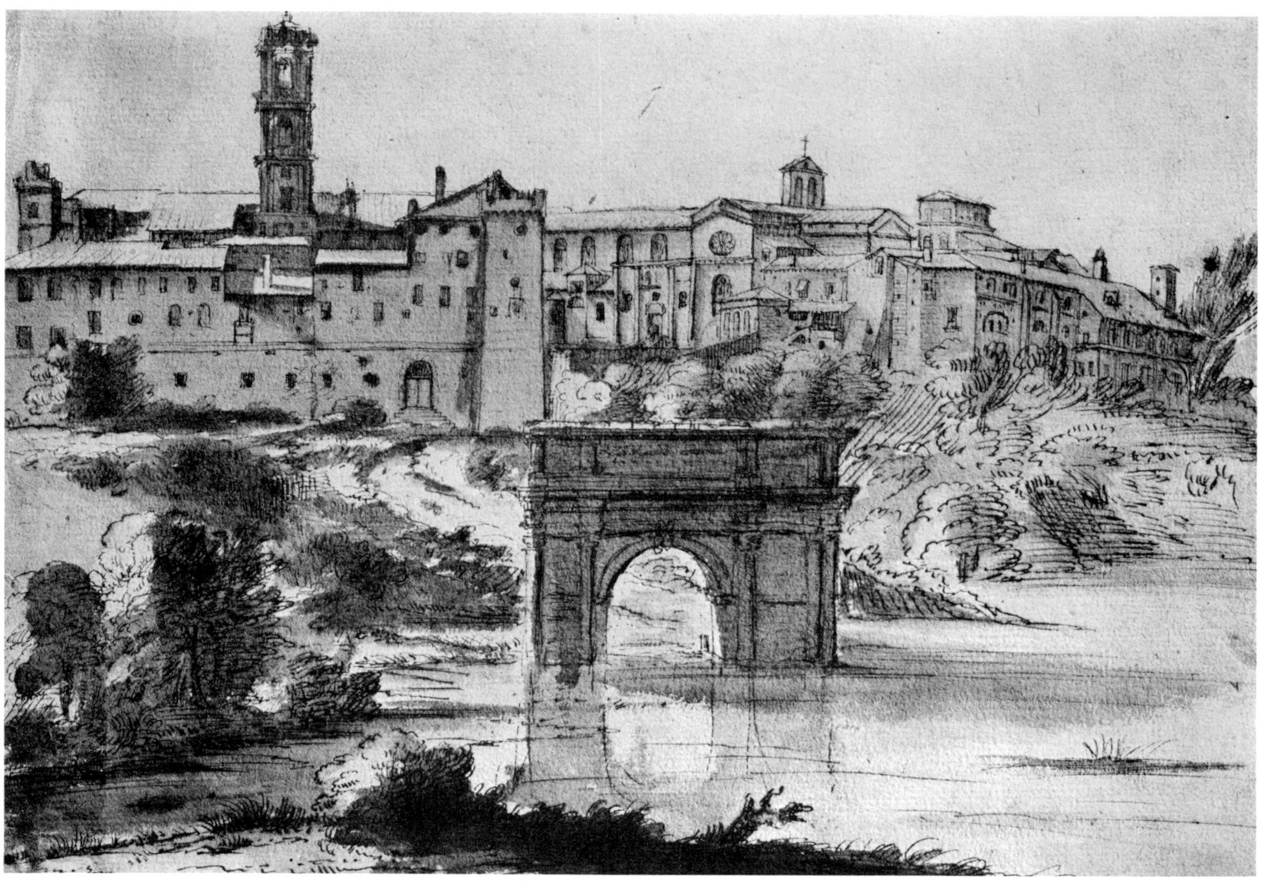

56. Arch of Septimius Severus flooded and Capitol, as of ca. 1650, Claude Lorrain, Oxford, Christ Church

safety and fleshpots of the imperial court, first at Ravenna, then at Constantinople, abandoning their estates and mansions in Rome. Among the poor as well, large numbers may have left to scrape out a living around the hill towns and in the countryside north of Rome, producing only enough to support themselves and too far away to allow for any effective provisioning of the city. Naturally, the population dwindled: still close to 800,000 by A.D. 400, it had dropped to 500,000 by A.D. 452 and to perhaps 100,000 by A.D. 500. After the Gothic siege, no more than 30,000 were left and possibly fewer, until by Gregory's time refugees from the Longobards swelled the figure to perhaps 90,000.

At the same time, the physical fabric of the city was deteriorating slowly but surely. Already by 500, the correspondence of Cassiodorus, Theodoric's chancellor, reflects their attempt to rescue the city; a few buildings, indeed, were patched up. But by and large, the letters convey a picture of utter shabbiness. Try as Cassiodorus might, his efforts to halt the erosion were in vain. Sewers were in need of repairs. So were aqueducts, and moreover water and maintenance personnel had been diverted for private ends. The public granaries had "collapsed through old age." Two bronze elephants on the Via Sacra were "falling into ruin. . . . Their crumbling limbs [should] be strengthened by iron hooks and their drooping bellies supported by masonry." Bronze statues all over were being looted, ". . . nor are they mute; the ringing sound they give forth under the blows of the thieves . . . wakes the dozing watchman." Marble, lead, and brass were looted from public buildings; the empty clamp holes all over the Colosseum yet testify to such pilfering, which continued from antiquity into the Renaissance. Temples, Cassiodorus complains, "have been

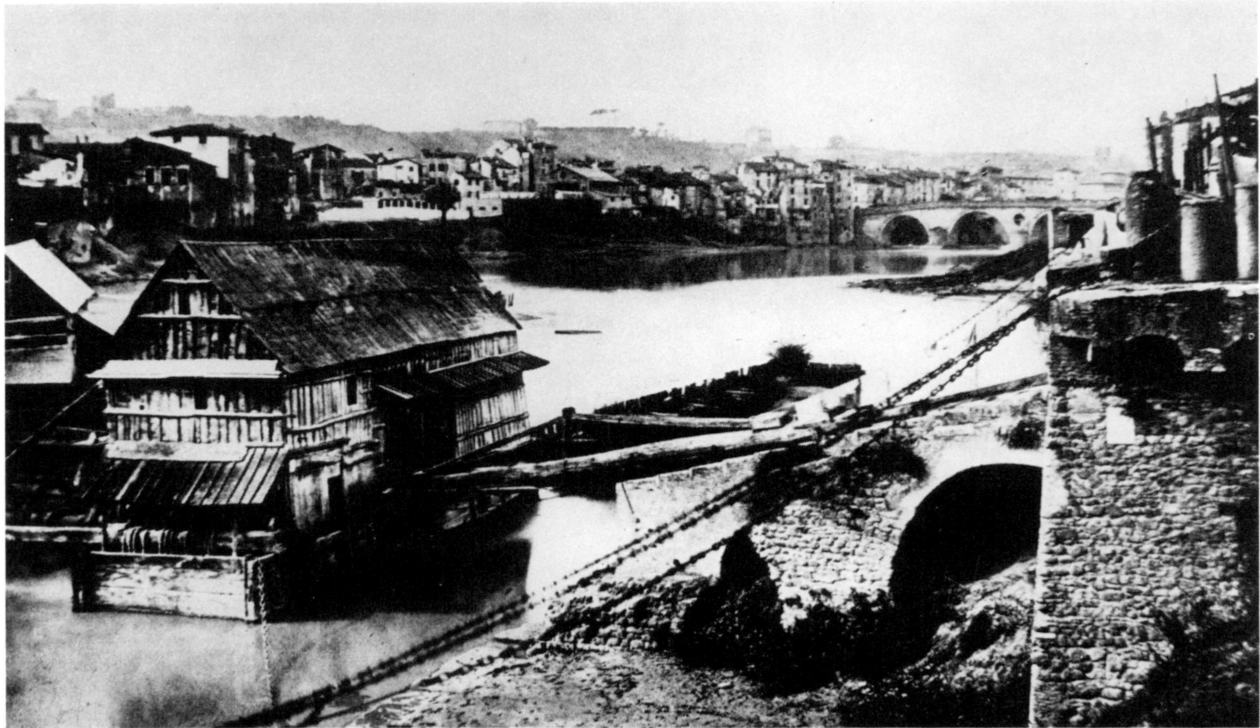

57. Floating mills on Tiber, as of ca. 1870, Museo di Roma

handed over to spoliation and ruin." Confiscated in 408, they had become government property; but no funds were available to keep them in repair. Many of the great mansions, too, had been abandoned; and, while here and there a community of pious men and women, or, from the sixth century on, a monastic congregation, would have settled down in one for a life of Christian contemplation, others became quarries. Colonnades would collapse, marble revetment would come off the walls, pavements would loosen, and the ruin would invite despoiling, notwithstanding ever repeated imperial vetoes. Indeed, in 459 spoliation was legalized where a structure, temple, public building, or mansion was "beyond repair," a phrasing that obviously allowed for the loosest of interpretations. Such pilfering of precious materials, to be sure, was age-old Roman custom; and from Constantine's day, the Church was its principal beneficiary and the main culprit. Spoils are plentiful in any church in Rome from Christian antiquity on through the Middle Ages and beyond: the column shafts, bases, capitals, and fragments of entablature assembled to build Old St. Peter's; the forty-two green marble columns, once in the aisles of the Lateran Basilica; the second-century capitals and columns and the marble revetment in S. Costanza; the set of twenty-four Corinthian columns at S. Sabina, and the twenty Doric columns at S. Pietro in Vincoli; and, as late as the sixth century, the columns in the east basilica of S. Lorenzo fuori le mura with their elaborate capitals (fig. 68). The physical collapse of the city from the fourth century on built Christian Rome.

Along with temples and statues, the public buildings and mansions, tenements and apartment houses would deteriorate: staircases would collapse, water conduits cease functioning, roofs and terraces leak, the upper floors become uninhabitable; but people would, as they did for another thousand years and more, find refuge on the lower floors or in abandoned mansions shored up as much as possible. No doubt, by Gregory's time large numbers, if not most, of the structures that had made Imperial Rome were in shambles. Nonetheless, Rome was not gone. The skeleton of the urban fabric had survived, shabby and damaged, but fundamentally intact. The city walls still stood, incorporating Byzantine repairs. The streets remained, albeit covered in places by an accumulation of earth and rubbish. But major thoroughfares and squares were kept free: the column set up on the Roman Forum in 608 to honor the emperor Phocas rises from the third-century pavement. The aqueducts functioned, at least in part, and some public baths were in working order; the aqueduct on the Gianicolo, repaired in 537 by Byzantine army engineers, still drove the mills on the hill slope; and the floating mills on the Tiber continued to work long after, even into the nineteenth century (fig. 57). People still came to the Forum to look at and buy new merchandise, including slaves, and to pass on the news; and the Forum of Trajan was used for literary reunions and survived into the seventh century. Cultured visitors would still tour the monuments of antiquity; when Emperor Constans II came to Rome in 667, a member of his retinue scratched the sovereign's name on the stairwell inside the Column of Trajan and on the Janus Quadrifrons. The palaces on the Palatine, too, were apparently kept in repair; various officers of the palace functioned there in Gregory's time; and a "curator of the palace" was in charge as late as 687. Public secular buildings were maintained, it seems, since they were imperial property, provided they were still of use and funds could be procured. Churches, as of old, were enriched by gifts. New ones had been built in the sixty years preceding Gregory's pontificate: SS. Quirico e Giulitta, in 537; SS. Apostoli, originally dedicated to the Apostles James and Philip, in about 560; S. Giovanni a Porta

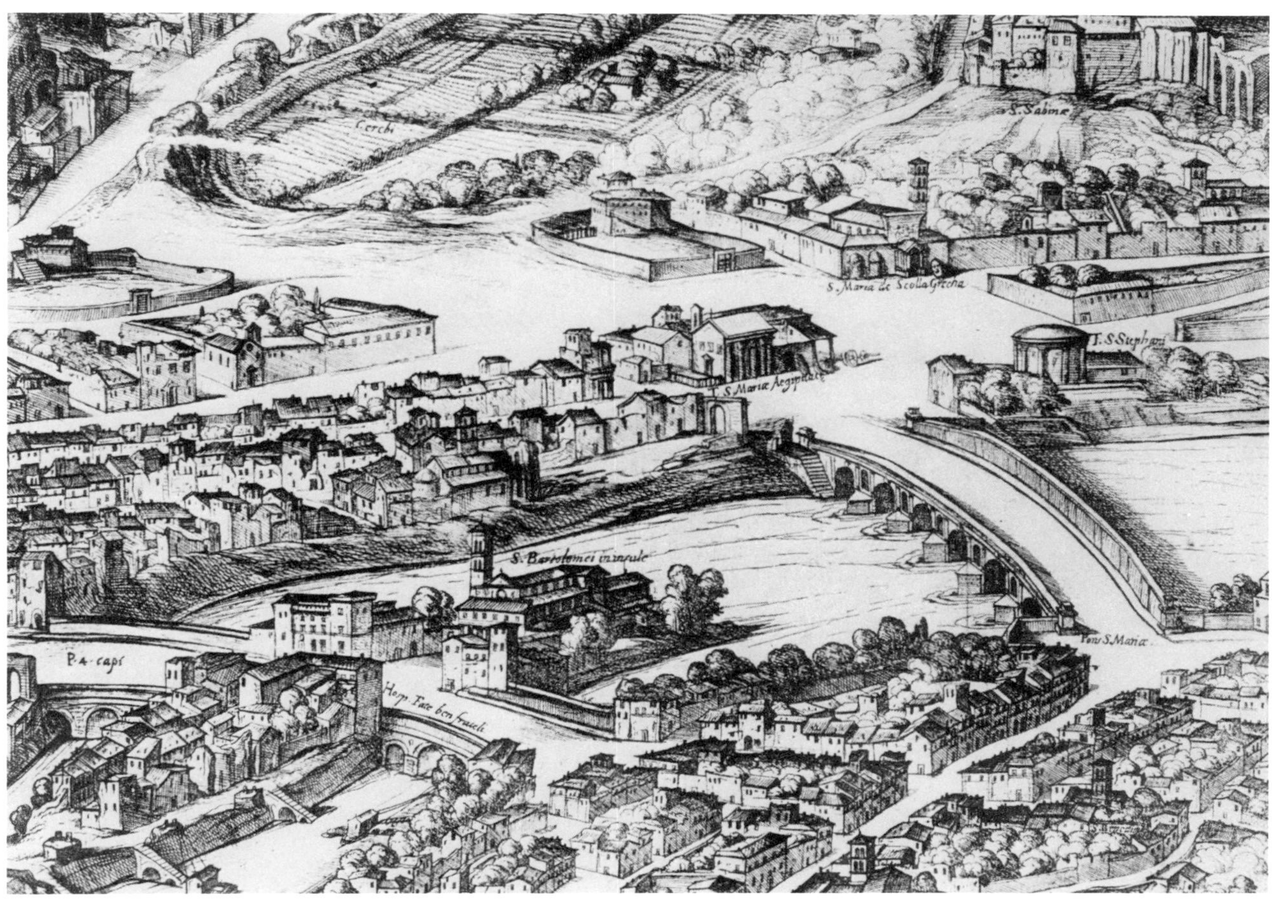

58. Map of Rome, 1593, A. Tempesta, detail showing Trastevere, Tiber Island with Ponte Fabrizio and Ponte Cestio, Ponte Rotto (Ponte S. Maria), S. Maria in Cosmedin, and (upper right) Aventine

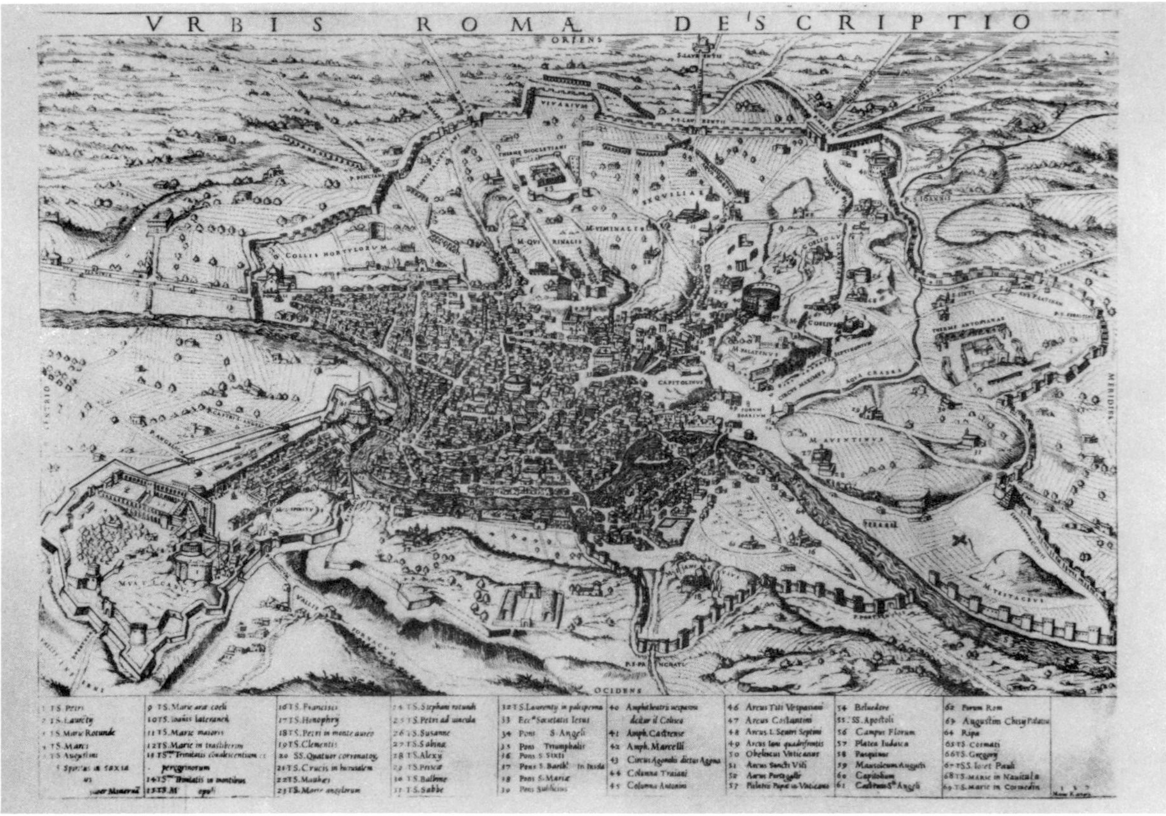

59. Map of Rome, 1575 ("Small Cartaro map")

Latina, far out near the walls, perhaps about 550; outside the walls, possibly about 600, the basilica over the graves of the martyrs Nereus, Achilleus, and Domitilla in the catacomb named after her; and, between 579 and 590, that over the tomb of St. Lawrence, now the chancel of the large church. All five date from the time of the Byzantine occupation and each is marked by some Eastern feature: a trefoil chancel at SS. Quirico e Giulitta and perhaps at SS. Apostoli; an apse, polygonal outside at S. Giovanni a Porta Latina; galleries over the aisles and inner narthex at S. Lorenzo, S. Agnese, and possibly in the Domitilla catacomb.

Housing, too, if patched up and near collapse, was available for the population. Reduced as it was, it may already have concentrated on either bank opposite the Tiber Island: in Trastevere and, on the east bank, between the Theatre of Marcellus, the foot of the Capitol, and roughly the line of today's Via Arenula, that is near the Tiber bridges and where Gregory placed his welfare centers (fig. 58). To the east, south, and north a wasteland extended to the walls, where formerly tenement houses had stood in popular quarters and great mansions had risen in the greenbelt. The contrast between the *abitato* and the *disabitato*, as the sixteenth century called them, had become apparent (fig. 59). Starting from the fifth century, and progressively ever more clearly marked, it persisted until the late nineteenth century: a large expanse of vineyards, fields, and ruins, interspersed with small settlements and a few farms surrounding a small densely populated nucleus (fig. 60). As late as the 1870s a vast stretch of vineyards, gardens, and groves covered the valley between the Palatine and the Celian Hill reaching from Porta S. Paolo, the old Porta Ostiensis, to the Colosseum (fig. 61). The smallness and compactness of the abitato within the vastness of the disabitato remains a constant factor in the picture of Rome far beyond the Middle Ages. By Gregory's time already it must have been marked—

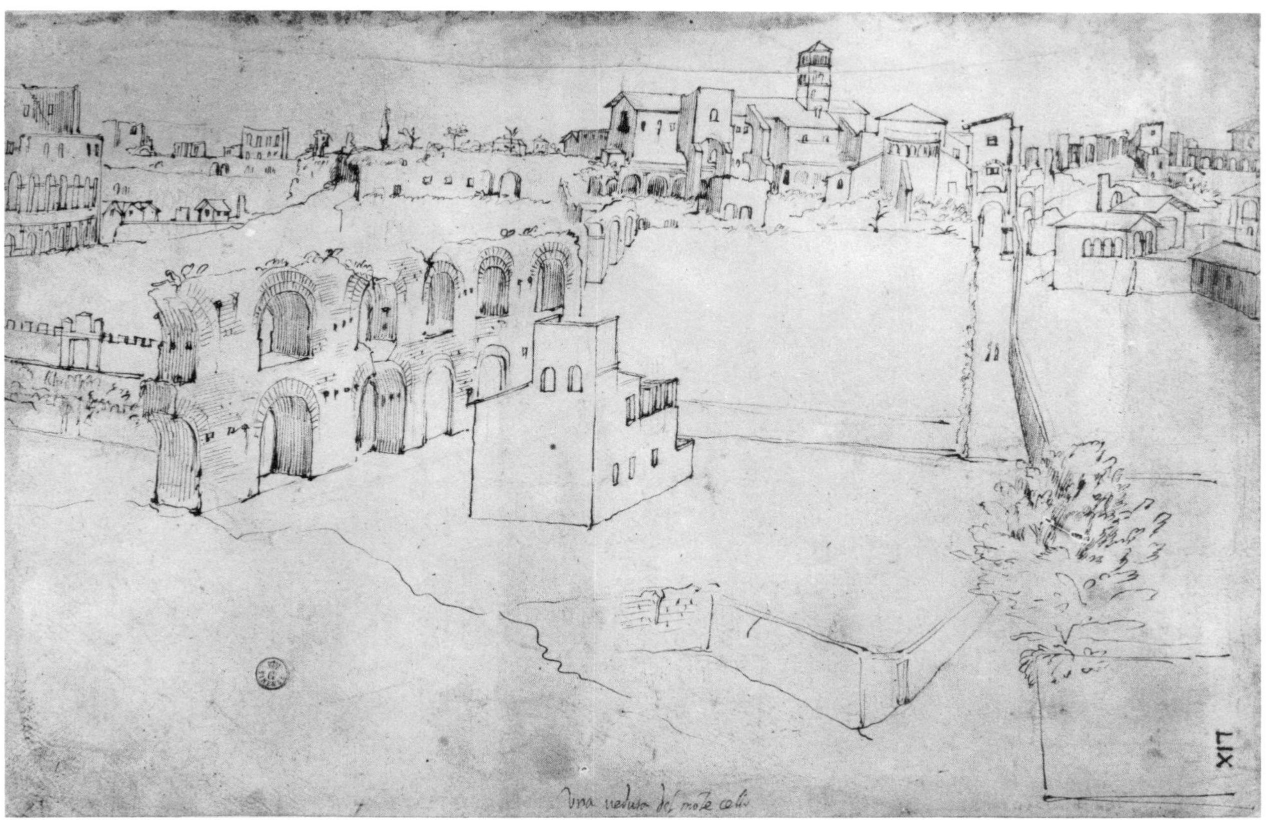

60. The disabitato from the Palatine toward the Colosseum, SS. Giovanni e Paolo, and (at right edge) chapels of S. Gregorio Magno, as of ca. 1560, G. A. Dosio, Florence, Uffizi

not as clearly as in the sixteenth century, perhaps, but marked. Nonetheless, shrunk as it was, this nucleus by 590 was not an empty shell; there was a foundation for Gregory to build on.

Like the physical skeleton of the city, a social and economic framework had survived, if deteriorated and badly in need of reorganization. The Byzantine government established at Ravenna had become powerless. Under the threat of the Longobards, its garrisons had withdrawn to a few strongholds: Ravenna and Rome, the temporal and spiritual capitals in Italy; Naples and Rimini, near the sea; and a stretch of inland territory intended to secure the route from Ravenna to Rome. Officials in Rome, cut off from Constantinople and often from Ravenna, had to rely increasingly on the local authorities, secular and ecclesiastical. The former could be of little help: the Senate, while reconstituted in 554, had only ceremonial functions; after 603, an informal advisory council appeared in its place, drawn from the leading families: a few of old Roman lineage, most others newcomers; Byzantine officials and army men, or Longobards, settled on new estates in or near Rome, quickly integrated in the local nobility and woven into the increasingly powerful papal administration.

The Church was the only efficient organization left to maintain the economic, social, and indeed the political fabric of Rome. From the fourth century on, she had acquired huge estates all around the Mediterranean, through donations and bequests from imperial and private sources, or through purchase and exchange. Those in the East, in Africa, Spain, and Gaul, were lost by the middle of the sixth century. But those in Italy remained: in the South; in Sicily and in Sardinia; the most important in Central Italy, where they extended in a loose chain from Rome across to the Adriatic coast and up into Tuscia, Tuscany, Liguria, and Romagna. The Church thus had become the largest and most powerful landholder in the Italian peninsula and

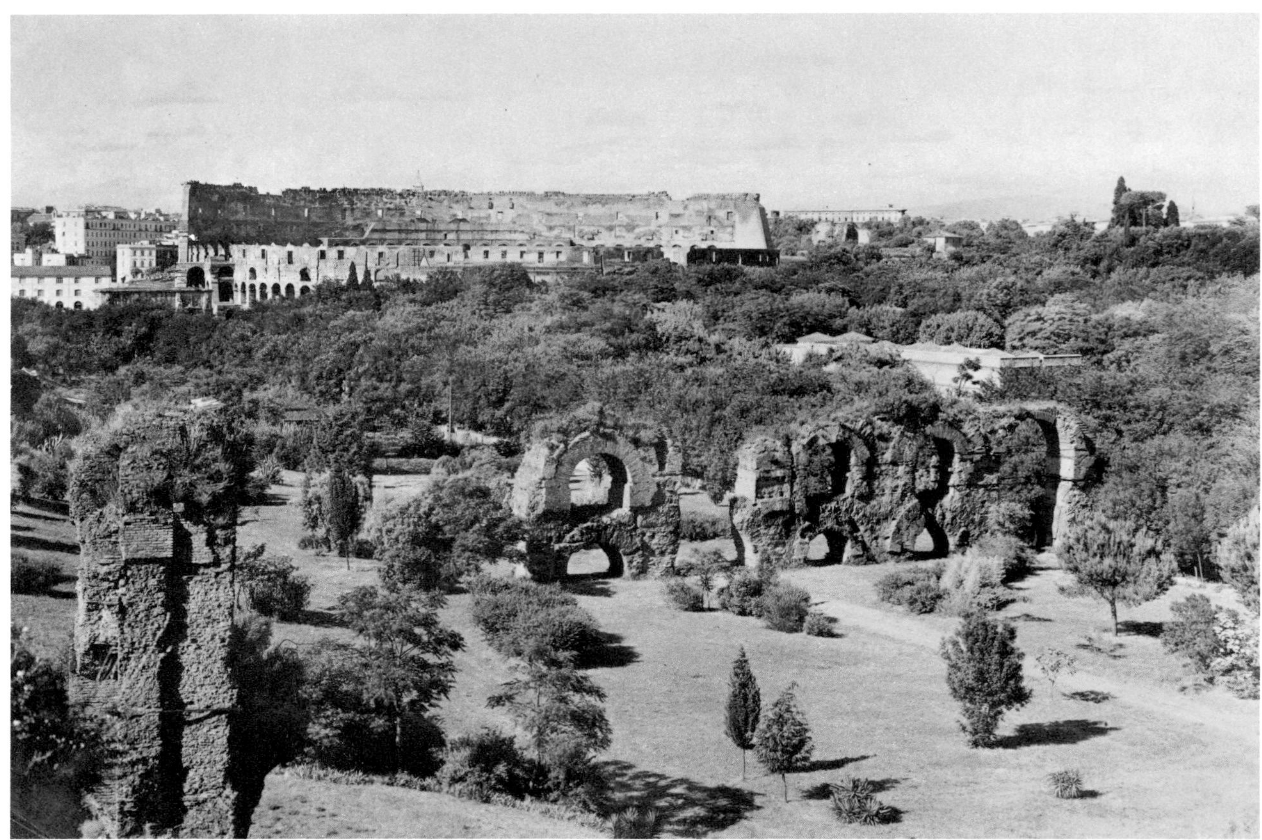

61. Part of disabitato, toward the Colosseum from south, as of ca. 1870

the nearby islands. The Longobard invaders endangered or occupied large parts of the Central Italian estates; but Gregory's negotiations saved many; those in the South and in Sicily were not threatened. Some of these holdings were locally controlled; the majority as early as the end of the fifth century were administered directly from Rome with great efficiency: a central accounting system was evolved in the papal chancery; and a budget was apparently prepared, one part of the income going to the papal administration, another to the needs of the clergy, a third to the maintenance of church buildings, a fourth to charity. These funds enabled the papacy to carry out through the fifth century an ambitious building program, including S. Sabina, S. Maria Maggiore, Sto. Stefano Rotondo and work in the Lateran complex. More important still, they soon placed the Church in a position to take over efficiently part of the welfare program heretofore run in a desultory way by the state to sustain the population of the city; to supplement or take on wholly, in times of famine, its provisioning; to erect, in the first years of the sixth century, hostels for poor pilgrims; and implicitly to gain ever greater political strength within the power vacuum of late-fifth- and sixth-century Italy.

Nonetheless, as the Gothic Wars, the Byzantine conquest, and the Longobard invasion successively swept over the country, the economic position of the Church and her efficiency obviously deteriorated; her landholdings shrank; and provisioning drawn from these lands grew less dependable and less plentiful in Rome. The wounds from the Gothic Wars were apparently healing in the twenty or so years following the Byzantine occupation of Rome. Funds for large and expensive church buildings were available; but they may have come, too, from private sources, as when SS. Apostoli was built, possibly by the Byzantine viceroy, Narses. Even after the Longobards swept through the countryside, a church as splendid as the new basilica of S.

Lorenzo fuori le mura could be set up by Pope Pelagius II, Gregory's predecessor; his dedicatory inscription mentions the threat of invasion. Much of the Church lands remained intact. A welfare program could be maintained within limits. The organization both for providing and distributing foodstuffs had presumably suffered, but its skeleton survived. With the progressive weakening of the Byzantine administration in the last third of the sixth century, the Church had to take on by herself, through force of circumstance, nearly the entire task of feeding the people of Rome; only rarely could the government assist in combatting the endemic threat of famine.

When Gregory ascended the See of Saint Peter, this situation was taken for granted. The Church rather than the Byzantine state, nominally still the legitimate government, was responsible for providing for the urban population. Concurrently, further governmental tasks had slid gradually through sheer default and went on sliding into the hands of the Church. The papal treasury, experienced and well organized, was the only one to function in Rome; the government's financial structure had broken down, and by Gregory's time the Church had to act as paymaster to the troops. Indeed, an energetic pope like Gregory would take a hand in military matters; he would negotiate a truce with the Longobards; or he would instruct his representative in Ravenna to urge in no uncertain terms the appointment of a papal nominee to take charge of Rome's aqueducts. In short, the Church increasingly assumed, and was forced to take on, the functions and responsibilities of a temporal, independent ruler of Rome and of the Lands of Saint Peter, from Central Italy and Tuscany to Sicily. By and under Gregory, this development was, if not completed, well advanced.

In the urban fabric of the city, the interplay of secular government and ecclesiastical administration and the gradual replacement of the former by the latter are first reflected in the Church takeover of public buildings. Maintenance funds from public sources or wealthy officials, starting with the sixth century if not before, were no longer flowing; the more so since many public buildings no longer filled any relevant function. After all, the importance of the central and city government had steadily declined. Prudence advised a shift in the burden of maintenance to the institution most able to carry it. As early as 526-530, under Pope Felix IV and still at the time of Cassiodorus and Theodoric, the sumptuous hall on the Via Sacra, presumably the audience hall of the city prefect, and its domed vestibule next to the the Basilica Nova were ceded to the Church (fig. 7). Converted into a church and dedicated to Saints Cosmas and Damian, the hall preserved its fourth-century wall-facing of *opus sectile* in colored marble until 1632. Pope Felix only added mosaics covering the arch and the vault of the apse to mark the new ecclesiastical functions of the structure: on the former, angels and the symbols of the Evangelists; on the latter, Christ at his Second Coming flanked by Peter, Paul, and the two patron saints, accompanied by another Eastern saint, Theodore, and by the papal donor.

Fifty years after SS. Cosma e Damiano, another public building, across the Forum at the northwestern foot of the Palatine, became a church: S. Maria Antiqua, as it was called as early as 635-642. Built in the late first century as a ceremonial hall, the structure by the mid-sixth century had apparently become a guard room to protect the ramp ascending to the palaces atop the hill, where the Byzantine governor then resided (fig. 62). As would befit the viceroy of the Most Christian emperor, the guard room was decorated with Christian murals, recalling Justinian's mosaics in the *Chalkē*, the Bronze Gate, the guard room of the imperial palace in Constantinople. From then on for another two hundred years, the hall, transformed into a church, was covered time and again with new murals, until a landslide in 847 buried the structure; discovered in 1702, its ruins were excavated and identified in 1900. Its rights and possessions after 847 were transferred to S. Maria Nova, now S. Francesca Romana, diagonally across the Forum and the Via Sacra. But the successive repaintings and their sealing off at that early time have turned S. Maria Antiqua into a repository of seventh- and eighth-century art in Rome, a regular *pinacoteca* reflecting the interplay of Western and Eastern elements in these early centuries.

Gregory himself seems to have been hesitant to take over public buildings for the Church. They were, after all, imperial property and given the delicate balance of his policy between Byzantines and Longobards, he may have refrained from asking permission; or he was reluctant to carry the expense of maintenance. Things changed in the thirty years following his death. Pope Honorius, between 625 and 638, turned the Senate House on the Forum Romanum into the church of S. Adriano, with but minor structural changes; possibly at the same time, the *secretarium senatus*, the High Court of the Senate, was converted into, or more likely replaced by, an oratory dedicated to S. Martina. All this was presumably done with imperial *placet*; as late as 630 or thereabouts, an imperial decree was necessary to allow the pope to move the bronze tiles from the Temple of Roma to St. Peter's. Likewise, large private buildings, abandoned or useless to the owners or too costly in upkeep, almost naturally fell to the Church; she was the only power left in Rome able to put them to new use and to afford maintaining them. Mansions were turned into monasteries, their reception halls into churches. Gregory, on the Celian, had set an example; a few decades later, Honorius I similarly appropriated the huge halls of two mansions: one, on the Esquiline, survives incorporated in the convent of S. Lucia in Selcis; the other, on the northwest spur of the Celian Hill, provided the foundation walls for the church of the Quattro Coronati.

It is far more incisive that in 609 for the first time in Rome, a temple was Christianized: the Pantheon, formerly dedicated to all the gods, was handed over by the emperor upon the request of Pope Boniface IV; consecrated to the Virgin Mary and all the martyrs, it became the church of S. Maria Rotunda (fig. 63). For a long time, it appears to have been the only major church to serve the eastward zone of what was later to become the inner city. Structural changes were minimal: an altar was placed in the main niche, surmounted by an icon of the Virgin and Child—the seventh-century original was recovered under layers of overpainting a

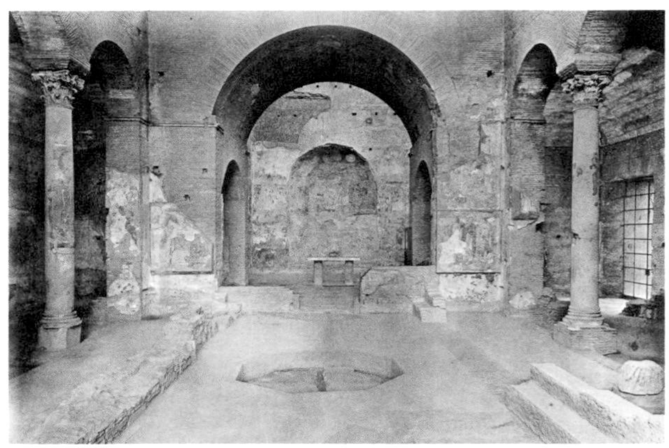

62. S. Maria Antiqua, interior

few years ago. It is strange that over two hundred years had elapsed after the closing by law of the pagan sanctuaries before a temple in Rome was converted; the more so, since Christians in the East as early as the fourth century had without scruple possessed themselves of pagan temples, and the West, too, in the sixth century had followed suit. But, for some reason, Rome remained reluctant. Even after the Pantheon was Christianized, nearly another three hundred years went by until one more temple, that of Fortuna Virilis on Bocca della Verità, was turned into a church, between 872 and 882; and, until the High Middle Ages, temples and indeed the sites of temples long since collapsed, were shunned in Rome by the founders of churches. Was it only in Rome that the belief in evil spirits haunting temple sites lingered on with such strength, and if so, why? Gregory time and again testifies to its prevalence. But late in life he also may have broken through it: "after considering the matter at length," he instructed the mission to England to reuse pagan sanctuaries as churches after destroying the idols; expediency seems to have won out over superstitious reluctance. Ultimately, he himself may have sparked off the idea of converting the Pantheon, and the medieval legend depicting him driving demons out of it may not have been far wrong. Legend, too, linked Gregory's name to the Christianization of Hadrian's Mausoleum. Ever since late Roman times, its huge cylindrical mass had served as a west-bank bridgehead to protect the access to the city across the pons Aelius, Ponte

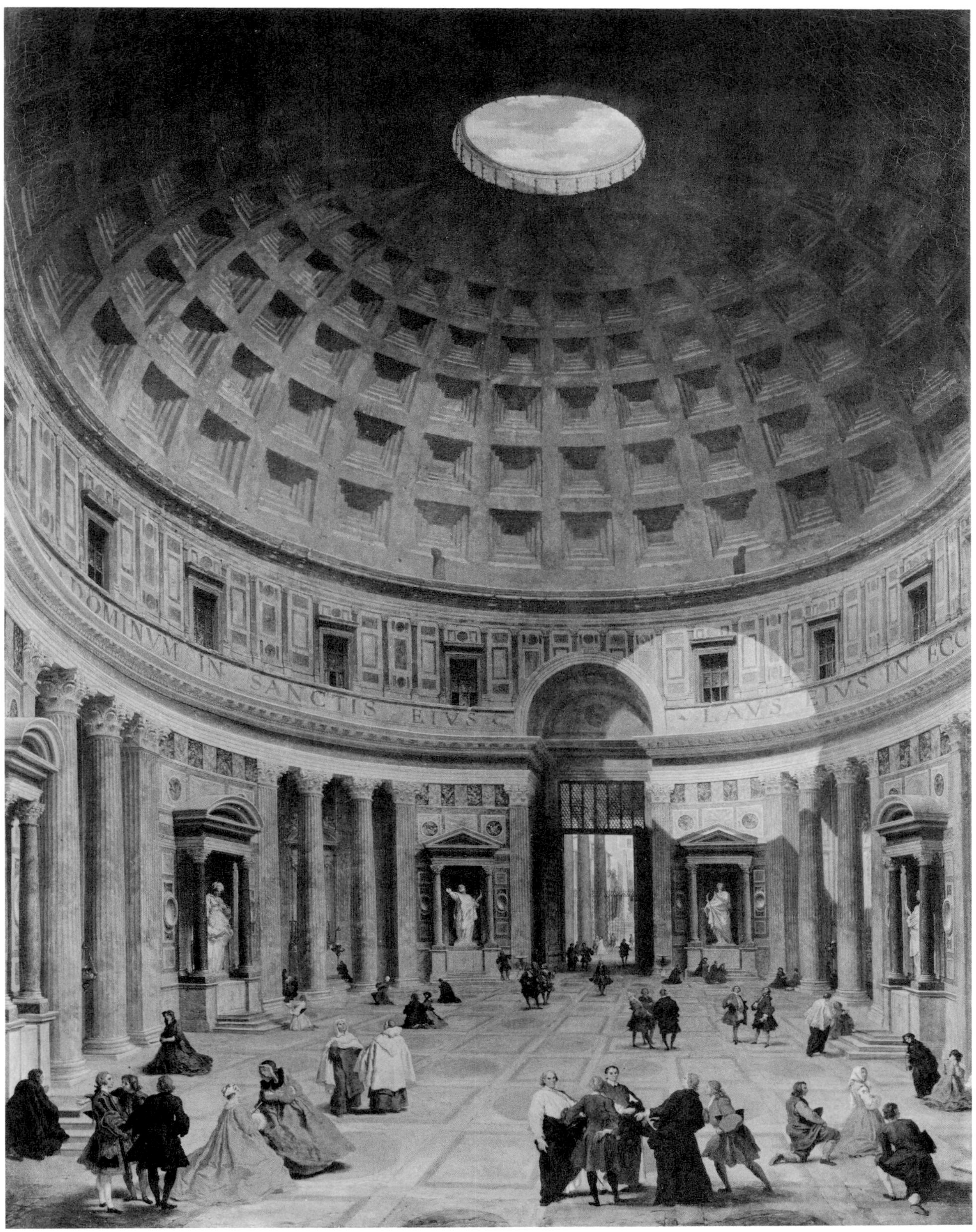

63. Pantheon, interior, as of ca.1740, painting G. P. Pannini, National Gallery, Washington, D.C.

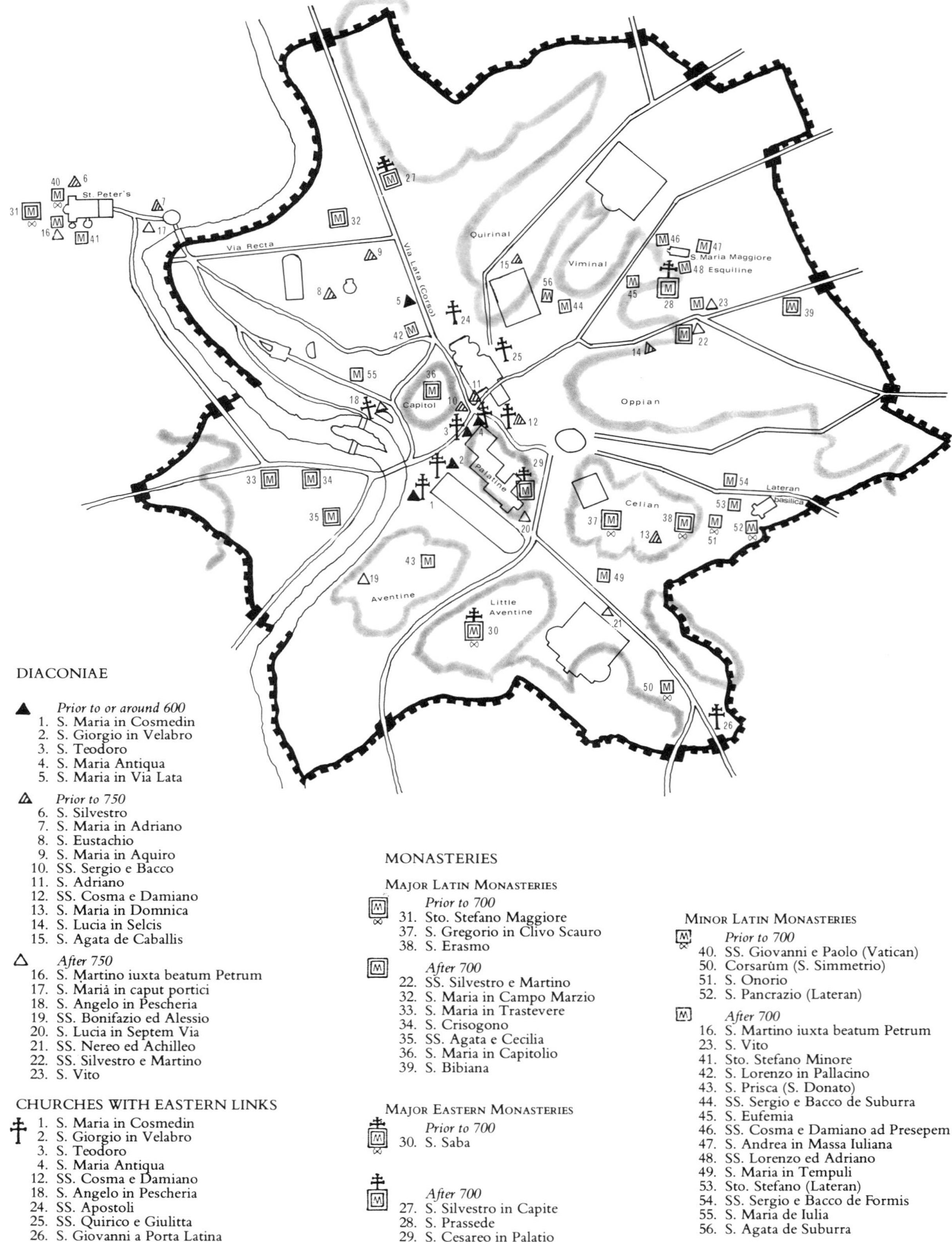

64. Map of Rome, seventh and eighth centuries

S. Angelo; in 536, the Byzantine commander defeated a *coup de main* of besieging Goths by having the statues on the tomb smashed and catapulted on the attackers. In 590, when Gregory led his processions to implore divine help against the disasters that hit Rome, the Archangel Michael was said to have descended to stop the pestilence. More likely, it was his successor Boniface's idea to crown the mausoleum with a chapel dedicated to Saint Michael. Given both its dedication and its position as a stronghold dominating and protecting both the city on the east bank and St. Peter's on the west bank, it eventually took its present name, Castel S. Angelo.

The majority of churches founded in the sixth century up to the time of Gregory and in the thirty years following were centered around the fora, the Via Sacra, and the Palatine, the very heart of Imperial Rome (fig. 64). The area was not and never had been densely inhabited; there was no need for places of worship for a sizable population. It was a showplace, then largely deprived of its former administrative and representative functions, and had thus fallen into disuse. Where its public buildings were turned into churches, the reason may well have been in part to shift the burden of maintenance to the Church. But along with such conversions, new churches in the sixth and seventh centuries were built all through the area; indeed, Christianization of the monumental showplace of ancient Rome was thorough. Beginning with the conversion of SS. Cosma e Damiano, it continued with the building of SS. Quirico e Giulitta behind the Forum of Nerva; with SS. Apostoli, north of the Forum and Market of Trajan; and with S. Maria Antiqua below the cliff of the Palatine. Between 625 and 638 S. Adriano and presumably S. Martina were installed in the former Senate buildings on the Forum. Later still, though also during the seventh century, a *diaconia*, or welfare center, was apparently set up near the Temple of Concord. On the hill overlooking the Forum of Trajan, near the present Torre delle Milizie, a chapel dedicated to Saints Cyrus and John and later known as S. Abaciro had been built by 680, it seems. Public buildings converted and newly built churches thus staked out a large Christian zone reaching from the foot of the Palatine to north of the Forum and the Market of Trajan, in and around the monumental show area of ancient Rome. Was the idea, then, also to consecrate to Christ the center of Old Rome, still filled with memories of pagan times, just as the Pantheon was turned from a temple of the gods into a temple of God? Where Constantine, two hundred and fifty years before, had shied away from letting the new faith invade the fora because of their pagan connotations, the Church now made the area her own with a vengeance. Still, it did take a quarter of a millennium to transform visually and ideologically what had been the hub of the empire.

The area thus became Christian, and it did so with strikingly Byzantine and Eastern accents. The cult of Cosmas and Damian, the miraculous healers from Cilicia, had reached Rome at the start of the sixth century, presumably through Constantinople. The veneration of Sergius and Bacchus, Syrian martyrs, also came from there, as did that of Saint Hadrian, a soldier saint. The cult of the martyrs Quirinus and Giulitta had spread from Tarsus in southern Asia Minor. Cyrus and John came from Egypt, where their relics were venerated still between 610 and 620 at a place near Alexandria. The joint veneration of the Apostles Philip and James, common all over the East, seems to have been unknown in the West prior to the foundation in Rome of the church built in their honor, SS. Apostoli. Below the southwest corner of the Palatine, the *titulus Anastasiae*, founded evidently by a lady of that name perhaps in the fourth century, two hundred years later took on the dedication to a homonymous saint much venerated in Constantinople. Such migrations of saints from the East to Rome were only natural in churches founded, dedicated, or remodeled under the eyes of the Byzantine authorities. Literally under their eyes: the palaces on the Palatine, overlooking the fora to the north, were, after all, potentially the residence of the emperor, if he ever came to Rome, or of his representative; and following ancient custom, the government offices would have been located there. The military commander seems to have been installed to the north of the Imperial Fora and not far from SS. Apostoli.

There, on Piazza Magnanapoli and adjoining the Market of Trajan, a thirteenth-century tower, Torre delle Milizie, stands today, linked by legend to Nero and the fire that laid Rome in ashes. The name suggests some early military establishment on the site. Indeed, the tower was added to an older fortification surviving at least till the late fifteenth century and known in 1130 as *Militiae Tiberinae*; the name may well allude to the "barbarians" formed into regiments bearing the name of the Byzantine Emperor Tiberius Constantine (578-582); or to the citizens' militia set up at that very time to defend Rome against the Longobard onslaught of 578. Possibly, too, the name *Magnanapoli*, corrupted from *bannum neapolis*, has military implications: the levy, *bannum*, from Naples; but this etymology is doubtful, and the reference to the Militiae Tiberinae can stand by itself.

Between the Palatine and the neighborhood of Torre delle Milizie, then, a Byzantine quarter seems to have grown up in the course of the sixth and early seventh centuries. It revived, though with a new meaning, the monumental and government area of Ancient Rome. The project, perhaps envisaged by the great fifth-century popes, to abandon that zone and focus the map of Christian Rome on the Lateran instead had failed. So had Cassiodorus' program to preserve and restore to their former glory, though devoid of meaning, Rome's ancient monuments. In the hundred and ten years between 530 and 640, between the conversion of SS. Cosma e Damiano and that of the Senate House, S. Adriano, a last effort was made to instil new life into the area by giving it a Christian meaning and turning it into a government quarter.

Gregory and the popes after him, it seems, were little involved, if at all, in this government compound north of the Palatine. No attempt was made to merge the government area with the quarters where the population by that time tended to live: in Trastevere; and, on the east bank, from the Theatre of Marcellus and the nearby bridgeheads of Ponte S. Maria, today's Ponte Rotto, and Ponte Fabrizio to the west foot of the Capitoline Hill and westward roughly to the line of the present Via Arenula. In this area of major concentration, the principal responsibilities of the Pope as the de facto ruler of Rome had to be discharged: feeding the people; maintaining essential services; building up an efficient administrative organization; keeping in touch with the urban masses. A second responsibility, no less important, was to provide Rome with a new raison d'être. Through the Christianization and re-Catholicization of Europe, she was being established as the Holy City of the West. The graves of the Apostles and martyrs became a focal point of veneration; they had to be kept accessible. Pilgrims by the thousands would be attracted to Rome and had to be taken care of. These were the main tasks and Gregory turned to them with all the energy of a top-flight administrator.

The population—residents, pilgrims, refugees from the Longobards, in the course of time foreigners permanently settled—had to be provided for. The landholdings of the Church, losses notwithstanding, were still large in Central Italy; in the South and in Sicily they were intact. Foodstuffs aplenty could be drawn from them. Where the organization had suffered during the troubled decades preceding his pontificate, Gregory restored, tightened, and improved it. As of old, the estates were administered under the direct control of the Papal See; they were regionally organized—the patrimony of Sicily, Tuscia, and so forth—and supervised by a staff dependent on Rome. Tenant farmers, serfs, and grain stores were vigorously defended against governmental encroachment; the harvest was collected in "Granaries of the Church"; if needed, additional grain was bought; and boats, owned or chartered by the Church, brought the supply to Rome, where it was again stored in Church-owned granaries.

Distribution to the urban masses in Rome was likewise well regulated. In the fifth century, one recalls, a central welfare organization had been set up at the papal palace, the Lateran. Gregory presumably reactivated and improved it. A roster of welfare recipients—churches, monasteries, individuals—was kept at the Lateran; it was preserved till the ninth century. Foodstuffs, seasonably available, were doled out on the first of each month—grain, wine, cheese, vegetables, lard, meat, oil, fish; mobile soup kitchens provided for the sick and infirm; notables were regaled with condiments; the clergy, monasteries, and churches received gifts in specie four times a year. However, the Lateran was far from what had become by Gregory's time the densely populated area of town. To supplement the Lateran center, welfare offices were set up nearer that zone; their name, *diaconiae*, has survived in the title of the Cardinal Deacons. Such centers were known in the East since the fourth century, and by the end of the sixth century they were common in the seaports of Ravenna, Rimini, and Naples. In Rome they are documented by name only from 684, when the monastic congregations servicing them were set apart as a group from the clergy and the service personnel attached to regular churches. Archaeological evidence, however, suggests that the first were established in the fifty years following the Byzantine reconquest, one perhaps preceding the pontificate of Gregory the Great. Whether or not they were initially connected with the quartermastering of the imperial militia remains open. Their functions, in any event—if only in the eighth century—are well documented: providing and distributing food, and thus supplementing the work of the central welfare administration; providing facilities for bathing, no longer obtainable in public baths; running hostels for pilgrims, for the poor and the sick—the three often coincided. Financial support for their work was provided by landholdings set aside for them by the Church or by wealthy donors. Given the Christian connotation of charity, their performance obviously was no longer a purely secular task, but interlocked with a Christian's duty to God and neighbor. Nonetheless, these welfare centers were not churches by any means. They were run by the Church and they each contained an oratory; but they were utilitarian and secular as much as ecclesiastical, and they inherited and continued an old government tradition: although serviced by monastic congregations, they were supervised by a lay official of the papal civil service, the *pater diaconiae*; and, more often than not, they occupied sites linked in Roman times to the administration, distribution, and storage of provisions.

In Rome, remains of early welfare centers have survived at S. Maria in Cosmedin, S. Giorgio in Velabro, S. Teodoro, S. Maria in Via Lata. In all four, the archaeological evidence points to a foundation date around 600 or earlier. All occupy sites linked of old to the administration or storage of food supplies. In all, the layout seems dictated by this ancient heritage, by their semi-ecclesiastical character, and by practical needs: a number of rooms offering storage and office space and living quarters for the monastic congregation in charge; and one larger room set aside as an oratory. Moreover, all were located in an area linked from ancient times to the task of feeding Rome. Close to the Tiber docks, below the cliff of the Aventine, it was filled with storehouses and markets; Ponte S. Maria, now Ponte Rotto, connected it with crowded Trastevere. This supply zone started at Piazza Bocca della Verità where, one recalls, the imperial official in charge of food supply gave audience at a loggia, the *statio annonae*. Northward, the area continued into the cattle market, the Forum Boarium, marked by the arch of the Janus Quadrifrons and the church of S. Giorgio in Velabro. Still further north followed the oil market, the Forum Holitorium, where since the eleventh or twelfth century the church of S. Nicola in Carcere has been standing. Below the west cliff of the Palatine, just east of the Forum Boarium, extended large granaries, and other *horrea* ran along the south stretch of the Corso. It was only natural for the early welfare centers to be set up in just that stretch, which extended from the river along the edge of the populous neighborhood that had formed there, spreading north to the Capitoline Hill and beyond in a northwesterly direction. In that zone, the welfare centers were easily accessible; also, they lay right under the eyes of the Byzantine authorities residing on the Palatine, and the garrison quartered, we conjecture, near the Torre delle Milizie.

S. Maria in Cosmedin, on Piazza Bocca della Verità, is the best example of such an early diaconia. Enlarged into a huge church in the eighth and again in the twelfth century, it was restored twice in the past seventy years and, incidentally, deprived of a charming eighteenth-

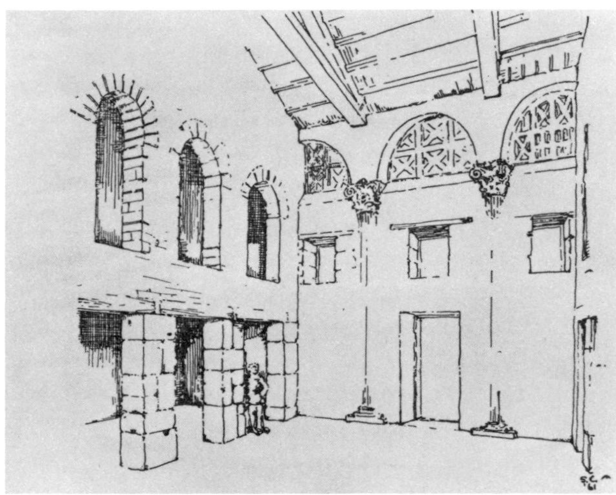

65. S. Maria in Cosmedin, diaconia hall, reconstruction Spencer Corbett

century façade. Today its walls enclose the remains of two earlier structures: the arcaded colonnade of the statio annonae; and, built across the depth of that loggia and well preserved in the nave walls in the front part of the present church, the side walls of a sizable hall (fig. 65). Apparently an oratory, this hall was flanked on either side by service rooms on two levels: those below, chambers or aisles; those above, communicating through windowlike openings with the main room. The plan, the tradition of the site as a center for provisioning and its function as a diaconia attested to from the eighth century, all make it likely that the hall and side rooms were built as a welfare center of the Church. Moreover, the masonry technique exhibits features unique in Rome, but common in sixth-century Naples; and the names of the church and its quarter, though documented later, suggest a Greek background, whether Constantinopolitan or South Italian: Cosmedin; the church of the Greeks; Greek street; or Greek compound, *schola graeca*—*schola* being the accepted term for foreign communities and their compounds in early medieval Rome. Presumably, then, the welfare center of S. Maria in Cosmedin was installed by Greeks from South Italy, perhaps traders, sometime after the Byzantine reconquest. Other centers followed a few decades later: one first mentioned as a church about 640 lies on the cattle market buried underneath S. Giorgio in Velabro—the present church dates from the ninth century. S. Teodoro, at the west foot of the Palatine and thus a few minutes walk from both S. Giorgio and S. Maria in Cosmedin, was installed over a Roman granary. The present church, round and domed, was built by Pope Nicholas V about 1453-54 (fig. 66). Around and below the rotunda extended the ruins of the granary, centered on an apsed hall of late-Roman date. The diaconia apparently occupied the granary rooms, its oratory arched over the late-Roman hall. The apse of the oratory survives; attached to the body of Nicholas' church, it carries a mosaic dating from about A.D. 600. Finally, at S. Maria in Via Lata on the Corso, the rooms of the welfare center survive below the splendid baroque façade. It, too, was set up in a granary of imperial times. Of six interconnected storerooms, one became an oratory; another was decorated in the early seventh century with a mural representing the Seven Sleepers of Ephesus.

Much as these welfare centers of the Church tell about conditions in Rome at the time of their foundation, their visual impact can only have been minor. They were modest structures, utilitarian in plan and appearance and, as often as not, installed in older structures adjusted as best possible. Most likely also, the increasing numbers of monasteries failed to catch the eye of the visitor to Rome. Of the four earliest, founded in the fifth century, three stood at the great sanctuaries outside town: at St. Peter's, S. Sebastiano and S. Lorenzo fuori le mura; the fourth, short-lived, occupied a now unknown site in town. By Gregory's time, a fifth must have existed at S. Paolo fuori le mura. By 630, their number had grown to seventeen, fifty years later to twenty-four. The majority were still out of town, clustered around the great pilgrimage centers and churches. Only eight stood within the walls and most occupied old mansions ceded by donors, pious and possibly unable or unwilling to maintain them. Gregory's monastery, set up on the family estate on the Celian, is but one such foundation. Others were established afterwards in their family mansions by Popes Boniface IV and Honorius I; earlier, Gregory's predecessor, Pelagius II, had installed an old-age

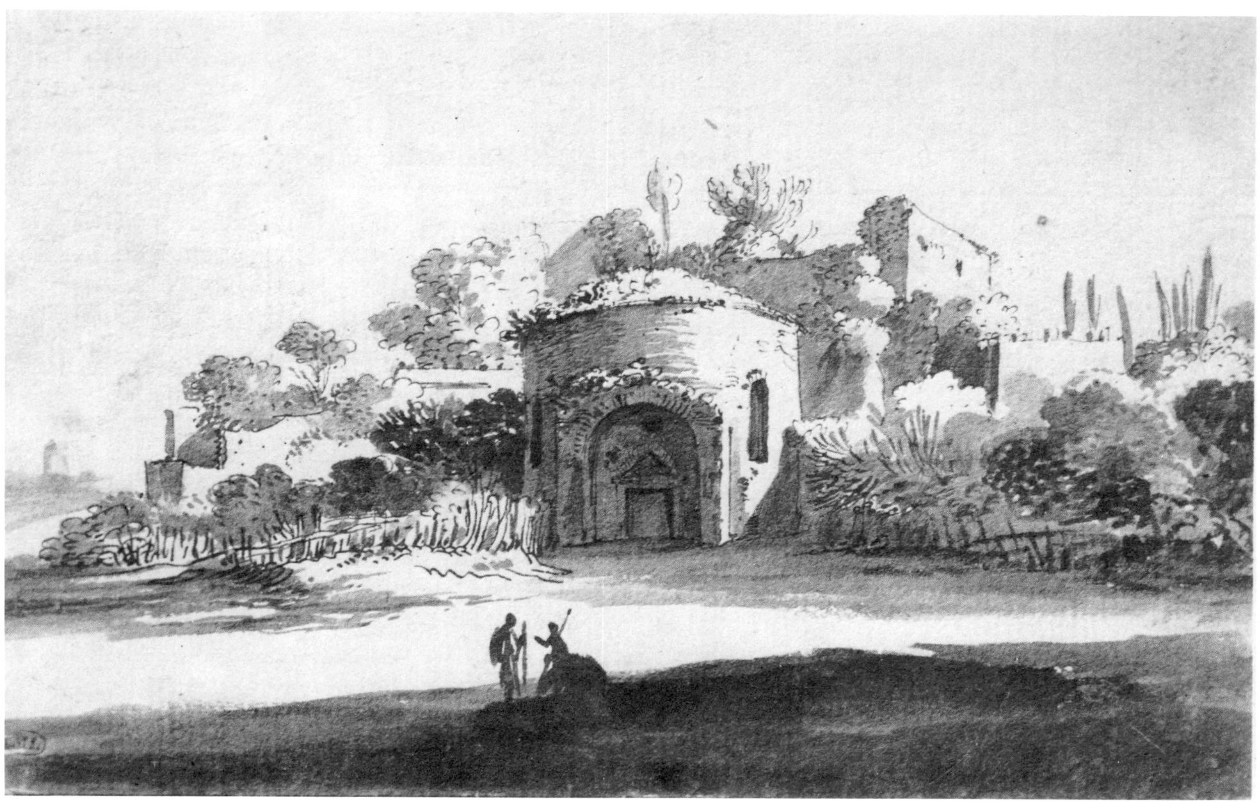

66. S. Teodoro, fifteenth-century church replacing old diaconia, as of ca. 1625, drawing, B. Breenbergh, Paris, Louvre

home in his mansion. The impact of monasticism on the ecclesiastical and civil administration of seventh- and eighth-century Rome was inestimably great. Monastic congregations served the Church in the highest and the most menial tasks. They supplied diplomats and theologians to handle both political and theological relations with Byzantium; their members acted as advisers and right-hand men to the popes, beginning with Gregory; as missionaries they opened up the West to Rome; they staffed the welfare centers; they served in the choirs of the great basilicas, the Lateran, St. Peter's, St. Paul's; and they acted as custodians of the martyrs' graves.

The allegiance of the Franks in Gaul to the Church of Rome ever since the late fifth century; the subsequent conversion from Arianism and paganism of Longobards, Bavarians, and Visigoths; and the mission dispatched by Gregory to the heathen of the North—England and the coastlands of France and the Low Countries; all had combined over a century to make Rome and the papacy into the spiritual center of Western Europe. Inevitably the Roman Church became a political power as well; and her seat, Rome, a focus toward which the newly converted barbarians and semibarbarians would look with awe. This actual prominence of Rome, moreover, was intertwined with and fostered by an older, powerful image: that of a magic center, a Holy City. From the second century on, Rome was to Christians the resting place of Peter and Paul. She was the burial ground of hundreds of martyrs, real and fictitious, whose graves attracted pilgrims. The opening-up to Catholic Christianity of new territories in Western Europe swelled the numbers of those eager to visit Rome; and this eagerness was combined with the ever stronger belief in miracles and the efficacy of relics. Always powerful among the faithful, this belief was inevitably strengthened by the influx into the Church of the new Christians from the hitherto pagan North. Among old and new Christians alike, it steadily increased in the sixth and seventh centuries, and was strongly favored by Gregory. The martyrs, in the first place, worked miracles; and burial near a martyr's tomb, preferably St. Peter's, had long been considered a guarantee of salvation. By the sixth century, relics were eagerly sought. To remove particles of bones had long been customary in the East. The West frowned upon the practice, which was contrary to Roman Law. Gregory himself took a strong stand. The Byzantine empress had pleaded for bone relics, the head of St. Paul and his shroud no less. To side-step the request, Gregory countered with a couple of gruesome tales: in his own time, the Abbot of S. Paolo had found bones near the Apostle's tomb, though these did not belong to it; daring to move them, he died after fearful omens. When Pelagius II attempted a minor structural change over Saint Peter's body, "although 15 feet distant," a terrifying portent occurred; and when, likewise under Pelagius, the tomb of Saint Lawrence was incidentally opened during building operations, the workmen who saw the martyr's body "without even touching it," all died within ten days. The most Gregory would grant the august petitioner were filings from the chains of St. Peter—a traditional relic distributed to VIPs. "It isn't the custom among the Romans" or in the West "to dare touch anything belonging to the corpse": linen strips lowered into the grave were just as efficacious; or, I might add, oil from lamps burning nearby poured into small bottles, such as those he sent to the Longobard Queen Theodolinda, which to this day are kept at Monza. The Eastern custom of revering and trafficking in bone relics Gregory found both ridiculous and disgusting, especially since, as he told the Byzantine empress, their authenticity was doubtful, at the least; two years before, he had caught Greek monks digging up bones in the cemetery, a largely pagan graveyard at that, near S. Paolo fuori le mura, intent on selling them as relics. This Roman reluctance to move martyrs' bodies or bones lasted with few exceptions until the eighth century; but by then, the West outside Rome had long acquired legally or by stealth masses of bone relics.

In any event, through its martyrs' graves, its miracles and relics, Rome in the sixth and seventh centuries grew to be the magic center of the West. When Jerusalem fell to the Muslims in 640, Rome remained the one Holy City of Christianity—focused on the graves and the cult of the martyrs: the "Thresholds of the Apostles," *limina apostolorum*, primarily St. Peter's. To the northerners he had become the foremost of the saints. Visiting his grave, being buried nearby, or touching his relics were sure guarantees of salvation. Rome was his see, which he continued to occupy in the person of his apostolic successors. Indeed, Rome, the papacy, and St. Peter all became identified with each other and were nearly synonymous. His grave became the center of veneration all through Europe, the depository of offerings and the guarantor of treaties placed upon and of oaths sworn before it.

Channeling and providing for the ever increasing stream of pilgrims to Rome thus became a major preoccupation of the Church from the sixth century on. Visitors had been coming to the venerated sites as early as the third and fourth centuries; many had scribbled their names on the walls of the shrine below S. Sebastiano and on the *memoria* of Saint Peter. By 400, whole villages from as far as Naples and Capua had come to pray at the martyrs' shrines. A century later the stream of pilgrims had become so copious and continuous that "houses for the poor" were set up at St. Peter's, S. Paolo fuori le mura, and S. Lorenzo fuori le mura—hostels for indigent pilgrims or almshouses for mendicants who gathered to draw on the pilgrims' charity. To these three great shrines, a fourth was added off the Aurelian Road, that of St. Pancras, S. Pancrazio, the avenger of perjury; Pope Pelagius I, to cleanse himself of any suspicion in the death of his predecessor, took a solemn oath at the martyr's tomb in the presence of the Byzantine viceroy. By the time of Gregory the Great and under his successors, pilgrimages to Rome must have reached flood proportions, and Western Europe's conversion to the Roman Church swelled the numbers further still.

Through the seventh and eighth centuries the flood of pilgrims vastly increased. Going the rounds of the major sanctuaries was *de rigueur* even on a state visit, like that of Constans II in 667, albeit combined with a sightseeing tour of the ancient wonders of Rome and a bit of looting. But then, objectionable though he was, Constans was an educated Easterner, steeped in the classical tradition. On the whole, pilgrims were simple folk, come for the sake of the pilgrimage only and for the benefit of their souls. The farther the distance and the more arduous the way, the greater the merit. And they did come from afar. Around 660, a group of Irish monks met in their hostel in Rome fellow pilgrims from Egypt, Palestine, the Greek East, and South Russia. But the largest number came from among the peoples recently converted in the West. Franks, Irish and English, joined in the eighth century by Frisians and South Germans, struggled over the Alpine passes on foot or horseback, singly or in groups; or more conveniently, though at greater expense, they traveled across France and by sea from Marseilles. Hostels were set up in Provence and North Italy to shelter them on the road, or hospitable convents or families took them in. Most came only once, but a few paid more than one visit—Benedict Biscop between 653 and 680 came five times from Northumbria. They formed a varied crowd: bishops combining business at the papal court with prayers at the tombs of the Apostles; clergy seeking to take home relics—by contact with a linen strip placed on the graves, rather than bones as customary from the late eighth century on—and information about dogma and ritual custom; missionaries, mostly British, about to convert the heathen in the Low Countries and Germany; many monks and nuns, led by a famous missionary bishop; chieftains and their retinues—Duke Theodo from Bavaria "with others of his tribe" or the disreputable Hunald from Aquitaine; nobles, like the lady who in 744 left her property to the monastery of Saint Gall in Switzerland in exchange for horses, blankets, and funds for a pilgrimage to Rome; and ordinary folks in large numbers. Inevitably, doubtful elements, such as "sex-hungry and ignorant Swiss, Bavarians, or Franks," to quote Boniface, the missionary to the Germans, in 749, mingled with the pious. A form letter, already a hundred years before, recommends the bearer as a *bona fide* pilgrim ". . . on his arduous road to the thresholds of the Apostles . . . guided by the Divine light, not, as so many make it a habit, as a loafer."

On arrival, pilgrims, genuine and counterfeit, found shelter, food and alms in the diaconiae (fig. 64); when, by the early eighth century, those existing proved insufficient or unsuitably located, new ones were founded: four by the early eighth century rose near St. Peter's with a fifth added before 806 dedicated to S. Pellegrino—the name speaks for itself—and a sixth, Sto. Stefano degli Abissini, in 817 directed "to take care of the pilgrims and footsore come from afar for the love of Saint Peter"; two more, S. Eustachio and S. Maria in Aquiro, were located near the Pantheon in the sector of the abitato closest to the northern city gate, Porta Flaminia; and others, by 800 if not before, strung out along the pilgrims' routes inside the walls leading to the great sanctuaries—three along the road to S. Lorenzo, one near that to S. Paolo at the southeast edge of the Palatine, a fifth on the way to S. Agnese. Many from their foundation in the eighth century serviced hostels: the one at S. Eustachio to house and feed one hundred poor, presumably pilgrims; two near St. Peter's of unknown size. Some served as hospitals; a form letter of the seventh or early eighth century charges the superior of a hostel in Rome to provide ". . . beds and sheets for the poor and sick, . . . medicines and all needed for the sick and to call doctors in." Yet others served as old-age homes for pilgrims or residents. However, a number of diaconiae established in the second half of the eighth century—to anticipate things a bit—retained the traditional function of storing and distributing food supplies, and were located within or frequently on the edge of the abitato. One was set up on or before 755 in the Portico of Octavia, when its church, S. Angelo in Pescheria, was consecrated. On the Forum, where S. Maria Antiqua may have been linked to a diaconia as early as around 600, two churches long converted from public buildings, SS. Cosma e Damiano and S. Adriano, had new diaconiae attached around 780, possibly because of the storage space available in parts of the structures not used for Divine Services; and, likewise on the Forum, the diaconia of SS. Sergius and Bacchus was shifted around 790 from the Temple of Concord, which threatened to collapse—the diaconia had been installed presumably quite some time before—to the Arch of Septimius Severus where its twice-rebuilt church stood until 1536. By the first years of the ninth century, then, the number of diaconiae had risen to twenty-four. Thereafter, they seem to have lost their welfare function and retained it only in the name.

Taking care of indigent pilgrims was costly, but repaid itself. Employment created by their influx and funds brought along by the well-to-do may have balanced the budget or left a surplus. The Tomb of Saint Peter was "enriched by the homage of many pilgrims"; customarily they deposited their gifts at the shrine upon arrival, as did Boniface and his companions in 718. Rich pilgrims come to stay became a source of permanent income. They settled near St. Peter's: Cadwalla of Wessex in 668; other British chieftains, Coinred of Mercia a generation later, Ina of Wessex in 726, finally Offa of East Anglia and with him "many of the English nobles and commoners, men and women, dukes and ordinary folk . . . " to spend their days ". . . in prayer, fasting and almsgiving . . . that they might be more easily received in Heaven." By the second third of the eighth century, Northerners of all kinds were permanently settled near St. Peter's. Large gifts poured in from home "for the relief of the poor and the maintenance of the lights of St. Peter's . . . ," as much as 365 marks annually from the King of Mercia alone. Eventually all the foreign colonies, the rich with their retinues, poor hangers-on, and hermits, moved together into tribal compounds. The first of such Northern scholae, perhaps as early as 726, was that of the Saxons, located on the site or near the present hospital and church of Sto. Spirito in Sassia: the name of the schola, *burgus Saxonum*, survives in the term *burgus*, Borgo, the name of the quarter across the river, leading to St. Peter's. Around 770, the schola of the Longobards was established north of the basilica of the Apostle, with its own church, St. Justin; toward the end of the century, the schola of the Franks south of the atrium grew up; finally, the compound of the Frisians rose on the site of S. Michele in Borgo, atop the hill southeast of Bernini's portico. By 799, all these scholae were organized as civilian and military autonomous entities. Only in the course of time were they absorbed into the life of Rome.

If the foreigners settling in Rome were gradually Romanized, those returning home became the main carriers of Roman influence in Western Europe. Bishops and clergy brought back, together with relics, the customs of the Roman rite. Benedict Biscop in 680 carried to England liturgical books, icons to set up on the chancel screen of his monastery church, and paintings, perhaps icons, to decorate its walls; and, with the pope's leave, the arch chanter of St. Peter's went to teach the English the Roman chant. Frankish bishops, too, from the late sixth century on, came or sent to Rome to learn and introduce in their dioceses the Roman liturgical usage replacing the older Gallican rite: by 590 Gregory of Tours had one of his deacons report to him in detail. English missionaries led by Boniface, always in close touch with Rome, carried the Roman liturgy to the lands newly Christianized, from Utrecht in Holland to Würzburg and Eichstätt in Southern Germany. When in 754 Pepin, clearly in accord with his papal visitor, Stephen II, decreed the Roman liturgy to be the only one permitted in the Frankish Kingdom, he merely capped a development long since prepared by returning pilgrims and missionaries. Starting with Gregory the Great, Rome grew to be the arbiter and ruler of religious dogma and practice for the Christian West. The See of Saint Peter's was the religious center of Western Christendom and became the arbiter and ruler of religious thought, dogma, and practice all over Europe. The pilgrims coming back from the tomb of the Apostle and the missionaries dispatched from his see were the ones bringing Rome's impact to churches of the West. At the same time they paved the way for her rising political importance and for the common identity of Rome, papacy, and Saint Peter.

The economic impact of the pilgrims on Rome, too, is easily gauged. Their influx brought money and employment to the im-

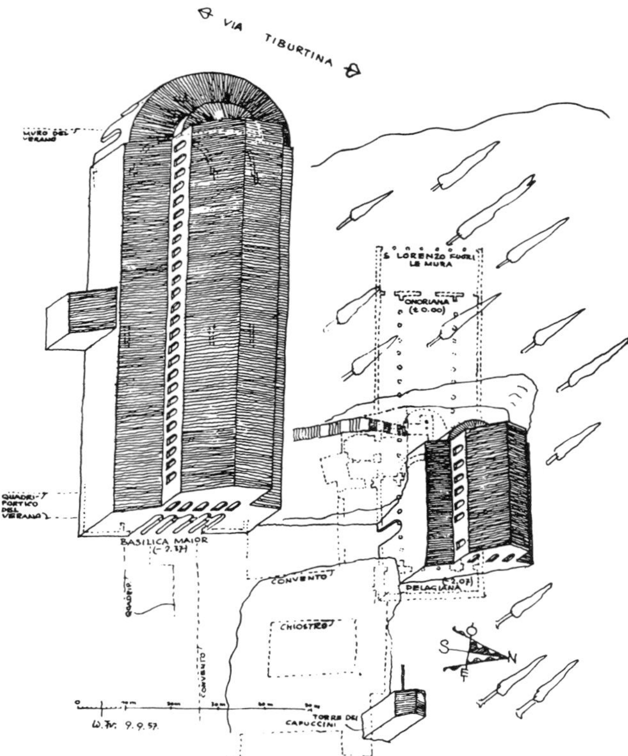

67. S. Lorenzo fuori le mura, covered cemetery and Pelagius' Basilica, reconstruction W. Frankl

poverished city and established one of the three industries that have supported Rome ever since—the tourist trade. The second supporting industry, the building trade, was likewise promoted by the influx of pilgrims. The increase in both tourist and construction trades is mirrored, the one in contemporary writings, the other in church buildings. The third, an overgrown bureaucracy, had survived from antiquity. It lives on to this day.

The tourist trade, meaning pilgrimages to Rome, reached a peak in the sixth and seventh centuries. It is not by chance that the three earliest surviving guides to Christian Rome date from the seventh century, two of them prior to 640. Addressed to pilgrims, the guides appeal to these visitors' belief in the miraculous powers of the martyrs' graves, and all follow the same scheme: proceeding along the roads outside the city walls, they list, often with legendary accretions, the venerated graves in the catacombs, the covered cemeteries, the small shrines, the great basilicas: "then on the Appian Way you come to Saint Sebastian, the martyr whose body rests in a place further down and there are [also] the graves of the Apostles Peter and Paul where they lay for forty years; and in the western part of the church you go down to where Saint Quirinus lies. . . . And on the same road further north [you reach] the holy martyrs Tiburtius, Valerian and Maximus . . ."; or else, "near the Tiburtine Road is the greater church of Saint Lawrence where his body formerly was buried and there is also the new basilica of admirable beauty where he now rests; there too, under the same altar, lies Abundus and outside in the porticus is the stone once tied to his neck when he was thrown in the well; and there are Herenaeus, Julianus, Primitivus . . ." and a host of other martyrs. One can practically hear the guides at each catacomb crowding in with their spiel for the pilgrims and the whining beggars and the coins dropping in their begging bowls; and one can imagine the gifts donated at the tombs and at the servicing monasteries and the sums left in the hands of innkeepers and tradespeople. Quite naturally, at that time within the city as well, legends were given concrete form: at the church of S. Lorenzo in Panisperna the pilgrims were shown the actual grill "where Saint Lawrence was roasted."

The flood of pilgrims forced on the Church new building activity at the graves of the martyrs. The covered cemeteries of Constantinian date, near the venerated sites, had been abandoned or reduced to secondary importance. The new type of pilgrim demanded more direct contact with the martyr. But a grave far down in the catacomb was hard to reach over steep stairs and through a maze of dark, narrow corridors; the situation was inconvenient, dangerous, and incompatible with the needs of the huge pilgrimage center Rome had become. A solution was found when Pelagius II (579-590) built within the hill alongside the fourth-century covered-cemetery basilica at S. Lorenzo fuori le mura a "new basilica of admirable beauty" to enclose the grave of the martyr in the catacomb (fig. 67). The new church of Pelagius, minus its apse and with its orientation reversed, survives as a raised chancel at the east end of the present thirteenth-century basilica; but its original level was much further down, roughly two meters below the

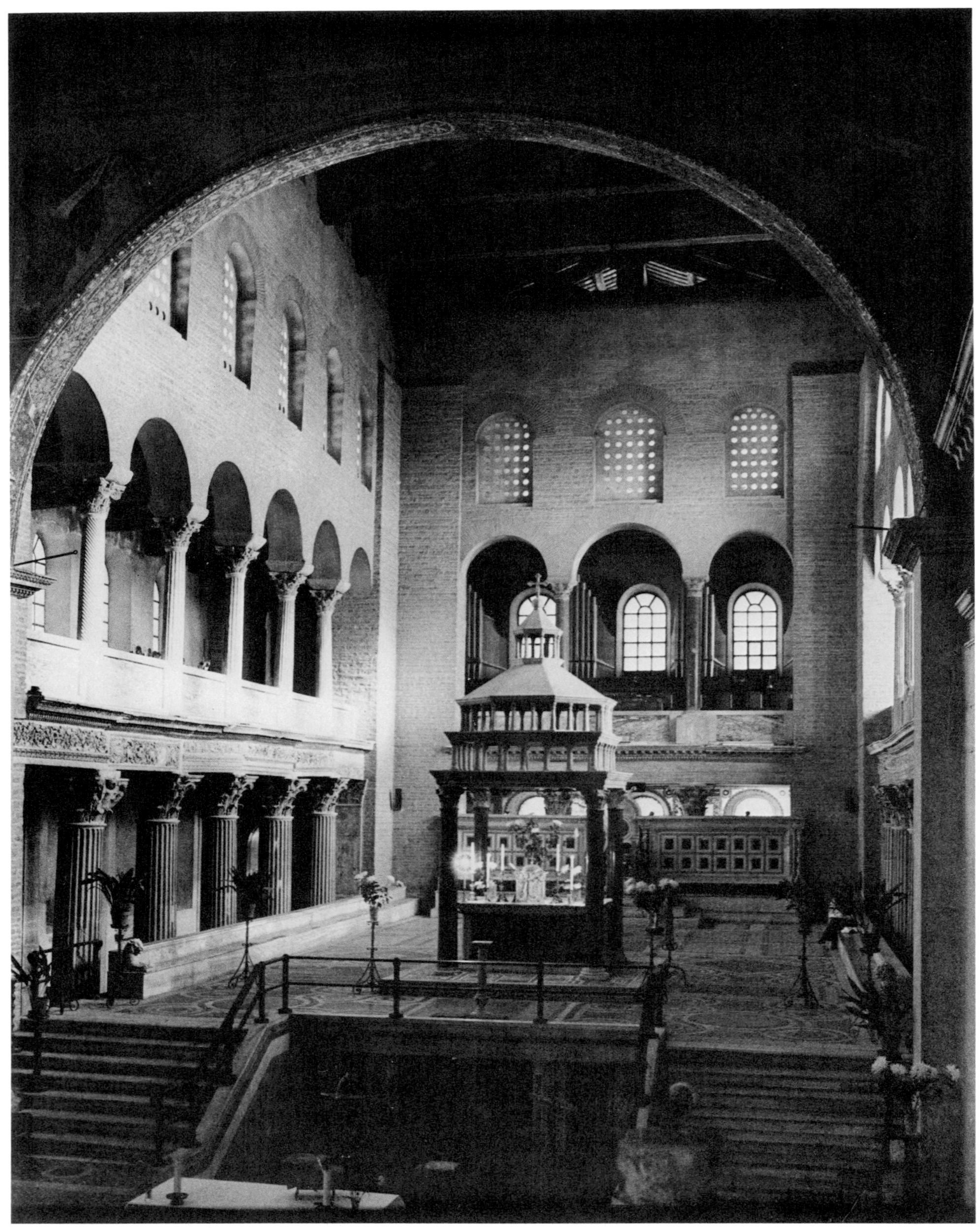

68. S. Lorenzo fuori le mura, Pelagius' Basilica, looking east

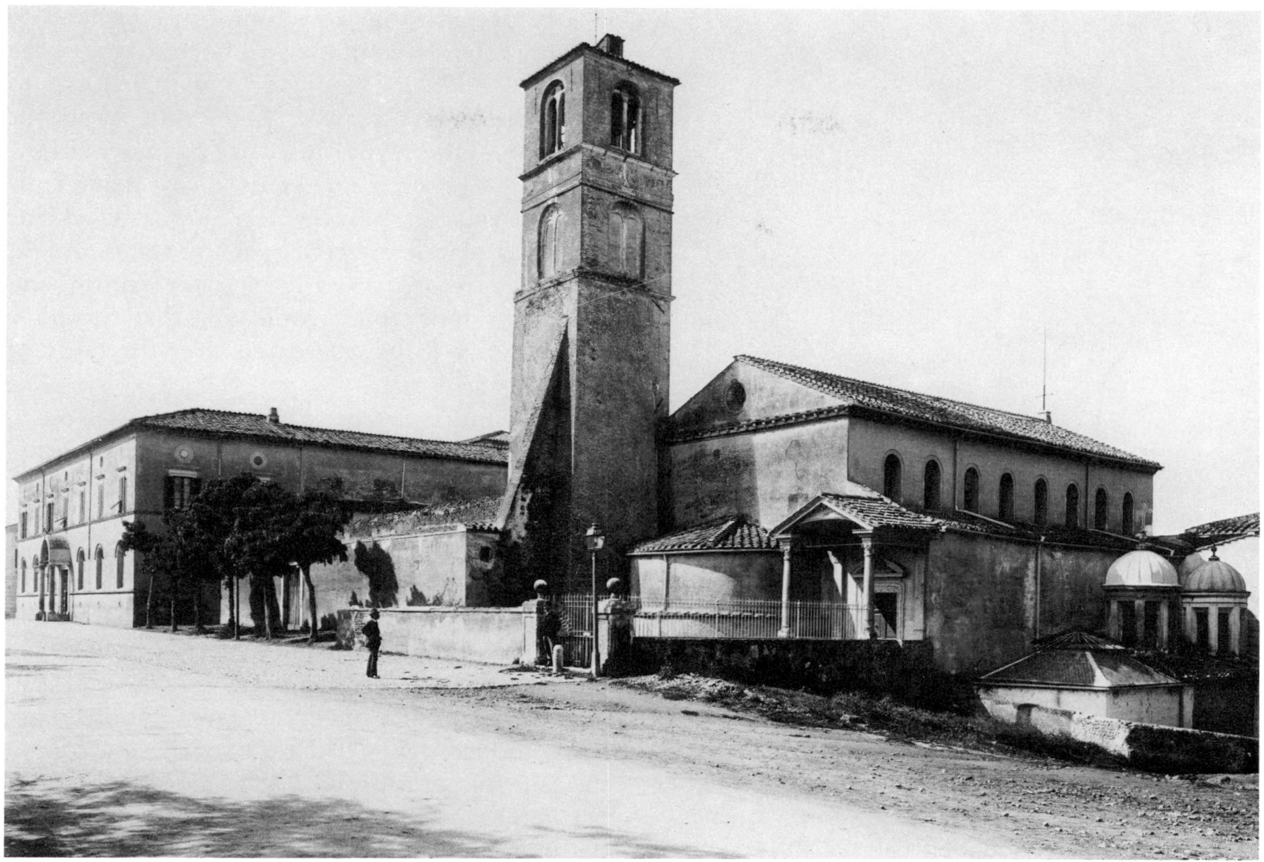

69. S. Agnese fuori le mura, exterior from road, as of ca. 1900

medieval nave level. Sunk into a pit hollowed into the hill of the catacomb, Pelagius' church had its floor level with the tomb of Saint Lawrence, which was isolated as the corridors of the catacombs round about were destroyed in the scooping operation. Aisles and galleries surround the nave on three sides; the aisles and nave were entered at the sides from the foot of the hill and the nearby covered cemetery, while the galleries were flush with and reached from the crest of the hill (fig. 68). The encasing hill at S. Lorenzo was long ago cut away. But it survives at Domitilla and, at least in part, at S. Agnese, where Pope Honorius around 630 built a church along the same lines: the hill scooped out; the nave and aisles, reached from the sides over stairs, level with the martyrs' tombs; the galleries, again on three sides of the nave, level with and accessible from the Via Nomentana behind the apse; and only the clerestory and galleries emerging from the hilltop (fig. 69). A third time the type was taken up when, presumably around 600, the grave chamber of the martyrs Nereus, Achilleus, and Domitilla, in the catacomb named after her, was enlarged into a sizable church.

The new basilica form was an ingenious solution to the major problem posed by the recent influx of pilgrims: the grave of the saint was made visible and easily accessible; the groundfloor of the church sunk in the hill would hold large crowds; the galleries, reached from the hilltop, offered space for the overflow and for those unable or unwilling to descend the stairs. Basilicas with galleries, to be sure, were not a new invention: they had possibly been known in secular reception halls in the fourth century in Rome, like the one incorporated into the church of S. Susanna; and they were familiar to Eastern church builders from the fourth century on. But in Rome prior to the sixth century, the type had never been absorbed into church architecture,

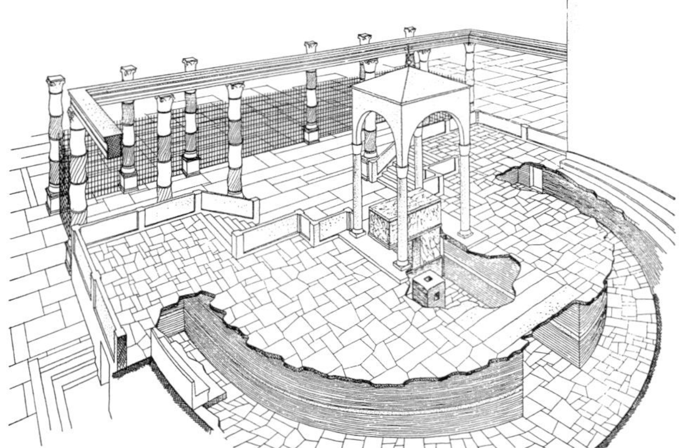

70. St. Peter's annular crypt, isometric reconstruction

and in the major centers of the East, too, it had by then gone out of fashion, though it survived in the provinces. That an eastern, albeit obsolete, type would be taken up in Rome during the first century of Byzantine occupation was natural. But Roman church planners, practical-minded, adopted it only for the functional ends it would serve in a catacomb church.

Equally ingenious was a second device evolved in the same years and to the same end—to regulate and control the approach of pilgrims to a venerated site, and concomitantly to link the shrine closely to the altar, where the Eucharist was celebrated. Where a site was on or only slightly below ground level, rather than in the depth of a catacomb, and had been enclosed in a basilica, as at St. Peter's, an annular crypt was installed: a few steps underground, a semicircular passage follows the inner curve of the apse; from its apex a straight corridor branches off and leads to a relic chamber—the venerated site—placed below the high altar on the chord of the apse (fig. 70). Pilgrims would enter the curved passage at one end, pause at the head of the straight corridor, offer their prayer, and proceed, leaving the curved passage at the opposite end. The device solved a number of tricky problems: it cleared the area around the altar; it channeled crowds of the pious into an orderly procession; and it prevented them from coming too close to the relic, thus keeping out of their way the temptation to break off a piece. A small window in the front or at the foot of the altar allowed VIPs to view the relic chamber more clearly, to throw in an offering in coin, and to procure relics by contact with linen strips (or the episcopal *pallium*) that were lowered down to touch the martyr's grave. At the same time, the insertion of the crypt caused the pavement in the apse to be raised a few steps above that of the transept and nave; on the new, higher level, the altar was placed directly over the tomb. At St. Peter's, it was covered by a silver canopy and Gregory's biographer could say that the pope caused Mass to be celebrated over the body of the Apostle.

The annular crypt is an eminently Roman type. It was first laid out, from what we know, at St. Peter's, inserted into the Constantinian apse; the floor level of the apse and the High Altar were raised, and the six Constantinian vine columns were rearranged as a trabeated screen in front. The arrangement seems to have existed by 590, and thus prior to Gregory's pontificate; but it is possible that as papal secretary he had devised it: it neatly fits his aversion to bone relics being moved—they had a way of disappearing if the faithful were allowed to come too close. At St. Peter's only traces of the crypt survive in the excavation area. Better than at St. Peter's, the new type of annular crypt is preserved at S. Pancrazio outside the Aurelian Gate on the Gianicolo; there, about 630, Honorius replaced the older oratory by a large church with a transept, apse, and annular crypt: a "copy" of St. Peter's on a smaller, but still large scale, impressive also in its baroque remodeling. In Rome, annular crypts reappeared between 731 and 741, when the fourth-century church of S. Crisogono was remodeled; and they became a commonplace feature of churches built in Rome in the ninth century. From the mid-eighth century on, too, annular crypts were a hallmark of early medieval church building in Western Europe. They spread first to other parts of Italy, Ravenna for instance, and soon north of the Alps, reflecting the close ties between church planning in Rome and in the Frankish territories under Carolingian rulers and their papal allies.

Church building on a considerable scale had been going on in Rome up to the very beginning of Gregory's pontificate. His immediate predecessor, Pope Pelagius II, had built the basilica over the grave of St. Lawrence. Much admired by contemporaries, it rested on twelve huge fluted columns, Corinthian capitals and entablatures on the ground floor and on equally precious, if smaller, columns and capitals on the gallery level—all spoils from different buildings and times; a splendid mosaic covers the apse arch; another in the apse vault is lost. Notwithstanding economic losses and the Longobard invasion alluded to in the apse inscription, funds were found and expended on a new and costly church building. Propitiating the wrath of Heaven and seeking protection from calamities was considered an essential duty of the papal ruler of Rome. Possibly, construction was also designed, as often in later centuries, to provide work; certainly it was meant to attract ever larger numbers of pilgrims, to provide through them additional employment, and to procure donations, as it did. Again, building on a large scale was taken up by Pope Honorius, a quarter of a century after Gregory's death. Indeed, Honorius was one of the great building popes; his work is seen all over Rome. To be sure, changing the Senate House, the Senate Court, and the reception halls of grand mansions into the churches of S. Adriano, S. Martina, S. Lucia in Selcis, and the Quattro Coronati was relatively inexpensive. But his new churches, S. Pancrazio and S. Agnese, were large buildings, lavishly decorated with marble columns—obviously spoils—marble revetment, and mosaics, and were provided with silver vessels and precious lighting fixtures. St. Peter's, too, was thoroughly repaired: sixteen roof beams were replaced; the roof was covered with bronze tiles removed from the Temple of Venus and Roma; the main doors were covered with silver; a gilded coffered ceiling was placed over the nave; and, possibly, mosaics were repaired or newly installed. All this must have cost a pretty penny. Funds obviously were available, not only for the needs of the papal administration and for welfare, perhaps on a scale less generous than under Gregory, but for a costly building program as well. Apparently, the income from the lands held by the Church was still large until the pontificate of Honorius: the remaining estates in Central Italy were secured through the truce negotiated by Gregory and annually renewed; and those in South Italy and Sicily were safe, enjoying even occasional exemption from Byzantine taxes. Honorius' policy of leasing Church estates, although eventually conducive to alienation, guaranteed a regular income in the short run. This, though, is less relevant in our context than Honorius' obvious willingness and eagerness to spend large sums on church buildings that were lavishly endowed, decorated, and furnished.

Gregory's policies differed thoroughly from those of popes before and after him. No church was built in his pontificate; only a few pieces of silver furniture were given to St. Peter's; inserting a crypt into its apse—whether it is Gregory's work prior to or after his election—or remodeling a few old granaries into diaconiae was inexpensive. Gregory clearly concentrated on what he considered the main tasks of a pope in his time: securing the Church, her possessions, and her capital city from invasion; relieving the inefficient Byzantine administration by having the Church take on the duties of a temporal government; reorganizing the running of the Church estates; maintaining essential services in the city; feeding the population; communicating with the masses on their own level and in their own language. Through the mission to the still pagan countries in the northwest, Rome became the goal of pilgrims from all over Western Europe and the Holy City of Western Christianity. All this was done, not so much in the name of a lofty ideal, as on an everyday administrative level. If, among the Western Church Fathers, Augustine is the great theologian, Ambrose the statesman, Jerome the fiery preacher and translator of the Bible, Gregory is the practical planner whose work affected the city of Rome and her place in the West.

CHAPTER FOUR

Rome between East and West

In the course of the seventh century, the political, economic, and cultural picture in Rome and all over the Mediterranean changed under the impact of events, both far and near. In 635, the Muslims conquered Syria and Palestine; Jerusalem fell in 640, Egypt in 641, Mesopotamia and Iran shortly after; by the end of the century, North Africa was in Arab hands; Spain was invaded in 711 and, except for the mountainous north, was swiftly overrun. The Mediterranean had become a Muslim lake. The Byzantine Empire, on the defensive against Islam in the south, against Slavs and Bulgars in the Balkans, and against the Longobards in Italy, was restricted to Asia Minor, Greece, and the Southern Balkans, with an insecure hold on South Italy, Sicily, and Ravenna, and an ineffective, though far from nominal, presence in Rome. In fact, Byzantium repeatedly strove to strengthen its hold on the Roman Church and the city. This effort reached its climax in the early eighth century in a reorganization that was to turn Rome into an administrative district, a duchy, under a Byzantine *dux*, a governor in charge of both civil and military affairs. The attempt failed, but the Emperor and his viceroy in Ravenna, the exarch, were still considered masters in Rome. Their authority as a very real constitutional and spiritual power, if remote and in everyday affairs inefficient, was never questioned. Imperial confirmation of papal elections until 731 was formally requested; at the Emperor's behest, the Pope would send legates or come to Constantinople in person; and Rome remained deeply embroiled in Eastern theological disputes. Emperor Constans II in 667 was ceremoniously received into the city by the pope, clergy, and notables. But the Byzantine presence took more real forms: Constans, clearly an objectionable character, took away with him after his twelve-day visit the bronze tiles from the Pantheon—Church property by then for sixty years; heavy taxes were imposed on the estates of the Church in Southern Italy; the exarch would interfere in papal elections; and Pope Martin I, refractory on a question of dogma—whether it was one or two energies operating through Christ—was arrested in 650 and shipped off for trial in Constantinople. All this was bound to lead to ever more exacerbating alienation between the Eastern Church and the emperor, on the one hand, the two being coterminal, and Rome and Italy on the other, meaning both Church and lay leaders. Still, time and again Rome and the East were forced by their common interests to cooperate, and relations between them continued to be ambivalent.

The impact of events around the Mediterranean on the city of Rome was not uniform. Economically, the new conditions meant disaster: North Africa and its grain were lost; sea lanes in the Mediterranean and the coastline of Italy were threatened; the South Italian possessions of the Church were overtaxed and menaced by Byzantium. In Central Italy a shortsighted policy, initiated already by Honorius I, had led to leasing Church-owned estates to private landholders and so to their eventual alienation. The resources of the Church thus dwindled over the second half of the seventh century, and provisioning Rome, always a problem, became more difficult still. Sanitary conditions were certainly poor, and in 680 the bubonic plague broke out: a mosaic icon at S. Pietro in Vincoli which shows Saint Sebastian as the protector from pests, made perhaps at about that time, has been linked to this epidemic. The adversities of the time, however, introduced new features into the picture of Rome. A short Persian onslaught on Palestine in 613 and subsequently the permanent conquest of the East and of North Africa by the Muslims drove refugees to the West. Among those who settled in Rome some apparently gained considerable influence. Theodore I, elected pope in 642, was the son of a bishop from Jerusalem. A generation later, from 678 to 741, a series of popes of Eastern background occupied the See of Saint Peter: eleven of thirteen were Syrian or Greek by descent, some born and reared in Sicily. Presumably, they were chosen for their familiarity with Eastern languages and affairs and their consequent ability to deal with current theological disputes. However, just because they or their families had fled from religious persecution, they were adamant in resisting Byzantine theological demands. Monastic refugees, too, came to Rome. By 645 a group of monks from the *lavra*, the convent, of Saint Sabbas in the Judaean Hills had settled on the Little Aventine in a mansion supposedly once belonging to Gregory the Great's maternal family. Its reception hall was converted into an oratory; its walls survive some way up the façade of the medieval church of S. Saba; below the floor of the oratory the monks laid out a regular Palestinian graveyard in double tiers of ovenlike graves. At the Tre Fontane, a monastic congregation from south-eastern Asia Minor had established itself by 641, bringing along the head of the Persian martyr Anastasius; their monastery has long since given way to structures of medieval date; and the site, which fifty years ago still rose in isolation outside the city, has been engulfed by apartment houses and office buildings. Still other Eastern congregations who came to Rome at the time are known only by name: a group of Nestorians from Syria or Mesopotamia, soon dissolved as heretical; two monasteries settled by Greeks, expelled from an unknown location; and an Armenian congregation. By the last third of the seventh century refugees from Muslim lands, by then fully Romanized, loomed large in spreading Roman dogma and liturgical custom to the barbarian countries of Western Europe: Hadrian, "by nation an African" from a monastery near Naples, and Theodore, a monk in Rome from Tarsus in Cilicia, were sent to England in 664 to strengthen and restructure the shaky young Church.

The refugees carried to Rome Eastern relics, feasts, and customs: besides the head of Saint Anastasius, they presumably brought that of Saint George—this latter perhaps in 682 but rediscovered at the Lateran only in the 740s—and the manger of Christ, installed at S. Maria Maggiore and first alluded to under Pope Theodore I, who came from Palestine; three feasts of the Virgin—her Nativity, the Annunciation, and her Dormition—were imported at the end of the seventh century by the Syrian pope, Sergius I; he also introduced the *Agnus Dei* into the Mass as an antiphonal song. Another custom, too, came to Rome at that time from the East and took deep roots: the transfer of martyrs' bones. Relics *ex ossibus*, customary in the East, had long been frowned upon by Rome; Gregory the Great had warned off the Byzantine empress with an atrocity story regarding the involuntary opening of Saint Lawrence's grave. That pope Boniface IV, Gregory's successor, brought to the Pantheon cartloads of martyrs' bones from the catacombs seems to be a late legend. The transfer of such relics is documented in Rome for the first time under two Eastern popes in the 640s: under John IV, who brought the remains of the local martyrs of Salona to S. Venanzio at the Lateran; and under Pope Theodore I, who transferred the martyrs Primus and Felicianus from their catacomb on the Via Nomentano to Sto. Stefano Rotondo. Another "Easterner," Pope Leo II, a Sicilian, brought to the city the relics of a group of martyrs from the catacomb of Generosa on the Via Portuense and deposited them in a chapel adjoining S. Bibiana. Iconographic elements, too, penetrated from the East. In the mosaic of the apse that Pope Theodore added to Sto. Stefano Rotondo, a jeweled cross is surmounted by a bust of Christ inside a roundel and flanked by two martyrs. Raised on three steps, it recalls the cross that rose in the courtyard at the Holy Sepulcher in the city of his fathers and as it was depicted, with Christ's head added, on hundreds of *ampullae*, small oil flasks sold as pilgrims' souvenirs: a personal memento, then, much like the graveyard of the monks driven from the *lavra* of S. Sabbas, and not having the permanent impact on the West asserted by the influx into Rome of Eastern saints, relics, and feasts.

This Eastern influence on liturgy and dogma led to changes in the furnishing and the decoration of Roman churches. A single stone pulpit, dated 705-707, was attached to the chancel enclosure of S. Maria Antiqua. Such ambones reached Rome apparently in the seventh century, when sermons also became a regular feature of the service in the West, as they had long been in Byzantium, Syria, and Palestine. The customary *solea*, the long pathway approaching the chancel, was reduced to a short but wider fore-chancel reserved for the singers, the *schola cantorum*. Frequently, too, the approach to the chancel was marked by a trabeated colonnade, a feature known to us first in the East. Such a freestanding colonnade appeared in Rome at St. Peter's around or shortly before 590. It was made up of the six vine columns of Constantine's baldacchino, fallen victim to the construction of the annular crypt and the concomitant raising of the apse area. A second row of vine columns brought "from Greece," meaning the East, in the fourth decade of the eighth century, doubled the arrangement. Icons, too, from around the early seventh century became a common feature in Rome. A very few, discovered over the last twenty years, survive and they are extraordinarily impressive: the Virgin and Child from the Pantheon, dating in all probability from the time of its consecration as a church in 609; perhaps around 680 the mosaic icon representing Saint Sebastian at S. Pietro in Vincoli; the colossal painting of the Virgin at S. Francesca Romana, possibly from S. Maria Antiqua, dating from 700 or earlier; or the Virgin flanked by angels from S. Maria in Trastevere, presumably of the early eighth century, though it has been dated also a century before and one after. All are Roman in style, yet iconographically linked to Eastern traditions. The custom of setting up icons, large or small, gained greater strength in Rome as from the early eighth century on the Eastern Empire evolved a policy proscribing the veneration of images. Leading the West, Rome resisted such iconoclast tendencies and, in protest, seems to have become a main center for the production, propagation, and veneration of icons. Hammered in silver relief or painted on panels, in which case they were sheathed in precious metals, icons are listed by the dozen among papal donations from the late seventh through the eighth centuries. Frequently—as the papal donation lists confirm—such icons were placed on trabeated chancel colonnades, either on top, or, if in metal relief, fastened to the architrave as had been done in Justinian's Hagia Sophia in Constantinople. Whether any of the venerated "Byzantine" Madonnas now encased in the baroque high altars of Roman churches still preserve an original early medieval layer under a later overpainting, as was the case with those at the Pantheon and at S. Francesca Romana, must remain an open question. But it does not seem unlikely.

Cultural links with Byzantium indeed remained close, as Rome, from the middle to the end of the seventh century, was trying to reconcile her own interests with Byzantine demands in politics and theology. The influx of refugees from Muslim-occupied lands, all Greek-trained, would reinforce such links: Hadrian and Theodore, sent to England in 664, were obviously bilingual. Nor did the cultural bonds weaken in times of political and theological dissent after the end of the seventh century. On the contrary, the series of popes from a Greek or Syrian background continued virtually unbroken from Theodore I till Zacharias in the middle of the eighth century, interspersed with but a few Romans. Greek-speaking theologians were more plentiful in Rome in the early eighth century than fifty years before; and translations from or into Greek—these latter for propaganda—were not infrequent from 680 to 750. In fact, this Greek presence made itself felt more strongly still when after 750 a new wave of refugees hit Rome, coming from the Byzantine Empire rather than from Muslim countries.

Friction with Byzantium nonetheless continued through the seventh century on political and religious matters, the two being coterminal. They reached a peak when in 726 the Eastern

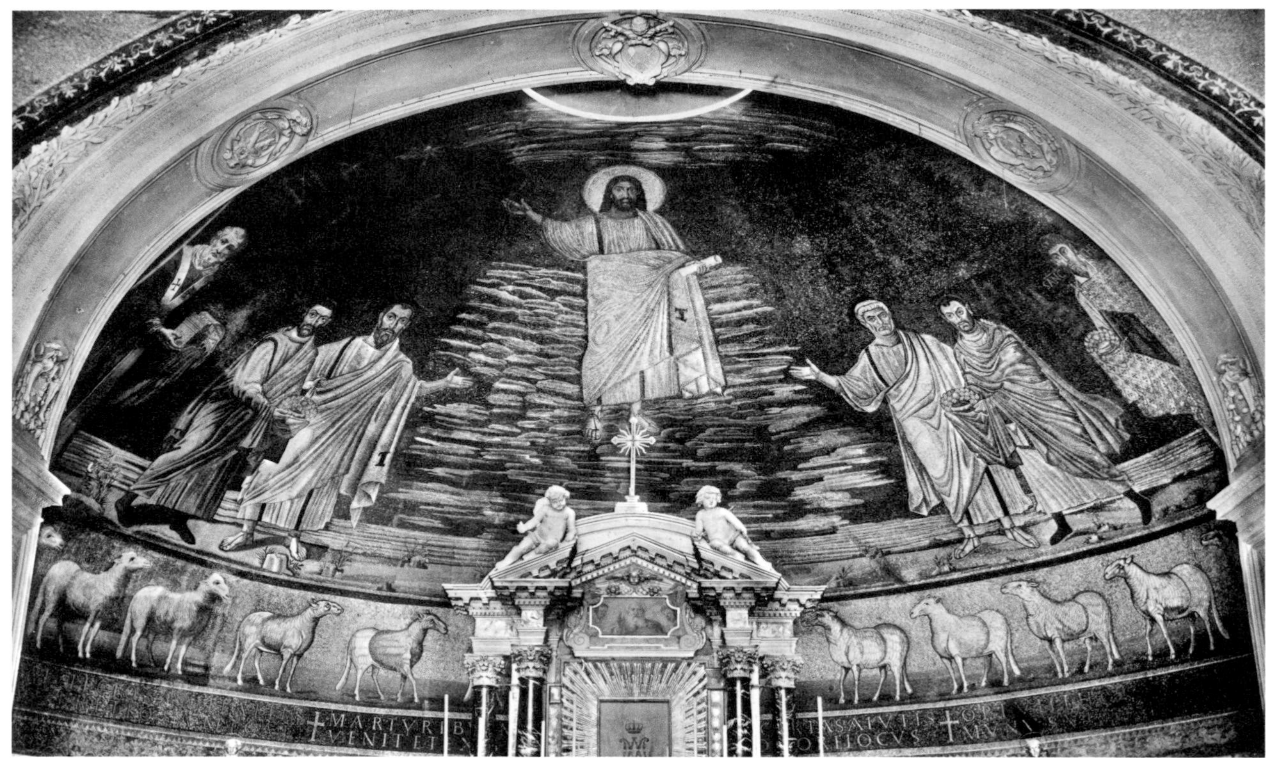

71. SS. Cosma e Damiano, apse mosaic

Church and Empire forbade the veneration of images—Christ, the Virgin, the Saints—starting on a policy of iconoclasm and pursuing it until 843 except for an interruption of thirty years from 786 to 816. The Church of Rome refused to comply, reaffirming the veneration of images and battling violently against iconoclastic encroachment. Meanwhile, ever since the 720s, hundreds of monks and hermits, who championed the resistance to the policies of the Eastern Church and government, fled persecution in the Byzantine Empire. The majority of refugees naturally turned to the Greek-speaking provinces of the West, South Italy, and Sicily. Two waves reached Rome: the first at the climax of the iconoclastic pogroms around 754; the second after their recrudescence in 816. Both groups, in accordance with prevailing papal anti-Byzantine policies, were received with open arms. There need not have been many such monastic refugees in Rome. But in the 750s they were allowed to take over a monastery as prestigious as Gregory the Great's own on the Celian Hill—one wonders why the Benedictines were forced out. And in 761 Greek monks staffed the convent founded by Popes Stephen II and Paul I in their family mansion at S. Silvestro in Capite. Likewise, the second wave of monastic refugees, arriving after 816, was welcomed to Rome and set up by the popes in some of the great monasteries. However, the refugees from the East, whether driven out of Palestine or Syria around 640 or expelled from the Greek Empire a century and more later, in their theological views and liturgical custom were quickly assimilated to Roman tradition; and they exerted, it seems, only minor influence on the formation of Rome's art from the seventh century into the ninth.

Links to Byzantium, especially of a political, theological, and cultural nature, though not always close, were never broken. At the same time a local Roman tradition remained alive, although its strength is sometimes hard to gauge. Rome's encounter with Eastern, in particular Byzantine, building types, iconographic schemes, and concepts of style and their reception, rejection, and transformation is a chapter

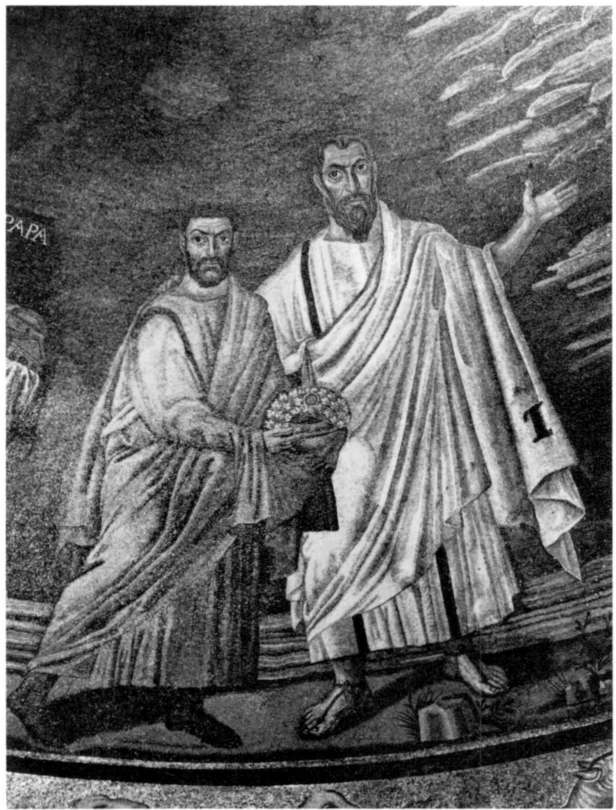

72. SS. Cosma e Damiano, apse mosaic, detail, Saint Paul and Saint Cosmas

in the history of Rome as fascinating as it is complex. In Rome this process of confrontation is reflected in mosaics and wall paintings, in icons and church plans. Much remains unclear, owing largely to the lack of evidence. No more than a few dozen mosaics, wall paintings, and icons survive, and only a handful can be safely dated; not a single building remains from the more than one hundred years between the construction of S. Agnese fuori le mura (625-638) and that of S. Angelo in Pescheria, 755. Questions about style and development of painting have been debated for the last half century and more: about the dating of the monuments; the immediate or indirect sources in the East; whether there was only one impact or repeated or continuous influences. We can only sum up the status of these questions and support it by focusing on a few monuments outstanding both in historical importance and in quality. It would be foolish to rush in where experts fear to tread—and disagree on questions of style and even on dating of the individual works by as much as a century.

The character of Christian art in Rome prior to the Byzantine conquest shows best in the mosaics in SS. Cosma e Damiano on the Forum (fig. 71). In the apse, against a dark blue ground marked with reddish pink, light blue and white clouds, Christ at his Second Coming floats from Heaven, flanked on earth by Peter and Paul, by Saints Cosmas, Damian, and Theodore, and the donor, Pope Felix IV—his figure and face restored; on the wall surmounting and flanking the apse, on a gold ground this time, angels and the symbols of the Evangelists guard the throne with the Lamb of Revelation, and the Four-and-Twenty Elders, mutilated in a rebuilding in 1632, offer their crowns. The apse composition, though the earliest of the type surviving in Rome, is presumably much older. One thinks of the lost apse mosaics at the Lateran and at S. Paolo, both presumably of fifth-century date. One or both may well have presented that

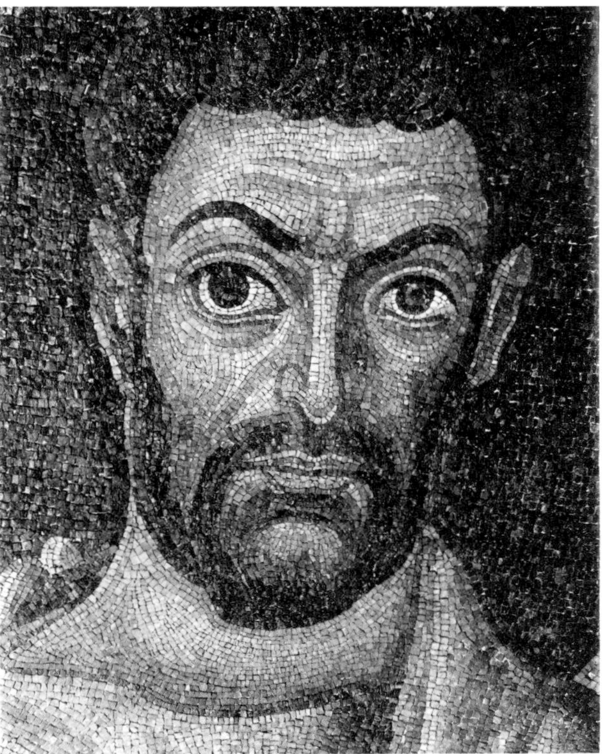

73. SS. Cosma e Damiano, apse mosaic, detail, head of Saint Cosmas

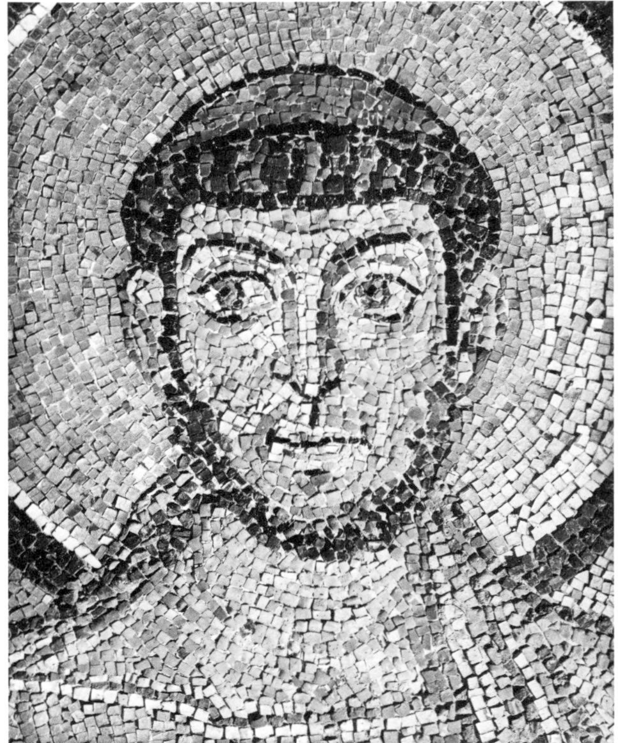

74. S. Lorenzo fuori le mura, Pelagius' Basilica, mosaic of triumphal arch, head of Saint Lawrence

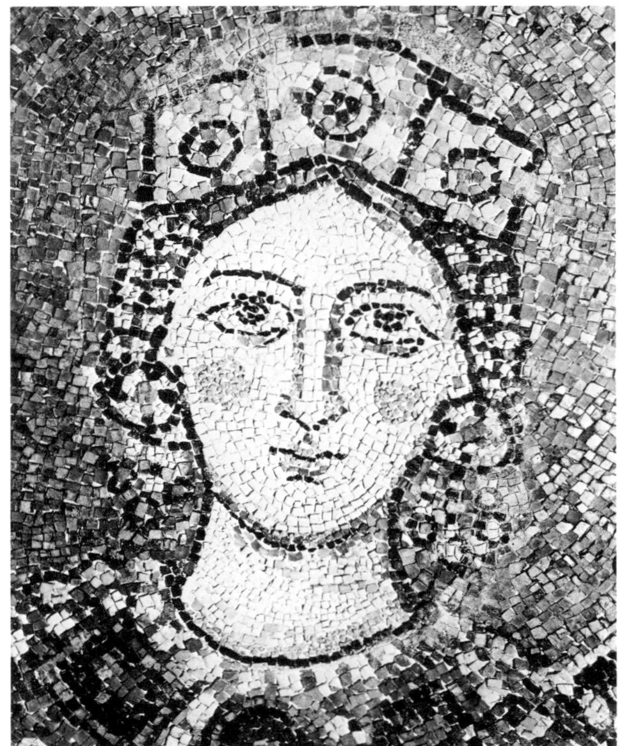

75. S. Agnese fuori le mura, apse mosaic, head of Saint Agnes

iconographic pattern; indeed, the mosaics surrounding the opening of the apse draw on that of the triumphal arch of S. Paolo, alike in all details except that there the bust of Christ takes the place of the Lamb. The figures at SS. Cosma e Damiano are monumental (fig. 72). The bodies are solid, their limbs articulate under the heavy drapery and move freely in a clearly defined, if limited, space. The mosaic tesserae are small and densely set. Faces are strongly modeled by light and shade; colors, on the whole subdued, are enlivened by bits of bright red or blue (fig. 73); and in the flesh tones glass cubes prevail, rather than marble tesserae. This feature has been claimed as indicative of Roman local workmanship; and indeed it marks the mosaics of S. Maria Maggiore and other fifth-century work in Rome. Whether or not the technique is really limited to Rome, the mosaics at SS. Cosma e Damiano stand in the tradition of the late antique Christian mosaics on the triumphal arch—formerly the apse arch—of S. Maria Maggiore. The monumentality of the composition and of the figures are comparable, as is the ease of movement. The illusionism of the earlier work, to be sure, had given way to more sculptural concepts; related to, though not necessarily dependent, it seems to me, on the style that in the same years came to the fore at Ravenna, possibly under the influence of that city's Byzantine contacts. Some fifty years later, a very different style made its appearance in Rome. At S. Lorenzo fuori le mura between 579 and 590, on the mosaic of the apse arch of the sixth-century church—it now forms the chancel of the basilica as rebuilt in the Middle Ages—stiff figures are lined up in an ill-defined nonspace; movements are insecure; bodies are barely rounded and outlined in black; draperies have been reduced to a linear if still voluminous framework, and while the colors are bright—brighter even than at SS. Cosma e Damiano—and the heads are still modeled in light and shade, the faces are dematerialized and marked by spotty highlights (fig. 74). The mosaic at S. Teodoro, heavily restored, may also date in its original parts to around

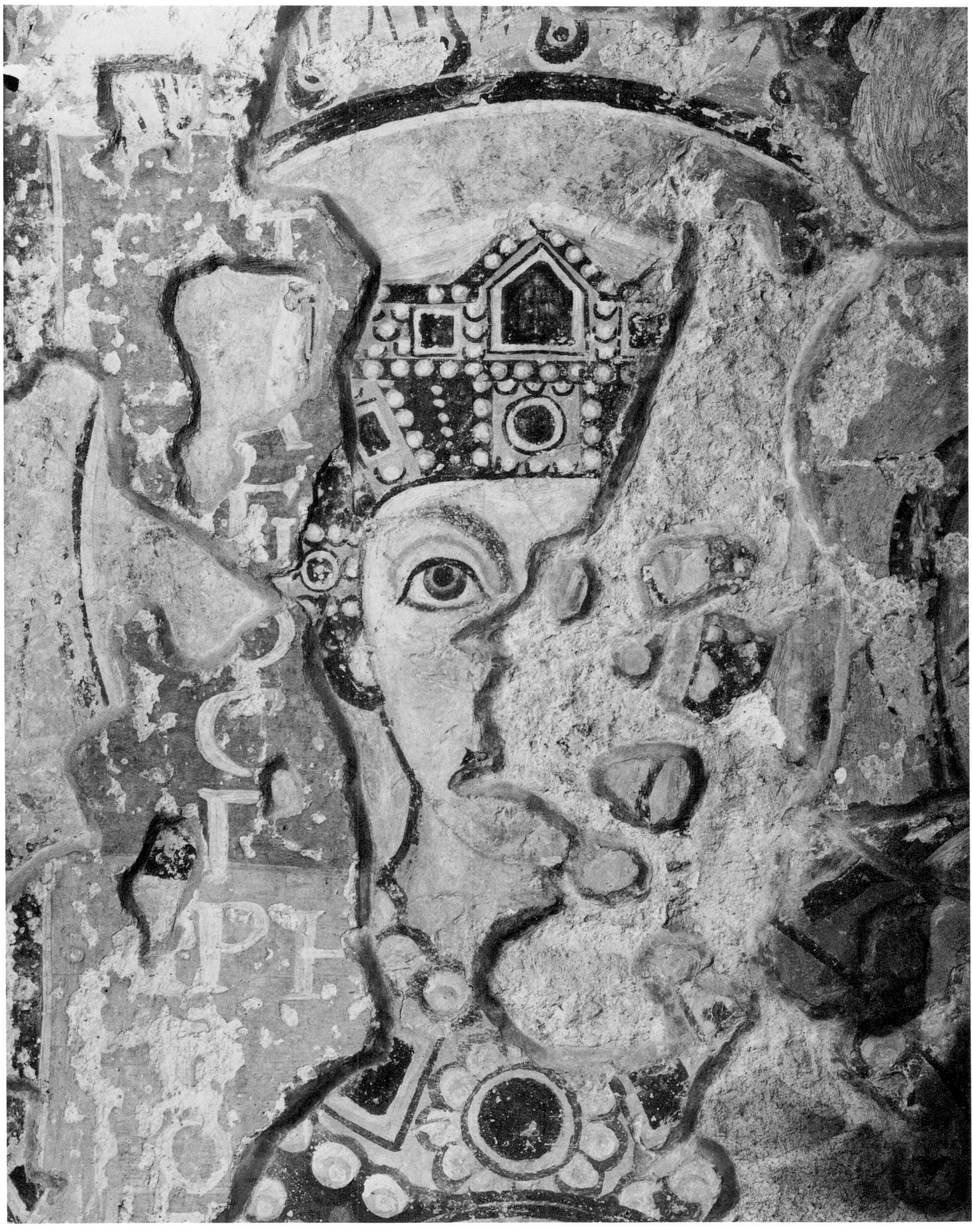

76. S. Maria Antiqua, *Maria Regina*, detail, head of Virgin

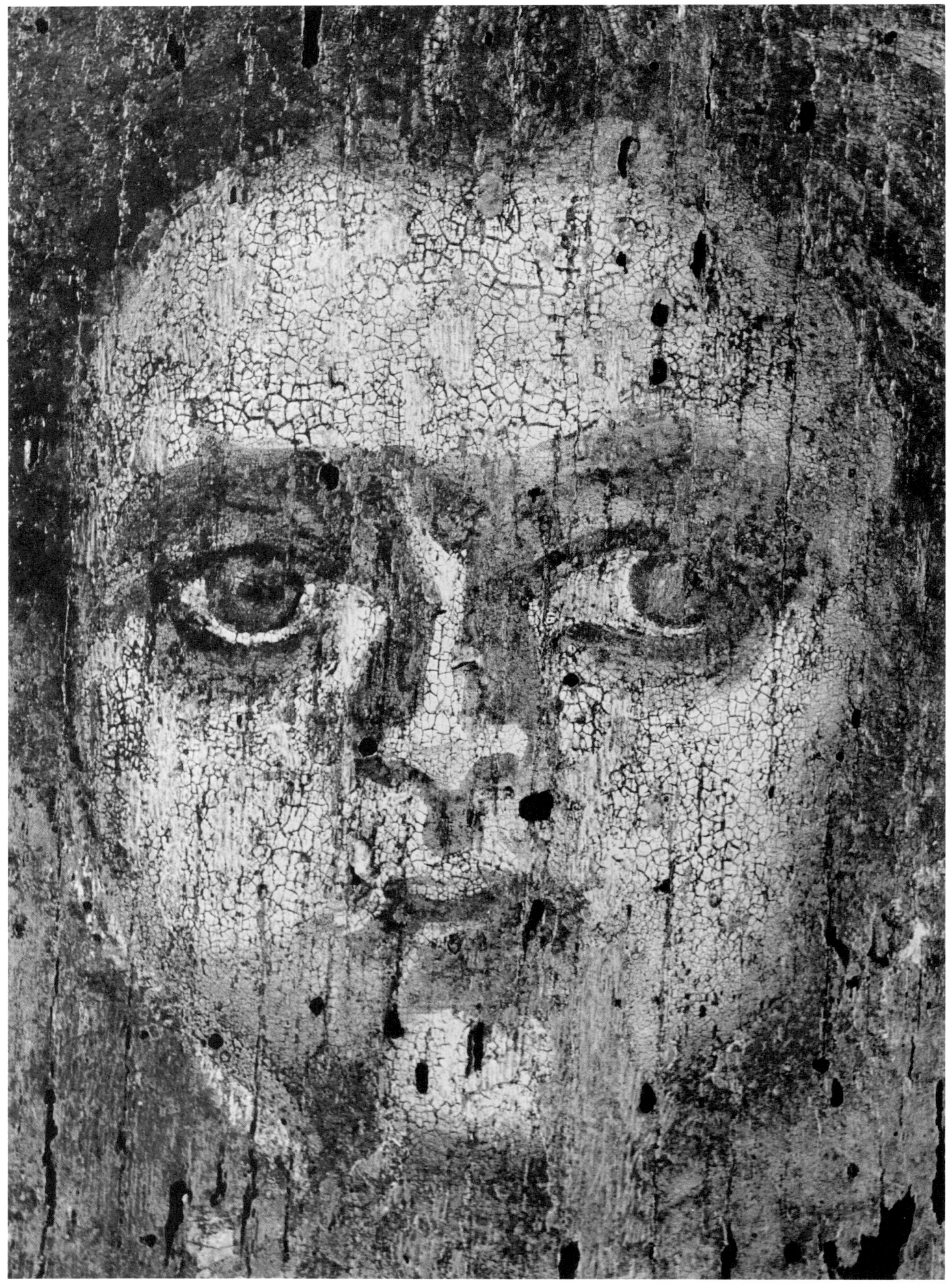

77. Madonna icon, Pantheon, head of Child

590-600. Another forty or fifty years later the figures in the apse vault at S. Agnese fuori le mura are stiff, as if flattened out against the gold ground. Modeling has disappeared, the bodies are dehydrated; the drapery, where it is not a heavy, almost metallic sheath, is articulated by just a few dark lines; the palette is somber, the coloring of a face rendered only by two yellowish-brown phthisic spots on the cheeks (fig. 75). None of this presupposes any impact from the East. But the gradual deformation of a grand monumental and sculptural style and of rational space took place in the Eastern Empire, too, in just the same decades.

Different forms and techniques in the figural arts are not easily compared. But one is inclined to view the earliest of the paintings preserved at S. Maria Antiqua as still close to the mosaic at SS. Cosma e Damiano. It is the so-called *Maria Regina*, a group of the Virgin and Child adored by two angels, only one of which survives (fig. 76). There are the monumental full bodies, the rounded faces, the huge eyes, their large pupils set off against broad bands of white; if anything, the forms are more crystalline, the facets of a cheek or brow more sharply set off; and, contrary to SS. Cosma e Damiano and closer to S. Lorenzo, the contours are marked in black lines. Indeed, the group has been dated as early as 530, and it must antedate the conversion into a church of what was formerly the guardroom of the Imperial Palace, for it was cut apart when the huge apse of the church was built to replace a small niche, presumably in or shortly after 576. The *Maria Regina* thus belongs to the decoration of the guardroom rather than of the church and it seems reasonable to attribute this decoration to the time of the Byzantine conquest of Rome, either 536 to 545 or, if it were stylistically possible, shortly after 550. On the other hand, the development does not run on a single track. A number of currents seem to flow side by side. Indeed, the fragment of an icon of the Virgin and Child still at the Pantheon, in all likelihood dating from the time the temple was dedicated as a church of the Mother of God in 609, seems to approach even closer, or rather to revive, the style of figures and heads in the mosaics of SS. Cosma e Damiano: the head of the Child is spherical, strongly sculptured in light and shade, the mouth small, the chin rounded, the pupils set off by white bands of changing width (fig. 77).

Different fields of art, though, do not necessarily develop along the same lines. While mosaic and painting through the sixth century seem to follow local traditions in Rome, church planners at the same time looked toward the East—not surprising at the height of the Byzantine occupation. As early as 538-545 SS. Quirico and Giulitta was laid out with a triconch chancel and a polygonal apse, a chancel type known from Constantinople and spreading from there all over the East; the church dedicated by Narses to the Apostles Philip and James, SS. Apostoli, may have had a similar chancel arrangement. At S. Giovanni a Porta Latina, around the middle of the century or even earlier, an apse with a three-sided exterior terminated the nave, another Byzantine feature. Again, basilicas with galleries, as they were adapted in the late sixth and seventh centuries by Roman church builders for use as catacomb churches, represent a plan common in the Byzantine capital and in Northern Greece, though obsolete there by the time it was carried to Rome. Workmanship, to be sure, remained strictly local; and architectural sculpture, capitals, and the like, were compiled from Roman spoils that were locally adapted. But the plans seem to have been imported straight from the East, either from Constantinople or from some provincial center, possibly by Byzantine army engineers.

The papery thin figures in the mosaics at S. Agnese were extreme for the seventh century. However, such a transposition into linear, disembodied figures seems to occur twice more in the artistic development of Rome in the early Middle Ages. The two saints flanking the Jerusalem Cross in Pope Theodore's mosaic at Sto. Stefano Rotondo, dating from between 642 and 649 and thus roughly ten years later, have been linked stylistically to the mosaics at S. Agnese fuori le mura, although their heads, it seems to me, notwithstanding the preponderant linear system, are more solidly modeled in fleshy colors (fig. 78). In the chapel of S. Venan-

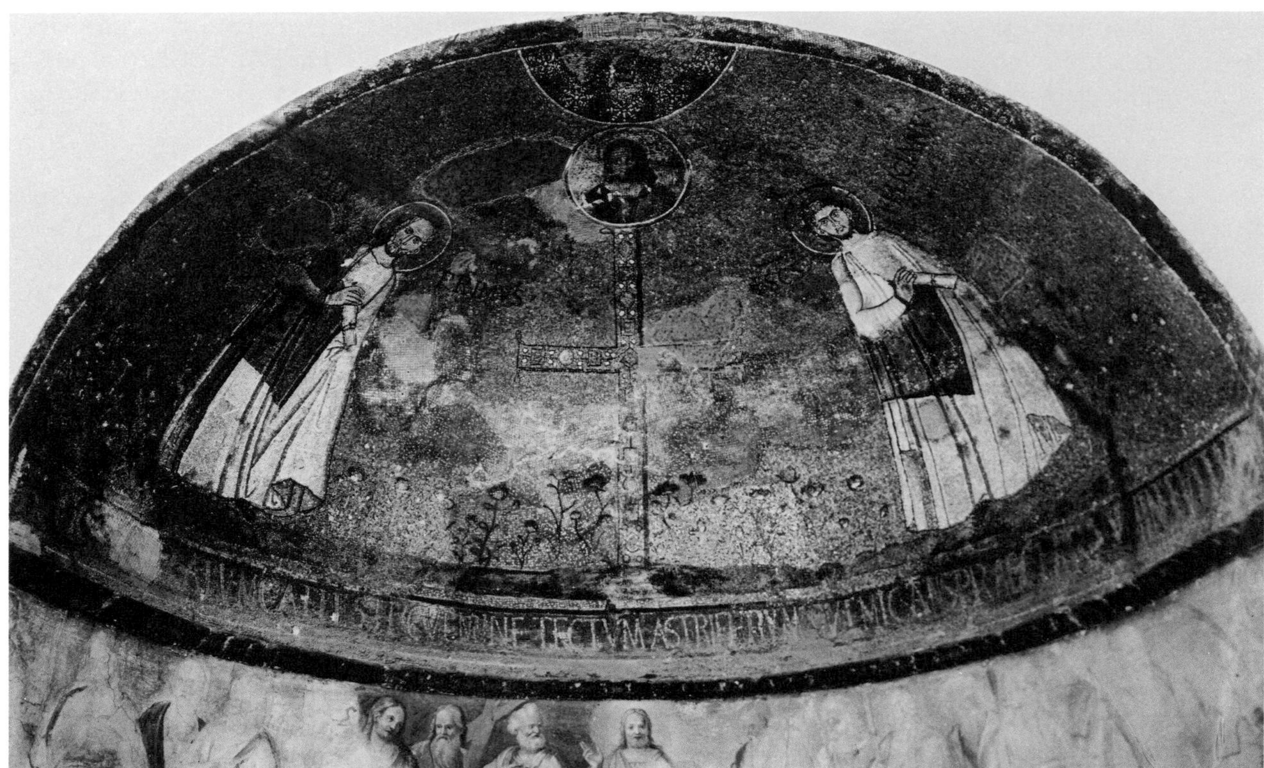

78. Mosaic from Sto. Stefano Rotondo

zio, installed off the Lateran Baptistery by Pope John IV, a cycle of mosaics including his portrait was donated by Pope Theodore. They show in the apse the bust of Christ flanked by angels and the Virgin with saints and Pope Theodore—an iconographic scheme that likewise has been linked to Eastern parallels; on the wall surrounding the apse appear the martyrs whose relics Pope John had brought from Dalmatia. Faces are framed in black; nonetheless they reflect traces of soft modeling and shading and of lively flesh colors; the figures of martyrs and saints, stiffly posed as they are, retain features of bodily mass, even though they are enclosed in the linear framework of a drapery formula.

The illusion of figures standing in space that these mid-seventh-century works create clearly draws on a style permeated by the concept of conveying bodily form through modeling the figures in light and color subdued by an atmospheric haze, the whole painted with easy brushstrokes and highlights. Such a style, closely linked to pseudoclassical features, prevailed in the early seventh century in Constantinople, notably in works produced for Emperor Heraclius, 610-641. Whether or not it was limited to Constantinople remains to be explored. In any event, an illusionistic style does appear at S. Maria Antiqua in Rome sometime within the fifty years spanning the sixth and seventh centuries. The *Maria Regina* group, mutilated when the structure was converted into a church, was painted over with an Annunciation, of which most of the angel and the face of the Virgin survive; further layers were superimposed, forming a "palimpsest wall" (fig. 79). Indeed, continually redecorated and repainted from the mid-sixth to the mid-ninth centuries, this church reflects the successive currents of painting in Rome during that period. The angel of the Annunciation is slim and erect, the head fully rounded and, both his and the Virgin's features are of a quiet "classical" beauty—hence the name *Fair Angel* or *Pompeian Angel* by which he goes (fig. 80). The mouths are small and gentle; the brushwork is loose; light and shade provide soft modeling and recall the illusionism of Pompeian painting in the first century, rather than

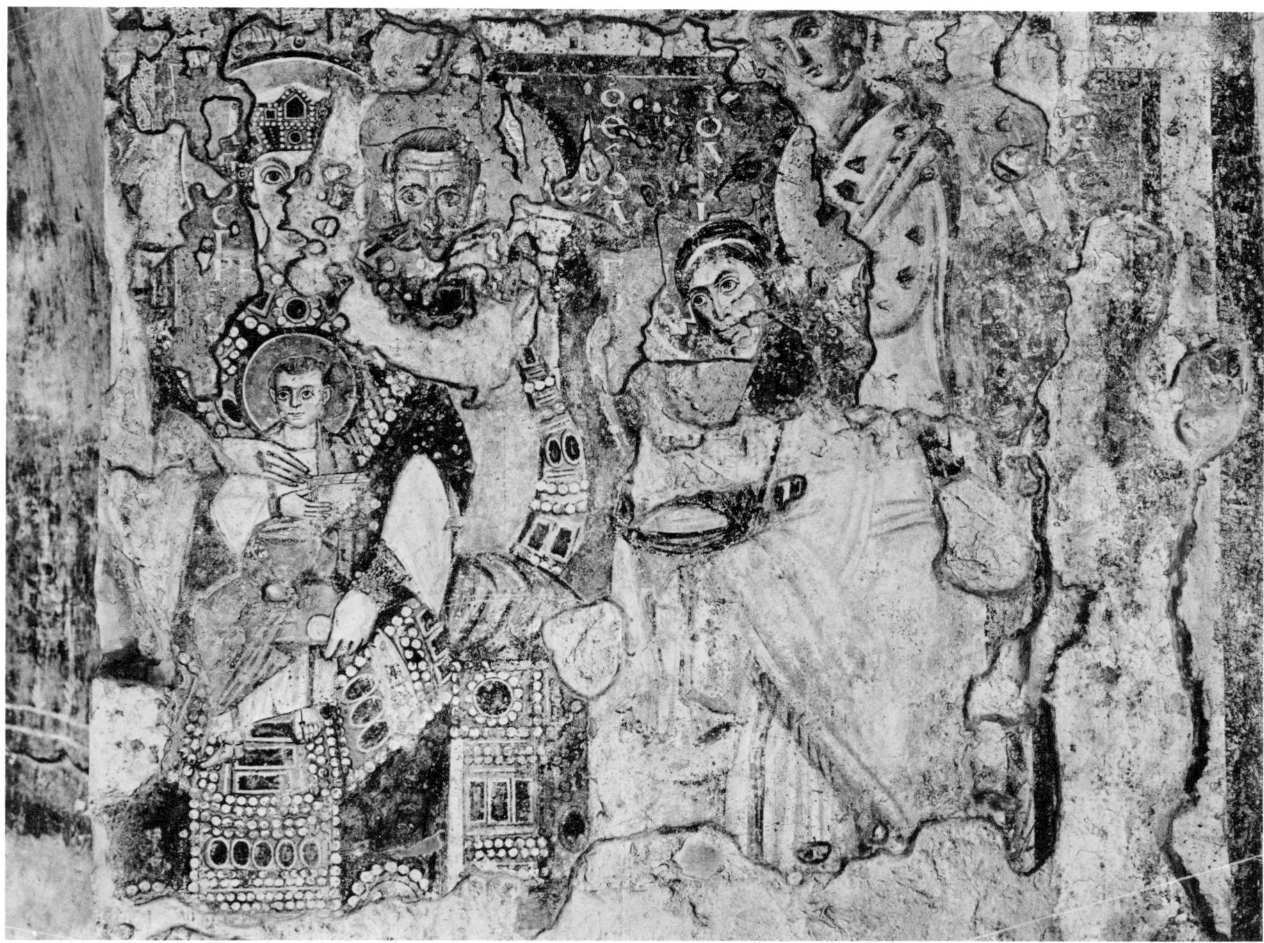

79. S. Maria Antiqua, palimpsest wall

that of late antiquity. The term *Hellenistic* for this style of painting seems appropriate. Scholars still disagree as to whether this Annunciation dates from 630 and thus reflects the peak of the style in the Byzantine capital, or whether it was painted fifty years before and thus mirrors a phase of "Hellenism" current before 600, either in Constantinople or possibly in Rome itself. I incline toward the earlier date, since I think a redecoration of the church shortly after its conversion is more plausible.

The *Fair Angel* is not an isolated phenomenon. At S. Maria Antiqua itself a fresco of Salome and her sons, the Maccabean martyrs, shows very similar figures and facial types, softly modeled and lightly moving in an airy atmospheric space, and more paintings of that group are on the church walls. All testify to an invasion of Rome by Byzantine contemporary art, to its taking root, being absorbed and quickly transposed into a local dialect. The new Hellenistic style, flattened and hardened, is still reflected in the Church Fathers, painted over the *Fair Angel* and the Virgin Annunciate between 649 and 653: cast into firmer forms and forced into a straightjacket of black lines and contours, the heads with their schematized highlights still recall the illusionism of coloring and the modeling of the Hellenistic current. The revived colorism and the schematic highlights of the mosaics at S. Venanzio might likewise be indebted to Rome's penetration by that Hellenistic wave. Such interlocking of hard, sculptured forms and dark outlines with features still reflecting neo-Hellenistic illusionism likewise characterized Eastern mosaics and painting—what little has

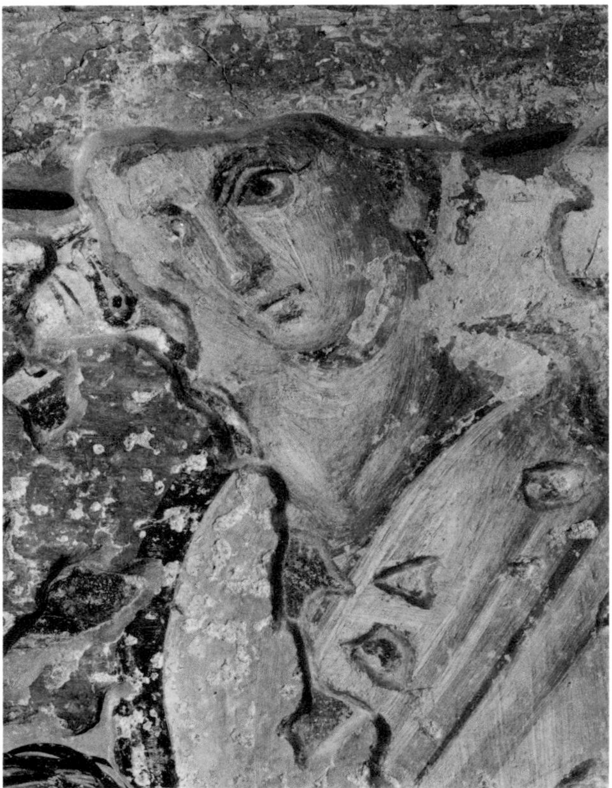

80. S. Maria Antiqua, *Fair Angel*

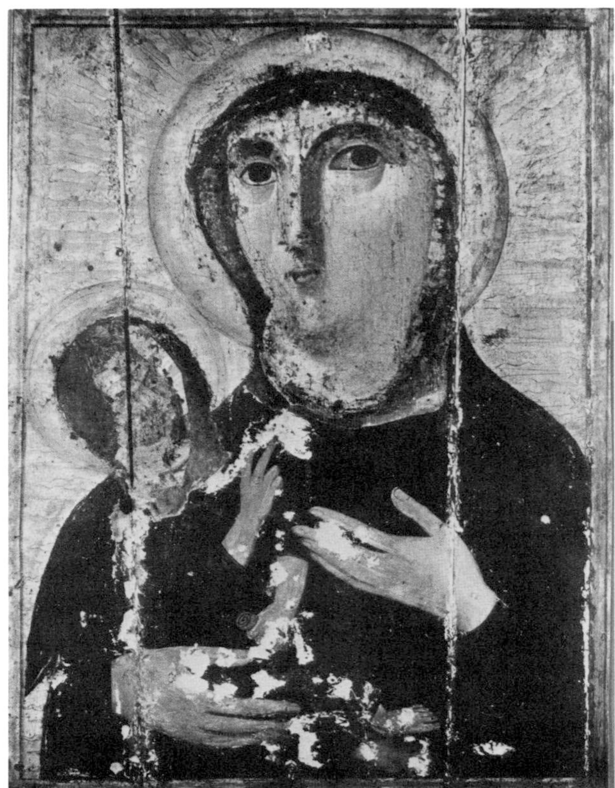

81. *Madonna* of S. Francesca Romana (S. Maria Nova)

survived—from the middle and second half of the seventh century. In Rome, the fusion also marks the large icon of the Virgin now at S. Francesca Romana, under its old name S. Maria Nova, since 847 the legal successor to S. Maria Antiqua. That the icon came from there is most likely; as to its date, the years around both 600 and 700 have been proposed and any intervening date is equally possible (fig. 81).

Reinforcing the persistent contacts with the Byzantine sphere, a second wave of Hellenism straight from Constantinople reached Rome under Pope John VII. It is no wonder, given his background: his father, Plato, after a long civil and naval career in the Byzantine service, had been *curator palatii*, governor of the Imperial Palaces on the Palatine—still the property of the Byzantine Emperors—and was buried at S. Anastasia, at the foot of the hill. John, in the short two years of his pontificate, 705-707, kept in close touch with the court at Constantinople. In the manner of a Byzantine grand seigneur, he became a great patron of art in Rome, thus ending fifty lean years of papal patronage; when the paving of the atrium at St. Peter's or the replacement of a wooden ciborium by a marble one at S. Susanna loomed large, his generosity must have looked fabulous to a city starved for splendor. In St. Peter's he installed a shrine against the inner façade wall of the outer north aisle: two vine columns carried a short barrel-vault surmounting the door; above the door, a mosaic extended the full width of the aisle façade; close to 9 meters long and 6 meters high, it showed a huge figure of the Virgin with the donor, framed by seven scenes from her life. Fragments of the mosaic survive in Rome, Florence, and Orte. At S. Maria Antiqua, his favorite church understandably, he had the chancel fully repainted and the *schola cantorum*, the singers' choir in the nave, newly laid out, decorated with Biblical scenes and provided with a pulpit. His plan to supplement or replace the Lateran by a new bishop's palace on the Palatine, presumably using part of the old Imperial Palace, was cut short by his death. Thirty years later Pope

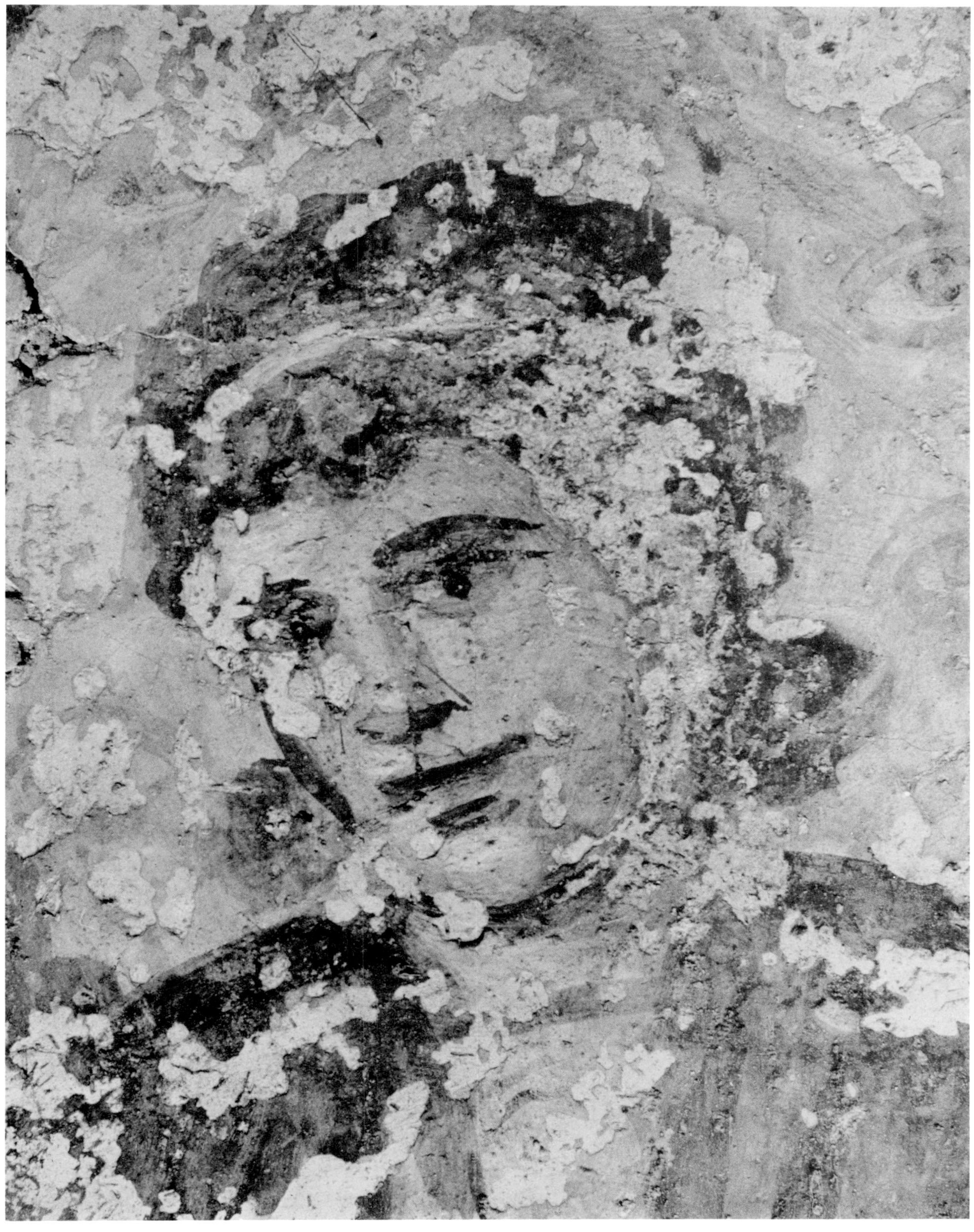

82. S. Maria Antiqua, Seraph's head

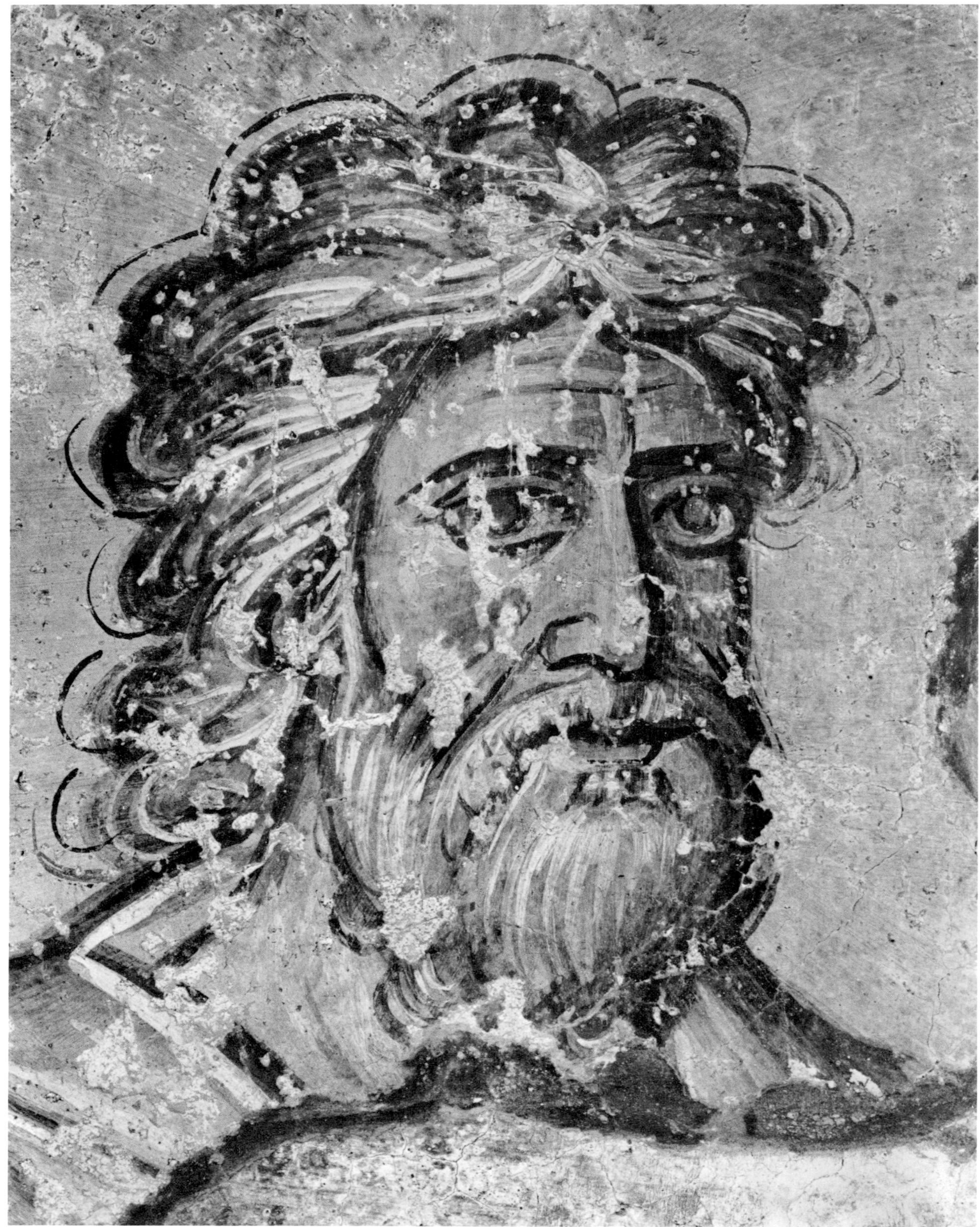

83. S. Maria Antiqua, head of Apostle

Gregory III, 731-741, and his successor Zacharias, 741-752, took up the tradition of lavish donations. Gregory placed in St. Peter's six vine-scroll columns, matching those given by Constantine; silver furnishings, altar vessels, and lighting fixtures were given to St. Peter's, S. Maria Maggiore, and to S. Crisogono, the latter for some reason close to his heart; at S. Crisogono he also constructed in the original church far below the level of today's twelfth-century basilica an annular crypt, recalling that of St. Peter's, and decorated it with murals. At S. Paolo fuori le mura and at S. Maria Maggiore, large roof beams were replaced, no mean technical feat. Repairs, too, went on at the Pantheon, in a dozen other churches, and in the catacomb chapels, which had long been neglected. For the flood of pilgrims, he set up and repaired, as his predecessor Gregory II had already done, hostels and diaconiae; to service the Lateran Basilica, St. Peter's, S. Paolo fuori le mura, and S. Crisogono, he restored and established monasteries attached to them. Between 741 and 753, Pope Zacharias restored, enlarged, and decorated with mosaics, marble, and murals parts of the papal palace at the Lateran, which he "found in great neglect." This magnificence has vanished with the palace; but the chronicler's account reflects the impression it made on contemporaries: the new triclinium, covered with marble, mosaics, and painting; the murals showing saints in the oratory of S. Silvestro and the portico; the porch in front of the archives and the tower with bronze doors and grills and the figure of the Savior above the door; and the triclinium on its upper floor with a map of the world and explanatory verses. The description recalls nothing so much as accounts of contemporary imperial-palace building in Constantinople. Would not the palace planned by John VII on the hill above S. Maria Antiqua have shown similar features?

The new links to Byzantium startle the eye in the paintings and mosaics surviving from the time of John VII. The head of a seraph on the chancel wall high above the apse at S. Maria Antiqua recalls the *Fair Angel*. Indeed, the seraph's head is painted even more loosely, with free, broad brush strokes (fig. 82). At the same time, the impressionism and illusionism of the rendering is supported, in contrast to the earlier Hellenistic wave, by a strong framework of black lines—contours, eyebrows, the nose, drapery where there is any—as traditional by then in both Roman and Eastern ateliers. A series of Apostle busts in the presbytery of S. Maria Antiqua bears witness (fig. 83). In an icon from S. Maria in Trastevere donated by John VII or his successor, the solid Roman forms and harsh outlines of the Virgin and Child enthroned contrast with the Byzantine subtle softness of the flanking angels, different "modes" of rendering being applied to different subjects. Similarly, in the mosaic fragments from the pope's chapel at St. Peter's—such as the *Birth of the Virgin* now at S. Maria in Cosmedin—coloration and modeling are framed by a linear system of black contours and drapery folds (fig. 84). The mosaic technique itself may testify to a new impact from the East: the artist worked with a mixture of glass and marble tesserae, the latter primarily

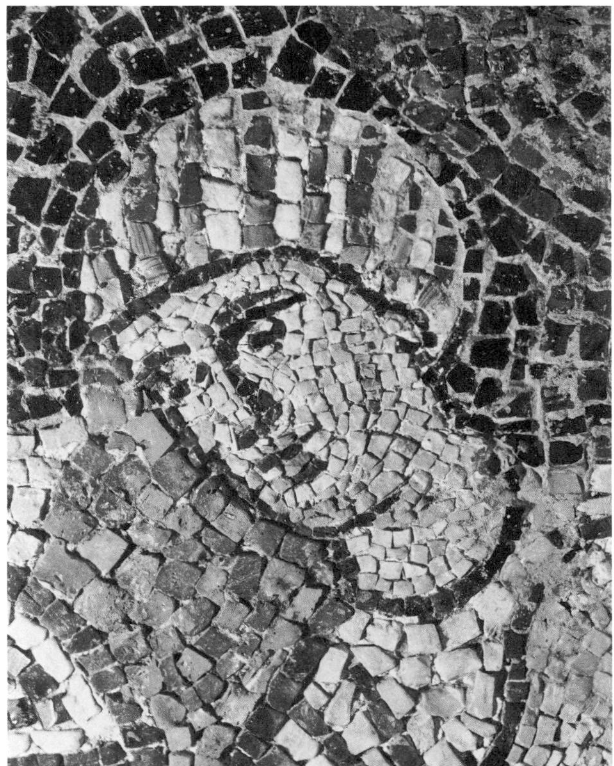

84. S. Maria in Cosmedin, mosaic, *Birth of the Virgin*, detail, head of attendant

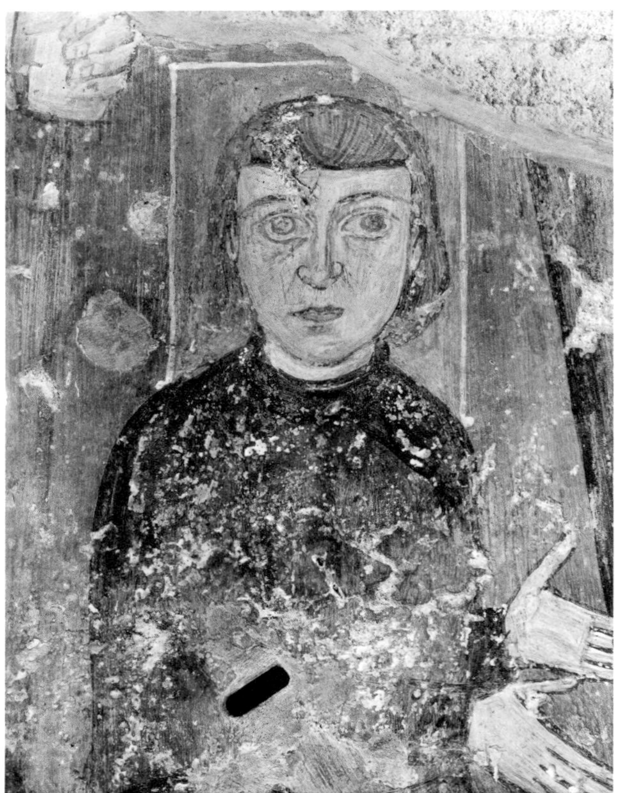

85. S. Maria Antiqua, Theodotus Chapel, head of child from donor's family

for the flesh tones, a technique attributed, rightly or wrongly, to Byzantine rather than Roman local custom. Very possibly John VII called in artists from Byzantium who may have returned home after the pope's death, but not before having trained local masters.

This second Hellenistic wave dating from the pontificate of John VII left its traces in Rome like the first had done a century before. Also like that first wave, the second soon changed into a linear formula. Only faint traces of illusionistic effects and impressionistic techniques survived within an ever-hardening linear framework; figures and busts, as in the wake of the earlier wave of neo-Hellenism, are dehydrated and stiffly posed against the neutral ground of a nonspace. The linear marking of the draperies has hardened into a few never-changing formulas to bring out schematically gestures, movement, and limbs. Heads, long and triangular, are distinguished by huge eyes, a straight nose, a small, sometimes petulant mouth, a firm chin. The formulas go far back in Rome and are ultimately derived from Byzantine prototypes of the sixth century. Examples in eighth-century Rome are: the murals, dated 731-741, in the annular crypt of the first church of S. Crisogono; those, possibly contemporary or a generation later, from the oratory now buried below S. Saba—the fragments are now in the convent; or those painted under Pope Paul I, 757-767, in the aisles of S. Maria Antiqua. The outstanding example of the style is found in the murals of the left-hand chapel flanking the chancel at S. Maria Antiqua, donated by the *primicerius* Theodotus, a leading civil servant of the papal administration, *dispensator*, that is, manager, and perhaps founder or financial backer of the diaconia connected by then with the church; and, incidentally, uncle of Pope Hadrian I. The date of the paintings, around 741, is provided by the portrait of Pope Gregory III, replaced while work was under way by that of his successor, Pope Zacharias. The portrait of Theodotus himself shows the style that had by then formed: a linear skeleton organizes figures, heads, and draperies, having nothing to do with modeling bodies or heads; but its schematized highlights still reflect faintly the Hellenistic style that invaded Rome from Byzantium (fig. 85). By the later third of the century, in the murals painted under Paul I, 757-767, in the aisles of S. Maria Antiqua and those done in the atrium under Hadrian I, 772-795, the linear style has become the dominant note: lively and often exciting, but lacking the effects of illusionism and the subtlety of the Byzantine touch. With new accents this style continues in wall paintings and mosaics of the ninth century.

The source of the Hellenistic influx around A.D. 600 and A.D. 700, and of Byzantine stylistic and iconographic elements in general, appears to have been Constantinople and its immediate sphere of influence, rather than some provincial center. At times, individual masters or workshops seem to have been brought to Rome straight from the Byzantine capital; the artists active under John VII were hardly an isolated phenomenon. It has been suggested that the Byzantine waves were carried to Rome by the monastic congregations that fled the East, either from the Muslim onslaught on the Syro-Palestinian and African provinces in the seventh century, or from the Byzantine heartlands after the middle of the eighth century and again after 820; but there is no proof. The monastic contribution appears to have centered on liturgical custom, theological dogma, and a few iconographic schemes. Late refugees from iconoclasm after 750 and after 816, these congregations may have produced a handful of manuscripts and scattered Greek epitaphs. But their contribution comes late and it is drawn from provincial Byzantine or Byzantinized centers in the West, rather than from Constantinople itself. In fact, a resurgence of Eastern, not necessarily Byzantine, elements comes to the fore briefly in Roman church building from the mid-eighth into the ninth centuries. At that time, a church plan with three apses comes into use, one each attached to the nave and aisles: at S. Angelo in Pescheria in 755; at S. Maria in Cosmedin, as rebuilt about 780 under Hadrian I, whose biographer stressed the unfamiliar feature of the three apses; finally, around 820 at S. Maria in Domnica. Undoubtedly of Syro-Palestinian origin, the plan had taken root in the West as early as the sixth century: the cathedral of Parenzo-Poreć is one example; the church of St. Martin at Autun, long lost but known from old sources, may have been another. From some such Western derivative the plan would have reached Rome. Likewise, another Syro-Palestinian feature, towers flanking the apse, would probably have come via some Western example: it appears in Rome only once, at SS. Nereo ed Achilleo near the Baths of Caracalla (fig. 86), built long after Syria and Palestine had been taken by the Muslims and all contact with the West was lost. In fact, all such imports in the eighth and ninth centuries remain isolated alien bodies. There is no continuity; and when basilicas with galleries reappear in Rome shortly before and after 800, they are best explained on purely local grounds: S. Maria in Cosmedin, as rebuilt with sham galleries around 780, takes up the motif of galleries in the old diaconia hall it incorporates; S. Susanna, in 798/9, was apparently remodeled from a fourth-century reception hall with galleries; and SS. Nereo ed Achilleo patently copied, in the city, the shrine of the martyrs, as built over their grave at the catacomb of Domitilla. In short, the phenomenon is both local and ephemeral.

The strength of the local forces in Rome is altogether remarkable, especially through these centuries of her closest links with Byzantium. Eastern elements penetrate—an Eastern saint, an iconographic scheme, Constantinopolitan neo-Hellenism, carried possibly by a workshop straight from Byzantium. But they are rapidly absorbed, transposed into a new language, and fused into the local Roman workshop tradition just as Eastern relics, feasts, and liturgical customs are assimilated and integrated into the Roman rite. Despite the Byzantine occupation, despite the continued close links to the East over two centuries and more, despite the sporadic influx of Easterners, Rome remained a Western city. In fact, just during the seventh and eighth centuries she grew ever more to be a mecca for Westerners, the spiritual capital and center of political power in the West.

The bringers of Rome's growing impact on

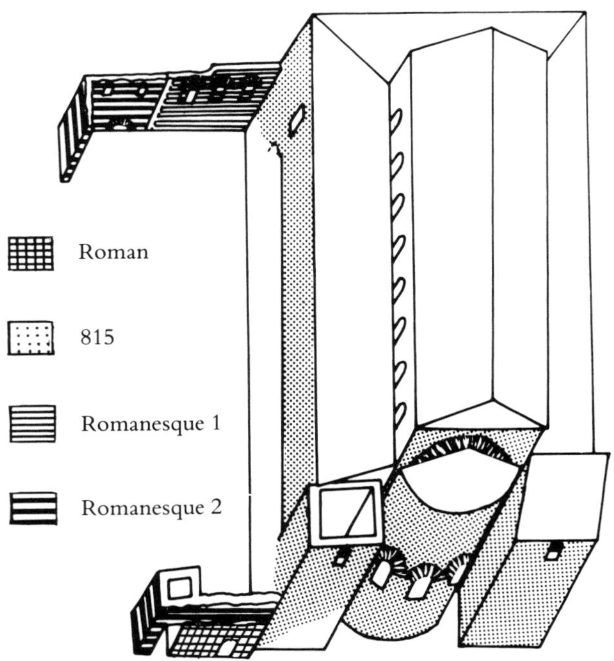

86. SS. Nereo ed Achilleo, rear, reconstruction Frankl-Krautheimer-Corbett-Lloyd

the West were missionaries sent to the barbarian countries and, even more, visitors to Rome. Returning from their pilgrimages, Northern bishops and clergy would bring home with the usual relics the customs of the Roman rite. Eastern elements, by then incorporated into Roman liturgical custom, inserted into the Roman calendar of saints, or absorbed into Roman church planning and decoration, would be swept along to the lands of the West and North. Benedict Biscop in 680 took back to England liturgical books needed for the correct performance of Mass; icons to set up on the chancel of his monastery church—an Eastern feature by then become part of Roman church design; paintings, obviously panels, either icons or Biblical scenes, but presumably the former; and the arch chanter of St. Peter's. Likewise, some Frankish bishops, prior to and during the first half of the eighth century, may have introduced Roman liturgy into their dioceses, including the Eastern elements it had absorbed, to replace the traditional Gallican rite. At the same time, English missionaries in frequent touch with Rome carried the Roman liturgy to territories newly Christianized. In the course of the seventh and eighth centuries Rome became the arbiter and ruler of religious dogma and practice for the Christian West, South, and North.

All this should be seen within the political context of the times. Papal policy from the sixth through the eighth centuries was necessarily torn between East and West. The need to cooperate with the Byzantine emperor and his representatives in Italy had to be balanced against the necessity to resist the Longobard threat or deal with it and maintain the safety and independence of the territorial possessions of the Church, of Rome, and of the papacy itself. Friction with Byzantium on points of dogma continued throughout the seventh century; and interference by the emperor and his representatives was frequent. But neither the power of the papacy nor its awareness of itself as a political force in the West allowed for effective resistance. By the early eighth century, the political climate had undergone a change. The papacy knew that it was a force to be reckoned with in the West; so much so that in 729 Pope Gregory II could warn the Byzantine emperor in so many words: "The whole West has its eyes on us . . . and on Saint Peter . . . whom all the kingdoms of the West honor. . . . We are going to the most distant parts of the West to seek those who desire baptism . . . [but] their princes wish to receive it from ourselves alone." At the same time ever since the mid-seventh century the papacy was aware of being backed up by an effective local force. As time went on, a new landholding class had formed, centered on Rome and her territory and linked by interest and family ties to the Church and her landholding institutions—churches, monasteries, diaconiae: Old Roman families in ever declining numbers; Byzantines and Longobards, acclimatized and Romanized within a generation or two. From among this class, local militias had risen to supplant the Byzantine army units; they were recruited from the smaller landholders and their tenants, led by local notables. These militias became the fulcrum of opposition to Byzantium and in support of the papacy, and were the spring of a movement striving for the independence of Rome and eventually all Italy. The militias of Rome and Ravenna in 649 or early in 650 resisted and for a few months prevented the arrest of Pope Martin; thirty-odd years later, the Ravenna militia, sent to arrest Pope Sergius I, mutinied and rescued the pope instead; and at the turn of the century, the united militias of "all Italy" (meaning at best Central Italy) gathered to protect Rome against the rebellious exarch. Concomitantly, the militia of Rome came to the fore in the last decades of the seventh century as a force, along with the clergy and the *populus*—the lay leaders of the great families—in electing the pope. Clergy, great families, and the militia provided an effective basis of support for the papacy as a temporal power and for its seat, Rome.

The ground was prepared for a break with Byzantium. But the empire was not going to give up easily its hold on Italy or its de jure sovereignty over Rome. A meeting in Constantinople between emperor and pope in 711, set to restore theological and political unity, failed. Nor was the attempt at reorganizing Rome and her territory into a Byzantine duchy (*ducatus*) successful. The open breach came in 726 over a question of dogma, the abolition of images, iconoclasm, decreed by Emperor Leo III. Rome's resistance led to reprisals: successive attempts by Byzantine officials to assassinate the ruling pope, Gregory II; heavy taxes imposed on the Church holdings in South Italy and Sicily; finally, confiscation of these holdings. Concurrently, the Longobards, who had been quiet for almost a century, invaded the lands of the Church in Central Italy and the Byzantine possessions around Ravenna. Through skillful negotiation Pope Gregory II persuaded the Longobard king, Liutprand, to deposit his arms at the tomb of Saint Peter. A new threat by the Longobards ten years later—the walls of Rome were hastily repaired—was similarly negotiated and, like any temporal sovereign, Pope Zacharias took over in person the frontier towns returned by the enemy. When the Longobards again moved against Ravenna in 743, the exarch and the population appealed to the pope as "their shepherd." Rome's diplomacy and her militias were factors to be reckoned with.

Peace was shattered again when the Longobards finally took Byzantine Ravenna and besieged Rome in 753, demanding surrender. Pope Stephen II temporized and managed to have the siege lifted, but at the same time the Byzantines appealed to him, presumably in his capacity as the highest legitimate Byzantine official still in power, to obtain in the emperor's name the Byzantine holdings under Longobard occupation. His request was refused, and Stephen turned to the only Western power able to cope with the Longobards, the Franks. In the winter of 753, he crossed the Alps. At Saint-Denis, Pepin the Short, who had usurped the throne a few years earlier with papal approval, was anointed, as were his sons. The legitimacy of his dynasty's rule as kings of the Franks was thus confirmed and he guaranteed on his part the safety of Rome and the possessions of the "republic of the Romans of God's Holy Church." As protector of Rome, he was appointed "Patrician of the Romans" by the pope, a title freely, if illegally, coined in analogy to that borne by the Byzantine viceroy. Once Pepin had obtained under armed pressure a Longobard promise to restore Church lands—a promise broken the following year—he marched in and made the Longobards cede with a donation to "Saint Peter and Holy Roman Church" not only these, but the ex-Byzantine territories as well. The legal position of the Byzantine lands, secured under the terms of the previous Byzantine request, remained undefined, as did the position of Rome. De facto, Byzantium had been eliminated from Italy north of Naples and had ceased to be a factor in European politics. In her place, Rome, represented by the Church and the great families, loomed as a major power in Italy. In a last uprising in 773 when the Longobards attacked Rome once again and the towns securing the road to Ravenna, the new pope, Hadrian I, appealed to Charlemagne, Pepin's son. Charlemagne moved in, conquered Pavia, the Longobard capital, and annexed their kingdom in 774. The Franks and the papacy together ruled Northern and Central Italy. As Patrician of the Romans, Charlemagne took on the protection of Rome and the Church. The papacy, no longer linked to the East nor looking primarily to the Mediterranean, had become both in fact and name a sovereign Western power—the spiritual ruler of Europe and the temporal ruler of a large territory in Central Italy. The Franks had turned into a crucial and potentially dangerous factor in its history. In the process, Rome had gained new status as both the spiritual and temporal capital of the pope, the successor of Saint Peter on his see and the ruler of his lands.

In this new image, the Church, Rome, and the figure of Saint Peter were all equated. The concept had been gradually developing since the fifth century. By the seventh and eighth centuries, it was fully formed. It was to Saint Peter's grave that pilgrims came from the North; to it that the Christian kings from the North sent their gifts; on his altar that the Longobard kings deposited their treaties. Pepin and Charlemagne's deeds of territory were made out to Saint Peter. It was his see that the head of the Church occupied; in his name that the English mission, in close contact with Rome, spread the faith to pagan Germany; in his name that Irish and Gallican monasticism and liturgy were reformed. Rome was his city, the Romans and those on the Church's lands his very own people—*peculiaris populus*; and the holdings of the Church were by equation his or the Church's *res publica*, or temporal commonwealth.

Indeed, from the time of Gregory the Great, the Church's estates in Central Italy, from Latium to Southern Tuscany, were fictitiously the property of Saint Peter—the *patrimonium Petri*. Its strongholds were the Castles of Peter, *castra Petri*; it was ruled by Saint Peter's See, the papal administration; its possessions made the papacy in fact, if not in law, a temporal power; and Rome was the capital of this de facto sovereign state. Territorial and municipal administrations were developed; whether based on those long customary within the Church, or newly created, or derived from Byzantine traditions, they were in any event sovereign. Militias were formed in Rome and through the territory of the Church, the one in Rome divided as early as the seventh century into twelve military districts. Headed by the pope and composed of clerics and laymen, the administration handled both foreign relations and the possessions of the Church in Rome and in the Patrimony of Peter. Local notables in the capital and the territory filled the civilian and military high offices: judgeships, municipal posts, and commands in the militia. Leadership in ecclesiastical, civilian, and military affairs obviously interlocked. The same families furnished high-ranking clerics, civil servants, and military commanders. Papal elections, too, were ultimately determined by these families. They were, after all, "the leaders among the civil servants, among the armed Roman militia, and among the clergy." Popes were elected by the "priests and high clergy and officers of the militia," supported by "the entire army and the respectable citizens and the whole assembly of the Roman people"—the latter presumably vociferous and, if need be, violent supporters of opposing families and their candidates, chosen most often from among members of the clan. Naturally, factions favoring Byzantine, Longobard, or Frankish interests clashed. Elections, peaceful after a restless time in the late seventh century when there was strife "as usual," were again violently fought over from 757 by the families ruling Rome and the small towns of the countryside. Attempts to codify the procedure by granting the vote to the clergy alone and the right of confirmation by acclamation and written consent to lay leaders and the militia failed to end hostilities. Notwithstanding such infighting, the great families in the eighth century gave Rome a permanent sound government based on the self-perpetuating administration of the Church, permeated as it was by their clergy and lay members. In theory, this government represented the Roman people; in practice, it was made up of members of the ruling families and their followers, whatever title was given them—*optimates*, leaders, Senate.

If the stress was primarily on independence for the Church, Rome, and the Patrimony of Peter, the three being synonymous, other overtones were noticeable. A loose federation in Central Italy was focused on Rome and the Patrimony. Sometimes allied with, at other times directed against, the Longobards, it always aimed at breaking Byzantium's remaining hold on Italy. The movement was decidedly antiforeign, if not proto-pan-Italian. Rome was its capital; the Rome of the papacy and of the great families; a Rome, moreover, where memories of ancient Rome resurfaced. Roman titles, long obsolete, were revived, intermingling with and replacing Byzantine ones. *Consul* became customary, along with the Byzantine titles *dux* and *comes*. *Senatus* was occasionally used to denote the great families—though the term became frequent only in the early ninth century. The Frankish king had the title *patricius Romanorum* bestowed on himself; and the commonwealth, heretofore simply *res publica*, became *Sanctae Dei ecclesiae res publica Romanorum*—both designations freely coined. Anti-Byzantine feeling was sustained by remembrance of Rome's ancient glory. The city of Saint Peter and the papacy, Christian Rome, was embraced by the memory of old Rome. She presented a new image to the world: her Christian past and present and the Rome of antiquity were the woof and warp of this image. The West and its legacy had gained the upper hand; the East had been eliminated from the new image Rome presented to the world.

CHAPTER FIVE

Renewal and Renascence: The Carolingian Age

The hundred years from 760 and 860 have strongly molded both the map of Rome and her image in contemporary thought. Buildings all over the city reflect her new vitality and her new place in the political picture of Europe; and, though her political power was soon lost, the memory of that power became the basis for an image of Rome that was to last for many centuries. The beginnings of this, the Carolingian Age, fall into the first half of Charlemagne's long reign (768-814) and into the pontificate of Hadrian I (772-795). This age climaxed in the first half of the ninth century under popes Leo III (795-816) and Paschal I (817-824), in the late years of Charlemagne and under the rule of his son, Louis the Pious. The end, roughly 840-860, coincided with the early reigns of Charlemagne's grandsons and with the pontificates of Gregory IV (827-844), Sergius II (844-847), and Leo IV (847-855). The decades from then till around 890 are marked by the figures of two great popes, Nicholas I and John VIII. Their political and religious concepts focused on the idea of a universal hierocracy; but the resulting actions, in the hard light of reality, came to nought. Nonetheless, revived centuries later, their concepts shaped the image of the papacy and her see, Rome, through the Middle Ages, but they no longer breathed the Carolingian spirit. Nor were they reflected, as were those of the popes over the preceding century, in buildings, mosaics, or wall paintings. To the modern visitor, no monuments in Rome recall that final third of the ninth century and its great pontiffs.

Pope Hadrian I, then, opens the Carolingian Age. He came from one of the Roman clans that for decades had served the Church, formulated and implemented her policies, given her popes, clergy, and lay servants, and dominated the city. The family mansion stood near S. Marco, on or near the site of Palazzo Venezia. His uncle and guardian Theodotus had been the high lay official who had established in 755 the diaconia of S. Angelo in Pescheria and had donated the paintings in the chapel named after him at S. Maria Antiqua. Hadrian was trained from his early years in the papal service and had served as *notarius regionum*, city-manager we might say. His family ties, training, and experience bound him to the traditions of both Christian and an older Rome, to the alliance between her ruling families and the papacy, and the need to defend her newly won independence and secular power. His biographer stresses his *romanità*, his being Roman to the core, "sprung from powerful Roman parents . . . defender of the faith, of his *patria* [the term connotes simultaneously birthplace, hometown, and fatherland] and the people entrusted to him . . . opponent of the foes of the Church of God and the commonwealth." Consequently he viewed the Franks' protection of the Church, of her territories, and of Rome as a necessity, but considered it equally essential to keep the protecting power at a distance. Charlemagne like his father, though *patricius Romanus* and protector of Rome and the papacy, still had to obtain the pope's permission to cross from St. Peter's—outside the walls—into the city proper, as a guest.

When Hadrian was elected, Rome was in poor shape. An improvement of economic conditions prior to the middle of the eighth century had been dealt a setback when in 752-755 Rome was twice besieged by the Longobards and the countryside was ravaged. The situation worsened after a breathing space of nearly twenty years, when new Longobard raids occurred in the first years of Hadrian's pontificate. Once again, estates outside the walls, private and Church property, were looted and burned; country folk and monastic congregations were driven into the city; supply and distribution of provisions had broken down. The aqueducts, neglected and partly destroyed in the Longobard sieges, functioned badly or not at all. The city was poorly defended against enemies and the elements; time and again the Tiber flooded the town and the fields across the river, the Prati. Buildings were in poor repair: of houses nothing is known, but the churches inside and beyond the walls, from the great sanctuaries of Saints Peter, Paul, and Lawrence to the chapels on and over the cemeteries, needed major repairs. The catacombs were decaying; Longobard raiders had carried off the bones of martyrs, genuine or putative; herdsmen in the campagna were using the underground cemeteries as shelters for cattle and sheep. Except for John VII in his two-year pontificate early in the eighth century and Gregory III shortly after, the popes had been more concerned with the needs of Rome's day-to-day political survival than with church building or decoration. Hadrian, in fact, was faced with the same problem that had plagued nearly all his predecessors since the later sixth century. But the context of the problems had changed. With the final defeat of the Longobards and the elimination of the Byzantines from Central Italy, Rome, under the protection of the Franks, was safe from attack. The lands held or reconquered by the Church provided a new sound economic basis. They also provided forced labor for what Hadrian seems to have considered his foremost task: to revive his city, Rome.

The remedies he applied to that end were rarely new, but he applied them with energy. Residents and pilgrims had to be fed: importing provisions from afar was next to impossible; the Church holdings in South Italy had been confiscated by the Byzantines, and long-distance hauling overland from Central or North Italy was difficult. So Hadrian strove to reactivate agriculture near Rome, building up large estates, Church-owned, Church-run, and under obligation to deliver set quotas for the maintenance of churches, clergy, the papacy, and welfare institutions. Such *domus cultae* as they were called had already appeared in the 740s, when Pope Zacharias set up four in the Campagna. Rather than scattered farms that were often days away like Church land under his predecessors, Zacharias' comus cultae were large holdings bequeathed to the Church, built up into huge estates by additional purchases and within easy reach of the city. They were decreed "forever and absolutely inalienable." Charters were issued for this "apostolic farmland"—*constituta apostolicae exarationis*. Oratories linked to the farm buildings were built or redecorated. A corporation of clergy was installed on each Church farm, one supposes to supervise operations. And at least one of these estates under Zacharias was set aside to provision the papal court. Zacharias, of course, may only have codified standing or half-forgotten Church practice going back to Gregory the Great or beyond, and Hadrian only revived existing custom when he established his domus cultae. One called Capracorum near Veii, north of Rome, took the place of an ancient Roman villa. Others still unidentified may have done likewise. In any event, Hadrian vastly increased the number of these Church farms, founding no less than seven in the twenty-three years of his pontificate. It appears he made them even larger than his predecessors had done and linked them to the city by locating them along the great cross-country roads; and he set apart the produce of Capracorum, one of the largest, "with its farms, lands, buildings, vineyards, olive groves and watermills," to supply the welfare system of Rome. Wheat and oats, wine and vegetables were to be shipped to the "Granaries of the Church" and stored separately; one hundred hogs were to be killed annually and the pork stored on its own, not mixed with the foodstuffs belonging generally to the Church. Out of these provisions, one hundred poor were to be fed daily at the Lateran "in the portico next to the stairs where these same poor are depicted"; one would love to know what the mural looked like and whether it dated from Hadrian's time or earlier. To each person were doled out a pound of bread, two cups of wine, and a bowl of meat. In short, Hadrian revived the systems of agricultural production and welfare distribution instituted by Gregory the Great that had fallen into disuse over the past two centuries. Naturally, too, these domus cultae would serve—like those under Gregory the Great—as political and economic power bases for the Church amid those big landowners, the great families or powerful abbeys. During the first quarter of the ninth century, Hadrian's successors increased the number and extent of these domus cultae by means fair and foul: purchases, bequests, confiscation from political opponents among the Roman nobility, illegal occupation of lands owned by abbeys, such as Farfa. Amid the inevitable friction, arson, and bloodshed by opponents, the Patrimony of Peter under Hadrian, Leo III (795-816), and Paschal I (817-824), grew into a powerful economic and political arm of the papacy.

Likewise, the increased number of diaconiae in Rome under Hadrian I and Leo III should be seen within the framework of recreating a "Gregorian" efficient welfare system and at the same time strengthening the papacy's hold on the urban masses and needy pilgrims. Three diaconiae were revived under Hadrian near St. Peter's to provide the local and foreign poor with alms—stipulating that they should take a weekly bath as well, an extraordinary measure for the time. Three more welfare centers, S. Adriano, SS. Sergio e Bacco, and SS. Cosma e Damiano, were installed or rebuilt on the Forum at the edge of the inhabited area, all richly endowed with land, vineyards, and serfs to provide food and "frequent baths," and all occupying ancient Roman buildings, long since converted into churches, but offering additional storage space; two more, SS. Nereo ed Achilleo and S. Martino ai Monti, were added under Leo III by substituting them for ancient tituli. Repairs on the aqueducts—one recalls Gregory's measures—formed part of Hadrian's program to provide for the city. The Sabbatina aqueduct feeding the mills on the Gianicolo, the fountain in the atrium of St. Peter's, and the bath nearby "serving the pilgrims and those in charge"—again the preoccupation with sanitary provisions—had been cut in the Longobard siege of 775, and the lead pipes leading to St. Peter's had been looted and damaged by sheer neglect. Early in his pontificate, Hadrian rebuilt a hundred arches that were miles out of town, and repaired the pipeline "so that the water flowed as of old, feeding the fountain . . . [and] the bath and driving the mills inside the city." The Aqua Claudia likewise was repaired. Crossing the Celian Hill from Porta Maggiore, in Roman times it fed the huge reservoir near SS. Giovanni e Paolo, the Claudianum, and continued to the Palatine, the Aventine, and Trastevere; at the time of Pope Hadrian, it appears to have served mainly the Lateran, its bath, the baptistery, and the churches on the Celian. The Aqua Jobia, too, was restored at the same time as the Sabbatina; a branch of the Marcia, it ran mostly underground along the Celian and ended at the river, near S. Maria in Cosmedin. Finally, the Aqua Vergine, like the Jobia almost all underground, was recommissioned so as to supply "nearly the whole city." Along with provisioning and restoring the water supply went measures to defend Rome against attacks, human and elemental. The Aurelian Walls, though far too extensive to be either defended or besieged along their full length by eighth century armies, had for some time been objects of concern. But whereas earlier attempts at restoration had been limited to preparations or hasty repairs, Hadrian rebuilt walls and towers where needed all along the circumference and "from the ground"—whatever that means. To safeguard the crowds of faithful rushing through the fifth-century portico along the Tiber from the bridge at Castel S. Angelo to St. Peter's, he built a protecting embankment.

All these enterprises were city planning on a large scale. They required vision, rational foresight, a clear aim and, for the construction work, a strong labor force. The latter was provided by levies drawn from the countryside, a device not mentioned, and perhaps not used, in Rome since late antiquity. Hadrian's levies worked in shifts and were recruited apparently from the neighborhood of the building site—those from Southern Latium, then called Campania, on the Claudian Aqueduct outside the walls. Wages, food for the laborers, and materials were provided by the administration at considerable cost—one hundred pounds in gold for the repair of the city walls. Technical difficulties were a challenge to be overcome and hence they were proudly listed by the papal biographer: spanning the naves of the huge basilicas, new beams were put in place—eighty feet long at St. Peter's; more than twelve thousand tufa blocks were used in the Tiber embankment near Castel S. Angelo; for rebuilding S. Maria in Cosmedin, a large temple behind the church was demolished by burning it, the whole operation taking a year. The aim of the whole of Hadrian's campaign was clear. Reorganizing agricultural production, restoring the welfare system, feeding residents and pilgrims, repairing the aqueducts, rebuilding the city defenses—all were part of an integrated, far-sighted, and practical program aimed at the physical renewal of Rome.

To make the city safe and livable was one of Hadrian's objects. Another was to restore the grandeur of her sanctuaries and to revive the veneration of her martyrs. Churches had been kept in reasonably good shape from the beginning of the eighth century onward, and new frescoes or icons were not rare: at S. Maria Antiqua, the mural cycles of John VII and of Theodotus had been complemented by the redecoration of the apse and triumphal arch under Paul I, Hadrian's predecessor; Hadrian later added wall paintings in the atrium. But Hadrian's vision was wider. If he did not, as his biographer claimed, "restore and embellish all the churches within and without the Walls of Rome," he at least set out on a consistent campaign to repair and refurbish as many as possible, especially where the need was greatest. Foremost were the great sanctuaries whose relics and memories attracted the flood of pilgrims: St. Peter's, where the atrium, pavement, and damage to the apse mosaic were taken care of; St. Paul's, S. Lorenzo, S. Pancrazio, SS. Marcellino e Pietro on the Labicana—all outside the walls; S. Maria Maggiore, which sheltered the manger of Christ; and the Lateran Basilica. S. Clemente was refurbished; so were SS. Apostoli, its apse repaired with metal clamps, and S. Marco, Hadrian's own church close to his family palace. Roof repairs were a primary task. The huge beams, requested from Charlemagne to span the naves of the major churches, came from the forests near Spoleto: thirty-five for St. Paul's, fifteen for the Lateran Basilica, fourteen for St. Peter's, twenty for S. Maria Maggiore. One thousand pounds of lead were to be provided by Charles for the roof of St. Peter's. The Frank Walcharius, archbishop of Sens and apparently an engineer long in the confidence of both the papal and Frankish courts, was to come to Rome as a consultant. In the end, the actual supervision was provided by a high-ranking member of the papal court, the *vestiarius Januarius*, with occasional assistance from Hadrian himself. Precious gifts were showered on major and minor churches: silver-covered icons to be placed on silver-covered beams at the chancel entrance; and masses of luxurious textiles—altar covers and sets of curtains for the doors, the triumphal arch, the chancel enclosure, and the intercolumniations of the nave—purple, silk, embroidered gold, and otherwise. Never before had such splendor been given so lavishly nor so proudly listed by the papal biographers; the new, secure landed wealth of the Church made itself felt. St. Peter's again received the lion's share: silver paving from the chancel doors to the foot of the high altar; a cross-shaped chandelier with one thousand three hundred and sixty-five lights to be lit at Easter, Christmas, the feast of Saints Peter and Paul, and on the pope's anniversary; a set of sixty-five curtains to hang between the nave columns; a large curtain for the main portal. St. Paul's with seventy curtains, the Lateran with fifty-seven, and S. Maria Maggiore with forty-two were not forgotten; S. Pancrazio received a twin set of thirty-eight, SS. Apostoli and Sto. Stefano Rotondo matching sets of twenty curtains each, all of linen and purple; the twenty-two titular churches then functioning were given sets of twenty, the sixteen diaconiae six curtains each; and altar covers were provided for all titular or other churches, diaconiae, and monasteries.

The catacombs and their chapels above or inside presented a problem. No burials had taken place there for some time. And ever since the Gothic Wars cemeteries above and below ground had fallen into a decay, only slightly delayed by repairs effected up until the time of Gregory the Great. The faithful in Rome, and the pilgrims from the North even more so, clamored to see and touch the martyrs' remains, and popular piety viewed as relics any bones found in the catacombs or sanctuaries outside the city. A last campaign in the 730s aimed at repairing chapels and cemeteries and thus reviving the martyrs' cult *in situ* came to nought. Looting, devastation, and general neglect forced a new policy upon the Church: the transfer of relics, individually and in cartloads, to within the safety of the city walls, a measure formerly frowned upon in Rome and practiced only by popes of Eastern background. The mid-eighth century made this foreign custom Roman. When Paul I in 761 completed the church and monastery of S. Silvestro in Capite, founded by his brother and predecessor, Stephen II, on the grounds of the family mansion, he brought "from the devastated cemeteries innumerable bodies of saints." The remodeled church still stands east of the Corso; the monastery has given way to the General Post Office. Hadrian, too, provided for a mass transfer of relics: when rebuilding S. Maria in Cosmedin, he placed a "hall crypt" below the chancel; a small underground basilica supported by columns and architraves, its walls were set with niches, halved by shelves (fig. 87), where the relics were to be sheltered and made accessible to pious crowds. Too accessible—ninth-century church planners at S. Prassede, SS. Quattro Coronati, Sto. Stefano degli Abissini, and elsewhere reverted to the maximum security of the annular crypt as first laid out at St. Peter's around 590. Unique in Rome, the Cosmedin crypt drew on models of a faraway past, both pagan and Christian: *columbaria*, their sides honeycombed with niches to hold ash urns; and luxurious mausolea of basilical plan. Among the latter, the best known in Rome till the fifteenth century was attached to the apse of St. Peter's. Designed in rich classical forms, it was built shortly after 390 for Anicius Probus, a Christian grandseigneur, an ancestor of Gregory the Great, and a member of one of the great families that had ruled Rome in the fourth century, as had Hadrian's and Paul's in the eighth.

Another aim, then, is revealed in the building program of the papacy in the later part of the eighth century. Rome was to be restored for the safety, welfare, and benefit of residents and pilgrims; but she was to be restored also to the ancient glory of Christian antiquity. Hadrian and Paul's activity and that of their successors through the better part of the ninth century explicitly and by implication proclaimed the aim of bringing Rome back to the position she had held four and five hundred years before. The glittering splendor showered on her churches—it continued through the pontificates of Leo III and Paschal I in the first quarter of the new century—emulated, consciously it seems, Constantine's gifts as recorded in the *Liber Pontificalis*. The transfer of relics into the city, individually and by the cartload from the time of Paul I to that of Paschal, placed before the faithful visual testimony to the glorious past of Roman Christianity. The presence among them, at S. Silvestro in Capite, of relics of three early popes, including Sylvester, Constantine's contemporary, stressed the traditions of the early papacy and its links to the Christian Empire. Its venerable age and its descent from Saint Peter were similarly emphasized when, under Stephen II and Paul I, the sarcophagus of a Roman lady, Aurea Petronilla, was brought from St. Peter's to the rotunda, attached around 400 as an imperial mausoleum to its south transept; popular belief turned her into the daughter of the Apos-

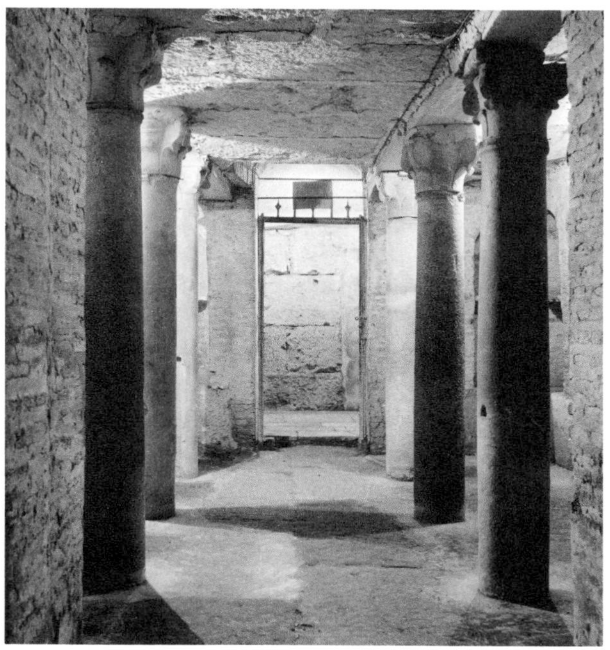

87. S. Maria in Cosmedin, hall crypt

tle; and the dedication in 760 of the mausoleum to the new putative saint as the chapel of the Frankish kings established a tangible bond between them, the Apostle, and his successors to the see. Early Christian and specifically Constantinian usage was revived even in the architectural terminology of the papal biographers. Early in the pontificate of Pope Hadrian, St. Peter's is termed an *aula* rather than plainly a church (*basilica*, *ecclesia*). Aula had been used before only in the solemn language of dedicatory inscriptions, the most obvious being those of Constantine at St. Peter's—on the arch of the apse, on the triumphal arch, on the gold cross, the latter reported in the biography of Sylvester in the *Liber Pontificalis*. The arch between nave and transept, before simply the "major arch," in the 820s and 830s was called the "triumphal arch" as it is even today. The term was heretofore rarely employed, even for Roman triumphal arches. In all likelihood it was freely coined in analogy to the dedicatory lines both on the Arch of Constantine and on the triumphal arch at St. Peter's, triumphs being referred to in either case. Title churches in the second quarter of the ninth century were occasionally given not the customary names linked to their patron saints—S. Prisca, SS. Giovanni e Paolo, SS. Quattro Coronati—but designations obsolete since the sixth century: "*titulus Aquilae et Priscae*," "*titulus Pammachii*," "*titulus Aemilianae*." Finally, a late-eighth-century guide, the Codex Einsidlensis, was written no longer for the pious pilgrim: its introductory anthology records inscriptions impartially, whether pagan or Christian, secular or ecclesiastical, while the itineraries through the city, whether worked out from firsthand knowledge or from a map, list indiscriminately Christian and ancient monuments as they present themselves to the visitor. The guide, then, is meant to appeal to a visitor who is Christian, but has antiquarian interests and knowledge. Ancient Rome reclaims her place in the image of the city, long turned Christian.

All such elements spring from concepts current in Rome from before the mid-eighth century onward and, perhaps slightly later, at the Frankish court. They are reflected first in that famous spurious document, the Donation of Constantine. They came to fruition in A.D. 800, in the coronation of Charlemagne as emperor, an event not envisaged at the start. The Donation, either composed entirely in 754 during Pope Stephen II's stay in France, or gradually developed until the end of the century, pretended to be a decree addressed by Constantine to Pope Sylvester. In it, so runs the thesis, the emperor granted to the pope and to all his successors as the heirs of Saint Peter a status higher than his own "secular throne," imperial honors and income, *insignia* and *regalia*; he ceded him the Lateran Palace, the city of Rome, and "all provinces, places and towns of Italy and the Western regions"; and, because of this cession, he moved his capital to the East. Other concessions were thrown in, foremost among them papal supremacy over the Eastern patriarchates. The political theory thus outlined relegates the Byzantine emperor's de facto rule to the East without denying in so many words his legal sovereignty in the West; and it claims for the pope imperial status, spiritual supremacy over all of Christendom, and temporal rule over Rome, Italy, and the West. The latter claim, vague as it is, had best be understood as defining the positions of the pope and the Frankish king, as viewed from Rome. A king, and a "barbarian" king at that, was implicitly subject to the imperial authority as invested, according to the Donation, in the pope; he would be, as was Charlemagne, a powerful but obedient defender of the See of Saint Peter and his city; he would be styled "patrician of the Romans," the title created for and conferred on him by the papal chancery from 754 on without any legal basis. The claim of the papacy to Italy rested on firmer ground; it meant the holdings of the Church, the Lands of Saint Peter, including the ex-Byzantine territories in Central Italy. The claim to Rome was the least ambiguous and for that reason central. Finally, all three claims were hallowed by the imprint of Constantine's name.

Hadrian, intent as he was on preserving papal independence, carefully maintained to the end of his pontificate a balance of power—Byzantine emperor, King of the Franks, pope. The equilibrium was thrown off the beam when Leo III, expelled by a putsch, returned to Rome in 799 under Charlemagne's protection. Cleansed from accusations and reconfirmed in his see, he crowned Charles emperor at St. Peter's on Christmas Day, A.D. 800. The step had apparently been prepared in meetings between Frankish and papal representatives and, Charles' biographer Einhard notwithstanding, the king must have been aware of its imminence: on approaching Rome, he was received with the ceremony accorded a Roman or Byzantine emperor rather than a *patricius*, as he had been on his previous visit; and the choirs of the Romans—clergy, civil servants, militia, nobles, and people—greeting him after the coronation as *Augustus* ("Majesty" is the best translation) were well rehearsed. But the character and extent of the new imperial sovereignty were left unspecified. The wish to spare Byzantine feelings may have been coupled with a lack of agreement on the significance of the step. The Frankish camp may have thought vaguely and idealistically of a "Christian Empire" of the West, based on the spread of Charles' power over nearly all of Christian Europe. The papal diplomats may have envisaged more concretely an *imperium Romanorum*, an empire of and for the Romans. Pledged to the defense of Rome and the Church, it would not have been too different from the "patriciate of the Romans" held previously by the Frankish kings and like it in the gift of the pope, as implied in the Donation.

The papal diplomats' view of Charlemagne as Constantine's heir and the protector of the Church, and their view of the pope as Saint Peter's successor and the fountainhead of both Frankish and papal rule, are reflected in a mosaic once in the Triclinium of Leo III and dating presumably from 798 or before April 799. The triclinium, a triconch hall in the Lateran Palace, was demolished in 1589, except for its main apse, and it is known only from descriptions and drawings. The main apse and its mosaic, thoroughly restored in 1625, survived until 1743, when the mosaic was transferred to a newly built niche behind the Scala Santa. In the transfer, what little was left of the original was so badly damaged and patched up as to leave only a copy, and not an entirely trustworthy one at that

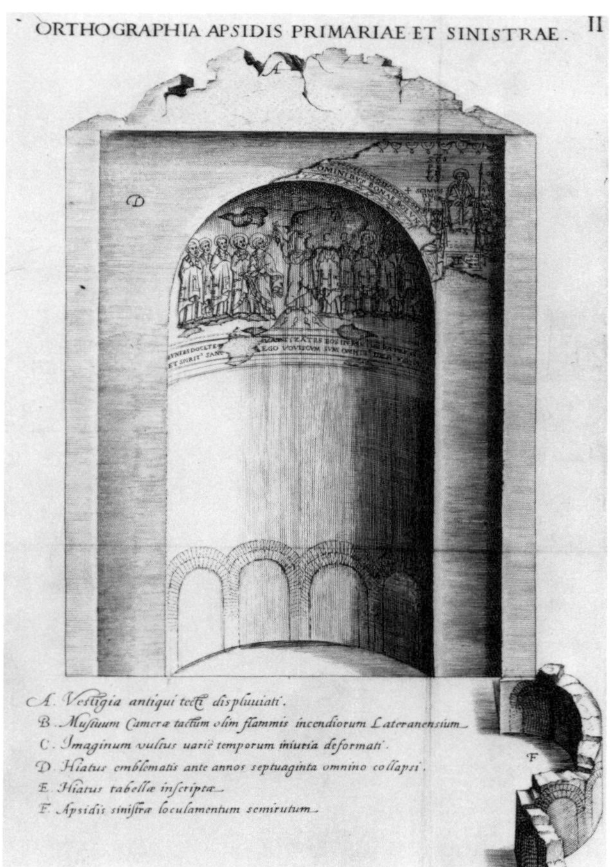

88. Lateran, Triclinium of Leo III, before 1625

(figs. 88, 89). Of the original, only the fragment of one head survives in the Vatican Library, yet the main elements remain. On the front arch, on the sides of the apse opening, two groups were depicted, each of three figures. To the right Saint Peter enthroned handed the pallium to Pope Leo and a banner to Charles—still king, not emperor (fig. 90). On the left, at present Christ hands the labarum to Constantine, the pallium to Saint Peter; in 1625 this group was restored or possibly re-created, we don't know on what precise basis. Sylvester may have been represented instead of Saint Peter and even an entirely different group has been suggested. I myself believe, as do most scholars, that the group was conceived from the outset as the antetype of the one to the right, in the spirit of the Constantinian Donation. Correspondingly, in the half-dome of the apse, the Mission of the Apostles was shown in the original, as it is in the copy, Christ flanked by the eleven disciples going to

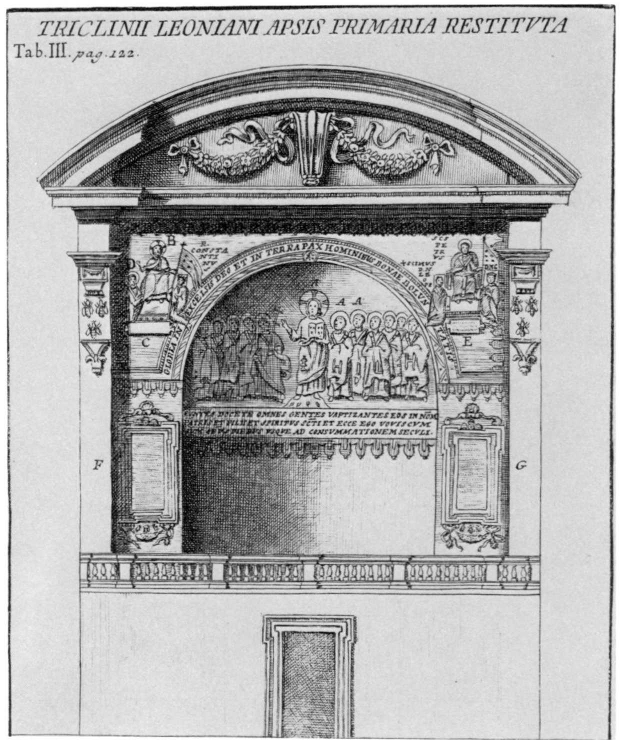

89. Lateran, Triclinium of Leo III, as restored in 1625

convert all the world. Clearly, the scene alludes to the policy of spreading the faith and strengthening the position of the Roman Church in Europe. In this policy the Church counted on the support of Charlemagne. This support she had received from Constantine in her mission to "resurrect the world under Christ's leadership," as phrased in the inscription on the triumphal arch at St. Peter's and as implied from the mid-eighth century on in the Constantinian Donation. Constantine was to be Charlemagne's model in supporting and protecting the Church. Details remain a matter of argument. But whatever the answer, the mosaic in Leo's triclinium seems to me the first visible witness in Rome of the Carolingian Renascence.

The coronation on Christmas Day 800, though not intended to do so, changed the political picture from that reflected by the mosaic. Leo III and his advisers may well have viewed the imperial crown as the mere seal on the old alliance between the pope and the *patricius Romanorum*. But the creation of the empire had political and ideological consequences not readily foreseen by contemporaries. By implication it denied any Byzantine claim to the West, previously unsubstantial but unchallenged. Beyond, the Western emperor claimed implicitly and explicitly to succeed the Roman emperors of antiquity: to succeed the Christian emperors explicitly, but implicitly their pagan predecessors as well. Charlemagne ruled large parts of what had been their domain, including their capitals "in Italy, Gaul, Germany"; he held Rome, the "Mother of the Empire, where Caesars and Emperors were wont to reside"; he and his successors adopted the titles *Caesar* and *Augustus*, as first used on Christmas Day, 800; documents were dated in consular years and *post consulatum*, in the Roman style; seals bear the legend

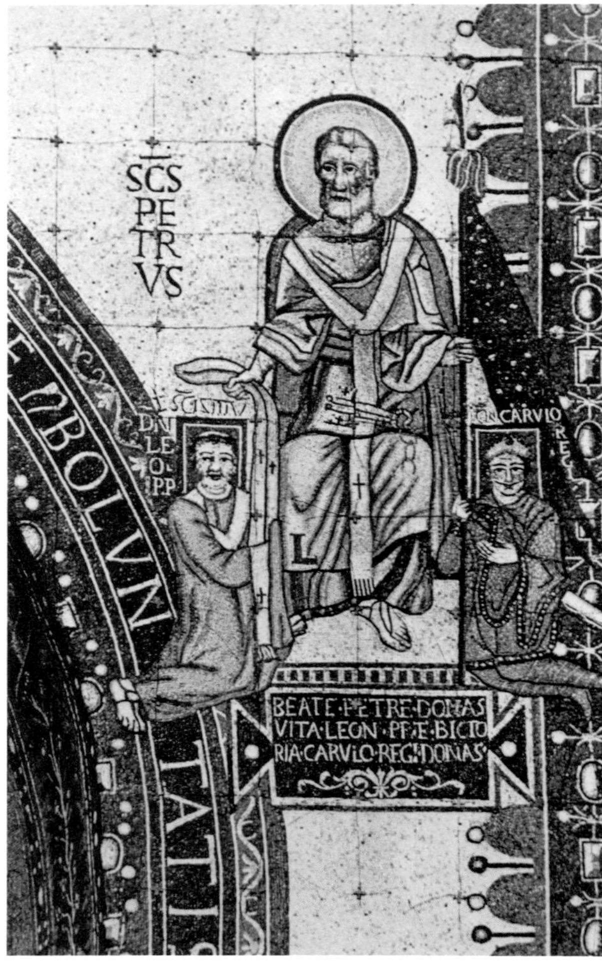

90. Lateran, Triclinium of Leo III, mosaic, eighteenth-century copy, detail of Saint Peter with Charlemagne and Leo III

Renovatio Romani Imperii, framing a symbolic image of Rome. Charles' court-poet, Alcuin, addressed him as *Flavius Anicius Carlus*, Flavius being the official name borne by Christian emperors from Constantine on. It is self-evident that within this framework the first Christian emperor was a key figure. As conceived by the Donation, papal diplomacy foresaw the revival of a new Christian Empire as focused on the figures of Constantine and Sylvester: at their time, so it was thought, Christianity and the empire were supposedly one, and the first Christian Emperor and Protector of the Church ruled in unison with his papal counterpart. The parallel between Charlemagne and Constantine, alluded to, I believe, in the mosaics of the triclinium in 798-799, became an integral part of the political theory. Time and again the papal chancery referred to Constantine as a model for Charlemagne, the "new Constantine." A crown believed to have been Constantine's was supposedly used for the coronation of Louis the Pious, Charlemagne's son, in 816. Possibly a piece of poetic fiction, the report nonetheless reveals contemporary concepts of the new empire. Ideally, if not in fact, Rome was both the capital of that empire and the see of the papal successors to Sylvester and to Saint Peter.

The situation was fraught with perils: for the papacy, that of surrender to an all-too powerful ally; for the empire, permanent involvement in the affairs of Rome, the papacy, and the family factions, who controlled both the city and the See of Saint Peter. As Charles' successors grew ever more conscious of the claims and obligations inherent in their imperial role, the Frankish and the papal sides became aware of the dangers. In 824 Lothar, Charlemagne's grandson, felt compelled to assert his authority over Rome; a constitution was issued both to break the revolt of a local Roman faction against Pope Gregory IV and to check the all-too strong papal reaction. The decree in effect established imperial suzerainty over the city and the papacy: papal elections, to be voted on by the clergy and consented to by the lay leaders, were to become valid only after imperial confirmation; the Roman nobility was granted protection against arbitrary papal action; and an imperial resident, a *missus*, was to act jointly with a representative of the pope as supervisor for Rome and the papal see. A separate agreement demanded an oath of allegiance to the emperor from the newly elected pope, the clergy, and the leaders among the citizens. Reacting against such imperial claims, the Roman clergy and lay leaders elected, over the following decades, a series of popes chosen from among the great Roman clans, all set on defending the independence of Rome and the Church and the hold of the local power elite on the papal see. Things came to a head when, in 843, the empire claimed the city of Rome and the Lands of Saint Peter as a fief subject to its subkingdom of Italy, which had been meanwhile established. Pope Sergius II, a Roman grandee, resisted the demand, notwithstanding a punitive expedition by the Italian king, Lothar's son; a rigged Church council set in motion against the pope failed. The breach was patched up: imperial confirmation of papal elections continued; the oath of allegiance to the emperor was sworn as before; and coronation by the pope remained a prerequisite of imperial legitimacy. But resentment against the Northern barbarians was strong among Romans, united in passive resistance, and it was deepened by the lessening of central authority within the Carolingian Empire. Raids by Saracen pirates in 846 and the looting of the churches of Saints Peter and Paul showed up the helplessness of the city and the lack of adequate imperial protection. Self-defense and independence became the goal of the Romans. The threat of a new raid was averted by the victory won in 849 by a naval coalition, which was headed by Pope Leo IV but drawn from Naples, Gaeta, and Amalfi.

Simultaneously, a program of fortification was carried out along the coast and inland. To secure St. Peter's and its treasures, the surrounding minor churches, monasteries, hostels, and foreigners' compounds, a wall was built enclosing the entire settlement that had formed around the basilica (fig. 91). Starting at Castel S. Angelo, this Leonine Wall ran due west to Porta S. Pellegrino, next to the passage that now leads from the north to Bernini's Piazza; from there it continued, it seems, to the foot of the hill behind the apse of St. Peter's so as to secure, together

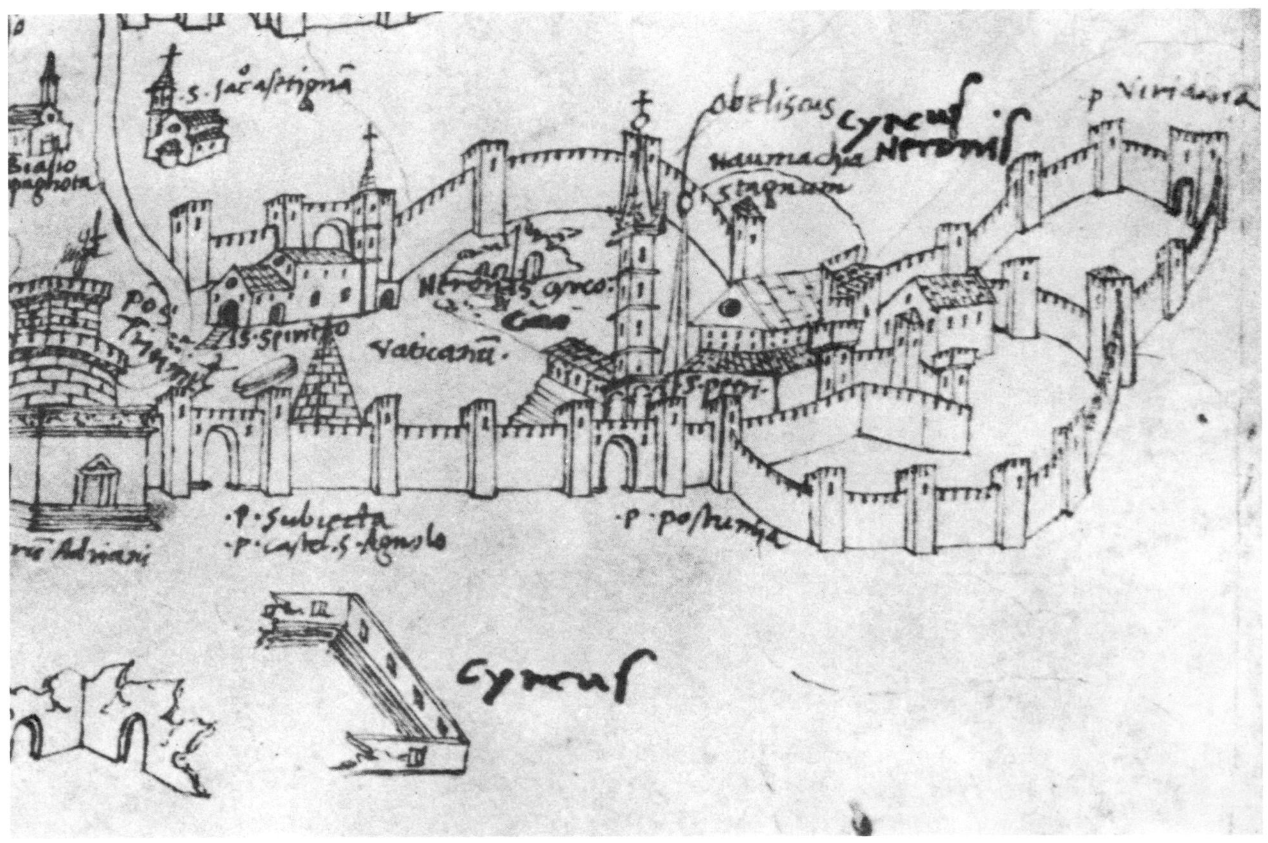

91. Map of Rome, 1474 (original 1450), A. Strozzi, detail of Borgo Civitas Leonina, with Leonine Wall, later enlarged

with the basilica, Sto. Stefano degli Abissini and the other churches and convents nearby. Then, the wall turned back east and by way of the Saxon Gate, near today's Porta Sto. Spirito, it reached the river bank. Of the north stretch, large parts survive; the major part carries the fifteenth-century *passetto*, the corridor linking Castel S. Angelo to the Vatican Palace; smaller fragments have been identified in the papal gardens north of New St. Peter's. The south wall of Leo IV seems to have disappeared in medieval times and its exact course is uncertain. It was rebuilt later, perhaps between 1277 and 1280 by Pope Nicholas III, a great builder, either on the original lines or slightly further south. One may reasonably assume that Leo's wall would have enclosed both the hill with the Frisians' compound, replaced in the twelfth century by S. Michele Magno, and the site of the hospital of Sto. Spirito, then the Saxon compound. Northward and westward, the land enclosed by Leo's wall was later enlarged and secured by new walls, as seen on the Strozzi map of Rome, copied in 1474 from an original dating back to 1447. Nicholas III built the northward loop to enclose the medieval Vatican Palace he had enlarged. A huge westward loop ascends the hill behind the basilica and carries on its crest Porta Pertusa; it is commonly attributed to Nicholas V, who from 1451 to 1455 began to strengthen the fortifications all around. The battened base of a huge tower of his, the Torrione, remains at the east corner of the northern loop. The Strozzi map does not show that tower, but it renders the big west loop of the wall behind St. Peter's, and therefore this loop may well antedate the fifteenth century. In the sixteenth century, all these defenses dating from the ninth to the fifteenth centuries were replaced by a modern system of fortifications with bastions—a system that to this day encloses Vatican City.

The wall of Leo IV had already been planned

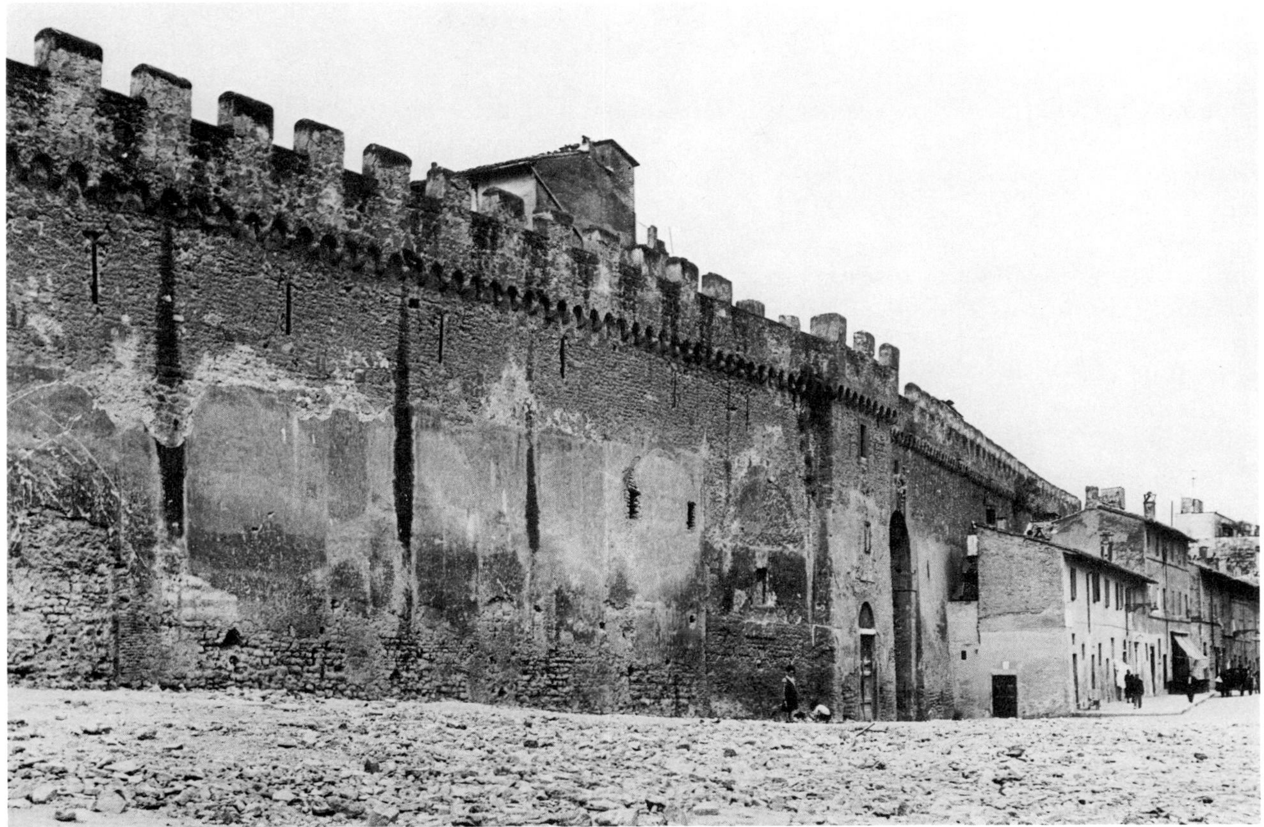

92. Leonine Wall, north stretch, detail as before 1938

half a century before his pontificate. Leo III had laid its foundations and assembled materials; they were subsequently stolen. The events of 846 shook Leo IV into action. The emperor's agreement was obtained. A meeting was called to organize the work. Levies, militarily organized militias, were drafted from the *domus cultae*, or Church farms, from independent churches, and from monasteries in the Campagna. Each militia was assigned a stretch of wall, identified by an inscription. Construction followed a new defense technique different from that of the Aurelian Walls. The remains of the Leonine Wall are hidden under later rebuildings, but its features remain clear. It was equipped with forty-six fortified towers, *turres castellatae*, each having a machicolated parapet, rather than the uniform type of merlon with traverse that was characteristic of the older wall (fig. 92). Begun in 847, work was completed by 853. On June 27 of that year, Pope Leo's new city, the Civitas Leonina, was solemnly consecrated, the pope accompanied by his clergy, all barefoot, with ashes on their heads, making the rounds of the wall, sprinkling holy water on the new construction. At each of the gates the Pope offered a prayer that the new city might be secure from the enemies against whom it had been built: the *new city*, for the Civitas Leonina was and for many centuries remained a separate town outside and different from Rome. Dedicatory inscriptions were placed over its four gates, that of S. Pellegrino, the Saxon Gate, the one near Castel S. Angelo, and a fourth of unknown location. The wording breathes a new spirit of pride and self-confidence: Rome is again "the head of the world, its splendor, its hope, Golden Rome"; and "Romans, Franks and Longobards" are called upon to admire the work of Leo. Similarly, when a fortification was built in the 880s to protect St. Paul's, called *Johannipolis* after its founder, Pope John VIII, against renewed Saracen threats, the inscription over the gate addressed itself to the "nobles, old and young, wearing the toga." With the building of the Leonine City and the victory over the Saracens, a new image of Rome began to take shape in the circles that determined papal policies. It lasted only a short while and, except for the wall and town of Leo IV, it has left no major visual record. Rather than this last phase, churches and their decoration in Rome splendidly reflect the apex of the Carolingian Renascence from the pontificate of Leo III to just after the middle of the ninth century.

The image of Rome that coincides with this Carolingian Renascence had many layers for contemporaries. As of old, she was the city of the martyrs, the resting place of Saint Peter, the goal of pilgrims. She was the See of Saint Peter and his successors and, in a very real sense, the capital and administrative center of his vast patrimony. However, she also connoted an imperial capital in a dual and, indeed, conflicting sense. Granted to Sylvester by Constantine, as the Donation had it, the possession of the city reflected the pontiff's imperial standing. At the same time, the new Western emperor, being heir to Constantine and to all Roman emperors, retained his title to Rome as his capital. She was the "Mother of the Empire" and her location within his domains was a strong argument supporting Charlemagne's claim to the new imperial crown. The handing over to him by Leo III of the city's banners symbolically demonstrated the handing over to the emperor of his capital. The emperor's coronation took place in Rome at St. Peter's, and only thus gained legitimacy. Time and again contemporaries insist on deriving the title to the empire from the possession of Rome and from election by the "Roman people." Old Rome reclaimed her place and the concepts of *Rome* and *Empire* became interchangeable and indivisible. But both concepts oscillate: Constantine's Rome and the Rome of the Caesars; the Rome of the papacy and the Rome of the Carolingian emperors; Old Rome and New Rome on the Bosphorus, the Eastern emperor's capital, which mirrored the old one.

All these images, jointly or singly, are reflected in the donations and the building activity of the papacy, from Leo III to his namesake, Leo IV (847-855), and perhaps beyond. To revive Rome in her old Christian splendor had already been a major aim of Hadrian I. It became the foremost goal of his successors, though with stronger political overtones, to give a visible sign of her grandeur. New churches were laid out to replace the last surviving community centers: ordinary houses remodeled or simple halls of early date, they no longer reflected the new image of Rome. Church furnishings and the decoration of papal palaces grew ever richer. Leo III's biographer endlessly lists churches repaired or newly built: new audience and banqueting halls in the Lateran Palace and near St. Peter's; mosaics and paintings, silver furnishings, textiles for altars and church naves, lighting fixtures—all papal gifts. One hundred and twenty silver chandeliers, from the largest to the smallest and graded according to the recipients' importance, were distributed in 806 or 807 to all churches, diaconiae, monasteries, and oratories then functioning in Rome. None of the previous *vitae* in the *Liber Pontificalis*, not even Hadrian's, had given in equal detail inventories of the riches showered on the city's churches—not since Constantine's days, and the parallel is not without meaning. Similarly, in the biographies of Paschal I (817-824) and Gregory IV (827-844) the stress is on their gifts and their buildings rather than on political events. Only afterwards and through the third quarter of the ninth century does papal largesse take second place in their biographies and, one suspects, in reality as well.

The Rome of the emperors mirrored in the living tradition of ninth-century Byzantium exerts a powerful impact, primarily on papal palace building. No major elements, except the mosaic of Leo III's triclinium, survive of the palace of the popes at the Lateran; and the extant records—descriptions, plans, and views prior to its demolition in 1589—give only an approximate idea. But it seems evident that its nucleus, parts antedating the cession of the building to the bishop of Rome, rose near and underneath the present Scala Santa, and that this nucleus grew westward as time passed. Likewise, it is clear that as early as the eighth century, if not be-

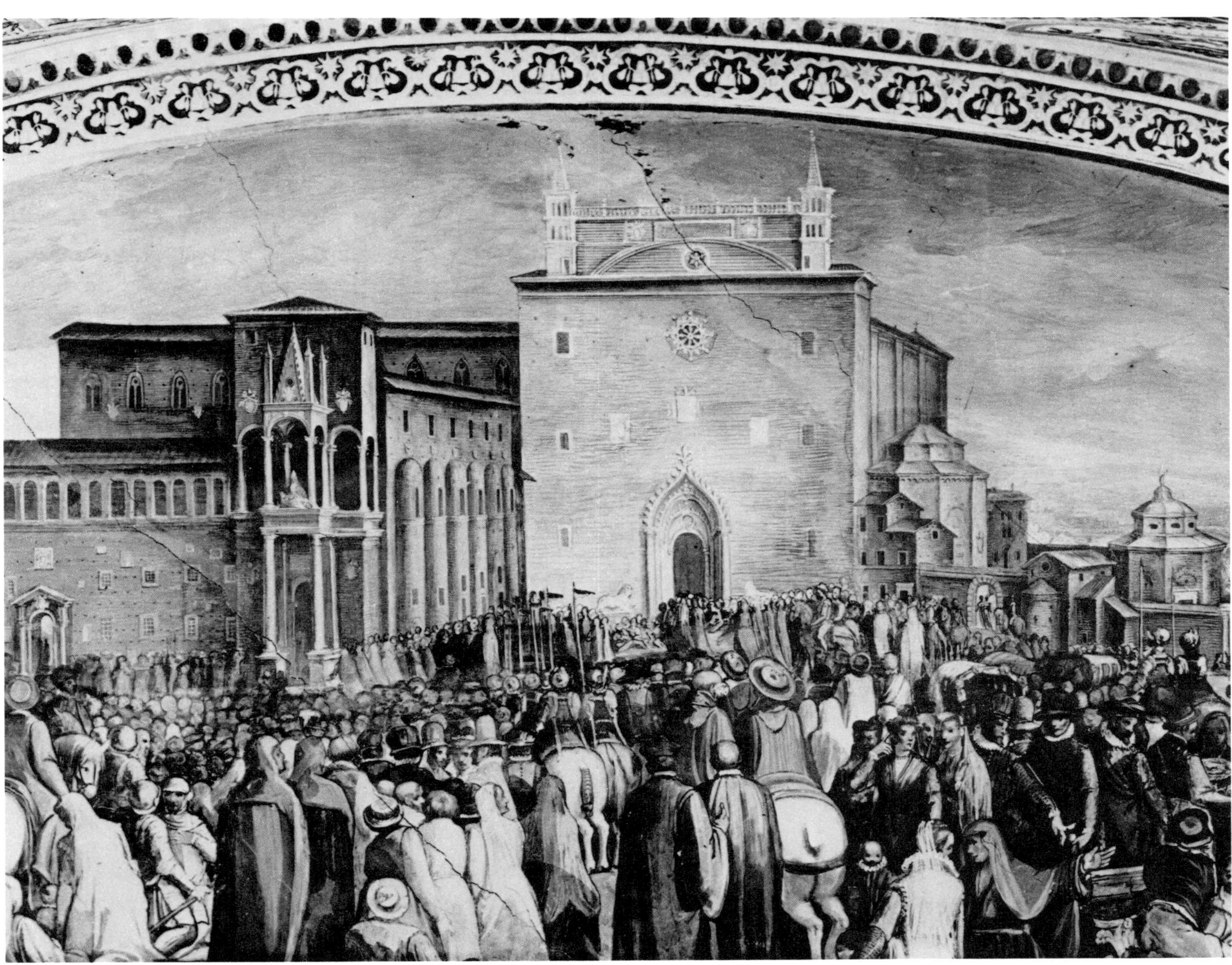

93. Lateran Palace and Church as before 1588, fresco, Vatican, detail showing banqueting hall and thirteenth-century transept of basilica

fore, the papal patrons were set on competing with the Palace of the Byzantine Emperors in the New Rome on the Bosphorus. When, shortly before the middle of the century, Pope Zacharias erected an entrance "tower" with a bronze gate surmounted by a portrait of Christ, it was unmistakably derived from the bronze gate, the Chalkē—the two-storied towerlike entrance to the Imperial Palace in Constantinople. Likewise, the triclinium that he built, decorated with marble revetment, mosaics, and murals, and provided with a portico, competed with similar elements in the Imperial Palace. Sixty years later, the intention of rivaling the palace of the Byzantine *basileus* is equally obvious in the structures added to the Lateran Palace by Leo III. The triconch triclinium, its apse carrying in mosaic the Mission of the Apostles and the two groups of pope and emperor, was "larger than all other triclinia"—it measured nearly 26 meters by 12.50 meters. Its walls were sheathed in marble; the entrance was supported by porphyry columns, white columns, and pilasters and preceded by a narthex, as it appears in a sketch done before 1588. The structure in plan, colorful decoration, and precious materials continued a tradition of triconch ceremonial reception rooms going back to antiquity. In Constantinople, the type lived on, as witness a triconch in the Imperial Palace of slightly later date, which had just the features of Leo's triclinium. A second triclinium, built by Leo III shortly after 800 in the Lateran Palace and restored fifty years later, likewise found its counterpart in the

Great Palace in Constantinople. Pictorial and written records antedating the demolition of the old Lateran Palace in 1588 give a fair impression of Leo's structure (fig. 93). A full 68 meters long and located on the upper, main floor of the palace, perpendicular to the northern flank of the Lateran church, the triclinium served as a state banqueting hall. A terminating apse and five conchs on either flank of the hall held tables and dining divans, *accubita*—apparently at such solemn occasions one lay rather than sat at table. The interior, like the triconch hall, was fitted with marble revetment and paving, a porphyry fountain and mosaics. From an anteroom, a canopied balcony projected north overlooking the area facing the palace; much restored or rebuilt, it still served even to 1300 as a focal point from which to impart the papal blessing *urbi et orbi*. A long corridor—it bore the Greek name *macrona* and was merely repaired by Leo III—linked the hall and balcony to the parts of the palace near the façade of the church. Dining halls with flanking conchs had been familiar, to be sure, since antiquity: in Constantinople; in Ravenna; in Rome, where Leo III himself had built another one adjoining the steps ascending the atrium of St. Peter's. However, the Lateran banqueting hall, in plan, decoration, furnishing, and function, was clearly meant to compete with the Hall of the Nineteen Divans in the Great Palace of the Emperors in Constantinople: size, location in and links with the rest of the palace, and function all correspond. It remains unclear whether the Great Palace of the Emperors in Constantinople was also mirrored in any of the other halls or oratories added to the Lateran Palace or refurbished in the ninth century: one more triconch hall and a comfortable living room—or was it an open loggia?—both built by Gregory IV; or the basilica of Nicholas I, with its three fountains, completed around 870. Links are more than possible; rivaling the Imperial Palace of Byzantium had been an aim of papal building in the Lateran Palace from before the middle of the eighth century. But the tendency gains new meaning in the context of Rome's revival as the imperial capital of both pope and emperor in the West.

The many-layered meaning of Rome to contemporaries is best seen in the ecclesiastical building program, not so much of Leo III as of his successors, from 817 till the middle of the ninth century. As it took twenty-five years for the concept of the revived Empire to consolidate fully, so it took time for the idea of the renascence to be reflected fully in church planning and decoration. Those laid out by Hadrian and the majority of Leo III's church buildings revert to Byzantine models or derive from Near Eastern church plans long rooted in the West; still under Paschal I, around 819 or 820, S. Maria in Domnica was laid out with three apses as S. Angelo in Pescheria had been sixty-five years before. But already in the first years of Leo III's pontificate, church plans and mosaic decoration start reverting to Early Christian, and specifically Constantinian, models. Beginning with Paschal I, the plans of churches, their decoration, and their number—nearly a dozen survive—speak not only of the vigor of a papacy intent on renewing Rome, but clearly of a program to renew the city and her monuments in the spirit of a rebirth of Constantinian building and decoration, genuine or putative. Nearly all the new churches of the first half of the ninth century replace community centers or churches no longer up-to-date and out of keeping with the dignity of a papal and imperial capital. The new structures were reasonably large, no longer hidden away, and clearly had the appearance of churches to the eye of any contemporary. They were meant to create a new image of Rome in planning, design, and masonry technique. Eastern church plans or purely local features, prevailing still in the pontificate of Leo III, disappear. The new churches and their mosaics unmistakably reflect the determination to revive the Christian past of Rome in its manifold aspects: the Rome of Constantine and Sylvester; the Rome of the martyrs; the Rome of Saint Peter, fountainhead of papal and Frankish power; the Rome of the church where he rested. Expressing a political creed, they patently go back to past prototypes. Inevitably, elements of classical pagan antiquity, whether decorative and thus neutral or prone to Christian reinterpretation, were fused into the compound. That the Carolingian Renascence, of which this Roman revival forms a part, was rooted and fo-

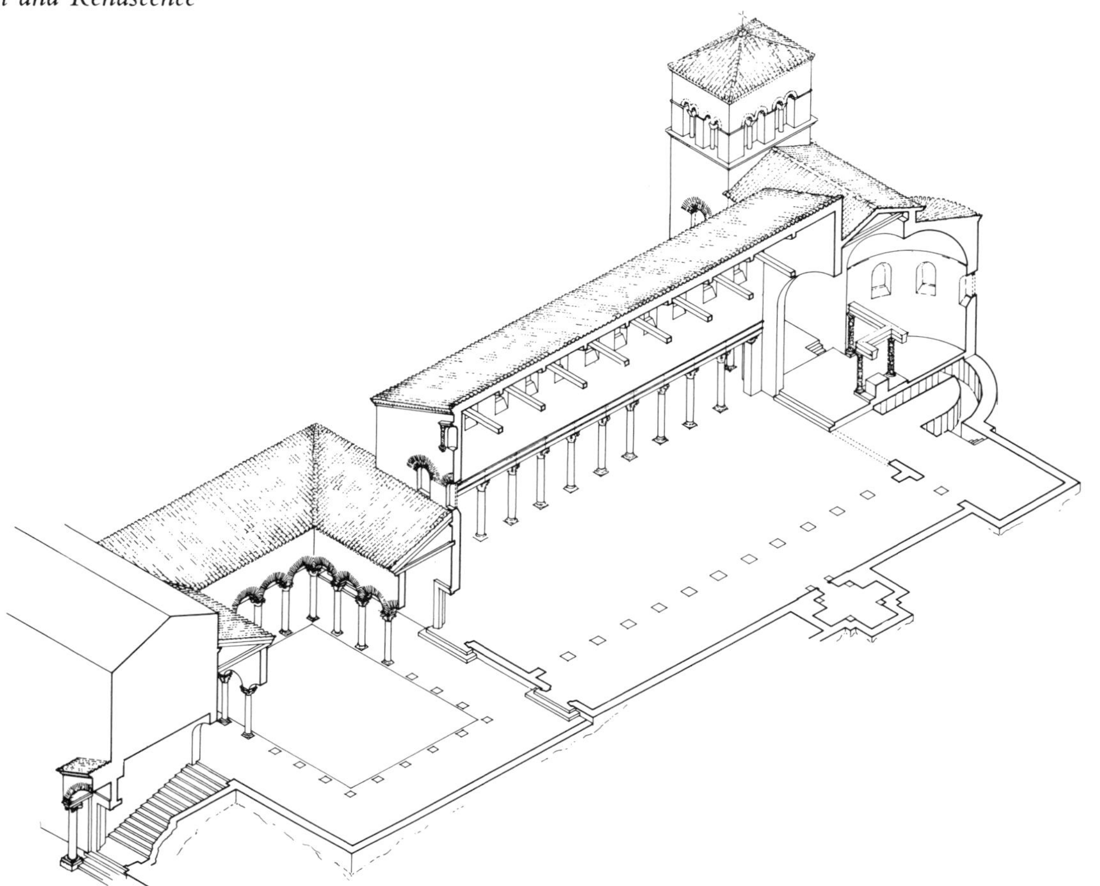

94. S. Prassede, isometric reconstruction Spencer Corbett

cused north of the Alps, places Rome in a new context: for the first time in all her history, she wants to be seen in a European, and no longer in a Mediterranean, perspective; even so, within the overall picture of the Carolingian Renascence, Rome carries a note of her own.

The Roman church type of Carolingian times is best represented by S. Prassede, as laid out and decorated by Paschal I (fig. 94). Replacing an old community center, it was built to shelter "many remains of saints lying in ruined cemeteries," collected by Paschal "so as to save them from neglect," and solemnly transferred into the city church. A long list survives in the church, giving their names, and the inscription below the apse mosaic, too, stresses the martyrs' theme. The plan of the structure clearly harks back, though on a vastly reduced scale and somewhat simplified, to Constantine's St. Peter's: a flight of steps ascending the atrium, once enveloped by four arcaded porticoes; a plain façade; the nave carried by trabeated colonnades (it was redecorated in the sixteenth century, when its ten small windows were blocked and replaced by four large ones, whereas the diaphragm arches across the nave and their supporting piers were inserted in the High Middle Ages); a narrow transept communicating with the nave through a triumphal arch; a single apse; underneath, an annular crypt like that which around 590 had been inserted into St. Peter's; the aisles, single rather than double, are linked to the transept by colonnaded and trabeated twin openings, recalling the corresponding triple openings in the Vatican Basilica (figs. 95, 96). The reduction in scale is as obvious as the resemblances: two instead of four aisles; eleven instead of twenty-two columns on either side of the nave; one instead of two columns screening the transept off the aisles. At the same time, the transept equals the

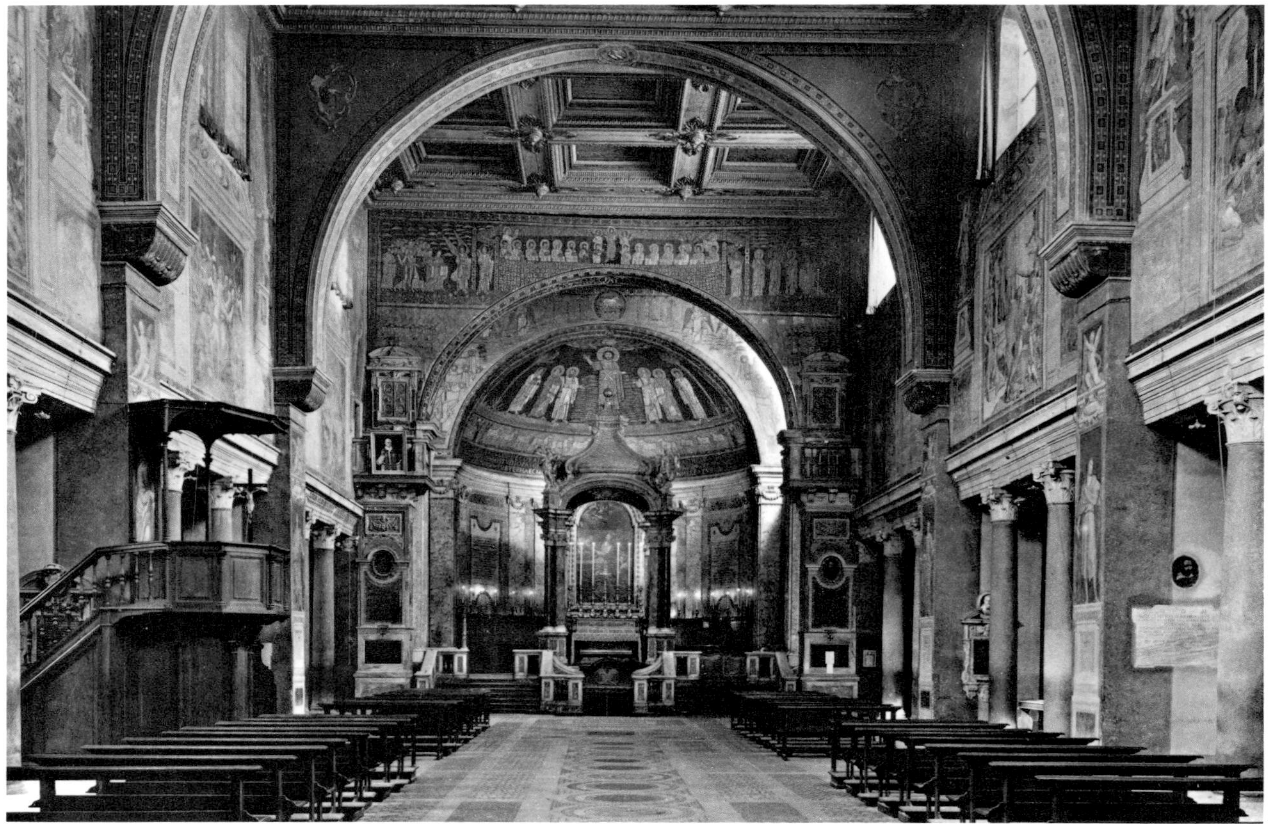

95. S. Prassede, interior

nave in height, unlike the original low transept of St. Peter's; moreover, it lacks the projecting exedrae. Other putatively Constantinian models, such as S. Paolo fuori le mura, were presumably on the mind of Paschal's architect. The technique of construction, too, revives fourth- and fifth-century custom: bricks are laid in more or less regular courses, though sloping, rather than with the poor workmanship seen in eighth-century Rome; the small original windows, now blocked, are surmounted by double relieving arches, recalling the doubled arches customary for far wider spans in ancient and in fourth-century structures, such as the triumphal arch of S. Paolo fuori le mura (fig. 97). Foundations are solidly laid—built, to be sure, not of heavy-faced concrete as four and five hundred years before, but of large tufa blocks quarried from the "Servian" city walls: at S. Silvestro in Capite, S. Prassede, the Quattro Coronati, along the flank of S. Martino ai Monti. Columns and architraves, although spoils, are selected and displayed with regard to size and material almost as carefully as in Early Christian times.

The decoration as clearly as the plan of S. Prassede reflects the character of early ninth century Rome. The wall of the apse is sheathed in marble—restored some fifty years ago—and the vault still carries the original mosaic, the whole reminiscent of Leo's Triclinia in the Lateran Palace. The reappearance of mosaic in Rome shortly before 800 was presumably stimulated by the wish to compete with imperial secular and church building in Byzantium. More decisively, though, it links up with Carolingian Rome's revival of Roman late antique Christian monumental art: Old St. Peter's, the Lateran Basilica, S. Paolo fuori le mura are the models that church planners, architects, and mosaic workers kept foremost in mind. The material employed by the Carolingian mosaicists, almost exclusively glass tesserae rather than the cus-

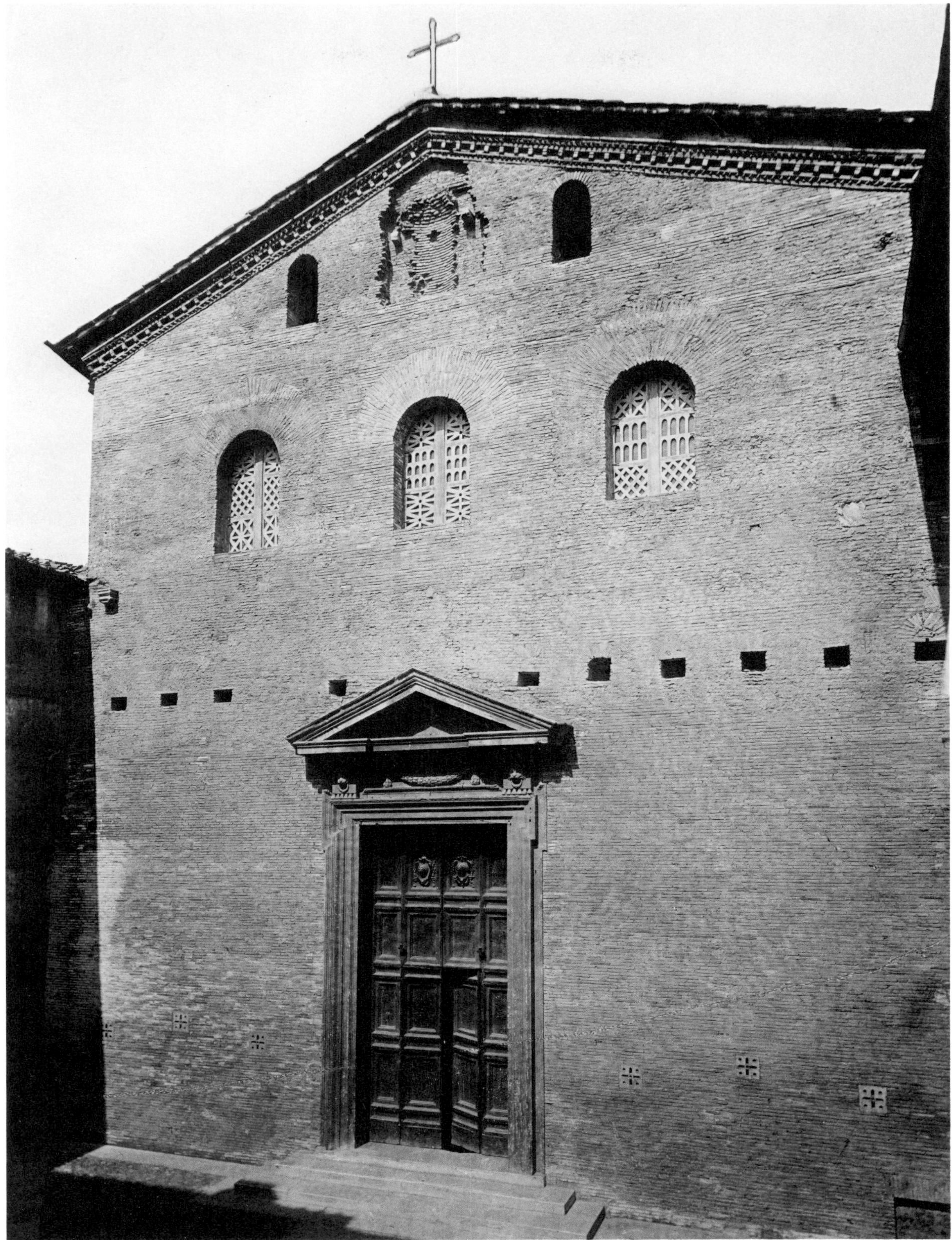

96. S. Prassede, façade

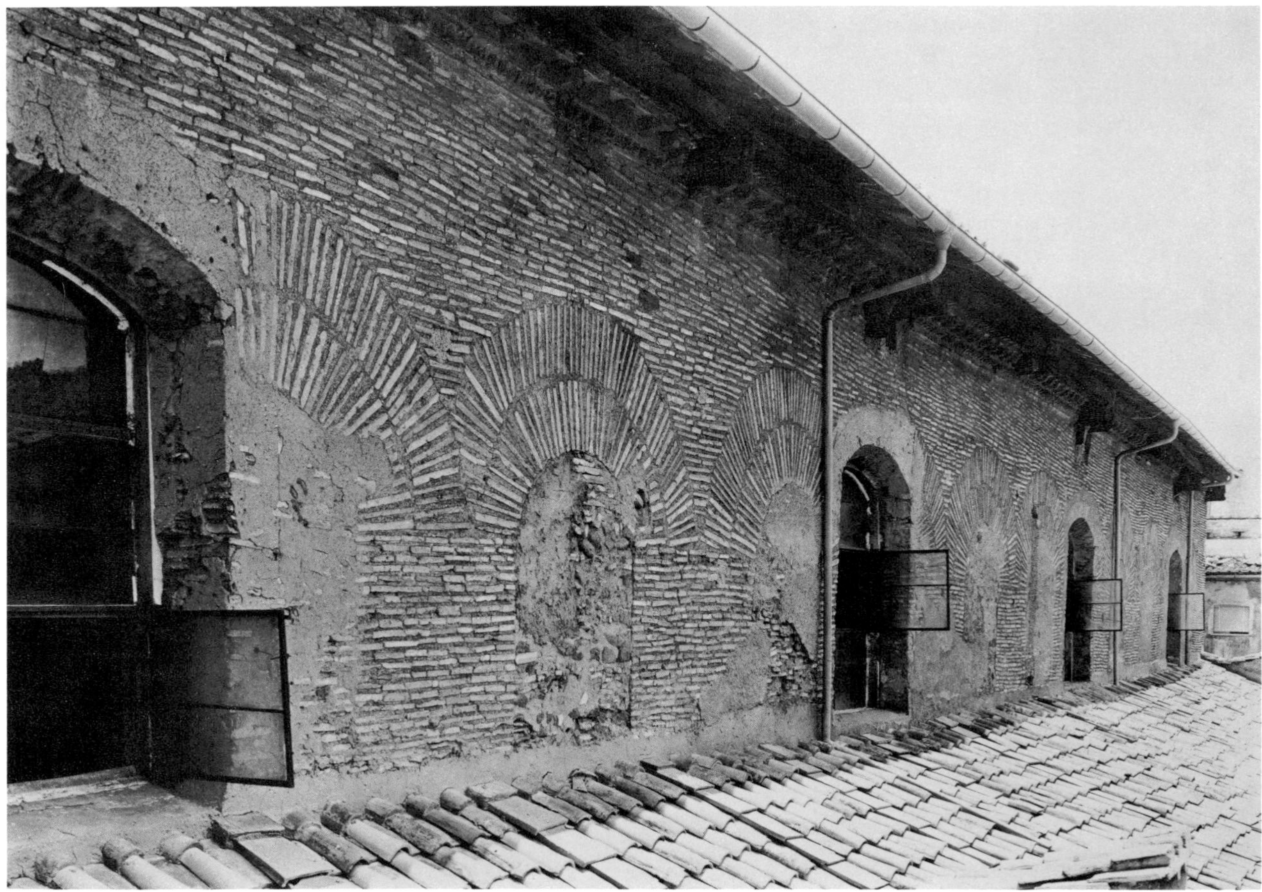

97. S. Prassede, clerestory wall

tomary marble and glass of Byzantium, was that used by their ancestors three and four centuries before; the glass cubes themselves, in fact, seem to have been taken from decayed ancient mosaics. Likewise, the iconographic schemes are drawn from the distant Christian past. At S. Prassede, Christ at his Second Coming floats in a deep blue heaven, enlivened by red, pink, white, and bluish gray clouds; placed on the green carpet of this earth, set with long-stemmed red flowers in twos and threes, Peter and Paul introduce the titular saint, Praxedis, her legendary sister Pudentiana, her brother and the founder-pope, the latter marked by the blue square halo assigned to the living; at the outer ends of the composition are palm trees, a phoenix nestling in one. The same scheme appears at S. Cecilia (fig. 98); it goes back to the Early Christian apse scheme reflected in the sixth-century mosaic of SS. Cosma e Damiano on the Forum—Christ, saints, founder, palm trees, phoenix, and all. The frieze of lambs underneath on gold ground goes back to the same model; so do the dedicatory verses below the lamb frieze, both in wording and lettering. Written in a beautiful antique script, gold on deep blue ground, they recall along with that at SS. Cosma e Damiano the fifth-century inscriptions both on the triumphal arch at S. Maria Maggiore and on the entrance wall of S. Sabina. No earlier dedicatory verses in mosaic survive in Rome; but those of the fourth century cannot have been very different. On the wall framing the apse arch at S. Prassede, the Lamb of Revelation is depicted, flanked by four angels and the symbols of the Evangelists, and adored by the Four-and-twenty Elders on gold ground. It is the composition that decorated the triumphal arch at S. Paolo fuori le mura, but in the same location in which it survives at SS. Cosma e

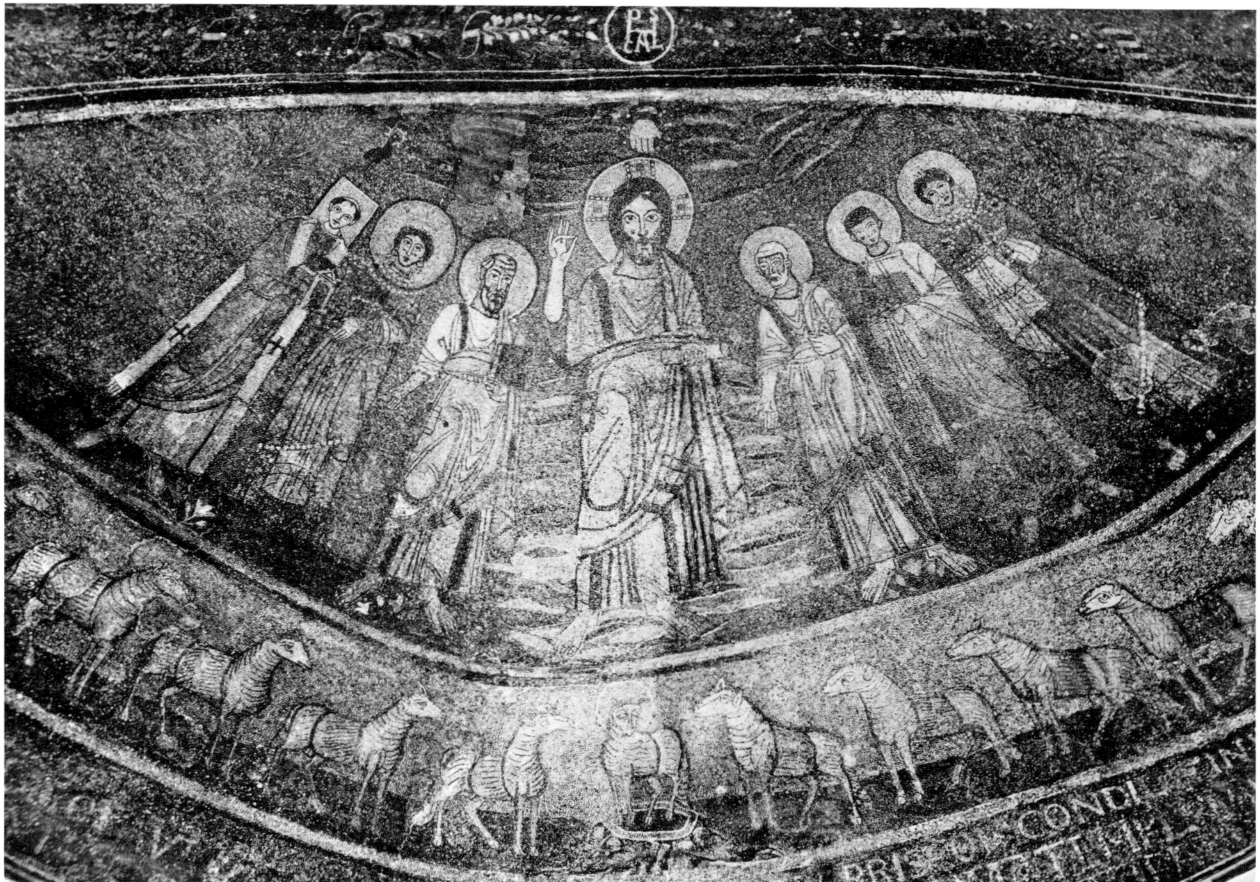

98. S. Cecilia, apse mosaic

Damiano. Throughout, then, the artists of Paschal I tended to substitute schemes drawn from Early Christian models in Rome or their sixth-century derivatives for those adhering to Eastern tradition so frequent in the preceding hundred and fifty years. Already the apse mosaic in the Triclinium of Leo III may well have gone back to an Early Christian Roman composition rather than to a Byzantine model as has also been suggested; and in any event that mosaic already reverts to the customary Roman technique of using predominantly glass tesserae. That technique, indeed, remains the hallmark of ninth-century mosaics in Rome: like that at SS. Nereo ed Achilleo from the last year of Leo III, 815/6; at S. Prassede and in the Chapel of S. Zeno, at S. Cecilia, and at S. Maria in Domnica under Paschal I, presumably in that sequence between 817 and 820 (fig. 99); at S. Marco under Gregory IV, roughly 829-830. Likewise, Early Christian compositions are taken up time and again: the Four-and-twenty Elders adoring the Lamb; the Apostles approaching Christ in a mandorla above the apse arch of S. Maria in Domnica—the scene appearing in the fifth century on the apse vaults of S. Agata dei Goti and S. Andrea in Catabarbara; finally in ninth-century apse vaults, as at S. Prassede, Christ floating or standing against the deep blue ground of Heaven, marked by colorful clouds and on either side of Him the Princes of the Apostles, the titular saints of the church, and, without fail, the papal donor. The scheme of composition, in fact, is among the first to be revived in Carolingian Rome. At the very end of the eighth century it appeared in the apse mosaic of S. Susanna—with two donors depicted, Leo III and Charlemagne; lost since the late sixteenth century, the donor figures are known from old descriptions and drawings.

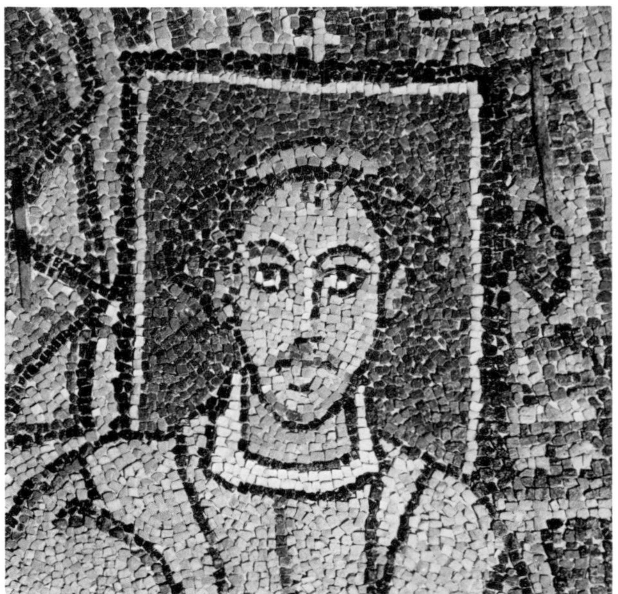

99. S. Maria in Domnica, apse mosaic, detail, portrait of Paschal I

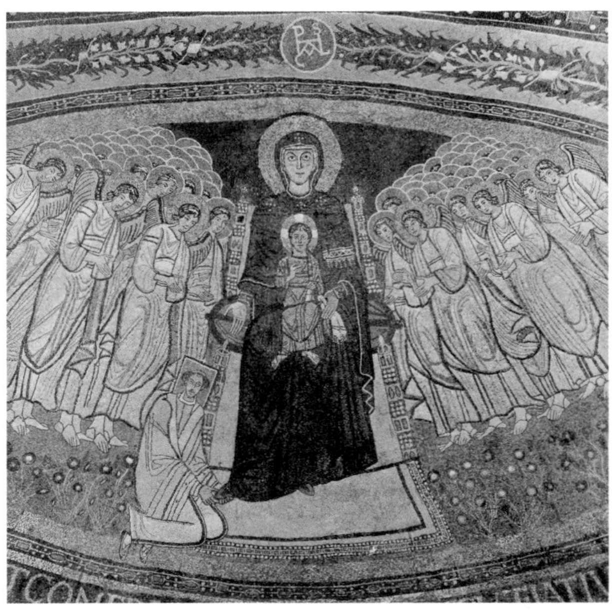

100. S. Maria in Domnica, apse mosaic, detail

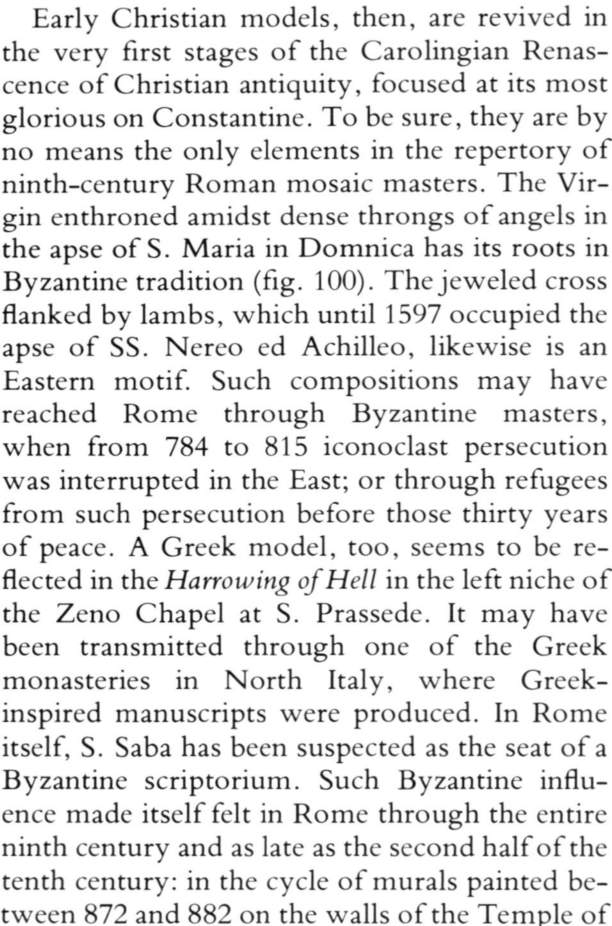

Early Christian models, then, are revived in the very first stages of the Carolingian Renascence of Christian antiquity, focused at its most glorious on Constantine. To be sure, they are by no means the only elements in the repertory of ninth-century Roman mosaic masters. The Virgin enthroned amidst dense throngs of angels in the apse of S. Maria in Domnica has its roots in Byzantine tradition (fig. 100). The jeweled cross flanked by lambs, which until 1597 occupied the apse of SS. Nereo ed Achilleo, likewise is an Eastern motif. Such compositions may have reached Rome through Byzantine masters, when from 784 to 815 iconoclast persecution was interrupted in the East; or through refugees from such persecution before those thirty years of peace. A Greek model, too, seems to be reflected in the *Harrowing of Hell* in the left niche of the Zeno Chapel at S. Prassede. It may have been transmitted through one of the Greek monasteries in North Italy, where Greek-inspired manuscripts were produced. In Rome itself, S. Saba has been suspected as the seat of a Byzantine scriptorium. Such Byzantine influence made itself felt in Rome through the entire ninth century and as late as the second half of the tenth century: in the cycle of murals painted between 872 and 882 on the walls of the Temple of Fortuna Virilis, reconsecrated to S. Maria Egiziaca; in a mural, again of the *Harrowing of Hell*, in the lower church of S. Clemente; and, dating from about 965, in the *Ascension of Christ* painted in the Tempio della Tosse in Tivoli, an ancient mausoleum turned into a church. The most outstanding example of Byzantine influence on Rome within the Carolingian Renascence, though, remains the program of the mosaic decoration in the Zeno Chapel, built between 817 and 824 by Pope Paschal I. The hierarchy of the overall scheme corresponds to that of Byzantine theology as reflected in Eastern churches; Christ supported by angels in the vault; in subordinate places, the Virgin and the Princes of the Apostles, saints and martyrs.

All this, though, needs to be seen within the framework of a rebirth of the Roman Christian heritage, as it had developed from the fifth and sixth through the eighth centuries. Indeed, it has been pointed out that the figures and faces, the draperies, gestures, and movements depicted by the ninth-century mosaic workers are firmly rooted in the traditions of the workshops that fifty years before had transposed a Byzantine heritage in the murals of the apse, aisles, and atrium of S. Maria Antiqua into the artisans' local dialect. Figures lack bodily volume; they stand

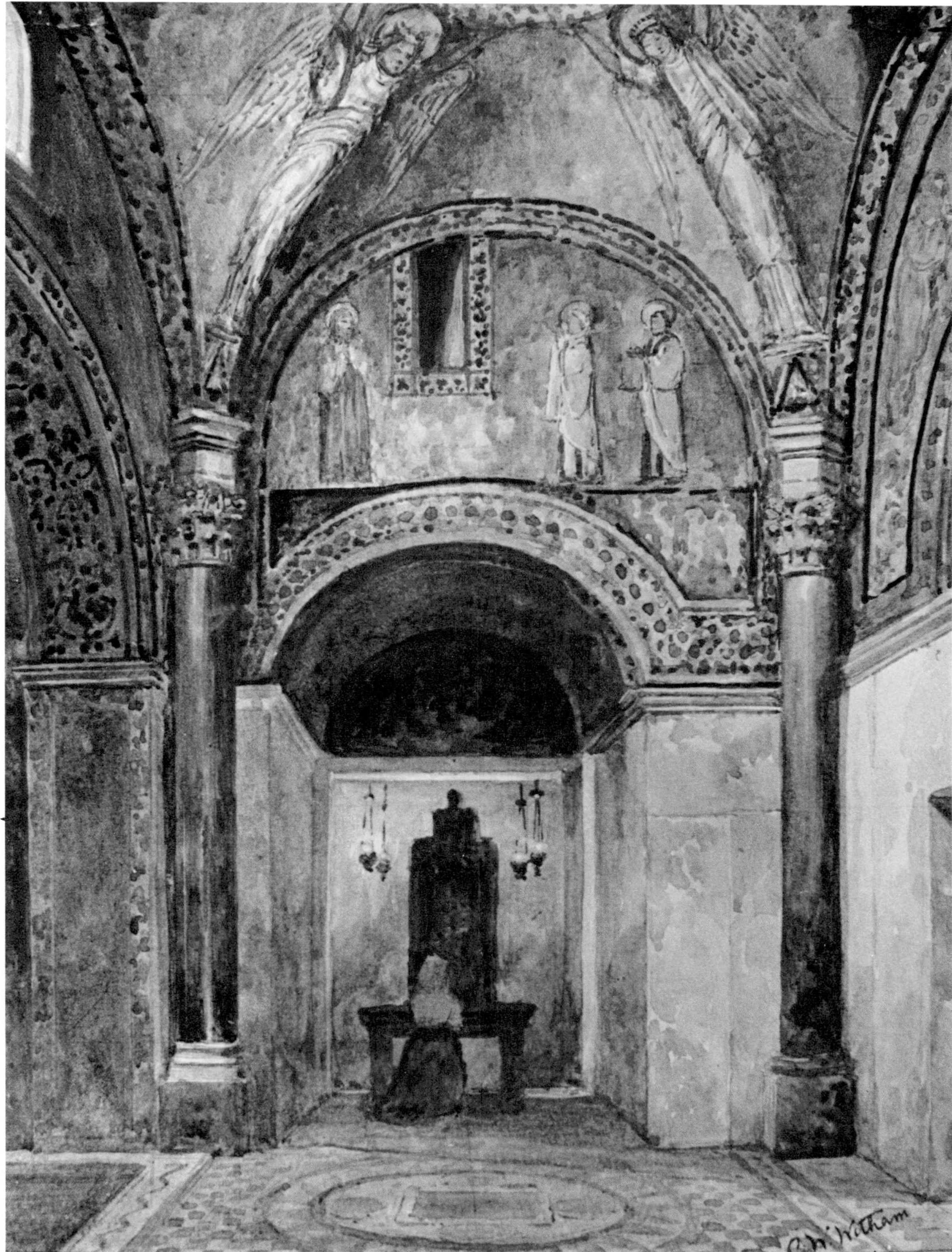

101. S. Prassede, Zeno Chapel, interior, watercolor, anonymous, private collection

stiffly, repeating the same pose over and over in a nonspace. Crowds are suggested, as witness the apse of S. Maria in Domnica, by heaping three or four rows of head tops or just halos atop the front row of figures. Draperies are marked by a framework of lines, faintly suggesting the articulation of limbs. Faces are oval or triangular, outlined by darker contours. All this has its prototypes in late eighth century work in Rome.

However, if the wording is similar, the pronunciation is utterly different. Nothing proves this better than the mosaics in the Chapel of S. Zeno. Attached to the right aisle of S. Prassede, and richly encrusted with marble revetment and mosaics, the chapel is associated with the memory of the pope's mother, Theodora Episcopa, and provided with relics of martyrs. In plan it is modeled after early mausolea, pagan and Christian, which still dotted the fields outside the city; cross-shaped, the groinvault supported on corner columns (fig. 101). One such mausoleum comes to mind; reputedly that of the martyr Tiburtius, it rises close to the basilical covered cemetery of SS. Marcellino e Pietro that was built by Constantine and linked to his and Helena's memory. Likewise, the decoration of the Zeno Chapel time and again draws on early models. The mosaic of the groinvault, four angels supporting the bust of Christ in a roundel (fig. 102) has its earliest known prototype in the mosaic placed by Pope Hilarus in the 460s on the vault of the now lost chapel of S. Croce near the Lateran Baptistery, where four caryatids—not angels!—carried the cross in a laurel wreath, evidently a fifth-century insertion into a pagan mosaic. The same scheme, albeit with variations

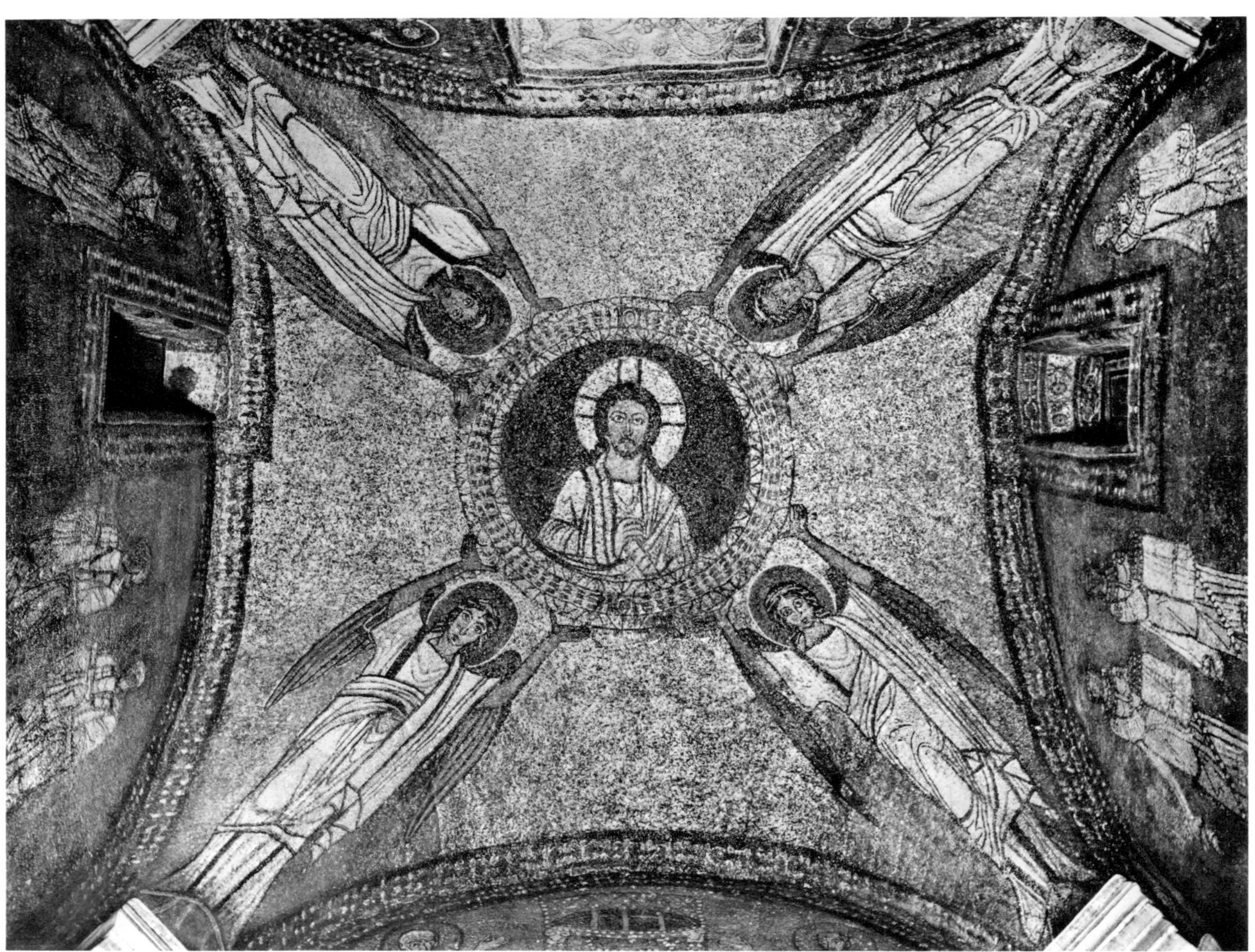

102. S. Prassede, Zeno Chapel, vault mosaic

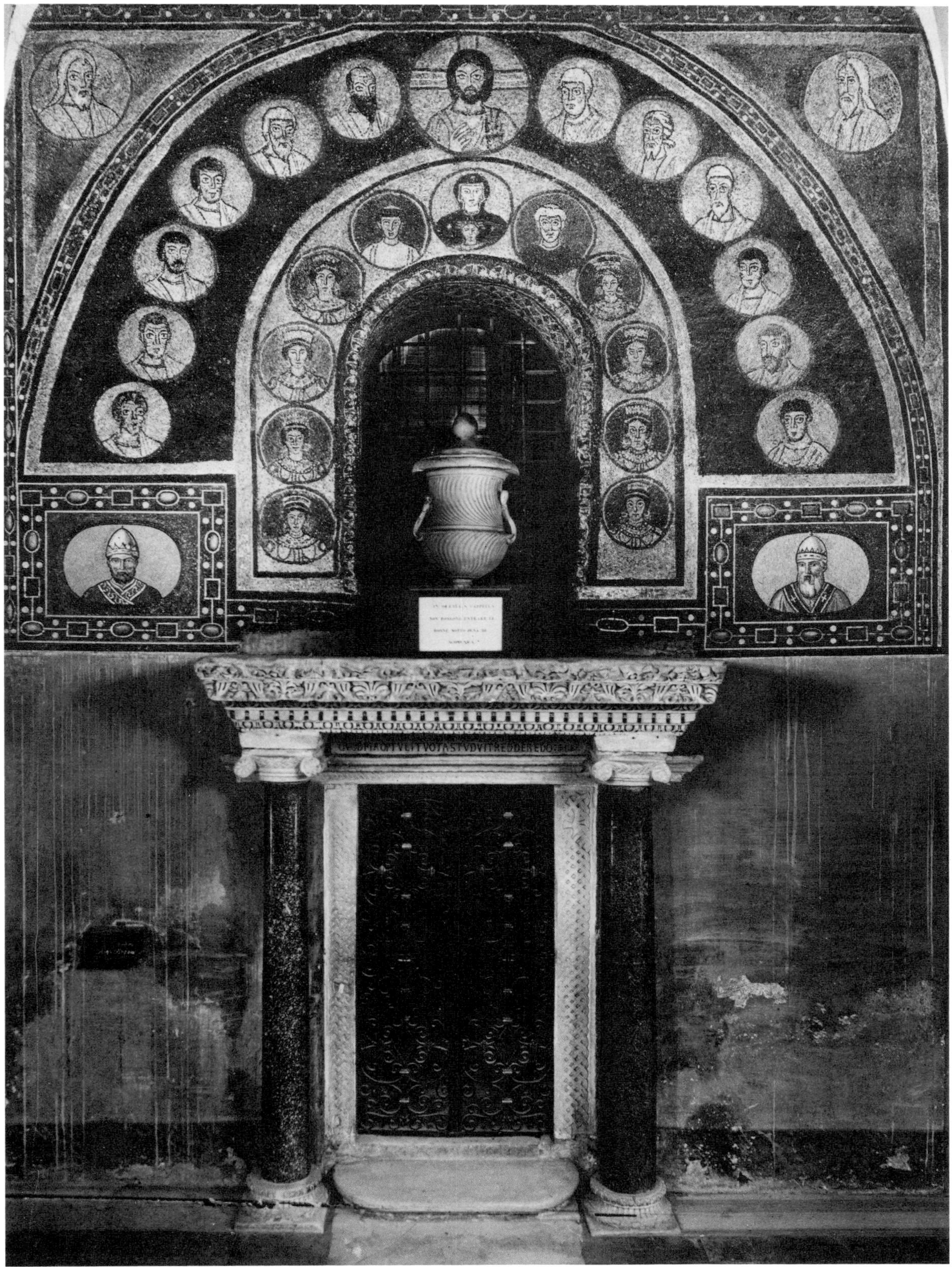

103. S. Prassede, Zeno Chapel, outer façade

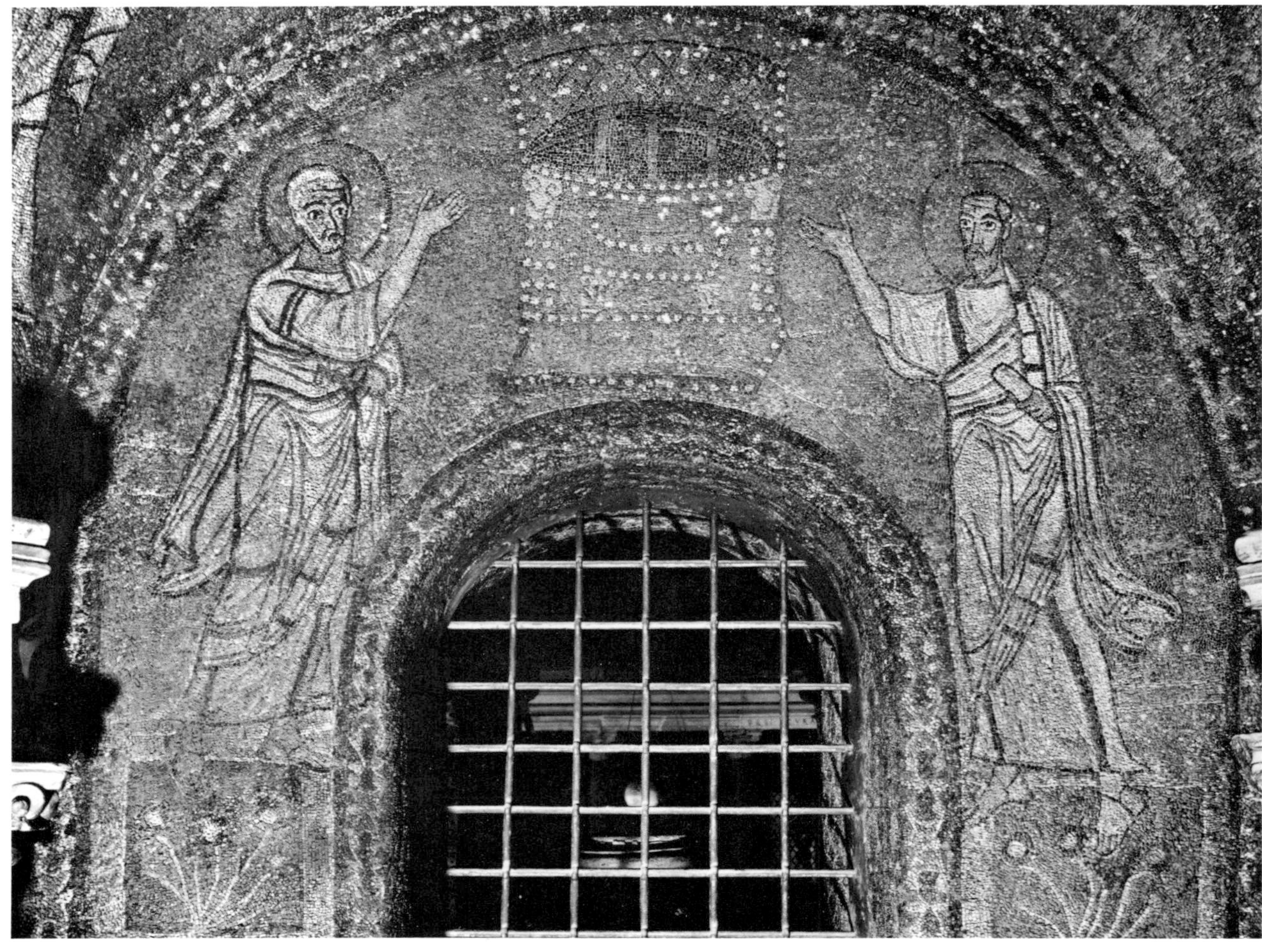

104. S. Prassede, Zeno Chapel, Saints Peter and Paul

in the central roundel, survives in the sixth century in Ravenna, both in S. Vitale and in the chapel of the archbishop's palace. But models earlier than the one at S. Croce in Rome may have disappeared without trace. The mosaics on the walls of the Zeno Chapel, too, draw on Early Christian motifs. On the outer façade above the portal, two concentric half circles of clipei with the busts of Christ, the Apostles, and martyrs frame a window (fig. 103) and recall those running along the fifth-century apse arch of S. Sabina and preserved until the eighteenth century. On the inner façade wall of the Zeno Chapel, Saints Peter and Paul point to a jeweled, empty throne surmounted by a cross (fig. 104): the same representation—the *etimasia*—on the fifth-century triumphal arch at S. Maria Maggiore (and possibly in the Lateran apse) come to mind. The soffit of the arch above the altar is decorated with an acanthus scroll *all'antica* with animals and birds, a "peopled scroll," recalling the fifth-century mosaics in the narthex of the Lateran Baptistery. All the figures—in the vault, on the side walls, and in the niches of the chapel, angels (fig. 105), saints, martyrs, and Theodora Episcopa, with her square halo—are cast in traditional poses and are marked by the linear framework of faces and draperies customary in Rome by then. But the coloring sets apart from that tradition these and indeed all the mosaics produced by the workshops of Leo III and Paschal. Rather than black, the lines marking the draperies are light and dark blue, green, and red. The beard and hair of Saint Peter are white and blue. Garments of female martyrs are done in the richest colors, with dark and light blue, yel-

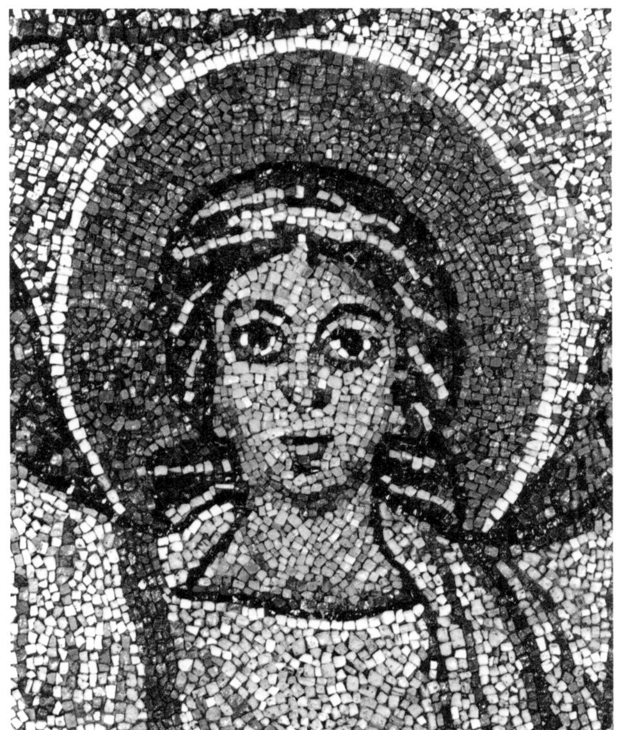

105. S. Prassede, Zeno Chapel, head of angel

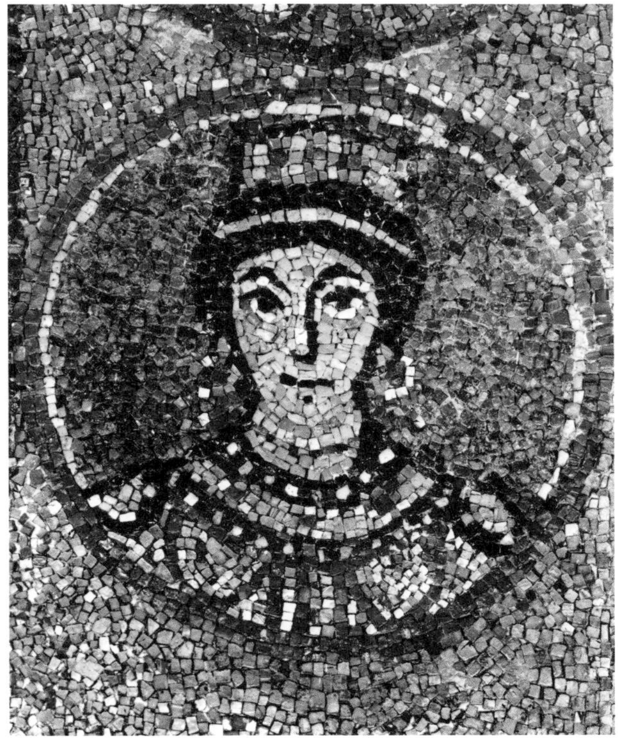

106. S. Prassede, Zeno Chapel, façade, head of female saint

low, green, white, red, and gold tesserae set closely; broad, jeweled gold collars mark the neckline (fig. 106). Bits of brick-red sketch a mouth or the height of a cheek. The outline of a face, a nose, a chin, is given in rusty brown or deep red. Halos of angels at S. Maria in Domnica alternate between gold and blue; Christ's golden halo carries a cross, its arms blue or green and outlined like the halo itself in red. And all is done in the shining glass tesserae that reflect the light of the candles and make the entire chapel resplendent with an amazing radiance. The color, the light, their impressionistic rendering, and the exclusive use of glass tesserae more than anything else link the mosaics of the Zeno Chapel and of all the related work to those of Christian antiquity in Rome; the handling of faces in the chapel, on the triumphal arch of S. Prassede, in the apse mosaics of S. Cecilia and S. Maria in Domnica, and already on the apse arch of SS. Nereo ed Achilleo, recalls nothing so much as the faces on the triumphal arch of S. Maria Maggiore. It is, indeed, a revival of Christian antiquity.

Under Paschal I, however, the renascence movement in Rome can no longer be understood along general lines alone. It takes on very personal features. His interest in the construction and decoration of the churches erected under his pontificate must have been extraordinary. In only seven years four large churches were built and provided with sumptuous mosaics: S. Prassede, S. Maria in Domnica, S. Cecilia, the Quattro Coronati. Wherever possible, his portrait appears, an elegant longish face; only once, in the apse mosaic of S. Prassede, does he appear to have grown a bit stout. Hazardous though it is, one cannot resist the temptation to read these features as those of a somewhat vain but highly sophisticated gentleman. It is hardly by chance that the artists he employed achieved a peak in shaping an equally sophisticated illusionistic style. Nor is it by chance that the figures in the mosaics done at Paschal's time are so superbly elegant and refined—overrefined, one is tempted to say. The female saints in particular, swaying and slender, with pert little faces, sumptuously decked out, seem teenagers of seductive charm—"Paschal's Lolitas," as the best connoisseur of these mosaics calls them off the record (fig. 107).

Inevitably, interwoven with the rebirth of Rome's Christian past were reminiscences of classical antiquity, genuine or putative. The plan of the Zeno Chapel obviously is that of a late-antique mausoleum, and cross-shaped chapels derived from such models time and again were attached to their churches in Rome by Carolingian architects. Two were joined to the ninth-century basilica of the Quattro Coronati and one survives in fairly good condition; even the impost blocks remain in place, splendidly worked Roman spoils (fig. 108). Antique elements naturally prevail in the neutral sphere of sculptural decoration. In S. Prassede six columns of extraordinary beauty and unusual design remain in the chancel; their fluted shafts are girded by four rings of acanthus and surmounted by densely bunched laurel leaves, held together by a knotted string (fig. 109). Roman spoils, they may well have been reused to form a colonnaded screen above and near the high altar, a *fastigium* much like that at St. Peter's. In the Zeno Chapel, too, capitals, column shafts, and the surmounting brackets are spoils; of the column socles, three of ninth-century date imitate clumsily but unmistakably the vine tendrils of a fourth, a late-antique, fifth-century spoil (figs. 110, 111). The portal, framed by a pair of porphyry columns and a surmounting first-century architrave, draws on a Roman prototype—one thinks of the colonnaded portal of the fourth-century rotunda serving as a vestibule to SS. Cosma e Damiano; on the sides, where the architrave was cut, a ninth-century sculptor copied the original design; and the ninth-century capitals surmounting the columns, though decorated with interlace, are Ionic, a type last used in Rome in the fifth century (fig. 112).

Full-scale "copies" after St. Peter's such as S. Prassede, reduced in size and, like all medieval copies, selective in the number and placing of their constituent elements, remain rare in ninth-century Rome. The only other one surviving, though badly mauled, is Sto. Stefano degli Abissini behind the apse of St. Peter's, built some thirty years after S. Prassede. But Constantinian, or in general Early Christian, basilicas with two aisles flanking the nave, remain the constant model for ninth-century church building in Rome. Their construction constitutes part of a vast program promoted by a succession of popes through the better part of the century. It is linked to the continued transfer of relics from the catacombs to the safety of the city walls; to replacing community centers or old-fashioned sanctuaries; and aimed at restoring the past glories of Roman Christianity and, implicitly, her imperial defenders. At the Quattro Coronati an atrium opens, protected by a huge tower; the nave, over fifty meters long, rested on trabeated colonnades—scant remnants of the architrave, Roman spoils, are incorporated in the walls of the forecourt of the present, much smaller twelfth-century church; an annular crypt and confessio are sheltered in the apse, as is a list

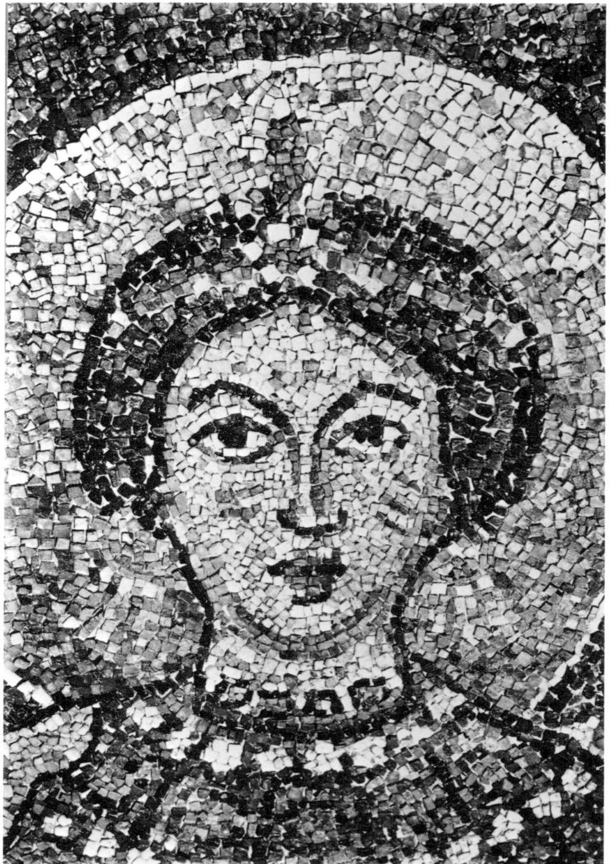

107. S. Prassede, apse mosaic, head of female saint

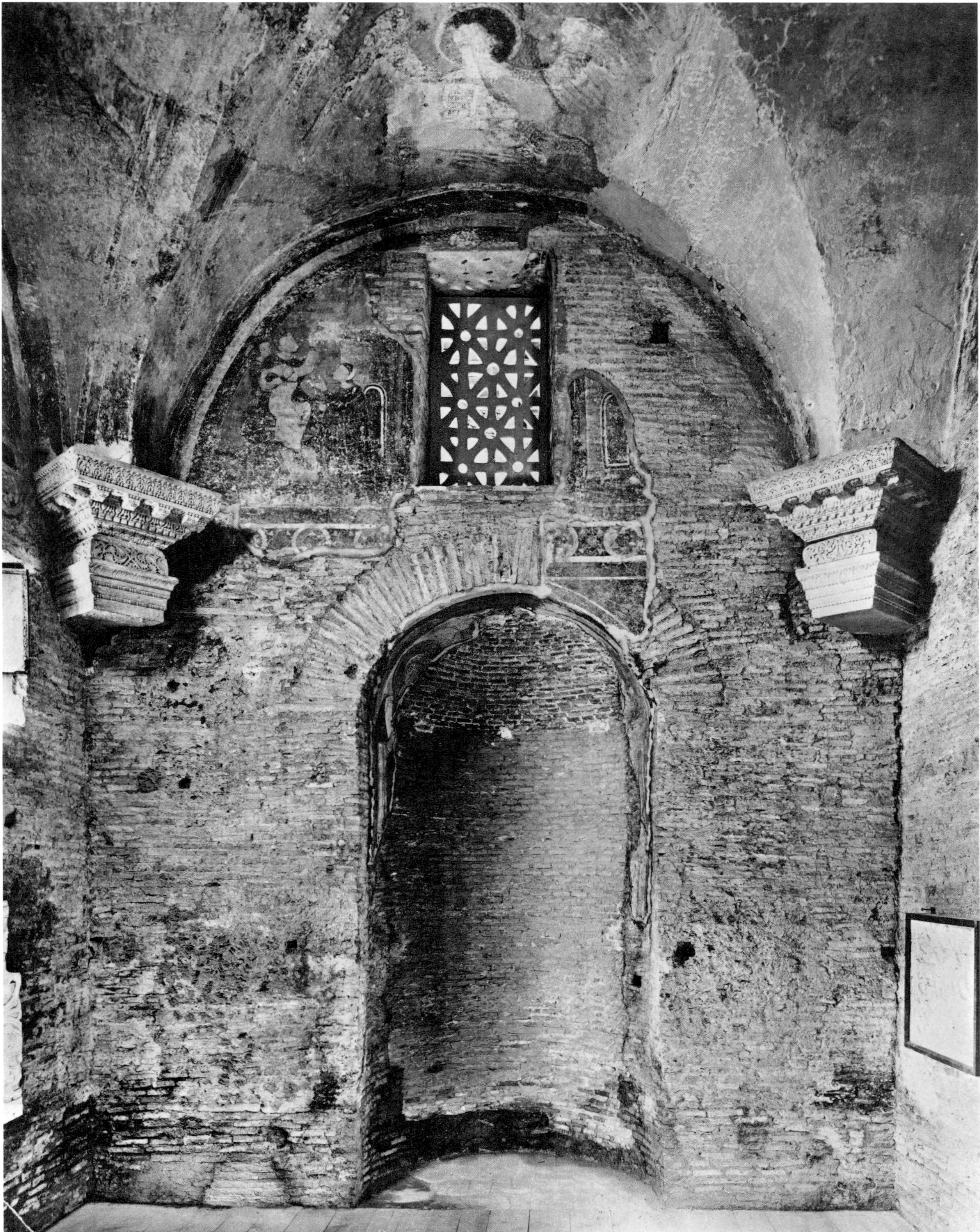

108. SS. Quattro Coronati, ninth-century chapel

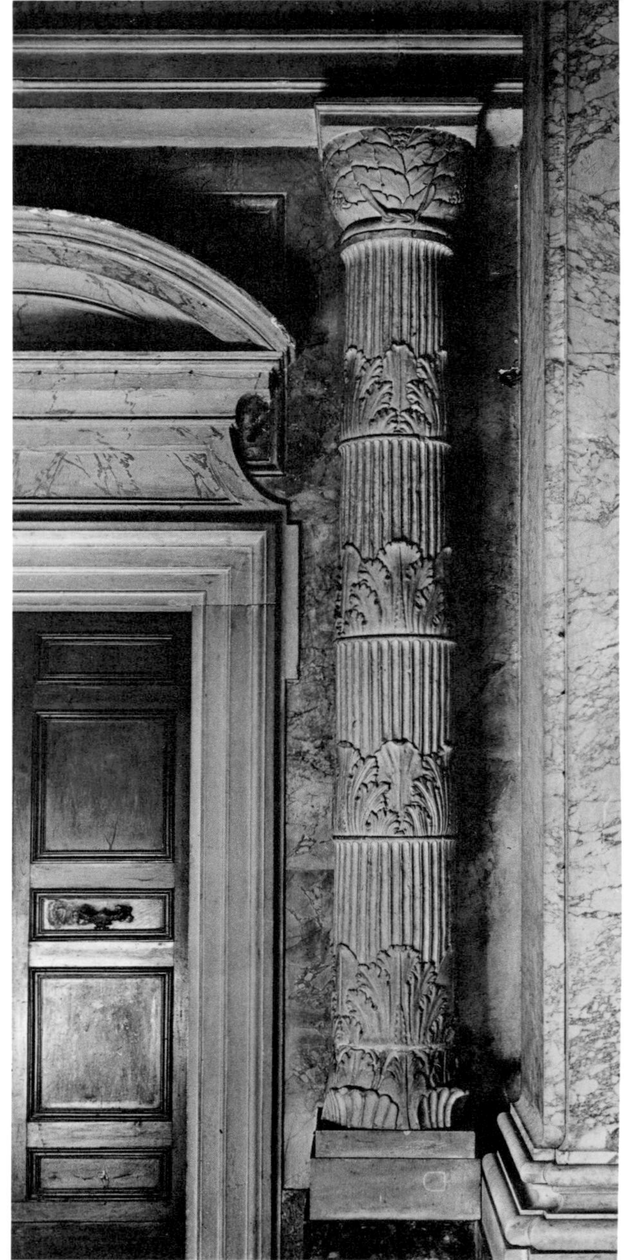

109. S. Prassede, antique column, presumably from fastigium

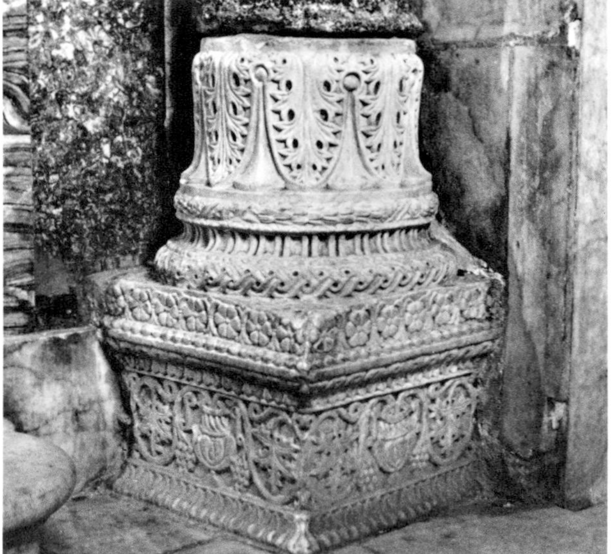

110. S. Prassede, Zeno Chapel, antique socle and reversed capital

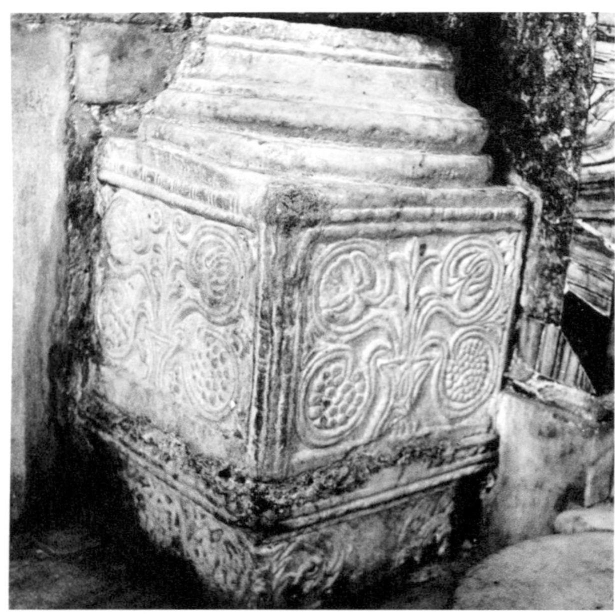

111. S. Prassede, Zeno Chapel, ninth-century imitation

of relics that were gathered from the catacombs by Leo IV (847-855); martyrs' chapels are attached to either aisle, one cross-shaped like the Zeno Chapel at S. Prassede, the other a domed quatrefoil. At nearly the same time, S. Martino ai Monti and S. Maria Nova were built: the former, originally with an atrium, annular crypt, and trabeated nave colonnades, survives, splendidly decorated around 1650, but fundamentally unchanged (fig. 113); the latter, now S. Francesca Romana, harder to trace below its baroque remodeling, was built at the eastern summit of the Forum to replace nearby S. Maria Antiqua, buried under a landslide in 847, and to

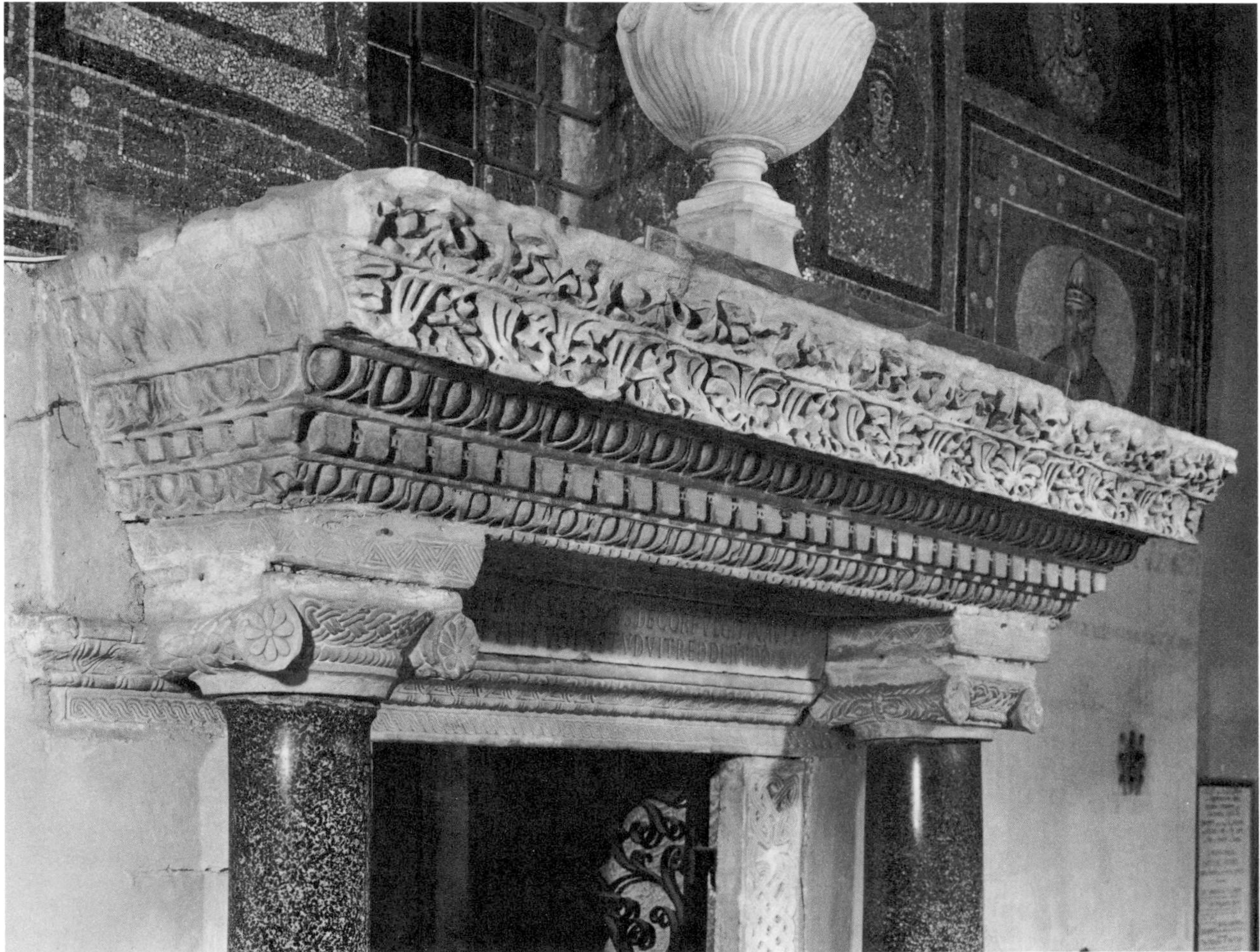

112. S. Prassede, Zeno Chapel, portal, showing Roman fragment with ninth-century reworking at side and ninth-century capitals

shelter its icon. The entire group of churches, characterized by trabeated colonnades, harks back either to S. Maria Maggiore or more likely to the Lateran Basilica, the latter reduced to a two-aisle scheme and deprived of "aisle transepts," devoid of function by then anyhow. But just as frequently the colonnades are arcaded rather than trabeated: examples are at S. Cecilia, S. Maria in Domnica, S. Giorgio in Velabro or S. Marco—this last a superb example of a ninth-century basilica, remodeled in the fifteenth and eighteenth centuries and at that time clad in a profusion of the richest materials and colors. In resorting to arcades the ninth-century builders may have thought of late-fourth- and early-fifth-century basilicas, such as S. Paolo fuori le mura and S. Sabina; or they may have used arcades simply because spoils of architraves were not easily available in the right sizes. Whether trabeated or arcaded and with or without a transept, all ninth-century churches in Rome adopt one post-Constantinian element with the Constantinian: the annular crypt and confessio, inserted in St. Peter's by the end of the sixth century. Naturally so: to provide both shelter for and easy access to the martyrs' relics was at any rate a major raison d'être of church building and planning in the Rome of Carolingian times; and ninth-century church planners in Rome and elsewhere evidently considered the annular crypt at St. Peter's an integral part of Constantine's basilica at the Vatican.

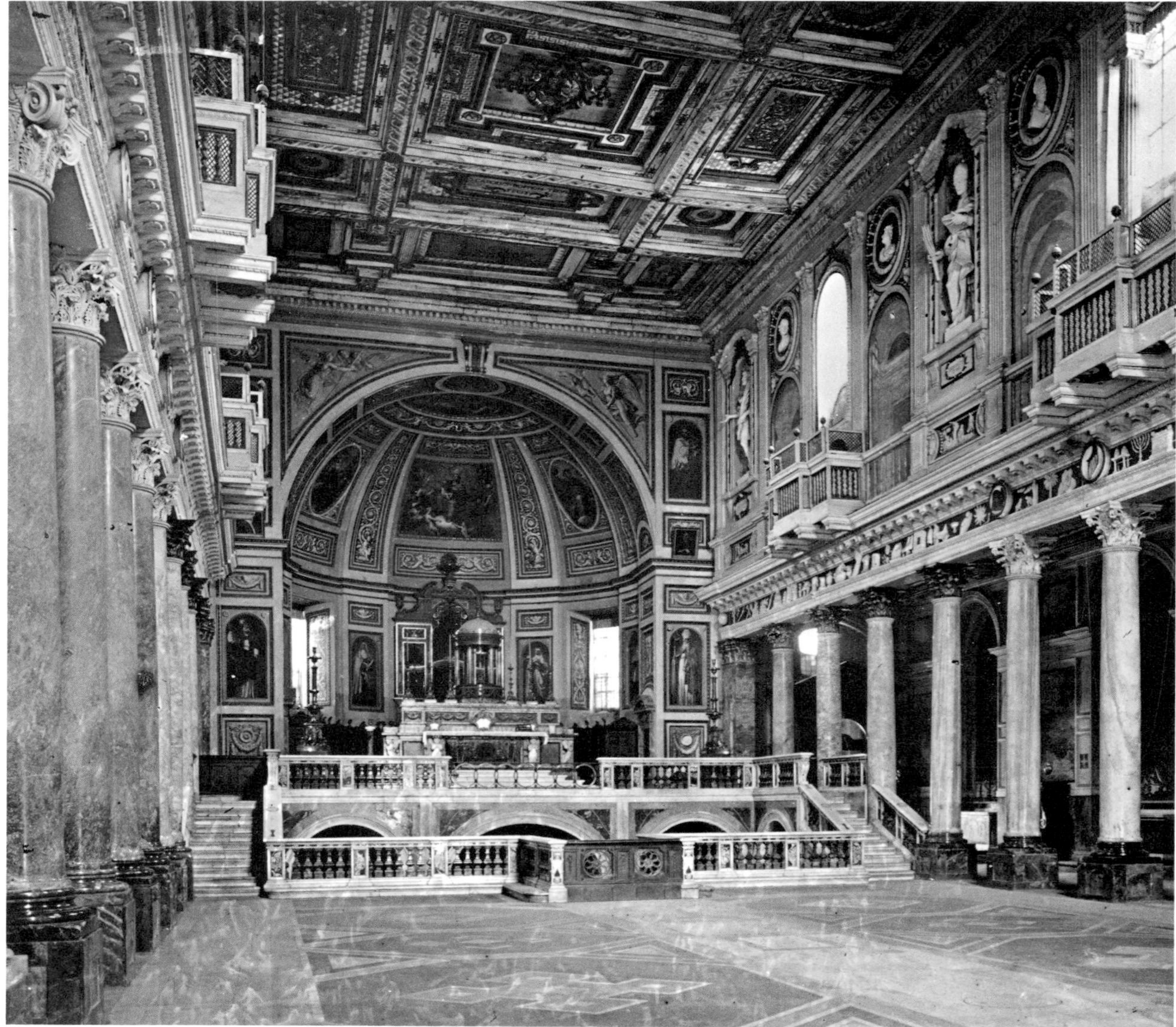

113. S. Martino ai Monti, interior, as remodeled ca. 1650

None of the churches newly built in the ninth century or indeed in the last third of the eighth century were located in what by then must have been the core of town—the Ripa from the Theatre of Marcellus to the foot of the Capitoline Hill and west to the Theatre of Pompey, the neighborhood of the Pantheon and the core of Trastevere. Rather, they are situated on the edge of the abitato, the built-up area, like S. Cecilia, S. Marco, or S. Silvestro in Capite. Or else they are located in the disabitato, like S. Prassede, SS. Nereo ed Achilleo, S. Susanna, S. Maria in Domnica, the Quattro Coronati. Replacing as they did old community centers or diaconiae, the congregations formerly served by these centers had long disappeared. But apparently that did not discourage papal founders. Continuing the tradition attached to the site was in itself important. In place of a parish congregation and its clergy, a monastic community would take care of the new church and its property, as at S. Prassede, S. Cecilia, S. Silvestro in Capite. At the same time, the new monasteries guaranteed ecclesiastical rather than secular control of large tracts of the disabitato. Consequently the new churches built between 760 and 860, though economically dominating the wasteland, were unconnected with and had no impact on the physical map of the town proper.

As we have seen, the revival of Early Christian church plans and decorations may well have begun in Rome prior to Leo III and indeed to Hadrian. S. Silvestro in Capite, founded shortly after the middle of the eighth century, could be an early example. Details remain doubtful. But the church was a basilica, large, colonnaded, and probably trabeated, in striking contrast to Roman church building from the sixth century onwards; there may have been an annular crypt; and the foundation walls, of huge blocks as in all churches of the Carolingian group, are among the first testimonies to the new solid technique of construction made possible by the quarrying of the "Servian" Wall. More than thirty years later at S. Anastasia, early in the reign of Leo III, aisles and nave—was it trabeated?—were added to a fourth-century transept left over from an older structure; by accretion, the new basilica thus took up the plan of Constantine's St. Peter's. The Roman house buried underneath—perhaps a community center—precluded the construction of an annular crypt; but the clerestory shows the brickwork and the small double-arched windows that mark the later buildings of the group. More important, these local beginnings are interwoven with parallel currents in church planning north of the Alps. In the very first years of the ninth century, the abbey church at Fulda in Hesse was replanned *romano more*, following Roman custom: the main apse in the west was preceded by a long, continuous transept, its ends partitioned off, perhaps by colonnades; to the east an atrium; the nave flanked by columns, whether carrying arcades or an architrave; the whole 120 meters long from atrium façade to west apse. Patently, the intention was to imitate and rival St. Peter's. It is equally obvious that no church in Rome follows the model of Constantine's basilica that early and that closely. Fulda, then, at first glance might seem to have sparked the movement that in Rome reached its peak from 817 to 855. Rome's links across the Alps had existed for some time: as early as 752-757 a wooden tower, a Frankish feature gilded and silver-

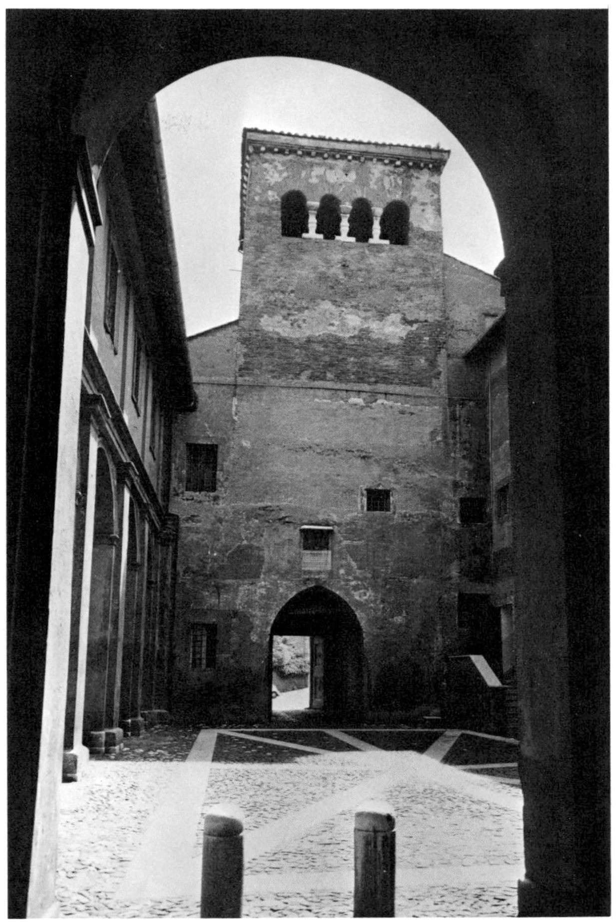

114. SS. Quattro Coronati, gateway tower

plated, rose from the roof of St. Peter's; a northern consultant, Walcharius, was to be employed to supervise the changing of roof beams at St. Peter's; at the Quattro Coronati, as late as ca. 850, the massive tower rising protectively over the entrance gate of the atrium is unique in Rome, but a feature familiar north of the Alps (fig. 114). Its window piers indeed have a purely northern, possibly English, flavor. However, such northern elements in Rome are rare and they are ephemeral. Vice versa, the plan of St. Peter's, pure as it appears at Fulda, takes no real root north of the Alps, except once at Seligenstadt; as a rule, it is fused with elements that never appear in Rome—west towers or westworks, for instance. In brief, the Constantinian church plan is not germane to the northern version of the Carolingian Renascence; whereas in Rome it is its salient feature.

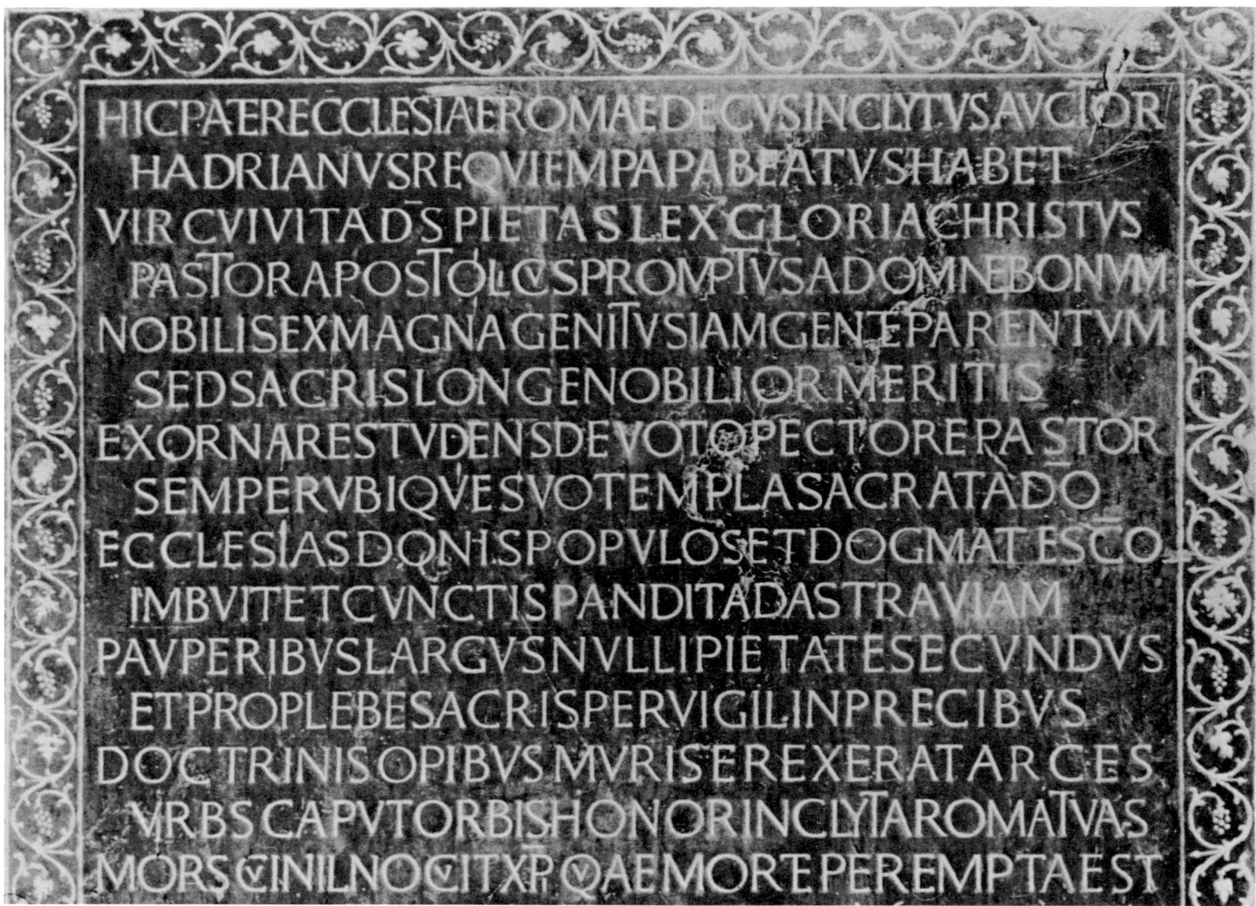

115. Tomb plaque of Hadrian I, detail

On the other hand, taken in a broad sense, the Carolingian Renascence has its roots decidedly north of the Alps, where it sprang from movements in Britain and Spain. In the last twenty years of the eighth century, scholars and poets from all over gathered at the court of Charlemagne—Alcuin from York, the Spaniard Theodulf, the Frank Einhard. They set about creating a new style in prose and poetry: schooled on Ovid, Horace, Virgil, Suetonius and, though strictly Christian in thought, permeated by allusions to Roman and Greek mythology. Scribes and painters in the northern and eastern convents of the Frankish realm at Trier, Rheims, Tours and at the Carolingian court produced illuminated manuscripts, filled with motifs purloined from classical and Christian antiquity; ivory carvers at Aix-la-Chapelle, Metz, and elsewhere, as well as goldsmiths followed the same lines; bronze casters in Aix by the end of the eighth century worked the railings and doors of the palatine chapel in the purest classical style. All this was long before anyone in Rome thought along similar lines: the tomb plaque of Pope Hadrian I, its hexameters composed by Alcuin, its lettering shaped after a second century *capitalis quadrata* and framed by an elegant classical tendril, was carved near Aix-la-Chapelle and shipped to St. Peter's in Rome (fig. 115). Indeed, while the movement around the Frankish court flourished through nearly the entire ninth century, much of it reached Rome relatively late, if ever. The Carolingian classicizing literary style came to the fore in Rome only in the later part of the ninth century and for a short time; the contemporary papal biographies composed or inspired by Anastasius Bibliothecarius, the correspondence of Nicholas I, the Life of Gregory the Great written by John the Deacon Immonides are the outstanding documents. The art of the northern scribes, illuminators, and ivory carvers, in fact, never reached Rome, save in the form of gifts brought by Carolingian rulers—such as the *cathedra Petri* and the Bible of St. Paul's, both donated by Charles the Bald at the time of his coronation in 875. The one exception would seem to be a mural at S. Clemente dating from the pontificate of Leo IV, the *Assumption of the Virgin*. The agitated figures of the Apostles and their terrified expressions recall illuminations in manuscripts of the Rheims school; but, then, a northern artist may well have painted the fresco at S. Clemente. No scriptorium, Latin or Greek, active in Rome during the ninth century and no "Roman" style of lettering or illuminating manuscripts have so far been identified with any degree of certainty.

The churches laid out in Rome and their decoration, dating from the pontificate of Leo III to that of Leo IV, or about 800 to after 850, reflect, then, a special aspect of the Carolingian Renascence. North of the Alps, certainly in its beginnings, the movement seems essentially an antiquarian, cultural phenomenon characterized by a revival—in poetry, prose, and the figural arts—of classical formulae purloined from the entire gamut of Roman art, pagan and Christian, from Augustan times to the fifth and sixth centuries. The architect of Fulda obviously could find a model only in Christian antiquity; the basilica of Saint Peter, goal of all pilgrimages from time immemorial and focus of piety for the peoples north of the Alps ever since their conversion, would offer itself as the natural prototype. No allusion to Constantine need have been involved. Political overtones in a broad sense—the concept of a Christian commonwealth, right government and the like, all derived from Gregory the Great—had pervaded northern thought as well at least from the time of Bede in the early eighth century. In a specific and narrower sense, it seems to me, the renascence movement in the north acquired its political resonance only with the establishment of a Western Christian Empire in 800 and the consequent search for a legitimate ancestry. But the cultural, antiquarian note survives undiminished. The movement never goes into depth; the image of antiquity, both pagan and Christian, remains diffuse; and, if political overtones are injected into it, they generally echo concepts long alive at the papal court.

In Rome, on the contrary, the renewal of the city and the rebirth of a new art are deeply rooted in her own late-antique imperial and emphatically Christian traditions. Their roots are sunk in the political ideology of the return to an imaginary Constantinian past cultivated for eminently practical reasons at the papal court from the mid-eighth century on. Eastern elements, inherited from a more recent past or newly penetrating, were quickly absorbed by the reborn Roman Christian tradition; a tradition powerful, if not on other grounds, by the very presence of its great monuments—St. Peter's, the Lateran Basilica, S. Paolo fuori le mura, S. Maria Maggiore. The art sprung shortly before 800 from this Christian antique renascence is reflected in dozens of major Roman buildings and mosaics through and beyond the middle of the ninth century, sixty years and more. As times of flowering in Rome go during the Middle Ages, this is a long span for sustained activity in building sizable churches in great numbers and decorating them extensively with mosaics, mural paintings, and marble revetments, with chancel screens and at the chancel entrance with colonnaded pergolas of marble or covered with hammered silver, most of them now lost but recorded by the papal biographers.

The length of this sustained effort in the ninth century and of similar periods through Christian antiquity and the Middle Ages needs explanation. It rests, I think, both with the general character of the papacy and its specific hallmarks at a given time. The papacy by definition from Constantine on has been an elective monarchy. Given the advanced or mature age at which, as a rule, the sovereign is elected, his reign normally is short—*non habebis annos Petri*. An effort, political or other, demands specific conditions to be sustained through a number of successive pontificates. One such condition in the Middle Ages was apparently that successive popes be chosen from a cohesive group: the administrative hierarchy of the Church and the great Roman families—the two being nearly synonymous in Rome from Christian antiquity through the thirteenth century. Only a pope backed by his clan and its allies and by their combined political and financial power linked to that of the Church could hope in the Middle Ages to carry through a large-scale building program; and only a succession of such popes, through both the cohesion and the competition of various clans within the group considered *papabili*, could effect an effort sustained over an extended time. The situation may well have obtained in Christian antiquity in the one hundred years from the pontificate of Damasus I (366-384) to that of Simplicius (468-483); but too little is known of the social background of the successive popes in that time. It certainly did obtain between 750 and 860, when a concerted program of church building and decoration was sustained by a succession of ten popes from Stephen II to Nicholas I, all chosen from great, wealthy, and, not least, Roman families.

CHAPTER SIX

Realities, Ideologies, and Rhetoric

Rome, as reflected in her monuments, underwent a process of renewal from the late eleventh century through the thirteenth. New churches sprang up, a new art was born twice, the map of the city was redrawn. Even as she remained faithful to her old traditions, Rome broke out of her isolation. To understand this rebirth one must have an idea of her history from the end of the Carolingian era through the High Middle Ages and of the economic and political realities, the ideological conceits, and the rhetorical claims at the basis of the successive medieval renascences.

After the Gothic Wars, Rome had become a rural town dependent on agricultural produce close at hand, within the Aurelian Walls or just outside. Traces of this rural character persisted up to modern times: no more than fifty years ago the cattle market was held twice a week at the Theatre of Marcellus and farm labor was hired at the Pantheon. In earlier centuries, whenever the Tiber flooded the Prati north of the Borgo and prevented sowing or harvesting, famine broke out. Communications overland or by river were poorly developed and did not make up for any serious deficiency in the city's supplies; the Church farms established by the popes of the eighth and ninth centuries to combat the situation soon fell into private hands. Through the early and the High Middle Ages the Church and the great families allied with it drew their resources and their political strength from estates in the Campagna and the hills north of Rome toward Viterbo and south toward Terracina. There was very little trade. Pilgrims, as they had done from early times, continued to bring business and occasionally extra pious donations. They needed lodgings, food, and other services, as did the papal bureaucracy and the nobles with their retainers, when residing in town. The craftsmen—blacksmiths, cobblers, butchers—provided for their needs, but remained linked to agricultural production and requirements. The papacy and its administration, interwoven with the great families, formed a superstructure. But it did not affect the hard reality of the city and its appearance, which was merely that of a respectable county seat.

The ambiguities of the situation—a bare subsistence level coupled with the worldwide claims of the papacy and ruling families—need to be seen against the overall political background. The weakening and eventual breakup of the Carolingian house and of the alliance between the papacy and the empire ever since the 840s left the popes and Rome in the hands of the great local clans. Feuds within and between these families and their partisans gave rise to blood-curdling violence within the city. At the same time Rome was threatened from outside; Muslim pirates raiding the coasts of Italy ventured far inland, sacking Roman churches beyond the walls, St. Peter's, and S. Paolo fuori le mura. They were defeated in 849 and 916 by the naval and land forces of Gaeta and Naples rather than by the Romans and their papal leaders; and though these victories gave new courage to the citizens and the papacy, they had practically no effect on deteriorating conditions. The papacy sank to ever lower depths, morally, politically, and financially. The *patrimonium Petri*, the Lands of Saint Peter, in Latium and Central Italy was lost to big landowners, private lords, or great monasteries like Farfa in Sabina. Papal power in the city shrank. Alberic, scion of a great family, as *princeps* and *senator omnium Romanorum* set up an efficient government in Rome and her territory in the second third of the tenth century. Upon his invitation, the congregation of Cluny, newly formed within the Benedictine Order, reorganized the monasteries in Rome and her territory; it is noteworthy that this monastic reform in Rome was instituted at the behest of a prominent layman and carried through by a church leader called in from the outside. Alberic and the noble families supporting him saw Rome realistically as their city, the Church as theirs to rule, and the papacy as theirs to dispose of; perhaps he even thought of fusing the two when on his deathbed he arranged for his son to be elected pope as John XII. That Alberic made Rome the leading principality in Central Italy, able to keep at bay would-be Northern invaders from this side of the Alps and beyond, and to negotiate as a near-equal with the Byzantine emperors, lived on in the memory of his fellow aristocrats; just as they remembered how he seized power by appealing to the Romans' hatred of and contempt for foreigners and to their glorious past.

Indeed, the image of Rome as determined by her past was to medieval man a reality no less powerful than politics and economics. Often sheer rhetoric, it nonetheless exerted its influence again and again on political events. Many strands, past and present, pagan and Christian, were interwoven in that image; but in all, Rome was viewed as head of the world, *caput mundi*, mistress of the nations, *domina gentium*, queen of cities, *regina urbium*. She was the resting place of the Apostles, Saint Peter foremost; she was his see and that of his successors and hence supreme. The claim made by Leo I in his effort to Romanize Christianity was renewed four hundred years later as Pope Nicholas I aimed at establishing primacy in the East and West for a papacy with imperial connotations; and with changing political and spiritual accents it was revived throughout the Middle Ages. However, medieval Rome was also the seat of the empire; only in Rome could the emperor by right be crowned. But it remained open whether this right was inherent in the pope or in the Romans, by whom he was or claimed to be chosen, or in the city herself, whence the emperors of old had ruled the world. Again, with different accents, the claim to world rule was made by the Romans themselves—by the grandees in the early centuries, by the Roman people later. Conscious of the past, the great took up ancient Roman titles and names: Alberic's father Theophylact styled himself *senator Romanorum*; his mother Marozia was the *senatrix*, who with a string of successive husbands occupied Castel S. Angelo; his son was named Octavian, presumably after the first Roman emperor. In the name of "the dignity of this city of Rome," Alberic incited the Romans to rise against the foreigners, "of old their slaves . . . who now would rule over Romans," for ancient Rome stood for freedom from foreign domination. Nationalist feelings mingled with such recourse to the past were appealed to at other times also by popes or German emperors to suit their aims. The papacy, the empire, and the Romans all made claims to world rule through holding Rome. At an early time the basis was laid for a three-cornered conflict that continued through nearly the entire Middle Ages.

The claims to the imperial crown and hence to Rome were raised anew by the emperors of the Saxon house. Otto I in 962 descended on the city to be crowned, and he quickly replaced Alberic's son, John XII, with a pope of his own choosing. More brutally realistic even than the Roman grandees, Otto saw both Rome and the papacy as pawns to be held by naked force, to insure possession of the imperial crown and to establish a kind of royal theocracy. Roman resistance, apparently from nobles and commoners alike, to the foreigners and their puppet-popes erupted in rebellion three times in twenty years and was suppressed with cold severity: the leader of the most serious uprising in 965, the city prefect, was hung by his hair from the statue of Marcus Aurelius at the Lateran, the pope's residence, after being led through town seated backward on an ass, and was then sent into exile; exile, too, was the fate of the consuls, the nobles; the twelve *decarcones de vulgi populo*, the leaders of the common people, were hanged—fine differences in justice. The *decarcones*—perhaps better *decariones*—incidentally, may have represented the *rioni*; if so, these medieval quarters of Rome, twelve east of the Tiber, one in Trastevere, and later a fourteenth in the Borgo, seem to be alluded to for the first time. Revolts continued under Otto's son and grandson, Otto II and Otto III, led by a great clan, the Crescentii. A Roman stands against an imperial faction. The last rebel, Johannes Crescentius, like Alberic before him, in the name of Rome's national traditions strove to set up an independent principality, taking on the style of patricius. In the end, defending Castel S. Angelo against the army of Otto III and a strong imperial faction within Rome, he was captured and executed in 998, his body exposed on Monte Mario overlooking the city. Dirges accompanied the long, drawn out collapse of the city. Shortly after 972, the monk Benedict lamented from a monastery on Mount Soracte: "Woe, Rome, oppressed and downtrodden by so many. Now the Saxon king has captured thee—and turned thy strength to nought. Thy gold and silver they have carried off in their bags. . . . Proudly at the height of thy might thou didst triumph over peoples . . . thou hast held the sceptre of supreme power . . . thou didst conquer the earth from south to north. . . . The Gauls have taken thee, thou wert too fair. . . . Woe, Leonine City." Rome and the papacy were at their nadir.

A new image of Rome, grand if ephemeral, emerged around the year 1000. Otto III strove to renew Church and empire jointly by the interlocking support of the ecclesiastical and temporal powers. More tightly linked than the alliance envisaged around 800 by Charlemagne and Leo III and closer to Byzantine concepts—Otto's mother was a Byzantine princess—he saw the papacy and the empire as a dual theocracy under the emperor's guidance. Rome was the fulcrum of that vision, capital of a universal monarchy whence emperor and pope in mutual accord would rule the Christian Empire. The conceit of such a joint capital, believed to have been realized by Constantine, had become part of a political theory by which the empire defended its claim. In Rome and only there, Empire and Church could be reborn. To Charlemagne's contemporaries already she had been the place "where the emperors always used to reside." To Otto she was not only "head of the world and mistress of [all] cities," but also in particular "worthy to house the body of Saint Peter," and therefore entitled "to create the emperor of the world" and "our royal city." This was all the more so as Otto came to see himself as both equal to the Apostles, *isapostolos*, like Constantine, and as their servant, responsible for the defense of the city and master of Rome. Not by chance did his teacher Gerbert, whom he appointed pope, take the name Sylvester, heretofore borne only by the Constantinian pope. Clearly, his aim, too, was to renew the Church and to reestablish Rome as the unquestioned spiritual mistress of the West. In Rome, Otto built up a court, fusing Byzantine with what were believed to be old Roman models and filling the posts with Roman nobles. Two pages from a Gospel Book in Munich, written in 1000 for Otto III, reflect the new concept far more clearly than any words (fig. 116). Otto, enthroned and flanked by the temporal and ecclesiastical powers, receives the homage of the "nations" composing the empire—Gallia, which was Rhenish Germany and the Netherlands; Germania, or the lands between the Rhine and the Elbe; Slavia, those east of the Elbe; all three led by Roma, his capital. The Romans were his favorites, to the disgust of his German and non-Roman Italian subjects. The "consuls of the senate and the people of Rome" take first place in his decrees, followed by the temporal and ecclesiastical dignitaries of the rest of Italy; in appealing to his Romans, he declares that he has led them into the farthest parts of the empire where even their ancestors when they ruled the world had never set foot; all this, to spread their name and glory to the ends of the earth. Rhetoric apart, nobles, clergy, and intellectuals in Rome were attracted by the underlying political concept, by the honors of his court, or by more substantial prospects, such as donations, possibly from the estates of the fallen Crescentii clan. An imperial faction was formed among Romans. For a mere five years—until the deaths of Otto in 1002 and Sylvester a year later—a new era seemed to have begun for Rome and a poet could break out in jubilation: "gaude papa, gaude Caesar, gaudeat ecclesia."

It was only a brief interlude. For almost fifty years after Otto's death, Rome and the papacy slid into the old groove: the city was dominated and the popes were installed first by a great family from the nearby hills, the Counts of Tusculum, and from the forties on by the German emperor, Henry III. No one questioned the le-

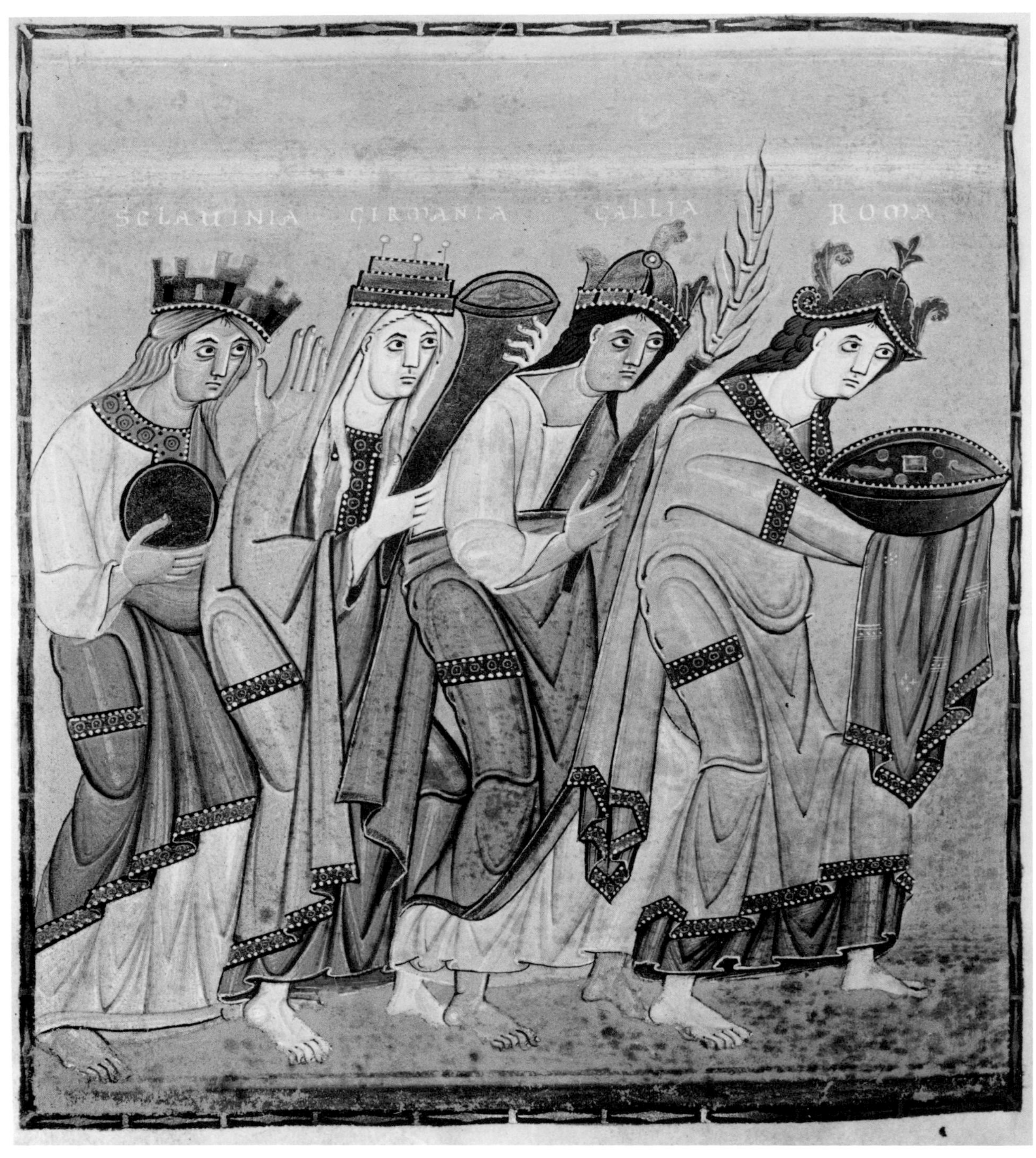

116. Obeisance of the realms before Otto III, *Gospels of Otto III*, Bayerische Staatsbibliothek, Munich, Cod. Monac. Lat. 4453, Cim. 58, fol. 23^{v}, 24^{r}

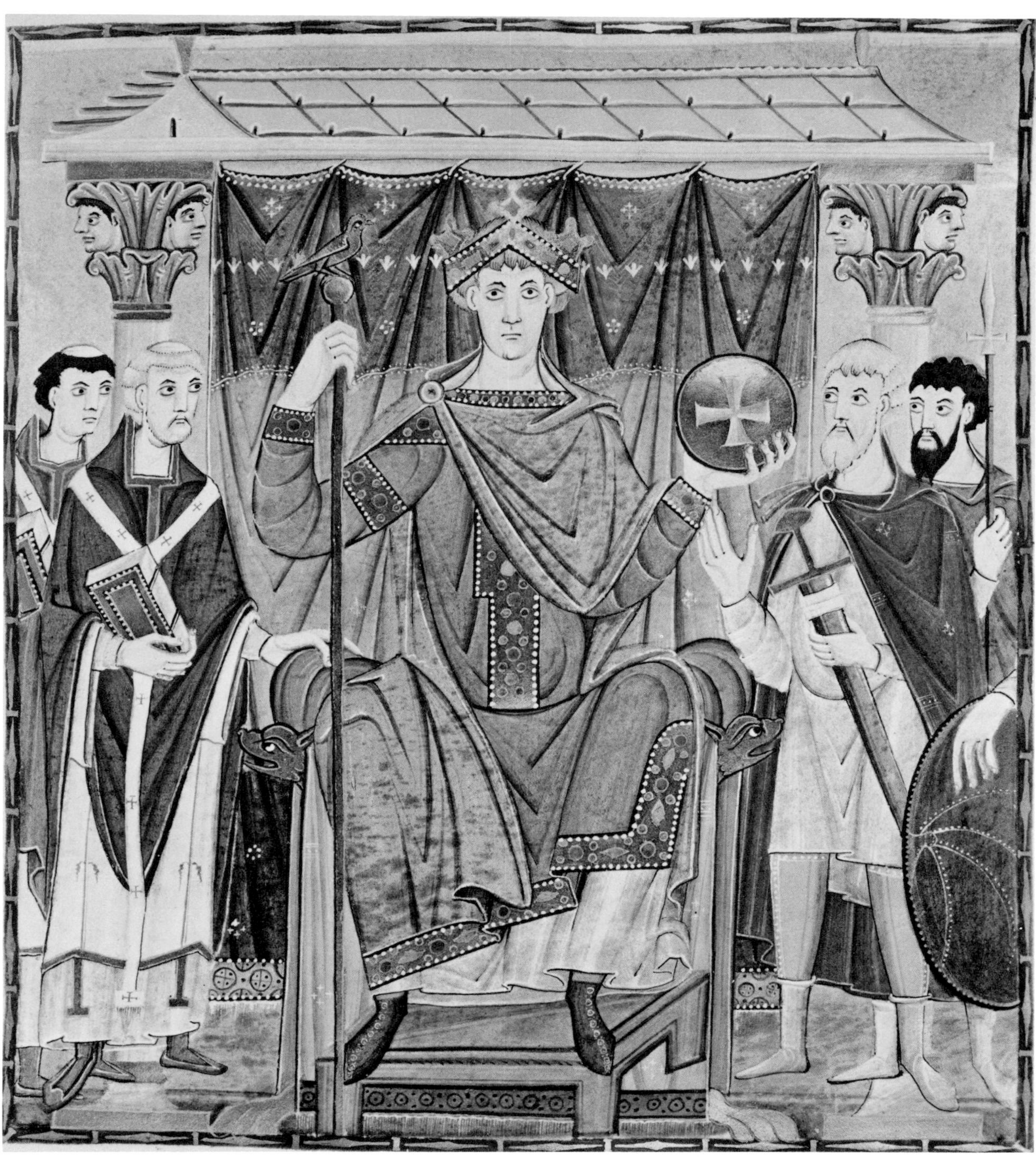

gality of the procedure: any bishop in France, England, or Germany was in fact installed by the ruler who invested him with the insignia of his office, the crozier and episcopal ring; not unjustly so, from the king's point of view, since the appointment was coterminal with the conferment of territorial possessions as fiefs and thus made the ecclesiastic a vassal of the ruler and a dignitary in the temporal realm also. Abuses were bound to mushroom: ecclesiastical offices were sold as a matter of course—the sin of simony; and clerics, likewise as a matter of course, were and behaved like worldly lords living in great style with their concubines and offspring and conferring on them ecclesiastical and temporal property.

Opposition by the early eleventh century rose from within a group of monastic congregations that for the last fifty years had initiated a renewal within themselves. Led by those from Lorraine and North Italy and, in the beginning perhaps to a lesser degree by that of Cluny, they raised the cry for reform of the Church, abolition of the sale of ecclesiastical offices, of the feudalization of the clergy and of the clerical concubinate; and they sustained the fight against moral and financial corruption. The clamor for reform was echoed by the urbanized restless middle and lower classes in the growing cities from North Italy to France and the Rhineland—the *pataria* in Milan stands out—occasionally allied with heretical movements. The underlying demands, leaving aside the specifically ecclesiastical complaints, were those repeated throughout the Middle Ages and after by Christian reformers and revolutionaries: social and economic betterment; return to the purity of an evangelical Christianity and to the simplicity of apostolic times; an inner religiosity free from dogmatism and intellectualism and coherent with action in daily life; and independence of the Church from temporal pressures so as to free her for her religious tasks.

Around 1050 these demands crystallized into an effective program and concomitantly the aim, character, and carriers of the reform changed. The evangelical and revolutionary elements, strong among early monastic and lay groups, were gradually defused. Attention was concentrated not so much on the moral renewal of the clergy and the abolition of simony, but on making the Church autonomous and free from temporal and specifically imperial interference. No longer confined to ethical issues, the conflict revealed its political nature. At the same time, new leaders arose. No longer cloistered monks in huge country abbeys, they were clerics from urban Cluniac convents and risen high in the Church, at the center of power, Rome: Cardinals Peter Damian and Humbert of Silva Candida and Archdeacon Hildebrand, from shortly after 1050 the not so very gray eminence behind the papal see. A conceptual thinker and moralist the first, pragmatic planners and men of action the other two, they carried the fight for the political independence of the Church against temporal, and especially the emperor's, claims to confirm papal elections or to invest bishops with the insignia of ecclesiastical office or otherwise to interfere in Church matters. To strengthen her hand in that "Investiture Struggle," the Church restructured and centralized her organization: papal elections were placed strictly in the hands of the cardinals, disregarding the imperial claim to confirmation; the right of temporal rulers to episcopal investiture was categorically denied; and from the mid-eleventh century on, the papal administration was molded into a tight bureaucracy. At the same time, ironically, the Church was forced to strengthen and expand her own temporal power. The Roman nobles were deprived of their stranglehold on the papacy and its administration, the Lands of Saint Peter were reformed and enlarged, and, again ironically, the Church had to increase her temporal power by herself turning feudal overlord. The Norman dukes, later kings, of South Italy and Sicily, were accepted as powerful and dangerous vassals and defenders. The great lords and eventually the towns of Latium were gradually taken into vassalage, all carrying along their minor feudatories. A feudalized state of the Church was forming, with the powerful papal vassals filling the big lay offices of the City of Rome as well.

The struggle for independence turned rapidly into a contest for the supremacy of the Church in the temporal as well as the spiritual realm.

Leadership fell increasingly to Hildebrand. Born from a great Roman family, he was perhaps related to the Pierleoni, big financiers and only recently converted from Judaism. He was trained at the Cluniac monastery of S. Maria in Aventino and was early drawn into the innermost circle of reformers. Filled with religious fervor, ambition for the Church, and political genius, he developed from the late 1050s on the policy of reform. He was unyielding, authoritarian—"he laid down the law for servants and lords alike"—and yet a political realist. Forced to some compromises both before and after his election to the papacy as Gregory VII, he sometimes fell short of his visions of the Church's place, if indeed these are represented by the *dictatus papae*—more of it anon. But he is one of the two greatest popes of the Middle Ages; the other, Innocent III, achieved what Gregory had laid down as the ultimate aim of the medieval Church.

The center of strife and the battlefield in the most literal sense was Rome. By 1061 the break with the empire—King Henry IV was a child—and with its bishops, unwilling to renounce their territorial fiefs, was inevitable. Against the somewhat irregular election of Pope Alexander II, forced by Hildebrand, they chose an antipope, Cadulus. Egged on by an imperial envoy, Benzo, whose report on his mission is a jewel of hilarious grandiloquence, a faction of Roman nobles called the antipope to Rome and occupied the Leonine City. Alexander and Hildebrand were at first defeated; but they won out in the end, backed by the Pierleoni and their money, and supported by Norman mercenaries. But in two successive years "fighting raged through the city [from Castel S. Angelo] as far as Campitelli," the region behind the Theatre of Marcellus. Street battles were renewed ten years later, when Hildebrand, now Gregory VII, pursued his aims undeterred. Kidnapped in the first year of his pontificate by a Roman magnate who was long his enemy, and held in the latter's mansion *in Parrione*, the very center of town, he was freed next day by the populace who stormed the building. A few months later—the date is uncertain—he laid down the *dictatus papae*, not so much perhaps the charter of his policy, as headings for a planned collection of canon law and hence not necessarily meant as guidelines for immediate political action. The Church was to be recognized as divinely instituted; the pope universal, speaking for the entire Church; the government of the Church absolute and in his hands, with the right to make new laws, to depose bishops and to overrule synods and Church councils; and all secular power subordinate to the Church, it being within the rights of the pope to depose kings and emperors and to wear the imperial insignia himself—an echo of the Constantinian Donation. It remains open whether or not this subordination of secular to ecclesiastical power was intended to imply vassalage, except in clearly stated cases—Hungary, Croatia, and far away Kiev; but at times it certainly was understood to mean just that, even by papal legates. Henry IV, unwilling and unable to accept such claims or to abandon the right to investiture, was excommunicated and formally deposed twice, interrupted by his brief submission in 1077 at Canossa. He in turn declared Gregory a usurper, "not a Pope, but a false monk." After being deposed a second time in 1080, he marched on Rome, laying siege to her three times. At the second try, in 1083, his troops occupied the Leonine City and St. Peter's—its gatehouse was damaged by fire; but Gregory in Castel S. Angelo prevented their crossing to the city proper on the east bank. The following year, though, Henry entered Rome, took the Lateran and had himself crowned at St. Peter's by the antipope he had chosen. Large numbers from among the anti-Gregorian nobles and the people, tired by three years of warfare, supported him. But Gregory's faction held the Septizonium, the ancient colonnaded show-façade at the southeast corner of the Palatine, at that time walled up; it also held on the Capitol the fortified mansions of the Corsi family; and when these were stormed by the emperor, the Tiber Island and Castel S. Angelo, where the pope had taken refuge, remained unconquered. A relief expedition of Normans led by Robert Guiscard drove Henry's troops out and rescued Gregory, at a price: widespread looting; many Romans carried off, supposedly to be sold into slavery; parts of the city laid waste—not quite as bad as contemporaries would have it, but bad enough—in the *disabitato*, the wasteland extending to the Aurelian Walls, and on the outskirts of the town proper, from the Lateran to the Colosseum and on the northern rim of the Campo Marzio from S. Silvestro in Capite to S. Lorenzo in Lucina.

Gregory died in May 1085 at Salerno among his rescuers. The fight between empire and papacy went on, focused less on what he had had in mind, the fundamental relation between priesthood and kingship, than on the symbolic act of episcopal investiture by the emperor. Claims, counterclaims, and bloody warfare continued for another forty years, and again Rome bore the brunt of it all. Popes and antipopes, the latter backed by the emperor, but both elected more or less canonically by rump colleges of cardinals, divided the clergy, nobles, and people alike in shifting alliances; imperial and papal factions fought street battles and held or conquered strategic points—the Lateran, St. Peter's and the Leonine City, Castel S. Angelo, the Tiber Island; and only the recurrent lack of funds to hire mercenaries or bribe factions, both in the popes' and in the emperors' camps, occasionally enforced a few years or months of truce. Pope Urban II, elected in 1088, was unable to enter the city for six years of his eleven-year pontificate. When he could, he sought protection in one or another fortified mansion of the Pierleoni, his main backers and bankers as they were Gregory's—on the Island or near (perhaps in) the Theatre of Marcellus; even his body had to be brought to St. Peter's for burial by way of Trastevere—Ponte S. Angelo was apparently held by the antipope's faction. His successor, Paschal II, fought all the nineteen years of his reign to subdue hostile strongholds in the Campagna or in the city—"always restive when the ruler is absent." He is said to have twice destroyed the stronghold of the Corsi on the Capitol, which, according to Gregory VII's biographer, a generation before had been destroyed by Henry IV in 1084—none of the successive destructions could have been very thorough, it seems. The latter half of his pontificate grew more turbulent still: Henry V, the new German king, invaded Rome in 1111, both to enforce his claims to episcopal investiture and to be crowned emperor; the pope, from the Tiber Island and protected by the Pierleoni, agreed to compromise by having bishops renounce all temporal fiefs; ratification at St. Peter's was prevented by a riot of the German bishops, who were unwilling to abandon such possessions; street fights once more raged through the city; Paschal, abducted by the king, under duress granted him the right to investiture, as claimed, and secretly crowned him at St. Peter's—concessions revoked once Henry left. A second invasion by Henry in 1117 drove Paschal out of the city and for a while Rome, from the Lateran to St. Peter's, was in the king's hands—or almost so; for Castel S. Angelo, held by papal partisans, hampered his triumphal march through the festooned city and he had to cross to St. Peter's by boat—the island bridges presumably were also closed to him by the Pierleoni.

Likewise, under Gelasius (1118-1119), Paschal's successor, the city remained a battleground dominated by hostile strongholds: at the news of the pope's and his electors' being kidnapped and mistreated by the head of the Frangipani clan, "the twelve *rioni* of Rome," the first clear reference here to the town on the east bank divided into districts, and "those from Trastevere and those from the Island" rose in arms, led by the great families from the Ripa quarter and Trastevere, the Pierleoni, Normanni, Tebaldi, Buccapecorini, Boveschi. But the Lateran and presumably parts of town and some outlying areas remained in hostile hands; the pope, though freed, had to flee the city. Peace returned to Rome only in 1122 when the question of investiture was solved by a compromise between Pope Calixtus II and Emperor Henry V, the Concordat of Worms. It was but a brief interlude though. In 1130 in a double papal election, Innocent II stood against Anaclete II: the former a Papareschi from Trastevere, supported by the Frangipani and backed by the German King Lothar; Anaclete, a Pierleoni and Cardinal of S. Maria in Trastevere. Supported by a majority of cardinals, nobles, and citizens, and by the Norman rulers of South Italy and Sicily, Anaclete held the city and the Lateran, reputedly looting the major churches, while Innocent hid in the

Frangipani fortifications on and below the Palatine and in the Colosseum, and in the Corsi strongholds on the Capitol; after a few weeks, though, he fled to France. Three years later he returned with the emperor, but could not drive Anaclete from St. Peter's and Castel S. Angelo. Consequently, the imperial coronation took place at the Lateran, and shortly afterwards Lothar and Innocent left the city again. A second attempt to capture Rome in 1137 was equally unsuccessful. Finally, in 1138 Anaclete died. Innocent was master of Rome, but for only five years. Then new trouble arose, this time from the citizens of Rome. It was overcome and seventy years later the popes ruled Rome and the Lands of Saint Peter both in fact and in law; the papacy could view itself as having risen to victory over the empire and would claim with full authority world supremacy.

Indeed, throughout the twelfth century the concept of the relation of Church to kingship as adumbrated by Gregory VII was consolidated and the underlying theses were formulated with ever greater consistency. The moral issues at the root of the reform movement had long been lost; so had the basic aim of Gregory VII, the subordination of temporal to spiritual authority. The papacy by 1130 saw the subordination of kings and emperors to the pope, ambiguous to start with in its meaning, increasingly in the legal terms of a feudal relationship. The conceit found expression in or after 1133 in a mural painted in the Lateran Palace, transmitted to us through a rough sixteenth-century pen sketch, together with its explanatory inscription: "The king stood before the gates vowing to safeguard the rights of the city. Then, liegeman to the pope, he accepts from his [i.e., the pope's] gift the crown." Whatever its actual meaning, it was widely interpreted in the broadest sense: both spiritual authority and temporal power belong by rights to the Church; temporal power is conferred by the pontiff on the emperor through the act of coronation; hence the empire is held as a fief from the papacy. The thesis was rarely stated outright by the papal jurists. But the claim of the popes to hold the supreme position on earth, to control by spiritual coercion temporal powers as the ultimate supervisory organ, to arbitrate their disputes, and in fact to hold imperial power themselves, was implied time and again, beginning with the reform papacy, in papal pronouncements, in unofficial contemporary statements, in the ceremonial, and even in the style of papal dress. The right to wear imperial insignia, claimed by the pope in the Constantinian Donation, was newly stressed by Gregory VII. The tall papal tiara was interpreted as an imperial crown and was provided with one diadem, most likely a golden rim, to represent "kingship from the hand of God." Occasionally a second was added to symbolize "emperorship from the hand of Peter"; it became the rule in the course of the thirteenth century. A red cloak was worn by the pope as "a sign of imperial status"; and Innocent II was addressed in panegyrics as "Caesar and ruler of the whole world," as "true emperor." Indeed, reinforced by the victory claimed over the empire, the concept of the pope's imperial position was stressed ever more strongly, reaching its climax under Innocent III in the form of a latitude in secular affairs and the fullness of power in spiritual affairs, embodied in the pope's office and person; and a century later, Boniface VIII added a third diadem to the tiara, making it a triple crown. His answer to the envoys of the German emperor Albrecht—"*I* am Caesar, *I* am emperor"—may be just an anecdote spread by malicious contemporaries, but like any good anecdote it sums up his true opinions as proffered, if less openly, in his letters and decrees.

The concept of the papacy as supreme in both the spiritual and temporal realms and truly imperial was naturally reflected in the place assigned to Rome in contemporary political thought. The age-old vision of Rome as head of the world, held through the Middle Ages, had many facets. Depending on the political context of the claims to be supported, the accents shifted. In imperial circles from the time of Otto III, the emphasis was primarily on Rome's place as the emperor's rightful residence; in 1033, for the first time to our knowledge, an imperial bull—the lead seal appended to documents—bears the inscription: "*Roma caput mundi tenet frena orbis rotundi*"—"Rome, head of the world, holds the reins of the globe"; the phrase, sheer rhetoric by then, nonetheless continued to mark imperial bulls to the end of the Middle Ages. The underlying concept was bound to be taken up most emphatically by the emperors as the struggle with the papacy reached its height, from the late eleventh through the twelfth centuries. On their side, contemporary popes and their spokesmen stressed Rome's preeminence within the context of the papal claims (if vaguely conceived) to secular supremacy and imperial power invested in the papacy; a claim possibly raised two hundred and fifty years before by Pope Nicholas I and his diplomats, though in a quite different context. To the popes of the twelfth and thirteenth centuries, the concept of Rome as head of the world was more than an empty phrase; she was, after all, their own imperial capital. They, rather than the German emperors, viewed themselves as the heirs of ancient Rome and her emperors; her past glories had been absorbed by the greater present glories of Christian Rome, the seat of a papacy, imperial and claiming world supremacy; and, very realistically if more prosaically, Rome was the administrative center of the territory in Latium and beyond ruled by the popes.

At that point, the third force claiming world supremacy as inherent in Rome came to the fore: the Romans. Poets and writers had always presented them as carrying the traditions of ancient Rome, heirs to her glories and virtues. And whenever it suited the politics of the moment, the phraseology of Roman antiquity, the memories of her past grandeur or lost freedom had been resuscitated by popes, civic leaders, and emperors: to Nicholas I in 860 the citizens of Rome were *Quirites*; the spokesman of Henry IV in 1061 addressed the assembled nobles as *patres conscripti*; and Henry, laying siege to the city in 1081, "built a New Rome of tents . . . and made new centurions, tribunes and senators, a prefect and *a nomenclator* . . . following ancient custom." All this was empty talk, and the Romans apostrophized were by no means the Roman people, but a few nobles to be won over by the emperor. Indeed, fifty years later, in 1130, it was still the Roman grandees listed by name who with "our consuls and palatine judges" invited King Lothar—with the pope's concurrence—to be crowned in Rome. But—and this is new—the invitation was coupled with the demand that the king "submit to the laws of Rome and refrain from disturbing the concord of her citizens"; that is, in this case, that he recognize Anaclete II. Self-reliance and overconfidence speak. But soon after, rhetoric gave way to consistent ideology and to action directed toward a political goal clearly envisaged. In October 1143, challenging the papacy's claim to sovereignty over Rome implied in Pope Innocent II's demand to receive in vassalage the town of Tivoli, recently subdued by the Roman militia, the Romans rose in revolt. "Pretending it to be for the good of the commonwealth," they "assembled on the Capitol and, desiring to renew the ancient dignity of the city, again set up the Senate, lapsed ages ago . . ."; this was in line with the ideas of Arnold of Brescia, just then come to Rome and long a leading revolutionary intellectual, "who wanted to resuscitate the senatorial dignity and the knightly order after the model of the ancients . . . and to rebuild the Capitol." Such revolutionary feelings, if dimly conceived, may have been simmering for some time. They were nourished by demands for self-government in Rome and power to rule over the surrounding territory coming from a citizenry grown wealthy but politically powerless, from small sub-vassals of the great lords, and from part of the clergy, though obviously not the hierarchy or those connected with the great families. In 1143, feelings crystallized into action directed against the pope, the high clergy, and the great nobles who in his name ruled Rome. A republic was proclaimed; a Senate was set up where none had existed since the seventh century; the titles of senator or senatrix used later on were honorific marks of nobility. The fifty-six members of the new Senate were chosen from among the citizens, liberally sprinkled with lawyers and lesser nobility. A *patricius* was appointed as top executive officer—Jordanus Pierleone, a brother of Anaclete II and a maverick in his family, which had switched to supporting the successors of Innocent II. Demands were made for the pope to abdicate to the *patricius* his temporal power and to live on tithes and donations, "like the ancient priests"; and "all nobles" were expelled from town, their mansions and the "splendid palaces" of some cardinals were looted. An attack on the Capitol undertaken by Pope Lucius in 1145 failed and a provisional compromise was reached between the exhausted contestants: the Romans dropping the claims and position of the *patricius*, the pope recognizing the republic and limiting himself to confirming the senators and accepting their oath of loyalty. Dissatisfied, both parties turned to the German king Conrad, the Senate offering to place on his head the imperial crown and inviting him to reside in Rome, "all hindrance from the clergy to be removed," and to bring back "the times of Constantine and Justinian, who held in their hands the whole world by the power of the Senate and People of Rome"—jurists in the Senate speak, hence the allusion to Justinian. But the Senate had no power and the king did not come; on the contrary, he negotiated with the pope, who with the support of the great feudatories and the Norman king prepared a new assault on Rome. Nonetheless the agreement of 1145 was renewed four years later. At the same time, though, negotiations between the papal diplomats and the new king, Frederick Barbarossa, in 1153 led to the emperor's promise to support the pope's temporal rule; a promise the more important since Pope Hadrian IV, elected the following year, was confronted with fresh riots in Rome and an invasion into papal territory by his former ally, the king of Sicily. Frederick came to Rome in 1155 and was again approached by the Senate, who offered him the crown, but he refused the offer in the rudest possible terms. Making short shrift of the claims made in the name of Rome's great past by "her wise and valiant citizens," he interrupted their speech, which, "as Italians do, they meant to draw out at great length with long sentences going round and round." Coronation by the pope at St. Peter's in July 1155 ended in the customary bloody battle with the Romans in the Borgo, and in the equally customary malaria epidemic, which forced a quick retreat on the part of the Germans.

Political realities and ideological claims soon broke the uneasy alliance between emperor and pope: the emperor interfered in Italian bishoprics, considered by the Curia as their sphere of interest; the investiture question flared up anew with the papal conceit hinting at vassalage for the imperial crown; the imperial side countered that temporal power had been conferred on the Church by Constantine only and hence ironically took up the revolutionary cry for the Church's return to evangelical poverty. Nonetheless, while bitterly fighting each other, emperor and pope—no longer Hadrian, but his successor Alexander III—each stood firmly against the demands of the Roman citizenry to share in the temporal rights and the resulting income of the administration of the Church, as well as their aspiration to expand the city's domination over towns in Latium, also claimed by the pope and the emperor. Clearly, Barbarossa's opposition to the Romans' demands coincides with his overall policies in his wars with the Lombard cities. At Monte Porzio, in 1167, a Roman army marching against Tusculum was smashed by German and mercenary cavalry and more than two thousand Romans were killed. Thereupon, turning against the pope, the imperial soldiery broke into the Borgo, burned the gatehouse of St. Peter's, and occupied the basilica, only to be decimated by malaria, throughout the Middle Ages a faithful ally of the Romans against northern invaders. The pope, apparently as wary of the emperor as of the citizenry, meanwhile hid in the Frangipani mansions and finally fled the city. Another ten years passed in the three-cornered war between emperor, pope, and city, complicated by the appointment of antipopes by the imperial faction, by inroads on the possessions of the Church by great feudatories, and by the seizure of churches and their property by the rebellious city. Reconciliations between two of the parties, never all three, were short-lived. Peace between Frederick and Alexander, concluded in Venice in 1177, failed to stop the conflict. However, in 1188 the pope, now Clement III, and the city of Rome reached a final, lasting compromise; that Clement was Roman by birth facilitated agreement. All temporal rights were restored to the pope; church property that had been seized was returned; the Senate and other representatives of the citizenry swore loyalty. In exchange, the city kept the right to make war or peace; she received an annual share in the papal income in the form both of a subsidy for maintaining the city walls and of "gifts" to its high officials; heavy indemnities payments were made for war damage both to the citizens of Rome and to feudal lords in town and country; and imperial influence in the city was reduced to appointing the city prefect.

Like any good compromise, the Concordat of 1188 made concessions to both sides and left room for further maneuvering. The pope saw his overlordship restored; the city had received recognition as a commune, comparable to those established ever since the late eleventh century in North Italy, France, and the Rhineland. An energetic leader on either side could achieve much. To gain strength, as a first move, the city replaced the unwieldy fifty-six-member Senate by a single *senatore* as top executive officer. Benedictus Carushomo, apparently not a noble, was chosen to fill the post and seems to have prepared a constitution; he also started to secure and expand the city's sovereignty over lands claimed by the Church as well. Both policies, domestic and foreign, might be called populist in character and were bound to lead to friction with the papal party. Indeed, difficulties continued for the next eighty years. Only a pope with the stature of Innocent III in the eighteen years of his pontificate, 1198-1216, could manage cautiously and forcefully to keep the situation in balance, helped by changes in the social and economic stratification in the city. The old families, aware "that everything must change if it is to stay the same," had made peace with the innovations initiated in 1143 and were liberally represented in the Senate; new families, the Capocci, Orsini, Annibaldi, had come to the fore, either sprung from among wealthy citizens (the Orsini from the Boveschi) or, like Innocent's family the Conti, moved in from the country. Well-to-do commoners' families continuously pushed into the ranks of the nobility. Within the ruling groups drawn from these various strata factions naturally formed: one, favoring an aggressive "Roman" policy, aimed at expanding the dominions of the city; the other, pro-papal and set on preserving the lands and power of the Church. Innocent ingeniously managed to avoid clashes for the better part of his reign and to keep the city both happy and under control. The last vestige of imperial claims was eliminated by making the city prefect liegeman of the pope. The *senatore*, too, was appointed by the pope. On the other hand, the city remained sovereign within limits, with the right to make war and peace, conclude treaties, and exercise its feudal privileges, including taxation of neighboring towns. No force was threatened; Rome was too valuable as "an independent commune possessing claims to rule a large area of Latium and having a prosperous community" to risk harming it. But Innocent made sure of a firm hold—"we hold it in our power," he wrote in 1201—by appointing as *senatore* a succession of nobles from families old and new, solidly anchored in Rome and Latium, and loyal to the Church: a Pierleone, Pandulf of the Suburra, a Tebaldi. The one big fight in his time between the papal and "Roman" factions seems to have been more vociferous than bloody; stones were thrown and towers demolished, but few, if any, men were killed. However, it was settled by papal arbitration and clearly by bribery; "the pope's money had defeated them," said the adversaries. Innocent's procedure in Rome fits in with his overall temporal policy: to hold, restructure, and expand the papal lands through Central Italy. Under him, the Church became a great feudal lord; by diplomatic and legal means he built up the papal state as it existed for centuries thereafter; and he secured it by granting large fiefs in key areas to his own and allied families. The firm hold on Rome, the consolidation of a papal state, an efficient administration reorganized, and a sound fiscal policy, all combined to form a strong realistic basis to support both his international policy and his claim to world supremacy in the temporal and spiritual realms.

The rise of the papacy, its ultimate victory over the empire, and the emergence of the city of Rome as a political entity are closely bound up with the social and economic changes that the town had undergone from the ninth into the twelfth centuries. An agricultural note prevailed for a long time: Romans, big and small, tended their gardens behind their houses; they kept and purchased land in the disabitato and beyond the Aurelian Walls, often far distant; the produce from fields and vineyards came to the markets; and craftsmen continued to work for farming needs. Also, the big landholders in the Campagna and the hills remained powerful in the affairs of the papacy and the city. Their influence, in fact, was rather strengthened by their becoming liegemen of the papacy in greater numbers during the eleventh and twelfth centuries. A majority of popes, cardinals, and other Church dignitaries still at the end of the thirteenth century came from the great country families near Rome. But other forces were at work as well from the eleventh and twelfth centuries on. On the one hand, foreigners increasingly penetrated the papal administration and the papacy itself: in the twelfth century, Frenchmen, like Urban II and Calixtus II; Hadrian IV, an Englishman trained in France; not to speak of the string of French popes in the thirteenth century. On the other hand, in Rome itself, new social and economic groups emerged strongly. Craftsmen already by the late tenth and early eleventh centuries had gained new strength, apparently by organizing themselves into *scholae* or guilds—cooperatives of entrepreneurs—to regulate prices and wages, negotiate with suppliers, and obtain rights of way and of loading and unloading: cobblers and tailors, market gardeners, vegetable dealers and butchers, blacksmiths, kettlemakers and goldsmiths; also at an early point shippers and shipbuilders, lawyers and the service personnel of churches, the *mansionarii*, presumably administrators of church property; later, cattle breeders, grain and feed dealers—really agricultural entrepreneurs; and in the twelfth century, overseas shippers and merchants. By then an economically strong citizenry had formed, and naturally they claimed political power. Allied with the minor vassals reacting against the big landholders and with discontented intellectuals, lawyers, and minor clerics, they carried the revolution of 1143.

The organizational framework for the revolt and the ultimate compromise between papacy and city likewise had existed for centuries. Ever since the earliest Middle Ages, the citizens had been organized militarily, possibly according to a seventh-century Byzantine military division of the city into defense districts; a similar division of Ravenna into twelve districts dates from roughly the same time. From then on, it seems, each section of Rome had its own banner, its own militia, its own leader or representative. When Charlemagne first came to Rome in 774, he was met outside the city by the *iudices* of Rome, each with a flag, as well as by all the groups of the militia, each with its leader, the children from the schools and the "venerandas cruces, id est signa"; this, says the papal biographer, was the traditional ceremony to receive the exarch. Later, emperors were met with a similar panoply of militia, flags, and banners. These also appeared in solemn papal liturgy. By the twelfth century the pope was preceded by twelve banners; "Ante crucem milites draconarii, portantes XII vexilla, quae bandora vocantur." Three hundred years before, when Emperor Otto I in 965 put down a rebellion, as we have seen, both the leaders of the nobles, "consules," and twelve representatives of the common people, "decarcones de vulgi populo," were harshly punished. These twelve leaders were very likely representatives of the twelve rioni into which the city was then divided; and it is likely that the twelve military ensigns likewise represented the twelve districts. Their military character was seen again in 1118, when at the election of Gelasius II the Romans—the Roman prefect, the noble families with their factions, the twelve rioni of Rome, and moreover the men of Trastevere and the Tiber Island, "regiones XII Romanae civitatis, Transtiberini et Insulani"—took up arms to defend the legitimate pope.

Grown as a framework of the military organization of the citizenry, the rioni at an early time functioned as civic districts of the city as well. Documents from the tenth century on refer to property located within specific "*regiones*" and close to conspicuous monuments or topographical landmarks. While different both from the seven ecclesiastical regiones, mentioned from early times in the *Liber Pontificalis* as well as from the fourteen regiones of Augustan Rome, the medieval city districts, the rioni, numbered fourteen. Their political function had come to the fore de facto as early as the tenth century, in the revolt against Otto I. With the establishment of the *comune*, the Roman republic of 1143, and its claim for civic independence in administrative and judicial affairs, the rioni, rather than being primarily military districts, became in law as well as in fact the basis of the political and civic organization of Rome. The fifty-six senators elected from 1143 would seem to have represented fourteen rioni, four for each. Twelve were on the east bank of the Tiber, the other two being Trastevere on the west bank and the Tiber Island, just as they were listed twenty years before in 1118. However, the exact limits of each rione, as well as the total number of rioni, fluctuated. In the fourteenth century there were only thirteen: Tiber Island apparently had disappeared as a separate district, and Trastevere was only then formally integrated in the overall administrative division of the city. The *civitas Leonina*, the Borgo, focused on St. Peter's and the Vatican, remained independent till 1586, when it became the fourteenth rione.

By and large, then, the citizenry, organized in rioni and composed of craftsmen and small traders, carried the rising Roman republic and finally achieved the compromise with the papal ruler of Rome. On the other hand, the great families, both landholders through Latium and a new, town-based aristocracy of entrepreneurs and financiers, took the part of the papacy. This unduly oversimplifies the situation; but roughly it holds. Moreover, the borderline between town-based entrepreneur and landed gentry became ever more fluctuating. The big landowners became merchants and overseas shippers on their own account. By the first years of the twelfth century, the lords of Tusculum, Ptolemy I and his son of the same name, who controlled the seacoast south of Rome, made treaties and business contracts with the republic of Gaeta and the monastery of Montecassino to secure partnership rights and openings for import and export in their territories. Such merchandising on a large scale, moreover, needed financing. Indeed, banking and financing on both small scale and large must have flourished early in Rome; by the eleventh and twelfth centuries, the city had become a great financial center. Money changers were needed to deal with the foreign currencies pilgrims carried. In a broader framework, bankers seem to have been called on to finance business ventures—why else would the gardeners' guild in 1030 elect a banker as its *prior* or chairman? The great country families, too, needed financial backing to enlarge their holdings and guarantee their marketing. Most of all, the Church was in permanent need of bankers. Income from her estates, from the fiefs and the subjected towns, was irregular and undependable. Occasionally subsidies from the Norman rulers of South Italy and Sicily or the Countess Mathilda of Tuscany would help, but daily needs required constant banking support: to take care of the administrative overheads of the ever-swelling Curia; to back the rise of the reform papacy, of Gregory VII foremost; to finance the wars of the popes during the Investiture Struggle; and, of course, to provide the bribes wanted to buy support from nobles and commoners, outbidding the imperial faction. On a larger scale still, backing from bankers was needed by the Curia to collect and transfer to Rome by credit operations, rather than in specie, the income from tithes, taxes, St. Peter's Pence, and other kinds collected in faraway lands, including bribes to influence papal and administrative decisions. Conversely, banks were necessary to remit Church funds from Rome to wherever they were needed. Only big firms with far-flung connections could handle these tasks for the Curia. From the thirteenth century on such *mercatores de curia* were mostly Sienese and Florentine companies. In the eleventh and twelfth centuries, on the other hand, the financiers of the papacy were apparently Romans. The Pierleoni stand out: time and again the chroniclers point out how Pierleoni money decided the struggle over Rome and the papacy. But they were not the only ones. The Frangipani, always close to the Pierleoni as allies or competitors, were apparently big creditors of the papacy by the middle of the twelfth century. Possibly other Roman families, too, were in trading or banking, or had started out there, the two businesses being coterminal—the Tebaldi,

Bracucci, Boveschi; the name of the last rather suggests that they were cattle breeders. In any event, none of these families need have started as landholders; it seems they only acquired land later on. Whereas the old clans ruling Rome had their strength in the countryside, the new families were town-based. But they quickly amalgamated with the older land-based families, and, as these latter increasingly bought, expanded, or built fortified mansions in town as well, the borderlines more and more disappeared.

Whether town- or country-based, the noble families in the course of the later twelfth and the thirteenth centuries penetrated the city administration as the compromises between Rome and the papacy evolved. At the same time, they formed a network which, though never recognized by law, was above the legal and administrative division of the city into rioni. From the ninth century on, Alberic's family, and later the counts of Tusculum, sat on the slope of the Quirinal. Their heirs the Colonna occupied the same site in the High Middle Ages, and from there dominated the Quirinal and the Esquiline. By 1167 they also held the Mausoleum of Augustus. Their territory, then, extended in large part over the rione Monti. The Frangipani, from the eleventh century on, held another sector of Monti, the Palatine, the Colosseum, the Circus Maximus and, for a time, Torre delle Milizie; it was a sector of great importance, since it controlled the main approaches to the Lateran and its papal residence. Similarly, the Conti di Segni from around 1200 on occupied the west slope of the Viminal and the area behind the Forum of Nerva, again in the rione Monti. On the contrary, other families controlled sectors of the abitato. The Pierleoni, in the eleventh and twelfth centuries, were dominant in Trastevere, on the Tiber Island, and in the Ripa. The Ripa, in particular, was undisputed Pierleoni territory by 1100; it was presumably under their patronage that S. Maria in Porticu was consecrated by Gregory VII, always close to the Pierleoni; that S. Nicola in Carcere was rebuilt or reconstructed—it was known as the "church of Petrus Leonis," the head of the clan around 1100; and that both churches shortly after were raised to the rank of diaconiae to be presided over by cardinals. In Trastevere, though, they shared power with the Normanni, the Papareschi, and the Tebaldi. The Crescentii at the same time controlled parts of the rione Ponte or Parione—one recalls the kidnapping of Gregory VII by one of that clan. Later, in the thirteenth century, the Orsini, who were descended from the Boveschi, held in the same sectors Monte Giordano in the rione Ponte and the Theatre of Pompey in Parione; the Savelli held sway over the Aventine, the river bank at its foot, and the Ripa with the Theatre of Marcellus; the Caetani took over control of the Tiber Island and Torre delle Milizie; the Annibaldi succeeded the Frangipani in the Colosseum, on the west spur of the Esquiline, and as far as the Celian Hill; and the Capocci dominated parts of the Quirinal and the Aventine.

Prepared slowly during the twelfth century, the medieval papacy reached its peak under Innocent III and his successor, Honorius III. In their pontificates, from 1198 to 1216 and then to 1227, the pope was truly, as he claimed, supreme. Spiritual power rested with him as ultimate authority. The Church, cardinals, bishops, lower clergy, and the monastic orders, including the newly founded Franciscans and Dominicans, were subordinate to him. In temporal matters, too, within the Church and beyond, he was the final arbiter of Europe. France, very much a rising power, nonetheless sought accommodations with the pontiffs through the first half of the thirteenth century. England, Hungary, the Scandinavian and Spanish kingdoms, were seen by the Church and, except for the first, largely saw themselves as papal vassal states. The Hohenstaufen emperors, notwithstanding the towering figures of Henry VI and his son, the great Frederick II, and despite the union of the imperial crown with Sicily and South Italy, Norman heretofore, were losing the battle against the papacy. No emperor was crowned in Rome for a century after 1220, and none was crowned by a pope from 1220 until 1432. Any claim to Rome as capital of a universal temporal monarchy was abandoned by the German emperors, late heirs of Charlemagne. Rather than through the imperial crown or through her citizens' declaiming it in grand language, Rome in the early decades of the thirteenth century was, in a very real sense, head of the world, *caput mundi* through the papacy, a power center in politics, in law, in finances. All legal business of importance in Western Christendom, whether or not within the Church or even between temporal powers alone, came to the papal court at some point. The court, indeed, was gradually restructured into the swollen bureaucracy of the Curia, staffed by hundreds of clerks and with many scores of lawyers and their scribes in the city representing litigants from abroad. Inevitably, political arguments came up or were brought before the pontiff and decided by him: the legitimacy of an imperial election, a royal succession, the title to a territory. Legal business, through fees and bribes, brought large sums to Rome, as did tithes and the purchase of ecclesiastical office. Thus the Church (we might as well quote verbatim) was "transformed into an enormous financial concern . . . with its collectors scattered in every corner . . . its deposits loading the houses of the Templars or the coffers of Tuscan bankers" (Sienese rather than Florentine at that time), "with its remittances and bestowals of funds" and the corresponding administrative organ in Rome, the papal *camera*. The control of episcopal elections and ecclesiastical benefices, increasingly centered on Rome, resulted in pouring untold sums into the hands of Church dignitaries at the Curia. Popes and cardinals amassed huge personal fortunes, and through economic and political pressure the reigning pope's relatives acquired riches and lands near their inherited estates in the neighborhood of Rome and through Latium. Such broad policies encompassing all of Western Christendom, both in the spiritual and in the temporal realms, were combined with a sound and indeed cautious policy in the city, which formed the center and seat of their world rule, Rome.

Innocent's policies, implemented by Honorius III, could not be continued for any length of time. In the international realm the papacy was threatened more than ever by Frederick II, heir to the Hohenstaufen emperors, Frederick Barbarossa and Henry VI, and heir through his mother to the Norman rulers of Sicily and South Italy. The counterweight sought by the papacy in the French royal house turned out in the long run to be more dangerous still. Concomitantly, already in the 1230s the claims of the city, too, were becoming more strident, and the weakness of the papacy, primarily the financial difficulties caused by its wars with Frederick II, encouraged ever greater aggressiveness in the Romans. The city even went so far as to claim the right to tax clergy and ecclesiastical property and to extend its jurisdiction over clerics. Delayed only for a while by strife in town, such aggressive policies led to the summoning of a strong man from outside to rule the city, Brancaleone di Andalò. As *senatore* from 1252 till his death in 1258, he immensely strengthened the commune: expanding its suzerainty over practically all of Latium; holding down the factions in town—one hundred and forty family towers were torn down and two Annibaldis were hanged; consolidating the organization of the guilds and their economic and political power; keeping in check the great feudal lords; and reducing to a nominal factor papal sovereignty. Rome under him became an important power, if only locally; realist that he was, he never seems to have taken up the old Roman claim to be *caput mundi*. Rhetoric meant little to him. After his death, politics in the city slid back into the normal state of confusion, with street-fighting between papal and anti-papal factions, city and papal claims to power. The search for a new strong man ended in 1263 with the election of Charles of Anjou, the French antagonist and successor to the Hohenstaufen as king of Sicily and South Italy. Through him the Anjou branch of the house of France became the dangerous protector of the Church, more dangerous still since it was close at hand and established in the city. For twenty-one years Charles of Anjou was in fact, if not always in name, in control of Rome and the papacy. From 1261 through 1277, six popes, French by birth or allied to France or the Neapolitan Anjou, followed each other. Among sixty cardinals created between 1261 and 1296, twenty-one were either French or Francophiles by birth or interest. To be sure, few if any were unrestrictedly controlled by France or the Anjou. They were absorbed into the Roman milieu and, allied to this or that great local clan, acquired economic interests of their own through capital investment or landholdings. Interlocked with the native Roman members of the Curia, they formed a complex international group.

The fight against this international element in both Church and city was waged by factions grouped around the great families of the time, with infighting among themselves. The Savelli, Orsini, Annibaldi, Capocci, Colonna, Caetani, Stefaneschi all had their fortified mansions in the city, their strongholds in the hill towns, landholdings through Latium, and large parcels of real estate in Rome; cardinals and canons sprung from their midst had amassed huge ecclesiastical benefices all over the West; and family influence, both financial and political, in the Curia and in Rome, was strong. In 1277 it led to the election of Pope Nicholas III, a Roman if ever there was one. In the three years of his pontificate he eliminated the Anjou power in the city and worked out an accommodation with the Romans by which the pope himself became *senatore*—it was modified by the pope's appointing a vicar. Nicolas was followed—except for the pontificate of the Anjou-oriented Frenchman Martin IV—by a series of Roman popes, all from or closely allied with great Roman families: a Savelli, Honorius IV; Nicholas IV, a Colonna protégé; finally, after the two-year pontificate of the inept hermit Celestine V (1292-1294), Boniface VIII Caetani. They in their turn created a bevy of Roman cardinals from among their own and related families; and both popes and cardinals helped themselves and their families quickly and unscrupulously to immense riches. The papal administration meanwhile grew into an unwieldy and stale bureaucracy, while litigants from all over the West poured legal fees and bribes into its courts. Tithes poured in by the millions: within three and a half years one single Florentine bank held over 137,000 florins worth of tithes in deposit; and pilgrims' offerings at St. Peter's in a normal year amounted to 30,400 gold ducats. Never before had the high dignitaries of the Church and their relatives been that wealthy. The policy of building up family fortunes and power by the reigning pontiff reached its peak under Boniface VIII—granted that he overdid his nepotism. In four years, the Caetani bought lands and towns up for well over half a million ducats—Sermoneta, Ninfa, S. Felice al Circeo.

At the same time, however, papal power was declining in matters international, domestic, and financial. French predominance, while temporarily reduced through eliminating the Anjou, remained a constant threat; the papacy, notwithstanding its enormous income, was in constant debt to its bankers; and rivalry between the Roman families was only strengthened by papal attempts to push their own relatives into power. Local family interest conflicted with the necessary accommodations sought with the city. At times such conflicts spilled over into the realm of international politics: in 1303 the Colonna, despoiled by the pope and his Caetani relatives, took league with the French to overthrow Boniface; the removal to Avignon was prepared. Prior to that event, though, neither Curia nor pope seem to have faced the changed world. Boniface VIII in the bull *Unam Sanctam* claimed world supremacy, both spiritual and temporal, as Innocent III had done a hundred years before. But where Innocent had based his claim on the very real fullness of power he held, Boniface VIII was no longer able to enforce the authority he claimed. As from the late twelfth century on, so after 1270, the popes and their advisers, except for the unworldly Celestine V, were great lawyers, organizers, and financiers. But lawyers and financiers are not always great statesmen or deep religious thinkers. Through the last two thirds of the thirteenth century, the Church was de facto weak, inside and out. The conflict between the riches and power of the Establishment Church and the longing of laymen and new religious orders for renouncing worldly goods in the name of a deep-felt inner religiosity remained unresolved. And on the political chessboard of Europe she was rapidly turning into a pawn of France. The papacy's claim to world supremacy with Rome as its capital was becoming empty.

It is within this context that the proclamation by Boniface VIII of 1300 as the Holy Year, the first of its kind, should be seen. Proclaimed upon popular demand, it corresponded, to be sure, to a deep-felt spiritual need of Western Christians—why else would two million pilgrims, give or take a few hundred thousand, have come, 200,000 staying every day? At the same time it was an attempt on the part of the Church to reconcile the religious fervor of the masses with her own spiritual and temporal aspirations. She administered, after all, and distributed to the faithful through indulgences, the treasure of salvation. Inevitably, to be sure, the celebration developed into a colossal publicity stunt; and likewise inevitably, it brought riches to the Church and to Rome. The well-organized provisioning of the masses of pilgrims awed those in a position to judge its inherent difficulties. Giovanni Villani, from a big business family in Florence, came to Rome on pilgrimage and reports that "all were provided with plenty of food, both men and horses, with much patience and without shouting and rioting." Another well-to-do pilgrim from Asti confirms that "bread, wine, meat, fish and oats were cheap" and apparently plentiful. Riches poured into the coffers of the Curia—annual offerings multiplied one hundredfold—and of individual churches and monasteries; at S. Paolo fuori le mura, the man from Asti saw "two clerics day and night at the altar, rakes in hand to gather the coins" thrown by the pious on the grave of the Apostle. Money naturally also flowed into the pockets of inn- and tavernkeepers, grocers, vendors of straw and hay, horse traders, and all those who drew a living from the tourist-pilgrim trade. Quite aside from this, the Holy Year and the influx of the faithful from all over the West made Rome and the papacy once more the very center of Christendom: the indulgences to be acquired by visiting the graves of the Apostles and the Roman martyrs, the many relics, the size and splendor of the churches, the riches of a bustling town, all brought in tangible form before the eyes of visitors and Romans the greatness of the pope and of Rome, the two having become as one. Rhetoric, ideology, and reality for once seemed to coincide—for the last time in the Middle Ages.

CHAPTER SEVEN

The New Rebirth of Rome: The Twelfth Century

The reality of Rome in the Middle Ages and the image contemporaries held of her were closely interwoven in their many and diverse facets, heterogeneous and often contradictory, and they are reflected in the visual context of the city: in the urban layout; in churches, convents, and secular buildings; in mosaics, paintings, church furniture; and in the meaning given by contemporaries to monuments surviving from Roman antiquity. All speak clearly of a second renewal of Rome, following the Carolingian Renascence and the city's subsequent decline. The changes in its urban aspect are dealt with in a separate section: the growth of the Borgo across the river from St. Peter's to Castel S. Angelo and its bridge into a pivotal point on the city map; the resulting westward expansion of the built-up town, the abitato, into the area enveloped by the Tiber bend and toward Ponte S. Angelo; and the resurrection, at the abitato's eastern outskirts, of the Capitol as a second pole on the city map, though ineffective at first. Like the overall urban development, the individual monuments, whether buildings, mosaics, or paintings, reflect this renewal.

Among churches and convents, three stand out, all from the early twelfth century: S. Clemente, S. Maria in Trastevere, and the Quattro Coronati. At S. Clemente, sometime between 1110 and 1130, a new church richly fitted with mosaics and liturgical furniture replaced the fourth-century basilica, five meters below street level by then and precariously shored up, though still in use, it seems, for another twenty years after the Norman raid of 1084. Entered through a gabled porch, a full-fledged atrium, whose colonnades are crowned with Ionic capitals somewhat crudely carved, repeats on a slightly smaller scale the fourth-century atrium buried underneath. The new church, under its attractive eighteenth-century decoration, is simple in plan (fig. 117): a nave flanked by two aisles—of different widths, since the new church occupies the site of only the nave and left aisle of the fourth-century basilica; ten arcades resting on two rows of four columns each, originally with Corinthian capitals, and on a longish pier in the middle, at the front of the clergy section; originally, ten tall, narrow windows, those near the sanctuary alternating with oculi; and a large apse to terminate the nave—the small trefoil

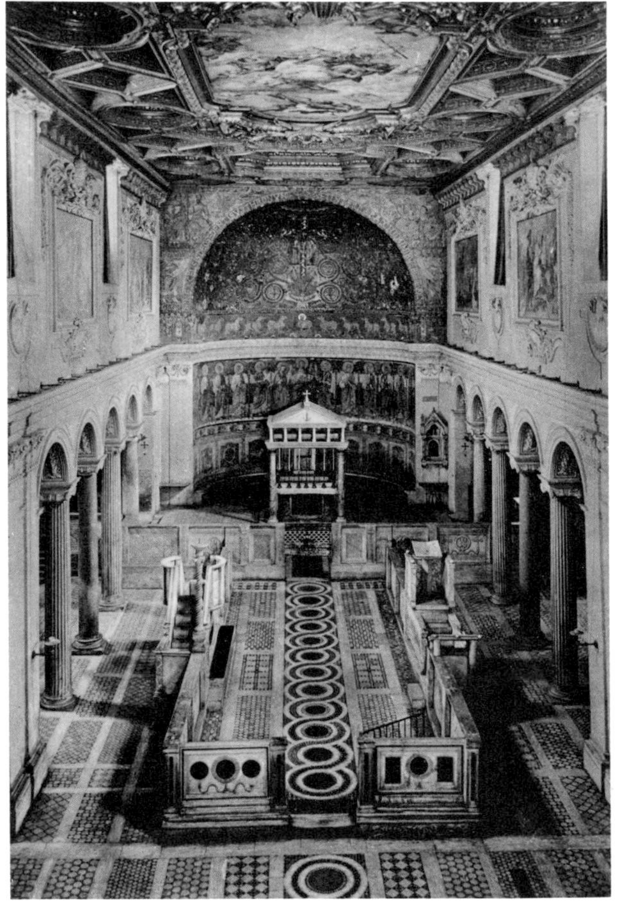

117. S. Clemente, interior

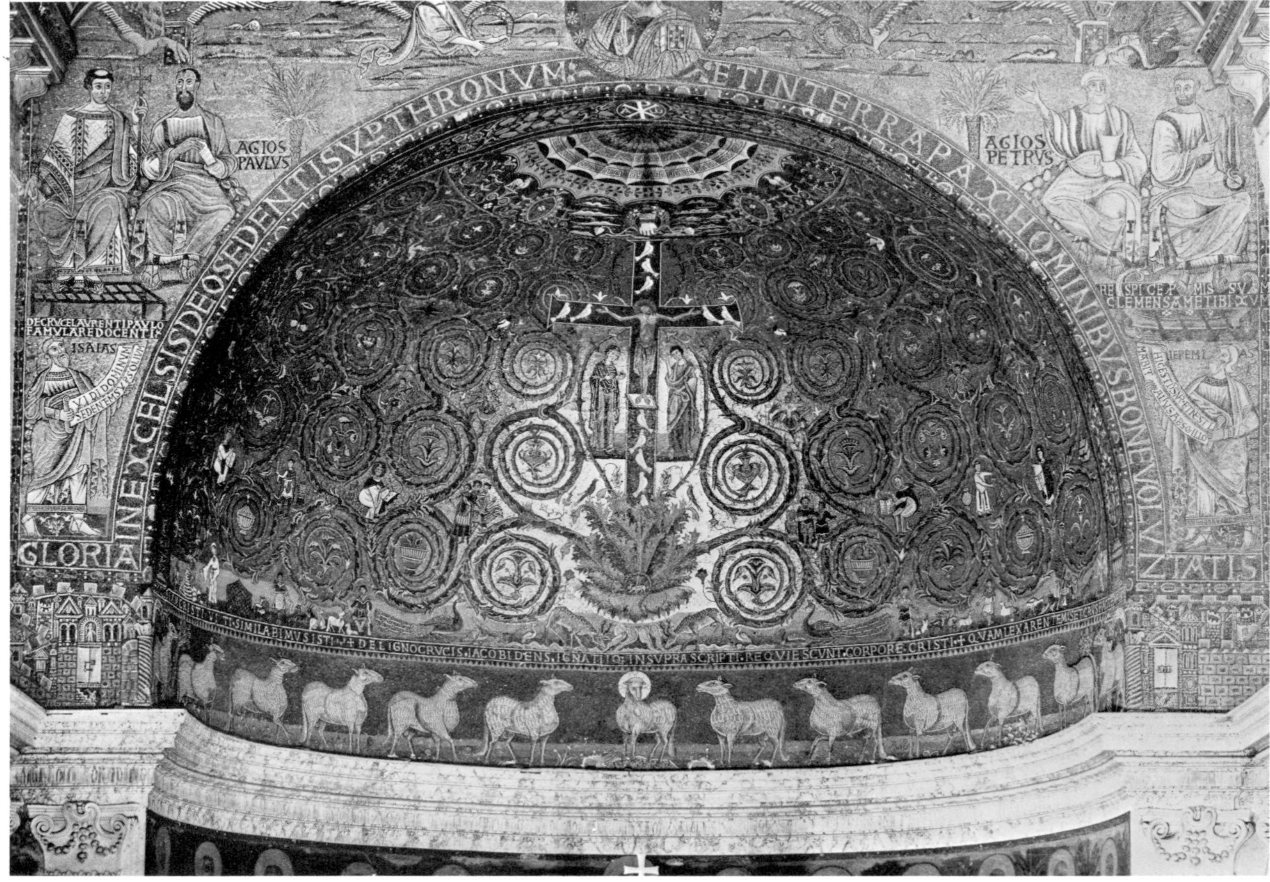

118. S. Clemente, apse mosaic

apse of the right-hand aisle was added later. Convent buildings to house the Regular Canons in charge flank the atrium and the front bays of the right-hand aisle. Built jointly with the new church, though subsequently enlarged and remodeled, they form solid blocks, two- and three-floors high, built of brick and lit by small arched windows and round oculi.

If the plan of the new church is simple, furnishings and decoration are lavish. A chancel projects from the apse, enclosing the high altar under its canopy; from the chancel a long enclosure provided with an ambo and lecterns extends as far as the nave pier to shelter the choir, the *schola cantorum*; and a papal cathedra—rather than a bishop's throne—rises in the apse. The plaques composing the enclosure, the pulpits, and parts of the cathedra were taken from the abandoned lower church, but their arrangement marks a departure in church furnishing. The pre-cosmatesque pavement—it long antedates the Cosmati clan of *marmorarii*—also presents a new and distinctive layout: a narrow carpet of roundels, worked in green serpentine and porphyry, bordered by a guilloche design along the length of the nave, links the portal to the entrance of the *schola cantorum*, the singers' precinct, and continues up to the sanctuary in the apse; it is flanked on the right and left by panels in multicolored geometric patterns. The decoration of the apse and the surmounting arch wall are equally new in style and iconography, about which more later—at this point an overall sketch must suffice (fig. 118). On the apse vault, a cross carrying the body of Christ and flanked by the Virgin and St. John grows from lush acanthus leaves, and is enveloped by vine scrolls and surmounted by the Dome of Heaven. Birds, hinds, putti, groups of people, baskets filled with fruit, scenes from a farmyard, shepherds with their sheep, a woman feeding chickens, are all scattered among and along the foot of the scrolls, details not seen in Roman church decoration ever since the fourth and fifth centuries (figs. 139, 141-44). A long inscription and a frieze of lambs mark the springing of the apse vault. On the wall on either side and above the apse arch there appear in four ascending tiers: Bethlehem and Jerusalem; Isaiah and Jeremiah, Christ's harbingers; Saints Peter, Paul, Lawrence, and Clement, the great martyrs of Rome and the patron of the church; finally, the symbols of the Evangelists, on either side of a bust of Christ Pantocrator. A sophisticated scheme has been evolved from new and old elements, and equally eclectic is its presentation in mosaic; a veritable breakthrough, it is after nearly three centuries the first example in Rome of mosaic work on a large scale. No expense was spared on the pavement, furnishings, and decoration of S. Clemente. Within the framework of the simplest architecture, innovations and traditional elements were joined to create a grand and opulent place of worship in the spirit of a new age.

The ambiance for such new departures—and new departures they are—is illuminated more sharply still a few years after S. Clemente by S. Maria in Trastevere, notwithstanding the remodeling it underwent a century ago—a superb example, if hard to swallow, of the *stile Pio Nono*. Replacing a structure of fourth- and ninth-century date, the present church may have been begun in the 1120s, possibly by its title-cardinal Pietro Pierleone, later Anaclete II—its lavishness suggests a rich patron; whether or not he was the founder, construction and decoration were completed, it seems, by his opponent, Pope Innocent II, in 1143. The size is large, one and a third that of S. Clemente, and comparable to major fifth-century basilicas, S. Sabina for instance. Equally impressive is the elaborate layout. Behind the narthex—simple, colonnaded, with Corinthian capitals, and trabeated before it was rebuilt in 1702—the nave façade rises high, topped by a projecting cornice—the latter, like similar cavettos in Rome, was probably added in the thirteenth century; the cornice is covered with medieval mosaics, and the murals of the façade proper date from the nineteenth century. A campanile towers to the right, built into the first bay of the aisle (fig. 119). Inside, the spacious volumes of nave and aisles open into a transept, originally, it seems, level with the nave (fig. 120). Two huge columns with granite shafts carry the triumphal arch at the end of the nave, framing the high altar; pairs of columns screened the aisles from the transept, as shown in a plan of fifteenth- or sixteenth-century date. The nave columns, eleven on either side, carry entablatures rather than arcades. With their bases and imposing capitals, they form an impressive medley of Roman spoils, all carefully selected and matched so as to mark the liturgical division of the nave into lay and clergy sections. The original windows were tall, narrow, and few, both in the aisles and the nave; the wide nineteenth-century windows, wall paintings, and pilasters clash with the original twelfth-century design as well as with the splendid seventeenth-century ceiling. The *opus sectile* pavement was relaid over a hundred years ago, replacing one that may have been of thirteenth-century date rather than original. Just as at S. Clemente, the apse vault carries a grand mosaic, which shows Christ en-

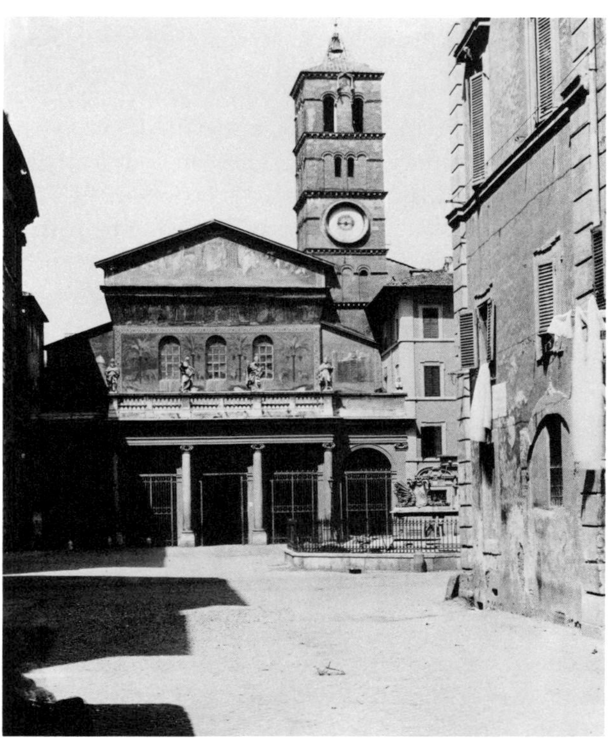

119. S. Maria in Trastevere, façade as of ca. 1900

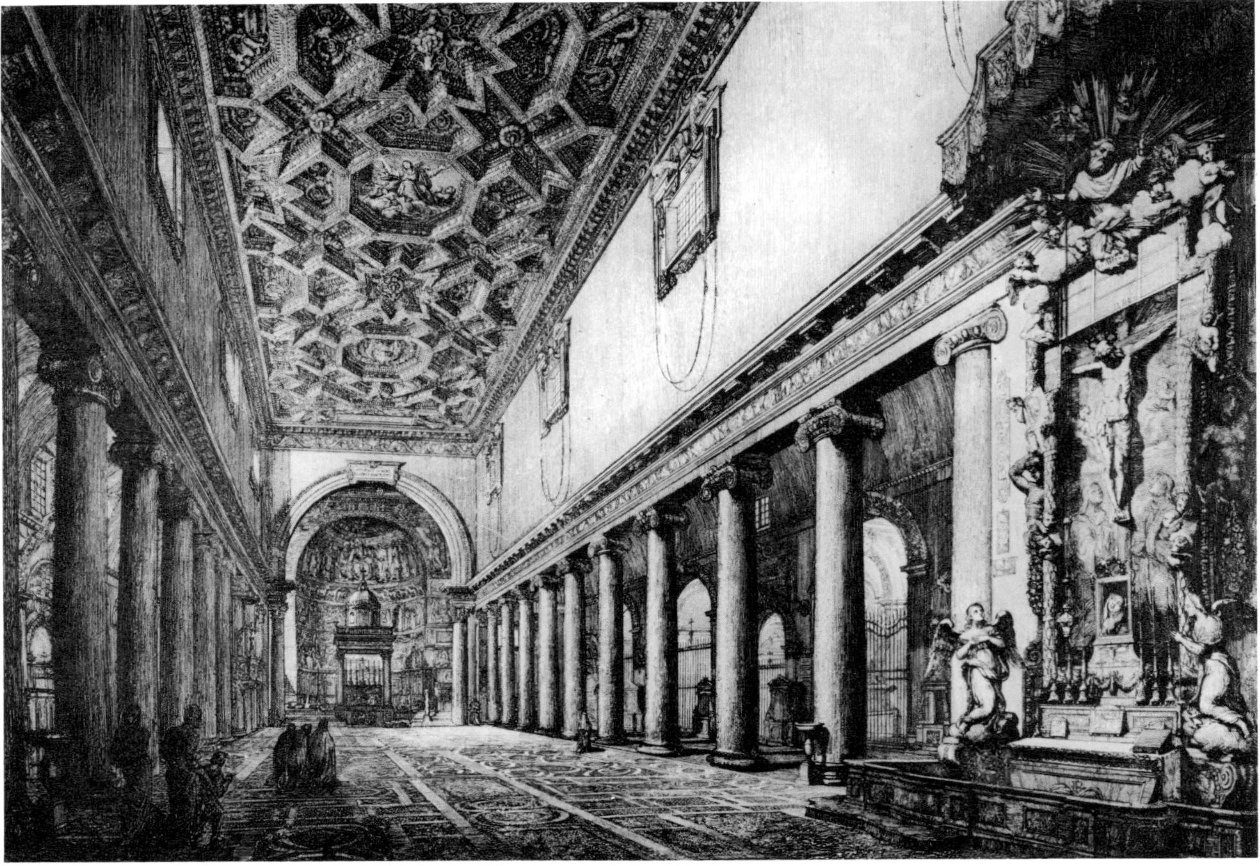

120. S. Maria in Trastevere, interior as of 1825, engraving Antonio Sarti

throned with the Virgin, both flanked by the saints associated with the church, led by Peter and followed by the donor, Innocent II (fig. 121). The theme of Christ and Mary enthroned, to be sure, is new in monumental design in Rome; but otherwise, the scene at S. Maria in Trastevere reverts to the scheme of saints and donors flanking Christ or the Virgin, traditional from Early Christian times and prevalent in Carolingian apses. At the side, the mosaic extends over onto the transept wall with the figures of Isaiah and Jeremiah forecasting the conception and sacrifice of Christ. Cavallini's mosaic panels on the apse wall, a century and a half later, completed the decoration of the chancel. Outside, the wall of the apse shows a design as impressive as, and perhaps more innovative than, the interior decoration. Nine blind arcades steeply articulate the wall carried by broad shallow pilasters; the arches spring from unadorned impost blocks marked by upper and lower stringcourses; three of the arcades shelter windows, later lowered to conform with the mosaics; halfway up the apse, a thin marble stringcourse, finely profiled, runs across the pilasters and intervals; marble brackets cut from a classical Roman cornice are interlaced with a brick cornice along the eaves-line. It is a design new and unique in Rome and without parallel elsewhere.

Finally, close to and nearly contemporary with S. Clemente, there is the church of the Quattro Coronati. The huge Carolingian basilica was burned down in 1084 by the Normans, and a first attempt at rebuilding it in its former size, made apparently by Pascal II in 1099 or shortly after, failed; it seems neither the funds nor the long beams needed to span the huge nave were available. Instead, a much smaller church was completed by 1116: nave, aisles, and

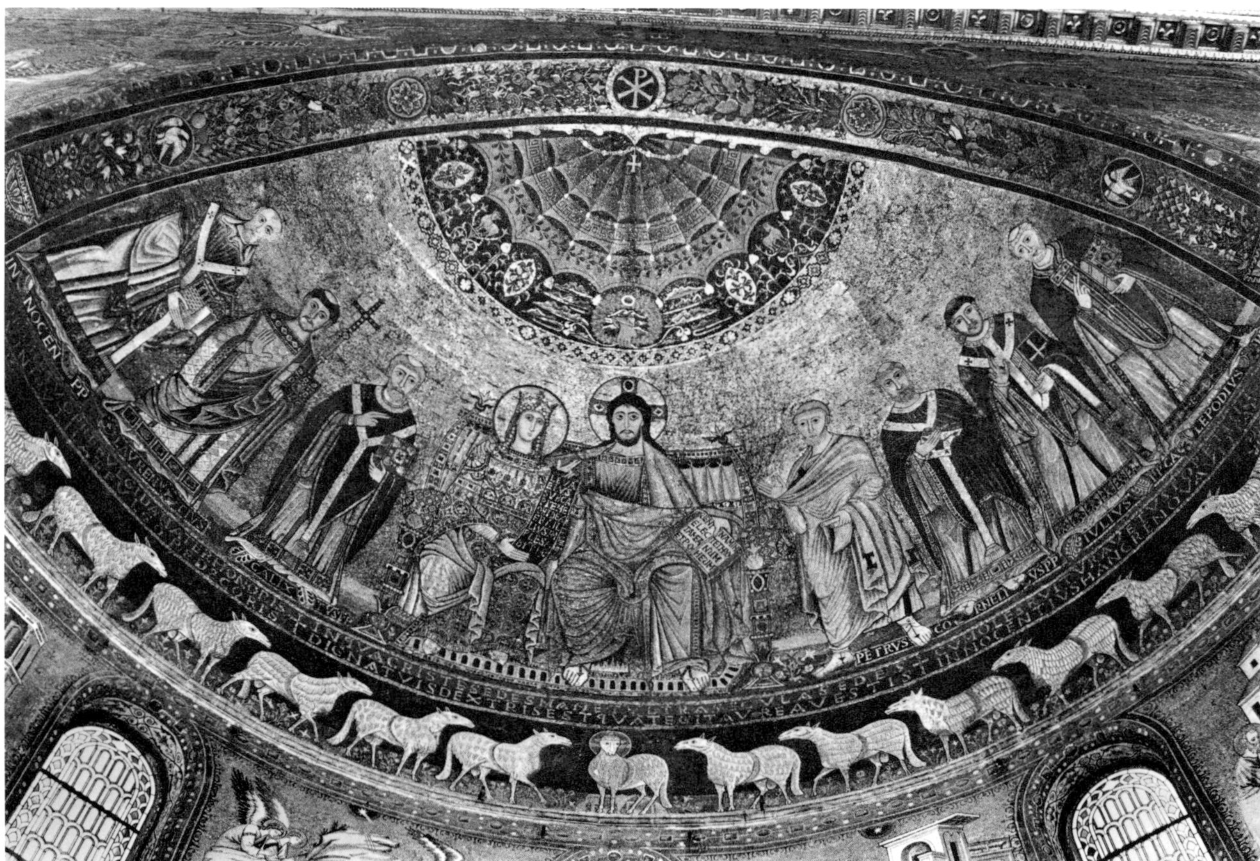

121. S. Maria in Trastevere, apse mosaic

transept were all inserted into the rear of the previous nave (fig. 122). Columns with Corinthian capitals, all spoils, carry the nave arcades on either side; above their five arches, two triple dwarf arcades, separated by a pier, open into a gallery that was probably not accessible originally. Rather, it appears to have been a sham gallery, designed to carry on its high wall a roof across the combined width of nave and aisles. A pre-cosmatesque pavement much like that of S. Clemente covers the floor of the nave and transept. On the left flank, contemporary with the church of 1116 and built in the same brick masonry, a new convent was laid out, perhaps replacing an earlier one; its long wing facing west was lit by small oculi like those seen in the church and convent buildings of S. Clemente (fig. 123). The cloister within the Quattro Coronati convent shows narrow arcades, grouped in eights on the long sides, in sixes on the short sides, and separated by piers set with finely fluted pairs of pilasters; the arches resting on paired, slender colonnettes with simple foliage capitals are surmounted by a double saw-tooth frieze and a row of brackets, the interstices filled with colorful cosmatesque mosaic (fig. 131). It seems to be one of the earliest cloisters surviving in Rome, maybe the first built in the city; earlier convents installed in older buildings close to the church offered no space for this feature, well-known by the eighth and ninth centuries elsewhere. Later, in the twelfth and thirteenth centuries, more convent buildings were erected at the Quattro Coronati along the opposite flank of the church and its forecourt, inserted into the site once taken up by the right-hand aisle of the large older basilica and of other ninth-century structures attached. The Chapel of St. Sylvester, dedicated in 1246, with its rich frescoes, stands foremost among these

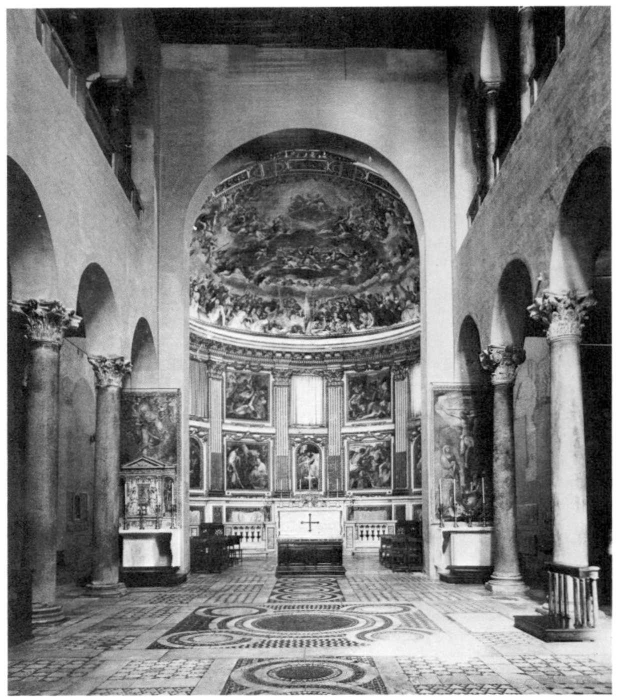

122. SS. Quattro Coronati, interior

additions. Twelfth- and thirteenth-century structures tower high on the cliff commanding the narrow road ascending to the Lateran.

In spite of their differences in planning and design, S. Clemente, S. Maria in Trastevere, and the Quattro Coronati stand apart from run-of-the-mill church building in the city as it seems to have prevailed from the late ninth century through to the twelfth. Once the wave of Carolingian architecture and decoration had ended around 850, church building in Rome seems to have nearly stopped. Chapels were ensconced in ancient ruins, such as the oratory of S. Agnese in Piazza Navona before 800, which is still accessible below the splendid Baroque church, though barbarously restored. Another, after 900, was S. Barbara dei Librai in a vault of the Theatre of Pompey. Temples were Christianized and decorated with cycles of murals—

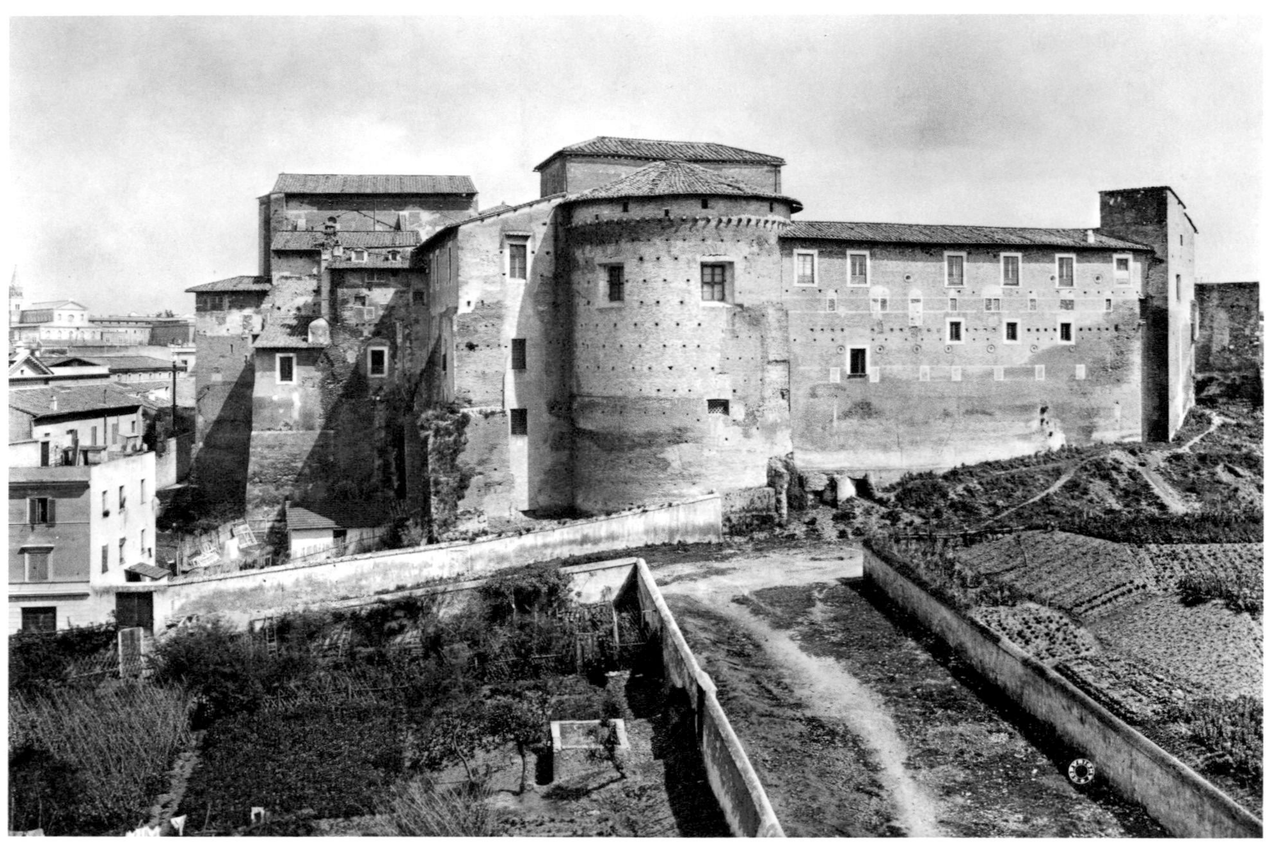

123. SS. Quattro Coronati, church and convent, as of ca. 1880

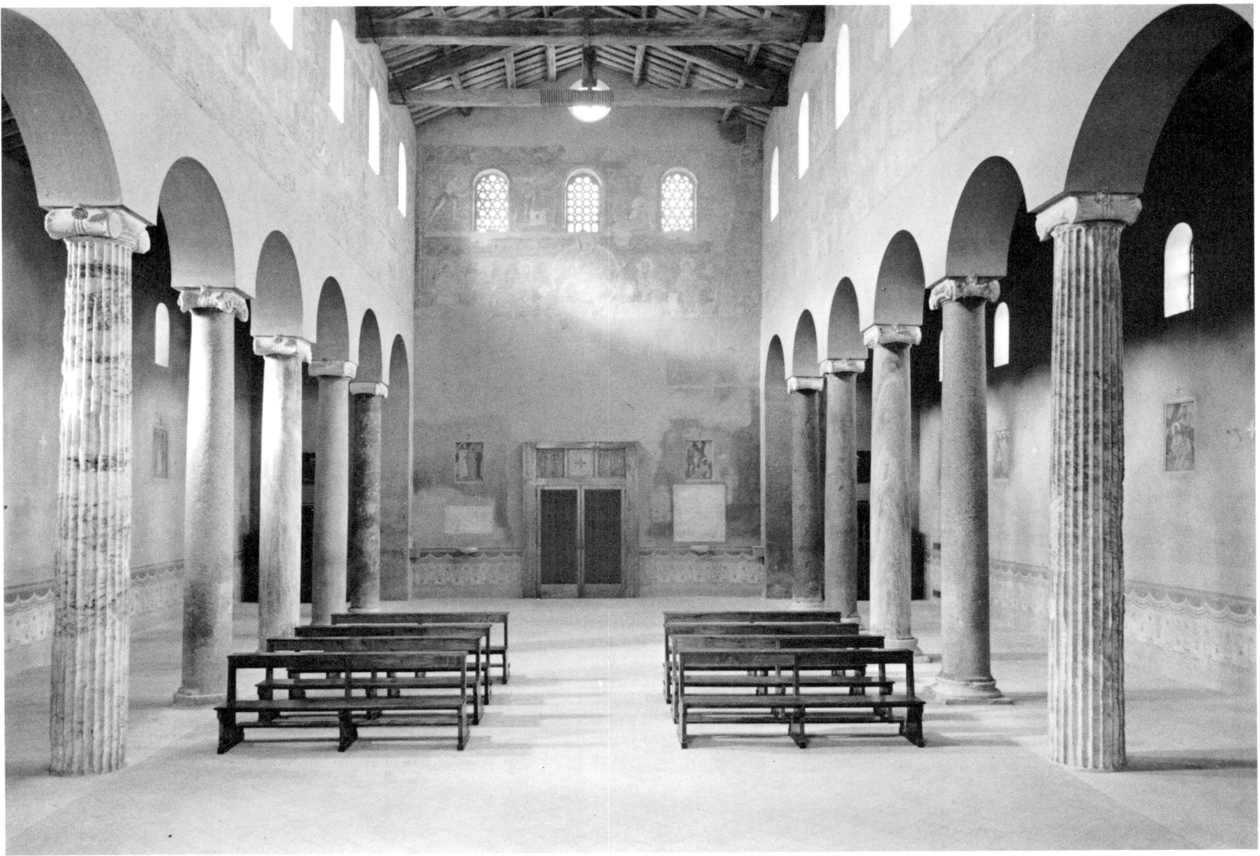

124. S. Giovanni a Porta Latina, interior

the Temple of Fortuna Virilis consecrated as S. Maria ad Gradellis, later S. Maria Egiziaca, between 872 and 882. Tiny single-naved apsed chapels were newly built: they were often attractive, like S. Maria in Pallara on the Palatine, now S. Sebastiano alla Polveriera, founded by the physician Petrus and covered with murals around 970; and, near the south end of Trastevere, S. Maria in Cappella, built in 1090—the date on its bell—or shortly before, and disproportionately enlarged some eighty years ago. Many may have been private foundations, serviced by a "house chaplain" for the benefit of a family—S. Barbara dei Librai, for instance; or they were handed over, like S. Maria in Pallara, to a monastic community.

Starting with the last third of the eleventh century, though, a veritable spate of churches sprang up *ex novo*. The majority were in the abitato, from the Corso to the Tiber bend, and were parish churches, the large ones serviced by congregations of canons or sizable monastic communities, the small ones by two priests or just one. The prevailing type was a smallish basilica, with a nave, two aisles, and an apse, timber-roofed except for the latter; it became standard for a century or more. Four to seven columns on either side carried arcades surmounted by the clerestory walls. Depending on the number of supports, the overall plan varied from a near square to a two-by-three rectangle and the height was comfortably low. Windows were small, keeping the nave and aisles poorly lit. Sto. Stefano del Cacco near the Piazza del Collegio Romano or S. Salvatore in Onda, both built around 1100, would be perfect examples, were it not for the thorough rebuildings they underwent, one in the seventeenth, the other in the nineteenth century. As things stand, S. Giovanni a Porta Latina represents the type best, notwithstanding its location far out near the Aurelian Walls, its function as a convent church, its

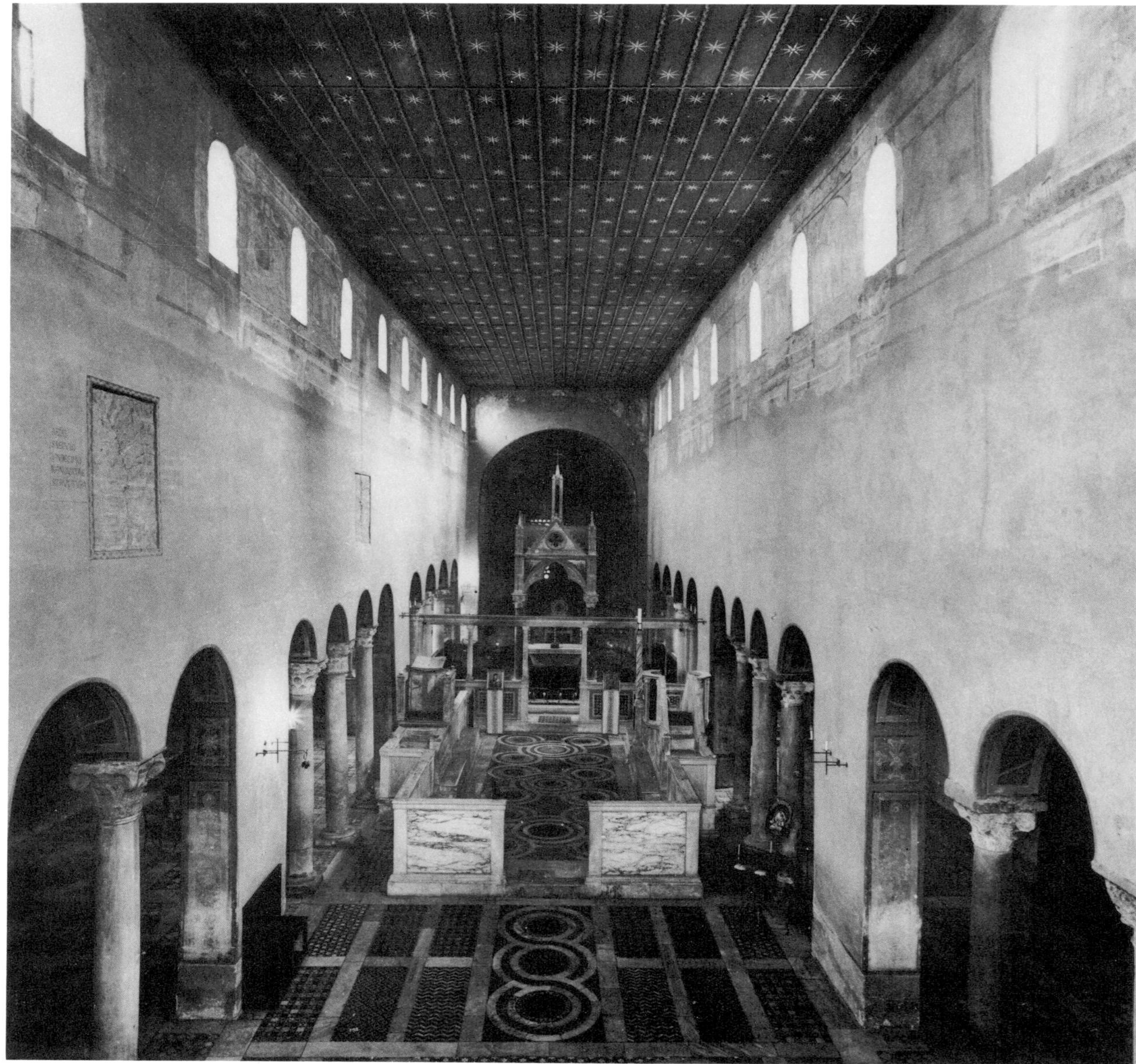

125. S. Maria in Cosmedin, interior

late date of consecration (1191), and the incorporation of a sixth-century forechoir, apse, and side rooms (fig. 124). Five columns flank the nave on either side; shafts of different lengths and materials, bases, and plinths are spoils; of the capitals, all Ionic, some are spoils, others twelfth-century work. The nave walls are covered with murals, the windows are small; part of the original cosmatesque *opus sectile* pavement remains near the high altar. An arcaded narthex extends along the façade; a campanile rises within it. Such modest churches, whether early or late, provide a striking foil for basilicas like S. Maria in Trastevere and its early-twelfth-century contemporaries, all monumental in plan, size, and richness of decoration and furnishing.

The new churches set new standards. Like S. Maria in Trastevere and almost identical in size, S. Crisogono, built between 1123 and 1130, has a nave and two aisles separated by eleven ancient columns carrying an entablature, a deep transept

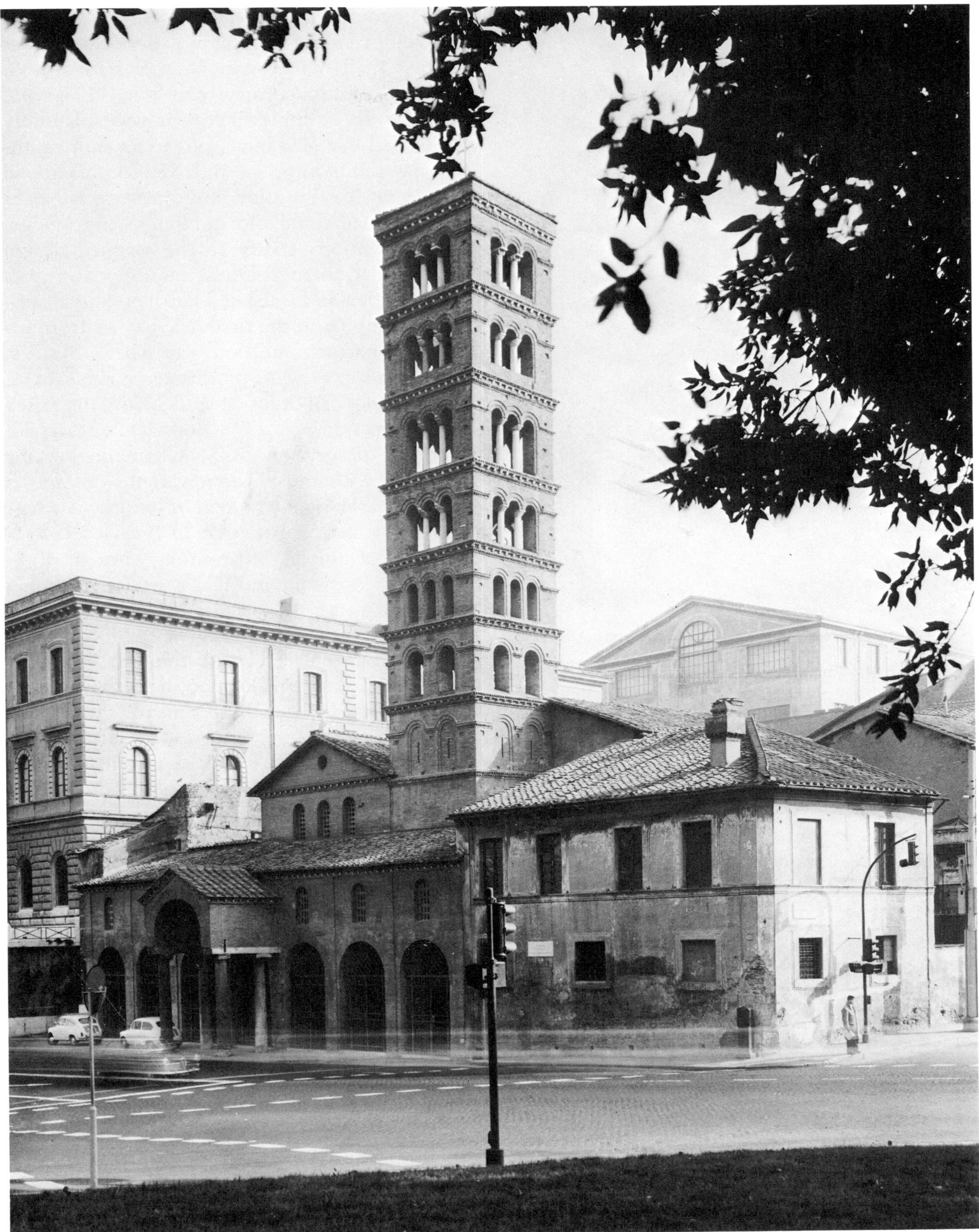

126. S. Maria in Cosmedin, exterior

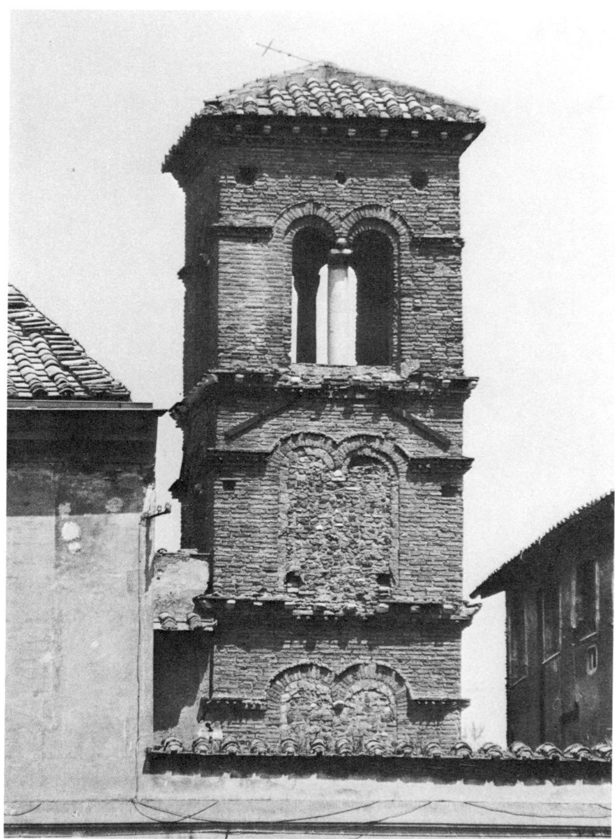

127. S. Rufina, campanile

framed in the center by a triumphal arch supported by columns, and an apse. The original decoration has vanished, but the overall splendor is the same, witness the spacious nave and the precious columns, including porphyry ones supporting the triumphal arch, and the rich *opus sectile* pavement, many times restored. S. Bartolomeo in Isola, though laid out on much the same plan as S. Crisogono and S. Maria in Trastevere, contains variations on the standard type. Built perhaps as early as 1113 or as late as 1160, it is but half the size of the two Trastevere churches; its nave columns carry arches; and below the transept, raised as it is five steps, extended a hall crypt, its vaults resting on columns. At S. Maria Nova (now S. Francesca Romana) on the Forum, the ninth-century church was modernized and enlarged before 1161 by adding a transept, apse, mosaic and campanile; two more remodelings in the seventeenth century have overlaid but not obliterated these medieval features. In another variant, a plan with transept and sham galleries like those of the Quattro Coronati became standard. S. Croce in Gerusalemme, rebuilt in 1144-1145, provided an example, before it was splendidly remodeled in 1743; and, prior to its eighteenth-century rebuilding, so did SS. Bonifacio ed Alessio on the Aventine, built perhaps as late as 1217. Remains and old drawings, engravings, and descriptions testify to the original design with arcaded sham galleries, a transept and apse, a colonnaded and trabeated narthex, and a campanile rising from the first aisle bay or from inside the narthex, at both churches. Besides, fragments of a cycle of murals survive at S. Croce, and a hall crypt extends below the raised level of the transept at SS. Bonifacio ed Alessio. Plan and decoration of S. Clemente became standard, with and without variants. Alfano, a papal camerlengo and a man of wealth, whether layman or cleric, around 1123 financed the rebuilding of the eighth-century church of S. Maria in Cosmedin and had it provided with a campanile, murals, a cosmatesque pavement, and furnishings (figs. 125, 126). The last included an altar canopy, replaced late in the thirteenth century by a Gothic baldacchino; preceding the altar, a colonnaded screen; screens for the chancel and *schola cantorum*; pulpits and lecterns; and a bishop's throne. Over-restored around 1900 and deprived of a ravishing eighteenth-century façade, the church has become the best-known medieval tourist attraction in Rome. In the nave, two longish piers break the colonnade into three groups of four arcades each and mark the liturgical sections of laity, *schola cantorum*, and chancel. The pavement, much as at S. Clemente, forms a pathway from door to altar, broken by a huge roundel, a *rota*, enveloped by guilloches. A narthex and foreporch, both rebuilt in the early part of this century on the original lines, preceded nave and aisles, and a campanile, built into the first bay of the aisle, towers to the right. In yet another important variant on the plan, diaphragm arches were thrown across nave and aisles, rising from pilasters attached to the longitudinal piers, as seen both in the abortive first remodeling on a large scale planned at the Quattro Coronati shortly after 1099, and in the re-

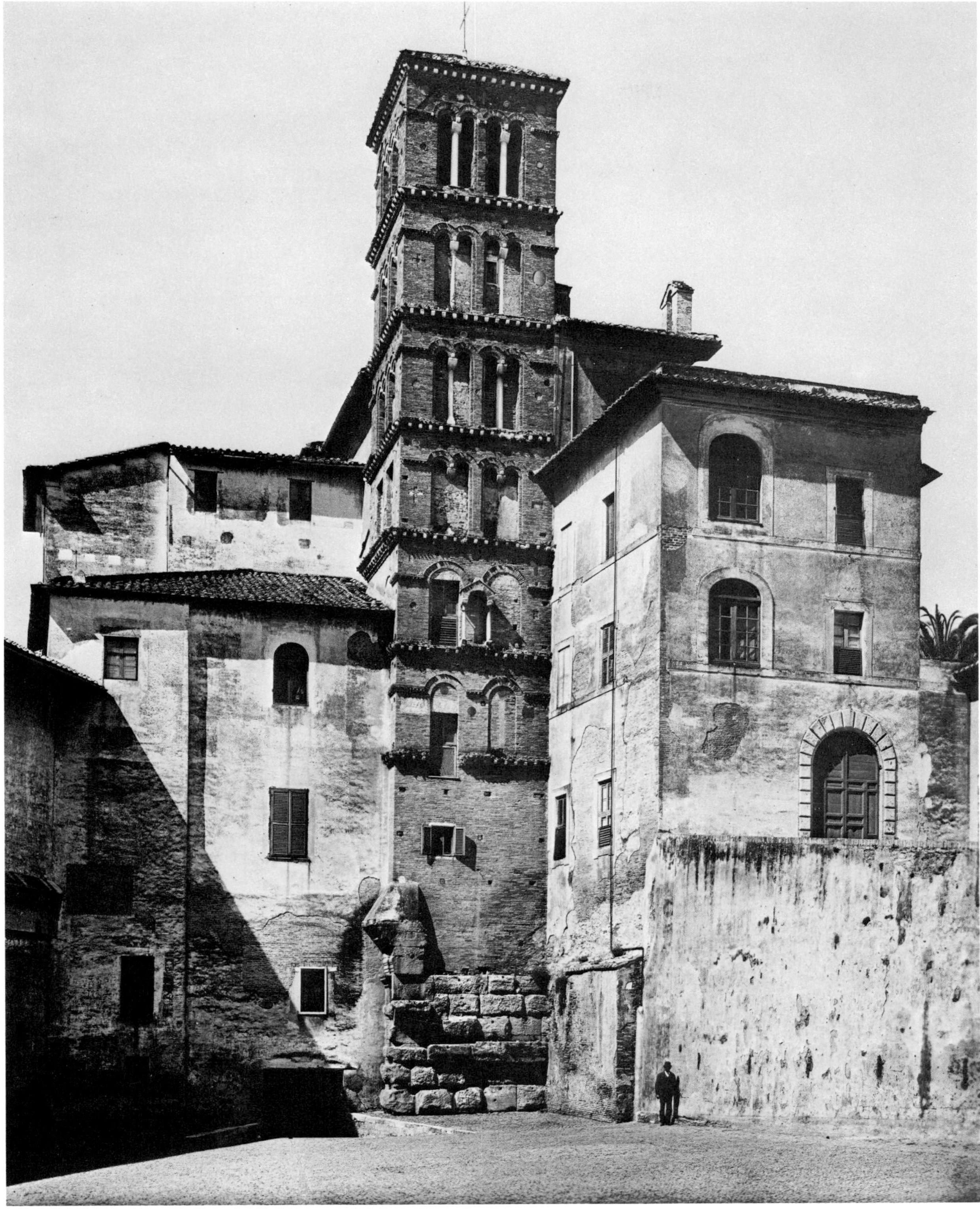

128. SS. Giovanni e Paolo, campanile, before restoration

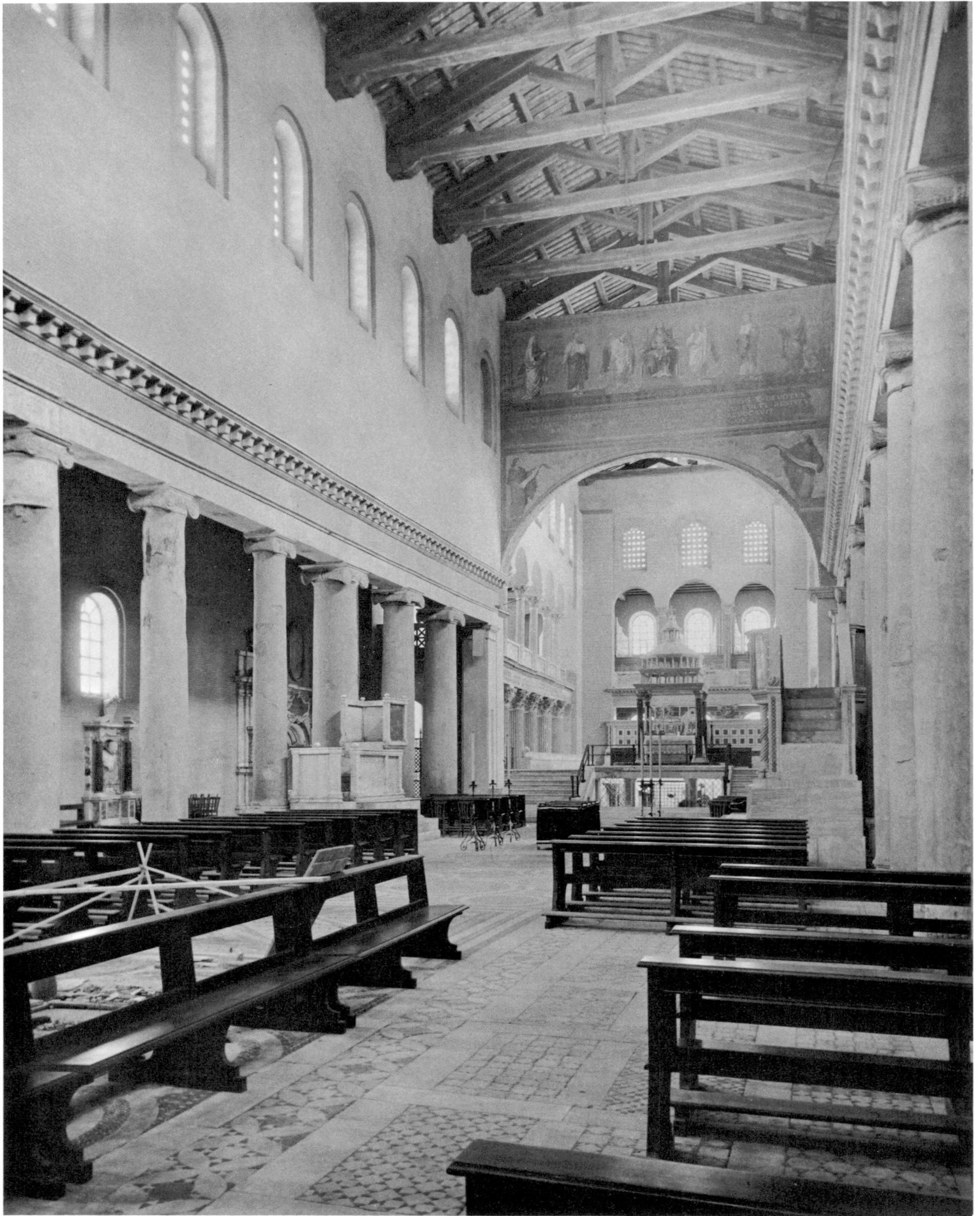

129. S. Lorenzo fuori le mura, nave, ca. 1200

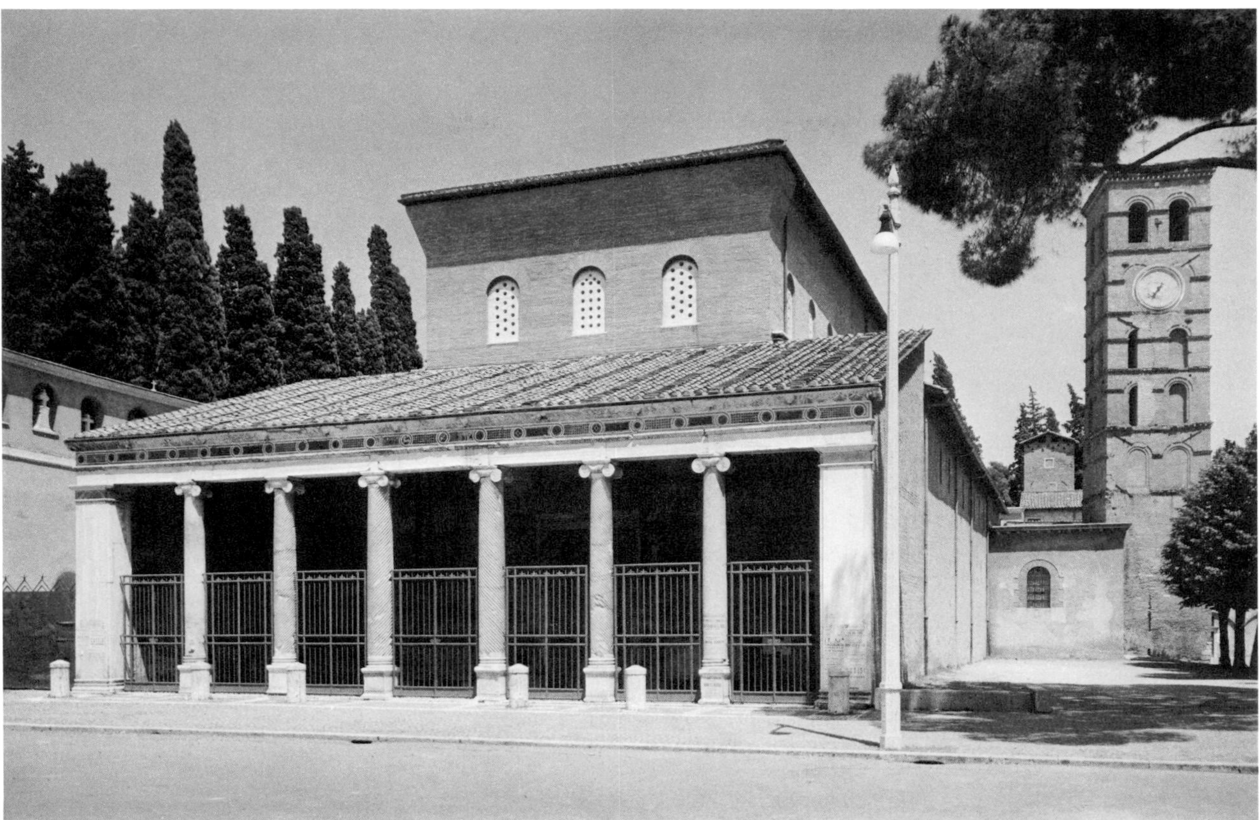

130. S. Lorenzo fuori le mura, façade and narthex

building campaign, presumably of 1116, at SS. Giovanni e Paolo; again they serve to mark liturgical divisions. Elsewhere, the basic modest basilical standard plan was modified, as at S. Gregorio Magno and S. Saba, where lateral apses terminate the aisles and thus flank the main apse. Again, isolated features inherent in the standard type were added to older structures by twelfth-century patrons and builders: nartheces with trabeated colonnades and Ionic capitals were set up at S. Lorenzo in Lucina in 1130, at SS. Giovanni e Paolo in 1154, at S. Maria Maggiore in 1145-1153, and at S. Giorgio in Velabro early in the thirteenth century, to pick four at random. Gabled porches on columns, like those at S. Clemente, were joined to an atrium or narthex at S. Prassede, S. Maria in Cosmedin, and S. Cosimato; hall crypts were built at S. Bartolomeo in Isola and SS. Bonifacio ed Alessio; and, from the late eleventh century through the thirteenth century and beyond, campanili were built together with new or older churches all over the city: huge ones, like that of S. Maria in Cosmedin, and tiny *campaniletti*, such as that of S. Rufina in Trastevere (fig. 127). They stood sometimes alongside the church—though there was hardly ever room; rarely opposite, as at SS. Giovanni e Paolo (fig. 128); atop a transept wing, as at S. Prassede; most frequently inserted into an aisle, in the first or last bay, as at S. Sabina, S. Pudenziana, S. Maria Nova and, even in the fourteenth century, at S. Maria Maggiore.

Dates are often difficult to gauge, as documentary evidence is not always reliable. Consecration often took place long after construction had terminated: S. Maria in Trastevere, completed together with its decoration by 1143, was not consecrated until 1215. Stylistic evidence only rarely provides a chronological clue. The plan and design of churches and the style of their decoration changed little through the following hundred years. At S. Lorenzo fuori le mura, a

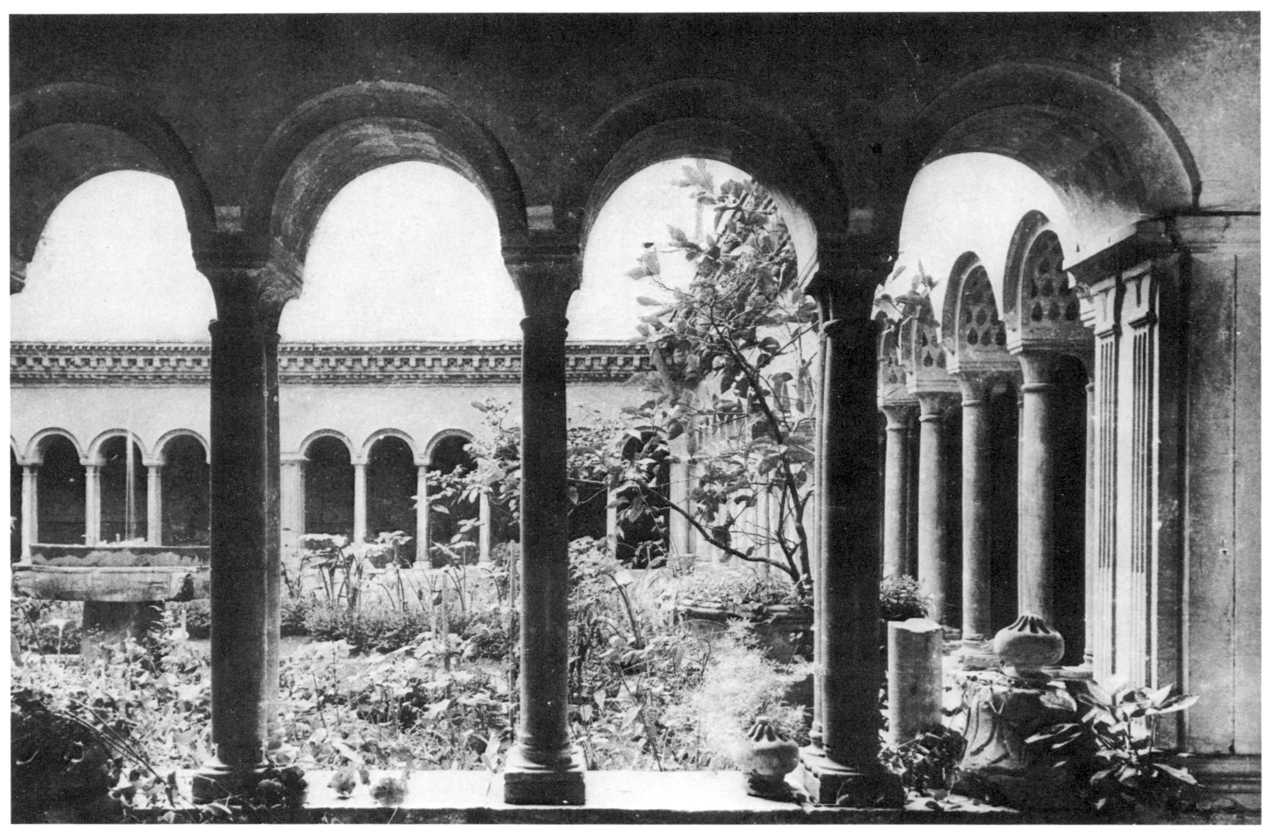

131. SS. Quattro Coronati, cloister

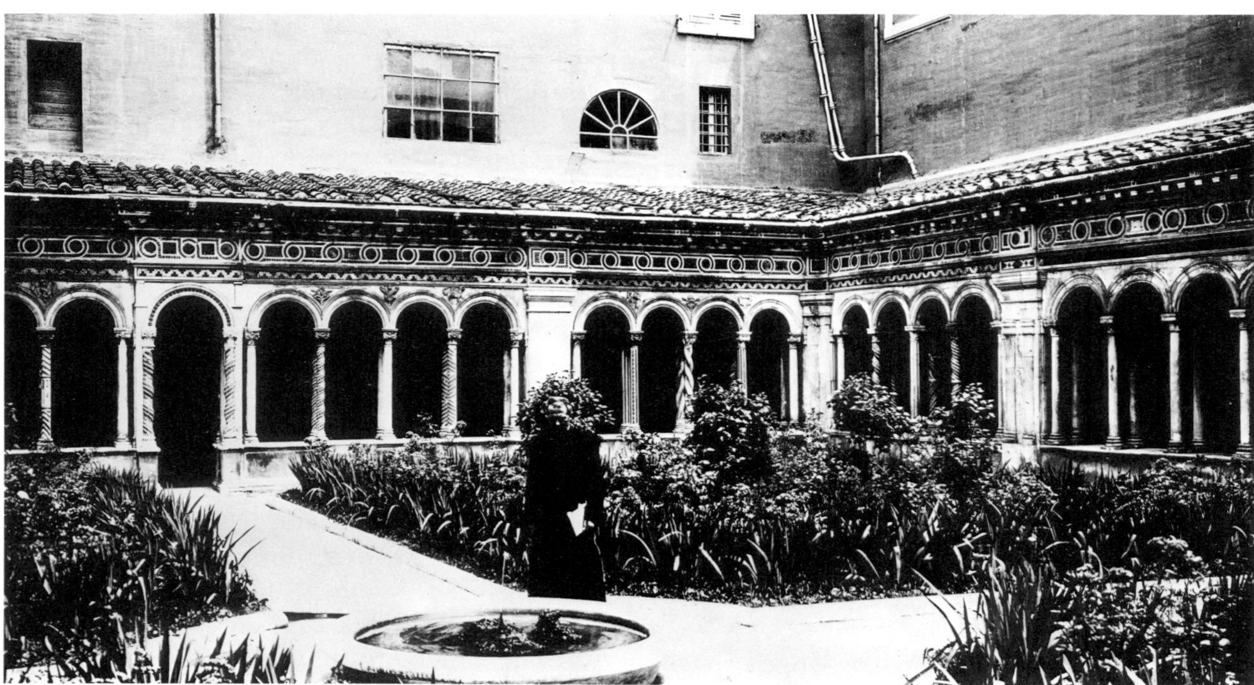

132. S. Paolo fuori le mura, cloister

large basilica was laid out at the end of the twelfth century by Cencius Camerarius, cardinal chancellor and later Pope Honorius III, and completed in the first quarter of the thirteenth. The sixth-century basilica with galleries, built by Pope Pelagius, was deprived of its apse and turned into the chancel of the new church, its ground floor half buried except for a small crypt, the new level raised nine steps over the new nave. The tomb of Saint Lawrence inside the crypt was restored and redecorated. The new nave (fig. 129), flanked by aisles of steep proportion, is supported by long rows of eleven columns on each side, carrying a trabeation. Windows are small, both in the nave and in the aisles. Columns and the trabeation seem to be spoils, evidently taken from the fourth-century cemetery, long in decay, which rose south of the church. After more than two generations, the type of S. Crisogono and S. Maria in Trastevere is here taken up again, albeit without a transept. A narthex, also trabeated, its frieze decorated with mosaic, precedes the new nave (fig. 130). It dates as late as after 1217; but it still much resembled that of S. Maria in Trastevere, which was nearly a century older. The Ionic capitals of both the narthex and the nave, except for a number of spoils, are of extraordinarily fine medieval carving. The canopy over the high altar, commissioned in 1148 by Hugo "*humilis abbas*" for the basilica of Pelagius, was apparently transferred to the new chancel, while the liturgical furniture with rich, colorful mosaic inlay—the clergy bench, the bishop's throne and ambo—date from 1254. As late as 1260, S. Maria in Aracoeli high on the Capitoline Hill retains the basilical plan and design that had again come to prominence in Rome early in the twelfth century: an arcaded nave of wide proportions, a continuous transept, originally a single apse, an open timber roof, a cosmatesque pavement. Only the vocabulary had absorbed a few Gothic elements. Apparently from the middle of the twelfth century on, continuous transepts as high as the nave seem to have been accepted as a standard element of any respectable basilica. In fact, the great Early Christian churches lacking them had regular transepts added: at St. Peter's in 1154, the low transept wings of Constantinian date were raised to nave height; at S. Croce in Gerusalemme in 1144, a transept was carved out by subdividing the old undivided hall; at S. Maria Maggiore, a regular transept, though narrow, was joined to the old nave and aisles; and at the Lateran in 1291, a continuous transept replaced the Constantinian low side chambers.

Church decoration, like church planning, in general seems to have been equally standardized far into the thirteenth century. In apse mosaics, the age-old scheme of the Savior or the Virgin flanked by saints and donors, once reestablished around 1140 at S. Maria in Trastevere, was retained for another hundred years with only slight variations in composition: at S. Maria Nova around 1161; at St. Peter's about 1210; at S. Paolo fuori le mura ca. 1218-1227. To be sure, the style of the figures and heads in thirteenth-century mosaics changed under the impact of foreign artists called to Rome from Norman Sicily at St. Peter's, and from Venice at S. Paolo. The real breakthrough to a new style occurs only two generations later, in the last third of the thirteenth century.

Standardized as they are, church planning and design, including major figural schemes in apse mosaics or murals, show few if any signs of change in Rome through the High Middle Ages. Only specific features—building techniques, liturgical furnishings, the design of pavements or cloisters, often dated—provide clues for tracing a development. Some changes are obvious: the *opus sectile* decoration of church screens, pulpits, bishops' thrones, and paschal candlesticks, simple and large-scale to start with, in the late twelfth and early thirteenth centuries grew more detailed and fussy; by the mid-thirteenth century, the porphyry and green and white marble began to give way to glass mosaic of gaudy red, blue, and gold in minute patterns. The furniture at S. Maria in Cosmedin (1123) provides an early example; the chancel screen at S. Saba from about 1235, and the cathedra and clergy bench at S. Lorenzo fuori le mura of 1254, exemplify the later phase. Equally clear in its general lines is the sequence of cloisters, from that of the Quattro Coronati (fig. 131) in 1116 or shortly after, to that at S. Lorenzo fuori le mura of 1187-1191, and finally to the elaborate ones at

S. Paolo fuori le mura (fig. 132) from after 1193 to after 1228, and at S. Giovanni in Laterano, 1220-1232. The grouping of arcades, the supporting pairs of colonnettes, the profiles of the arches, the terminating cornices, all plain and neat to start with grew ever more elaborate. In the later cloisters the colonnettes are twisted and inlaid with mosaic; cornices are carved with rich foliage and masks, lion heads, and palmettes; friezes appear with geometrical patterns of marble inlay: all part of a vocabulary whose changes should help to assign undated cloisters at S. Cecilia, S. Cosimato, and S. Sabina their appropriate place. But no serious study has been undertaken so far. Nor have the precise nature and possible development of building techniques used in Rome during the High Middle Ages been explored enough to assign undated or insecurely dated buildings to a particular time on the basis of a stylistic or archaeological analysis.

Nevertheless, this does not change the mainstream of the argument. Church building and decoration in Rome from the early twelfth century into the thirteenth presents a remarkably uniform picture. Marked by a number of constant features, it is somewhat monotonous. Certainly it is unexciting when viewed in the context of the great Romanesque churches that in these same years, and often one or two generations before, rose in Normandy, England, and Burgundy, along the pilgrimage roads of southwestern France, in the Rhineland, in Lombardy, and in Tuscany: St. Etienne in Caën (1064); the third abbey church at Cluny (1085); St. Martin at Tours (997-1050); St. Sernin at Toulouse (1096); the cathedral of Speyer, as first built between 1030 and 1061, and as remodeled after 1080; S. Ambrogio in Milan, rebuilt as at present, after 1090; Durham cathedral and its rib-vaulted chancel (1093-1104); and the Early Gothic façade and chevet of St. Denis, built in the same years as S. Maria in Trastevere. The great majority of these churches in France, Germany, and England are vaulted; but even when timber-roofed, the nave, aisles, transept, crossing, and bays are clearly set off against each other; the supports are articulated, the walls accentuated both vertically and horizontally by stringcourses, blind arcades, and pilaster strips, half-columns, or shafts. Throughout, clear articulation of volumes, masses, and surfaces prevails inside and out, combined with the compact design of steep interior spaces. In Rome, such features are merely marginal. Proportions, unless conditioned by preexisting elements—old foundations or rising walls reused—are comfortably wide. Space flows easily—diaphragm arches, rare at that, lack the organizing function of those found as early as 1060 at S. Miniato in Florence. Walls, unarticulated by horizontal or vertical membering, are given over to mural painting, as was customary ever since the fifth century; the supports are columns, rather than multiform, compound piers; shafts, bases, and frequently capitals are spoils. Only rarely was a purloined feature from the Romanesque vocabulary incorporated in the fabric of a Roman church: the Lombard or Rhenish dwarf gallery placed atop the Early Christian apse of SS. Giovanni e Paolo remains forever an alien body (fig. 133). In short, in the Middle Ages, Roman church planning remains notably isolated from the great movements that from the early part of the eleventh century reshaped architectural thinking from the Atlantic to the Elbe and from Lund and Durham to Florence and Compostella. It is insular and uninventive, and it seems conservative and retardataire when compared with the developments north of the Alps. With but minor variations it uses the same standard types; time and again it harks back to the same models. Still, to brush aside Roman medieval church building and its decoration as monotonous, conservative, and of indifferent quality seems too simple a way out.

Granted, no lengthy discussion is needed to show that all or nearly all the twelfth-century standard plans in Rome go back to Early Christian local prototypes. Transept basilicas, such as S. Maria in Trastevere and S. Crisogono, call to mind first and most obviously St. Peter's, ideally the focal point through the Middle Ages of any revival of Early Christian or, in particular, Constantinian church building. However, a major feature of St. Peter's, the narrow, low transept and its exedrae, experimental as it was, as early as the late fourth century had given way at S. Paolo to a high, continuous transept, its

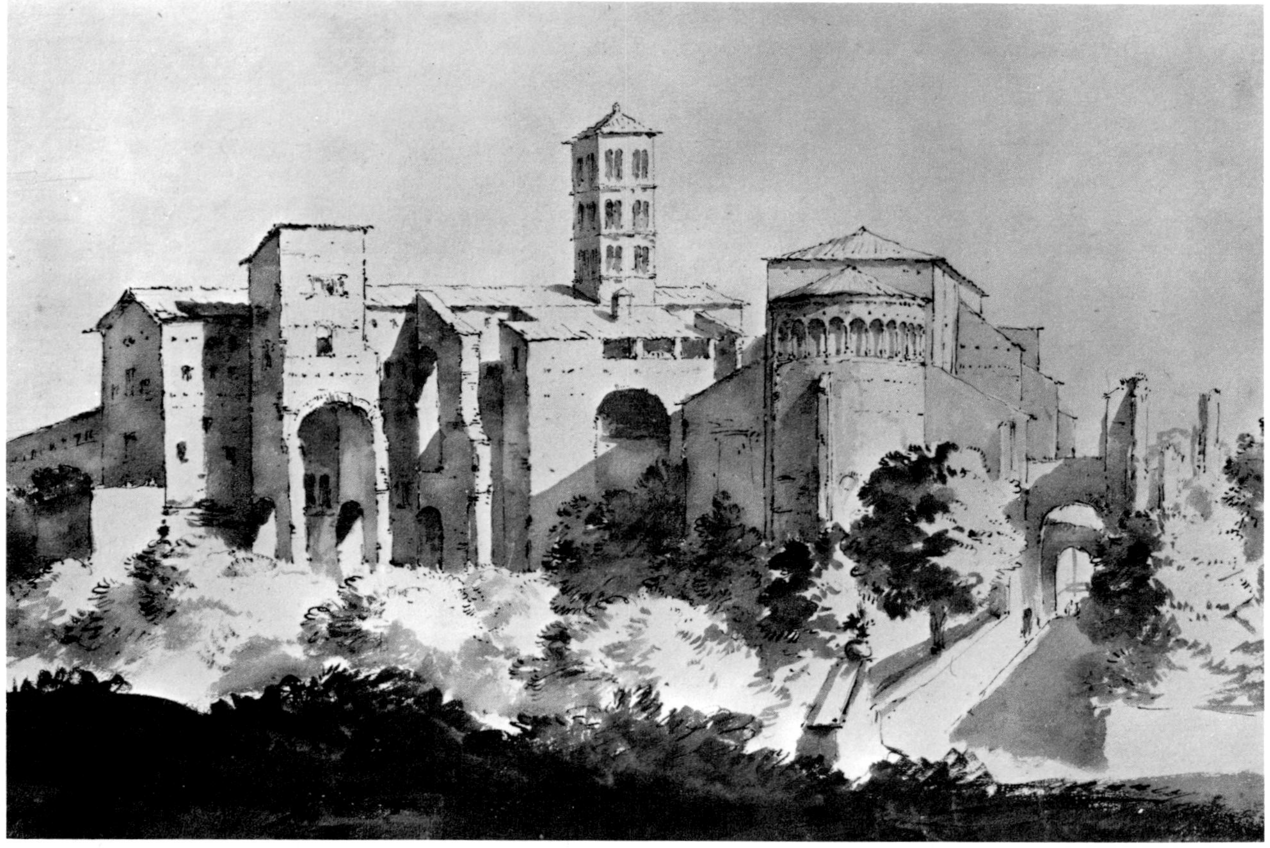

133. SS. Giovanni e Paolo, rear, as of 1654/5, drawing Jan de Bisschop, Albertina, Vienna

end walls in line with the aisles. In that form the transept was taken up in Carolingian times, though not consistently; in the twelfth century it became the rule. It seems as if medieval church planners had accepted as a norm the S. Paolo type and had conceptually superimposed it on the uncanonical plan of St. Peter's, the basilica that nonetheless ideally remained the archetype of all medieval church building in Rome. On the other hand, reduced to the smallest scale, a plan like that of S. Sabina or the Lateran Basilica, which had no transept prior to 1291, would seem to underlie the modest standard basilicas of the twelfth century, such as S. Salvatore in Onda; while churches with sham galleries, like that of the Quattro Coronati as rebuilt in 1116, may well have drawn on Early Christian basilicas with galleries, such as the east basilica, now the chancel, of S. Lorenzo fuori le mura, or S. Agnese. Surely, medieval church planners and patrons in Rome from the eleventh century on looked back to the monuments of centuries past. Rome was weighed down by her history; and the weight she carried kept her out of Europe. She remained very much aware and was daily reminded of her great Christian tradition and her place at the head of the Christian world, the only world conceivable to the Middle Ages. She was conscious of being the seat of the papacy, founded on Saint Peter; of sheltering the graves of the Princes of the Apostles and the relics of very many martyrs; of being the magical center that attracted pilgrims from all over the West. All this grandeur was present in her great Christian monuments. The Lateran Basilica sheltering the papal see, Old St. Peter's, and S. Paolo, all built or believed to have been built by Constantine, were permanent and very active reminders. They had been revived once before in Carolingian times. They and their Carolingian descendants were bound to determine church plans and decoration in Rome simply through their overwhelming presence and their inherent connotations. The new-fangled concepts, evolved north of the Alps, had no place in a city with her past.

Still, the revival of Early Christian models in twelfth-century church planning and decoration did not make its first appearance in Rome until shortly after 1100. Half a century before, Abbot Desiderius had built and adorned a new abbey church at Monte Cassino. It has long since gone, but a fairly clear picture is gained from excavations, old plans, a detailed description written in 1071 at the time of consecration by Leo of Ostia, and from the numerous filiations spreading during the late eleventh century all over South and Central Italy, from Salerno to Bari and Trani, and as far as Castel S. Elia near Nepi north of Rome: a nave, supported by colonnaded arcades, two aisles, the transept raised, the triumphal arch resting on columns; an atrium enclosed by arcaded porticoes and with two towers in front; a freestanding campanile, left of the nave façade (fig. 134). A pre-cosmatesque pavement covered the floor of the nave—multicolored discs surrounded by guilloches along the axis, though not a neat pathway to the chancel, and flanked by geometric panel designs; murals on the walls, mosaics on the triumphal arch, the apse, and the arch above. The mosaics, as brought out by Ernst Kitzinger, are most likely reflected in the mosaic fragments surviving at Salerno—the symbols of the Evangelists flanking the bust of Christ, the *veronica*. A *schola cantorum* extended far into the nave, enclosed by multicolored and white marble plaques; a chancel in the transept was surrounded by bronze screens set with silver-plated columns in front of the altar; an Easter candlestick of marble rose near the pulpit, which, strangely enough, was merely of gilded wood. In the major filiations of Monte Cassino, a hall crypt extends the full width and depth of the transept; in the mother church, the rocky site and the need to leave undisturbed the grave of Saint Benedict forbade it. Filial churches of smaller size—S. Angelo in Formis may be representative—drop the transept; nave and aisles end in apses; and the atrium gives way to a narthex, arcaded and with the center arch stilted and gabled. Rich murals in the nave, apse, and narthex probably echo the decoration at Monte Cassino.

Desiderius clearly sought the model for his church in Rome. Columns, capitals, bases, and marble were bought there; the inscription he placed in the apse echoed the one in the Lateran Basilica and that on the triumphal arch of St. Peter's. Plan and design were close to S. Paolo: arcaded nave, raised transept, columns at the triumphal arch, the atrium, and the mosaic with the symbols of the Evangelists and the bust of Christ. Monte Cassino, then, in 1066 had reverted to the Early Christian models of Rome; Desiderius, disciple of Gregory VII, would tend to cast into visual form the concepts of the Reform Papacy and its reversion to the Christian past. No wonder either that Desiderius would single out S. Paolo as his model—the basilica was entrusted to the greatest Benedictine abbey in Rome, reformed by Gregory VII himself, then Abbot Hildebrand. Needless to say, the early model at Monte Cassino was transposed into eleventh-century terms: the size much smaller, the proportions steeper, the liturgical arrangements changed, three apses in the place of one due to the need for more altars.

To carry out his program, however, Desiderius had to look elsewhere. No pavement in *opus sectile*, no major bronze or silver work, no mosaic had been composed in Rome after the mid-ninth century. Leo, the chronicler of Monte Cassino, was well aware of Desiderius' having made a new start. As he expressly states, the arts of working mosaic and laying *opus sectile* pavements, which the *magistra latinitas* had not practiced for five hundred years and more, were brought back to Monte Cassino by artists from Constantinople called in to decorate the new church; one of the brethren was sent there to supervise the execution of an altar antependium with enamels and other fixtures in precious metals; a bronze door like the one Desiderius saw in Amalfi was ordered in 1066 for the old church—it still survives, enlarged and installed in the new church he built; and a school was founded for training craftsmen to keep alive the renewal of the arts. The West, then, to revert to Leo of Ostia, had taught these arts to the East, and the East had returned them after a lapse of five hundred years since Early Christian times—Carolingian mosaics seem to have been held in

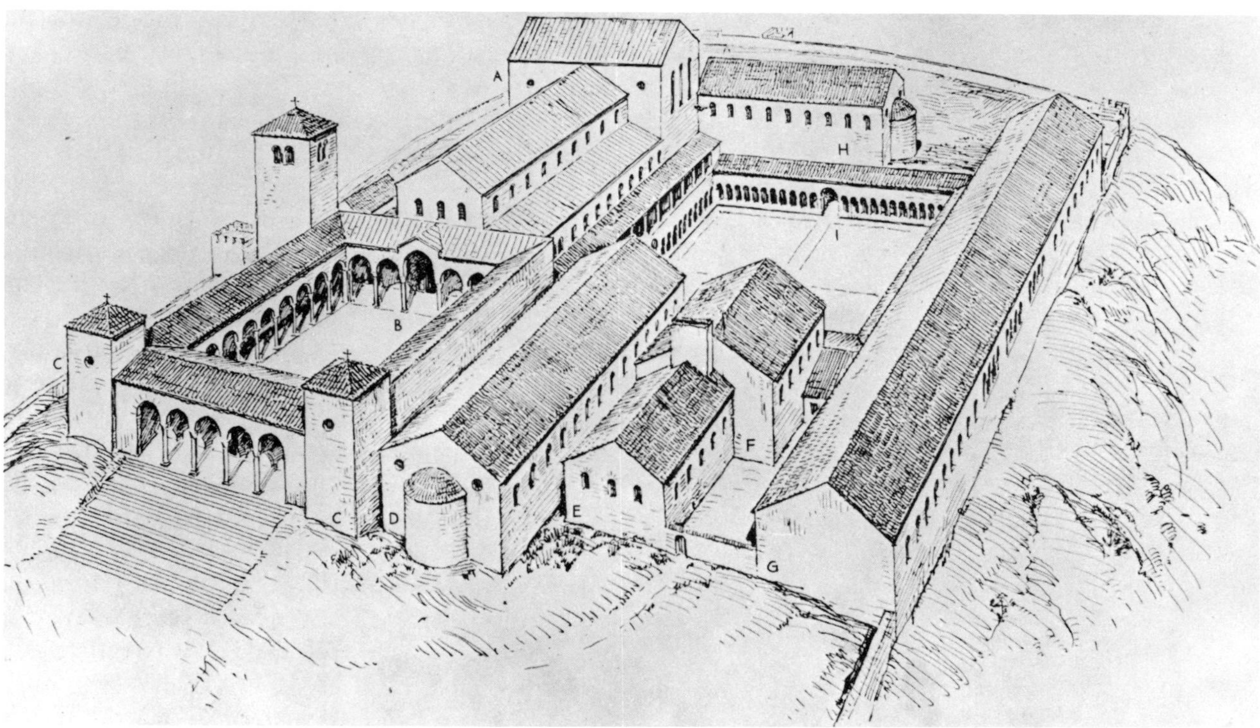

134. Monte Cassino as of 1100, isometric reconstruction Conant and Willard

small account by the chronicler. It has been suggested that Byzantine trained artists from South Italy may have played a part along with those called in from Constantinople. Art in medieval parlance means craft, technique; but inevitably the artists, whether from Constantinople or South Italy, brought along with their skills contemporary Byzantine designs: the pavement patterns and the ornament of the bronze doors, like those on the earlier door in Amalfi and on later doors through South Italy, reveal their Byzantine origin. The program of the doors, to be sure, is Western and the figural plaques, in contrast to the ornament, show markedly Western features. Drawings may have been sent East, as they no doubt were for the enamels showing the Life of St. Benedict on the altar antependium made in Constantinople—no Byzantine models could possibly have existed for that eminently Western saint. Even more clearly, the program and style of the mosaics at Monte Cassino, as reflected at Salerno, appear to have broken away from Byzantium and sought their models in the early apse mosaics preserved in Rome.

Preserved, but apparently unused by Roman church planners, in the last thirty-five years of the eleventh century these Roman mosaics attracted Desiderius and his South Italian confrères. Gregory VII and the Roman circle of reformers remained aloof, one gathers, from giving visual expression to their concept of a Church Renewed by reverting to Constantinian Roman archetypes. Among the bronze doors commissioned and wrought in Constantinople at the time for clients in the West, only those ordered in 1070 for S. Paolo fuori le mura under the abbacy of Hildebrand-Gregory, and financed by the same Pantaleone who had provided those for his native Amalfi and for Monte Cassino, remain strictly Byzantine in design, subject matter, and inscriptions, except for the Latin dedication (fig. 135). The stimulus both to turn to Early Christian models and to strengthen the monastic features in church and convent planning thus seems to have reached Rome from Monte Cassino, with a delay of one or two generations. The Benedictines, indeed, were evidently the "main propagators of the renewal of Early Christian church planning and decoration

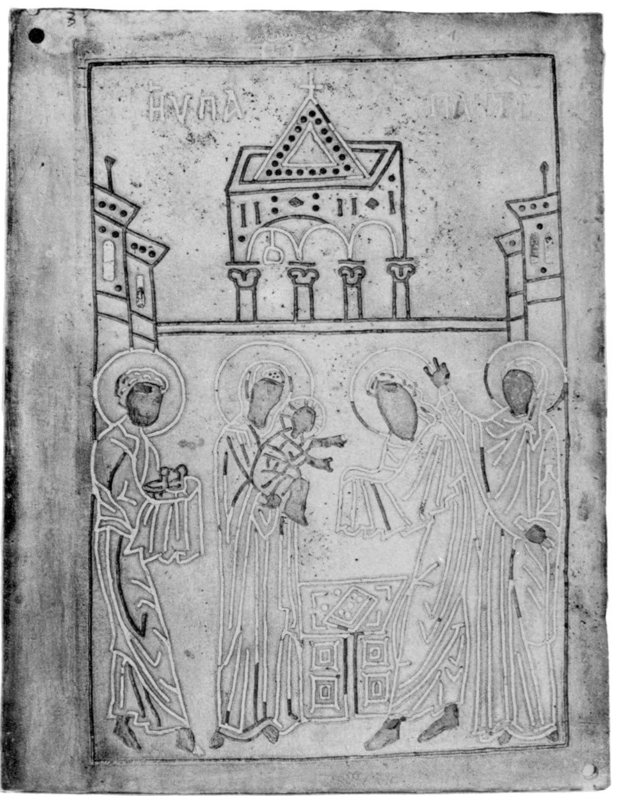

135. S. Paolo fuori le mura, bronze doors, detail, *Presentation in the Temple*

from the late eleventh century on." In Rome the greatest convent of the Order at S. Paolo fuori le mura naturally took the lead. Monte Cassino remained the direct and closest model for Roman church planners. But S. Paolo exerted a collateral influence. From about 1120 on, under their combined influence, basilicas in Rome were laid out with a transept raised above nave level, their triumphal arches carried by columns. Indeed, the earliest seedlings of Monte Cassino in Rome, S. Crisogono and S. Maria in Trastevere, within a ten percent margin, equal Desiderius' church in size. From Monte Cassino, too, Rome seems to have adopted: freestanding campanili alongside her churches, a veritable hallmark of the Roman High Middle Ages; cloisters in her major convents, whether monastic or canonical; in minor churches, the three apse plan without transept, as customary among smaller Monte Cassino derivatives; and occasionally, as in large Monte Cassino filiations, hall crypts extending below transepts. Nartheces, too, arcaded or trabeated, may have come to Rome out of the Monte Cassino school. Church furniture and pavements stand within that same tradition: chancel screens, *scholae cantorum*, lecterns, ambones, Easter candlesticks, altar canopies, and episcopal thrones, all finely carved and inlaid with discs and other patterns of colored marble. Very likely the alumni of the art school started by Desiderius taught their craft to Roman artists, and through the twelfth and into the thirteenth centuries they evolved dynasties of marble workers—the Cosmati, Vassalletti, Romani. Stimulated by Monte Cassino, Rome revived her great tradition of mosaics; those on the apse arch of S. Clemente, so close to Salerno, speak for themselves. To be sure, Monte Cassino, from the last years of the eleventh century on, seems to have had an impact on the rebirth of mural painting in Rome. Around that time, the lower church of S. Clemente was precariously shored up and decorated with murals: textile patterns filled with lively birds, floral candelabra frames, and scenes full of life and emotion, such as the miracle of the child found alive and kicking in a church of Saint Clement that had been submerged for a year in a sea filled with every kind of fish (fig. 136). Composition, design, and colors seem to have been traditional among artists who, at or even before Desiderius' time, illuminated manuscripts at Monte Cassino; or else, the painters of S. Clemente adapted, parallel to their confrères at Monte Cassino, South Italian and possibly Byzantine elements to a specifically Roman style. Certainly, the classicizing elements, such as long-stemmed plants growing from urns and the intertwining rinceaux, reveal a Roman tradition reviving the vocabulary of late antiquity.

Roman church planners of the High Middle Ages, then, under the stimulus of Monte Cassino, turned to models of late antiquity. The movement was carried to Rome probably by the Benedictines and the high clergy associated with them. In Rome, however, their contact with the archetypes was more immediate. They went more deeply into the richness of late antique art, Christian and pagan; they developed a strong feeling for its style; and they absorbed, together

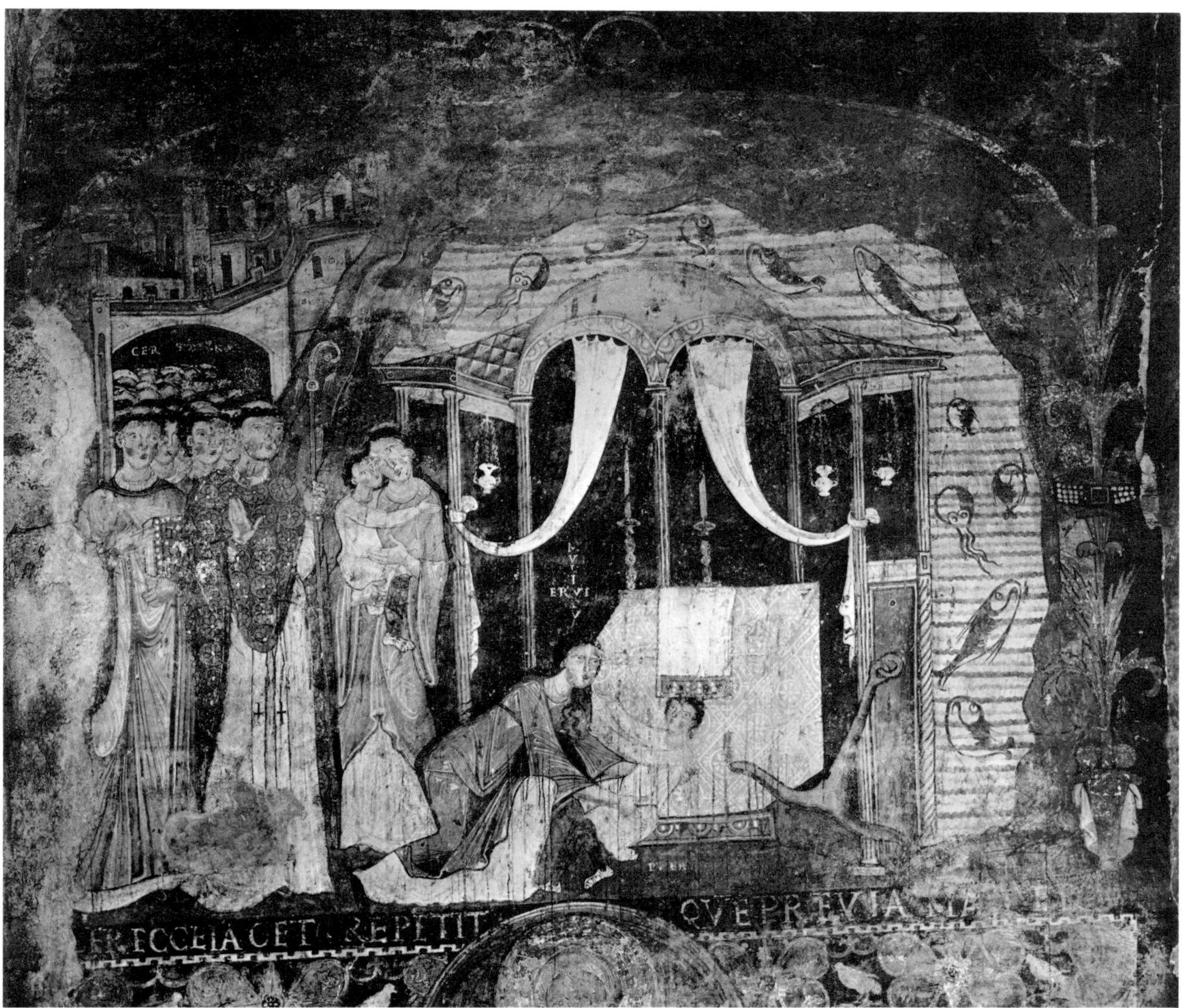

136. S. Clemente, lower church, *Miracle of the Child*

with Christian features, neutral or indeed pagan elements. Thus, they evolved in Rome a revival with markedly local overtones. Transepts, rather than reaching higher as was customary in the Monte Cassino group, are the same height as the nave; instead of three apses, there is only one; naves are quietly proportioned rather than steep; colonnades are frequently trabeated rather than arcaded; capitals, shafts, and bases are chosen with care—naturally, given the surfeit of spoils available in Rome; the Roman workshops early turned to producing Ionic capitals on their own, adapted from classical models and often highly refined (figs. 137, 138). Foreign to Monte Cassino, all these features seem to be drawn straight from early models in Rome, or possibly from their Carolingian "copies": St. Peter's, S. Paolo, S. Maria Maggiore; or else, S. Susanna or S. Prassede. Only atria, the hallmark of fourth- and ninth-century Roman basilicas and eagerly adopted by the Monte Cassino school, are rare in Rome, of all places. Those at S. Clemente, the Quattro Coronati, and S. Gregorio Magno are exceptions, and the first two are, anyway, copies of earlier predecessors. But, then, all three were located in the emptiness of the disabitato. In densely built-over Trastevere or Parione, space for atria was scarce.

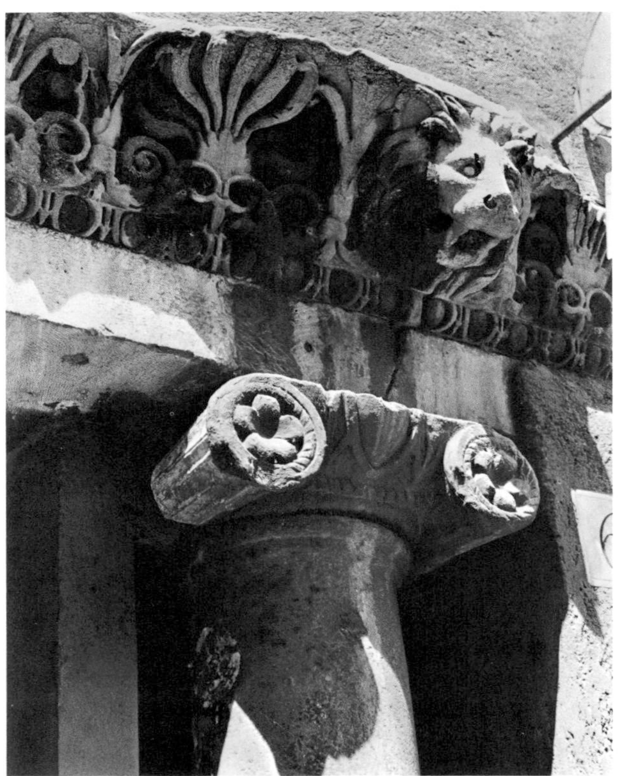

137. Ionic capital, twelfth or thirteenth century, via S. Celso 61

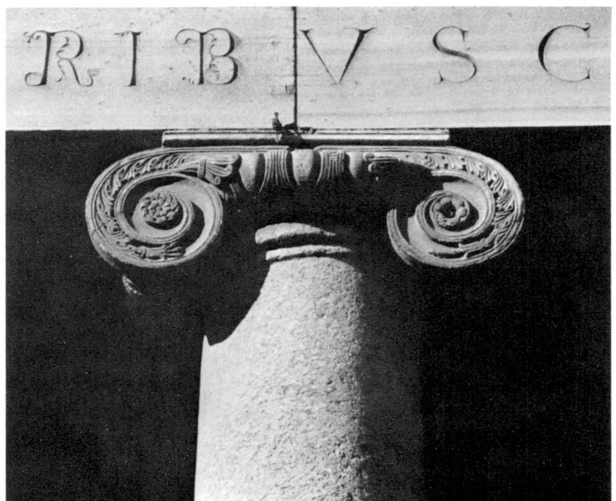

138. Ionic capital, 1154, SS. Giovanni e Paolo, narthex

Likewise, the mosaics at S. Clemente and S. Maria in Trastevere drew directly on local models, six or seven centuries old by then. Other mosaics no doubt existed but are lost. The great mosaics of Early Christian Rome, especially those linked, albeit mistakenly, to the name of Constantine at St. Peter's and S. Paolo fuori le mura, had been the models from which Desiderius at Monte Cassino and the artists trained under his abbacy had drawn their programs of church decoration. To their Roman followers in the early twelfth century—and the Benedictines again may have been instrumental—not only these mosaics but also Early Christian and late-antique models in general (fig. 139) became a far richer and inexhaustible source. From them, whether Christian or pagan, elements of subject matter, style, and at times entire compositional schemes could be adapted, selected, and newly combined. All these elements, to be sure, were adapted to high medieval modes of presentation and meaning, as may be seen in the handling of bodies, faces and draperies, plants and animals; and the interpretation in terms of contemporary theological symbolism of the foliate cross, the rivers of Paradise, the peopled acanthus scrolls, and details such as the caged bird or the chicken and her chicks. In the context of the revival and renewal of twelfth- and thirteenth-century Rome, through a reversion to late-antique sources, the location of these early models is of primary significance. As at S. Clemente, acanthus scrolls spread in tiers over the dark blue, not gold, ground of the right-hand apse vault in the narthex of the Lateran Baptistery, believed in the Middle Ages to have been not only built as it was, but also decorated, by Constantine rather than by a fifth-century hand (fig. 140). The crucifix growing from a lush acanthus plant at the center of the S. Clemente apse vault may be a variant on the cross in the apse mosaic of the Lateran Basilica, naturally ascribed to Constantine and presumably echoed, if modified, in Torriti's mosaic of 1293; the clipeus with Christ's head, the famous *veronica*, floating over the Lateran cross, was moved higher up at S. Clemente to the apex of the apse arch; and the doves on the stem and arms of the S. Clemente crucifix may have taken the place of the jewels on the Lateran cross. The Canopy of Heaven,

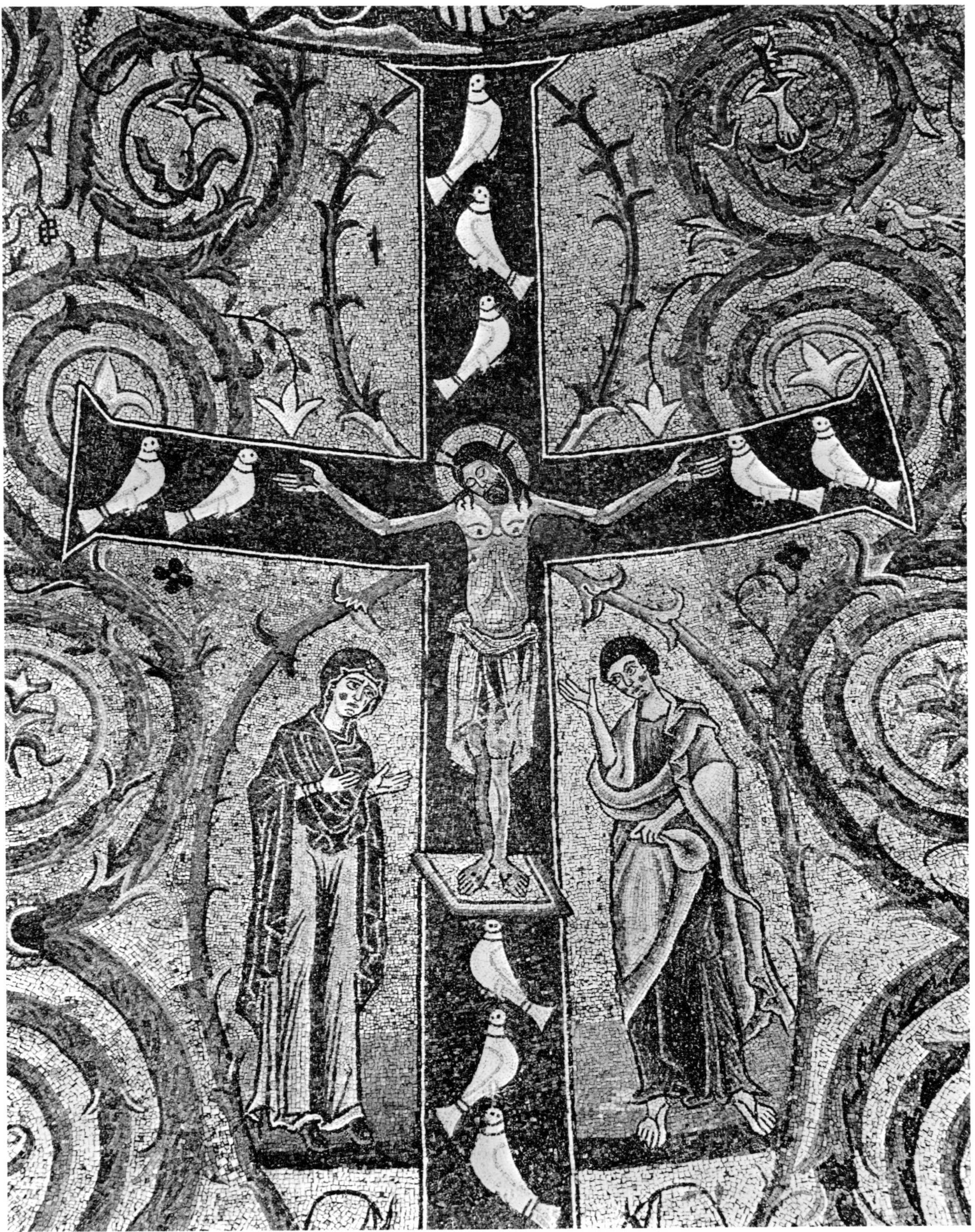

139. S. Clemente, apse mosaic, detail, the Cross

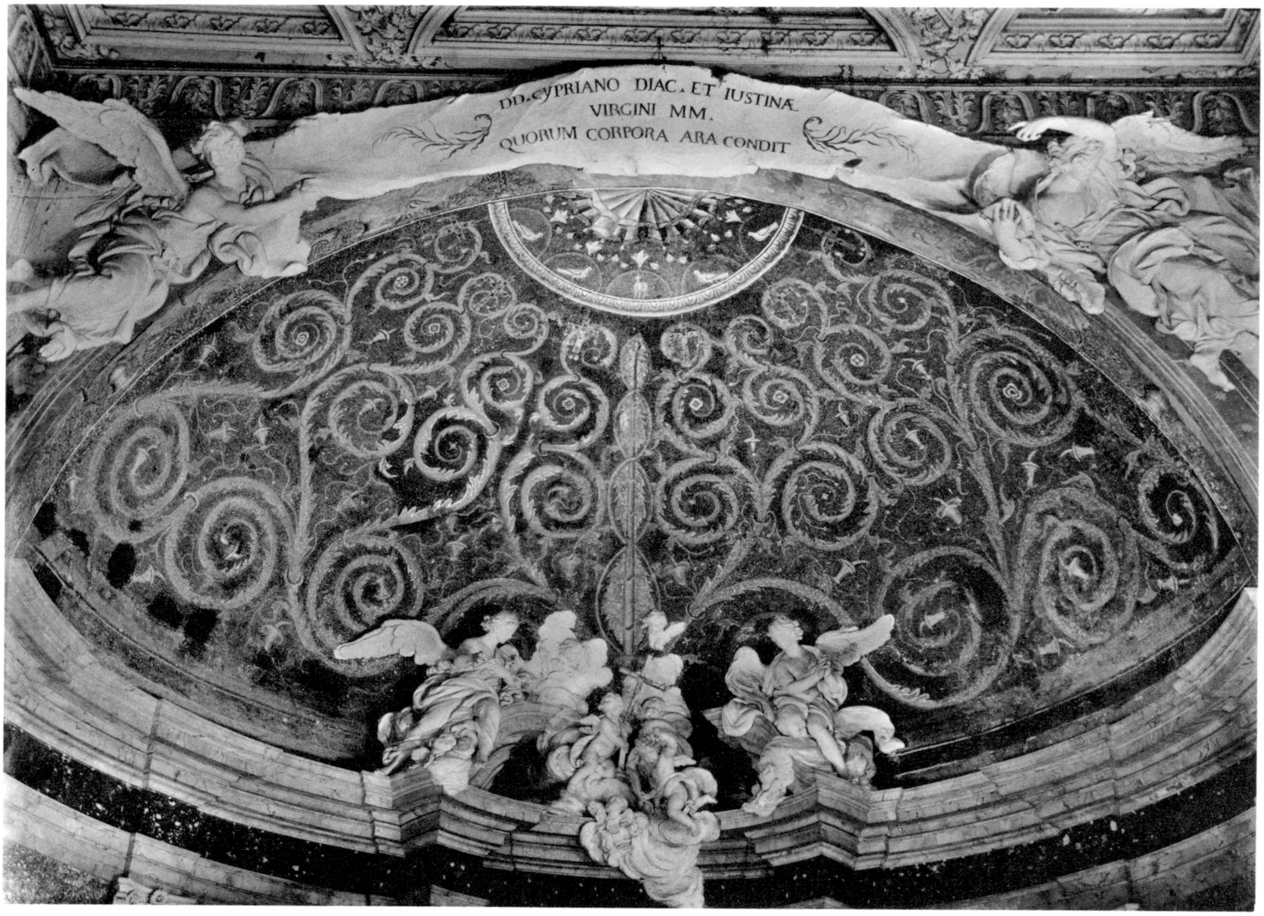

140. Lateran Baptistery, narthex, apse mosaic

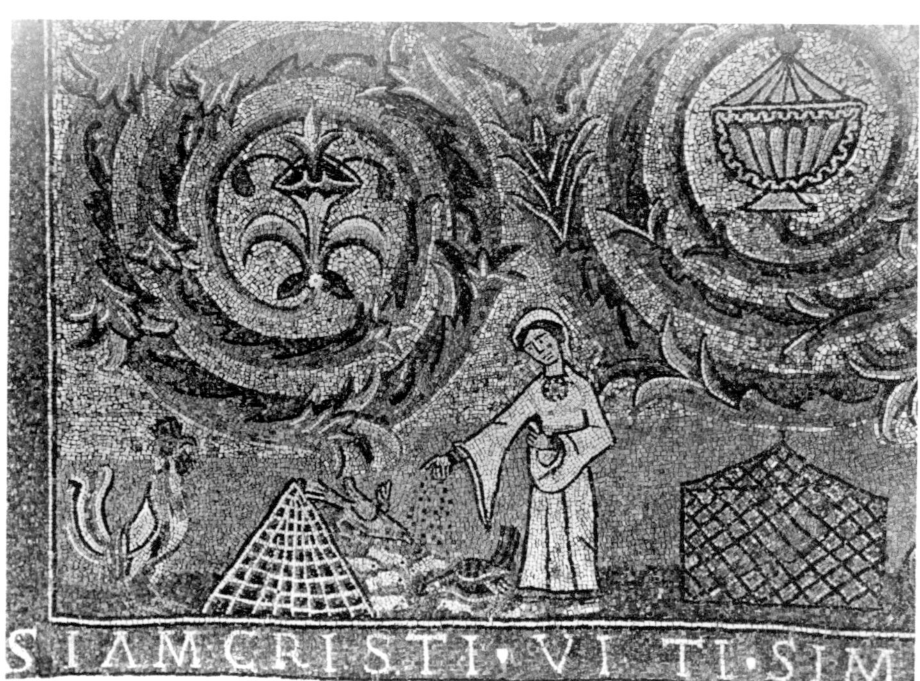

141. S. Clemente, apse mosaic, detail, woman feeding chicks

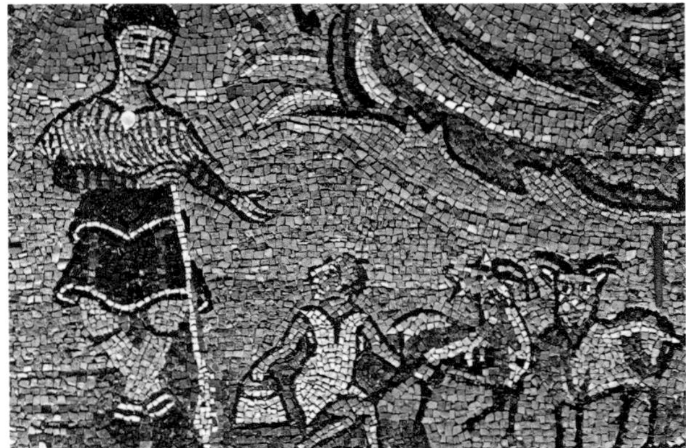

142. S. Clemente, apse mosaic, detail, shepherd and slave

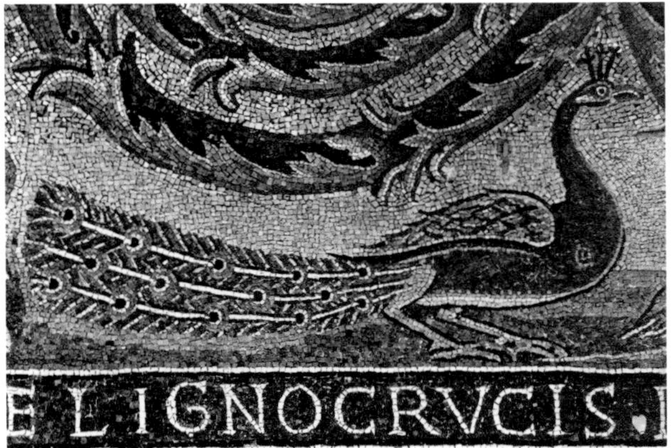

143. S. Clemente, apse mosaic, detail, peacock

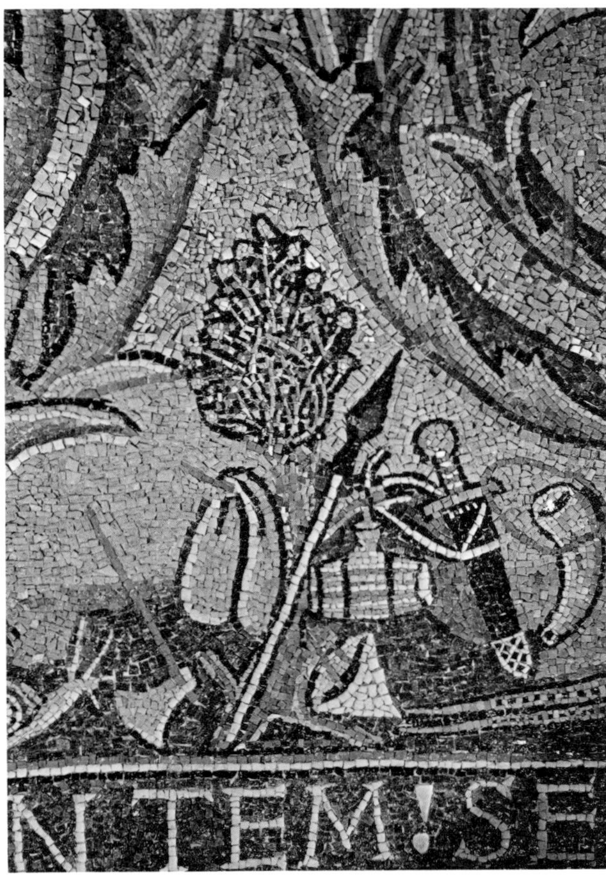

144. S. Clemente, apse mosaic, detail, hunting outfit

which floats fanlike at the crown of the apse vault, finds its counterpart nearly feature for feature in the narthex vault of the Lateran Baptistery. All such elements, to be sure, were presented in a style unmistakably medieval. Still, the rendering, at S. Clemente anyway, is shot through with elements of technique and design schooled directly on late-antique models, all impressionistic features reminiscent of fourth- and fifth-century mosaics—S. Pudenziana or S. Maria Maggiore: highlights on flesh and drapery; folds marked in strips of white marble tesserae bounded by strips of black and gray glass cubes—the age-old Roman technique; eyes composed of one white and one black cube; no sharp outlines anywhere. More hardened than at S. Clemente, the forms in the mosaics at S. Maria in Trastevere still reflect such late-antique Christian models; models more often than not linked to the name of Constantine.

Not all the elements in the mosaics of S. Clemente or S. Maria in Trastevere are Christian in content. Integrated already in the compositions of their Early Christian models were genre scenes: the mosaic in the left-hand apse in the narthex of the Lateran Baptistery, long lost, was populated along its rim by cowherds and shepherds, lambs, birds, a chicken coop, and a woman feeding birds. All reappear at S. Clemente (fig. 141), enriched by further genre elements of late-antique flavor: water fowl, as once pictured along the rim of S. Costanza's dome; loosely strewn vine leaves, grapes, and gamboling putti; and the garland inside the apse arch, as in the apses and aisle vaults of S. Constanza and other early churches in Rome. The master of S. Clemente drew on elements of this kind from other unidentified late-antique sources: a goatherd and his dwarflike ugly slave, with a milking pail (fig. 142); a bird feeding its young; a stork pouncing on a lizard; a splendid peacock (fig. 143); the still-life of a hunting outfit (fig. 144); a putto playing with a dolphin (fig. 145), another trumpeting. A sower, a monk, and a layman feeding birds; a group of three men, one richly dressed, appear in medieval attire, but their movements and grouping suggest late-antique sources for them as well, albeit perhaps transmitted by Carolingian manuscripts. Similarly, at S. Maria in Trastevere, pairs of putti hold drapes filled with flowers and a huge urn (fig. 146); remains of murals from S. Nicola in Carcere, preserved in the Vatican Museum, show a heron (fig. 147), a parrot, dolphins, a lion-headed monster, an antique mask. At S. Maria in Cosmedin a frieze crowning the nave walls is composed of roundels filled with fauns' heads and ornaments *all' antica*—rinceaux, coffered friezes, candelabra rising from vases, scattered flowers, fruit and birds, drapery, and cornucopia, hard to see at present, except in photographs taken early in this century (fig. 148). Such antique models pervade medieval church decoration in Rome from the late eleventh cen-

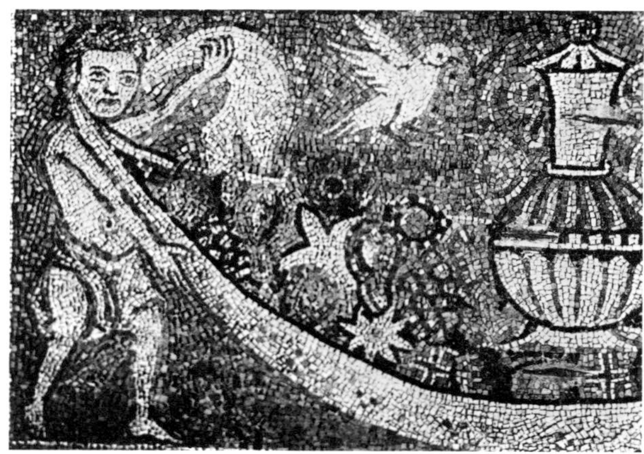

146. S. Maria in Trastevere, putto with drape

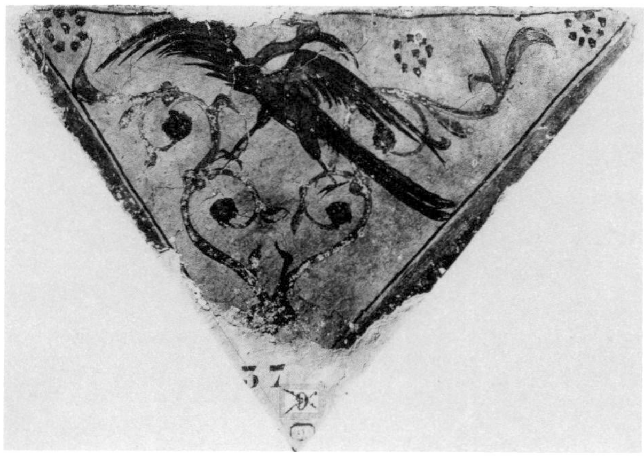

147. Heron, Musei Vaticani, from S. Nicola in Carcere

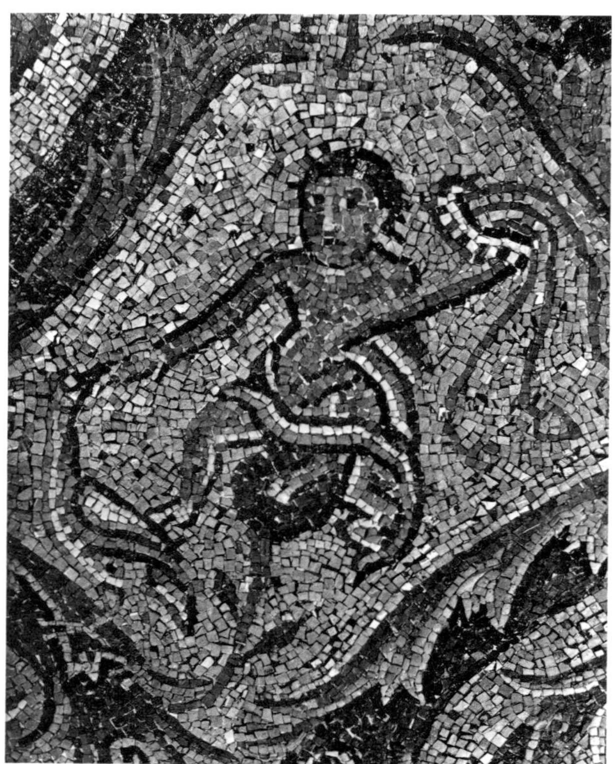

145. S. Clemente, apse mosaic, putto playing with dolphin

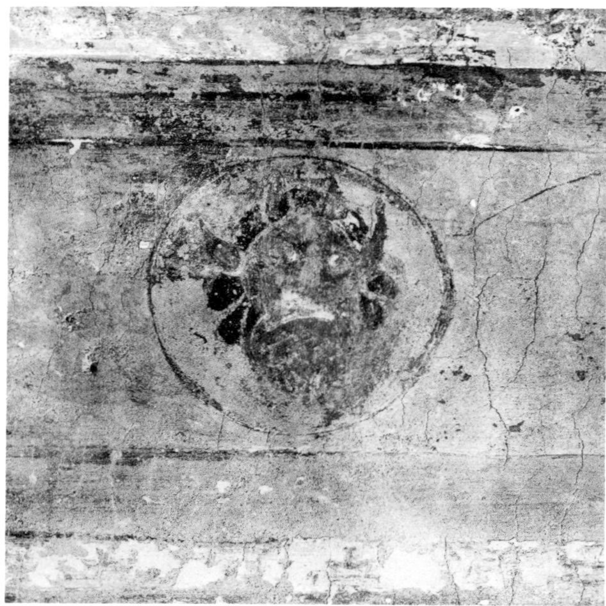

148. S. Maria in Cosmedin, faun's head

tury through the first decades of the twelfth. Lifelike as they were, although insignificant in themselves, they would be substitutes, in the eyes of medieval man, for the representation of reality, striven for but unattainable.

By the early twelfth century, the lure of antiquity and its reflections in medieval art were neither new nor linked exclusively to Rome. From the late eleventh century and for a hundred and fifty years more, writers, artists, and their patrons from France, England, or Italy absorbed and employed the phraseology and vocabulary of classical antiquity; they gradually began to think in its language. Within the context of this medieval rebirth of antiquity, they flouted their learning and savored the elegance of a phrase plucked and adapted from a Roman writer; they enjoyed and emulated the refinement of an ornament, the naturalness of a genre scene, the graceful movement of a bird or a body, the convincing likeness of a gesture or a human head, as seen in a Roman mosaic, Christian or pagan, a mural, or an ancient statue. Clearly this renascence had many facets. Panofsky, the first to see it as a whole, contrasted two main trends: in the North, grown from a soil not nurtured by love of the ancient world's tradition, it took the form primarily of a literary movement, leading to a rediscovery of nature in prose and poetry, but absorbing the language of ancient statuary late, though with all the vigor of the masters of Rheims; on ancient soil in Provence and Italy, on the other hand, the figural arts readily incorporated an antique vocabulary in the ornament and statuary of church façades and portals, such as at S. Gilles and Modena. Whether or not such differentiation can be fully sustained, the classical elements reemployed were either integrated in the medieval program of a church façade and thus made void of their original meaning or they were neutral to start with, a curiosity to be savored for its rarity, naturalness, and beauty—an ornament, a genre scene, a heron, a putto—as in Rome at S. Clemente and in the fragments of S. Nicola in Carcere.

In this medieval revival, Rome held a unique position. She had no need to search for the remains of antiquity. They were ever present: the Pantheon, the Colosseum, the theatres of Marcellus and of Pompey; the ruins of the great thermae and of the palaces of the Palatine; the remains of the temples on the fora and the Campus Martius; the fora themselves, those of Nerva, Augustus, Trajan; the triumphal arches and the monumental columns of Marcus Aurelius and Trajan; the mausolea of Hadrian and Augustus; the obelisks, especially the one then along the south flank of St. Peter's; the pyramid of Cestius and the other pyramid that till the fifteenth century stood near the Mausoleum of Hadrian. Ancient sculpture, too, was plentiful: the reliefs on the triumphal columns and arches; the river god, the *Marforio*, then near S. Martina on the Forum and now at the Capitoline Museum; the horse tamers, the *caballi di marmo* on the Quirinal and along with them two river gods and three standing barbarians; the Trofei di Mario; and others, mentioned by medieval visitors but now gone. Wall paintings, mosaics, and stucco decoration must have been accessible in the ruins of the Golden House, on the Palatine, in the vaults of the Colosseum—many lost to us but surviving in their medieval reflections. Likewise ever present and kept in good repair were the great monuments of Christian antiquity: the basilicas of St. Peter's, S. Paolo, S. Maria Maggiore, and at the Lateran, and their mosaics and murals. Contact with the classical past and its survival in pagan and Christian monuments was an everyday experience in Rome. To Romans of the Middle Ages, whether native or adoptive, antiquity was an integral part of their environment. It was not distant history, but a live and very real element. Such familiarity bred diverse and vastly divergent attitudes. Roman statuary or architectural materials habitually went into the lime kilns—from late antiquity into the sixteenth century: lime, probably from burning ancient marble, went into repairing the city walls in the eighth century. The quarter around what is now Largo Argentina took its medieval name, *de calcarariis*, as early as 1023 from the lime burners' shops, and other kilns were worked near the Mausoleum of Augustus, in the Thermae of Agrippa behind the Pantheon, on the Forum, and wherever else marble was near at hand. Or else, again a custom continued ever since antiquity, architectural elements were reused as spoils, either as they were or slightly altered, in new buildings: bases, column shafts, capitals, entablatures, piers or pilasters, votive altars, inscriptions, or just ordinary building blocks. Just as in Christian antiquity—one recalls S. Sabina—or in Carolingian times, the colonnades of medieval churches in Rome were built wholly or in part from such spoils; spoils, too, form the brackets of a cornice, the cornice itself, the plaques of chancel screens and pulpits. Likewise, houses, some of which survive, often used ancient columns in their ground-floor porticoes, surmounted occasionally by fragments of an ancient frieze: one carved with lion heads and palmettes is still to be seen on the corner house opposite Ponte S. Angelo (fig. 233), another in Via Capo di Ferro 10. Lime burners and stonecutters would keep in their workshops deposits of marble spoils, statuary and architectural decoration, capitals, friezes, brackets. More than a dozen such shops ranging from late antiquity, it seems, to the Renaissance, and filled with ancient spoils, have been identified. Occasionally the pieces may have served the owners, the *marmorarii Romani*, as models. More frequently they went into the limekilns; or they were in demand for sale, reworked or as they had been found, to builders from Rome and afar. Just as Desiderius bought marble and other materials for the construction of Monte Cassino, Suger of St. Denis planned to procure them from Rome for building his abbey church, with the difference that his ambition, tiny man that he was, aspired to nothing less than columns from the Thermae of Diocletian and other baths—even how to convey them by ship right to the building site was carefully worked out. The *marmorarii* of Rome were, I think, no less famous as marble workers than as dealers in architectural spoils and other materials; and once in a while one of them would carve his name on the ancient piece not so much as proof of ownership as to advertise the firm, often passed down from father to son and grandson.

Obviously, the ancient ruins and their decoration, the antique statues and reliefs, held a fascination, beyond their practical use and reuse, for men of the Middle Ages. But their attitude toward these witnesses of a world so foreign to their own remained ambiguous and many-layered. The hoi polloi of Romans and visitors, especially pilgrims, would be overwhelmed by the sheer size of a building or a colossal statue surviving in fragments and spin strange yarns about it: the Colosseum was the Temple of the Sun and had formerly been covered with a huge dome; the *pigna* in the atrium of St. Peter's had stood atop the opaion of the Pantheon, God knows how; wriggling through the four bronze supports below the obelisk near St. Peter's secured forgiveness of sins, and the bronze globe on top of the obelisk was said to contain the ashes of Caesar (fig. 149). In short, all ancient statuary and buildings were filled with magic. Popular fancies and magical fear crept into learned descriptions of Rome as well.

At the same time, though, these elements, the ancient structures, the remains of ancient art salvaged from the limekilns or surviving in murals,

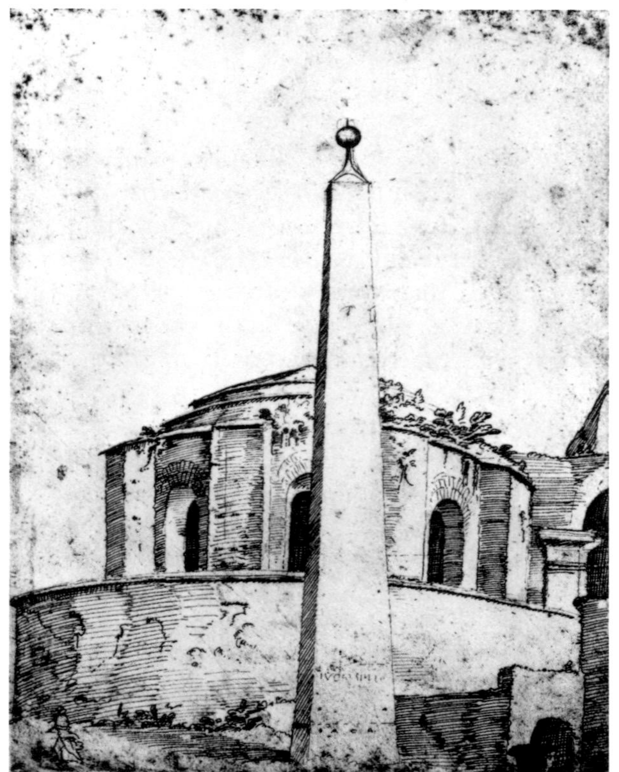

149. Obelisk at St. Peter's, as of 1534-1536, drawing Marten van Heemskerck, Berlin, Kupferstichkabinett, 79 D2A, fol. 22v

stucco, mosaic, and marble, whether Christian or pagan, held a very different fascination for cultivated men of the Middle Ages. To them these artifacts were, other connotations notwithstanding, a source of pleasure and admiration. They enjoyed their lifelikeness and grace, their monumentality and liveliness, their elegance and the technical skill of execution. The pagan elements could be given a Christian meaning; but just as often they were disregarded. Whether pagan or not, these relics were viewed simply as quotations, like those employed by contemporary writers to flout their own learning and for the sheer enjoyment of their tasteful richness and refinement. Their pagan character was largely irrelevant; more often than not, they seem to have been considered void of content. For purely decorative elements such absence of meaning is self-evident. However, the cultured prelates and monastic congregations responsible for designing the decoration of S. Clemente or S. Nicola in Carcere apparently felt no reluctance at integrating non-Christian motifs in their programs. Paganism was dead; a putto or even a faun's head was by now an empty shell, a mere phrase; harmless, it could be prized for its lifelike immediacy and its perfection as a work of art: "better than nature," as later medieval artists put it, amazed that human nature could rise to such heights of craftsmanship.

One likes to think that there would always have been Romans impressed by the city's ancient remains. Perhaps more frequently, so would visitors have been, who were less familiar with and therefore more curious about buildings, sculpture, monuments, paintings, and mosaics. At the end of the eleventh century and into the early twelfth, the evidence for this becomes overwhelming. Nothing shows it better than the decorations and antique motifs incorporated in the paintings and mosaics of the churches built or rebuilt in Rome at the time, or in the sumptuous Roman columns, capitals, and bases reused at S. Maria in Trastevere; clearly, these elements were chosen by the artists employed at the command, or with the consent, of their clerical patrons: sophisticated gentlemen, steeped in the writings of the ancients and often trained abroad, in Paris for instance, as was Anaclete II Pierleone. Sometime between 1145 and 1150, Henry, bishop of Winchester and brother of the English king, Henry II, on a business trip to Rome was buying up ancient sculptures to take home with him. So set on his quest was he as to go about the city seriously, his beard unkempt, like many an avid collector. He was ridiculed for this whim of his by native Romans. But John of Salisbury, who tells the story, saw clearly that the pieces he bought were "produced by the subtle and diligent, rather than intentional, error of the heathen"; their pagan content, though damnable, was separate from their aesthetic qualities. There was most likely no regular dealing in antiques. But if a stonecutter had a good piece around, as did the one in whose workshop a well-preserved statue of Antinous was found among column shafts and other spoils ninety years ago, he would part with it, were a mad Englishman willing to pay. Another English visitor to Rome, Magister Gregory, around 1200 was filled with enthusiasm and curiosity when seeing the wonderful remains of antiquity: he paced off the width of the Pantheon at 266 feet—he must have had small feet; in the Thermae of Diocletian the columns stood so high that he couldn't throw a pebble up to their capitals—who but an English don would try?; he washed his hands in a hot sulphur bath contained in a bronze tub, one assumes antique, and tipped the attendant, but did not bathe because of the stench; in front of the Lateran Palace he saw with fascination the statue of the thornpicker, "that ridiculous Priapus," supposedly looking down at his large genitals—they are of perfectly normal size; and "driven by some magic or I don't know what," he went to the Quirinal three times to see a naked Venus of rosy marble "as if ashamed of her nudity"—representations taboo in medieval art, but with a particular attraction of their own. Indeed, Magister Gregory saw magic in all the weird art of the ancients—his treatise, after all, is entitled, *Tale of the Marvels of the City of Rome, whether Produced by Magic Art or by Human Labour*: one could not be sure. He believed a good number of the fancy stories then current. But he was critical of others told by and to pilgrims—whom he disliked—and informed himself by talking to the prelates at the papal court. Nonetheless, he shows great admiration for ancient works of art. He was deeply impressed by the high quality of the bronze head of Constantine at the Lateran: its colossal size, its workmanship, "the merit of the artist"; the beauty, "no human head . . . has anything of perfect beauty that is missing here"; the softness of hair achieved in hard bronze; its fidelity, "if you look at it with your eyes half-closed, it seems to move and speak."

Ancient art, then, was attractive, but dangerous; admirable, but of an uncanny perfection that only evil spirits could achieve. It became safe only when understood either as a Christian symbol or a political one. The Christian interpretation of motifs purloined from antiquity and incorporated in a mosaic, as at S. Clemente, has been discussed previously, at least in passing. In Rome and within a milieu permeated by political overtones, as was the case in the twelfth and thirteenth centuries, the revival of late-antique models and formulas and the attraction of ancient monuments or statuary would necessarily have had political overtones as well. Ever since Virgil the idea of Rome and her past was bound up with the consciousness of her place as mistress and head of the world. The recollection of what she had been remained a goal to be striven for; or, since the goal was beyond reach, it remained a vision ever kept alive. The search for the glory and power she once held remained in medieval Rome inseparable from politics in its many aspects: rhetoric, aspirations, the reality of power and action. It tinges the laments over her downfall in the chronicle of Benedict of Soracte; the quest for freedom from foreign rule and the successive revolts led by Alberic, the Crescentii, and the Pierleoni; the dream of Otto III of a universal monarchy ruled from Rome; the concept pervading the entire Middle Ages of a better, because Christian, Rome which had conquered and replaced the pagan, though glorious, city; the conviction ever recurring from Nicholas I in the ninth century to Innocent III in the thirteenth of her being mistress of the world as in ancient days, through being the seat of the papacy, heir to Saint Peter and the Roman emperors and thus supreme both spiritually and temporally; or else, the thought of Rome as the stronghold of a free republic resisting temporal rule by either emperor or pope. By 1122, the papacy had emerged victoriously from the Investiture Struggle. The German emperors were vanquished; the Church had won freedom from temporal interference; indeed, she had forced the temporal powers to acknowledge her superiority. From the third decade of the twelfth century on, the popes could see themselves increasingly in the image first adumbrated by Gregory VII: both spiritual leaders of Christendom and overlords of all temporal rulers in the West. The concept found visual expression in murals and mosaics and their inscriptions, once in the Lateran Palace and on the narthex of its basilica. Known from late copies, they all referred to the victorious termination of the Investiture Struggle by the Concordat of Worms, to the triumph of the papacy over antipopes nominated by the German emperors, to its claims to temporal supremacy in a very real feudal sense, and to the historical basis supporting these claims. In one mural, the Virgin, Queen of Heaven, appeared flanked by Popes Anaclete I and Sylvester I, the former believed to have been ordained by Saint Peter himself and to have set up his memoria, the latter Constantine's counterpart and the alleged recipient of the Donation. At her feet knelt Calixtus II and Anaclete II Pierleone who was later declared antipope, apparently the donor of the mural cycle sometime between 1130 and 1138. In a lower tier, finally, were ranged the great popes of the early centuries, among them Leo I and Gregory the Great, and opposite them those victorious in the Investiture Struggle. Another mural showed in three scenes the coronation in 1133 of Emperor Lothar III by Pope Innocent II—his oaths to the city of Rome and to the pope, then his coronation—explained by an inscription; it broadly hinted at the emperor's being liegeman to the pope, his crown's being a papal fief and, by implication, the pope's being the supreme spiritual and temporal ruler. Lastly, a mosaic on the narthex of the Lateran Basilica, probably built between 1159 and 1181 or slightly later, illustrated the foundation of the claim by showing Constantine handing to the pope the charter of the Donation, and thus transferring to him the imperial insignia, prerogatives, and actual rule over the West; similarly, the fresco cycle in the Cappella di S. Silvestro in the convent of the Quattro Coronati, completed in 1246, shows Constantine offering to Pope Sylvester the imperial headgear, the *phrygium* (fig. 150). The pope—and this is the official view of papal partisans in the High Middle Ages—controls empires and kingdoms as well as the Church. He is the successor to Constantine and the Roman emperors as well as to Saint Peter.

These several traditions—the Petrine, the Constantinian, and that of imperial Rome as mistress of the world—constitute a matrix within which the revival of antiquity in medieval Rome, in papal circles at any rate, became pregnant with political implications. Quite naturally, Old St. Peter's, Constantine's foundation and monument of the Apostle, would be the great model for church planners in medieval Rome, *idealiter*, anyhow. *Realiter*, one recalls, ever since Carolingian times a standard type had been developed: the transept plan of St. Peter's, unconventional by then with its low roof and still lower exedrae projecting beyond the aisles, was replaced by that of S. Paolo fuori le mura, as high and wide as the nave. St. Peter's itself seems to have been viewed as following that norm, and indeed in 1154 it was brought closer to it by raising at least its exedrae—or perhaps only the northern one—to the height of the transept roof. Or else the gallery scheme of S. Lorenzo or S. Agnese fuori le mura, both evidently believed to have been Constantine's original churches on the spot, may have served as prototypes for the sham galleries of the Quattro Coronati or at S. Croce as rebuilt in 1144/5. Mosaic designers, one recalls, time and again drew on genuine or putative Constantinian models—at the Lateran Baptistery, at S. Costanza, possibly the old mosaic of the Lateran Basilica, in all likelihood attributed to the imperial founder despite its fifth-century date. Early Christian churches of a classical hue, such as S. Maria Maggiore, may well have been absorbed by twelfth-century builders into an ideal picture of "Constantinian" architecture to serve as an overall standard. (Did the set of fifth-century Ionic capitals once in S. Maria Maggiore spark the resurrection in high medieval Rome of a capital type hardly ever used after Early Christian times?) In any event, the adaptation of such models apparently reflected or supported the claims of the popes to be legitimate successors to both Saint Peter and Constantine. One may speculate whether their aspiration to be the heirs of the Roman emperors too effected the absorption in twelfth- and thirteenth-century church decoration of non-Christian, or even decidedly pagan, elements. Indeed, it has been suggested that the Roman spoils—be they leonine armrests, gamboling putti, or rinceaux—were incorporated into pontifical thrones set up in the early twelfth century at S. Maria in Cosmedin, S. Lorenzo in Lucina, and S. Clemente, just because of the imperial connotations claimed by the papacy. Whether or not this holds for antique motifs in general, beyond, that is, their already having been incorporated as harmless genre scenes in Early Christian compositions, is a moot point. After all, such elements abounded in stucco reliefs, wall paintings, and pavement or wall mosaics in the imperial residences on the Palatine, in the Domus Aurea, or in the Thermae, all known in the Middle Ages as palaces of the Roman emperors. Certainly, though, recourse to an antique vocabulary became a fad in twelfth- and thirteenth-century Rome. In the work of the Cosmati and other dynasties of Roman marble workers, motifs *all'antica* abound, often surprisingly close to the original:

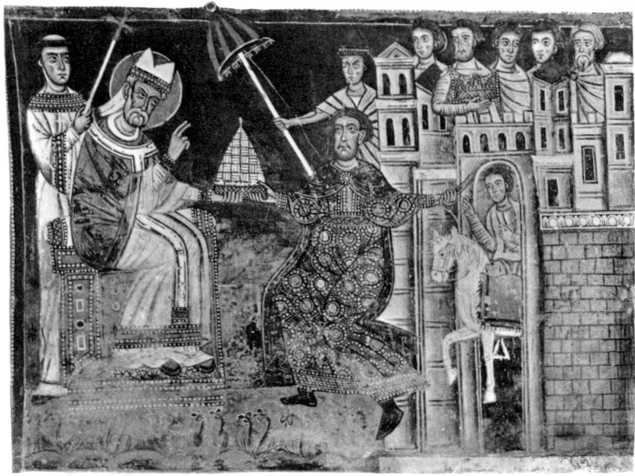

150. SS. Quattro Coronati, Capella di S. Silvestro, detail, Constantine offering phrygium to pope

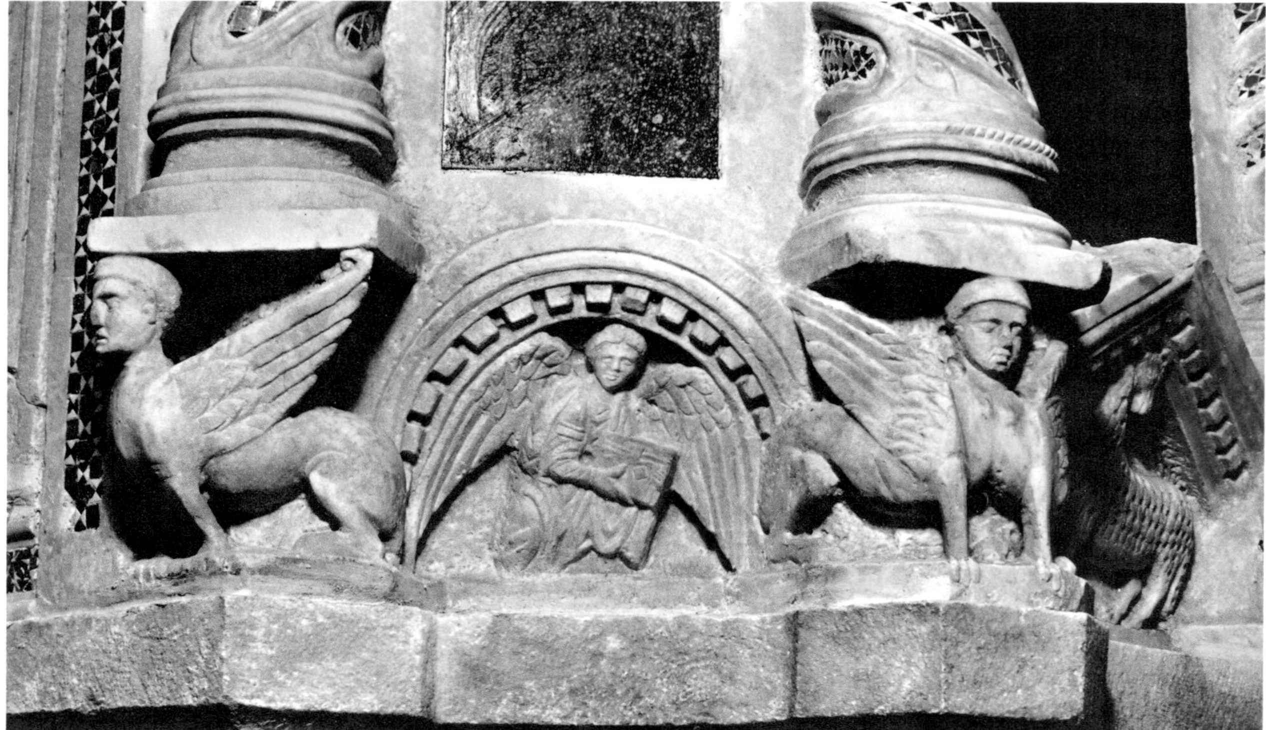

151. S. Cesareo, pulpit, detail

sphinxes, lions and griffins, all fashionable quotations and without political or other ideological motivation. The pulpit at S. Cesareo, wherever it came from, is one of many examples of this pretentious but crude art (fig. 151).

Is it possible that the ancient statuary assembled at the Lateran Palace, the papal residence through the Middle Ages, was interpreted, at least from the eleventh and twelfth centuries on, to support papal claims to be heirs to the tradition of ancient Rome? By then a number of bronze sculptures had been gathered under the porticoes and in front of the palace: the *lupa*; the equestrian Marcus Aurelius; the tablet with the *lex Vespasiani*; the thornpicker; Constantine's colossal head and hand—the last three placed on columns; a ram or ram's head spouting water, below the *lupa*. A selection from among the pieces is depicted, fantastically transposed, in a fifteenth-century manuscript (fig. 152). The "palace of our imperial rule at the Lateran, which excels all other palaces on earth," was listed in the Donation as one of the principal gifts of Constantine to the pope. The equestrian statue of Marcus Aurelius was viewed as establishing the pope as the legitimate ruler of Rome and the West, as the Donation would have it. Moved at an unknown time from the emperor's ancestral villa, under what is now the hospital of S. Giovanni, to a site near the northeast corner of the older part of the papal palace, the statue was apparently set up on a new base carried by columns and lions, some time in the twelfth or thirteenth century (figs. 153, 154, 260). As early as the tenth century it was believed to represent Constantine—an opinion not doubted until the twelfth century—and like the *lupa* it was a place of judgment: in 963, as noted, the unfortunate city prefect who led a revolt against emperor and pope was hung by his hair from the statue. At that time, then, it was a symbol of papal, and originally perhaps imperial, jurisdiction, a monumental reminder of the legitimacy of papal temporal rule, as established by the Donation. By the middle of the tenth century or the end, if not already the first thirty years, of the ninth, the bronze *lupa* marked the site where in a portico of the palace the emperor's permanent resident in Rome, his *missus*, sat in judgment (fig. 155). Originally on the Capitol and in 65 B.C. struck by a bolt of lightning that evidently broke its feet and destroyed the group of the twins, the she-wolf seems to have been hidden with other sacred statues in the vaulting of the Capitol and from there brought to the Lateran at an unknown time. The reason for the transfer, on the other hand, appears obvious: "Mother of the Romans," as she was, the *lupa* would be the symbol of the ruler of Rome. With the disappearance of imperial power from the mid-eleventh century on, she would stand, in conformity with the reinterpretation of the Constantinian Donation, for papal jurisdiction and rule over Rome. A third witness to papal rule was the bronze tablet "before the *lupa*," the *lex Vespasiani*; inscribed in a beautiful *antiqua*, it bore part of a decree through which the Senate and People of Rome transferred to Vespasian the imperial *potestas* as previously exercised by Augustus. First mentioned by Magister Gregory, who found it hard to decipher, the tablet may have been there long before; its lettering is likely to have been legible when *antiqua* was in use in the ninth and possibly tenth centuries. Thus it would have closed the circle: Senate and People transferred to the emperor jurisdiction and rule over Rome; and Constantine, having made Rome and the empire Christian, passed them on to the pope. Along with the *lupa*, the Marcus Aurelius, and the *lex Vespasiani*, a bronze head and a hand carrying a globe, both from a colossal statue of Constantine, also stood in front of the Lateran palace. They clearly held political implications. Popular belief, from before the 1100s and into the thirteenth century viewed the fragments as remains of a giant Samson. Magister Gregory, on the other hand, or his acquaintances at the Curia, saw the political note; the

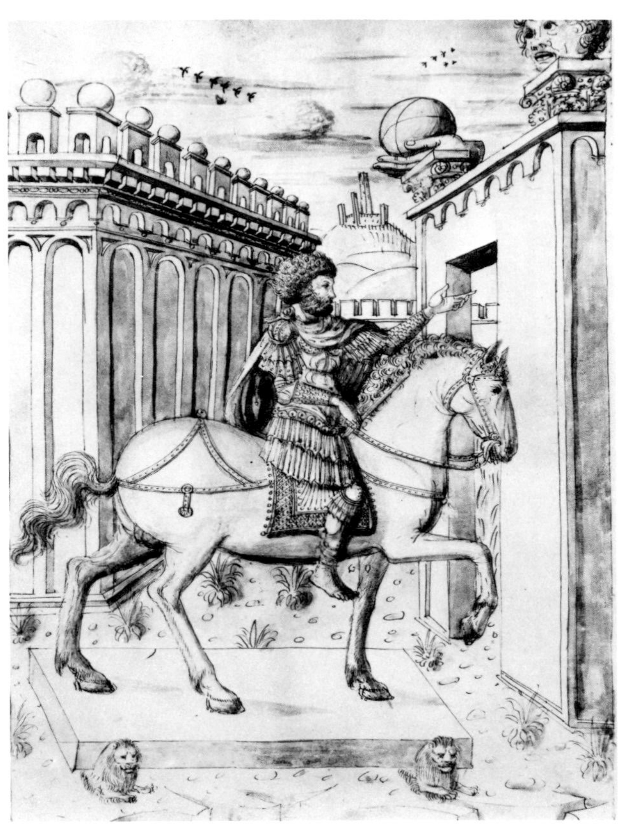

152. Collection of antiques at Lateran in fantastic setting, Giovanni da Modena (?), Modena, Biblioteca Estense

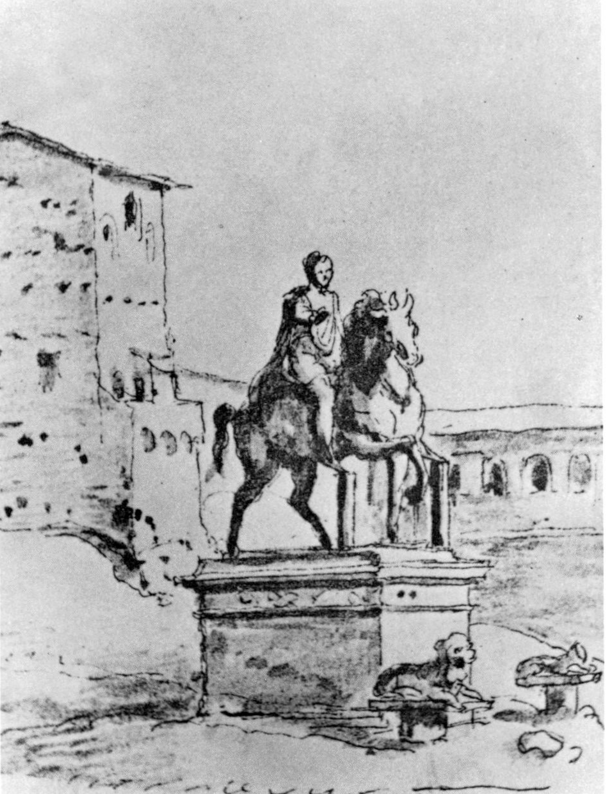

153. View of Lateran, detail, showing statue of Marcus Aurelius as set up in the fifteenth century, and twelfth-century lions, as of 1534-1536, drawing Marten van Heemskerck, Berlin, Kupferstichkabinett, 79 D2, fol. 71^r

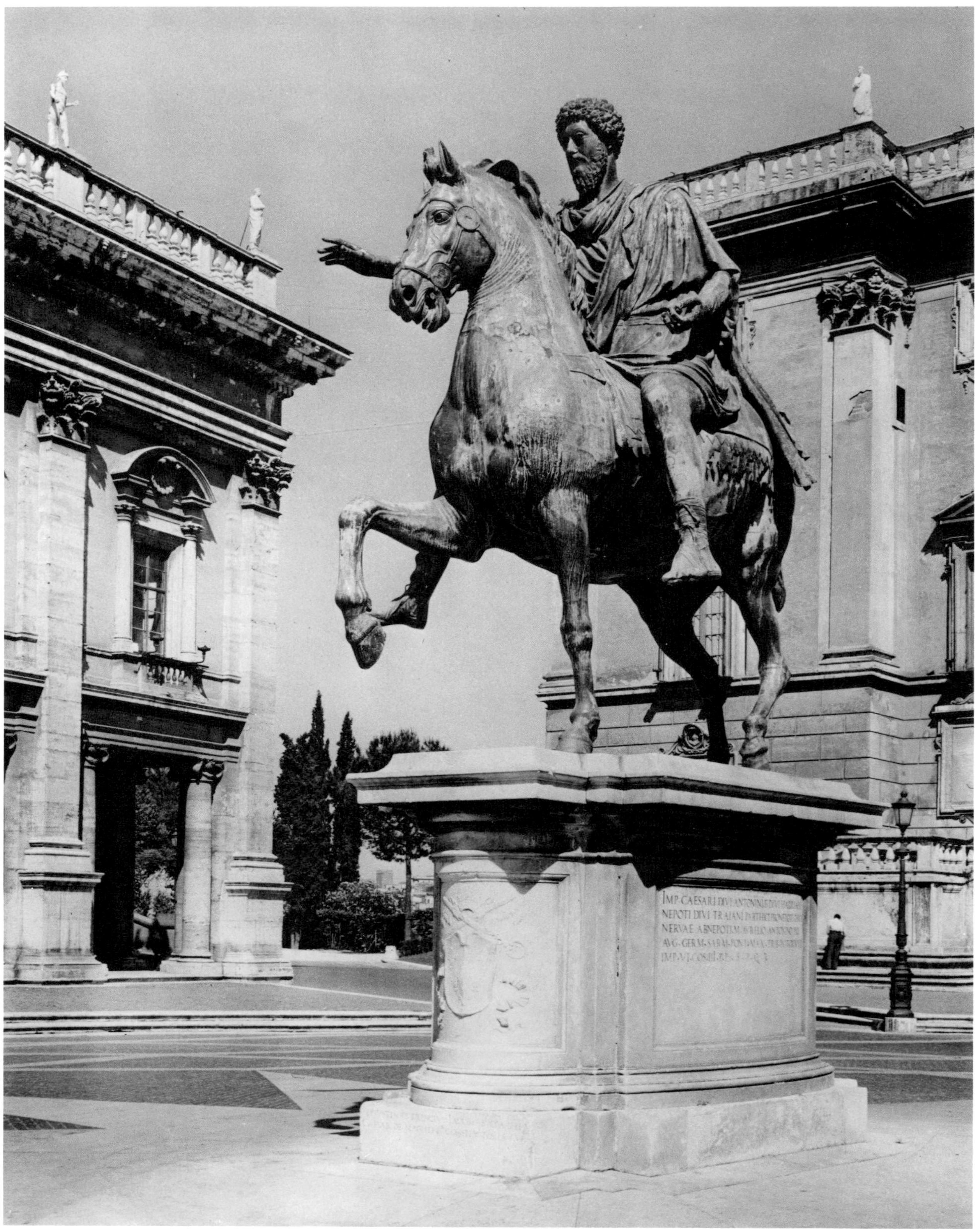

154. *Marcus Aurelius*

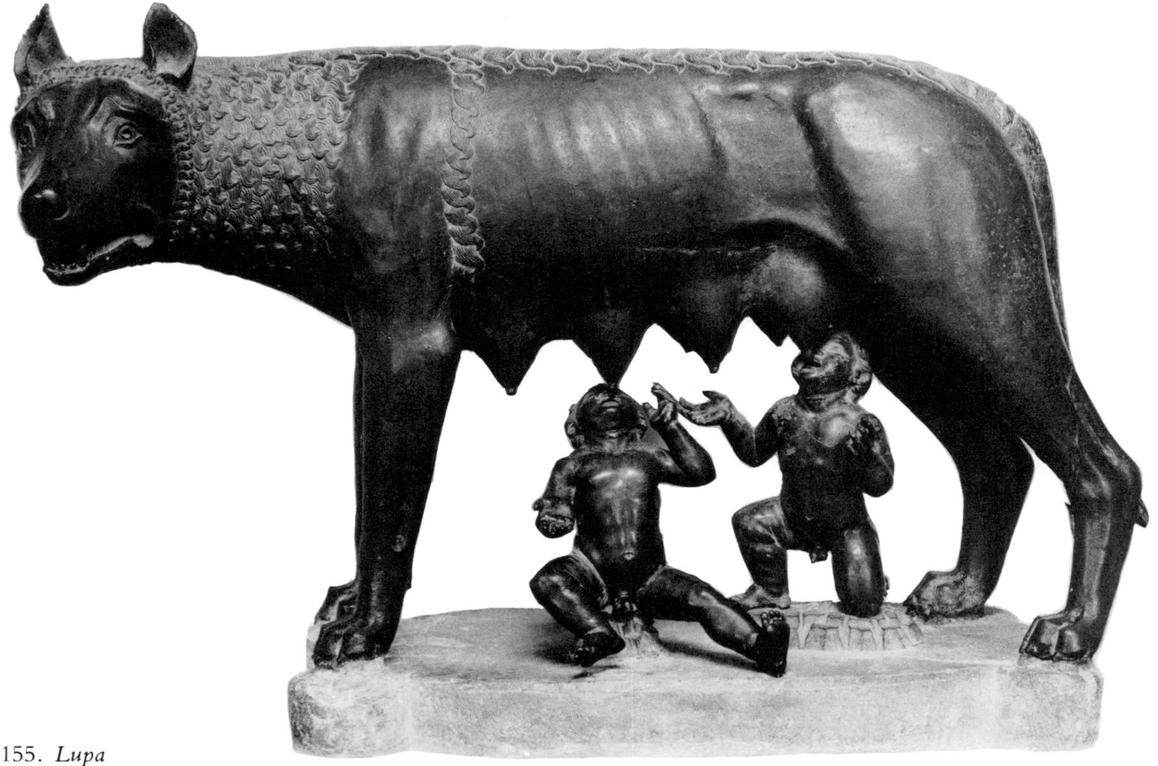

155. *Lupa*

globe meant the world and the power to hold it. He believed the pieces to have belonged to a colossal statue atop or near the Colosseum—he had read both Suetonius' *Life of Nero* and the late-antique gazzetteers; to him it represented the Sun God, venerated by the ancients as a symbol of Rome and covered, he says, with "Imperial gold." To the learned, it seems, these colossal fragments signified the power of Rome, her sway over the world, and her imperial splendor.

However, other meanings as well were seen in all this statuary assembled at the Lateran. Popular exegesis went its own way—the "Samson" is one example, the Marcus Aurelius, as we shall see, another. Placed on columns, as were several of the pieces, they could also have been interpreted as idols, as Heckscher suggested. Certainly, the thornpicker, one would think, was such a heathenish thing, laughable in the sight of Christ's victory and the sway He held through his vicar, residing in the palace (fig. 156). Yet, exposed to ridicule, these pagan

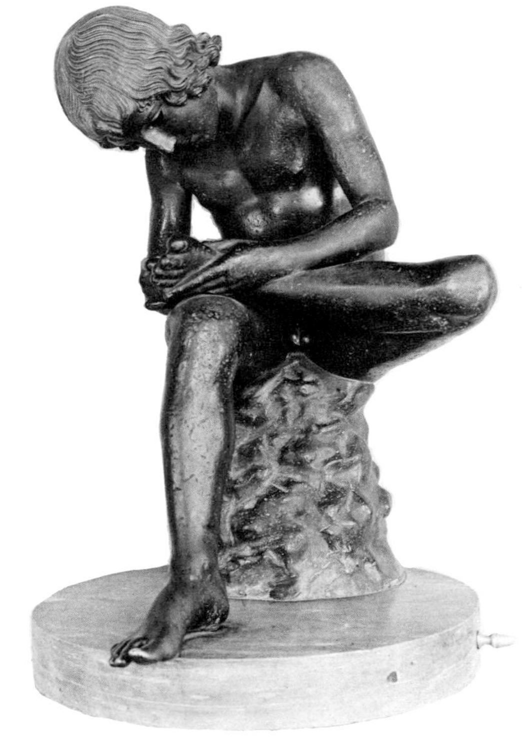

156. *Thornpicker*

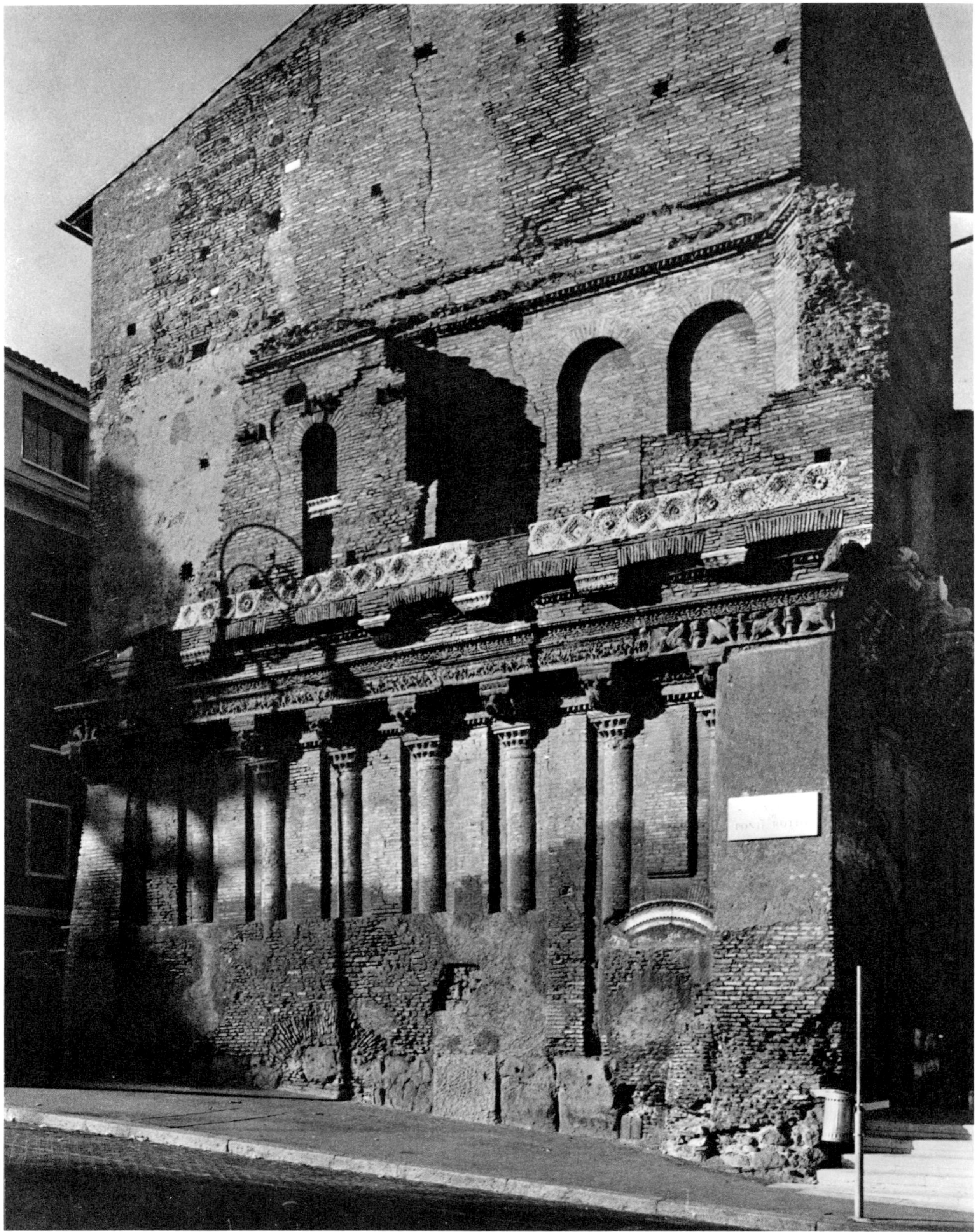

157. Casa di Crescenzio

"idols" were awesome as well. The colossal head and hand were, according to Magister Gregory, "of frightening size"; and their technical perfection and lifelike beauty, too, were somewhat scary. Nonetheless, meanings aside, all this sculpture assembled at the Lateran over the centuries had another facet as well. A great lord, like the pope, would have taken pride in and enjoyed the possession of so many rare, curious, and beautiful, not to mention precious, objects. That they had political overtones was one thing; that they impressed visitors and the people, another; and another yet that the cultured prelates at the papal court just liked them.

The political overtones Roman antiquity and its revival held for the papacy reflect one aspect of the picture. Another aspect is reflected in the connotations this revival had for the Roman Republic, revived along medieval lines in 1143/4 by the Senate and People of Rome. But this republican rebirth is rarely mirrored in surviving buildings or their decoration. The installation of a Senate palace around 1150 on the Capitol was certainly a tangible symbol of the city's freedom, precariously and ephemerally won. But that building may simply have used the mansion of the Corsi clan set up on the ruins of the Tabularium; and its thirteenth-century successor, now enveloped by the structure as redesigned by Michelangelo, held no antique overtones in plan or design. The only surviving monument to reflect visibly the spirit of antiquity antedates, it seems, the formation of the republic by decades, perhaps as much as half a century—the so-called Casa di Crescenzio (fig. 157). Based on the style of the lettering in the inscriptions, a date "between the late eleventh and the middle of the twelfth century, but closer to 1100" has been plausibly suggested. Built by one Nicolaus, son or descendant of a Crescens and a Theodora—both names recall the family of Alberic, Rome's tenth-century master—it rose, originally as a tower, in the midst of what in the Middle Ages was the densely built-up quarter near the river between the Theatre of Marcellus and S. Maria in Cosmedin. However, it differs vastly from the usual run of towers. At present, only the ground floor and a fragment of the upper story and its arcaded loggia remain, isolated in the asphalted clean-up of the area effected half a century ago. Seven segmented column shafts, half swallowed by the wall, all built of brick and flanked by brick piers, weakly articulate the façade. Two rows of bricks, diagonally inserted, crown the shafts in place of capitals, while the entablature and the supporting brackets represent a collage of architectural fragments—volutes, foliage, putti, sphinxes, coffering—purloined from ancient Roman buildings, with a few medieval copies in between (fig. 158). Poorly constructed, the building forecasts the connotations of antiquity revived, as they were prevalent at the height of the Roman republic in the middle of the twelfth century. The inscriptions placed by the owner all over his mansion strengthen these implications. Interwoven with the theme, whether Christian or Stoic, of the passing of all earthly glory and the inevitability of death, they stress his pride in

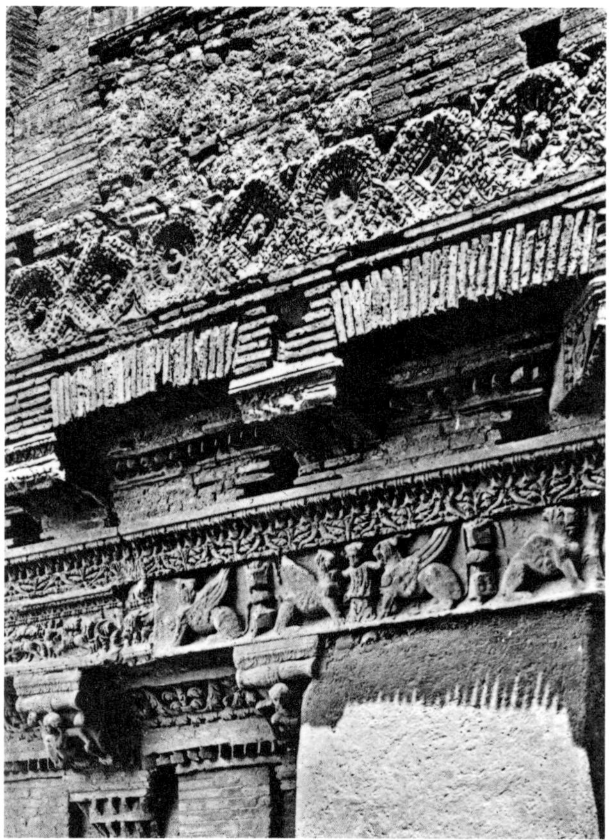

158. Casa di Crescenzio, detail

his ancestry and his aim to renew Rome's ancient grandeur, the house doing the Roman people proud. Nor is it by chance that the passers-by are called "Quirites," the long-obsolete ancient name for a citizen of the Roman Republic.

The Casa di Crescenzio, if indeed it dates around 1100 or shortly after, highlights the situation. The spirit that in 1143 led to the formation of the republic had been alive presumably among intellectuals and litterateurs long before it crystallized into political action. Sparked off as it was by their readings of the ancient writers, the revival of antiquity and its political interpretation was naturally reflected as much in literary as in visual form. It is hardly by chance that, as in ancient Rome, repairs of a purely practical nature—on the city walls in 1157; on the Bridge of Cestius in 1191-1193—were commemorated by inscriptions, naming officials responsible—the Senator Benedictus Carushomo on the bridge. In 1119, S. Silvestro in Capite's possession of the Column of Marcus Aurelius was still confirmed simply in terms of the monastery's property rights to both the Column and the attached chapel and its income. On the contrary, by 1162, the Column of Trajan, while still the property of SS. Apostoli—although the attached chapel belonged to the nunnery of S. Ciriaco in Via Lata—was placed directly under the protection of the Senate, in honor of that church, and the People of Rome in its entirety; this was to ensure that the column should "remain whole and undiminished as long as the world lasts," any violation to be punished by death and confiscation of property. Sometime between 1150 and 1250—I incline toward the earlier date, but others, possibly better informed, prefer a later one—an obelisk from Roman times was repaired and set up at the northeast corner of the Capitoline Hill, on a base resting on four lions of medieval workmanship; both obelisk and lions are in Villa Mattei on the Celian, transferred there in 1582. On the Capitol, the obelisk was placed between the medieval Palazzo del Senatore and the twelfth-century church of S. Maria in Capitolio (fig. 159), which until about 1260 rose on the site of the transept of the present church of S. Maria in Aracoeli. Thus, the obelisk may well have stood as a symbol of the *comune* and the Senate, the Roman Republic revived.

The concept of ancient Rome reborn and interpreted along the lines of contemporary political aspirations and realities comes forth most clearly in a guidebook, completed by Benedict, a canon of St. Peter's, between 1140 and 1143, and revised the following year. Written by a scholar much alive to the political constellations of his day, for men as learned and as much political animals as himself, the *Mirabilia* drew on many different sources: fourth-century gazetteers; passions of saints; pilgrim guides of the seventh century; passages from the *Liber Pontificalis*; and, more relevant still in our context, legends woven ever since late antiquity around the monuments and sites of ancient Rome and newly interpreted; and, in a periegesis through the city, references to temples and ancient sites plucked from Roman literature, in particular Ovid's *Fasti*. All this has been set in a structure very different from any of the earlier Rome guides. A glance at the periegetic section will tell. The pilgrim guides had led the faithful to the relics of the saints in catacombs and churches, naturally so. The Einsiedeln sylloge and itinerary had indiscriminately listed inscriptions, pagan or Christian, and temples and churches along the routes traversing the city. On the contrary, the author of the *Mirabilia* centers attention exclusively on ancient Rome; churches serve only to locate the presumed site of an ancient building or sanctuary. Thus he leads a systematic tour through the ancient city, always focusing on the monuments; their identification from literary references, though important, is secondary. Starting at the Vatican, he lists the obelisk—its globe contains, as Benedict is the first to say, Caesar's ashes; the two mausolea—one presumed to be a Temple of Apollo; and the *pigna* and its canopy in the atrium. Thence he moves to the Mausoleum of Hadrian and other ancient monuments nearby; across the river to the Mausoleum of Augustus, the Pantheon, and the other temples of the Campus Martius; and as the climax, to the Capitol and its long-lost temples, to the Forum and the Palatine. A tour of ancient monuments

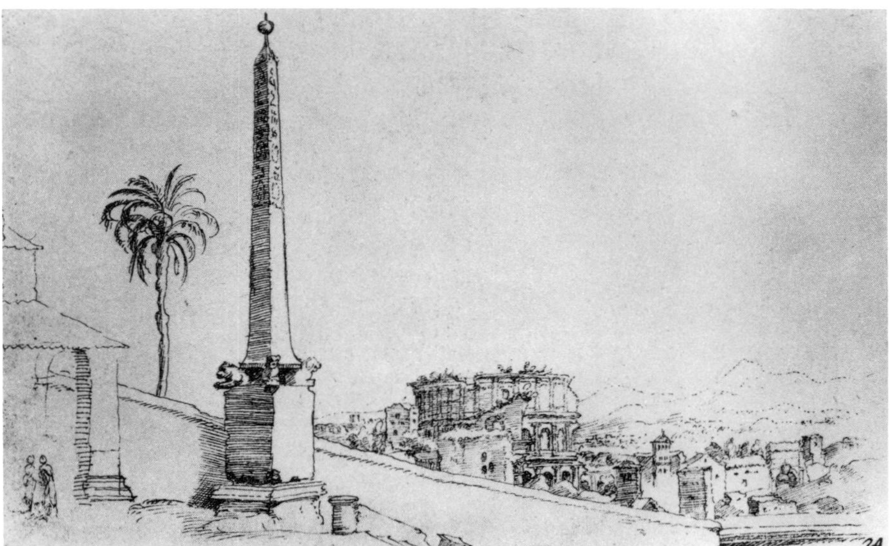

159. Obelisk on Capitol, with view of Colosseum in distance, as of 1534-1536, drawing Marten van Heemskerck, Berlin, Kupferstichkabinett, 79 D2A, fol. 11r

in the disabitato—the Celian Hill, the Esquiline, Quirinal, and Aventine, ending in Trastevere—terminates the survey.

The aim of this evocation of ancient Rome, and of the entire treatise, is revealed in the selection of legends recounted, in their interpretation and that of the monuments, in the overtones of the telling and in the terminating summary. Time and again an event is said to have taken place "at the time of the consuls and senators," this rather than the emperors; the building of the Pantheon is linked to "the subjection to the Roman senate of the Swabians and Saxons and other nations in the West"—an obvious dig at the German emperors of the early twelfth century, the Hohenstaufen Konrad II and Lothar of Supplinburg—and of the Persians in the East; Augustus was given his name *ab augendo rem publicam*, because he increased the commonwealth; and the Capitol was the *caput mundi*, "where the senators and consuls sat to rule the world." The age-old legend of the *salvatio Romae*—the seventy statues on the Capitol, each with a bell to warn of any disturbance in the lands subject to Rome—gains new prominence. The statue of Marcus Aurelius at the Lateran "is said to be Constantine's; but this is not so"; instead, it represents a squire who "at the time of the consuls and senators" freed Rome besieged by a king from the East, and captured him; the slap at Constantine, whose Donation had established the pope at the Lateran as temporal ruler, seems as unmistakable as his replacement by a folk hero. Just as significant may be the omission of the other bronze statues at the Lateran—"there are many to admire, but we must not write of them," possibly because they were symbols of papal rule—but were they all, even the thornpicker or the ram Magister Gregory saw? The last paragraph of the book finally sums up the sources, methods, and political aims of the author: "These and many more temples and palaces of emperors, consuls, senators and prefects were in pagan times in this city of Rome, as we read in the old annals and see with our own eyes and have heard from our elders. How beautifully they shone in gold and silver, bronze, ivory and precious stones, we have taken care to sum up as best we could for the remembrance of future generations."

Clearly, such a summoning forth of Roman antiquity drew its meaning from the political aspirations and passions of the time, and was kindled by intellectuals, such as Arnold of Brescia. But this gives a lopsided picture. None of the scholars or political figures involved in the movement, always conscious and enamored as they were of the memory of ancient Rome, her grandeur and her monuments, forgot that this past was pagan. The Middle Ages were Christian and those enthused with antiquity, whether or not in a political context, were as good Christians as anyone else. Their love for the ancient past of Rome would go hand in hand with their sincere conviction that this past, since pagan, had been overcome by the Christian traditions of the city; that its destruction, indeed, was God's punishment for its long, sinful, heathen history; and that holy men, lending a hand in the work of destruction, had acted rightly. The same John of Salisbury who without disapproval recounts Henry of Winchester's collecting ancient sculpture, tells almost approvingly of Gregory the Great's having burnt the ancient libraries because Holy Writ was ever so much better. Thirteenth- and fourteenth-century chroniclers enlarged on the legend: by then, Gregory had "caused the heads and limbs of the statues of demons everywhere to be truncated, so that the root of heretical depravity would be ripped out and the palm of ecclesiastical truth more fully raised." Hildebert of Lavardin's long double poem brings out in superb verse the interweaving of this love of ancient Rome, of her divinely preordained destruction and the victory of Christ, a true love-hate relationship:

Par tibi, Roma, nihil, cum sis prope tota ruina;
Quam magni fueris integra, fracta doces.
Longa tuos fastus aetas destruxit, et arces
Caesaris et superûm templa palude iacent.
Ille labor, labor ille ruit, quem dirus Araxes
Et stantem tremuit et cecidisse dolet;
Quem gladii regum, quem provida cura senatus,
Quem superi rerum constituere caput;
Quem magis optavit cum crimine solus habere
Caesar, quam socius et pius esse socer;
Qui crescens studiis tribus hostes, crimen, amicos
Vi domuit, secuit legibus, emit ope;
In quem, dum fieret, vigilavit cura priorum,
Iuvit opus pietas hospitis, unda, locus.
Materiem, fabros, expensas axis uterque
Misit, se muris obtulit ipse locus.
Expendere duces thesauros, fata favorem,
Artifices studium, totus et orbis opes.
Urbs cecidit, de qua, si quicquam dicere dignum
Moliar, hoc potero dicere: Roma fuit!
Non tamen annorum series, non flamma, nec ensis
Ad plenum potuit hoc abolere decus.
Cura hominum potuit tantam componere Romam,
Quantam non potuit solvere cura deûm.
Confer opes marmorque novum superûmque favorem,
Artificum vigilent in nova facta manus.
Non tamen aut fieri par stanti machina muro,
Aut restaurari sola ruina potest.
Tantum restat adhuc, tantum ruit, ut neque pars stans

Here follows a translation of the crucial lines:

Rome, without compare, though all but shattered;
Your very ruins tell of greatness once enjoyed.
Great age has tumbled your boasting,
The palaces of Caesar and the temples of the gods alike lie smothering in the mud.
Fallen, fallen the prize of all that effort
At whose power the dread Araxes once trembled.
Whose prostration he laments today.
She, whom the swords of kings, the caring foresight of the Senate,
And the gods themselves established at the head of all creation. (1-8)

Fallen the city of which, were I to attempt a worthy phrase,
I'd say—Rome, she was. (19-20)

Here, the gods admire their images in her
Longing to resemble those sculptured faces;
But nature could not fashion gods in that form
By which man shaped such marvelous statues of gods.
With those features, these gods were honored,
Rather for the skill that shaped them than for their deity. (31-36)

She indeed is a blessed city who is free of masters,
Or if she have them, if it but be held ignoble that her masters lack the Faith. (37-38)

Aequari possit, diruta nec refici.
Hic superûm formas superi mirantur et ipsi
Et cupiunt fictis vultibus esse pares.
Non potuit natura deos hoc ore creare,
Quo miranda deûm signa creavit homo.
Vultus adest his numinibus, potiusque coluntur
Artificum studio quam deitate sua.

One reads the warm elegiac lines, filled with a sad love of Rome in ruin, and too easily forgets that there is a sequel, a second poem to go with the first:

Urbs felix, si vel dominis urbs illa careret,
Vel dominis esset turpe carere fide!
Dum simulacra mihi, dum numina vana placerent,
Militia, populo, moenibus alta fui;
At simul effigies arasque superstitiosas
Deiiciens, uni sum famulata Deo,
Cesserunt arces, cecidere palatia divûm,
Servivit populus, degeneravit eques.
Vix scio, quae fuerim, vix Romae Roma recordor,
Vix sinit occasus vel meminisse mei.
Gratior haec iactura mihi successibus illis;
Maior sum pauper divite, stante iacens.
Plus aquilis vexilla crucis, plus Caesare Petrus,
Plus cinctis ducibus vulgus inerme dedit.
Stans domui terras, infernum diruta pulso;
Corpora stans, animas fracta iacensque rego.
Tunc miserae plebi, modo principibus tenebrarum
Impero; tunc urbes, nunc mea regna polus.
Quae ne Caesaribus videar debere vel armis,
Et species rerum meque meosque trahat,
Armorum vis illa perit, ruit alta senatus
Gloria, procumbunt templa, theatra iacent,
Rostra vacant, edicta silent, sua praemia desunt
Emeritis, populo iura, colonus agris;
Durus eques, iudex rigidus, plebs libera quondam
Quaerit, amat, patitur otia, lucra, iugum.
Ista iacent, ne forte meus spem ponat in illis
Civis et evacuet spemque bonumque crucis.
Crux aedes alias, alios promittit honores,
Militibus tribuens regna superna suis.
Sub cruce rex servit, sed liber; lege tenetur,
Sed diadema gerens; iussa tremit, sed amat.
Fundit avarus opes, sed abundat; foenerat idem,
Sed bene custodit, si super astra locat.
Quis gladio Caesar, quis sollicitudine consul,
Quis rhetor lingua, quae mea castra manu
Tanta dedere mihi? Studiis et legibus horum
Obtinui terras; crux dedit una polum.

While I delighted in idols and false gods,
I boasted civil and military might with impregnable defenses;
But once throwing down idols and their pagan altars
I made submission to the one true God,
My power dried up, my temples fell to ruin,
My people sank to servitude, my knighthood wasted.
I hardly know who I have been:
I, Rome, can scarce remember Rome! (39-45)
But now, more than the eagles of the legions,
The standard of the Cross has gifted me;
More than Caesar, Peter;
More than armored princes, the common people;
And all this without resort to arms. (49-50)
The Cross now pledges other mansions, different honors,
Opening to its knights a kingdom in Heaven. (65-66)
Which Caesar gave me possession of such riches with his sword,
Or consul's vigilance, or speaker's skillful tongue,
Or which, indeed, of my military camps?
From these, by their heedful government, I won the earth;
From the Cross all Heaven. (71-74)

Pagan Rome, then, had given way to a better, since Christian, Rome, the only Rome imaginable to medieval man. This, of course, was the view generally held all through Western Christendom; to the ordinary visitor, and even more so to the pilgrim come to seek salvation, Rome was *The* Christian city, and her Christian sanctuaries were what counted; her ancient ruins were strange survivals of a bygone world, suspect because of its pagan, devilish connotations. Men such as Hildebert of Lavardin took a different view: pagan Rome had been defeated, Rome was a Christian city; but in defeating paganism, Rome had made the pagan monuments her own. The pagan city had been fused into and become an integral part of Christian Rome. Such men were obviously a small group; but they shaped the image of Rome held by an educated class into the fifteenth century. This image from the late thirteenth century on is reflected time and again in "abbreviated views," in which Rome is represented symbolically by a few selected buildings: Cimabue's at Assisi, from about 1280, shows the city walls, with their gates and towers—recalling the first sections of the *Mirabilia* and their late-antique forerunners; St. Peter's and S. Maria in Aracoeli, with the arms of the Commune; Torre delle Milizie and, perhaps, Tor de' Conti; Castel S. Angelo, the obelisk at St. Peter's, the Pantheon, and what may be the Colosseum. More clearly, the Golden Bull of Louis the Bavarian, 1328, presents the walls, towers, and gates of the city, as well as the Tiber; the Pantheon and the Column of Marcus Aurelius; perhaps the Mausoleum of Augustus; the Palazzo del Senatore, the Colosseum, a triumphal arch, the Pyramid of Cestius; the Lateran; and across the river, Castel S. Angelo guarding the bridge, St. Peter's, the obelisk and, downstream, S. Maria in Trastevere (fig. 160). The merger of pagan Rome into Christian Rome could not be more clearly evident. Rome's essential duality disappears only when in about 1460 a Florentine *cassone* painter reduces Rome almost exclusively to non-Christian symbols (fig. 223): Castel S. Angelo, its bridge, the many-towered city walls, a triumphal column, the Pantheon and the Colosseum, and the Capitol with the Palazzo del Senatore; naturally so, given the themes—the Aeneid and Caesar's triumph. Likewise, naturally, the Christian sanctuaries are omitted, except for S. Maria in Aracoeli—its status as a civic symbol along the Palazzo del Senatore, together with its legendary link to Augustus, explain the intrusion. But by then the Middle Ages have ended and with them the easy fusion of ancient Rome with Christian Rome, so obvious to Hildebert of Lavardin.

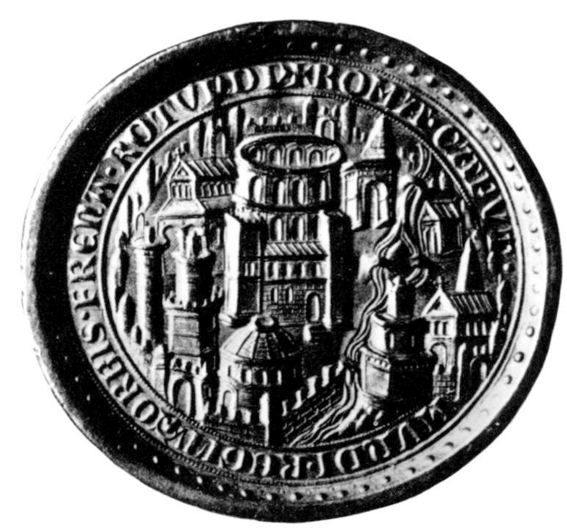

160. Seal from Bull of Louis the Bavarian, enlarged, Munich

CHAPTER EIGHT

The Thirteenth Century: An Epilogue

Three times in the thirteenth century Rome aspired to greatness. In the beginning, with Innocent III and his successor Honorius III on the See of Saint Peter, she became, through the papacy, capital of the Christian world in a very real sense: seat of pontiffs, successors to Constantine as well as to the Apostle, and hence the supreme authority in matters both temporal and spiritual, making and unmaking kings and emperors; a focus where legal and diplomatic decisions were made for the West; a financial power of the first magnitude; at the same time, capital of a papal state, peacefully cooperating with her ruler, the pope. This image of Rome held by medieval man tallied with political reality or nearly so, for thirty years. After the middle of the century, for a short six years, Brancaleone di Andalò, aiming far lower, made Rome into what was almost a free city, capital of a large territory in Central Italy, well organized and economically strong. Reality came sharply into focus against the hazy background of Rome's traditional image. Again, in the later years of the century, from 1277 to 1303, a line of emphatically Roman popes strove to make Rome head of the world, as she had been in the beginning of the century. They failed to do so; political and economic realities fell short of the grand image. Instead, they turned Rome for these twenty-six years into a cultural capital of Italy, if not of the world; the center of a new art which stands beside that of Siena, Florence, and Venice. But, in the end, political events cut short this final flowering of the city, the last in the Middle Ages.

The peak of papal power in the beginning of the century and of Rome's place in the medieval world has left few visible traces in the urban fabric or in surviving monuments. Innocent III, when still a cardinal, rebuilt his title church, SS. Sergio e Bacco on the Forum; it was a very minor construction adjoining the Arch of Septimius Severus; restored again two hundred years later, it was drawn by Heemskerck just before it was demolished in 1536. As pope, Innocent was sparing in subsidies for church building. A list of his contributions survives in his biography: they are small, except for those going to churches and convents of the Cistercian Order then under construction near Rome—Fossanova and Casamari. To be sure, he gave textiles and altar vessels to dozens of churches in Rome and the hill towns; numerous, precious, and colorful though they were, the expense was small in the overall papal budget.

For secular building, on the other hand, he spent large sums—for practical and humanitarian-social ends and for reasons of prestige, both of the papacy and his family. The old Lateran Palace was strengthened and patched up, and a small infirmary was set up. In the Borgo, just across the river and south of Castel S. Angelo, Sto. Spirito in Sassia was established by him in 1198 as both hospital and hostel. Finally, a hundred meters or so north of Old St. Peter's and higher up the Vatican Hill, he built in 1208 a fortified residence for the papacy, the core of the present Vatican palace; today it is enclosed in the corner of a tiny courtyard, the *Cortile del Papagallo*. Built in small *tufelli* blocks, *opus saracinescum*, it rose as a solid block, three floors high, with a five-storied corner tower—its top floors now shelter the chapel frescoed by Fra Angelico (fig. 161). Towers protected a forecourt; they have disappeared, as have a number of office buildings listed and supposedly attached to or contained in the main block: the chaplain's apartment, chapel, and chamber; the bakery, wine cellar, and kitchen; the smithy; and houses for the chancellor, treasurer, and almoner, all obviously with their staffs. It was a structure, "honorabile et utile," representative

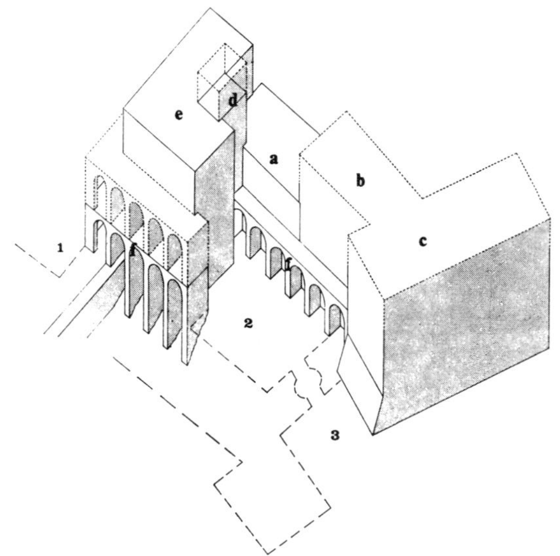

161. Vatican Palace, as of ca. 1280, isometric reconstruction Redig de Campos

and useful, as his biographer described it. For his family, he began in the very first year of his reign building Tor de' Conti (fig. 162), the huge blocky tower behind the Forum of Nerva "in height and width surpassing any other tower," as contemporaries noted, adding that the hospital of Sto. Spirito was built to make up for such pride. The tower, of course, did not stand by itself; rather it protected a fortified compound to shelter the Conti and their retainers, a safe and threatening fortress outside, yet dangerously close to the abitato.

Church building, it seems, Innocent left to others. His Cardinal-Chancellor, Cencio Savelli, later elevated to the papacy as Honorius III, already some years before Innocent's election had started work at S. Lorenzo fuori le mura; during Innocent's pontificate he seems to have continued building, and as pope himself he completed the large church over the shrine, though possibly with funds provided from outside, at least in part—the figure of a layman, perhaps a donor, appears in the mosaic frieze of the portico. An impressive if old-fashioned structure—we spoke of it before—it still stands along the road to Tivoli, its plain nave resting on columns and architraves, all spoils from older buildings nearby (figs. 129, 130). Nave and aisles were joined to the old sixth-century church turned into a raised chancel, and the whole church reaches a full seventy-five meters in length. Presumably, Honorius' aim was to have the rebuilt S. Lorenzo compete with the other large basilicas within and beyond the walls of Rome, venerable either for their age or the martyrs' shrines they sheltered, or for both—St. Peter's, S. Paolo fuori le mura, S. Maria Maggiore, S. Sebastiano, where Honorius had an oratory decorated. His successor, Gregory IX, built near the Lateran "a noble palace for the uses of the poor"—a pilgrims' and visitors' hostel or a poorhouse and possibly a hospital all in one, like Innocent's foundation at Sto. Spirito.

On the whole, Innocent III and his two successors focused on politics, administration, legislation, and finances rather than on church building. When they built, they concentrated on commodiousness and protection for themselves and their families in strong palaces; and they provided social services for Romans and visitors—poorhouses, hospitals, hostels. A third related

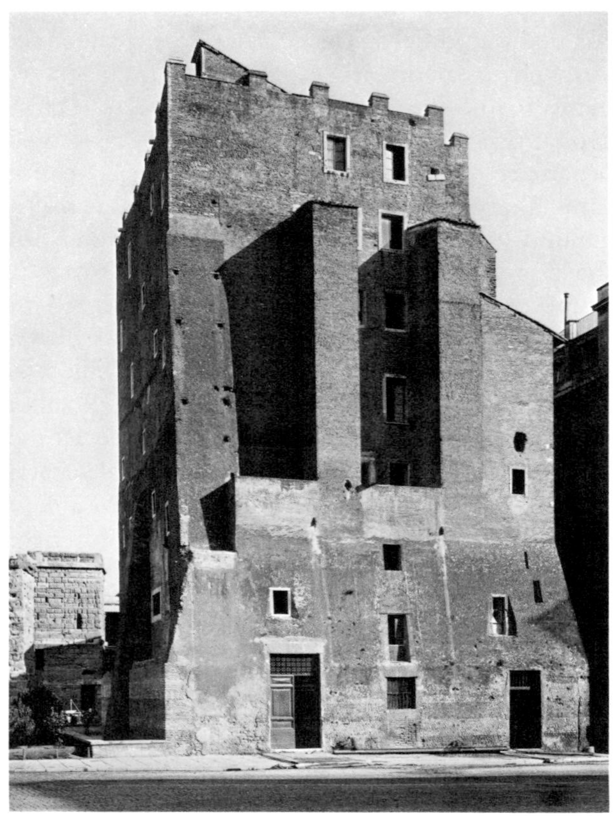

162. Tor de' Conti, as of ca. 1880

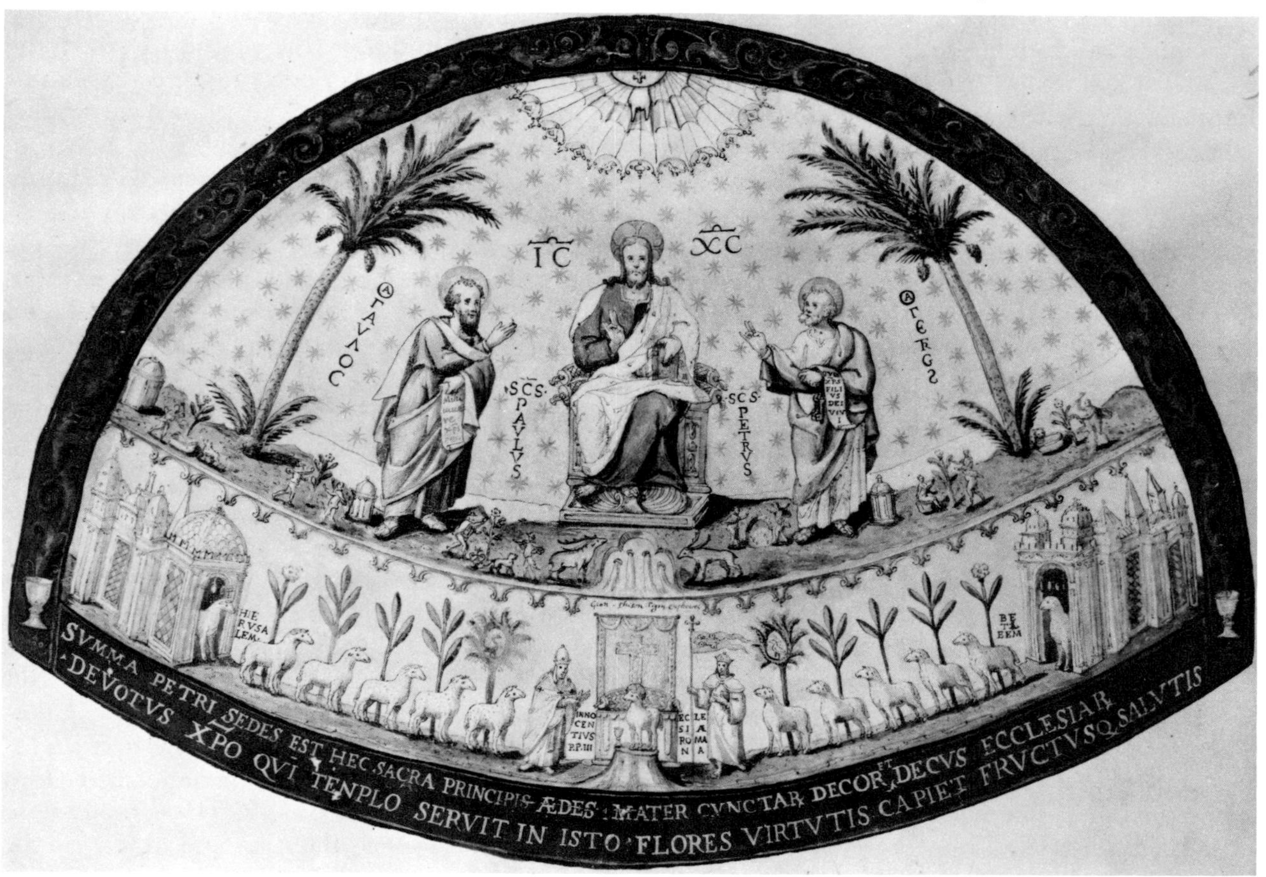

163. St. Peter's, apse mosaic, Giovanni Grimaldi, Biblioteca Vaticana, Arch. S. Pietro, Album, fol. 50

aim was obviously to impress Rome's visitors with the grandeur of her palaces and fortifications and with the lavish decoration of the churches they would likely see; all were donations of the ruling pontiff, bringing glory to himself and to the institutions for which he stood, the papacy and the Church. With glorification in mind, large mosaic decorations were begun by Innocent and completed by his two successors, both at St. Peter's and at S. Paolo fuori le mura. Innocent's apse mosaic at St. Peter's remained in place until the late sixteenth century, when it gave way to the building of New St. Peter's (fig. 163). It showed Christ enthroned, flanked by the Princes of the Apostles, a palm tree at either end. At their feet spread a landscape set with small round and domed structures, huge flowers, dwarf lions, and tiny figures, evidently pigmies—one cutting a flower with an axe; a river apparently flowed below the main scene, suggesting a "Nilotic" landscape, frequent in antiquity. In a lower register, along the rim of the apse vault ran a frieze of twelve lambs, proceeding from Bethlehem and Jerusalem respectively, and separated by palm trees, a phoenix resting in one; at the center, the Lamb of God on a mountain was flanked by the Church of Rome—*Ecclesia Romana*, thus the inscription—banner in hand, and by the pope, standing; his head, that of *Ecclesia*, and the phoenix are the only fragments to survive. The main figures in the apse vault, Christ, Peter and Paul, the palm trees, the Nilotic landscape, and the frieze of lambs may well have repeated the late-fourth-century mosaic that Innocent replaced, if significantly modified: Christ, in the Early Christian mosaic, would have been standing between Peter and Paul, handing the Law to Peter—the formula of a *Traditio legis*; and the figures of Innocent III and the Church were obviously not part of the earlier scheme. But their appearance and placing in Innocent's composition carry significant implications. True, papal donors had regularly appeared in apse mosaics in Rome from at least the sixth century into the twelfth. But, at SS. Cosma e Damiano, at S. Prassede, at S. Maria in Trastevere, the pope had stood alongside the Princes of the Apostles and the patron saints of the Church, a denizen of the Heavenly realm, introduced by these intercessors into the Presence; or he had been kneeling, as at S. Maria in Domnica, at the feet of the Virgin amidst the Heavenly Host. At St. Peter's, Innocent and the Church with the Apostles occupy a separate sphere: the world where Christ, the Lamb of God, became flesh and sacrificed Himself, lower than Heaven, but higher than daily life. Nor is Innocent marked as donor, holding a model as customary. Rather he is *The* Pope. He and the Roman Church are equal and coterminal; they mirror on earth the Apostolic Succession adumbrated both in the Heavenly sphere and by the pope's being placed among the lambs, the Apostles—*isapostolos*, one is tempted to say. The inscription under the apse mosaic stressed the same theme of Apostolic Succession and papal supremacy: "This is the See of Saint Peter, this the Temple of the Prince [of the Apostles], the glory and mother of all churches . . ."—Innocent usurping for Saint Peter's the title claimed by the Lateran, the cathedral of Rome and hence traditionally "Mother of all Churches."

The apse mosaic at S. Paolo likewise may have been begun in Innocent's pontificate. Largely executed under Honorius III, though completed after his death and badly damaged in 1823 when the church burned down, it survives, heavily restored. But its theme, the glorification of Christ enthroned in majesty among Apostles and Evangelists, with the Cross and symbols of the Passion in the lower register, is apolitical. The mosaics at St. Peter's stressed time and again the greatness and age of the Church of Rome and the papacy, whereas those at S. Paolo were neutral in that respect; and, significantly, the tiny figure of Honorius III kneels at the feet of Christ, below and outside the Heavenly sphere, a donor and a mortal.

Papal power and consciousness of it had declined by the middle of the century. Instead, the power of the city was rising, and it is within this context that the most conspicuous communal building was created: the Palazzo del Senatore on the Capitol. Whether it was erected or simply rebuilt in this period is uncertain, for a first palace of the commune was in use as early as 1151 when the city council met in the "new assembly hall of the palace of the Senate." This hall, as I said before, had possibly been installed in the old fortified mansion that the Corsi family by the eleventh century or before had raised over the ruins of the Tabularium, the arcaded Roman structure at the east cliff of the hill overlooking the Forum. Whatever that early palace of the commune looked like, it was thoroughly rebuilt or indeed replaced a hundred years later by a *palatium novum*, a new palace, on the same site. Construction campaigns and dates of this new Palazzo del Senatore remain to be clarified. But it seems as if work had started while Brancaleone was *senatore*; in 1257 for the first time a new and an old palace are distinguished from one another. Construction may have made slow progress. However, the plan and aspect of the new palace as it appeared by 1306 have been convincingly sketched, hidden as they are to this day under two major remodelings: Michelangelo's, begun in 1538 and completed by others by 1612; and a previous one, shortly before and after 1400, which turned the structure into a four-towered fortress with all openings blocked. The core of the tall rear tower likewise seems to date about 1400, while the loggia and the false façade still seen in 1550 went back to a mid-fifteenth-century remodeling. The thirteenth-century palace, on the contrary, opened its façade—possibly from the pontificate of Boniface VIII on—in three tiers of low arcades, resting on piers and columns surmounted by Ionic capitals (fig. 164). Inside, three superimposed halls occupied nearly the entire main block; an entrance ramp ascended on the right, stairwells filled the rear; the right end was given over to smaller rooms, whence the *senatore* attended capital executions performed halfway up the ramp; on the left a tower projected from the northwest corner, whence joint assemblies of

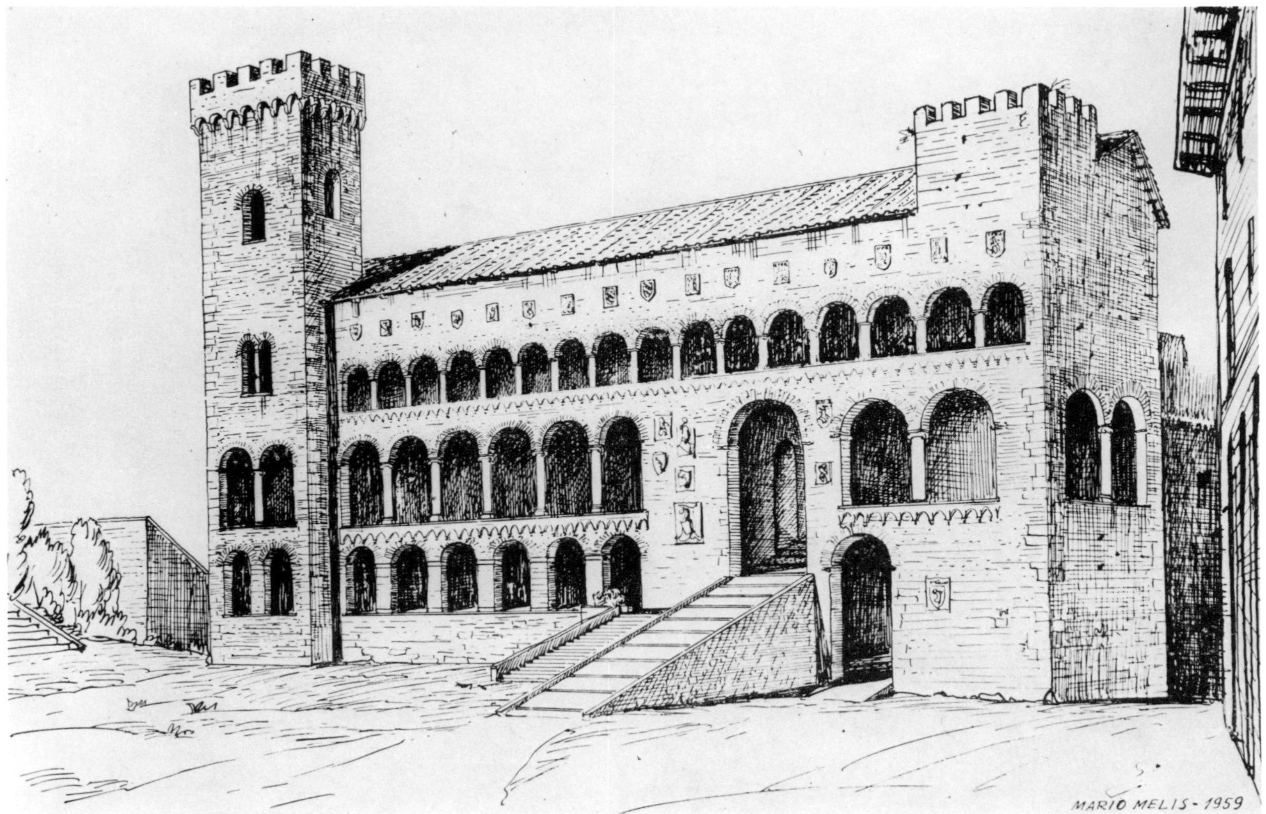

164. Palazzo del Senatore, as of ca. 1300, isometric reconstruction Pietrangeli

the People and Senate, the former in front of the palace, would be called at "the sound of trumpets and the ringing of the bell." The right corner was later raised so as to form a second front tower as it appears by the early fourteenth century. It seems that the body of the thirteenth-century structure filled the length, width, and height of Michelangelo's palace. The design harks back to town halls commonly built by the North Italian communes a century and more before—with a typical Roman time lag. Still, the palace in the thirteenth century must have been an imposing structure, dominating the hill and, beyond, the eastward parts of the abitato.

If the peak of papal authority in the early decades of the thirteenth century and the resurgence of city pride around the 1250s are scarcely reflected in surviving monuments, on the contrary the popes from Nicholas III to Boniface VIII, from 1278 to 1303, reveled in beautifying Rome. Popes and cardinals rebuilt and redecorated churches, furnished them with precious textiles and altar vessels, set up elaborate sepulchral monuments, and built and lavishly decorated their palaces. The papal court luxuriated in ostentatious splendor. Precious stones, textiles, and goldsmith work accumulated in the treasuries of popes and cardinals, in the Lateran Palace, and in churches and convents in Rome and the hill towns. Inventories abound with descriptions of liturgical vestments embroidered with gold thread, set with pearls and jewels resembling, or in fact, imports from England, Cyprus, or Sicily, and donated by successive popes and foreign kings. All too few survive in Rome, in Anagni, in Veroli. Never before had the high dignitaries of the Church and their relatives flaunted their wealth so conspicuously. Roman born and bred, popes and cardinals and their families rivaled each other—one thinks of the similar situation in Carolingian times—in building up a continuous tradition, redecorating churches and filling their treasure chambers, all with the aim of turning Rome into a resplendent

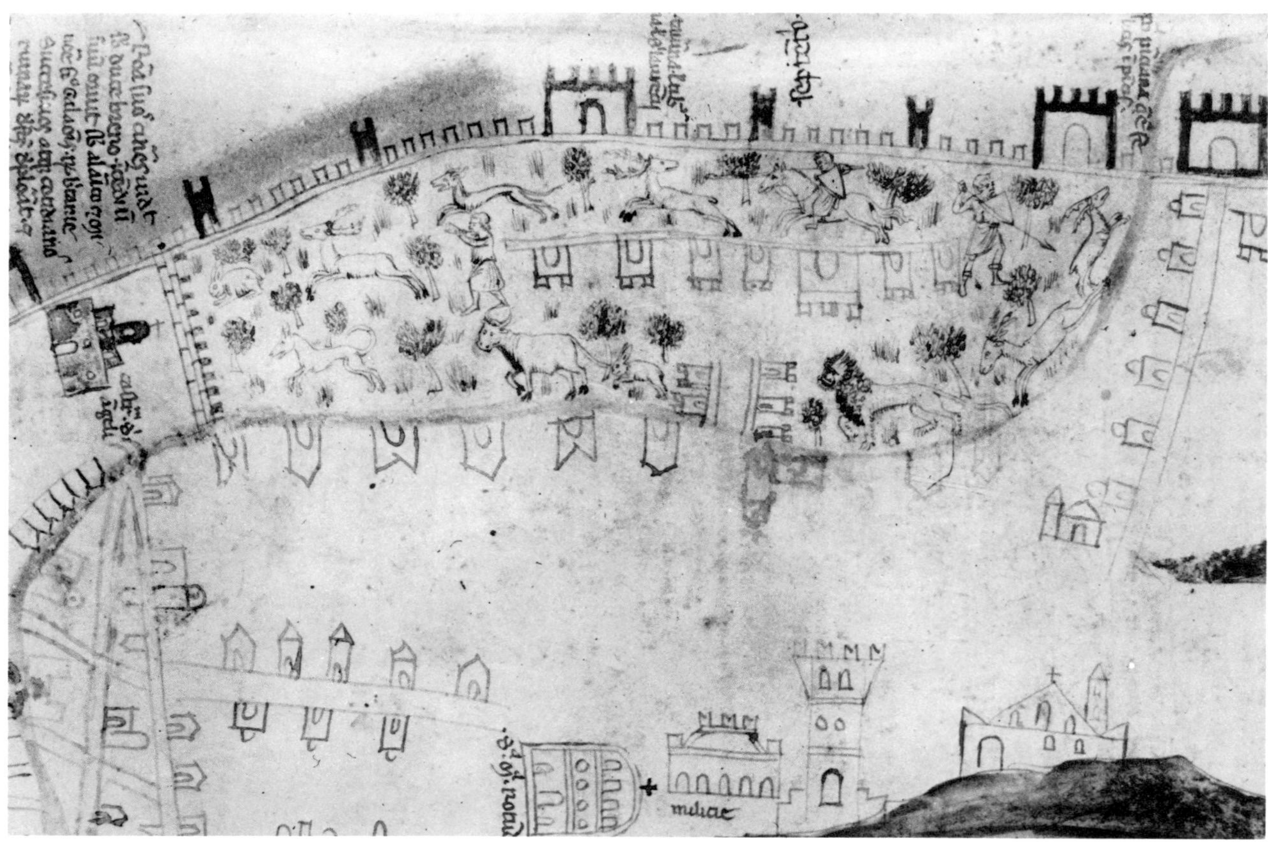

165. Vatican deerpark, Fra Paolino da Venezia, Map, 1323, Biblioteca Vaticana, Vat. lat. 1960, fol. 270v

capital of the world. Large sums went into the program: to honor the saints, to benefit the souls of the donors, and to impress the faithful. Two Colonnas financed work at S. Maria Maggiore, building the transept and apse and covering the walls and the apse vault, as well as the old façade, back and front, with mosaics and murals. Cardinal Jean Cholet took care of redecorating S. Cecilia—murals all over, and an altar canopy. Bertoldo Stefaneschi, a Caetani nephew, donated the mosaic cycle from the life of the Virgin on the apse wall of S. Maria in Trastevere. His brother Cardinal Jacopo without batting an eyelid put down 8,000 gold ducats for work at St. Peter's—2,200 for Giotto's *Navicella* mosaic, 800 for his altarpiece, and 5,000 for his painting the apse. A score of showy tombs, built and sculptured in and around Rome, were paid for by popes, cardinals, and their relatives in these same years.

The palace erected by Innocent III on the Vatican Hill was turned into a luxurious papal residence by Nicholas III and his successors up to 1300, and, like Innocent's, the late-thirteenth-century structures survive, albeit remodeled and enclosed by later buildings within today's palace. Where Innocent had set up a plain three-story block with a corner tower, forecourt, and perhaps small office buildings, Nicholas and his successors added a number of wings, surrounding the present Cortile del Papagallo and extending into the adjoining sixteenth-century parts. An impressive loggia, still to be seen incorporated in the Cortile di S. Damaso, faced the Borgo; mural paintings decorated the rooms and some fragments survive, removed to the storerooms of the Vatican Museums—birds of all kinds, sea monsters, flowers, niches in perspective, all in a colorful impressionistic technique recalling late-antique painting. North of the palace a large, walled garden reached, it seems, as far as the north end of the hill, where since 1483 the Belvedere has stood; a map of 1323 suggests that it was a deerpark (fig. 165). In the old Lateran Palace, Nicholas rebuilt the Chapel of the Sancta Sanctorum; and Boniface VIII, probably in 1299, recast the old balcony projecting from the large Triclinium of Leo III, the *accubita*, into an airy *loggia di benedizione*, facing north whence the pope would bless the crowds assembled in the square (figs. 93, 260). Along with S. Maria Maggiore, the Lateran church, and the other great basilicas, St. Peter's and S. Paolo fuori le mura, were remodeled and provided with mosaics and murals, altar canopies, altarpieces, sculptured tombs, and precious vestments. It would be tempting to view all or some of this activity as preparatory for the Holy Year of 1300. But temptation, unfortunately, must be resisted; the decision to declare a Holy Year was taken only in February 1300, albeit not as unforeseen as the contemporaries presented it. Hence, the splendor spread over Rome and her old sanctuaries by the succession of popes since Nicholas III must be understood, to be sure, as a continued program to present the city, her churches, and the papal palaces at their most impressive and glorious, but with an eye to the ever-increasing stream of visitors, whether pilgrims or prelates and laymen come on business—*ad limina apostolorum* or *ad limina curiae*.

The eagerness to refurbish the city coupled with the riches available drew artists from afar. Cimabue came from Florence as early as 1272. Where he worked, if at all in Rome, remains unknown; one speculates whether he might have taken a hand at some of the newly painted papal portraits at S. Paolo fuori le mura. But the simple fact that he came to Rome, called there or uninvited, shows the growing importance of, and the expectations placed in, the papal court as a center of art patronage. Around the same time, indeed, Arnolfo di Cambio, another Florentine, settled in Rome for nearly twenty-five years. Assisted by a large workshop, he furnished the bulk of the sculpture wanted by Roman patrons in the city and the temporary papal residences, Viterbo and Perugia. In Rome, there remain the altar canopies at S. Paolo from 1284 and at S. Cecilia, dated 1293-1296. There are numbers of tombs, such as that of Cardinal Riccardo Annibaldi, done about 1276—its remains survive in the Lateran cloister (fig. 170). There was the tomb chapel of Boniface VIII at St. Peter's, completed by 1300 and known from drawings done prior to its demolition in 1618 (fig. 171). Fragments survive, some in the Grotte Vaticane, others in the papal apartments. For S. Maria in Aracoeli he did, perhaps still in the 1270s, the statue of Charles of Anjou, lord-protector of Rome—it is now in the Palazzo dei Conservatori on the Capitol. His, too, are the bronze statue of Saint Peter in his basilica, executed about 1296 it seems, and the figures of the crêche at S. Maria Maggiore, though presumably assistants' work. Giotto was called in by Cardinal Stefaneschi to work at St. Peter's, whether in preparation for the Holy Year 1300, or much later, or both, remains under discussion. The murals he did in the apse are lost, and the mosaic of the *Navicella* on the inner façade of the gatehouse facing the atrium of the old church is known only from poor copies. But the monumental triptych for the high altar remains in all its greatness in the Pinacoteca of the Vatican. More important still in the context of a profile of Rome, at this time a group of great Rome-based artists came to the fore. Cavallini led the movement, though he had not necessarily started it. Jointly with as yet unknown artists he repainted the fifth-century murals at S. Paolo fuori le mura from 1277 to 1290; lost scenes he replaced with compositions of his own. Destroyed when the church burned down in 1823, the bulk of these murals is known only from seventeenth-century copies; but a few of the papal portraits survive and show, it appears, a different hand along with Cavallini's. The mosaics and murals, donated by Pope Nicholas III between 1278 and 1280, in the Sancta Sanctorum chapel of the old Lateran Palace—now atop the Scala Santa—have also been attributed to Cavallini as an early work; but this wants further proof. Certainly he designed and executed at S. Maria in Trastevere on the apse wall between the windows, probably by 1291 and not later, five scenes in mosaic from the life of the Virgin. At S. Cecilia, large parts survive of a mural decoration painted by him with the help of his workshop, between 1291 and 1293 or somewhat later, a Last Judgment on the inside façade and fragments of Old and New Testament cycles on the nave walls, the latter clearly modeled after those at S. Paolo; also as at S. Paolo, a series of papal portraits surmounted the nave arcades, whether in the spandrels of the arches or in a frieze running above. Finally, at S. Giorgio in Velabro in or after 1296 he painted for Cardinal Stefaneschi Christ and four saints on the apse vault. But all this is a fraction of his work. On the inside façade of St. Peter's, he and his workshop placed between the windows eight giant figures, Saints Peter and Paul, two other Apostles, and the Four Evangelists—they were still there in 1611 when the last parts of the old basilica were torn down. It remains an open question whether Cavallini's workshop or another also painted the similar colossal figures of saints once on the clerestory walls; but like the series of papal portraits over the colonnades—which also survived until 1611—they were part of the late-thirteenth-century program of redecorating the church of the Apostle. At S. Crisogono, Cavallini painted the entire nave—Ghiberti records it, as he records the work at St. Peter's; and at S. Paolo, if Ghiberti was right, Cavallini did part of the mosaic on the façade, started perhaps by Innocent III though completed only around 1325—but then Cavallini lived far into the new century. In any event, he was the leading and most sought after painter *al fresco* and mosaicist in Rome in the last quarter of the thirteenth century.

Along with Cavallini, Torriti dominates the Roman scene in the 1280s and 1290s. Most likely not a native Roman, he was nevertheless from the late 1280s on based in Rome. At S. Maria Maggiore, he created and signed between 1290 and 1295 the mosaic of the Coronation of the Virgin in the apse vault and the cycle from her life below it; likewise, the apse mosaic in the Lateran Basilica, also signed by him, was executed before 1292, but ruined in 1878 when it was replaced by what is to all intents and purposes a mere copy of the original. Outside Rome, his hand has been recognized at Assisi, in one of the painted nave vaults and in some of the Old Testament scenes in the Upper Church. Filippo Rusuti, the third Rome-based master known by name, with the help of assistants did the mosaics on the upper façade of S. Maria Maggiore, probably between 1293 and 1297. But along with these three, other so far anonymous masters, though of the highest quality, worked in Rome these same years. One possibly trained in Assisi, and distinct from both Torriti and Cavallini, painted floral ornament in the transept of S. Maria Maggiore, with niches in trick perspective and busts of prophets in roundels. Also in the 1290s, another master, close to Torriti, Cavallini, and Giotto yet distinct in his own right, executed an encyclopaedic cycle with secular scenes, fishermen, a caged bird, and the Barlaam story, on the wall of an upper loggia in the convent at the Tre Fontane—it came to light only ten years ago. Other cycles may well be recovered. But whatever remains is only a fraction of the painting, mosaics, sculpture, goldsmith work, and textiles scattered over Rome in the short span of time from 1278-1303. Rome, for a short moment, was one of the great centers where in the West a new art was shaped, supported by a succession of rich and splendor-loving popes and cardinals and by their relatives, as under different auspices occurred elsewhere in Italy and Europe.

It was no more than a moment, though. Neither the political nor the economic basis of the papacy was as strong as Boniface VIII believed. Defeated by France and the rightly revengeful Colonna, whom he had humiliated and deprived of a large part of their possessions, Boniface was overthrown in 1303. His death a few months later was followed after another two restive years by the removal of the pope and Curia to Avignon. Art patronage and employment ceased in Rome. The artists left. Cavallini went to the Anjou court at Naples—he may have returned later to Rome. Of Torriti's or Rusuti's whereabouts nothing is known; they and other masters not known by name may have joined the team working in Assisi, or they may have gone to Avignon. The thirty-odd years prior to 1303 became a last chapter in the history of medieval Rome, as reflected in her monuments: a beautiful short Indian summer.

Nonetheless this aftermath throws into sharp relief a problem recurrent in the history of Rome. Basically she was conservative. Her past, Christian and pagan, was her pride; but it weighed her down. The mistress of the world, see of the successors to Saint Peter, did not take easily to new ideas. Not by chance did she never house a medieval university. Bologna, not Rome, developed Roman law; Paris developed scholasticism. Similarly, for long periods patrons and artists remained untouched by new concepts of art evolved elsewhere in Europe. In the course of Rome's long history, whenever political constellations finally forced her to confront such alien concepts, there grew from the interplay of innovative and traditional forces time and again a surprisingly strong, new, and eminently Roman art. It happened in the ninth century under the impact of the Carolingian Renascence born north of the Alps and the political ambitions of both Charlemagne and the papacy. It happened again at the turn of the eleventh century and in the twelfth, when an art from abroad penetrated and was absorbed and transformed concurrently with the resurgence of the papacy in its struggle for reform and its victory over the empire, and with the rebirth of the Roman Republic. It happened again in the last decades of the thirteenth century with the backing of a papacy convinced of its supreme place on earth. Each time the upsurge of a new art was linked to a political revival; and it was interwoven with a rediscovery of the Roman past, Christian and pagan, rejuvenated. The alien ideas only took root when wedded to the living tradition. But a plainly conservative undercurrent lazily moved along beneath the recurrent upsweeps.

The conservative undercurrent ever present clearly prevailed in the thirteenth century among Rome's builders and their patrons. The abitato grew more and more crowded, planless it seems. Domestic building is likely to have been considerable. Cardinals, clerics, lawyers, and businessmen, from bankers and big cattle merchants to small traders, were in constant need of housing. But the type of houses, from what little we know at present, seems scarcely to have changed. The history of domestic building in medieval Rome remains to be explored. Two monumental poles at the rim of the abitato had been set by the twelfth century: at the Vatican, the old papal quarters adjoining St. Peter's and the palace of Innocent III; on the Capitol the first palace of the commune, whatever it looked like, the church preceding Aracoeli and the market on the hill. The thirteenth century developed and extended them, but added no new elements to the map of the city.

Nor did church building show any major innovative features. At a time when Gothic architecture for nearly a century and a half had held sway north of the Alps, Italy and more especially Rome resisted its assault. The Chapel of the Sancta Sanctorum, the only part to survive of the old Lateran Palace, was rebuilt on the solid walls of an earlier ground floor, one recalls, between 1278 and 1280. Triforium arcades, pointed clerestory windows, and rib vaults are all part of its Gothic vocabulary. However, the model chosen by the papal founder and his architect, Magister Cosmatus, was the transept of S. Francesco in Assisi, then fifty years old and a provincial derivative of churches in provincial western France. Contrary to the steep, airy naves of the Gothic heartland, the Sancta Sanctorum chapel, like its prototypes in Assisi and France, is low in proportion, the walls are solid, the windows small; the Gothic elements are overpowered by the marble revetment, mosaics, and murals, basic by then to Roman architectural thinking, if more than usually splendid in this papal chapel. The outside walls, built in brick and articulated only by round-headed blind arches and a bracketed cornice, are scarcely distinguishable from any structure built in Rome one hundred and fifty years before. The mendicant friars' Roman churches shunned even more obviously what elsewhere was considered fashionable or progressive. S. Maria in Aracoeli, around 1260, was laid out like any major transept basilica of the early twelfth century, save a few Gothic elements out of context. At S. Maria sopra Minerva in the 1280s—it was altered beyond recognition between 1848 and 1855—the builders, whether or not Florentine Dominicans as Vasari would have it, clearly turned to the Order's church in Florence, S. Maria Novella, then under construction, but they reduced the

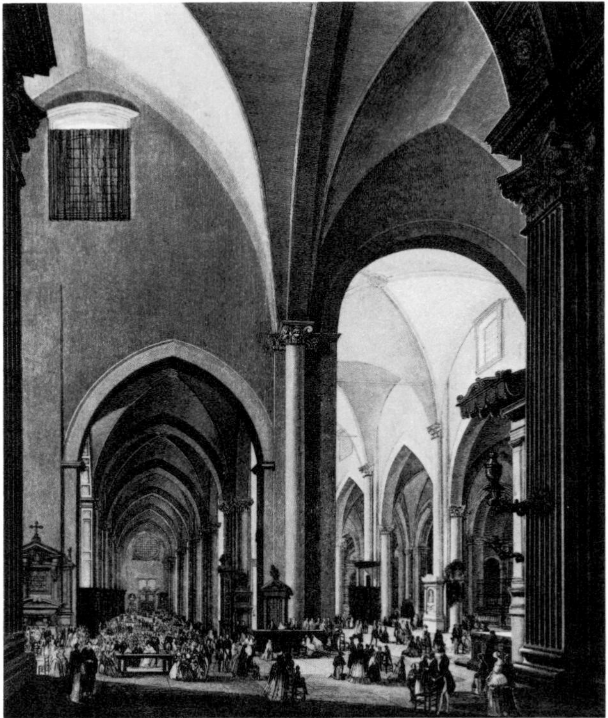

166. S. Maria sopra Minerva, as of ca. 1840

model to what might be called a basic mendicant-friars' Gothic (fig. 166): pointed arches, quatrefoil compound piers, shafts on responds against bare walls, small windows, and an open timber roof; the aisles were vaulted only in the fourteenth century, the nave in 1453.

Rome, then, both proudly conscious of and weighed down by age-old traditions, refused to take more than fleeting notice of the newfangled style evolved beyond the Alps. Even its Tuscan adaptation went too far for Roman taste. When, under Pope Nicholas IV, the Lateran Basilica and S. Maria Maggiore were thoroughly altered, the former in 1288-1290, the latter in 1288-1296, only a few Gothic features were scattered over the parts newly built: pointed windows, without tracery at that; a rose window in a façade; a pointed corbel table frieze along an eaves line; a rudimentary ambulatory enveloping the Lateran apse and recalling only in its function—to shelter additional altars—the *chevet* of a French cathedral. Placing twin towers on the north façade of the Lateran Basilica, facing the Piazza and the approach from town, recalls towered façades of Norman churches in Apulia or Sicily from the late eleventh and twelfth centuries rather than Gothic ones. The apses of the Lateran and of S. Maria Maggiore, articulated by round-headed blind arches on responds and shafts, look Romanesque provincial more than anything else. Fundamental in any event to the patron and his architects were not such frills but the plan and extent of the remodelings. In both venerable churches, the old chancel part was replaced by a transept as high and, at the Lateran, as wide as the nave (fig. 167)—at S. Maria Maggiore the sloping hill forced the builders to curtail its width. The old basilicas, then, were molded into the norm accepted ever since Carolingian times and through the twelfth century as "standard Early Christian." The pope and his advisers must have felt that they were only rectifying deviations from a norm established by the old planners. Bringing up to date and renovating the Lateran Basilica, as far as a medieval pope was concerned, simply could not mean making it into a Gothic cathedral, even if funds and trained workmen had been available. A Roman church had to conform to the pattern hallowed by age, by its links to St. Peter's successors, and therefore had to be normative in and for Rome. Innovation in church planning could be but incidental. Renovation was the true concern of Roman church builders and their patrons in the thirteenth century. The basic pattern had been set a thousand years before; and as so often in Rome, the oldest was also the newest.

Where models venerable by tradition were lacking, innovative concepts and outside influences were more readily accepted. No sculpture worth the name had been produced in Rome since late-antique times. It played no part in architectural contexts or in tomb design. The decorative friezes and capitals of the Cosmati workshops, active from the mid-twelfth century through the thirteenth, their sphinxes, lions, and monsters, are artisans' rather than artists' work. Throughout the Middle Ages, the great were buried in ancient sarcophagi: Emperor Otto II in 985 in the atrium of St. Peter's—the sarcophagus is now in the Grotte Vaticane under St. Peter's and the porphyry lid, removed from Hadrian's Mausoleum, Castel S. Angelo, serves as a baptismal font in St. Peter's; Innocent II in 1143 in Hadrian's porphyry sarcophagus, brought to the Lateran and lost when the roof of the church collapsed in a fire in 1308; Anastasius IV in 1151, likewise at the Lateran, in the porphyry sarcophagus of Saint Helena—a battle sarcophagus originally intended presumably for Constantine; Cardinal Guglielmo Fieschi in 1256 at S. Lorenzo fuori le mura in a wedding sarcophagus sheltered by a gabled canopy; Luca Savelli, father of Pope Honorius IV, in 1263 or shortly after at S. Maria in Aracoeli in a sarcophagus decorated with youthful genii carrying festoons (fig. 168). Dozens of other ancient sarcophagi survived in Roman churches until after the Renaissance as burial places of other now forgotten dignitaries, or as reliquary shrines, or as fonts. Or else, a wall tomb was built, like that of the chamberlain Alfaranus at S. Maria in Cosmedin round 1123, with a front plaque articulated only by pseudoclassical pilasters and surmounted by a gabled wall canopy like the more elaborate ones over the Fieschi and Savelli tombs.

By the last third of the thirteenth century, though, both French popes and cardinals and their Italian counterparts, whether residing with the migratory Curia at Viterbo, Orvieto, Perugia, or in Rome, demanded a tomb design more up to date. Derived, it seems, from French models dating around the mid-century, it was transmitted supposedly by French artists or French patrons to Roman workshops. It was quickly taken up by Arnolfo di Cambio, the Florentine sculptor and architect active in Rome from about 1275 on, first in the service of Charles of Anjou and for another twenty years

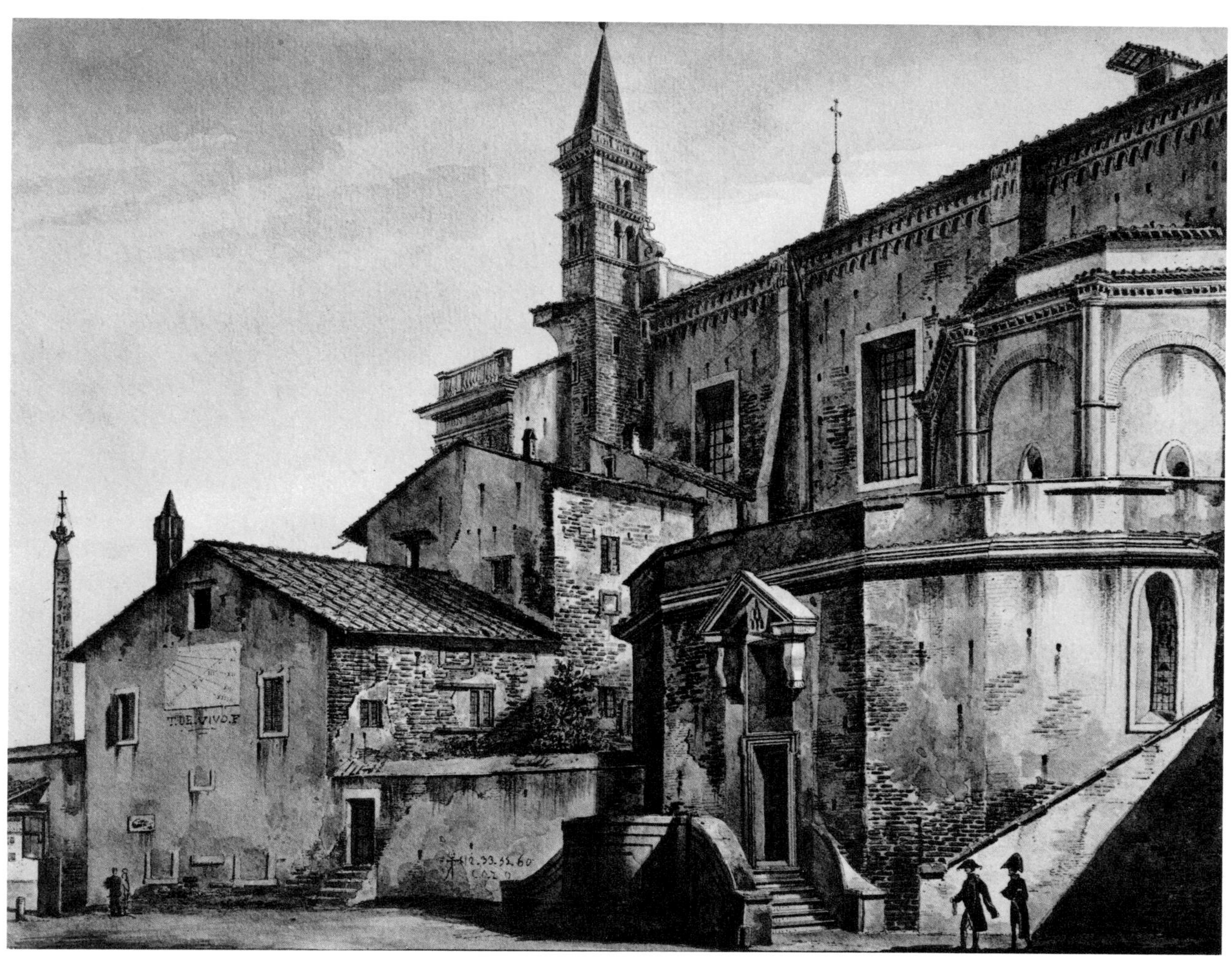

167. Lateran apse and transept as of ca. 1800, De Vico, Gabinetto delle Stampe, Rome

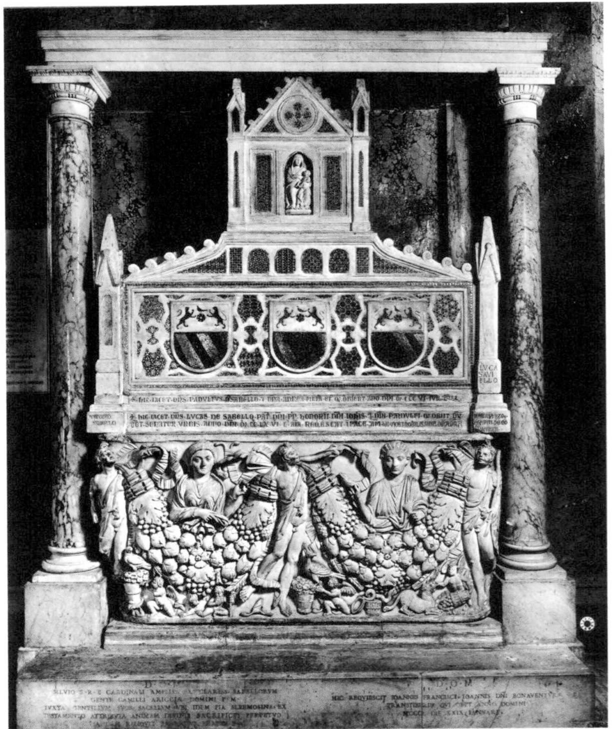

168. S. Maria in Aracoeli, tomb of Luca Savelli

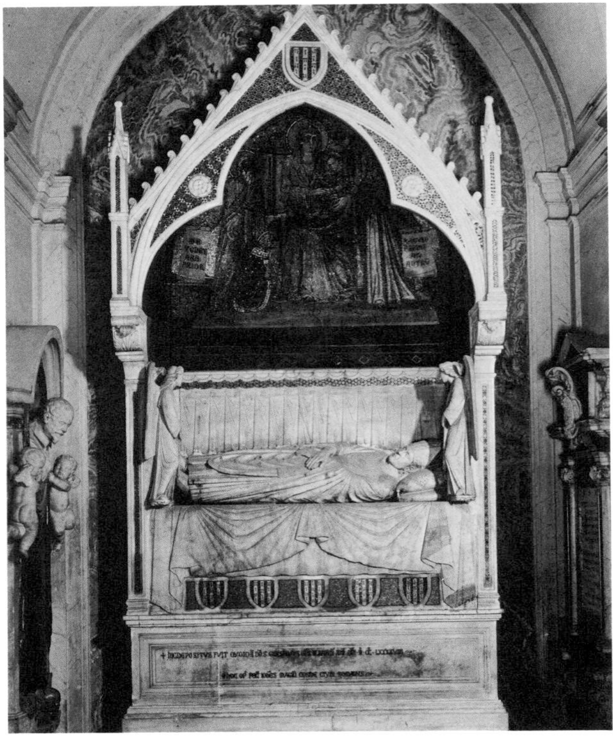

169. S. Maria Maggiore, tomb of Cardinal Consalvo Rodriguez, Giovanni Cosmate

or more head of a large workshop, dividing his time after 1284 between Rome and Florence. Arnolfo established among patrons and sculptors in the Roman milieu the new French tomb type: in its simplest form, a base carrying the sarcophagus with the figure of the defunct, the *gisant*, on top; above, against the wall, the Virgin flanked by saints, painted, in mosaic, or sculptures, the whole under a wall canopy with pointed arches and gables set with finials and crockets. The monument of Cardinal Rodriguez in S. Maria Maggiore from around 1302 is a late example, by the hand of a follower of Arnolfo, one of the Cosmati who took up the new style (fig. 169). Where funds were plentiful, the type was easily expanded: in the monument of Cardinal Riccardo Annibaldi in the Lateran—it is Arnolfo's earliest work surviving in Rome, around 1276—deacons or angels draw back curtains from the *gisant* and a procession of clerics, elegantly wrought, passes behind him (fig. 170); only fragments remain in the cloister. The monument of Boniface VIII, once at St. Peter's and completed in 1299 long before the pope's death, was a canopied chapel, crowned by an eight-sided dome, with sixteen finials and as many miniature gables, flaunting its Gothic vocabulary. Inside, it sheltered an altar and against the rear wall the sarcophagus with the effigy of the pope, eyes closed (fig. 171); the mosaic in the rear wall, showing the Virgin flanked by Peter and Paul, was done by Torriti; a half-figure of the pope looked down from a side wall; only this, the *gisant*, and his sarcophagus, remain, the first in the papal apartments in the Vatican, the latter two in the Grotte Vaticane. The mastery of a Gothic grammar, albeit slightly out of date by then in France, likewise appears in Arnolfo's altar canopies, one for S. Paolo, 1285, and another for S. Cecilia, 1296. Concomitantly, his sculptures reflect a French Gothic style, modified from that prevailing thirty years before in the work of his master, Nicola Pisano; thus whereas the latter had transposed contemporary French work into his personal idiom, Arnolfo's interpretation of such models was twice removed and by the end of the century hopelessly out of date. As in Nicola's work, to be sure, Arnolfo's figures are solid, their heads firmly shaped; they stand on or at least suggest a credible enveloping space; draperies mark the body and frame the limbs; and, as with Nicola, their folds break in sharp angles, rather than sweeping in easy curves or heavily falling, as they would in France. However, Arnolfo's modeling is finer than Nicola's, the proportions more slender, the movements more elegant: the clerics from the Annibaldi tomb; Charles of Anjou, seated, now on the Capitol; the kings from the crêche at S. Maria Maggiore, workshop production like, it seems, the Anjou statue. And there are his ever more exquisitely carved late works in Rome: the crouching prophets and evangelists on the canopy of S. Cecilia (fig. 172), fluid and sophisticated, are much removed from the angular figures on the altar canopy of S. Paolo fuori le mura; and Boniface VIII resting on his sarcophagus, finished before 1299, shows a full, tough face with a sensitive, fine mouth, a portrait superior to any other nearly contemporary papal portraits (fig. 173).

Trained under Nicola Pisano, Arnolfo was open to the beauty and verisimilitude of ancient Roman sculpture from the outset. Quotations from the antique, plucked from his master's pattern book or that of a Frenchman (one thinks of Villard de Honnecourt) pervade his work at an early time—witness the two figures of Eve on the S. Paolo canopy, both variants on a Venus. The longer he stayed in Rome, in daily contact with her monuments, such formulas gave way to a genuine understanding and feeling for the spirit and form of antiquity, a feeling so strong as to become second nature to him. The bronze statue of Saint Peter, seated and giving his blessing, in his basilica—by Arnolfo's own hand, we are confident—as late as the 1950s was taken for a fourth-century work (fig. 174). Creations

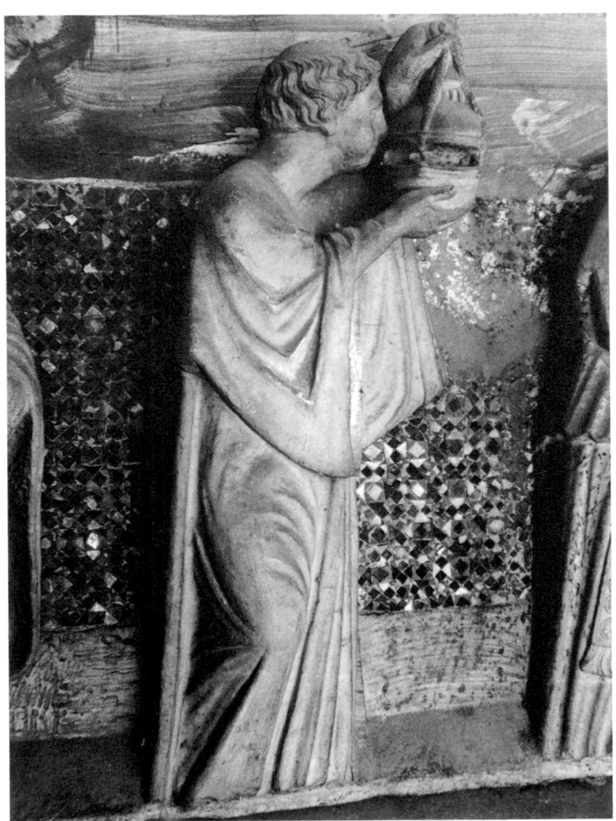

170. S. Giovanni in Laterano, cloister, tomb of Cardinal Riccardo Annibaldi, cleric, Arnolfo di Cambio

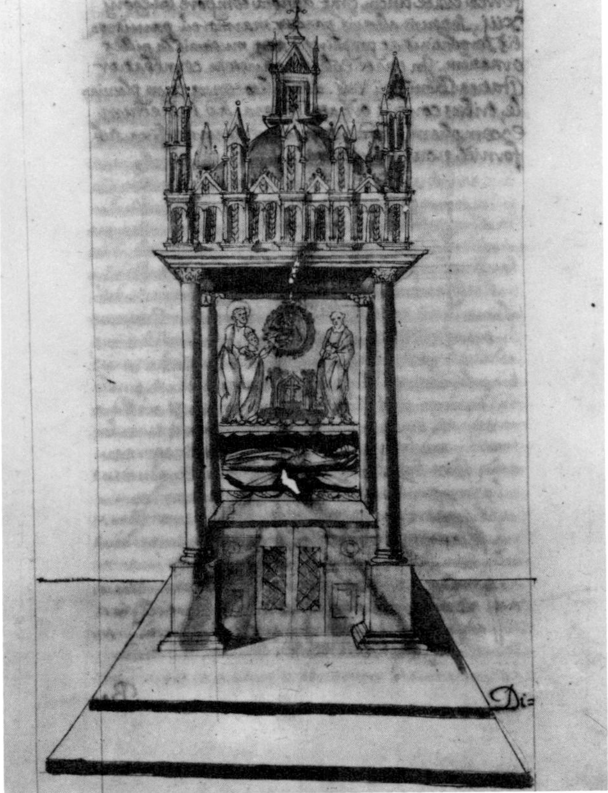

171. Tomb chapel of Boniface VIII, Giovanni Grimaldi, Biblioteca Vaticana, Barb. lat. 2733, fol. 8r

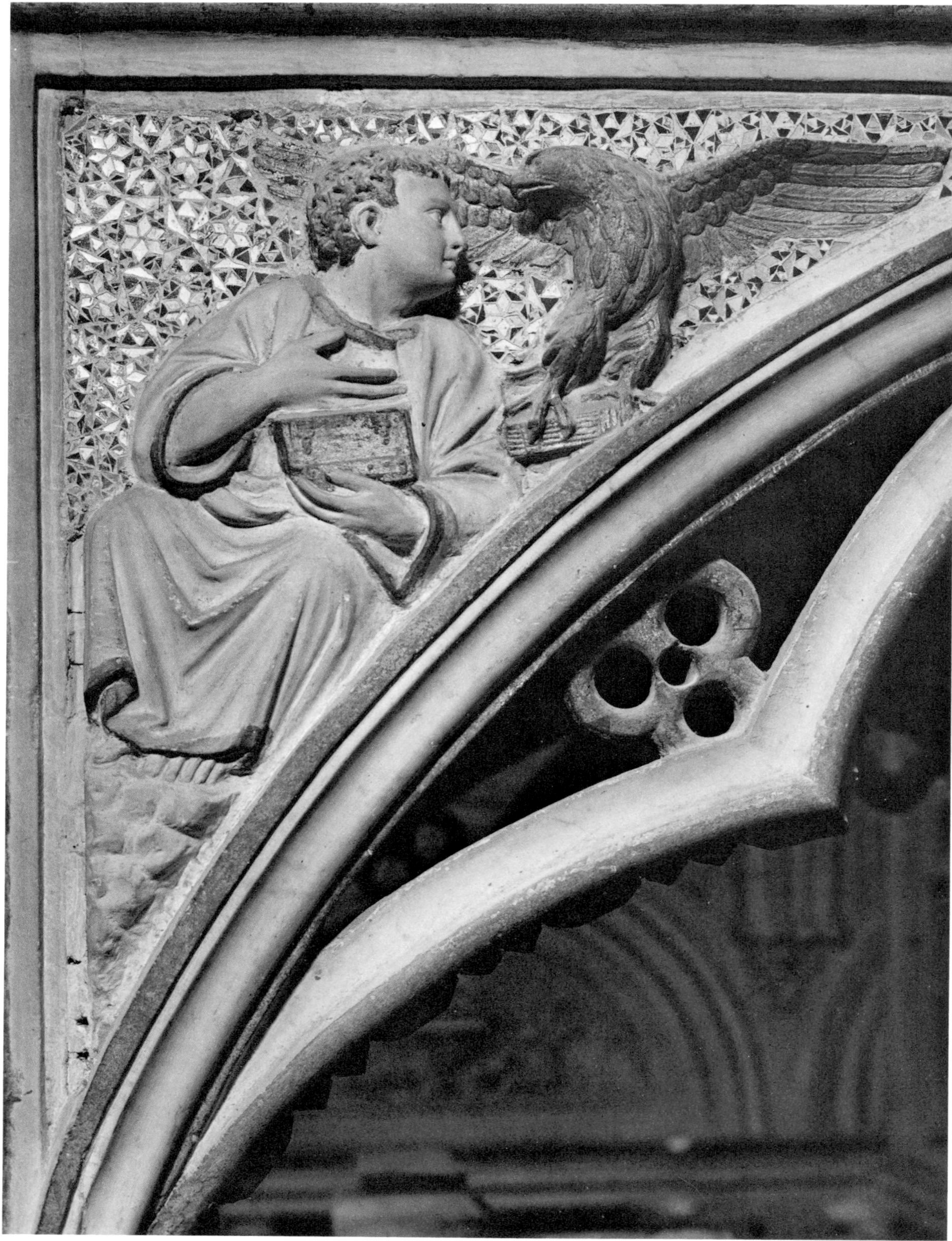

172. S. Cecilia, canopy, detail, Arnolfo di Cambio

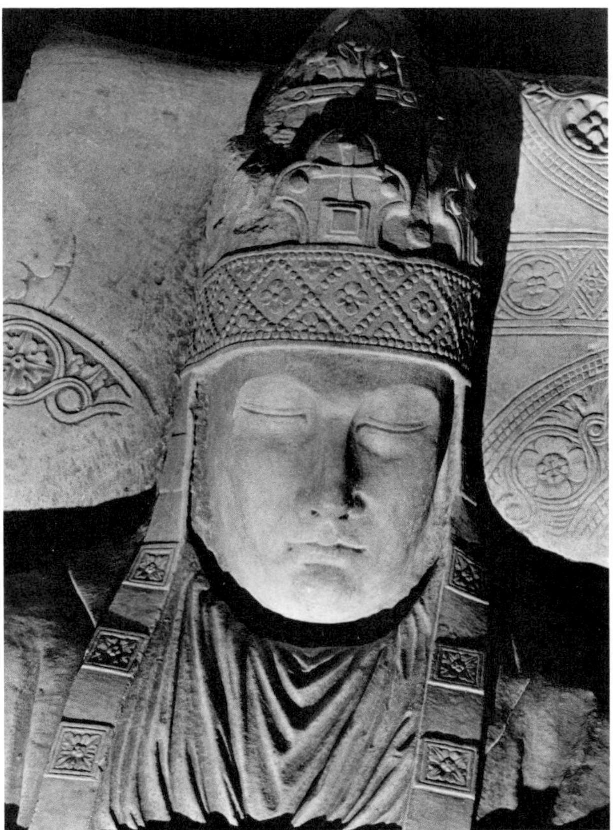

173. Grotte Vaticane, Tomb of Boniface VIII, detail, head, Arnolfo di Cambio

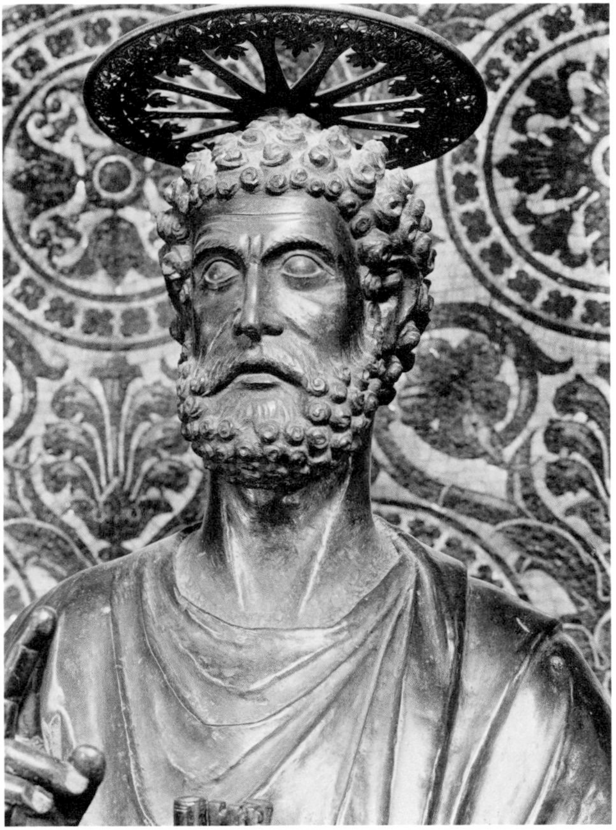

174. Bronze statue of Saint Peter, detail, head, Arnolfo di Cambio (?)

all'antica, like this, fitted into Rome at the end of the thirteenth century; they were welcomed by Arnolfo's patrons, all cultured gentlemen: Boniface VIII, the canons of St. Peter's, Jean Cholet, the title cardinal of S. Cecilia—French cardinals and popes, it seems, were quickly Romanized. And, not irrelevant in our context, the antique character of his work seems to have disappeared from Arnolfo's oeuvre once he returned for good to Florence around 1298, to a milieu not yet impregnated with the Roman feeling for antiquity.

Rome, then, shaped Arnolfo's work even more than she allowed herself to be shaped by him. She accepted willingly the French tomb type and a sculptural style derived from France by way of Tuscany and a bit out of date. But she did not really absorb the alien elements; whether she would eventually have done so, had not the catastrophe of 1303 interfered, is a futile question. In the mosaic and mural cycles of the three leading masters in Rome at the time—Cavallini, Torriti, and Rusuti—the interplay of forces becomes far clearer and the background broadens: the confrontation with concepts of art brought in from outside; their rejection or absorption; their blending with the Roman inheritance; and the resulting formation of a great Rome-based art in less than three decades preceding the fatal year 1303. It is not within the scope of these pages, nor within my competence, to unravel questions discussed for many years by those qualified in that field: the relation of Florentine to Roman painting of the time, of Cimabue to Cavallini or of Cavallini to Giotto; the role of S. Francesco at Assisi as a crucible; the identity of the Isaac master at Assisi and his links to Cavallini, Torriti, and Giotto; the impact of Cavallini on Torriti or their independence from one another; the place of Rusuti; the distinction in

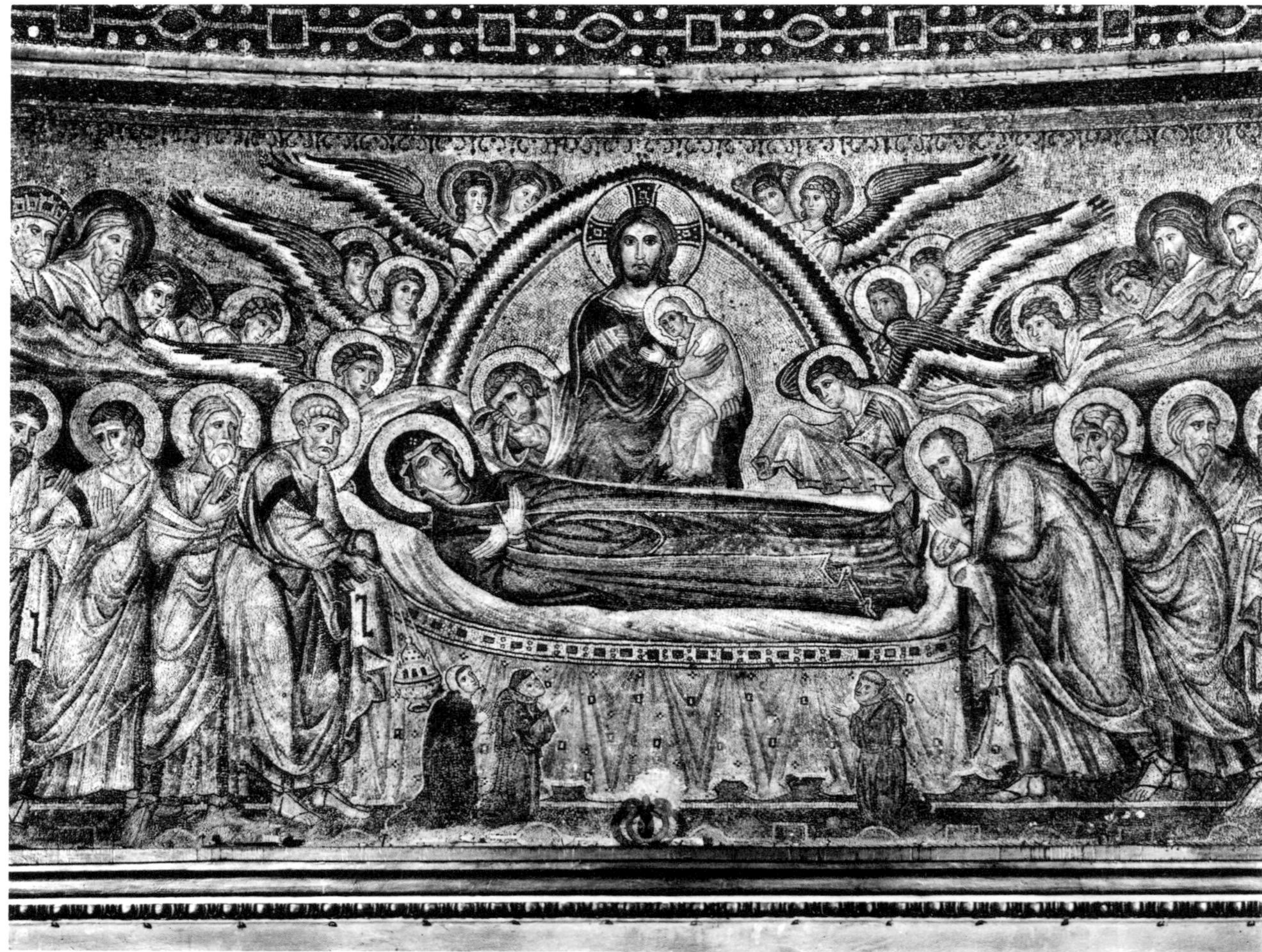

175. S. Maria Maggiore, *Dormition of the Virgin*, Jacopo Torriti

the oeuvre of the three Romans between works by their own hand and those done by assistants and followers; finally, the identity of yet anonymous, though clearly distinguishable, masters of the highest quality. The points that count most in the present context have been brought out by other scholars over the past ten to fifteen years, convincingly to me, and I gratefully accept and present them though they are not my own.

Cavallini, Torriti, Rusuti, and their workshops all differ greatly in manner and quality; but they and their unknown assistants stand within the frame of a style alien heretofore and utterly revolutionary in the Roman milieu. One only need place Torriti's mosaic of the *Dormition of the Virgin* in S. Maria Maggiore (fig. 175)—and I choose this rather than a work by the even more rebellious Cavallini (fig. 176)—against one of the scenes in the Chapel of S. Silvestro in the atrium of the Quattro Coronati (fig. 150) to see clearly the break with the local past. Dated 1246, the latter made up the richest mural cycle painted in Rome at that time. Its political message, to stress the supremacy and independence of the papacy as implied in the Donation of Constantine, makes it one of the great monuments in the war of propaganda waged by the papacy against the emperor, Frederick II. But it is not, so it seems to me, a great monument of art: the scenes are poorly composed, almost artless; crowds appear as rows of heads heaped above a row of figures lined up in a front plane and cut as if from cardboard; linear patterns

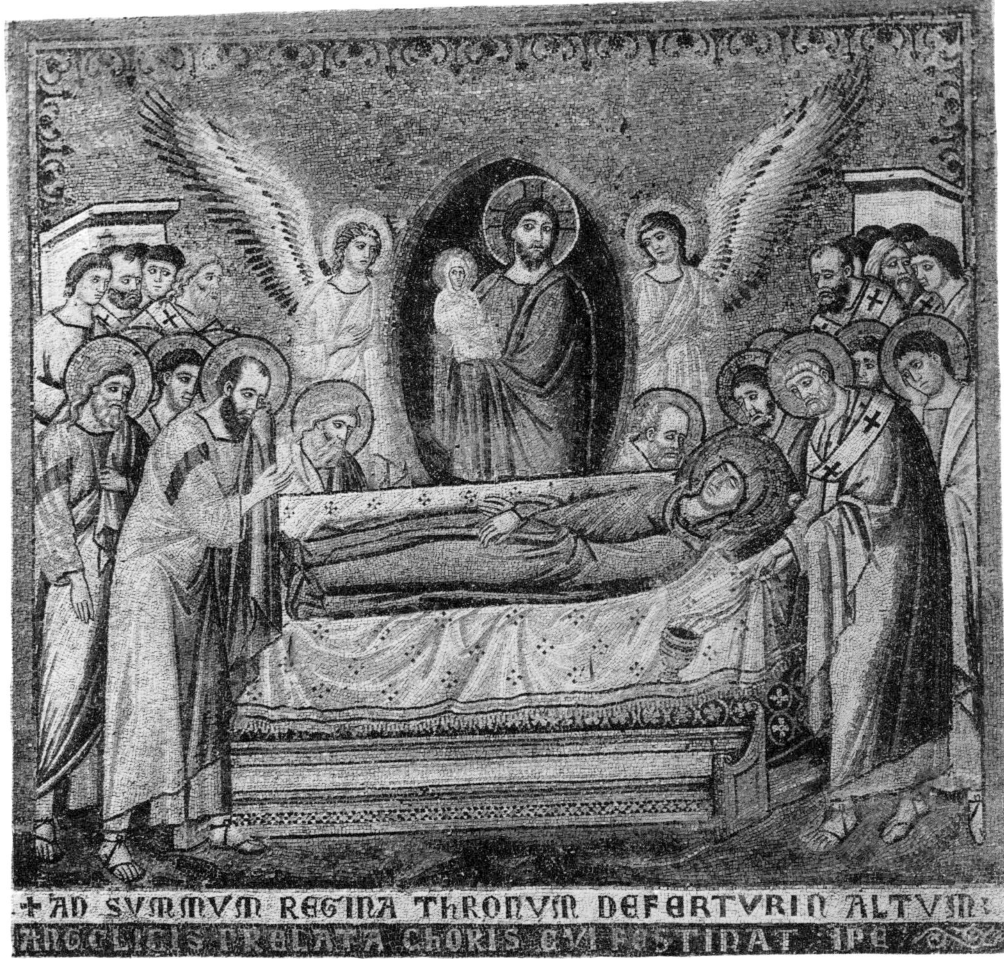

176. S. Maria in Trastevere, *Dormition of the Virgin*, Pietro Cavallini

mark the draperies; outlines are harsh, colors shrill; the backgrounds are flat, whether they represent an empty ground or architectural props lined up. It is hard to believe that a style as elegant and sophisticated as that from which around 1100 the frescoes in the lower church of S. Clemente had sprung could have degenerated to that level. But the murals of the Sylvester legend are no isolated phenomenon; the frescoes in the crypt of the Cathedral at Anagni, a decade or so earlier, are not so very different. It is this provincial art that by the second third of the century had come to prevail locally in Rome and Latium. Nothing could bring out more clearly the freshness and newness of the art that emerged in the last third of the century. In Torriti's *Dormition of the Virgin* at S. Maria Maggiore, the figures are full and rounded, their limbs outlined by the rich, heavy folds of their draperies; the Apostles overlap one another, moving back and forth on a stage, albeit shallow; behind the Virgin, on her bed and clearly set back from the front plane, rises the figure of Christ placed against the background of the mandorla, further back still; and even further in depth, behind the props of a rocky landscape and layers of clouds, figures of saints and angels look down, the latter supporting the mandorla. Space then extends sideways, backward, and upwards; the gold ground gives an impression of infinite depth; gestures and movements express the drama enacted. The scene rather than being confined to its frame links up with the *Coronation of the Virgin* above it in the apse vault, enveloped by scores of angels that repeat and continue those in the lower scene. The angels' outspread wings seem almost to support the cornice of the vault; the mandorla in shape and position takes the place of a central window in the apse. By these means Torriti harmonizes his dramatic, shimmering, and brilliantly colored composition with its architectural setting.

It is a masterpiece, it is fresh, and it represents a new style that is to dominate Rome from the 1270s on. Its origins remain to be explored in detail. But broadly speaking, it seems to have sprung from three roots: Byzantine art, as revitalized in just these decades, which penetrated the West by many roads and in many forms; the art of the Gothic North, as it found its way to Rome through patrons from France and the artists they attracted; and antiquity, always alive as an undercurrent in Rome, and linked to renascences as they occurred elsewhere. Rome in the last third of the thirteenth century opened herself up to all these sources. The masters that shaped her new art made elements and concepts carried in from abroad their own; they wedded them to the heritage of antiquity, deeply rooted in the Roman milieu; they revitalized that heritage and gave it new life by making it a tool to see afresh the world around them. But they broke decidedly, it seems to me, with the workshop traditions dominant in Rome until the middle of the century and often beyond.

The Byzantine component is obvious, both in Torriti's mosaics at S. Maria Maggiore and in Cavallini's at S. Maria in Trastevere. Formulas of iconography and concepts of design of Middle Byzantine art as it had evolved from the tenth century onward had been transmitted to the West, starting with the late eleventh and twelfth centuries: by eastern mosaic workers active in Sicily and Venice, both veritable outposts of Byzantium; by western artists visiting the East; and, more important still, by pattern books, icons, and manuscripts. Contacts grew even closer as a new sophisticated style, permeated by reminiscences *all'antica*, evolved in the Byzantine areas at the very time Constantinople was occupied for the nearly sixty years from 1204 to 1261 by French knights and Italian merchants. Indirect links between Rome and the art of Byzantium had existed from the early thirteenth century. For the apse of St. Peter's Innocent III had apparently brought in mosaic workers, from Sicily it has been suggested, certainly Byzantine trained; and for the apse mosaic at S. Paolo Honorius III employed Venetians, obviously from the Byzantine-schooled workshop active at S. Marco—a letter of his to the doge survives, dated 1218, thanking him for sending a mosaicist and asking for two more to be dispatched. True, mosaic work on a large scale had been revived in Rome in the early twelfth century probably under the influence of Monte Cassino where Byzantine artists a few decades before had rekindled the craft. But in the later half of the twelfth century it seems to have died out in the Roman milieu; just as it died out again after 1230 or thereabouts when the masters from Venice had done their work and presumably returned home to other employment. Torriti and Cavallini, two generations later, had to learn the technique anew, whether by going to or calling for assistance from the Byzantine sphere—Venice, Salonica, Constantinople. Iconographically, too, their cycle of scenes from the life of the Virgin both at S. Maria Maggiore and S. Maria in Trastevere draw on models long current in Byzantium. Iconography and technique aside, though, their works are shaped, if in different degrees as brought out by Kitzinger, by concepts of style that by the last third of the century in Byzantium and her outposts had evolved successively and concurrently diverse "modes" of presentation. Hence to some degree the obvious differences in the works of the two masters. Torriti's figures are voluminous, their draperies hard; they move quietly on a shallow, somewhat ambiguous stage; and a backdrop of landscape and architectural props runs parallel to the front plane—all features common in Byzantine contemporary art. In contrast, Cavallini's figures in his *Dormition of the Virgin* or in the *Nativity* at S. Maria in Trastevere (fig. 176), though equally full-bodied, are draped in heavier, softer stuffs; they act dramatically in a convincing if limited space, a space suggested by the action moving diagonally into depth with landscape and architectural props breaking, as it were, into the gold ground. Where Torriti suggests reality,

Cavallini makes reality convincing. But his scenes no less than Torriti's find parallels, perhaps even models, in the sophisticated art which just at that time came to prominence in some major centers of the Byzantine sphere of influence. A mural painted in the 1260s at Sopoćani in Serbia presents the Dormition scene even more dramatically than Cavallini; and his *Nativity*, in the composition of figures and landscape props, closely recalls one of the Moses scenes in the atrium of S. Marco in Venice, done at roughly the same time, including figures and motifs clearly purloined from antique prototypes.

It is obvious that such reminiscences of antiquity would be welcome and eagerly taken up in Rome. Her antique past, time and again, had been a stimulus in the Roman milieu, revived to shape a new art—in the fifth, in the ninth, and again in the early twelfth centuries. Indeed, Torriti's *Coronation of the Virgin* at S. Maria Maggiore, as has been suggested, may well have drawn on medieval local models: for the *Coronation* itself, perhaps the apse vault of S. Maria in Trastevere, where Christ shares his throne with the Virgin; for the acanthus scrolls bordering the main scene, the apse of S. Clemente. Nonetheless, models from antiquity proper then extant in Rome, pagan or Christian, seem to have acted more forcefully on Torriti. At S. Maria Maggiore, the rinceaux are more fleshy than those at S. Clemente—rather like those in the fifth-century narthex of the Lateran Baptistery; and the quails, herons, peacocks, rabbits, and parrots entwined in their coils likewise seem to go back to a late-antique source. A riverscape runs along the foot of the apse carrying boats with putti gamboling, fishermen and a boatsman, waterfowl and fish, a river god in the corner; and a similar "Nilotic" strip marked the rim of the apse mosaic in the Lateran. Both are drawn straight from late-antique sources such as the mosaic still seen by the sixteenth century in the dome of S. Costanza; or possibly even from the Early Christian mosaics once in the apses of St. Peter's, the Lateran Basilica, and S. Maria Maggiore. Elements inherited from late antiquity and revived abound also in Cavallini's oeuvre; the shepherd playing his flute, the dog watching

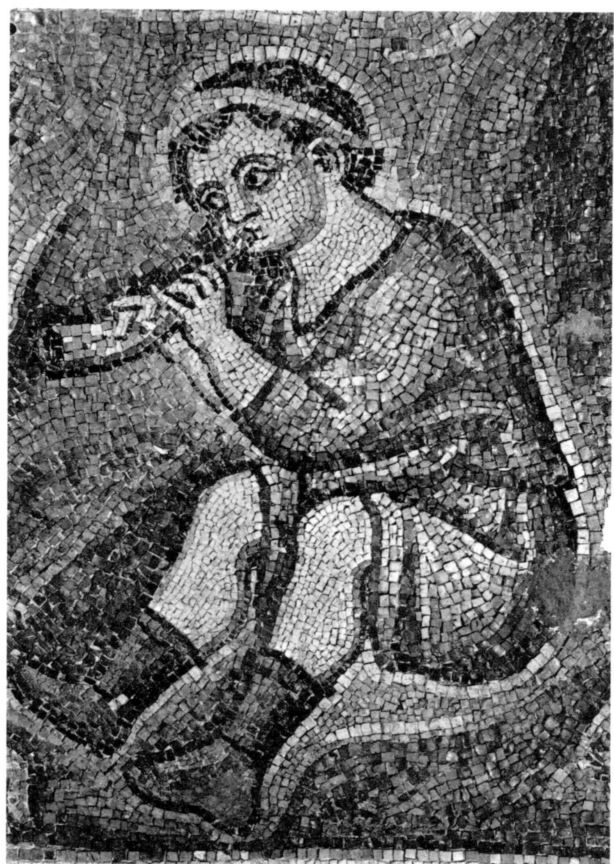

177. S. Maria in Trastevere, *Nativity*, detail, shepherd, Pietro Cavallini

him in the *Nativity* mosaic at S. Maria in Trastevere (fig. 177) might have been taken from any late-antique pastoral scene; likewise the attendant women preparing the bath in the *Birth of the Virgin* might have been drawn straight from antique models. Just such motifs, however, had long been part of the late-antique heritage of Byzantine art and came to the fore with new strength in the last decades of the thirteenth century. Cavallini could as well have known them through Byzantine pattern books. But to him, antiquity—and antiquity as he was familiar with it in Rome—meant not just incorporating in his work individual motifs, even in great numbers. To him it meant understanding overall concepts of late-antique art: its feeling for the fullness and convincing articulation of a body; for the fall of a drapery; for credible space, achieved by placing into depth figures and architectural props; for atmosphere and light; for dramatic action and monumental figures. Such concepts had become part of his own thinking probably ever since comparatively early in his life, when he had restored and complemented by compositions of his own the fifth-century murals at S. Paolo fuori le mura. When over twenty years later he painted a series of Biblical scenes on the nave walls of S. Cecilia—one still makes out fragments, parts of the story of Jacob—the placing of figures and props and the telling action are clearly drawn from corresponding compositions at S. Paolo (fig. 178). True, the wide space of the Early Christian originals (to judge by the copies surviving and by other fifth-century work, such as the nave mosaics at S. Maria Maggiore) has been restricted to a more limited stage at S. Cecilia, as to be expected in the medieval transposition of a late-antique model; the late-antique colonnettes framing the scenes at S. Paolo have been replaced by typically medieval twisted Cosmati ones. Similarly at S. Giorgio in Velabro, Cavallini or his workshop—it does not matter which in this context—goes back to an Early Christian apse composition to this day surviving at SS. Cosma e Damiano—Christ in the heavens and flanked by saints—this rather than the Carolingian derivations of the type; that the figures have been transposed into a late-thirteenth-century idiom goes without saying. Late antiquity, as he knew it in Rome and revived it, was deeply ingrained in Cavallini; more deeply so than in Torriti and far more deeply than the motifs *all'antica* appropriated from Byzantine models in Cavallini's mosaics at S. Maria in Trastevere would suggest.

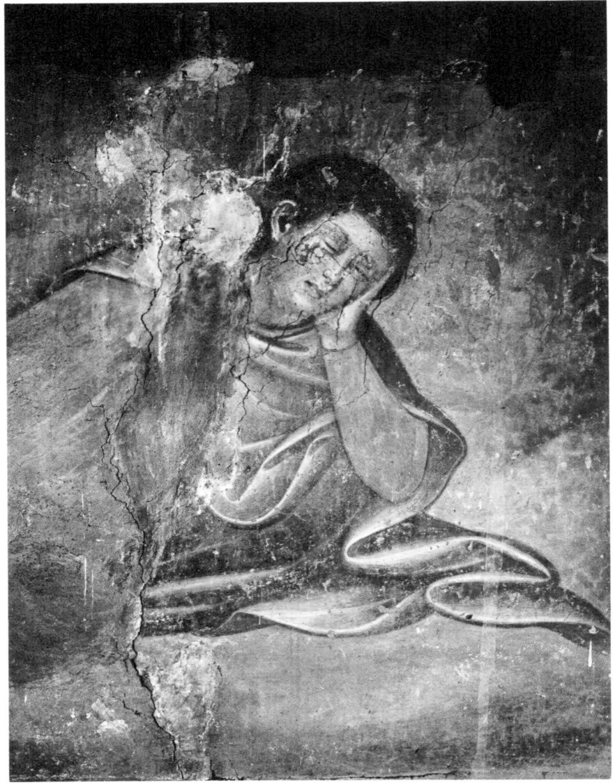

178. S. Cecilia, *Jacob's Dream*, detail, Jacob asleep, Pietro Cavallini

However, much in contrast to the twelfth-century renascence, the approach to antiquity and its revival in late-thirteenth-century Rome cannot be seen on just one level. In the twelfth century, Rome, as it were, rediscovered her own past in an antiquity Christianized—a few pagan elements having been rendered innocuous and absorbed. Essentially, the movement is a local Roman phenomenon, notwithstanding the stimulus provided by Monte Cassino. In Rome, the ancient models on which architects and painters drew were exclusively works of late, preferably Christian, antiquity, locally surviving. Nor does this renascence in the visual arts find any contemporary parallels in the West outside Rome. The twelfth-century revival of antiquity in prose and poetry north of the Alps was exclusively literary in nature. The Roman movement, on the contrary, was both visual and literary. Finally, it was motivated by local political forces: the papacy, victorious in the Investiture Struggle; and the intellectuals who prepared the way for the rise of the citizenry in the Roman Republic of 1143.

In the thirteenth century, the revival of antiquity in mosaics, paintings, and sculptures, as scattered all over Rome, offers a far broader spectrum. True, the thirteenth-century masters, like their ancestors a hundred and fifty years before, focused their attention chiefly on the late-antique monuments, pagan and Christian, surviving locally. But they reached further out. The vocabulary *all'antica* at their disposal was wider in range than that of their predecessors. No twelfth-century artist seems to have drawn either on Nilotic landscapes or on corbel table friezes in trick perspective, as they were to be seen in late-antique monuments such as the Basilica of Junius Bassus and S. Costanza. But just such motifs marked the art of the thirteenth century in Rome: Nilotic landscapes run along the foot of the apse vaults at St. Peter's, in the Lateran Basilica, at S. Maria Maggiore; and perspective niches topped the walls of some rooms in Nicholas III's Vatican Palace around 1280; ten years later they appear on the transept walls of S. Maria Maggiore. As the vocabulary broadened so did the sources far and near on which the new Roman school drew. Along with the antique models before their eyes in the city, local twelfth-century "neo-antique" models seem to have exerted their influence, if but occasionally and collaterally—the apse vaults at S. Clemente and S. Maria in Trastevere. At the same time, though, and far removed from Rome, Byzantium, the old "deep freeze" of a late-antique vocabulary, contributed to the Roman masters Torriti, Cavallini, and others, elements *all'antica* to effect a revival of antiquity.

Presumably, though, the Roman renascence of the late thirteenth century should be seen in a wider frame still. After all, throughout the thirteenth century, renascences abound all over the West, contemporary with or a generation earlier than the one in Rome: the reproduction of antique models with remarkable fidelity by the "Gothic" sculptors at Rheims cathedral between 1225 and 1230, perhaps stimulated, if indirectly, from Byzantium; the rebirth of antiquity around 1240 in South Italy, centered on the figure of Frederick II, politically motivated with strong Augustan overtones, impressive, isolated, and ephemeral; the classical revival in the oeuvre of Nicola Pisano in Tuscany around the middle of the century, apparently inspired by the Rheims workshop, but having at its disposal richer vocabulary and striving for a deeper understanding of the art of antiquity, rather than copying and incorporating isolated elements *all'antica*—a head, a draped figure—as did the masters of Rheims and those of Frederick II. I feel the Roman renascence of the late thirteenth century had best be viewed in this broader framework.

Through Nicola's pupil Arnolfo di Cambio, as one recalls, and perhaps through model books, French Gothic tomb types reached Rome in the 1270s—with a time lag of a generation or so; so did scattered motifs *all'antica* from Nicola's pattern book—the Eve-Venus on the S. Paolo canopy. The painters, it would appear, were by then familiar with more up-to-date French work. Torriti's color scheme, with its saturated reds and blues, has been linked to France as the ultimate source; the direct sources may well have been stained-glass windows painted for Assisi in the 1280s when Torriti worked there on the murals of the Genesis cycle. Cavallini, too, would seem to have been familiar with French art as it had developed shortly after the middle of the century: a quiet and monumental style fused into a Gothic idiom, without any of the features *all'antica* proudly flouted a generation before, but so "classical" as inevitably to call to mind Roman and Greek antiquity; the sculptures on the inner façade of Rheims cathedral, such as the Abraham-Melchizedek group represented the new grand manner at its best. Cavallini would likely have known it from pattern books; and, in any event, it seems to be reflected in his *Last Judgment* on the inner façade of S. Cecilia (fig. 179). True, the Byzantine elements are by no means lost; the jeweled stoles, *loroi*, worn by the angels; their soft rounded faces; the bearded individualized characteristic heads of the Apostles (fig. 180); the savage Baptist—all recall contemporary painting in the eastern Mediterranean; the angels looking up to Christ (fig. 181), the beardless face of John among the Apostles find their almost exact counterparts in the Sopoćani murals. Still, the dominant note in Cavallini's *Judgment* is rooted in the Northern Gothic tradition; the quiet, yet free grouping of the figures; the monumental, though far from hieratic poses of Christ and the Disciples; their thick woolen draperies falling in heavy folds; the firmly modeled faces; all find their counterparts in contemporary Gothic works presenting a semblance, without the actual vocabulary, of antiquity. Like Arnolfo di Cambio in his late Roman years, Cavallini at S. Cecilia at the same time had evolved a great new style in which the components, no longer distinguishable as such, were fused into a simple grandeur that breathes a spirit recalling, though

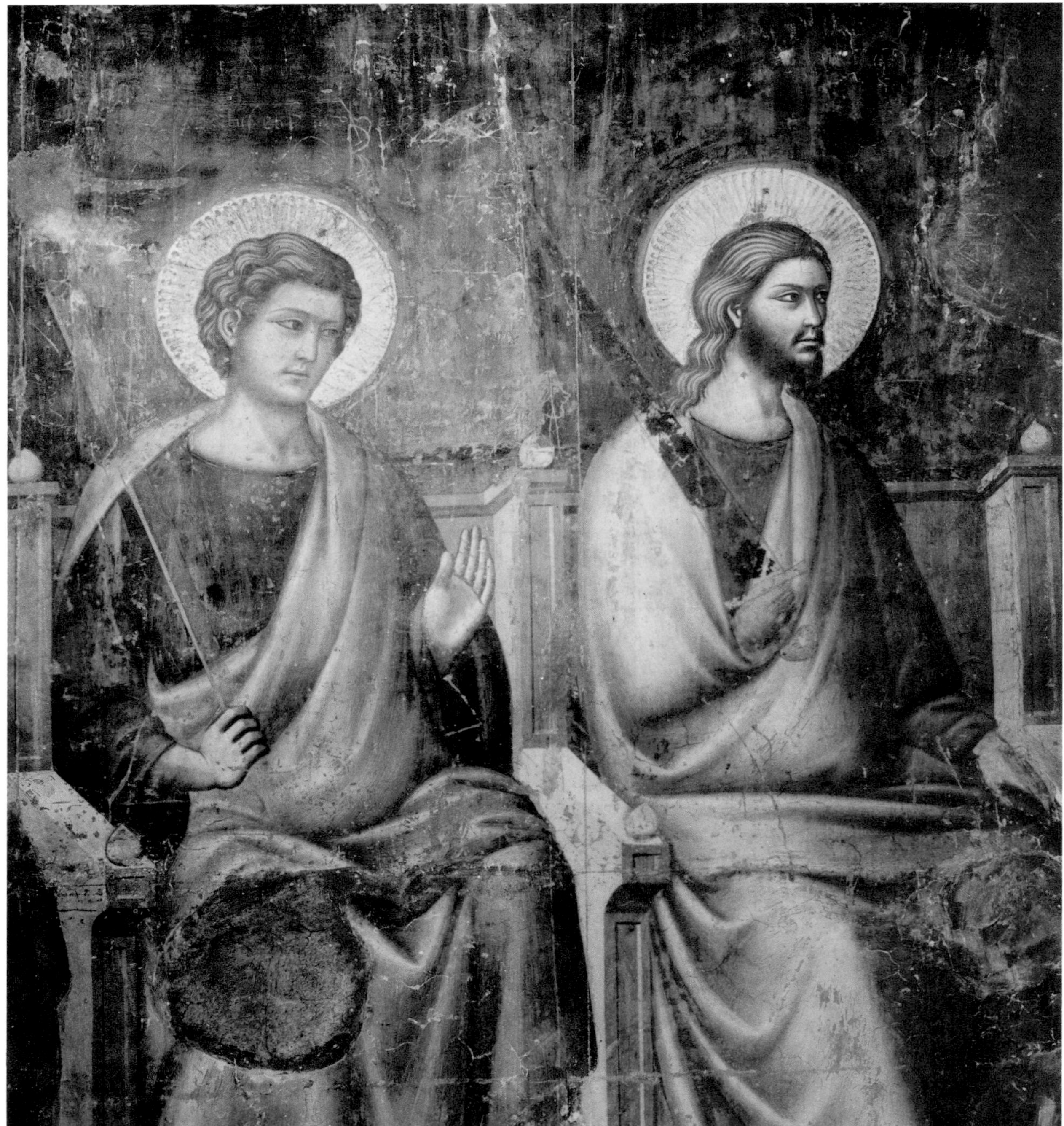

179. S. Cecilia, *Last Judgment*, detail, Apostles, Pietro Cavallini

not to be confounded with, that of classical antiquity. Giotto's Roman oeuvre should be seen along similar lines regardless of the dates it is assigned: the *Navicella* mosaic with its elements *all'antica*—the wind gods, the angler, the lighthouse—and with the monumental figures of the Apostles; and the Stefaneschi altar, free of antiquish motifs, and more monumental still. Both have been variously assigned dates prior to and long after 1300. If the latter were true, the persistence of concepts shaped in Rome during the last years of the century in the work of a

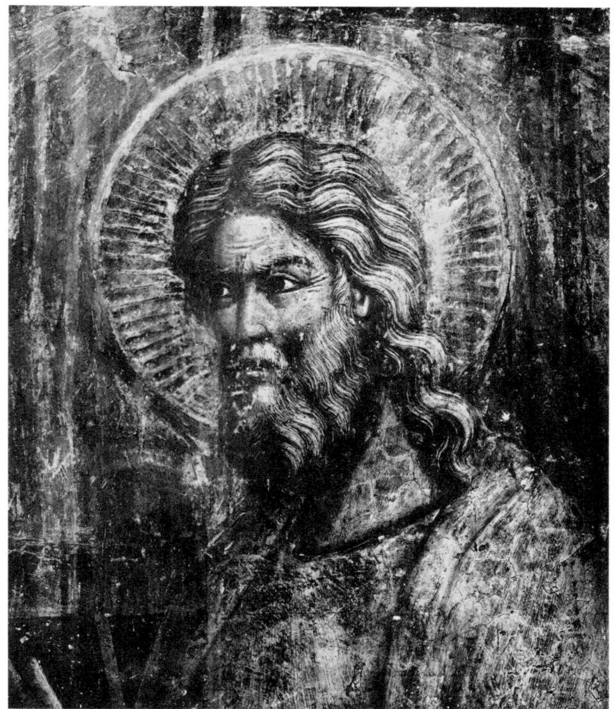

180. S. Cecilia, *Last Judgment*, detail, head of Apostle, Pietro Cavallini

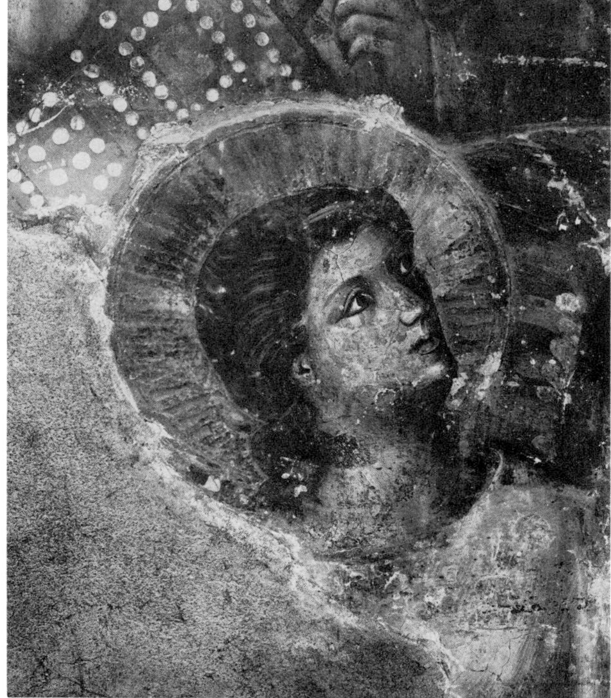

181. S. Cecilia, *Last Judgment*, detail, head of angel, Pietro Cavallini

master as Florentine as Giotto would be more amazing still.

The contemporary art of both Byzantium and Gothic France would seem to have contributed to and strengthened the new revival of antiquity as it was shaping up in the 1270s in Rome. But in its essence that renascence, like all those preceding it in Rome, remained emphatically Roman, based on the monuments of late antiquity extant through the city. To be sure, the Roman masters—and that distinguishes them from their twelfth-century great-grandfathers as well as from their predecessors in Rheims in the 1230s and from Nicola Pisano—cope with an infinitely broader range of antiquity, no longer a single head, a putto, a bird, but entire compositions. Almost nowhere but in Rome (and in Byzantium; but that is a different tale) were such compositions from late antiquity easily accessible: the familiarity with Early Christian mosaics and murals gained at S. Maria Maggiore and S. Paolo fuori le mura by Torriti and Cavallini and their circle would have opened to them the world of antiquity and led them to think anew in its spirit. They were confronted with the need to explore for themselves the problems of making figures act credibly in a credible space and thus to present a convincing near-reality. Setting aside their medieval training from pattern books, they had to learn afresh. Whereas the masters of S. Clemente in the first quarter of the twelfth century and those at Rheims around 1230 had substituted elements from antiquity for a reality unattainable by other means within a medieval vision of the world, to Cavallini, Torriti, and Arnolfo di Cambio in his last Roman years, antiquity was a guide toward exploring and a key to open reality. Inquiring into the nature of antique models led these artists to look directly and freshly at the world around them. Antiquity became a vehicle for conquering the visual world.

In the context of the political and cultural situation obtaining in Rome during these years, the background, fertility, and character of the new art fall into place. The patrons who commissioned the immense programs of decoration in churches and palaces (and of the latter we know but little) were evidently not only rich, they were, one suspects, highly cultured and open-minded. The influx of foreign dignitaries and their households no doubt played its part. They would have brought along works of art, vestments, textiles, enamels, goldsmith work, small sculptures, perhaps a portable icon, and quite possibly among their retinue a goldsmith or a painter. The Roman-born and Roman-bred high clerics would quickly have assimilated this new taste and broader vision. Like the French and English cardinals, they began to look beyond Rome: to Paris and the East, to Florence, Pisa, Siena, and Assisi. Like their confrères from abroad they were fascinated by the new art, with its overtones *all'antica*, which was sprouting, if ephemerally, at so many spots all over Europe. But they were equally fascinated by the gorgeousness of the materials, gold, precious stones, a vestment of gold thread set with pearls, the gold ground, one suspects, and the rich colors of a mosaic. The political framework of the Roman revival in the decades before 1300 becomes equally clear. Its main theme is the age of the Church and the supreme authority of the papacy rooted in the Apostolic Succession. This theme reappears time and again. The old venerable churches of Rome are remodeled, refurbished, and redecorated: St. Peter's and S. Paolo, sheltering the graves of the Apostles; S. Maria Maggiore, founded according to legend in the fourth century, a papal church in the proper sense of the word, where the pope celebrated Christmas; the Lateran Basilica, the see of the papacy as of old; and in the same context, the papal palace at the Lateran whence the pope would give his blessing *urbi et orbi*.

Over and over, the age of the Church and its foundation through Christ on the rock of Saint Peter are emphasized. Both Giotto's *Navicella* and his high altar of St. Peter's, the Stefaneschi altar, allude to these themes: Christ saving Saint Peter and the vessel of the Church, endangered; and Saint Peter enthroned in the scarlet cloak of the pope facing the congregation from the high altar in his basilica. It matters little in this context whether such allusions antedate the Holy Year of 1300 or are Cardinal Stefaneschi's nostalgic reminders of the papacy's proper place in Rome, rather than in the Avignon exile. The same themes show in the cycles of papal portraits decorating the ancient churches and stressing the Apostolic Succession: at S. Paolo a new series was placed in the spandrels of the arcades reaching from Peter to Boniface I and thus restating the oldest series placed above the arcades, dating partly from the fifth century, partly from the late seventh or early eighth centuries. Similarly at St. Peter's Nicholas III added on the entablature over each column a series of papal portraits, again restating the very beginnings of the papacy as reflected by the older series above the entablature, evidently also started in the fifth century. A third series of papal portraits was placed by him in the Lateran, but disappeared presumably in the fire of 1308. Finally, a fourth series was newly created, one may assume on the pattern of S. Paolo, by Cavallini at S. Cecilia, probably in the 1290s.

Such stress on the age of the Church had come to the fore brilliantly already at the century's start in the apse mosaic and the inscription Innocent III had placed in St. Peter's. Nonetheless, the approach of the popes from Nicholas III to Boniface VIII differs from Innocent's. Where he identified himself with Saint Peter and focused on his church—there is purpose in his building a palace there—the popes from Nicholas III on took a more comprehensive view. Not only was work at S. Paolo taken up again by refurbishing and complementing the old fifth-century murals; the perpetual continuation of the Apostolic authority was demonstrated *ad oculos* by the series of papal portraits in the three major basilicas, not to speak of S. Cecilia. At the same time, the Lateran, traditional see of the papacy, was reinstated in its old rights. Returning from their residences in Orvieto, Perugia, Viterbo, temporarily occupied in the mid-thirteenth century by the migrating Curia, the popes of the last twenty years of the century concentrated attention again on the Lateran as the official residence of the pontiff and on his cathedral. The palace at the Vatican was enlarged by Nicholas III, to be sure. It was more conveniently located for practical needs; it was fortified and easily defensible; and its position on the hill made it healthy. But it remained decidedly an auxiliary residence. The official seat of the papacy remained the Lateran. Nicholas III rebuilt the Sancta Sanctorum chapel and splendidly redecorated it; in the church he placed the series of papal portraits. Less than a decade later Nicholas IV had the old apse mosaic replaced by a new composition. Finally, Boniface VIII, the Caetani pope, emphatically stressed the importance of the old papal palace at the Lateran, ceded to the church, as legend had it, by Constantine. Boniface, after all, rebuilt the *loggia di benedizione* facing the square where the crowds would gather. He was shown there in a fresco once in the palace—a fragment survives in the church—proclaiming the Holy Year *urbi et orbi*, to the city and the world.

The stress on the age of the Church and of the papacy, on the Apostolic Succession, on the supremacy of the pope both as universal spiritual ruler and as claimant to universal temporal overlordship were long established themes by the end of the thirteenth century. Concepts and claims were accepted as being embodied in the office of the pontiff. Gradually ever since Innocent III, and more emphatically from the pontificate of Nicholas III on, the accent was shifted to the person of the pope. Nicholas seems to have been the first to allow, or at least not to have objected to, having a statue set up in his honor—it was at Ancona, a token of gratitude for his mediation in a quarrel of the city with Venice. A decade later another was erected for Nicholas IV; it has tentatively been identified with the badly mutilated portrait statue of a pope of late-thirteenth-century date in the collection of Palazzo Venezia. The pontificate of Boniface VIII, finally, marks a climax unparalleled for the next two or three hundred years. Now it was the Caetani pope himself who demanded that such statues to him be set up in prominent places: three marble statues at Bologna—the commune instead decided on a single statue in bronze—in recognition of his arbitrating a dispute with the marquis of Este; two over the city gates of Orvieto recalling similar arbitration; one at Amiens, of gilded silver, as a penalty in deciding a law suit between chapter and bishop; others still at Anagni and Padua—the last never executed, but this, too, planned for favors received; one more in Florence, formerly on the façade of the cathedral, now in the Opera del Duomo, again as a token of gratitude for his having contributed to the building fund; finally, one at the Lateran, likewise commemorating a decision in favor of the canons. Except for this last and presumably the one at Amiens where his statue was paired with that of the Virgin, they show him either standing or enthroned; all commemorate his role in secular matters—as arbiter, donor, protector of the town, possibly temporal ruler. Indeed, the tradition of setting up honorary statues, comparatively new by the late thirteenth century, was decidedly secular. In Rome, the first such statue was that of Charles of Anjou erected by the senate in 1276 for the new *senatore* for life. That he was ruler of South Italy may well have played its part in the senate's decision. It was there that the custom had been established by Frederick II—at Capua, Acerenza, possibly elsewhere—one may assume as part of the revival of antiquity such as he viewed it in the frame of his political ideology, a rebirth of the Rome of the Caesars in whose honor such statues had been set up as a matter of course.

When around 1280 the popes began to take up the custom, they did so as temporal sovereigns. But the role of a pope as spiritual ruler was hard to separate from the temporal one; time and again statues of Boniface VIII show him blessing. It is this secular/religious dual role that forms the framework within which the Rome and the papacy of the late thirteenth century must be seen. The pope is the spiritual ruler of Christendom. He claims overlordship over the temporal rulers of the West and himself rules Rome and a territory large in medieval terms, as a secular sovereign. In both these last two roles he is also the heir of the Roman emperors. In this vein, during the decades from 1278 to 1303 a series of Rome-bred popes and cardinals and their families attempted to turn Rome into the resplendent capital of the papacy, and its court into the true head of the world. Her churches, refurbished and renewed, were witnesses of her Christian past, of the saints who had lived and died for this past and hence of the age, legitimacy, and greatness of the living Church and of the pontiff in power who stood for and ruled it.

But the pope stood as heir to the Roman Empire as well; Christianized, to be sure, but empire nonetheless. Through the pope, Rome was in every sense the capital of the world. In this capital reborn, a fresh eminently Roman art had come to the fore and made Rome for a short while into one of the new centers that just then were shaping in Central Italy, in Pisa, Siena, Florence. Among them Rome stands out as a major center prior to 1300. With the removal of the pope to Avignon, she ceased to be that; Siena and Florence took her place.

Rome altogether, without the papacy, lost her raison d'être. She could not continue to exist as she had through the thousand years gone by. The bond between her and the papacy ideally had never been broken. Notwithstanding the many times when popes were forced, or chose, to take up residence elsewhere, Rome until 1308 remained the pope's capital. The move to Avignon was different. The papacy and Rome ceased to be one. Rome, for nearly a hundred years to come, would no longer be *caput mundi*.

The situation is reflected in the monuments, or the lack of them, in the fourteenth century. Papal activity by remote control was limited in the extreme. The Lateran Basilica, badly damaged by fire in 1308 and again in 1361, though not destroyed as Petrarch claimed with a poet's exaggeration, was twice repaired—the last campaign drawn out into the fifteenth century; during this last campaign, in 1368, a canopy was commissioned from the Sienese workshop in charge of repairs—Rome had no sculptors left, it seems. Late in the century, the Palazzo del Senatore, a papal stronghold by then, was fortified. All this should be viewed against the background of the political and economic situation. The better part of the century was filled with family wars and revolts against the papal vicars sent from Avignon. The last third saw sporadic and unsuccessful attempts by the popes to return. Economically, too, the picture was black. The papal bureaucracy and the income it brought to the city were gone; building, except for domestic structures put up at no great expense, came practically to a standstill. In short, two of the three industries that carried the economy of Rome had dried up. The third, the tourist trade, continued. Pilgrims came, perhaps in smaller numbers, until the Holy Year declared for 1350. Then their numbers swelled again, to perhaps as much as they were half a century before. Indeed, with the last half of the century an economic recovery seems to have set in: witness the growing importance, politically and economically, of the great cattle breeders and dealers, the *bovattieri*, and of the merchants' guild, the *arte dei mercanti*; the renewal of imports from Tuscany and further north; and the setting up, though mostly after 1400, of Florentine banking branches in Rome.

There is but one great monument in Rome known from the fourteenth century: the grand stairs leading to Aracoeli from the rim of the medieval abitato. Built in 1347, they reflect the fantastic dream of Cola di Rienzo to establish a Roman republic, superior to Emperor and Pope, with its seat on the Capitol from which the world was once ruled. We no longer see in Cola di Rienzo the great historical figure who fired the imagination of nineteenth-century liberals—Gregorovius allotted him close to one hundred and fifty pages—nor the hero, for different reasons, of Italian fascists in this century. His rhetorical ramblings had no basis in reality and no impact on or relation to the politics of the time, and his dream of a rebirth of Rome collapsed as it was bound to after a few years. He does not compare, it seems to me, with his great forerunner, Arnold of Brescia, an intellectual with clear concepts of a new relationship to be established between the city of Rome and the papacy. Cola's significance, I feel, lies elsewhere. He must be understood in the context of the early humanism of the fourteenth century, of Petrarch and his fellow litterateurs who formed a new picture of Rome over the second half of the century and opened the path to the Renaissance.

But this, like the economic recovery of Rome at that same time, is a different tale. For us, the year 1303 marks the end of the Middle Ages in Rome.

Part II

Forma Urbis Romae Medievalis

CHAPTER NINE

The Evidence

We simply lack the evidence to trace a map of Rome in the centuries from the Gothic Wars through the times of Charlemagne and his successors. Churches and papal palaces built and decorated at that time reflect the image of Rome and the political background rather than its reality. The welfare centers developed and maintained give but the vaguest hints of the areas to which the population had withdrawn or where pilgrims congregated, of the street system, the provisioning with water, the housing. What little is known we have discussed in the pertinent chapters preceding. This second section, then, deals with the map of Rome in the Middle Ages proper, from the tenth through the thirteenth centuries when evidence is less nebulous.

Even so, evidence for reconstructing the map or envisaging the aspect of Rome in the Middle Ages is not easy to come by. The medieval town, of course, like Rome of imperial times or Republican Rome, is all there, but overlaid by later buildings. Few elements are clear to the unaided eye and most of them are monumental buildings: churches, towers, cloisters. Of houses and streets few traces are left and documentation is skimpy. Even the size of the population remains in question. Lists of foodstuffs distributed to every inhabitant or every family, like those recorded for the fourth and early sixth centuries, are lacking; so are census rolls, baptismal and death lists, as they survive from the sixteenth century on. What we do know is that the number of inhabitants, still close to perhaps as much as 500,000 in the fourth century, rapidly shrank. Procopius' tale that only 500 men were left at the end of the Gothic Wars sounds unlikely. But even after the return of those who fled, the figure apparently remained small. At the time of Gregory the Great it swelled to perhaps 90,000 when refugees, many of them monastic congregations, were driven from the countryside into the city by the Longobards. But this influx was temporary. The breakdown in provisioning in the seventh century led to more depletion; and though the improvement of supplies under Pope Hadrian I and his successors seems to have led to some increase in the population, the final collapse of the welfare and supply system at the end of the ninth century, followed by political and economic disintegration in the tenth century, resulted in a new drop. From then through the twelfth and thirteenth centuries, the population figure is said to have oscillated around 35,000, which seems right, in the absence of firm evidence. If 20,000 people in the city—these the exact words of the sources—really died of malaria in 1167, one would reasonably guess that the inhabitants numbered 40,000 and more. But the chronicler is likely to have exaggerated the number of victims, and the actual population figure was proportionately lower, though large for a medieval town. Indeed, the size of the Roman army, 30,000 strong at the Battle of Monte Porzio that same year just before the plague struck, conservatively suggests a population of somewhat below 200,000 for Rome *and* her district, whence the levy was jointly drawn. Based on the proportionate figures of district and town population as they obtained after 1400 for Rome and her territory, one to ten, we could deduce that the city population was below 20,000. However, in the twelfth and thirteenth centuries, Rome and her district were presumably more densely populated than just after 1400. All over Italy the population appears to have dropped during the fourteenth century, owing to a generally deteriorating economy and frequent plagues. In Rome the decimation was worsened through the removal of the Curia to Avignon. Indeed, Rome's population at that point may have been as low as

17,000. But in the twelfth century both the district and the city itself were flourishing, and continued to do so through the following century. All the evidence suggests that Rome participated in the population explosion that hit the urban centers of the West at that time. Hence the proportionate figures of district and city may well have been closer to five to one than ten to one; and Rome would have counted any number between 30,000 and 40,000 inhabitants. Granted, she was not a center of industrial production and large-scale commerce, such as Florence, Cologne, or Bruges. But she had developed resources of a different kind: the vast income of the Church—St. Peter's Pence, tithes, fees and gifts from all over the West; the swollen bureaucracy of the Curia; the city's place as the foremost legal center of Europe with lawyers, clerks, and scribes attracting business; the flux of pilgrims and the resulting growth of commercial activity; the banking operations of and connected with the Curia. All would have led to an increase in the population; and this seems to be confirmed by evidence of vast building activity and the expansion of the built-up areas, the abitato, starting with the eleventh century and continuing through the thirteenth. The dozens of churches newly built, parish churches at that, can only mean a considerable increase in population; and the many hundreds of houses mentioned in deeds of sale, lease, or donations point in the same direction. Certainly, none of this proves the exact or even an approximate figure for the population of Rome. But the estimates proposed so far by economic historians and demographers also appear to be guesswork. There is nothing sound to go on prior to the first real census made in 1527 when Rome counted over 55,000 inhabitants—this after a century of rapidly rising prosperity and expansion. For the Middle Ages we may just as well admit that so far we know the size of Rome's population only in the vaguest terms.

Clues for envisaging the map of the city, on the other hand, are more promising, but they, too, are far from providing solid proof. The system of streets, as far as it survived a hundred years ago and still survives in parts, provides some evidence; but in it, streets from ancient, medieval, and later times intermingle. The bridges across the Tiber in use through the Middle Ages hint at the probable location nearby of built-up areas. Other clues are the foundation, maintenance, or rebuilding of churches, convents, and diaconiae, whether surviving or known only from documents, in neighborhoods that were populated, rehabilitated, or abandoned. Damage to and repairs of aqueducts provide supplementary clues of the areas to be serviced: papal residences, pilgrimage centers, and densely populated quarters. Occasionally, the accounts of a natural catastrophe, such as a Tiber flood, allow for a glimpse of the importance, functional or social, of a city quarter hard hit. The documented location of markets, mills, landing stages, and harbors, all by necessity near populated areas, furnishes further evidence. The location of great family mansions is indicated, if approximately, in papal biographies and elsewhere. The clearest and the most vivid evidence is furnished by legal documents. The registers of great abbeys such as Farfa and Subiaco refer to their real estate owned in Rome, its nature and location. Finally, many thousands of deeds of sale or lease from the archives of Roman churches and monasteries list the position and appearance of houses, lots, and gardens in their possession. Large numbers of these documents have been published, the majority in the *Archivio della Società Romana di Storia Patria*; others still await publication. These deeds more than anything else give a real picture of housing in the Middle Ages from the tenth century on. Houses are described in great detail: the location—such and such a quarter of the city; the boundaries—the house or property of so-and-so to the right, of so-and-so to the left, to the rear, in front; a garden in the back, the street; the type of house, one-storied, two-storied, an outer staircase in front or along the flank, a fireplace and chimney; the building and roofing materials, shingles, bricks, or tiles, the roof often thatched; the trees in the garden—apples, olives, a fig tree, a vine over a pergola. One gets a vivid impression of houses and neighborhoods.

There is further evidence, though of late date and hence to be exploited only with caution. The archives of Roman confraternities preserved in the Archivio di Stato contain their *catasti*—surveys of their real estate property—starting shortly after the mid-sixteenth century. These give hundreds of plans and occasionally elevations or even sections of houses owned by the confraternities all over town. Clearly, such houses may have been built or remodeled at any time prior to the survey. Still, simple house plans change little, and many, if not actually from medieval times, seem to represent medieval types. Sometimes, the elevation of a house façade reveals with some dependability its medieval character; or an inscription on the survey gives the date, back in the fourteenth or fifteenth century, at which the building became the property of the confraternity and thus provides a *terminus ante* or *ad quem*.

Important though these chartularies are, they give a lopsided picture in that they list only property owned by ecclesiastical institutions. Private property in the hands of great families or small householders is, for the better part of the Middle Ages, poorly documented. Deeds of sale or lease dealing with such property would have remained with the parties involved, and would by now be lost. A copy would have been kept in the files of the executing notary; and such notarial files in Rome do not seem to go back before the mid-fourteenth century. Only an occasional glimpse of the large private real estate holdings in Rome is gained through deeds of gifts made by laymen to churches and convents or through a rare document that has strayed into an ecclesiastical archive.

Maps and views of Rome, *vedute*, are, of course, all late. Nonetheless, they are helpful in building up a picture of the medieval town and its surroundings. The earliest map to survive—not counting maps drawn in pure symbols—is the one done by Fra Paolino da Venezia in 1323; but based as it is on a text of the *Mirabilia* dating from 1280, the map likewise may go back to a thirteenth-century original (fig. 182). Within the framework of medieval concepts of cartography, it gives quite a precise picture of the town as seen by a contemporary: the Aurelian Walls, albeit in the shape of an oval; the winding course of the Tiber and its island; some of the hills; the outstanding buildings—the Palazzo del Senatore on the Capitol, the Colosseum, the Pantheon, Torre delle Milizie, the Lateran Palace with its collection of ancient statuary (the Marcus Aurelius and Constantine's head and hand are shown), S. Giovanni in Laterano, the aqueduct on the Celian Hill, St. Peter's, Castel S. Angelo, the medieval Vatican Palace and its deerpark, Sto. Spirito in Sassia. More relevant to envisaging medieval Rome, the map shows the main streets, the city quarters—Trastevere, the Borgo, the built-up area in the Tiber bend, the Ripa—and houses lining the streets, singly or in rows. In short, it provides a picture of the medieval town far more real than the fifteenth-century maps, which show only churches and ancient monuments, starting with Taddeo di Bartolo's map in Siena and that of the Limbourg Brothers in the *Très Riches Heures du Duc de Berry* or with their apparent fourteenth-century prototypes. Fra Paolino's map is intended to present a true picture of medieval Rome; and in that respect it differs fundamentally from contemporary, earlier or later, ideal representations of the city such as Cimabue's fresco in Assisi or the Golden Bull of Louis the Bavarian of 1328. There, based on the *Mirabilia*, a few monumental structures—hardly changing in the long series of derivatives—stand for the grandeur of Rome, past and present, pagan and Christian: the towered and crenelated walls; the Tiber, its island and bridges; Castel S. Angelo, St. Peter's, the obelisk; S. Maria in Trastevere; the Pantheon, Palazzo del Senatore, the Colosseum; a triumphal arch, Constantine's or Titus's; the pyramid of Cestius; the Column of Trajan and what appears to be the Mausoleum of Augustus; finally, S. Giovanni in Laterano (figs. 160, 223).

The painters and draughtsmen, on the other hand, who from the fifteenth century on did *vedute* of Rome, either panoramas or individual buildings, aimed decidedly at showing the town as they actually saw it: Masolino around 1435; the Escurial draughtsman late in the fifteenth century; Marten van Heemskerck in Rome between 1532 and 1536; even Wijngaerde's and Naldini's panoramas in the 1550s and 1560s. Notwithstanding their postmedieval date, they render faithfully both the overall picture and individual elements that at their times either had

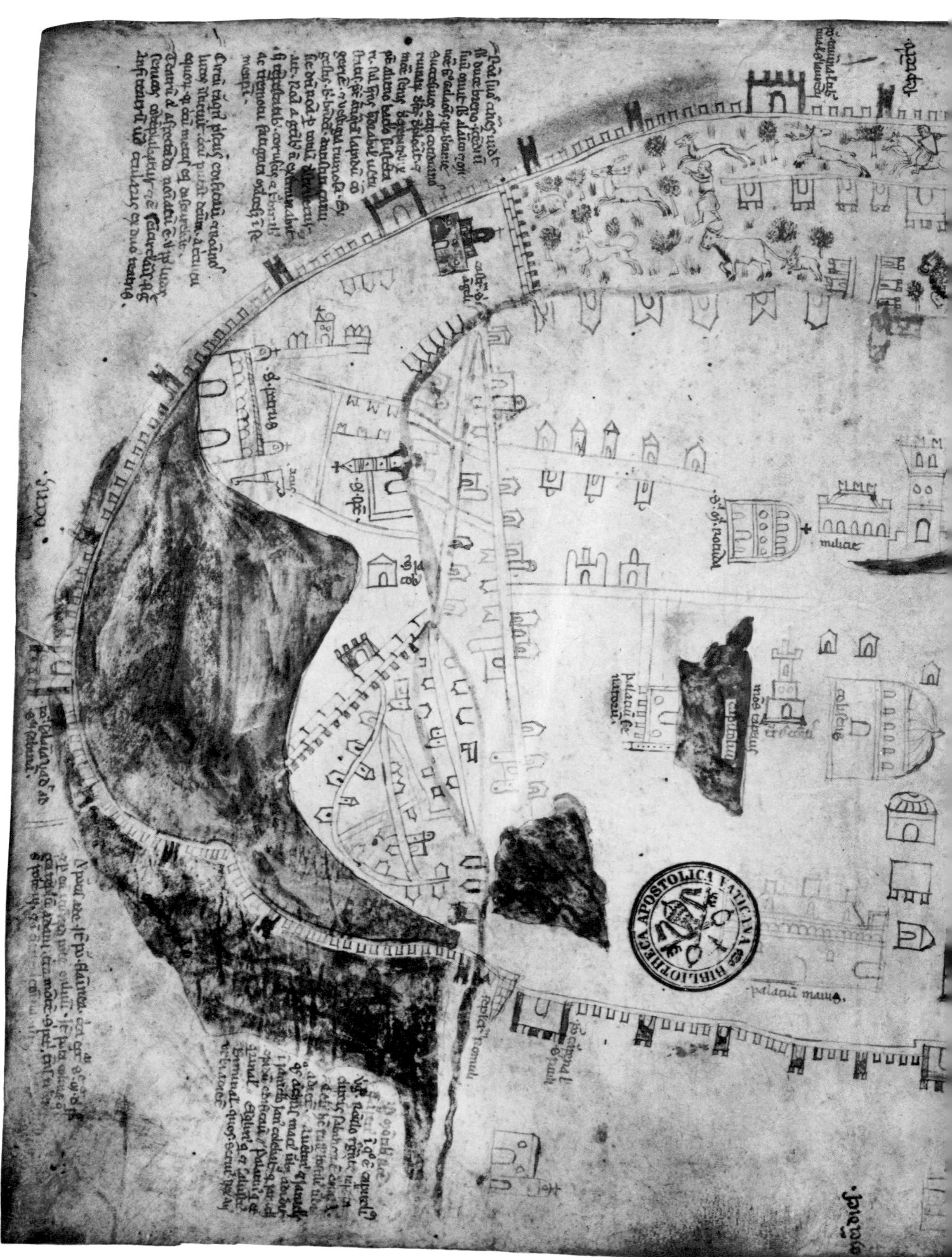

182. Map of Rome, 1323, Fra Paolino da Venezia, Biblioteca Vaticana, Vat. lat. 1960, fol. 270v

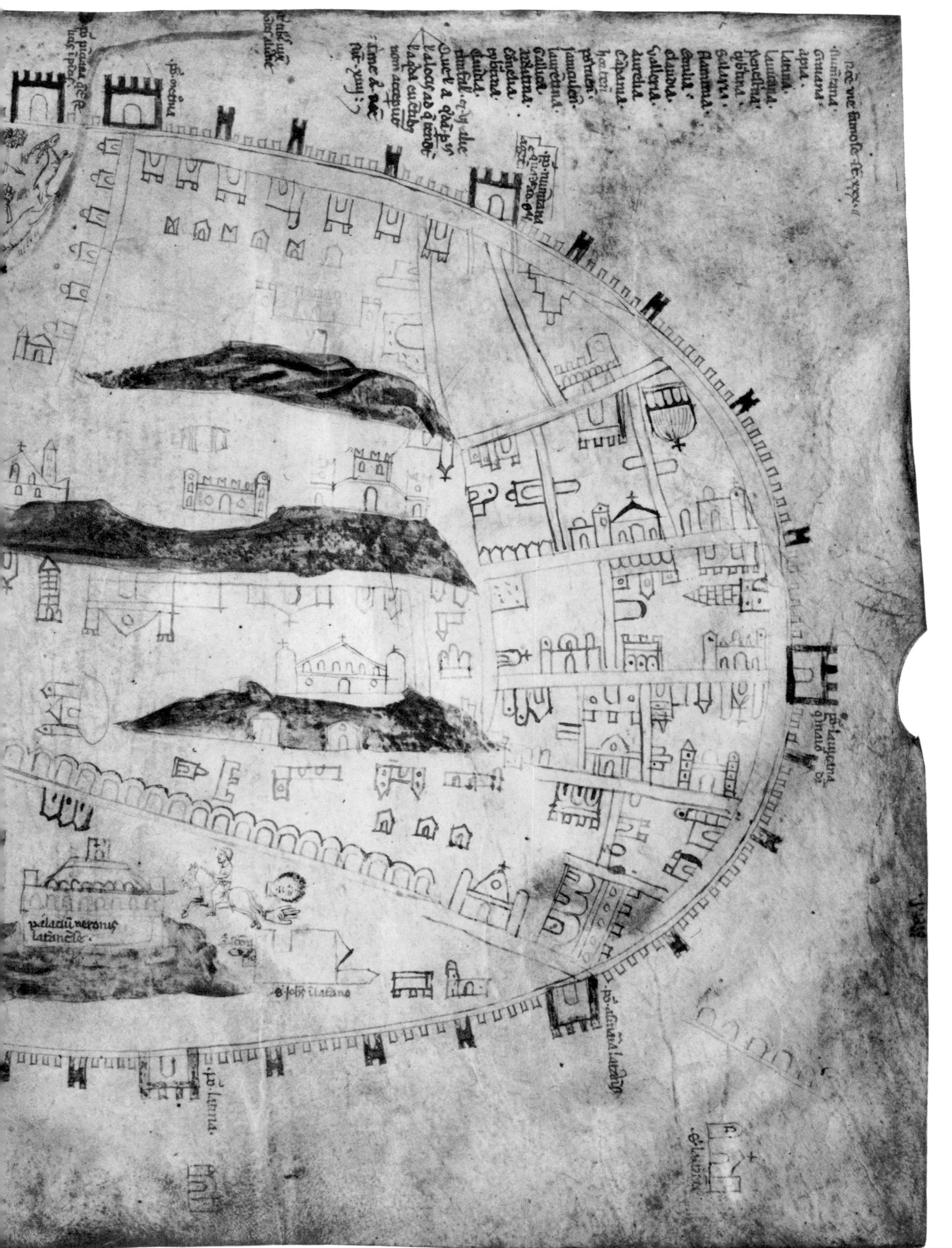

survived from medieval times or were based on a medieval layout: the contrast between the built-up area and the surrounding land, whether or not cultivated, and extending to the Aurelian Walls; the dense crowding of houses, churches, towers, and ancient monuments emerging from the abitato; ruins, fields, and vineyards in the disabitato; the sloping river banks; houses, just as they are described in deeds of sale from the tenth century on, and thus probably medieval; a group of family towers; and the like.

Even so, such hints suggest only the general outlines of a Roman map in the Middle Ages. The layout, growth, and aspect of the medieval town obviously must be seen within a structure in which political and economic conditions intertwine with inherited elements that are constant or at least slowly changing determinant factors: the terrain of hills and valleys, the winding course of the Tiber with its huge westward bend; the Roman inheritance—the Aurelian Walls; the main arteries of the Roman street system within and the highways outside the walls; the bridges spanning the river; some of the great Roman ruins, such as the buildings on the Capitoline Hill, the fora, or Castel S. Angelo; the foremost Christian sanctuaries, St. Peter's and the Lateran; finally, the areas where the shrunken population of Rome settled after the catastrophes of the sixth century and where the new Rome slowly and painfully grew over the subsequent four hundred or five hundred years. Nature, ancient Rome, and early medieval Rome, these last two turned, as it were, into nature, form the inheritance on which Rome was built in the High Middle Ages.

CHAPTER TEN

The Inheritance

The Aurelian Walls, militarily speaking, had never had much defensive value. Far too long to be either attacked or defended in their entirety by late Roman times, they gave protection against partial attack; gates were opened through treachery, but the walls were rarely if ever scaled by invaders. What was true in late antiquity was truer still in the Middle Ages when armies were even smaller. Nonetheless, the walls remained a deterrent to would-be attackers. Indeed, they were occasionally repaired still in the High Middle Ages, as witness an inscription near Porta Metronia dated 1157. Given the vast area they encompassed, they had no direct impact on the development of the medieval town: the built-up areas—the abitato—were tucked away inside and mostly far from the walls. The Leonine City around St. Peter's remained until the High Middle Ages a separate township across the river. Only rarely did the fields, and nowhere but at the Leonina did the abitato, extend beyond the walls. The situation had changed little by the mid-sixteenth century (fig. 183). The Aurelian Walls, enclosing both the town on the east bank and Trastevere, continued to form the boundary of Rome, legally through the eleventh century and visibly until about sixty years ago.

Inside the walls, the terrain obviously shaped the growth of medieval Rome just as it had determined the map of the ancient city. However, there was a fundamental difference. In antiquity the hills where the air was healthy, the Pincio, Viminal, Esquiline, Oppian and Celian, the Aventine and, across the river, the Gianicolo, had carried in a huge crescent the greenbelt of the big mansions; the low land was the great show area, from the Tiber bend reaching as far east as the Colosseum and enveloping the Capitoline and the Palatine, whence Rome had first grown; all over, the tenements of the lower and middle classes pushed into the gaps between the show area and the greenbelt, following with preference the valleys separating the hills and their lower slopes. But in medieval Rome, the hills no longer counted, except where they carried outlying clusters—on the Celian, the Esquiline, the Aventine. The abitato moved into the unhealthy low land, the *città bassa* near the river, the ancient show area. Ancient Rome had grown from the settlements on its hills and it remained centered on the Forum, the Capitoline, and the Palatine. Medieval Rome was anchored to the Tiber.

The Tiber, indeed, was the basic element in the growth of the medieval town. True, it remained a threat. Two and three times every century, but sometimes thirty or forty, and at other times only two or three years apart, the river flooded the town, in the area of the Tiber bend, as it had done in ancient Rome: the scenes that were recounted, one recalls, in lively colors, if in ritual terms, by papal biographers from the eighth and ninth centuries, were repeated through the Middle Ages and in more recent times until 1870. On February 1, 1231, to punish the Romans for having expelled Pope Gregory IX, or so contemporaries concluded, "the Lord opened the cataracts of Heaven and the flood of the Tiber rose in the houses up to the roofs, killing men and beasts, ruining grain and vine, and carrying off to sea beds and masses of large vessels; when the waters fell, they left heaps of big snakes within the city and their rotting caused a plague attacking men and beasts; some died, others fell ill." In that flood, too, what is now Ponte Rotto collapsed for the first time. In December 1277, the high altar inside the Pantheon was more than four feet under water. A similar flood is recorded in a nineteenth-century engraving (fig. 184); and other inundations are likely to have occurred. A marker in 1277, the oldest to survive, records the crest of the flood near the

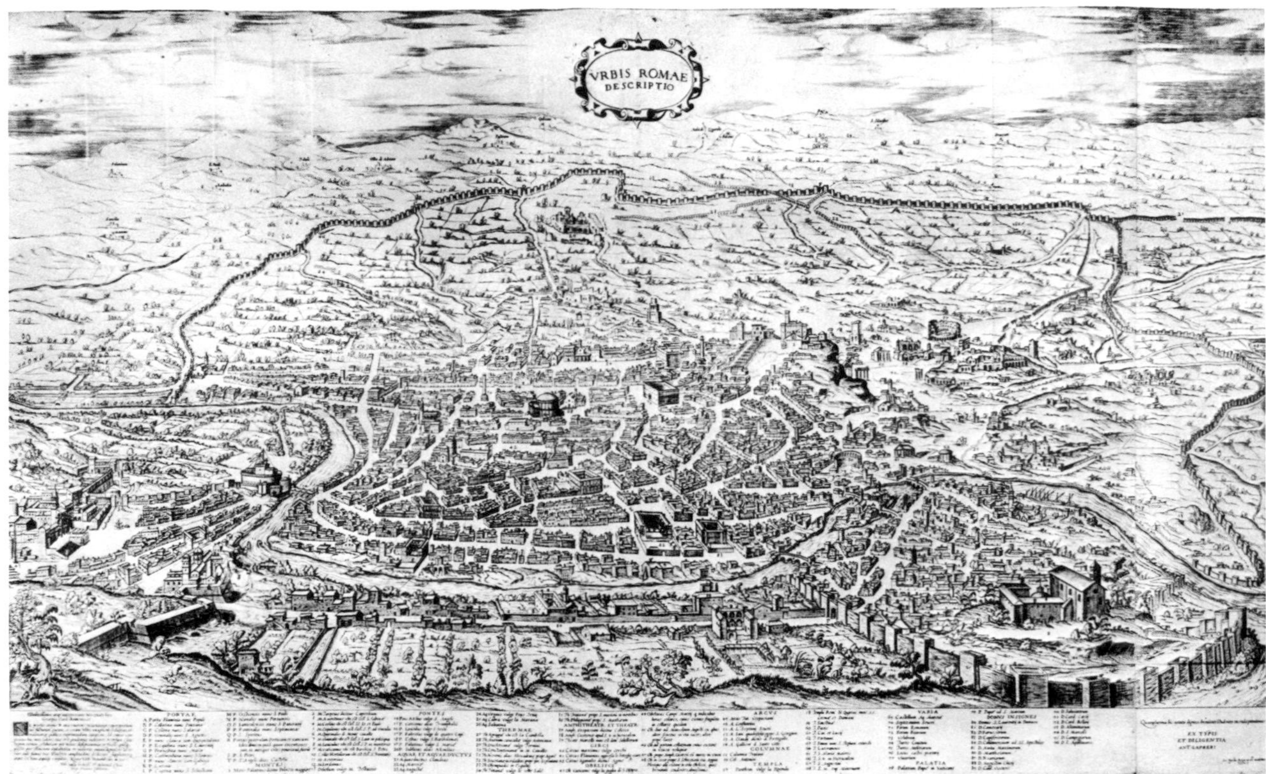

183. Map of Rome, 1555, Ugo Pinardo

Banco di Sto. Spirito, a hundred and fifty meters from Ponte S. Angelo. Even today, the protecting embankments notwithstanding, the Tiber in flood can look fearsome (fig. 185).

Despite all this, through the Middle Ages it was the very lifeline of the town. The banks opposite the island, north and south, remained key points as after the Gothic Wars the population, then decimated, withdrew to a few built-up clusters; and as the town took more cohesive shape, it spread over the Roman show area, the Campus Martius, enclosed by the great river bend. The river through the Middle Ages became the principal route to the outside world and the means of communication between the parts of town on either side. Of the old Roman bridges, four remained in the Middle Ages: northernmost, Ponte S. Angelo, the only link to St. Peter's; across the island, Pons Fabricius and Pons Cestius, connecting the southern end of the built-up area on the east bank with Trastevere (fig. 186); and the Ponte Rotto, in ancient times the Roman Pons Aemilius, later called Ponte S. Maria, which linked the southern end of Trastevere to the area near S. Maria in Cosmedin. Ruptured in 1557 and repaired in 1574, it collapsed again in 1598 and since then has retained its present name; in the early Middle Ages it was known as *Pons Maior*, the Great Bridge, either for its size or its importance or both. Other Roman bridges had collapsed by the eleventh century: the Pons Agrippae (or Aemilianus, misnamed Antoninus in the Middle Ages), which crossed to the very north of Trastevere in the eighth century and was replaced further downstream in 1475 by Ponte Sisto; and, at the foot of the Aventine, crossing to the southern part of Trastevere, the Bridge of Theodosius, ruined prior to 1018. Their remains made shipping more perilous than even the natural hazards (fig. 187). The navigable channel was narrow at best, hemmed in by the banks sloping gradually upwards and by sandbanks, one, the *isoletta*, just northeast of the island. One easily forgets the radical changes wrought by the building of the embankments, around 1900, but

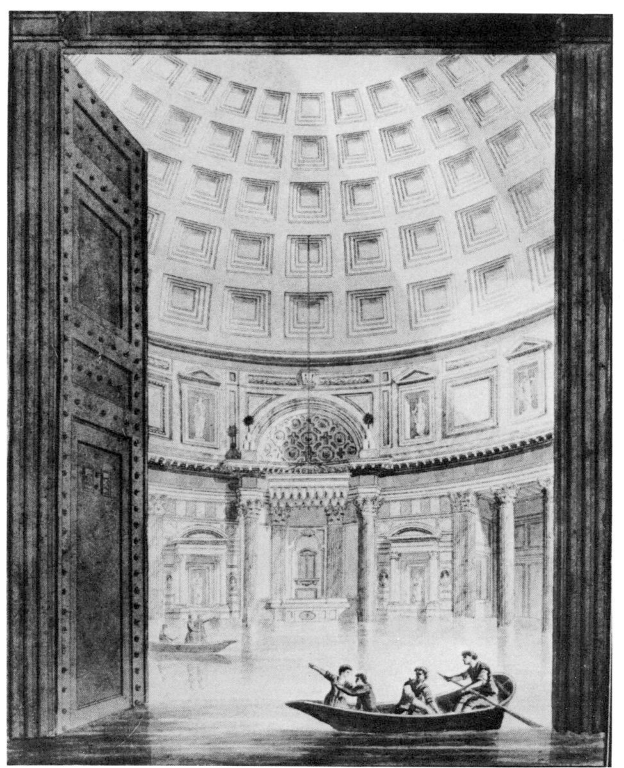

184. Pantheon flooded, anonymous, ca. 1800

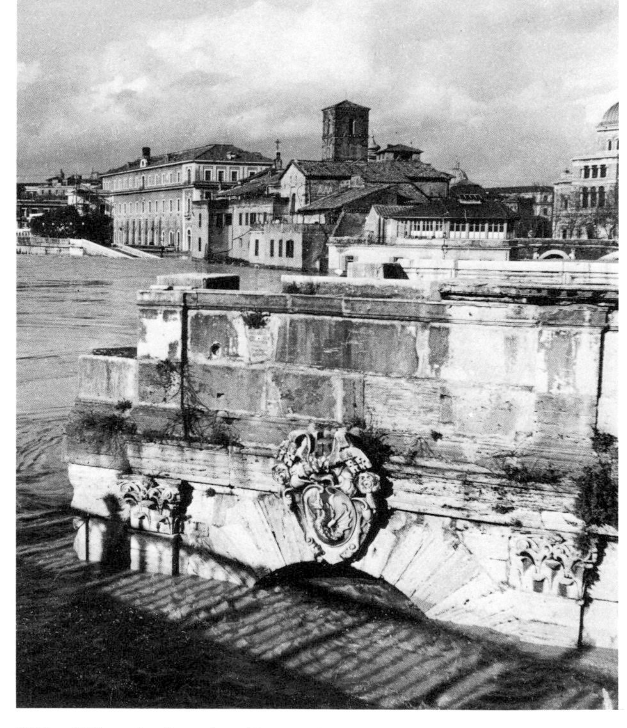

185. Tiber in flood at Ponte Rotto

any photograph or drawing prior to that conveys the idea. Along the northern stretch, too, as far down as Ponte Sisto, the remains of the Aurelian Walls skirted the river and early in the Middle Ages may have carried housing.

On the southern stretch, the ancient Roman port on the Marmorata had long been abandoned. A new port, the Ripa Grande, had been formed on the west bank of the Tiber, certainly by the ninth century when Leo IV (847-855) blocked the river to Saracen pirates with a chain and three towers, two at Porta Portuense, a third at the harbor. A church, S. Maria in turri trans Tiberim, marked the spot, and a flight of steps, first noted in the fifteenth century, ascended the steep river bank (fig. 188). The Ripa Grande remained the principal harbor for seagoing ships into the eighteenth century; as late as a hundred years ago, smaller craft used to dock there, including in 1870 three Italian gunboats. Another jetty existed on the east bank, south of Ponte Rotto at the Temple of Fortuna Virilis. It was turned into a church, S. Maria Egiziaca or popularly S. Maria ad Gradellis; the name referred to steps ascending from the river. From Ponte S. Maria to Ponte S. Angelo navigation was blocked. A small landing stage for the traffic coming downriver, at the Ripetta far above Ponte S. Angelo, went back possibly to Roman times; more likely, it was formed in the Middle Ages and remained in use into the late nineteenth century; its beautiful sweeping steps, built in 1701, remained in place till bodily transferred upstream to the west bank of the river in 1890.

If the river was a basic factor in provisioning Rome, it was also an important source, though not the only one, for drinking water, horrible as that may sound to a century familiar with bacteria, typhoid fever, and cholera. Living close by was a convenience; households further away had to rely on wells, and these were apt to dry up in the summer. The river, too, supplied fish. From the tenth century on, monasteries leased and sold fishing rights on the river banks and in midstream. Fish pools, fishing jetties, eel

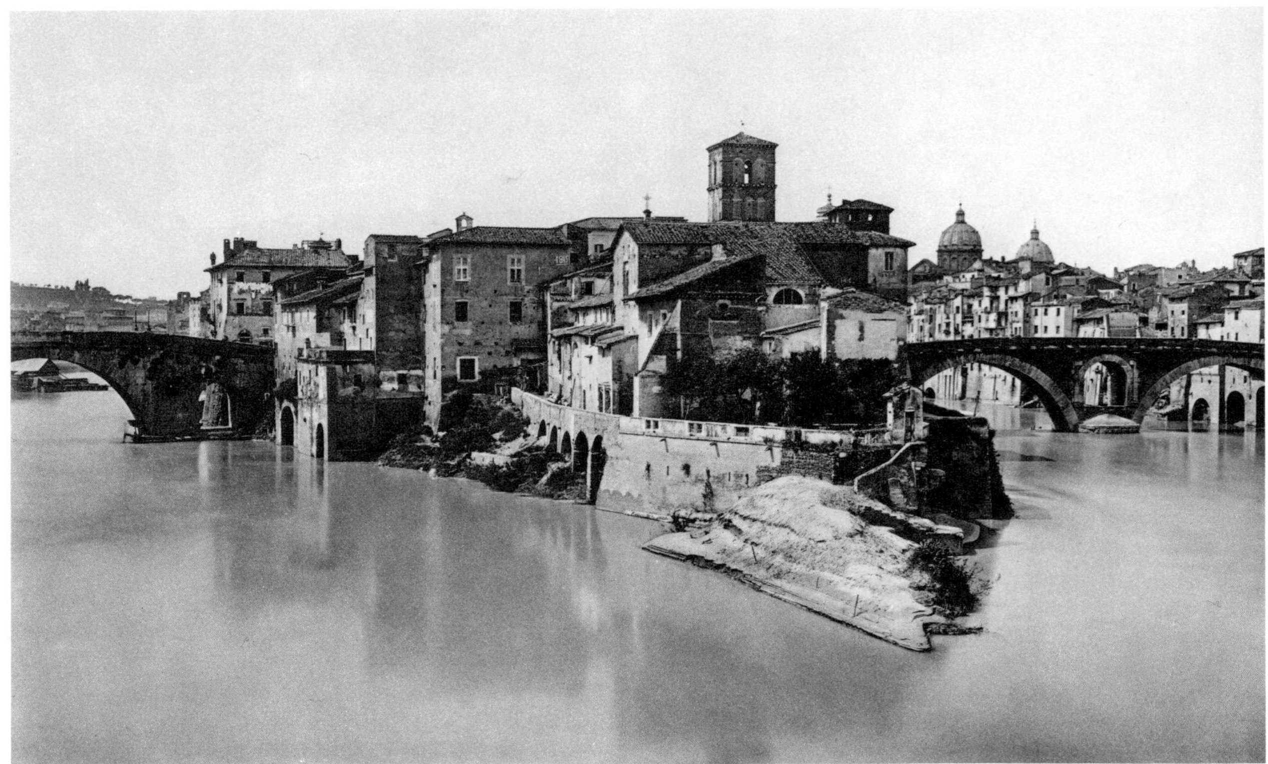

186. Tiber Island and Bridges as of ca. 1880

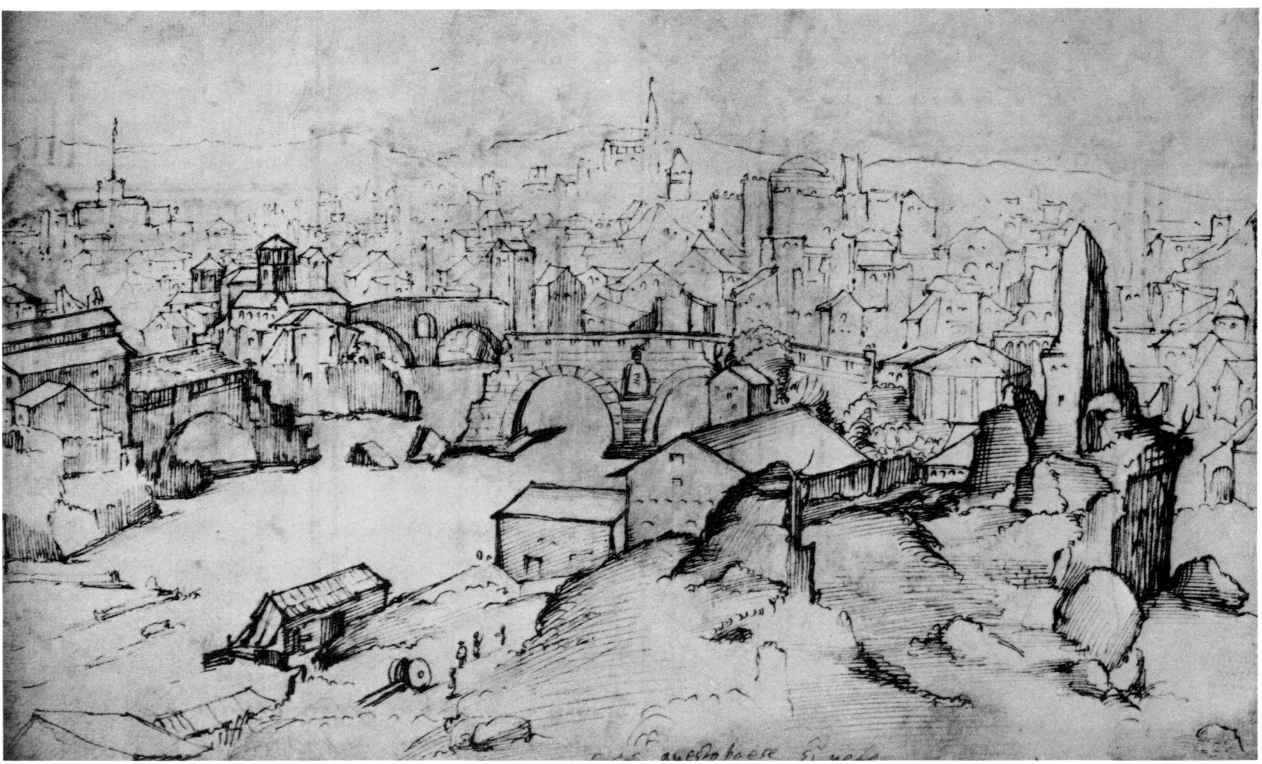

187. View of Tiber and city from Aventine, between 1557 and 1564, drawing Battista Naldini, private collection

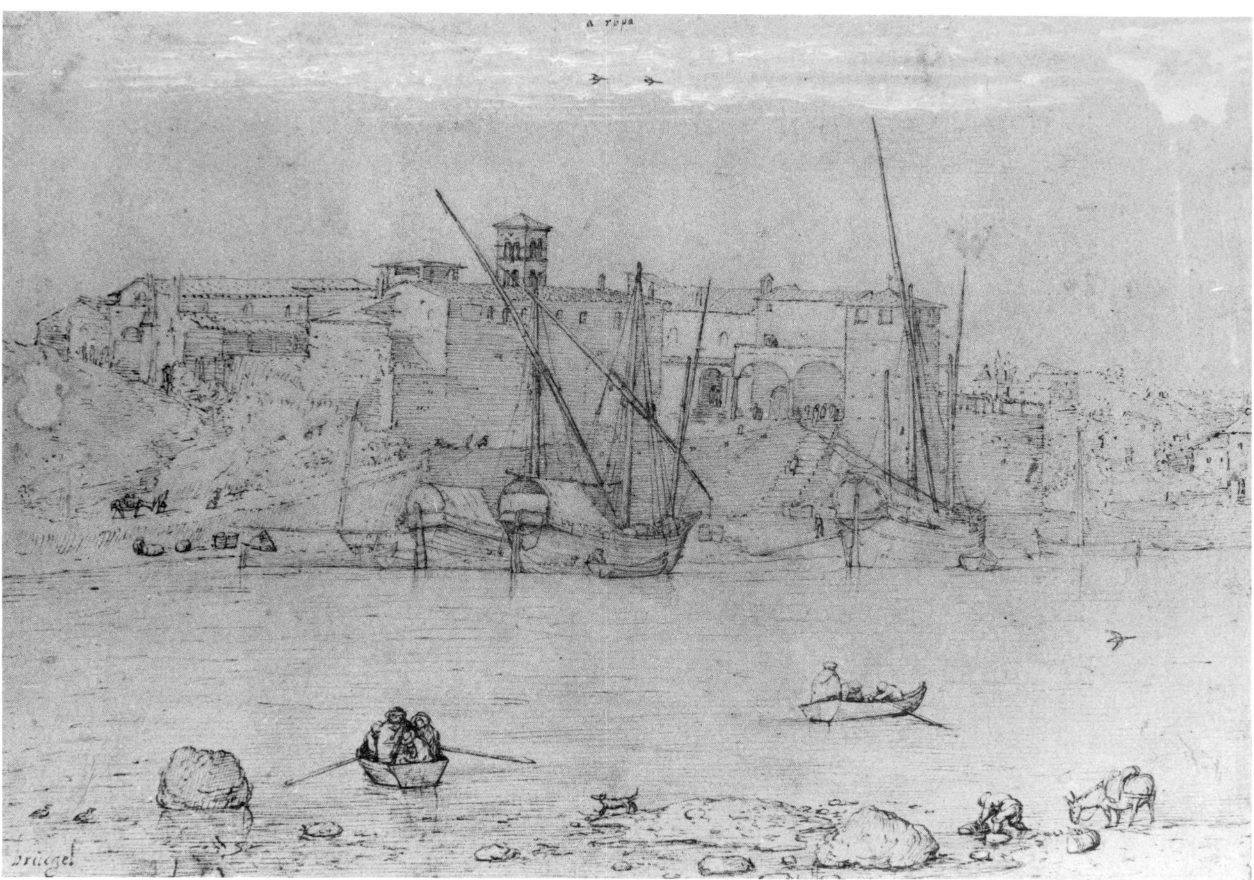

188. Ripa Grande, as of ca. 1560, drawing Pieter Breughel, Chatsworth, Devonshire Collection

pots, and other fishing baskets—whatever *piscaria* may mean in the documents—were laid out on the banks of the Tiber Island and rafts with fishing nets, permanently anchored, and fishing baskets, *giornelli*, were still to be seen there eighty years ago, as a photograph taken prior to 1870 attests (fig. 189). Lastly, the river carried the floating mills that ground the grain needed to provide for the population. From Roman times on and reinstalled by Belisarius during the Gothic siege, these mills had functioned; and they continued to function through the Middle Ages and later (figs. 187, 190). As early as the tenth century the monastery of SS. Cosma e Damiano in Mica Aurea, located in Trastevere, sold and leased water rights and anchoring sites for floating mills at the Tiber Island and on the Trastevere bank. By the twelfth century two churches on the east bank opposite the northern tip of the Island were called "*in capite molarum*." A drawing from the Codex Escurialensis of about 1490 shows a large group of mills in that neighborhood, where in the narrows the current was strongest; others were anchored as far upstream as Ponte S. Angelo, and such mills continued to function into the late nineteenth century.

If the river's impact on the growth of medieval Rome is clear, the influence of Rome's ancient remains is less easily determined. To be sure, the great monuments of antiquity rose in ruins, greater in number and more conspicuous than today: the temples and basilicas on the Forum; the palaces on the Palatine; at its southeast corner the three-storied colonnade of the Septizonium, until 1588/9; the Colosseum and the Golden House of Nero; far out, the Thermae of Diocletian and those of Caracalla; on the Quirinal the Baths of Constantine and the ruined temple of Serapis. Rising as

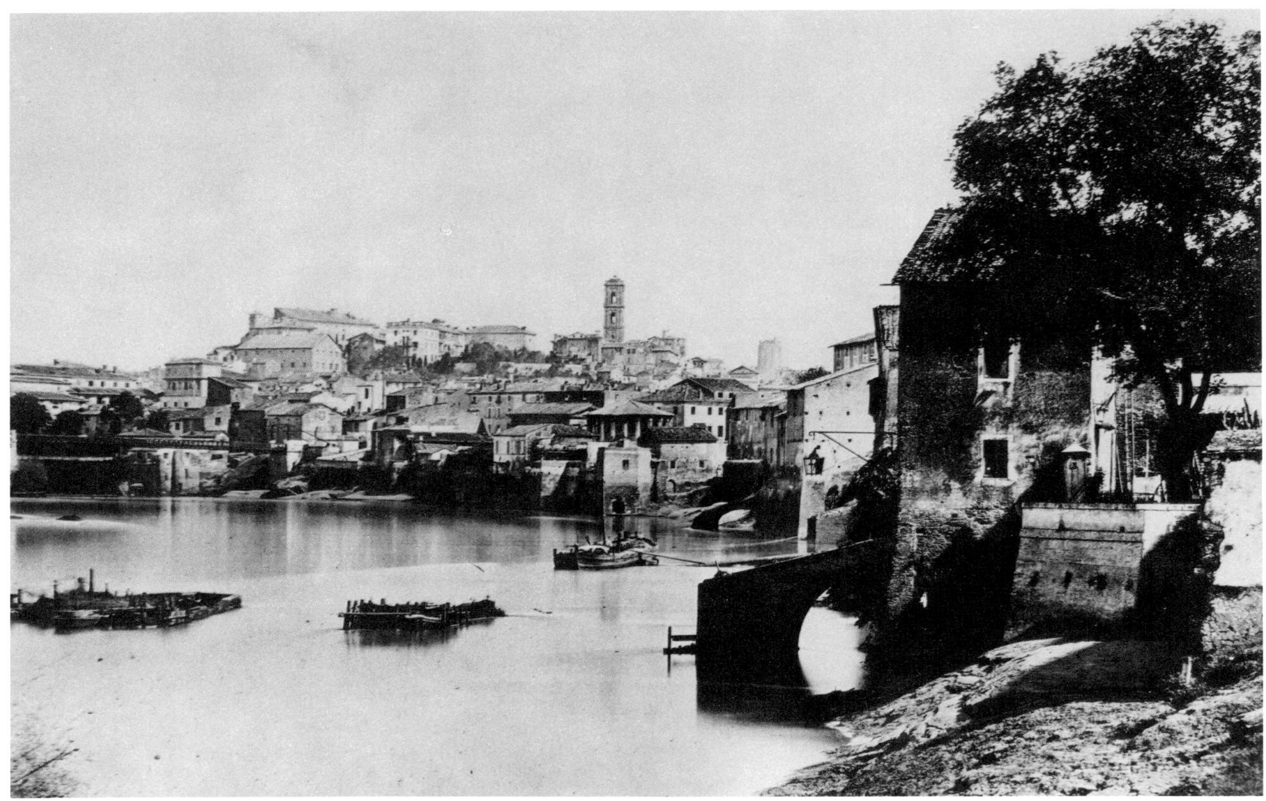

189. View of Tiber toward Capitol, before 1870, showing giornelli, Museo di Roma

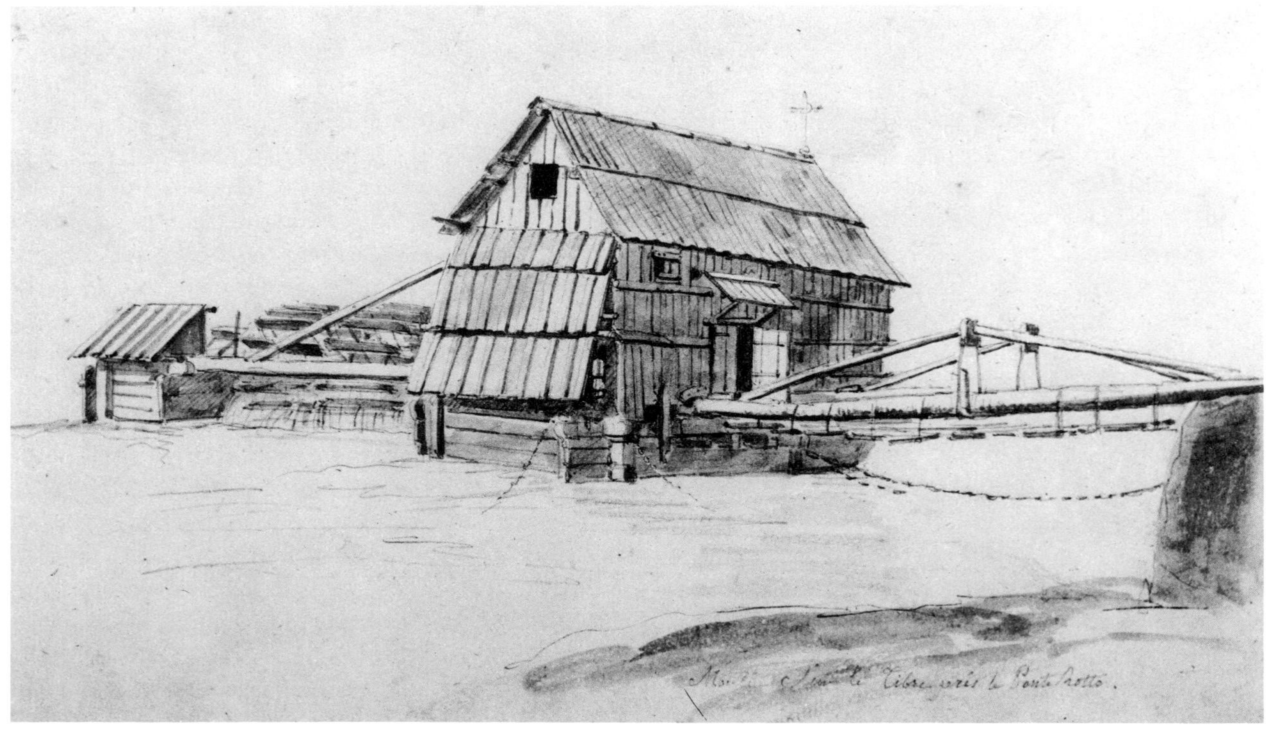

190. Floating mill on Tiber, watercolor D. N. Boguet, ca. 1650, Rome, Gabinetto Nazionale delle Stampe

they did in the disabitato, these monuments in no way determined the growth and aspect of the built-up area. However, even the monuments that stood inside the abitato counted surprisingly little in the city's expansion. Most were simply ignored; or, swallowed up by the medieval town, they served as convenient shelter. Occasionally, a structure since destroyed would have retained its ancient decoration: at the eastern end of Via dei Banchi Vecchi near S. Lucia del Gonfalone, there still stood in the twelfth century what was then known as "the palace of the Prefect Cromatius . . . a temple supposedly made, through mathematical skill, all of mosaic (*olovitreum*), of crystal and gold, where astronomy was represented with all the celestial signs." But most were in ruins. The broken walls and vaults of the Stadium of Domitian were not yet built over by the palaces, houses, and churches bordering Piazza Navona; only small oratories and, one supposes, some dwellings were ensconced in its vaults; the grand expanse of the Piazza itself remained an unused space until the fifteenth century. Only in the seventeenth century, when the church of S. Agnese, Palazzo Pamphili and the Four Rivers Fountain were erected, was it transformed into the grand monumental space it is to this day (fig. 191). East of Piazza Navona, the ruins of the Thermae Alexandrinae were likewise invaded by dwellings and minor chapels, as were the Thermae of Agrippa and the temple area in Largo Argentina, all south of the Pantheon. The Theatre of Pompey (fig. 192) was from all sides engulfed by the abitato; its vaults were exploited for housing, storing, and shops, presumably from an early time, as they still are now—one need but walk around it by Piazza del Paradiso, Via del Biscione, Piazza dei Satiri. Only a few great sites of antiquity became anchor points of medieval Rome: the Mausoleum of Hadrian, transformed into Castel S. Angelo and protecting the approach to St. Peter's across Ponte S. Angelo at the northwesternmost tip of the town area; the Theatre of Marcellus, at its southwest corner, likewise fortified early and dominating the three bridges to and from the island and Trastevere; and the Capitol. The latter, though, until the twelfth century was not anchored within the medieval town, nor was it an integral part of it. Located at the very rim of the built-up area, this, the very heart of ancient Rome, had early become part of the disabitato. Only to the west, where the hill sloped down toward the abitato, a market linked it to the inhabited area. To the compiler of the Einsidlensis Itinerary about 800, the Capitol was merely a cartographic landmark. In any event, it exerted little if any influence on the growth of the medieval abitato. Understandably so, as in antiquity it faced east overlooking the Forum, from which it was approached. The access from the west, from town, was developed only in the High Middle Ages and after, to be turned into a monumental approach by Michelangelo. Rather than attracting the medieval street system, as did Ponte S. Angelo and the Theatre of Marcellus, the Capitol deflected it.

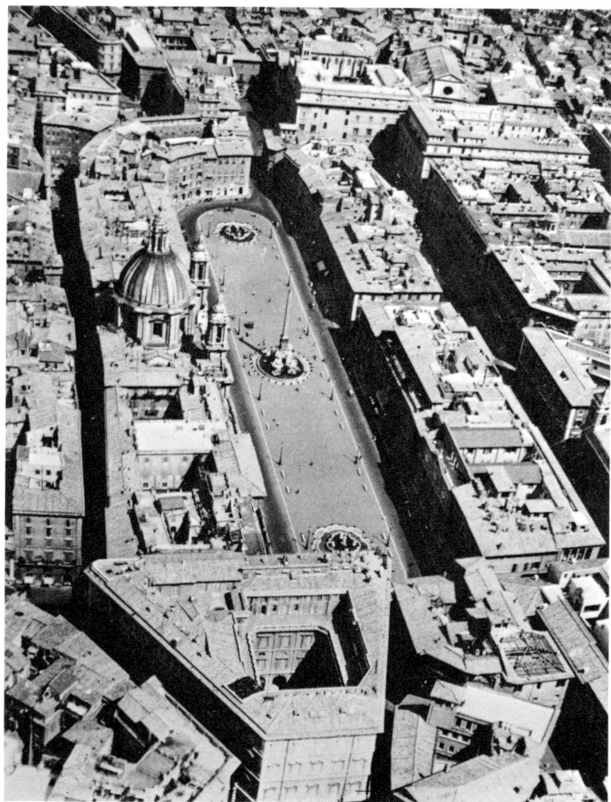

191. Piazza Navona, airview

Nonetheless, Roman antiquity, pagan and Christian, did help to shape medieval Rome. Its functional structures continued to make the

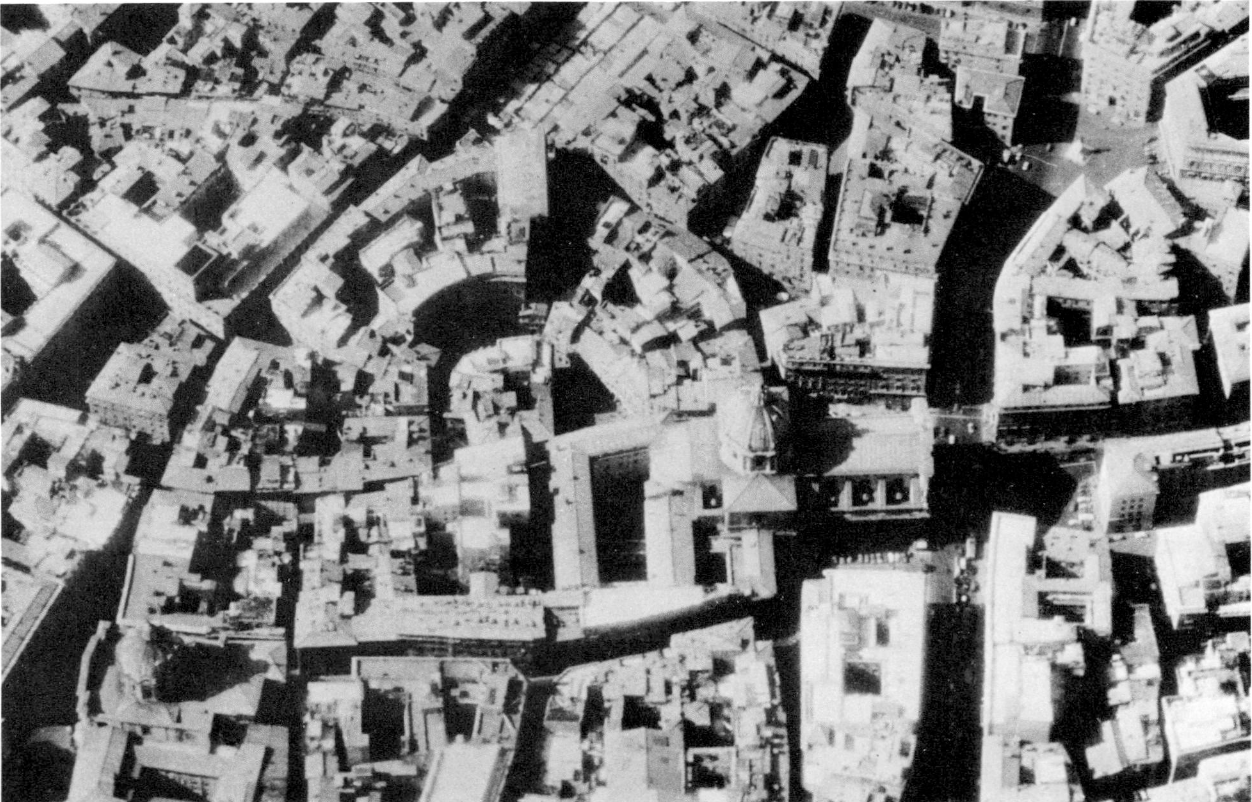

192. Theatre of Pompey, airview

town work: the bridges, which maintained traffic and tied together the east bank, the island, Trastevere, and the Borgo with St. Peter's; the streets; and to a lesser degree the aqueducts. The main arteries inherited from antiquity cross and delimit the area of medieval Rome and still stand out in any sixteenth-century map. Much remains unclear, and the attempt to reconstruct the map of medieval Rome and its growth must remain largely conjectural (fig. 193a, b). But some elements appear beyond doubt. The boundaries within which the medieval town gradually grew are set by two major Roman thoroughfares. To the east, Via Lata—the Corso—running from Piazza del Popolo to the northern foot of the Capitoline Hill, marked a line rarely crossed in the Middle Ages by built-up areas. Where it met the northern cliff of the Capitoline Hill, that is roughly where the Monumento Nazionale now piles up its mass of white marble, the Via Lata veered east; one branch crossed the Forum; the other, still skirting the east cliff of the hill, turned south toward S. Maria in Cosmedin and across Ponte S. Maria, now Ponte Rotto, connected the town with Trastevere. To the north, the area was similarly delimited by the Roman Via Recta, nowadays Via dei Coronari, and its eastward continuation. Originally starting from the Bridge of Nero, somewhat downstream from Castel S. Angelo, it was reached after the early collapse of that bridge by a short street from Ponte S. Angelo, the one remaining bridge between the city and St. Peter's. From these the Via Recta crossed the old Campus Martius in a straight line from west to east, until it met the Corso at the Column of Marcus Aurelius on Piazza Colonna. The quadrant thus delimited by the Via Recta, the Corso, and the bend of the Tiber was crossed east and west by three streets of Roman origin, roughly parallel to Corso Vittorio Emanuele, and all converging on Ponte S. Angelo. The street farthest south started at the Roman bridge, the Pons Fabricius—Ponte Quattro Capi in the Middle Ages—which, pro-

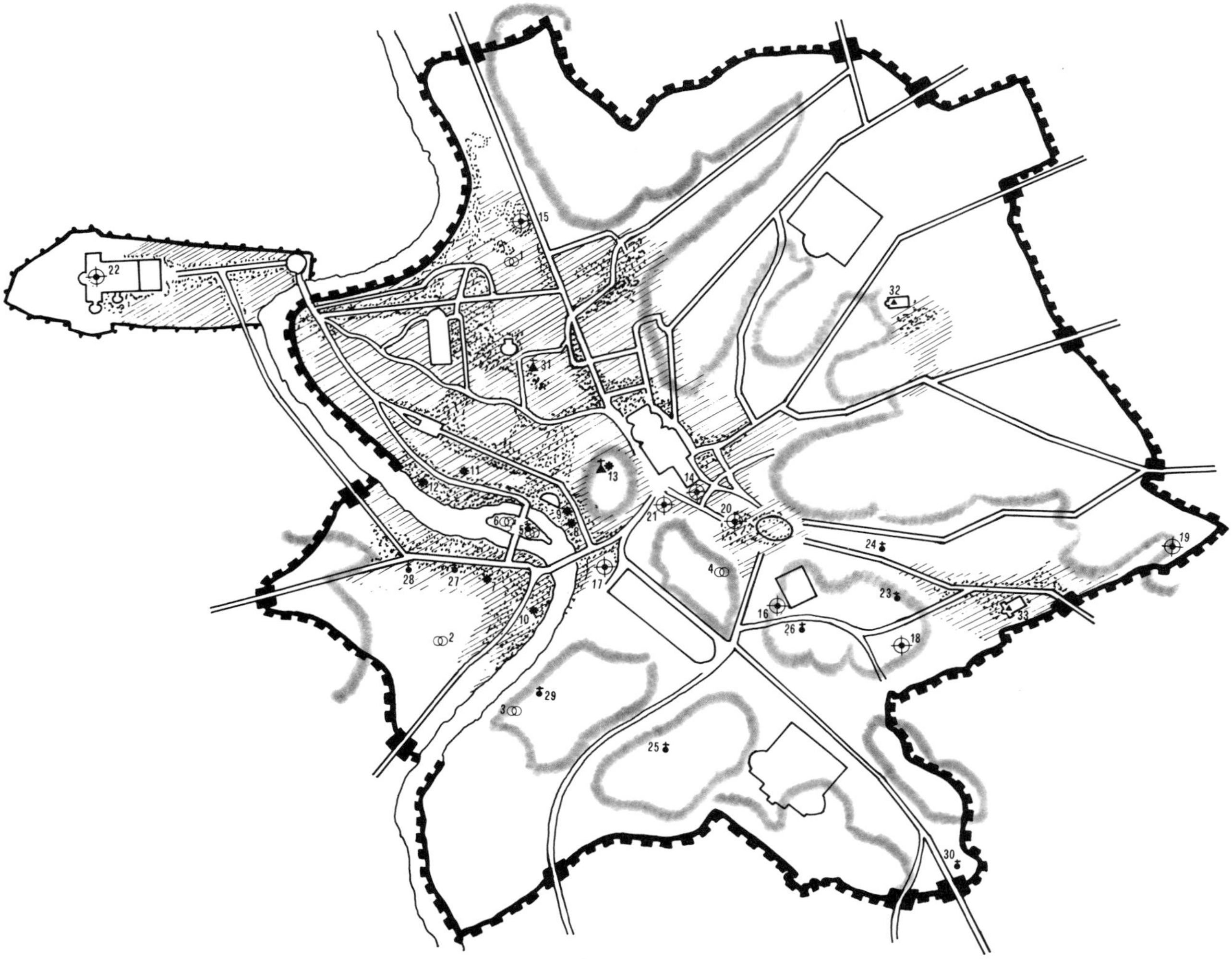

NEW FOUNDATIONS, ca. 900–ca. 1050
1. S. Maria in Campo Marzio
2. SS. Cosma e Damiano in Mica Aurea
3. S. Maria in Aventino
4. S. Maria in Pallara
5. SS. Adalberto e Paolino
6. S. Giovanni Calabita

NEW FOUNDATIONS, ca. 1050–ca. 1227
7. S. Benedetto in Piscinula
8. S. Maria in Porticu
9. S. Nicola in Carcere
10. S. Maria in Capella
11. S. Maria in Monticelli
12. S. Salvatore in Onda
13. S. Maria in Capitolio

EARLIER CHURCHES ALTERED, ca. 1050–ca. 1227
14. S. Adriano
15. S. Lorenzo in Lucina
16. SS. Giovanni e Paolo
17. S. Maria in Cosmedin
18. Sto. Stefano Rotondo
19. S. Croce in Gerusalemme
20. S. Maria Nova
21. SS. Sergio e Bacco
22. St. Peter's

EARLIER CHURCHES REBUILT, ca. 1050–ca. 1227
23. SS. Quattro Coronati
24. S. Clemente
25. S. Saba
5. S. Bartolomeo in Isola (formerly SS. Adalberto e Paolino)
26. SS. Andrea e Gregorio in Celiomonte
27. S. Crisogono
28. S. Maria in Trastevere
29. SS. Bonifazio ed Alessio
30. S. Giovanni a Porta Latina

NEW CHURCHES, ca. 1227–ca. 1308
13. S. Maria in Aracoeli (including part of S. Maria in Capitolio)
31. S. Maria sopra Minerva

EARLIER CHURCHES ALTERED, ca. 1227–ca. 1308
32. S. Maria Maggiore
33. Lateran Basilica

THE ABITATO BEFORE ca. 1050

THE ABITATO AFTER ca. 1050

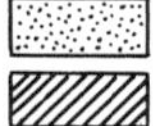

193a. Map of medieval Rome showing main streets and growth of abitato (hypothetical)

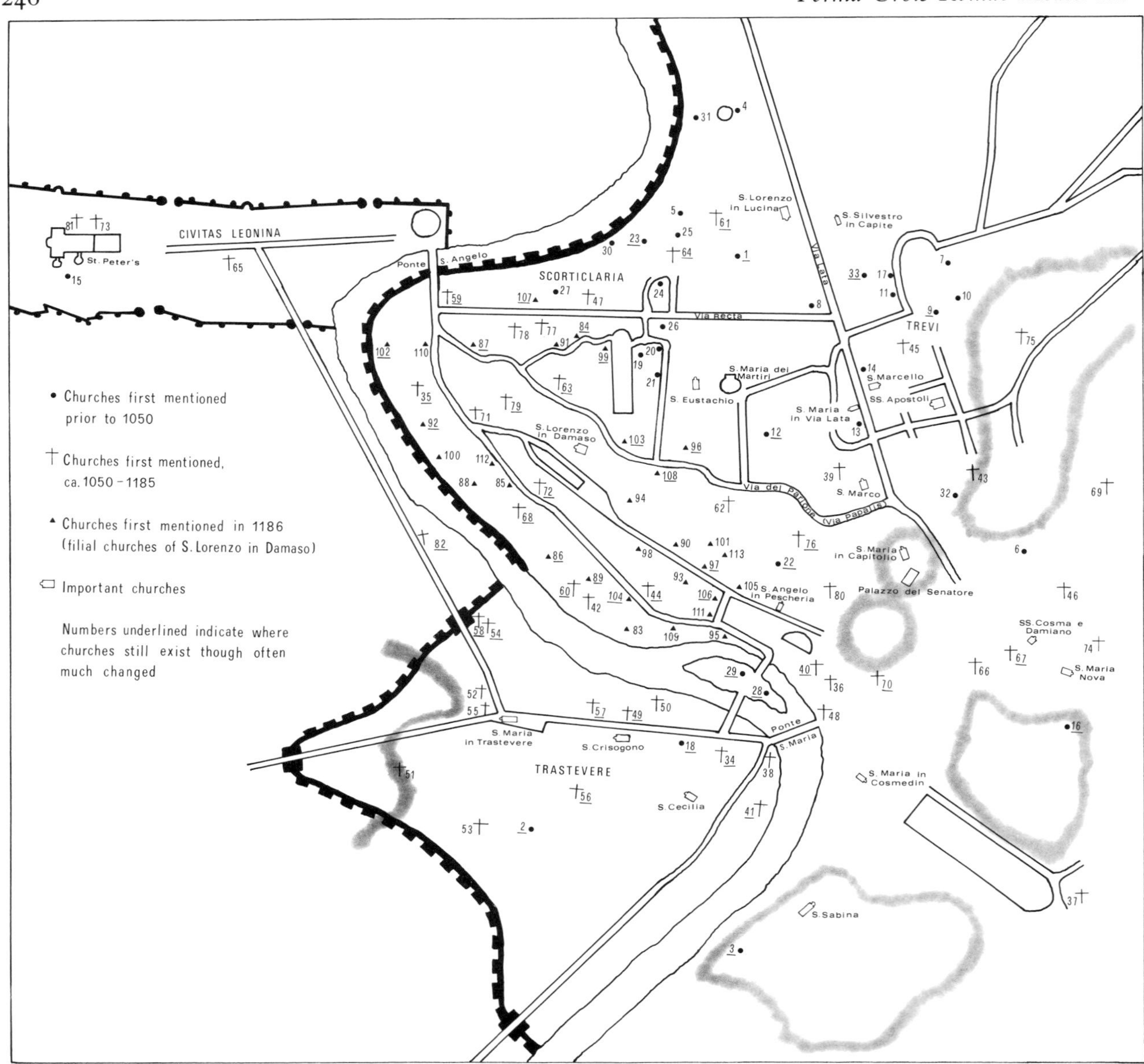

193b. The abitato and its churches, 937-1186

THE ABITATO AND ITS CHURCHES, 937-1186

Information for this map regarding medieval churches has been taken primarily from Huelsen, *Chiese*, *passim*. We have tried to number the churches as far as possible in chronological order and we give before the name of each church the date it is first mentioned. It should be noted however that the church may well have existed before it first appears in documents and inscriptions. Where a church still exists—although radically changed in shape and size and possibly with a new dedication—the number given on the map and in this list has been underlined, and if the church has a new name, this is given in parentheses.

• CHURCHES FIRST MENTIONED PRIOR TO 1050

1 937 S. Maria in Campo Marzio
2 936-939 SS. Cosma e Damiano in Mica Aurea
3 939 S. Maria in Aventino (now S. Maria del priorato)
4 955 S. Angelo *de Augusta*
5 955 S. Biagio *de Penna*
6 955 S. Basilio
7 955 S. Nicola *de Arcionibus*
8 962 S. Andrea *de Columna*
9 962 S. Anastasio *de Trivio*

10	962	S. Ippolito *de Trivio*
11	962	S. Maria *de Arcionibus*
12	962	S. Giovanni *de Pinea*
13	before 972	S. Ciriaco *in Camilliano*
14	973	SS. Cosma e Damiano *iuxta Viam Latam*
15	974	Sto. Stefano Miccini
16	before 977	S. Maria in Pallara (now S. Sebastianello)
17	before 989	Sto. Stefano *in Senedochio*
18	985-996	S. Salvatore *de Curtibus* (now S. Maria della Luce)
19	998	S. Benedetto *de Thermis*
20	998	S. Maria *Cella Farfae*
21	998	S. Salvatore *de Thermis*
22	ca. 1000	S. Maria *Domnae Rosae* (now S. Caterina dei Funari)
23	1002	S. Lucia *Quatuor Portarum* (now S. Lucia della Tinta)
24	1006	S. Trifone
25	1006	Sto. Stefano *de Pila*
26	1011	S. Andrea *de Fordivoliis*
27	1017	S. Simeone
28	1018	SS. Adalberto e Paolino (now S. Bartolomeo in Isola)
29	1018	S. Giovanni Calabita
30	1026	S. Maria *de Posterula*
31	1026	S. Martino *de Posterula*
32	1029-1032	S. Nicola *de Columna*
33	1042	S. Maria in Via

† CHURCHES FIRST MENTIONED ca. 1050-1185

34	1069	S. Benedetto in Piscinula
35	1072	S. Biagio *de Captu Secuta* (now S. Biagio della Pagnotta)
36	1073	S. Maria in Porticu
37	1073-1085	S. Leone *de Septem Soliis*
38	1073-1085	S. Salvatore *de Pede Pontis*
39	1083	S. Lorenzo *a Ciriaco*
40	before 1090	S. Nicola in Carcere
41	1090	S. Maria in Cappella
42	1096	S. Cesareo alla Regola
43	1090-1100	S. Salvatore *de Militiis*
44	1099-1118	S. Maria in Monticelli
45	1104	S. Maria *de Cannella*
46	1113	S. Pantaleo *Trium Clibanorum*
47	1113	S. Salvatore *de Primicerio*
48	1118	S. Maria *Secundicerii*
49	1121	S. Agata *trans Tiberim*
50	1121	S. Bonosa
51	1123	S. Angelo in Gianicolo
52	1123	S. Biagio *de Curtibus trans Tiberim*
53	1123	S. Giovanni *in Mica Aurea*
54	1123	S. Giovanni *de Porta Septimiana*
55	1123	S. Lorenzo *in Curtibus*
56	1123	SS. Quaranta *trans Tiberim* (now SS. Quaranta Martiri ed S. Pasquale Baylon)
57	1123	S. Rufina
58	1123	S. Silvestro *de Porta Septimiana* (now S. Dorotea)
59	1127	SS. Celso e Giuliano
60	1127	S. Salvatore in Onda
61	1131	S. Cecilia *de Posterula* (now Madonna del Divino Amore)
62	1132	S. Nicola *de Calcarariis*
63	1139	S. Tomaso *de Parione*
64	1130-1143	S. Andrea *de Montanariis* (now S. Ivo dei Brettoni)
65	1143	S. Lorenzo *de Piscibus*
66	ca. 1150	S. Antonio *prope S. Maria Antiqua*
67	ca. 1150	S. Lorenzo in Miranda
68	ca. 1150	S. Maria *in Catarina* (now S. Caterina della Rota)
69	ca. 1150	S. Maria *de Puteo Probae*
70	ca. 1150	S. Salvatore *de Statera* (now S. Omobono)
71	ca. 1150	Sto. Stefano *in Piscina*
72	ca. 1150	SS. Trinità *Scottorum* (now St. Thomas of Canterbury in the Venerable English College)
73	1151	S. Vincenzo in Vaticano
74	1156	S. Maria *de Cambiatoribus*
75	1160	S. Saturnino *de Caballo*
76	1174	S. Salvatore *in pensilis* (now S. Stanislao dei Polacchi)
77	1177	S. Salvatore *de Inversis*
78	1178	S. Maria *in Monticelli in Ponte*
79	1179	S. Maria in Vallicella (now Chiesa Nuova)
80	1180	S. Nicola *de Funariis*
81	1159-1181	S. Ambrogio in Vaticano
82	before 1185	S. Giacomo in Settignano

▲ CHURCHES FIRST MENTIONED IN 1186 (FILIAL CHURCHES OF S. LORENZO IN DAMASO)

83	S. Anastasio *de Arenula*
84	S. Andrea *de Aquarizariis* (now S. Maria della Pace)
85	S. Andrea *a domo Iohannis ancillae Dei*
86	S. Tomaso *de Hispanis* (now SS. Giovanni e Petronio dei Bolognesi)
87	S. Angelo *a domo Egidii de Poco* (now S. Giuliano)
88	S. Austerii
89	S. Benedetto *de Arenula* (now SS. Trinità dei Pellegrini)
90	S. Benedetto *in Clausura*
91	S. Biagio *Archariorum*
92	S. Lucia *ad Flumen* (now S. Lucia del Gonfalone)
93	S. Maria *de Cacabariis*
94	S. Maria *de Crypta Pincta*
95	S. Maria *a Capite Molarum*
96	S. Maria in Monterone
97	S. Maria *de Publico* (now S. Maria in Publicolis)
98	S. Martino *de Pannarella*
99	S. Nicola *de Cryptis Agonis* (now S. Nicola dei Lorenesi)
100	S. Nicola *de Furcis*
101	S. Nicola *de Mellinis*
102	S. Pantaleo *ad Flumen* (now S. Giovanni dei Fiorentini)
103	S. Pantaleo *de Pretecarolis*
104	S. Paolo *de Arenula*
105	S. Salvatore *de Baroncinis*
106	S. Salvatore *de Caccabariis* (now S. Maria del Pianto)
107	S. Salvatore *de Lauro*
108	S. Sebastiano *de Via Papae* (now S. Andrea della Valle)
109	Sto. Stefano *de Caccabariis*
110	Sto. Stefano *de Ponte*
111	S. Tomaso *in Capite Molarum*
112	S. Giovanni *in Agina*
113	S. Valentino *de Balneo Miccine*

tected by the stronghold of the Theatre of Marcellus, crossed to the Tiber Island. Running close to the river bank—a stretch disappeared when the embankment was built—it crossed Via Arenula (we give the modern street names), it continued along Via Capo di Ferro, traversed Piazza Farnese, and through Via di Monserrato and Banchi Vecchi reached Ponte S. Angelo. A second major thoroughfare still can be traced from Ponte Rotto (Ponte S. Maria) to the northern edge of the Theatre of Marcellus, from there along the Porticus of Octavia, in the former Ghetto, and again beyond Via Arenula, through Via dei Giubbonari, across Campo dei Fiori, until from there in two branches, Via dei Capellari and Via del Pellegrino, it reached Ponte S. Angelo, through Via dei Banchi Vecchi. A last major east-west artery linked Ponte S. Angelo to the south end of the Corso; through Via del Governo Vecchio, known until the sixteenth century as Via del Parione, it passed by the southern end of Piazza Navona; corresponding more or less to the east stretch of Corso Vittorio Emanuele, it crossed Largo Argentina and, through the Botteghe Oscure, reached the northern face of the Capitoline Hill, to continue east into the disabitato. North-south streets of Roman origin within the area were apparently rare; the many that crisscross the area today—there were many more as recently as a hundred years ago—appear to be of medieval date. As far as it was determined by its Roman heritage, the street system of the medieval town thus ran east and west and was anchored to three points: the Theatre of Marcellus and the bridges to the Tiber Island and Trastevere; Ponte S. Angelo, connecting with St. Peter's and the Leonine City; and the southern end of the Corso below the northern cliff of the Capitoline Hill.

Linked to the remains of inherited town engineering—streets and bridges—the great Christian sanctuaries outside the abitato nonetheless became key points in shaping the medieval layout and townscape: the Lateran and St. Peter's foremost; and to a lesser degree, S. Maria Maggiore, and the pilgrimage centers beyond the walls, S. Lorenzo, S. Agnese, S. Sebastiano and S. Paolo (fig. 194). St. Peter's and the Lateran, became anchors of the medieval street system in spite of their location far beyond the built-up area. The three Roman streets crossing the abitato east to west, all leading to Ponte S. Angelo, were the only approaches from the town on the east bank of the Tiber to St. Peter's. Moreover, the northernmost street, Via del Parione, from the point where it met the northern foot of the Capitol continued across the Forum to the Colosseum and, ascending the Celian Hill by Via S. Giovanni, terminated at the Lateran Basilica and the papal palace. It was the closest approach from town to the cathedral of Rome, Mother of all Churches, and to the papal residence and its administrative offices. Coming as it did from St. Peter's, it formed the one direct link between the two great Christian sanctuaries; and it became the most important route across the overall area of medieval Rome, trod by all pilgrims and followed by papal processions throughout the Middle Ages. Hence its names: "Via del Papa" for what is now Via del Governo Vecchio for a large stretch in town; "Via Maior" for what is now Via S. Giovanni, running from the Colosseum to the papal palace. The other Christian sanctuaries, too, were reached by way of old Roman thoroughfares. The pilgrim, on his way to the Lateran and before reaching the Colosseum, might turn left to the Forum of Nerva and, passing through it, ascend the Esquiline over one of two Roman streets: one, the Suburra, would take him to S. Maria Maggiore; another, crossing the hill south of that church, brought him to Porta Tiburtina and along the Tivoli highway to S. Lorenzo fuori le mura. Or else, starting from the north cliff of the Capitoline Hill, the pious would follow the route to S. Agnese, along the crest of the Quirinal and, beyond the city gate, Via Nomentana, always using the Roman street system, whether through the disabitato or outside the walls. Again, Roman streets, starting from the south end of the area built-up in the Middle Ages, took the pilgrim between the west cliff of the Aventine and the Tiber to Porta S. Paolo and the church of the Apostle. Or, continuing from the same southern tip of the abitato, along the south slope of the Palatine and further on to the Thermae of Caracalla, he would reach Porta Appia and S. Sebastiano. Throughout, the great

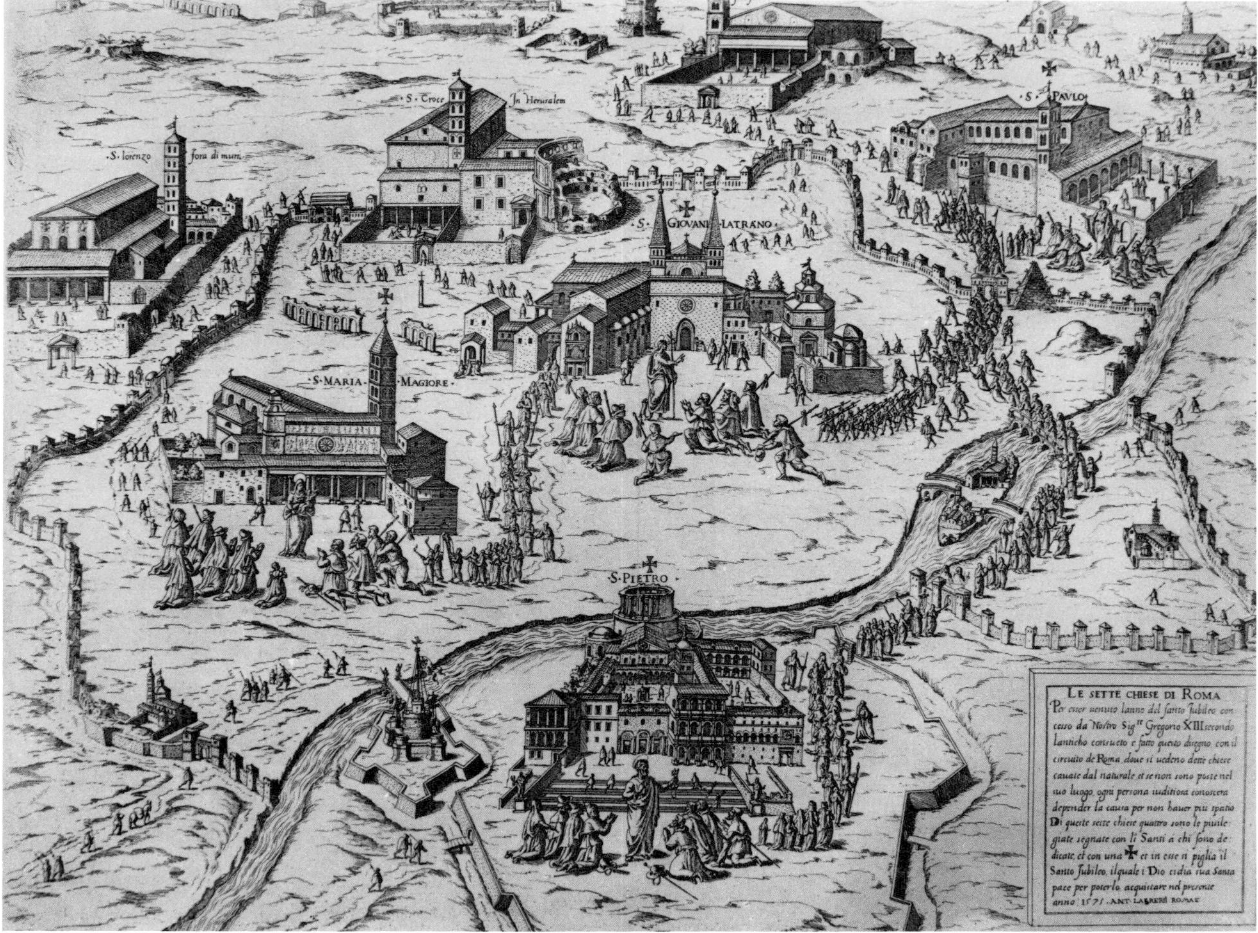

194. Sette Chiese, 1575, engraving A. Lafréry

Christian sanctuaries were tied into the old street system; naturally so, since all had risen in late antiquity with the system fully functioning. In the Middle Ages the streets survived; but they ran through the disabitato and were figuratively tacked on to the rim of medieval Rome, with one exception: three streets led through the abitato to St. Peter's—the only ones to link the town and its life to what quickly became its most venerated sanctuary and a powerful focus to attract the ever-growing medieval town.

The catastrophes hitting Rome from the sixth through the eighth centuries—the Gothic siege, the Byzantine conquest, famine, epidemics, the difficulties of provisioning, the resulting decrease in population, and the consequent change to a rural or semirural economy—all were bound to change fundamentally both the map and the aspect of the town. Only parts of the vast expanse within the Aurelian Walls would still have been settled by the time of Gregory the Great. The inhabitants would have retreated to a few sectors conveniently located on either bank of the river, the main line of communication and provisioning. Or they would settle near wells in the plain of the river bend, avoiding the waterless hills, except the Aventine, which was close to the river. But in any event they stayed far from the Aurelian Walls. The map of Rome, coherent and widely spread in antiquity, shrank and was radically transformed. It should be visualized in the early Middle Ages not so much as a coherent unit, but as a conglomerate of built-up clusters separated by large ruins, gardens, and stretches of wasteland, with only scattered houses linking the clusters.

The survival and maintenance of the Roman bridges, streets, and aqueducts, the location of diaconiae, monasteries, and churches of early date, the placement of markets, and other documentation all suggest that one such densely populated area—dense in medieval terms—had either survived from before the Gothic siege on the east bank of the river opposite the Tiber Island, or had been newly formed by the time of Gregory the Great (fig. 193a). Its core seems to have enveloped the southward spur of the Capitoline Hill and extended south to the Theatre of Marcellus and S. Maria in Cosmedin, to thin out along the Marmorata below the west cliff of the Aventine. Northward, skirting the west slope of the Capitol, it apparently reached up the southern stretch of the Corso to S. Maria in Via Lata. Westward it occupied the area of the Circus Flaminius, not very far beyond the Porticus of Octavia, where the church of S. Angelo in Pescheria now nestles; but among the early ecclesiastical foundations in that neighborhood, none were established west of Via Arenula; only in the eleventh century, evidently following the population, do churches and monasteries seem to have spread further west toward the Theatre of Pompey and gradually beyond. The Theatre of Marcellus, the Capitoline Hill, the south end of the Corso, and the Tiber bridges formed anchor points. This was only natural; three of the Roman bridges serving the town through the Middle Ages crossed from near the Theatre of Marcellus into Trastevere: two at the island; and Ponte S. Maria (Ponte Rotto), downstream. From the heart of the area, too, one recalls, the three main streets through the abitato, all of Roman origin, issued west leading to Ponte S. Angelo and St. Peter's. From the north, two streets crossed the quarter, both branching off the south end of the Corso and skirting the

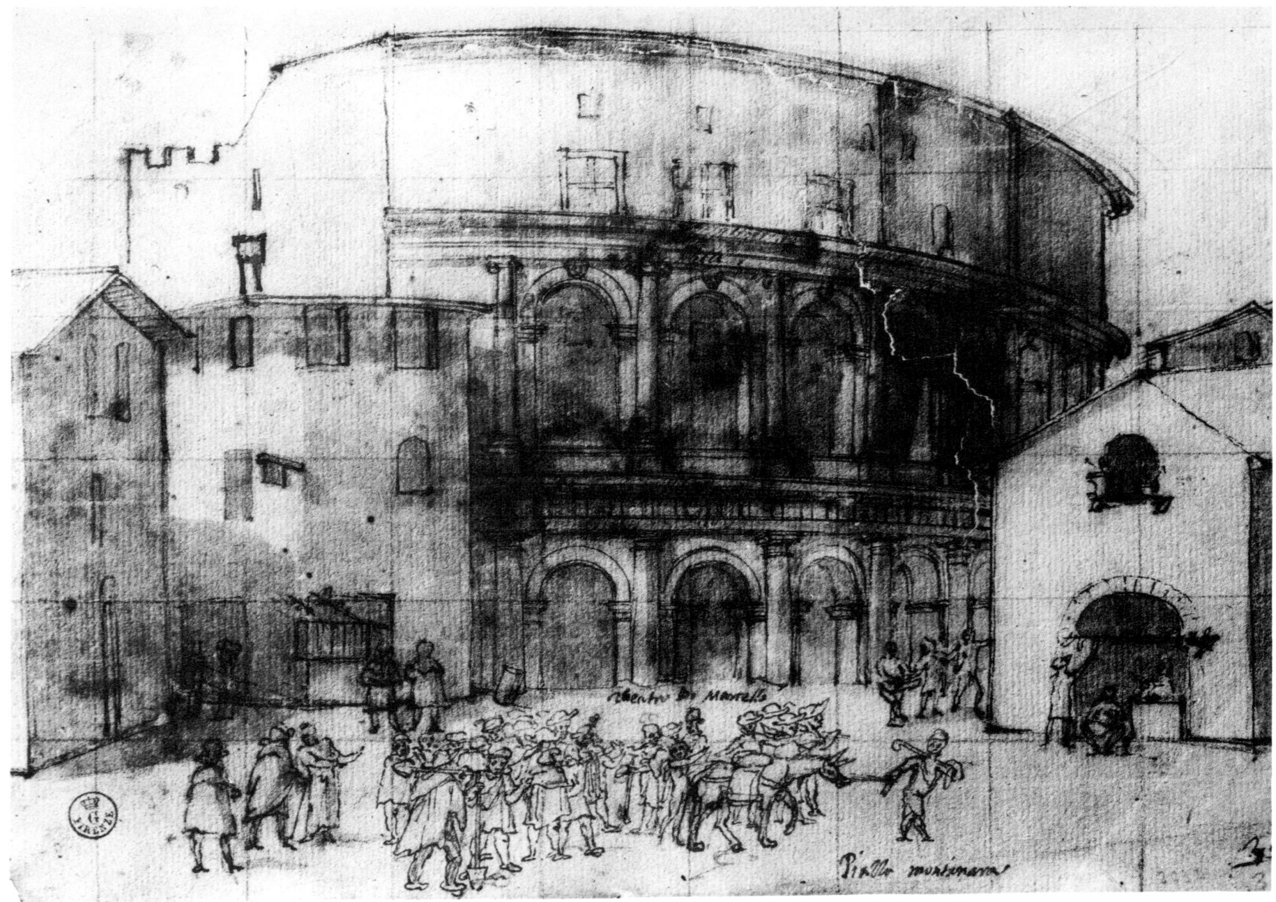

195. Theatre of Marcellus and meat market, as of ca. 1560, drawing G. A. Dosio, Florence, Uffizi

Capitol. One ran southwest toward the Theatre of Marcellus. The other, the *Canapara* ("Granary Street"), ran east of the Capitol and continued south; passing by S. Teodoro and S. Giorgio in Velabro, it led to Ponte Rotto and S. Maria in Cosmedin. Together with S. Maria in Via Lata on the Corso, these churches, one recalls, mark the location of the first diaconiae, the welfare centers established from the sixth century on to meet the needs both of pilgrims and the resident population (fig. 58). A late-comer, S. Angelo in Pescheria was installed in 755 behind the porch of the Porticus of Octavia west of the Theatre of Marcellus. Rebuilt in the sixteenth century, its church still survives behind the colonnaded Roman porch. Reinforced by huge arches as early as the third century, that porch until a hundred years ago sheltered a fish market—hence the name of the church. In fact, the entire area had long been a market area and remained so. A market was held on the Capitol by the fifth century; by the twelfth century it had shifted down the west slope of the hill to what became Piazza Aracoeli. By 998 a meat market was held at the Theatre of Marcellus, presumably to the north, and a butcher shop still functioned there in the sixteenth century (fig. 195); another butcher shop existed by the twelfth century near S. Teodoro. The fish market at S. Angelo in Pescheria, too, was probably held early, given its closeness to the river; the marble slabs on which the fish were displayed and their brick supports inside the Roman portico fronting the church and extending west along the Porticus of Octavia, in what became the Ghetto, survived until the end of the last century (fig. 196). Grain from the floating mills anchored below and above the Tiber Island and fish from the river were probably sold in the nearby markets, while the river port at the Ripa Grande supplied provisions from further away.

Alleys crisscrossed the quarter, and small piazze were scattered in between. Extending as far as Piazza Paganica and Piazza Mattei, it was apparently settled by citizens of some standing, rather than members of great families; witness documents referring to the neighborhood from the tenth century on. Ancient ruins provided shelter or building materials for structures installed in or near them: such were the Theatre of Marcellus, first listed as a stronghold in the eleventh century, though likely fortified earlier; the Porticus of Octavia sheltering, from the eighth century on, two convents and S. Angelo in Pescheria; the Circus Flaminius, nearer the river, housing one more convent. Among the ruins of the Capitoline Hill, yet another monastery, built prior to S. Maria in Aracoeli, had been installed by 934. Till the eighth century, fresh water was plentiful in the neighborhood. One of the aqueducts recommissioned by Pope Hadrian I in the late eighth century, the Aqua Jobia, led from Porta S. Sebastiano through the valleys of the Passeggiata Archeologica and the Circus Maximus "usque ad ripam"—mostly underground and hence presumably in rather good shape. The Einsiedeln monk who reported on it may well have intended the term *ripa* to cover not just the riverbank near S. Maria in Cosmedin, but to extend to the Theatre of Marcellus and perhaps further west and north, as it was used later in the Middle Ages.

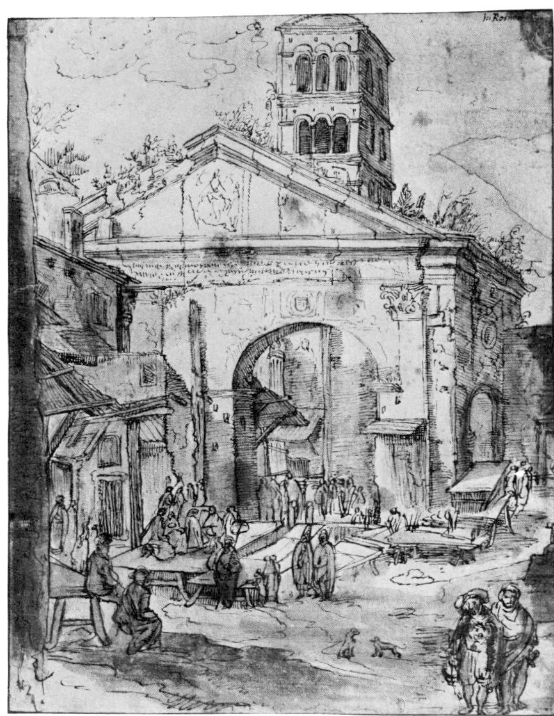

196. Fish Market in Porticus of Octavia, drawing, ca. 1650, Jan Miel, Paris, Louvre

Time- and labor-consuming as they were, and consequently stressed by papal biographers, the maintenance and repair of Roman aqueducts provide clues for the location of areas to be serviced. They need not have been the most populous quarters. The interest of the papal clerks who compiled the *Liber Pontificalis* was centered on needs of the neighborhood of the Lateran, where they were installed. Another focus of attention for them was the area around St. Peter's, with its welfare centers, the quarters set up for papal visits and those prepared for foreign dignitaries from the sixth century on. Thus, around 775, the repair of the Aqua Claudia was specified by Hadrian I's biographer as intended to supply water to the Lateran—the bath in the palace, the Baptistery—and other churches nearby "at Easter," and probably to the monasteries established near the papal palace. In keeping with this function, the aqueduct from 800 on was popularly known as the "Forma Lateranensis" and was restored again twice in the twelfth century. Similarly, reporting the repair of the aqueduct on the Gianicolo across the Tiber, Hadrian I's biographer stresses that its function was to supply, through a pipeline branching off to the north, water for the fountain in the atrium of St. Peter's and the bath nearby, both aqueduct and pipeline being repaired anew a generation later.

At times, though, the repair of an aqueduct was clearly intended to supply a populated quarter. The Aqua Vergine, recommissioned by Hadrian I, ran mostly underground like the Jobia, from Porta Salaria down the Pincio to what became the Trevi Fountain and further east of the Corso, to cross it near S. Maria in Via Lata and continue toward the Pantheon. The water, Hadrian's biographer claims, was "so abundant as to supply nearly the whole city." The "whole city" had best be interpreted, it seems, *totum pro parte*, as a densely populated section of town. Indeed, by the beginning of the seventh century at the latest, an area in the eastern section of the river bend seems to have been built up and well settled a few hundred meters west of the Corso around the Pantheon; the conversion of the temple in 609 into a church presupposes, after all, a populated neighborhood. So does the early establishment close by of diaconiae: at S. Eustachio, well before 715-731; and at S. Maria in Aquiro, the latter with a hospital of one hundred beds for the needs of both residents and pilgrims. The ruins of the Thermae of Alexander Severus west of the Pantheon sheltered the diaconia at S. Eustachio; a Roman temple housed that at S. Maria in Aquiro. Southeast of the Pantheon, a smallish oratory by A.D. 800 nestled in the ruins of the Temple of Minerva, where five hundred years later the Dominicans built their large church and convent, S. Maria sopra Minerva. Between the Corso and what is now Piazza del Collegio Romano, the old diaconia, S. Maria in Via Lata, gained new importance when in the tenth century the wealthy nunnery of S. Ciriaco was attached to it. Still, the neighborhood was focused not on the Corso, but on the Pantheon and S. Eustachio, where from the tenth and eleventh centuries on one finds the houses of a great clan, "those of S. Eustachio." Southward, the quarter around the Pantheon may or may not have been linked to the neighborhood extending north from the river bank and west from the foot of the Capitol. South of the Pantheon, the Thermae of Agrippa and the ruins covering Largo Argentina may have formed a barrier, until later on the kilns and housing of the lime burners formed the connecting quarter of the Calcararium.

How far north housing reached into the present Via de Campo Marzio remains to be seen; but prior to the tenth century and perhaps as early as 806, a nunnery had been installed at S. Maria in Campo Marzio; and by the early eleventh century the Campus Martius was inhabited, whatever specific location the term referred to at that time. To the west, the built-up area appears early to have incorporated Piazza Navona and Piazza S. Apollinare; in the ruins of the Thermae of Alexander Severus, by 998 three oratories and some monastic cells had been set up, bordering on vaults, a garden, and a courtyard in private hands; nearby, in 1006 a church and hostel dedicated to S. Trifone were rebuilt behind the present site of S. Agostino; an oratory of S. Agnese was ensconced by the end of the eighth century in a vault of the Stadium of Domitian at Piazza Navona—it survives, all rebuilt, below the splendid baroque church; and a sanctuary was set up perhaps as early as the seventh century or as late as the ninth north of Piazza Navona, where at present the large, if not very inspiring, church of S. Apollinare stands.

Somewhere in that neighborhood was a street or a few alleys that became known from the late tenth century on as the *Scorticlaria*; the name is supposed to derive from *coriarii*, the skinners and tanners, and one would like to think of them and the pollution caused by their trade a bit on the outskirts of the abitato, westward along Via dei Coronari where the quarter had expanded by the eleventh century. It may have been earlier, for, in all likelihood, since early medieval times a knoll just south of that street, near its western end and thus not far from Ponte S. Angelo, was settled. Known from the thirteenth century on as Monte Giordano, it was protected from the Tiber floods; and it commanded strategically one of the approaches to and from the bridge and beyond to St. Peter's. True, the hill is mentioned first in the mid-twelfth century when, most likely fortified, it was in the hands of one Giovanni di Roncione, lord of Riano Flaminio, and bore his name. A hundred or more years later it had fallen to the Orsini clan and a mansion there was the residence of Cardinal Giordano Orsini, whence the hill took its present name. Today a maze of palaces and houses dating from the fifteenth century through the eighteenth blanket it (fig. 242). But among them rises a small twelfth-century church, S. Simeone e Giuda, now desecrated and previously known as Sta. Maria in Monticello or de Monte Johannis Ronzonis; and by 1178 two more churches, S. Simeone and S. Salvatore de Inversis, the latter with gardens in the *Scorticlaria*, stood close by. None need antedate the eleventh- and twelfth-century westward expansion of the abitato into the Tiber bend. Nor are the secular buildings on the hill, as listed among Orsini property in 1262 and 1267, documented prior to those dates: a main tower and mansion at its foot; a loggia added to that mansion around the middle of the thirteenth century; and "two cottages inside the enclosure at the foot of the mansion and of the tower called *faiolum* (distinct from the main tower) all located in the quarter or street of the bridge of St. Peter's and the *Scorticlaria*." Indeed, enclosed by a crenelated wall and with several towers, the fortified hill appears on Strozzi's map—its original seems to go back to the middle of the fifteenth century (fig. 207). Presumably, though, these structures were remodeled from much earlier ones. In fact, another tower, which was demolished in 1536, rose at the southern foot of the hill on or near what is now Piazza dell'Orologio and the corner of Via del Governo Vecchio. Owned as a condominium by a number of families in 1262, it was bought by the Orsini. But its name, Turris Stefani Petri, leads one to speculate whether it might not be the very tower *in Parione*, the old name of Via del Governo Vecchio, where Cencius Stefani Prefecti in 1075 kept Gregory VII prisoner; the more so since Cencius lorded it over that area up to Ponte S. Angelo. In short, the early existence of a built-up cluster in that neighborhood commanding the east bank bridgehead at the northwest end of the river bend seems a plausible working hypothesis.

In the southern part of the Tiber bend, southwest of Piazza Navona, one single ecclesiastical foundation has survived from early times: the fourth-century title of S. Lorenzo in Damaso; it remains buried below the courtyard of the Cancelleria. Whether still the original mansion newly adapted to Christian use, or a regular basilica, in the early Middle Ages it seems to have stood low in the pecking order of the Roman churches, to judge by the small gift it received in 806/7, when all Roman churches and monasteries were provided with new chandeliers by Pope Leo III. The church and abbey of S. Biagio *de captu secuta* on the river bank, roughly where the remains of Bramante's Palazzo dei Tribunali rise off Via Giulia, must date comparatively early, since it needed restoration by 1072. On the whole, though, the westward area enclosed by the river bend, later the very core of medieval Rome, seems to have been thinly settled prior to the eleventh century. There would have been some houses, to be sure; but the neighborhood until the High Middle Ages seems to have been on the fringe of the abitato.

The Tiber Island in early medieval times sheltered only a few hermit cells and fishing jetties or fishing pools. It was built up only after 997, when Otto III founded the first church dedicated to his cousin, Saint Adalbert, on the site of S. Bartolomeo in Isola. By 1037, an apartment for the bishop of Silva Candida in the Campagna existed next to the new church. On the other hand, Trastevere, teeming and crowded in antiquity, remained populated through the Middle Ages. In the midst of the Gothic siege, Belisarius as a first relief measure repaired the aqueduct ending at the top of the Gianicolo, Trajan's Aqua Sabbatina, to have the water drive the mills on the slope of the hill. Pope Hadrian I, two and a half centuries later, followed in his footsteps. It is only reasonable to think of the water from the mills being channeled down the slope to supply the population. The extent of the built-up area, though, is hard to determine. The bridgeheads of both Ponte Rotto and Ponte Cestio, the latter coming from the island, seem to anchor a densely settled zone near S. Benedetto in Piscinula, the site of another fish market, to judge by the name. From there two medieval streets started: Via della Lungaretta, running due west toward S. Crisogono and S. Maria in Trastevere; and Via dei Vascellari going south to S. Cecilia and beyond, to a branch leading to the Ripa Grande. To be sure, Trastevere was not always as populated as it was in the twelfth century and is to this day. Even three and two hundred years ago the built-up area filled only the Tiber bend on the west bank; shallow, it was never more than three streets deep from the river bank. In the early Middle Ages, one would like to think of an extended area concentrated near the bridgeheads in the easternmost sector of Trastevere. From there it may well have thinned out toward and beyond S. Cecilia, an obsolete community center until the ninth century. To the west the sector reached out toward S. Crisogono, it, too, an old-fashioned structure until replaced in the twelfth century by the present church. At the northern tip of Trastevere around the church of S. Maria in Trastevere, another cluster of housing seems to have existed at an early time. The Roman bridge somewhat north of Ponte Sisto, the pons Aurelius, had collapsed by 1050, perhaps even as early as 792, cutting off that part of Trastevere from the east bank. The church until the ninth century retained its fourth-century plan, whatever that was. With the ninth century, though, a consistent attempt was made to rehabilitate Trastevere, presumably linked to its expansion south and north. The two old tituli, heretofore neglected, were rebuilt and supported by attached monasteries: S. Cecilia as a regular basilica between 817 and 824, and S. Maria by 850. By the eleventh century, housing was dense around S. Maria in Trastevere; houses, gardens, the tower of a noble family, fishing jetties, are documented from the church to Porta Settimiana where Vicolo dei Moroni is still flanked by houses of medieval type, if not medieval date. Still, the site of S. Maria marked the northern outskirts of Trastevere as late as 1600. Far beyond, among fields and vineyards, as early as the mid-ninth century, stood the new monastery of SS. Cosma e Damiano in Mica Aurea. Replaced in the thirteenth century by S. Cosimato, SS. Cosma e Damiano throughout its existence possessed great wealth. Correspondingly, from the late ninth century on, substantial citizens appear in documents as witnesses who probably resided in Trastevere. In short, Trastevere seems to have been flourishing early.

There is no evidence for the location in the early Middle Ages of great families' residences in the abitato—if indeed they resided there. In fact, much seems to suggest that they preferred the outskirts: there was more space to expand their mansions, retainers could be easily accommodated, fortifications could be built, and more land round about was available for cultivation. One such neighborhood seems to have been formed by the eighth century near the south end of the Corso, the old Via Lata, not far from the north cliff of the Capitoline Hill and extending eastward toward Piazza SS. Apostoli and the Imperial Fora. The family mansion of Hadrian I, where he grew up as a ward of his uncle Theodotus, the Consul, *dux* and *primicerius*, stood near the church of S. Marco; and a number of other popes in the ninth and tenth centuries, all from great families, came "de regione Via Lata" or from the Clivus Argentarius, the street linking the southern end of the Corso to the Forum, or from somewhat further behind the Imperial Fora toward the west slope of the Viminal. And did perchance the social prominence of the Via Lata quarter lead papal biographers of the eighth and ninth centuries to recount in detail the Tiber floods hitting that part of town?—just as reports four and five hundred years later would focus on the flooding of the Campo Marzio, the Pantheon, and the Borgo, the areas of concentration where the chroniclers themselves lived. In the early centuries anyway, the great families had settled, it seems, on the eastern edge of the abitato and further out. Near S. Maria in Via Lata, by the early eleventh century, stood a *domus maior*, presumably a large mansion. Beside it and the nearby convent of S. Ciriaco a number of small dwellings were sold or let at the time, possibly housing for retainers, serfs, and craftsmen drawing a livelihood from the lord of the manor. Other big families lived along the Canapara, east and southeast of the Capitol; while northeast, adjoining SS. Apostoli, the family of Alberic, *princeps* and *senator* of all the Romans, had settled from before the time of his grandfather Theophylactus. Around 900 they already occupied a compound enclosed by the imposing walls of a huge staircase of third-century date, descending from the Temple of Serapis, high up on the western spur of the Quirinal, to where the church of SS. Apostoli and the Colonna palace now rise. On the west slope of the Quirinal itself, near the group of the Horse-tamers, around 963 was the residence of Crescentius "at the marble horse," *a caballo marmoreo*, probably ensconced in the remains of the Temple of Serapis. The high walls, both of the staircase enclosure and of the temple cella, offered marvelous defenses and space for the mansion with its attached dwellings, stables, and the like. Overshadowed by the rear wall of the Temple of Serapis—the Middle Ages called it the Gable of Nero—*frontispicium Neronis*—as late as the sixteenth century a small palace still stood on the site, though remodeled in the thirteenth century and again in the fifteenth century by the Colonna family (fig. 197).

On the upper stretch of the Corso, the northernmost of these great houses seems to have been the family mansion of Pope Paul I, in 761 turned into the monastery of S. Silvestro in Capite, on the present Piazza S. Silvestro. It, too, was rooted in a huge ancient structure, the high walls and vast space of a temple precinct, possibly the Temple of the Sun. The two mausolea of Augustus and Hadrian were, needless to say, particularly well suited for defense. That of Augustus, far north and off the Corso, occupied a position of little strategic importance, and it seems to have been used as a fortress only briefly in 1002, by the powerful city prefect, Stephanus de Augusta.

On the other hand, Hadrian's mausoleum, Castel S. Angelo, had served as a fortification possibly from the late third century; its defense in the Gothic Wars is one of the high points in its history. From the ninth century on, it was taken over successively by the Roman families in power; first by that of Alberic, later by the Crescentii. Indeed, it retained the name "Tower of Crescentius," *turris Crescentii*, as late as 1084, when Pope Gregory VII was beleaguered there until rescued by Robert Guiscard. But, just because of its eminent strategic position, it never remained in private hands for long. Either the papal or the imperial faction was forced to secure this, the strongest point in Rome, commanding the approach from St. Peter's to town and vice versa.

The Aventine, dominating the bridgehead of Ponte Rotto and S. Maria in Cosmedin and the river downstream, was another preferred quarter of the great families in the early Middle Ages. "More than any other of the hills of the city," a tenth-century observer records, it had "elegant mansions and its plateau rising high rendered the summer's heat tolerable and made it a good place to live" (fig. 198). There stood the "Palace of Euphimianus," consisting of a summer and a winter palace: the former, adjoining SS. Bonifacio ed Alessio, presumably overlooked the Tiber, "at the end of the hill . . . near the *horrea publica*"—this the medieval name for the site below the western cliff of the Aventine; the winter palace stood "in front of the church," slightly downhill one suspects. Legend, as reflected in a spurious tenth-century document, would have Euphimianus the father of Saint Alexius; but when this was written, the mansion must have been old, possibly a domus of Roman

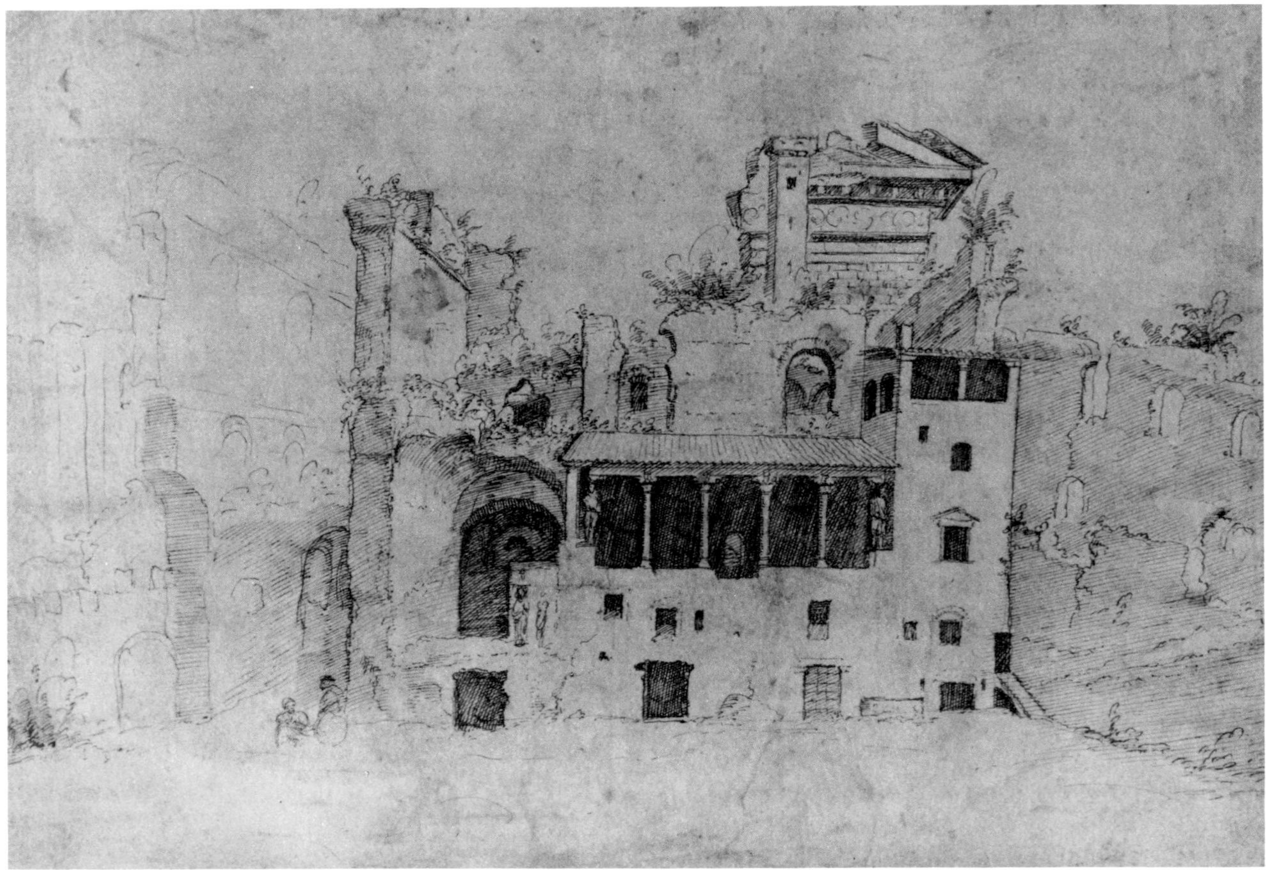

197. Early Colonna Palace and Temple of Serapis, Quirinal, as of 1534-1536, drawing Marten van Heemskerck circle, Kunstmuseum, Düsseldorf

times, as were others nearby. In the mid-ninth century, one Gregory, who was military commander and civil governor of the papal palace, and his son-in-law George, both members of a great family—though a bit unsavory—lived on the Aventine. Alberic, too, was born there around 900 in a mansion long owned by his family; it was situated on the site of the gardens of the Cavalieri di Malta; around 940 Alberic gave it to the Cluniacs, who transformed it into the monastery of S. Maria in Aventino. Whether or not Otto III resided on the Aventine "in an ancient palace," as some chroniclers say, is not quite certain. Others place his residence on the Palatine in the "Palace of Julian in the city"—perhaps one of the imperial palaces—which "he began to remodel into a grand palace for himself" and where medieval antiquarians located a "Temple of Julian," any large ancient building being to them a temple.

Beyond the populous quarters and the big mansions, the disabitato extended north, east, and south to the Aurelian Walls, given over mostly to fields, vineyards, and pastures. Amid them rose the ruins of Roman thermae, aqueducts, mausolea, and palaces; an occasional farmhouse or a laborer's hovel; and scattered clusters of houses, crowding around some church or monastery and making use wherever possible of nearby ruins. Any view taken as late as 1870 or thereabouts still conveys the same impression (fig. 199). Far out in the remote southeastern corner of the disabitato, close to the Aurelian Walls, remained the Lateran, the residence of the popes and their cathedral. Early, perhaps by the sixth and seventh centuries, it became the focus of a cluster of housing. To the north and west, where the obelisk now stands, extended the "campus Laterani," a vast irregular piazza facing the approach from the far away abitato, along

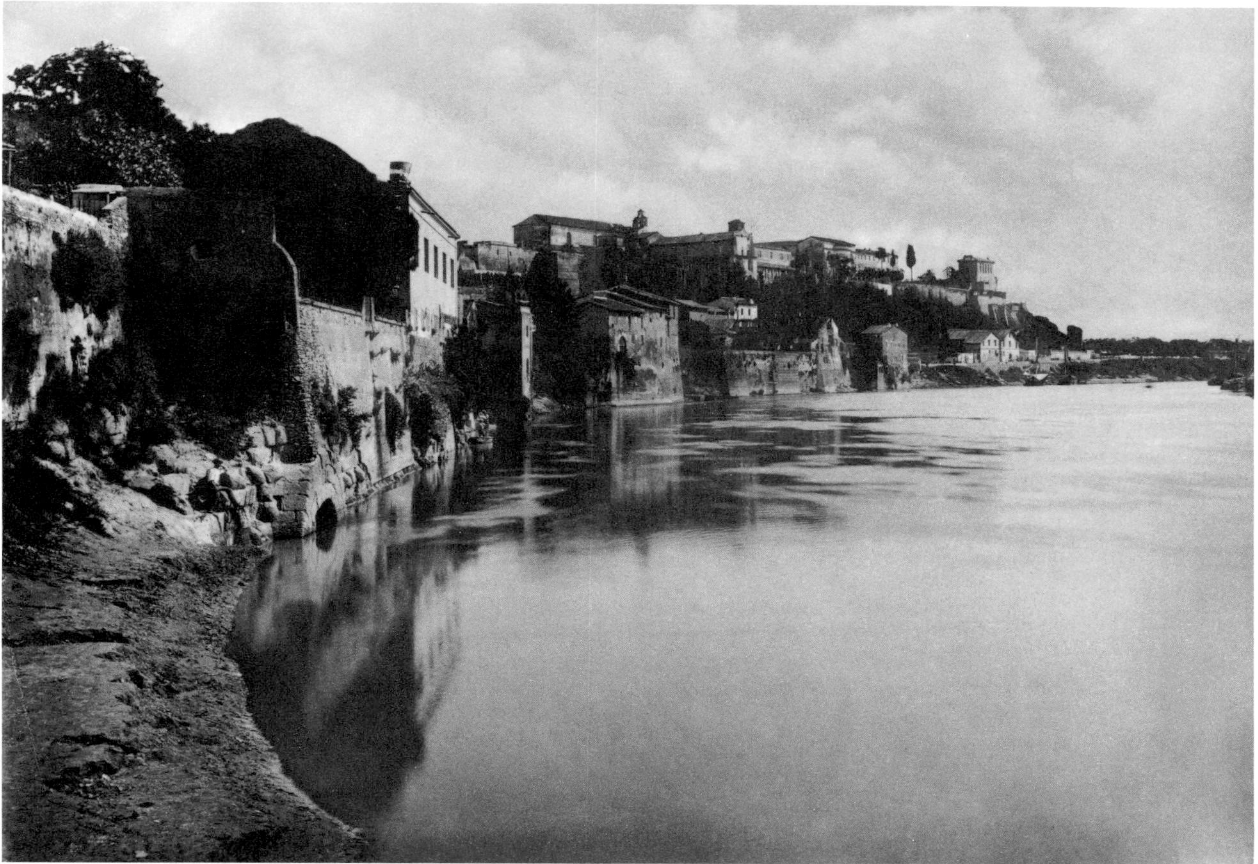

198. Aventine as of ca. 1870

the Via Maior, which ascended from the Colosseum. The palace to the north of the basilica by the ninth century was composed of an intricate agglomeration of structures, extending north and east of the basilica and more or less parallel to its main axis: reception halls, chapels, and papal living quarters, resplendent with mosaics, marble pavements, and revetment—one recalls the triclinium and the banqueting hall, the *accubita*, of Leo III (fig. 200, also fig. 93). Kitchens, larders, storerooms, stables, and a treasury listed by the early eleventh century would have existed long before. There also would have been quarters for the administrative staff and the servants, and all buildings were linked by corridors and probably by inner courtyards. Some documents, indeed, seem to suggest that buildings belonging to the palace extended west and south of the basilica as well, as far as the city walls. The main palace to the north through the High Middle Ages was kept in good repair, its halls and chapels redecorated and occasionally rebuilt in parts, like the two-storied Chapel of the Sancta Sanctorum and the façade and loggia of the accubita of Leo III, both added in the late thirteenth century; Heemskerck in 1536 marked them, the first at the left edge, the latter right of center of his view (fig. 260). But large parts of the complex, when in 1586-89 it gave way to the structure of Sixtus V, seem to have been of early medieval date.

The Lateran palace and church, then, by the early Middle Ages had grown into an impressive residence and administrative center. Other buildings sprang up around the palace. Houses to shelter members of the papal household or craftsmen and tradesmen drawing a living from it would have crowded about, as they are listed in far greater numbers in the High Middle Ages. Four monasteries from the sixth and seventh cen-

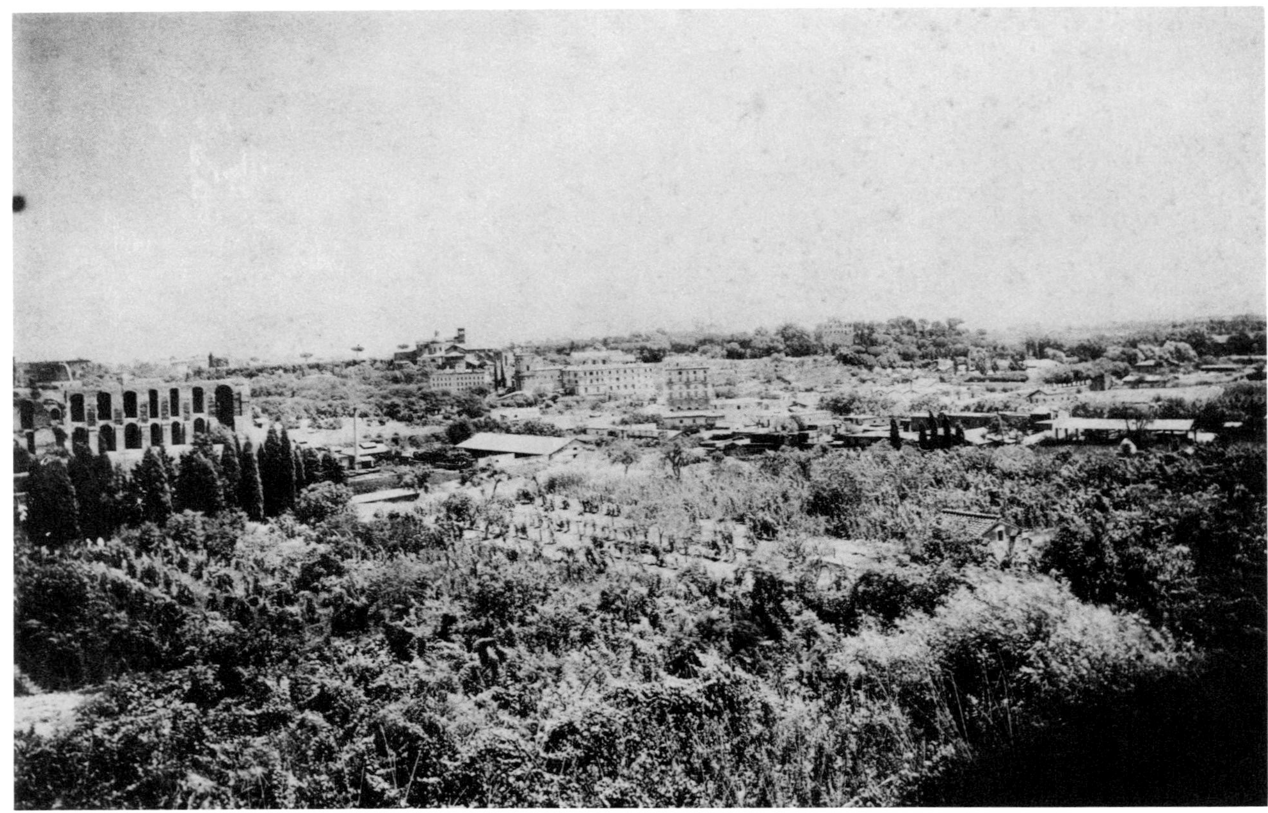

199. View from Aventine toward Palatine and Celian as of 1870, showing disabitato, Museo di Roma

turies on were installed close by: one in a mansion formerly owned by Pope Honorius; two more housed possibly in the remains of other mansions near the palace and the baptistery; the fourth, a late-comer in the ninth century, sheltered under or close to the arches of the aqueduct across the square north of the church. But the Lateran and the surrounding buildings remained far from the abitato, all isolated from contact with the living city of Rome. To the north along Via Merulana, coming from S. Maria Maggiore and slightly diverging from its present track, were the early community centers of S. Matteo and SS. Marcellino e Pietro—it was previously known as the titulus Nicodemis; by the eighth century both had been abandoned or were in poor repair. Only much later were they replaced by medieval churches. East of the Lateran likewise only fields and farms extended; S. Croce in Gerusalemme, in spite of being a Constantinian foundation and of large size, by the early Middle Ages ranked low among Roman churches: through the eighth century it was in poor repair, and the lighting fixture it received as a gift in 806/7 was no larger than fixtures assigned to minor chapels. Further east still, a cluster of farm buildings with a minor church are documented from the early tenth century on at Porta Maggiore. West of the Lateran the crest of the

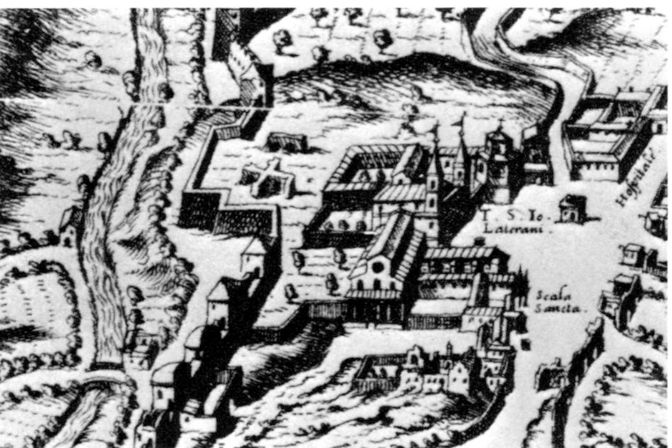

200. Map of Rome, 1575, Du Pérac-Lafréry, detail, Lateran Basilica, palace and surroundings

Celian Hill was similarly deserted. The convent of S. Erasmo east of Sto. Stefano Rotondo, flourishing since the seventh century, by 937 was deserted; it was rehabilitated by being handed over to the abbey of Subiaco and it lived on for another two hundred years. By the tenth century, though, only a few churches, farms, and cottages (*domicellae*) were loosely strung out along the track of the old Via Celimontana and the aqueduct passing by Sto. Stefano Rotondo, S. Maria in Domnica, SS. Giovanni e Paolo, and Saint Gregory's monastery, now S. Gregorio Magno, and descending between these two along the old street, the Clivus Scauri, to the valley at the foot of the Palatine. Such desertion of the Celian Hill in the Middle Ages was simply natural; the Via Celimontana no longer connected with any built-up area. If the installation of a diaconia at S. Maria in Domnica by 800 and the building of the church shortly afterwards, and the raising of Sto. Stefano Rotondo to the rank of titulus by the tenth century, were intended to bring new life to the area, they all failed. The churches remained in desolate isolation as recently as a hundred years ago, half-ruined structures in the disabitato. The palace and cathedral of the Lateran with the houses, convents, and minor churches crowded about, had become a residence and administrative center, separate from the city it ruled.

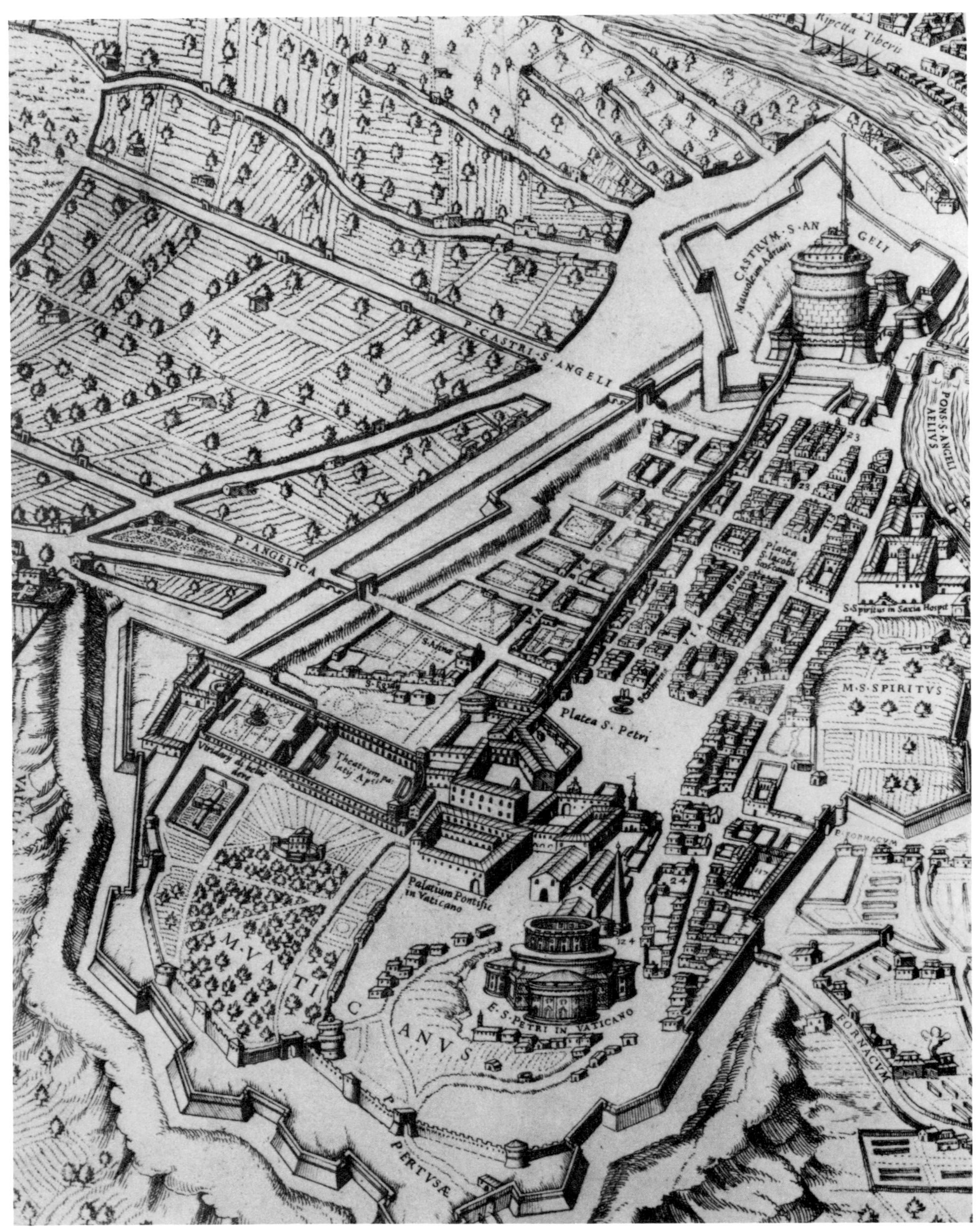

201. Map of Rome, 1576, M. Cartaro ("Large Cartaro Map"), detail, showing Borgo

CHAPTER ELEVEN

Growth of the Borgo

While the Lateran, in the southeastern sector of ancient Rome, grew ever more isolated from Christian antiquity through the early Middle Ages, a new epicenter had been forming since the fourth and fifth centuries at the northwestern edge of the city. Situated beyond the Aurelian Walls, across the Tiber and thus outside the ancient city, St. Peter's and the suburb extending to the river and Ponte S. Angelo became a pivotal element in changing the map of Rome. In popular feeling, the basilica had outranked the cathedral at the Lateran ever since Constantinian times. It was the shrine of the Apostle whose successors sat on the papal throne. To him pilgrims flocked in ever larger numbers. In his name Europe north of the Alps was Christianized. At his tomb treaties were sworn and deposited. In his church the emperors were crowned. Through his intercession Romans and foreigners from all over the West implored and expected salvation. Thus, around his church, from the fifth century through the ninth, a large settlement—large in medieval terms—had grown up: five hostels to provide for pilgrims, extending from the church to Ponte S. Angelo; six monasteries to serve both the basilica and the hostels, one in particular set aside for the footsore; cells attached to the basilica, for the poor and probably hermits also; a poorhouse; and at an early time, adjoining the atrium of the basilica, houses likely for clergy and laymen serving the churches; on the square in front of the basilica, a fountain and a lavatory. Small churches and oratories, aside from those connected with the monasteries, crowded about, some ensconced in the Roman mausolea south of St. Peter's. The one attached to the transept of the basilica in the eighth century was dedicated to Saint Petronilla, the legendary daughter of Saint Peter—a Roman lady's sarcophagus found at the time gave rise to the belief and the mausoleum became the oratory of the Frankish kings and the Carolingian House; until the building of New St. Peter's it was the chapel of the Kings of France. The times of Charlemagne, of his son and grandsons, and the contemporary popes mark a peak in developing a representative architectural focus around the basilica. Papal reception rooms were built: one by Leo III, a trefoil structure like the one at the Lateran; another "a structure of marvelous grandeur and beauty" with a State Banqueting Hall; and temporary quarters "for the pope to rest his weary limbs after morning prayers or Mass"—it was a long way to come from the Lateran. These buildings were still in use a century and a half later. Other quarters were set up for visiting dignitaries, among them the "palace" of Charlemagne—outside the city, one notes—perhaps installed in some older building and possibly on the site of today's Campo Santo Teutonico. It, too, continued to be used by the German emperors and their local representatives and envoys until the tenth century. Near the basilica rose the compounds of the foreigners, the Anglo-Saxons, Franks, Lombards, and Frisians. The Mausoleum of Hadrian, Castel S. Angelo, commanded the only approach from the city across the Tiber bridge Ponte S. Angelo. Whoever held it dominated the sanctuary of the Apostle and the surrounding settlement; he provided at once both powerful protection and a potential threat. From the settlement a single street ran south toward Trastevere, squeezed between the river and the foot of the Gianicolo. By 1576 the Borgo had been regularized (fig. 201). A new street, Via Alessandrina, had been laid out in the north sector, parallel to Via del Borgo Nuovo. Construction at New St. Peter's was well advanced; and outside the Leonine Wall to the north a suburb had been laid out by Pius IV, Borgo Pio. But essentially the situation was un-

202. View of Borgo from Monte Mario, as of ca. 1495, drawing, *Escurialensis*, fol. 7v, 84

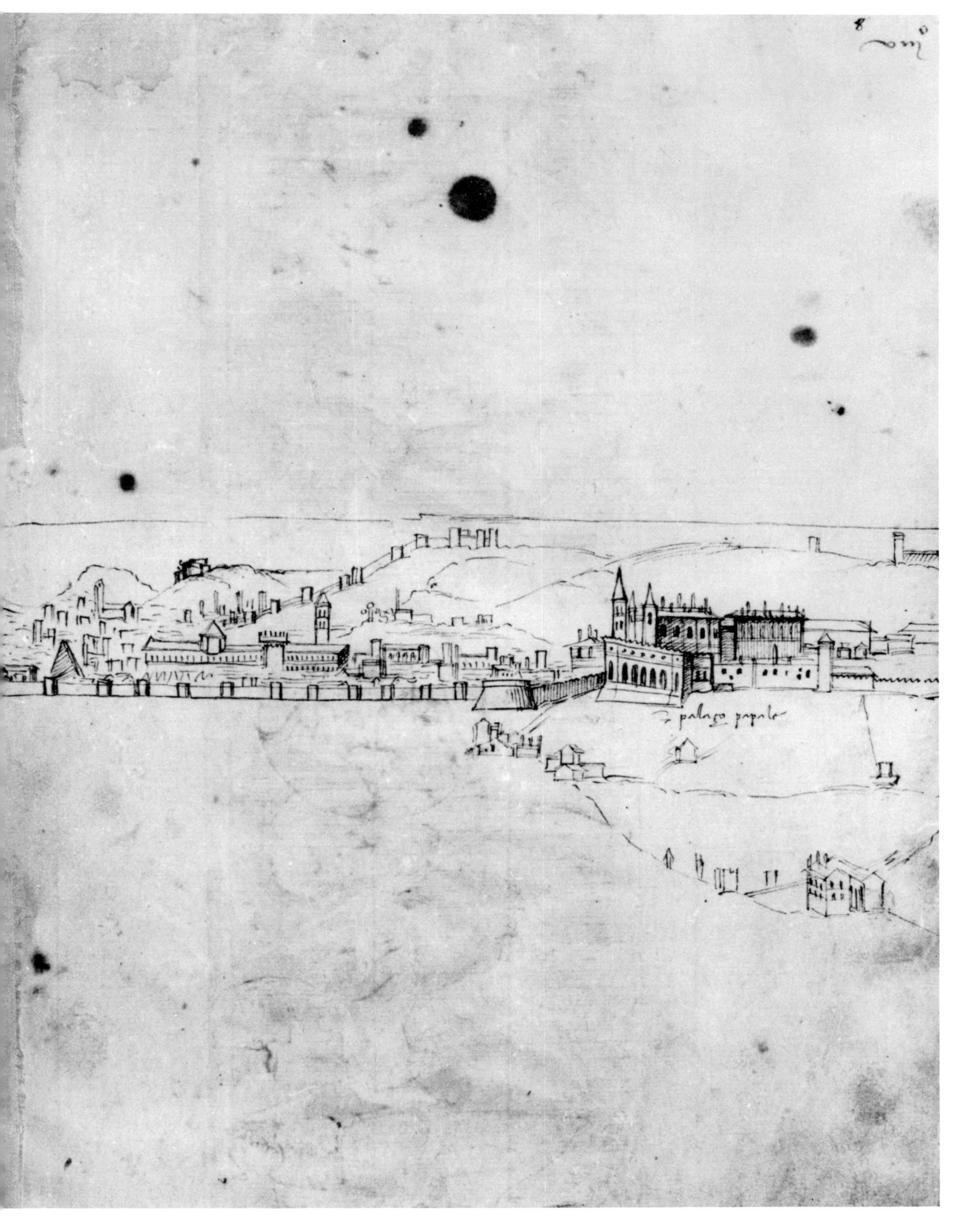
palazo papale

changed from that obtaining in the Middle Ages: inside the walls of Leo IV, St. Peter's and the minor churches; the convents and hostels, many grown from the foreigners' compounds, gone since the ninth century; outside to the north the Prati, the fields on which to a large extent depended the provisioning of Rome.

St. Peter's by the ninth century was the focus of veneration for the entire West. Situated outside the city, it was nonetheless the most important sanctuary of Rome. Treasures untold had accumulated in the basilica and its sacristy. The raid of the Saracens in 846 demonstrated with urgency the need for protection. Security was provided by the walls of Leo IV, built in 847-853. Running from Castel S. Angelo to behind St. Peter's and back to the river bank near where the hospital of Sto. Spirito now stands, this Leonine Wall made the area into a fortified compound, a new city that took its name from the founder, the Leonine City. It sheltered the great basilica and its treasures, the smaller churches and monasteries, the living quarters of the clergy, the papal apartments, the scholae of the foreigners, the houses and gardens of the people settled nearby, the diaconiae and the pilgrims' hostels. But it also turned the Leonine City into a township of its own, different from the town across the river and its suburbs inside the Aurelian Walls. Far into the Middle Ages, contemporaries remained aware of the distinction between Rome and the *civitas Leonina*. Benedict of Soracte in the tenth century bewails separately the fate of Rome and of the Leonine City: "Woe to you, Rome. . . . Woe to you, Leonine City"; in the Chronicle of Rudolf Glaber around A.D. 1000, Castel S. Angelo appears as "a tower outside the city, beyond the Tiber"; throughout the eleventh century, the "New Leonine City" is legally set apart in documents; and both by law and in public opinion it remained separate for nearly three hundred years; indeed, its juridical independence continued to some degree until the late seventeenth century.

By the eleventh century, the Borgo—from *burgus*, a small fortified settlement—had long taken the shape it retained far beyond the Middle Ages and essentially until 1938 when Via della Conciliazione broke through the old network of streets to Piazza S. Pietro. Maps and views from the sixteenth through the nineteenth centuries and documentary evidence give an eloquent picture. Enclosed by the Walls of Leo IV and enveloping St. Peter's and the neighboring sanctuaries, convents, and mausolea, it had continued to grow. Outside the walls, still in the fifteenth century, there were nothing but fields. A *veduta* by the Escurial draughtsman shows the view visitors to Rome would see when approaching from Monte Mario along Via Cassia (fig. 202): the Leonine Wall; the *meta Romuli*, a pyramid demolished in the sixteenth century; the Hospital of Sto. Spirito, as rebuilt by Sixtus IV, 1471-1486; St. Peter's and the papal palace; far back, the Gianicolo and the Wall of Trastevere; to the left, part of the city, marked by the Pantheon, S. Agostino, and the Palazzo del Senatore on the Capitol; and in the foreground, the fields, the Prati. Late in the nineteenth century these fields spread north of the Vatican Palace as far as Monte Mario and beyond (fig. 203). Inside the Leonine Walls, the somewhat shapeless square called *cortina S. Petri* or *Platea Sancti Petri* extended in front of St. Peter's and its atrium steps (fig. 204). From there, the settlement ran all the way to the river and Castel S. Angelo—minor churches, foreigners' compounds and houses, gardens, workshops, and stores. Houses with porticoes, one supposes to shelter shops and stands, lined the square and the streets approaching the basilica; between and behind them were gardens and an occasional empty lot. Two major thoroughfares, though comparatively narrow, were linked to the street system of antiquity. From the north, following an old Roman highway known as the Via Triumphalis, came *ruga Francigena*, Rue de France, whence first the Franks and later other travelers from north of the Alps entered the Leonine City through the Porta Sancti Petri. As they descended Monte Mario along the Via Cassia, they would get their first sight of Rome, "with its crowded mass of towers, and more palatial structures than man can count"—so wrote Magister Gregory around 1200 to his confreres in England. From the east, as marked on Bufalini's map of 1551, two or three streets approached St. Peter's, all starting from the narrow bridgehead

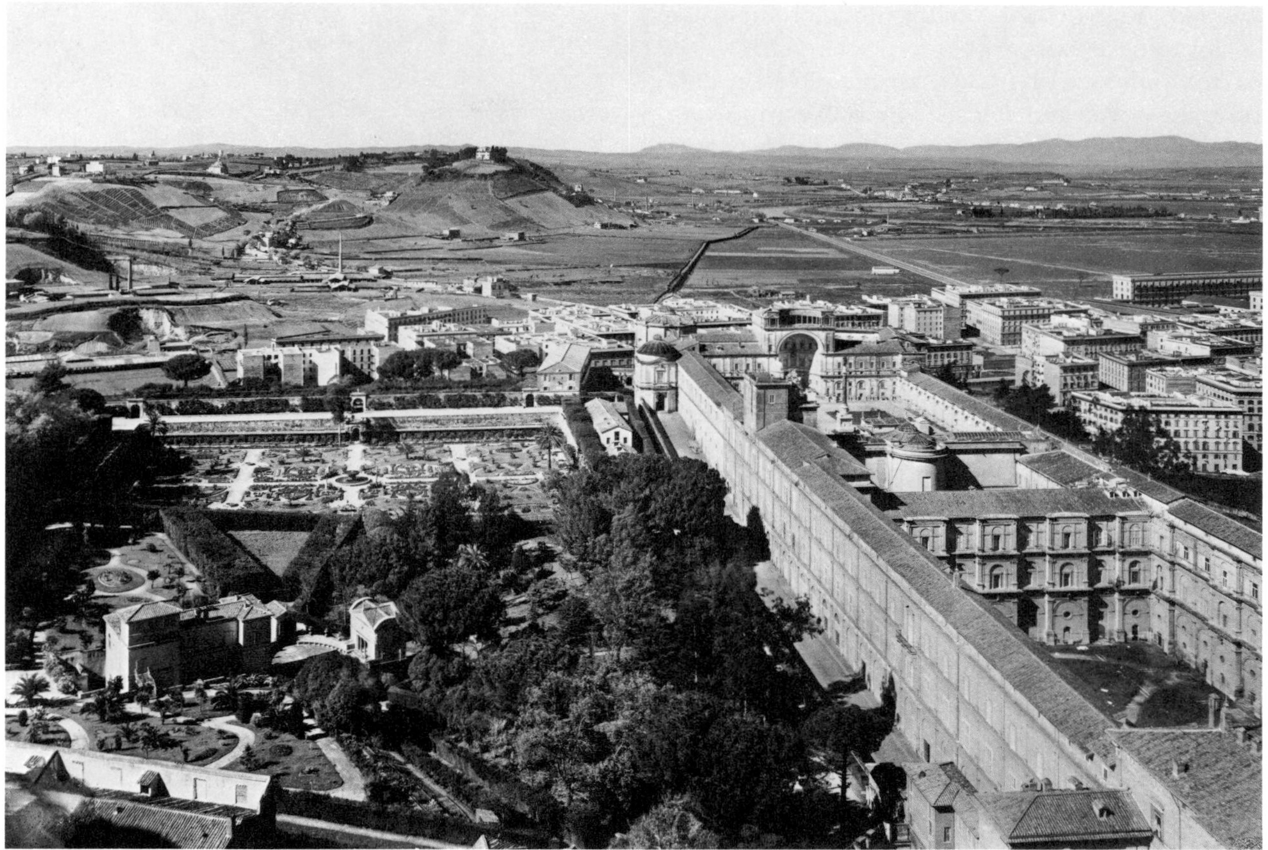

203. Prati and Monte Mario, as of ca. 1880; foreground, sixteenth-century Vatican Palace and Gardens

at Castel S. Angelo (fig. 205). Borgo Vecchio, most likely of Roman origin, was the major thoroughfare. Coinciding probably with the portico of St. Peter's of Christian antiquity, it ended at the southeast corner of the atrium steps; in 1938 it fell victim to the southern rim of Via della Conciliazione. A minor Roman road, the Via Cornelia, continued it, skirting the mausolea and the circus south of the basilica. Further east, what is now Borgo Sto. Spirito passed by the Anglo-Saxon compound on the site where Innocent III in 1198 first laid out the hospital and church of Sto. Spirito in Sassia, rebuilt in the fifteenth and sixteenth centuries. By and large, the street continued parallel to Borgo Vecchio, as it did until 1938. A third street, evidently of medieval rather than ancient date, may have run along the northern wall of the Leonine City. Whether any medieval street approached the square along the fifteenth-century Borgo Nuovo, roughly on the center

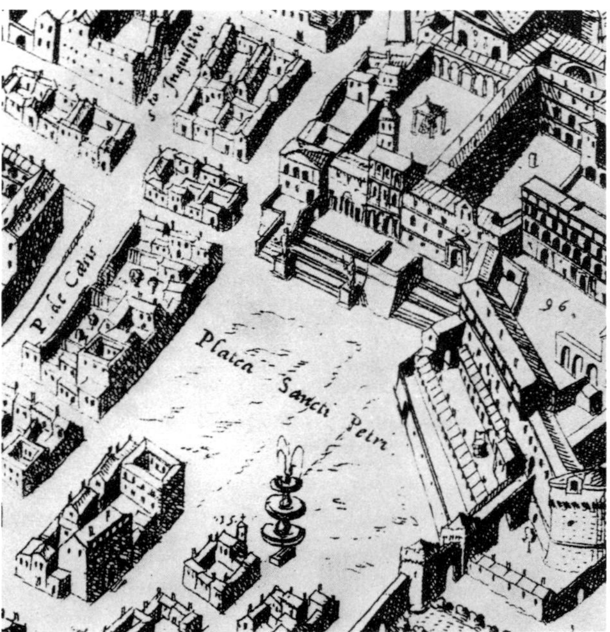

204. Map of Rome, 1577, Du Pérac-Lafréry, detail showing St. Peter's Square, atrium, and nave of old basilica

line of Via della Conciliazione, remains in doubt. These east-west streets were crossed by narrow alleys and streets, all medieval in date, running north and south. The most important, passing Sto. Spirito in Sassia, led to the Saxon Gate in the Leonine Wall, whence a country road went on to Trastevere. Traversing that quarter to near its south end, the pilgrim crossed Ponte S. Maria, Ponte Rotto, and proceeded below the cliff of the Aventine to Porta S. Paolo and thence to S. Paolo fuori le mura. Housing by the early eleventh century near St. Peter's Square, the *cortina*, must have been quite dense; in 1030 a two-storied house was sold, "with its stable and porch and a wooden staircase," bordering on three other houses. In between there were building lots; and on the outskirts of the Borgo near the walls, fields, and vineyards remained through the twelfth century.

Inside the Leonine City, the streets from St. Peter's to the bridge were the important traffic lanes and a major shopping center for visitors and pilgrims. By 1041, if not before, business must have been thriving; at that time a house was sold, "with two shops to do business . . . with a pergola and courtyard in front," in the Saxon compound; two years later, two double-storied dwellings were sold, "one linked to the portico [the porticoed street?] with shops inside the portico for business"; and in 1127, "a heated room, a *caminata*, with shops in front and a cottage at the back." In fact, as early as 854 houses with storerooms and cellars, wells, gardens, and vineyards extended between St. Peter's and the river. By the mid-eleventh century, too, shopkeepers or innkeepers, *tabernarii*, were listed among the inhabitants of the Leonine City, as were waiters or shop assistants, *servientes*. Two hundred years later, the Borgo apparently had become so much the tourists' quarter, the Via Veneto of medieval Rome, and the innkeepers and owners of lodging houses so powerful an economic factor, that they not only claimed a monopoly in that field, but went so far as to steal each other's guests by physical force. Brancaleone, the strong-man senatore of the thirteenth century, put in his veto and gave the pilgrims the right to lodge and buy their food wherever they wanted—perhaps egged on by innkeepers established across the river in Rome proper.

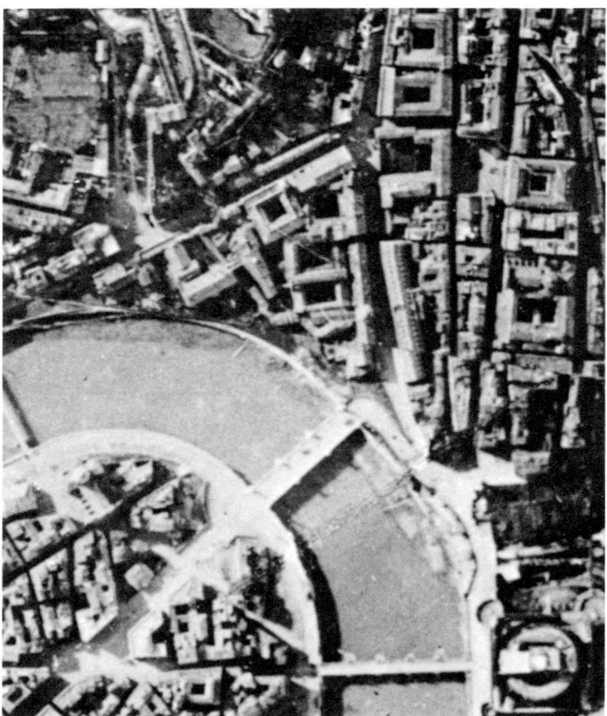

205. Streets of Borgo prior to 1938

Money changers, as one would expect, crowded near the basilica by the twelfth century and probably long before; by the early fourteenth century they had set up forty-nine stands, all owned by great Roman families, on parts of the square and the atrium steps. Along their stands, the straw vendors, ever since the twelfth century or earlier, provided bedding. In the atrium of St. Peter's booksellers had set up their stalls; one fourteenth-century book dealer was a Jew. Along the streets and on the square were the booths of the vendors of religious souvenirs, the painters of icons and ex-votos, the sellers of phials—filled, one assumes, with oil from lamps burning near Saint Peter's tomb—goldsmiths, and rosary makers; the cobblers, cloth merchants, and sellers of purses; and the small merchants of *generi alimentari*, fruit vendors, vegetable dealers, vendors of oil and spices, fishmongers. Indeed, as early as the mid-thirteenth century the tradespeople had invaded the steps leading to St. Peter's, the atrium, the narthex, and even the interior of the church, apparently with the consent of the canons in charge, who drew fat rents from them. The municipal administration attempted to check the practice—in vain, needless to say. In short, by the High Middle Ages, the main thoroughfares of the Borgo, the square in front of the church and the atrium and its steps had become one big bazaar.

The needs of the Borgo and its population, seasonally swelled by pilgrims, from early times required hostels and hospitals; one recalls the hostels set up by the eighth century with the diaconiae of S. Silvestro and S. Maria *in caput portici*; the hospital of S. Gregorio on St. Peter's square; the deed of Sto. Stefano degli Abissini charging the monks to take care of the footsore. Such needs, one surmises, were among the reasons for founding in 1198 the Hospital of Sto. Spirito in Sassia. It was replaced in the fifteenth and in the sixteenth centuries by new constructions; the first in 1474 was the splendid wing of Sixtus IV, still fully intact today, as it extends from the river bank all the way to Porta Sto. Spirito, the old Saxon Gate, and the street of that name. The twelfth-century hospital took over the Anglo-Saxon compound, the *schola Saxonum*, by then long out of use, and presumably enlarged the existing site, given the manifold tasks assigned to the foundation: a hostel for visitors of rank, a poorhouse, a foundlings' home and orphanage, a maternity ward, and a refuge for fallen women. Finally, the hospital was specifically charged "to seek out once a week through the streets and public squares sick paupers, to bring them to the houses of Sto. Spirito, and to nurse them carefully." Whether or not set up by Innocent III to make up for the sin of pride underlying the building of Tor de' Conti, the biggest family tower in town, the tasks and organization of the Hospital of Sto. Spirito reflected a grand design. But we have to rely entirely on imagination to visualize its plan and aspect.

The brotherhood of the hospital, according to its charter, operated all over Rome rather than in the Borgo alone. By 1200, then, a new relationship seems to have developed between the Borgo, the Leonine City, on one hand, and Rome, the city proper, on the east bank of the Tiber. Legally, the Leonine City remained separate from Rome. But from the viewpoint of contemporaries it came to be viewed increasingly as an integral part of the city of Rome. It sheltered, after all, Saint Peter's grave and it had grown around and, as it were, from his basilica. His church was the most venerated sanctuary in Rome, far more so than the cathedral at the Lateran. From the eleventh century on, the canons of St. Peter's claimed precedence for their church over the Lateran. The controversy raged back and forth for centuries, in pamphlets published by the canons of both churches. Inevitably St. Peter's won. Innocent III, one recalls, put his official seal on it when in his inscription on the apse mosaic of St. Peter's he called the basilica Mother of all Churches, the traditional title of the Lateran. After all, the Apostle and the pope, his successor, were identified with each other, and both had become synonymous with Rome. Necessarily then, St. Peter's and its suburb, the Leonine City, were no longer conceived of as separate from Rome herself. In the High Middle Ages, general opinion, if not the law, located St. Peter's and, with it, the Borgo, in Rome.

Nonetheless, within the urban context of Rome, the Borgo through the High and late Middle Ages retained features of its own. Its location protected it from Roman mobs and from any occupying power that might have taken over the city; Castel S. Angelo and the walls of Leo IV provided defense, if not always effectively, against hostile attack from the outside. In particular, the Borgo housed the basilica of the Apostle whose name was synonymous with the papacy. Hence it became a refuge for his successors: a fortified and sacred precinct; an integral part of Rome, yet on the edge of the city; easy to defend and a convenient springboard for counterattack. Popes in times of stress sought safety in the Borgo: they might enclose themselves in Castel S. Angelo, as did Gregory VII in 1084, when both the Leonine City and Rome were in enemy hands; or they might move to St. Peter's, as did Eugene III and Hadrian IV around the middle of the twelfth century when cut off by the Roman Republic from the Lateran, to stay in the old papal quarters as they had been set up in

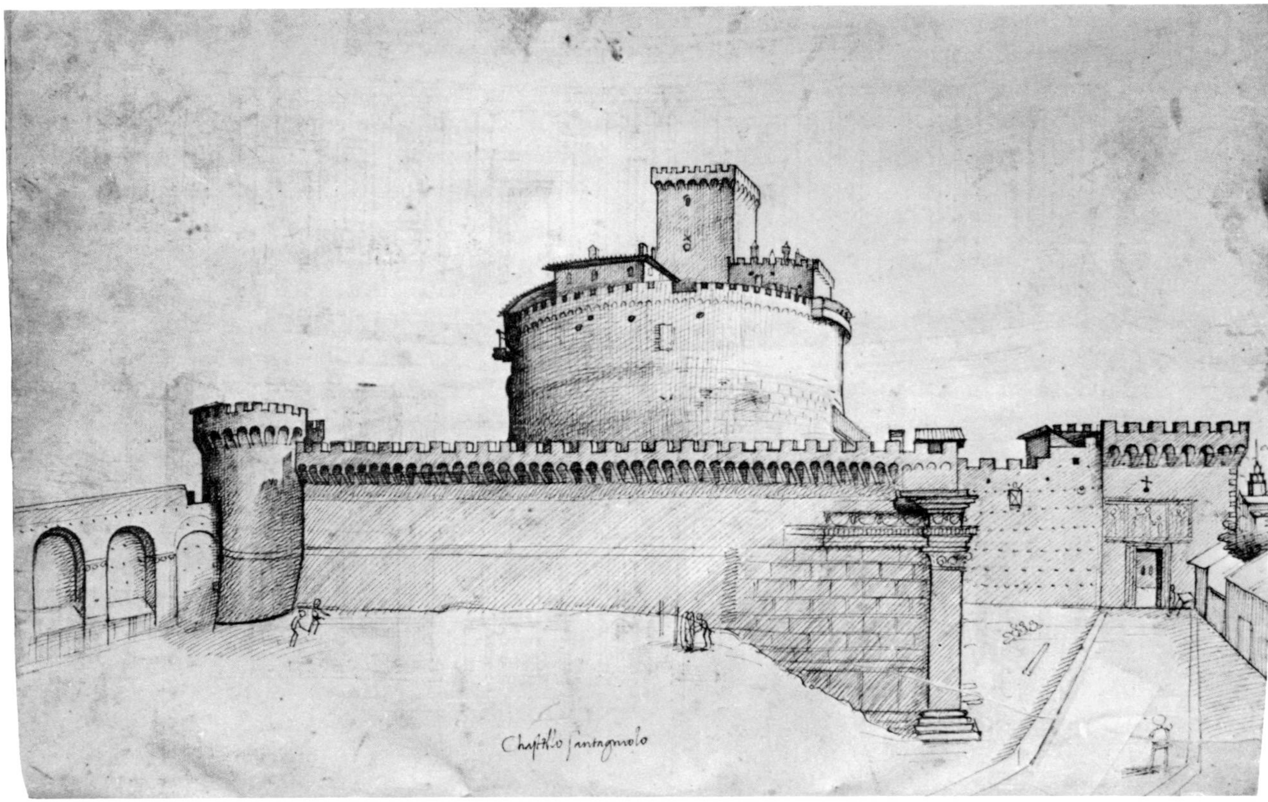

206. Castel S. Angelo from south, as of ca. 1495, drawing, *Escurialensis*, fol. 30v

the fifth and ninth centuries, evidently south of St. Peter's on the site of or near the Campo Santo Teutonico, and to the north attached to or separated by an alley from the flanks of the atrium and church. By the twelfth and thirteenth centuries such accommodation, designed hundreds of years earlier for temporary use, was in bad repair and inadequate to house the vastly swollen papal court and bureaucracy for extended residence. New quarters were needed, strong enough to withstand a siege, if necessary. A start may have been made shortly before 1150, when a "new palace" was built by Eugene III; if indeed it adjoined the basilica, as one document has it, no trace is likely ever to turn up. On the other hand, the nucleus of the palace, erected about 1208 by Innocent III and enlarged two generations later by Nicholas III and his successors until 1300, survives north of the church on the hill, incorporated into and hidden by the sprawling present Vatican Palace, but essentially well preserved (fig. 161). By the early fourteenth century, then, a large medieval papal residence stood on the Vatican Hill overlooking the Borgo and, across the river, Rome. Heavily fortified, it was still a refuge more than anything else; the walls of the Borgo, while not enclosing it, provided additional support; and jointly, palace, Borgo, and Castel S. Angelo represented a formidable defensive quarter: a stronghold for the popes, protection for St. Peter's and the people plying their trades in the Borgo, and a threatening memento to the ever rebellious Romans.

A key point in the defense of the Vatican was, of course, Castel S. Angelo, as it had long been in the defense of St. Peter's and the Borgo (fig. 206). Its value in defending the papal stronghold grew, as by the late twelfth century it became undisputed papal property instead of changing hands as before among war-mongering clans. Its fortifications had been constantly improved and work on them continued for another four hundred years. A tall tower as early as the eleventh century rose above its cylindrical mass; crenelated, it is seen on the earliest surviving map of Rome, that drawn by Fra Paolino in 1323 but possibly based on a thirteenth-century original (fig. 182); and, rebuilt in 1379, the tower with the square base, and the round core of the mausoleum with the towered bridgehead in front became hallmarks of Roman *vedute*, starting with Fra Paolino's map and the Bull of Louis the Bavarian of 1328 (figs. 160, 207, 208, 223), and continuing with the more precise but later views of the Escurial draughtsman at the end of the fifteenth century (figs. 206, 225).

The medieval Vatican Palace and the Borgo, protected by the stronghold of Castel S. Angelo and by the Leonine Walls, were essentially defensive and cautiously closed off against the city across the river. The permanent residence of the papacy until the mid-fifteenth century remained, ideally anyhow, at the Lateran. Nonetheless, ever since the eleventh century the Borgo and St. Peter's had become a magnet that drew unto itself the expansion of the abitato across the river; a pull strengthened immensely in the twelfth and thirteenth centuries. The shift of hierarchical rank from the Lateran Basilica to St. Peter's; the gradual building up of a papal residence nearby; the closeness to the medieval town on the east bank of the Tiber; the commercial importance of the Borgo and its strong defenses—all ever more powerfully attracted the abitato toward Ponte S. Angelo and into the bend of the Tiber. Saint Peter's grave and basilica and the Borgo were the major focus in developing and changing the map of medieval Rome.

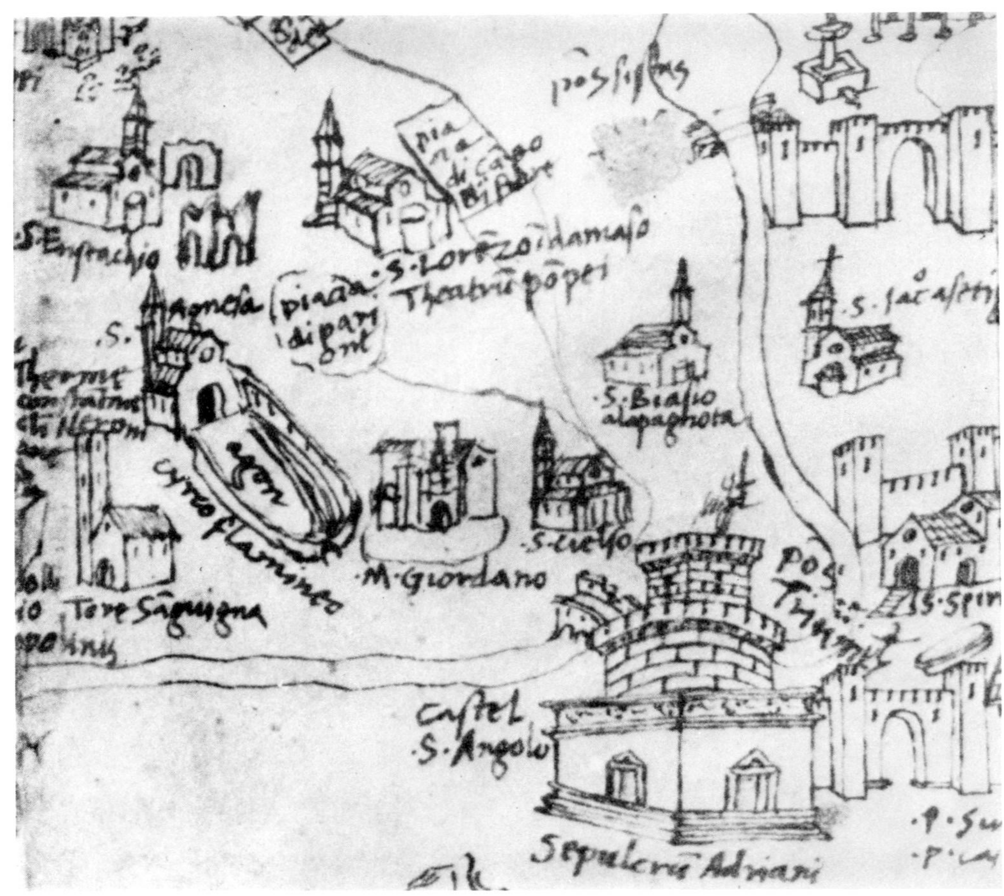

207. Map of Rome, 1474 (original ca. 1450), Alessandro Strozzi, detail, showing churches and fortified mansions in Tiber bend, Florence, Bibl. Laurenziana

CHAPTER TWELVE

The Abitato

The map of Rome and the appearance of both the abitato and the disabitato were gradually but thoroughly changed from the eleventh century through the thirteenth by the city's rise as a great administrative center and as the seat of the Supreme Court of the West, and the resulting population explosion. The three areas built up in the earlier Middle Ages east and west of the river grew into a coherent and, it would seem, densely populated town. In Trastevere minor churches, convents, and housing, heavily built up already by the early eleventh century, edged north to S. Maria and Porta Settimiana. The Tiber Island became a fortified link between Trastevere and the east bank. There the two early-developed areas, the Ripa spreading from the river's edge to the northern foot of the Capitol and the area from around the Pantheon to Piazza Navona, were fused and jointly pushed westward to fill the entire river bend. At the same time, the town spread northward far into the Campo Marzio and eastward to the foot of the Quirinal and what became the Trevi Fountain. At the edge of the abitato, the Borgo and St. Peter's to the west and the Capitol to the east became new foci of the Roman townscape. In brief, the abitato took on the aspect it preserved at least till the Renaissance, and which in parts of town essentially survives to this day. Further out, clusters that from early times seem to have formed around churches, such as S. Maria Nova—now S. Francesca Romana—at the eastern end of the Forum, and S. Maria Maggiore, developed into sizable suburbs, loosely linked to the abitato proper. Lost in the disabitato, a large settlement around the Lateran became a real satellite town, and all through the wasteland farmhouses multiplied, together with fortified convents and family mansions with towers.

The area within the Tiber bend, reaching from Piazza Navona and Campo dei Fiori west and south to the river, more or less the present rione Ponte and parts of the rioni Parione and Regola, seems to have been filling up from the late eleventh century on. New foundations of churches and monasteries serve as guide posts. Where until 1050 only a few oratories and minor churches had been erected—one on the hillock of Monte Giordano; another, S. Lucia della Tinta, off the river bank to the north on Via di Monte Brianzo—a veritable spate of churches rose in the course of the eleventh and twelfth centuries. The old titulus of S. Lorenzo in Damaso, rarely mentioned after the early ninth century, was apparently raised to prominence: an almost uninterrupted series of title cardinals reappears shortly after 1000; the borderlines between S. Lorenzo and the old diaconia of S. Eustachio, also grown powerful, were redefined between 1173 and 1176; and by 1186, when its title cardinal became Pope Urban III, S. Lorenzo would seem to have been the foremost church in the Tiber bend. No less than sixty-five churches and chapels were then under its jurisdiction, spread over the entire southern and western sectors of the area, from near Ponte S. Angelo to opposite the northern tip of the Tiber Island. Some of the churches listed in 1186 survive, replaced by splendid structures of later date, or modest basilicas retaining their original plan, even if badly restored; among the former, S. Agnese in Piazza Navona, S. Maria in Vallicella, S. Salvatore in Lauro; among the latter, S. Tommaso in Parione, S. Salvatore in Onda, S. Maria in Monticelli near Via Arenula, and S. Nicola dei Calcararii (also, dei Cesarini) on the site of Largo Argentina and demolished, except for the apse foundations and crypt, in 1932. To be sure, quite a few of the sixty-five churches subject to S. Lorenzo may have been standing for some time when listed in 1186; but those dated by inscriptions or otherwise documented seem to have all been founded not too long before; S. Maria in Monticelli between 1099 and 1118, but consecrated 1143; S. Salvatore in Onda prior to 1127; S. Nicola dei Calcararii, consecrated 1132; S. Tommaso in Parione 1139. Others in the same area, though undated, were apparently built or rebuilt at that time. S. Celso, near Ponte S. Angelo, serves as an example. First mentioned in 1127 and later rebuilt in the sixteenth and eighteenth centuries, it appears just to the left of Castel S. Angelo in a fresco by Benozzo Gozzoli (fig. 208): a good-sized basilica, preceded by a narthex and obviously of twelfth-century date. Likewise, the apse of the small church of Monte Giordano, SS. Simeone e Giuda, seems to date from a twelfth-century rebuilding. It looks as if a program of rehabilitation had been carried out consistently in the area, beginning in the eleventh century and continuing far into the twelfth. The great number of parish churches and the lawsuits concerning parochial boundaries point to the density of population and of housing all over the area. By the last third of the fifteenth century, the Strozzi map records the main features in the area of the Tiber bend: churches; towered mansions, such as Monte Giordano; piazze—Piazza Navona, Campo de' Fiori, Piazza di Parione, presumably today's Piazza S. Pantaleo; and the streets converging toward Ponte S. Angelo (fig. 207). At the same time, Gozzoli's fresco renders vividly the crowding of buildings in that quarter of town, overshadowed by the Pantheon and, far back, the Capitol and Aracoeli (fig. 208).

The expansion of the abitato westward into the Tiber bend in the course of the eleventh and twelfth centuries was but a natural development. The Borgo magnetically drew the town on the east bank toward Ponte S. Angelo, the only connecting link. The Borgo sheltered Saint Peter's grave and his basilica; it was there that pilgrims were lodged and fed; its booths, stands and shops formed the commercial center of Rome; money-changers and bankers were to be found along its streets; and, from the early thirteenth century on, the papacy had established a residence there. Business on the east bank naturally would be attracted in the direction of Ponte S. Angelo opposite the commercial center in the Borgo. Indeed, one would like to think that Piazza del Ponte, the square on the left bank of the Tiber opposite Castel S. Angelo, and the neighboring streets were taken over by merchants and bankers long before they are listed there from the late fourteenth century on; that Via dei Banchi Vecchi was Merchants' Street, *Via Mercatoria*, continuing the business district of the Borgo two or three hundred years prior to the documented appearance of the name; and that inns had started to open up in the neighborhood. While first mentioned in the fourteenth century and crowded in the area in the fifteenth, the monopoly claimed by the innkeepers of the Borgo in 1235 suggests unwelcome competition from the east bank of the Tiber.

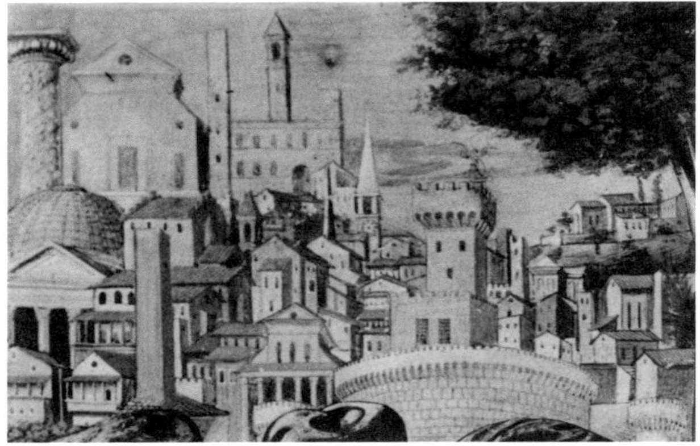

208. View of abitato inside Tiber bend, as of 1465, Benozzo Gozzoli, S. Gimignano, S. Agostino, detail

As the abitato expanded westward, filling the Tiber bend, the built-up areas around the Pantheon and from the Ripa to the foot of the Capitoline and westward to Via Arenula and the Theatre of Pompey gradually fused, grew more densely settled, and expanded. The Ripa, from the river bank opposite the Tiber Island to the south foot of the Capitoline Hill, and the island itself from the eleventh century on, flourished anew under the powerful patronage of the Pierleoni. S. Maria in Porticu was consecrated in 1073; a small church, sheltering a venerated image of the Virgin, it was transferred in 1665 to a site nearby and replaced by the splendid large church of S. Maria in Campitelli. Another church, S.Nicola in Carcere, was consecrated in 1128, apparently in place of an older sanctuary. At the northern tip of the island, the church of S. Giovanni Calabita, extant as early as 1018, seems to have been rebuilt in the first half of the twelfth century (fig. 209). Southward, the old and seemingly small church of S. Bartolomeo, founded by Otto III, gave way, whether in 1113 or half a century later, to the large basilica that exists there today, redecorated but substantially unchanged. Close at hand, by the early eleventh century the bishop of Porto owned a manse, a *curtis*; around it must have developed a densely built-up settlement. A hundred years later the Pierleoni took over and fortified the island, and it remained a stronghold for many centuries. A view done by the Escurial draughtsman shortly before 1500 shows the church of S. Giovanni Calibita and the tower of S. Bartolomeo rising behind the crenelations of a tall, fortified mansion with a tower facing the Ripa and commanding the bridge, the ancient *Pons Cestius*, called *Ponte Quattro Capi* in the Middle Ages or *Pons Judeorum*. The tower, first mentioned in 1192, and at least part of the mansion survive to this day (fig. 240) and the brick masonry of the tower suggests a twelfth-century date. It may have been built by the Pierleoni; by 1300 it fell to the Caetani.

Like the core of the abitato on the east bank, and the settlement on the island, Trastevere seems to have expanded and become more densely built up from the eleventh century through the fifteenth. The successive stages of its growth are not as clearly documented as those of some neighborhoods east of the river. Around S. Maria in Trastevere, as early as 1038 houses were built wall to wall, and by the twelfth century all of Trastevere seems to have been closely settled—but one wants to recall how shallow and short the built-up area remained till the sixteenth century: nowhere, ex-

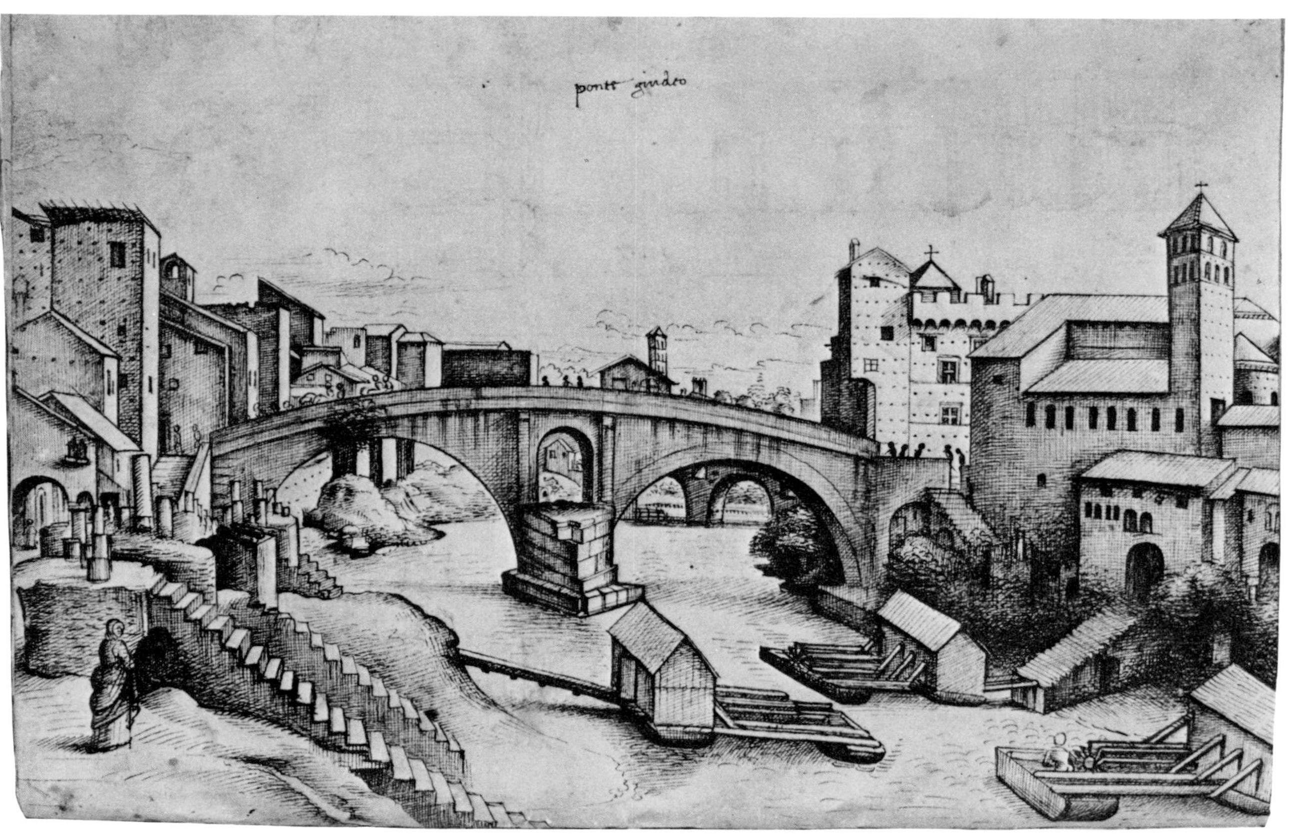

209. Tiber Island and Bridge of Fabricius, as of ca. 1495, looking downstream, with floating mills in foreground and, right, medieval church of S. Giovanni Calabita, drawing, *Escurialensis*, fol. 27[v]

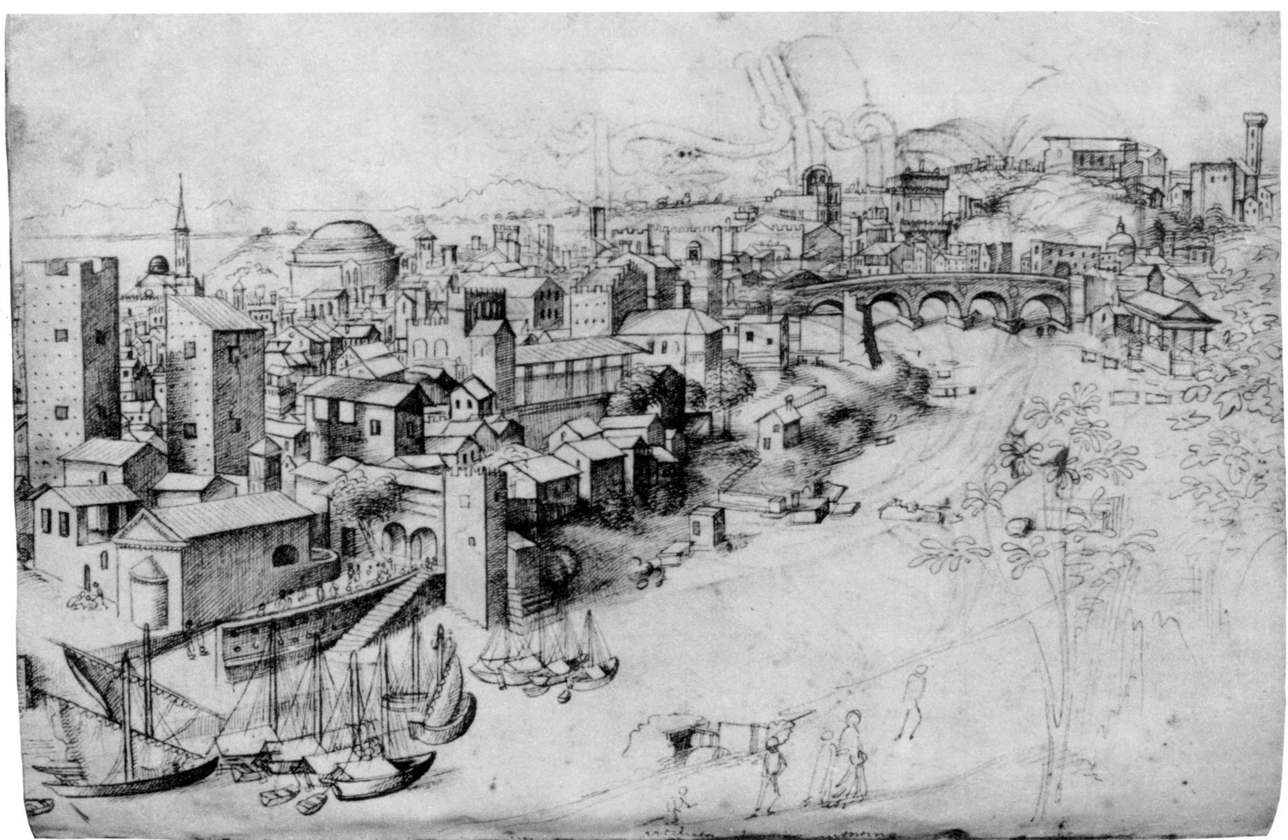

210. View from Aventine toward Trastevere and, in background, left bank abitato, as of ca. 1495, drawing, *Escurialensis*, fol. 56v

cept at its northern end behind S. Maria in Trastevere, did it reach to the foot of the Gianicolo; the old convent of SS. Cosma e Damiano in Mica Aurea, now S. Cosimato, and S. Francesco a Ripa were far out in the fields; no houses extended west of S. Cecilia; and downstream from the Ripa Grande there were only gardens along the river bank. Within the settled area, though, big mansions and towers owned by great families must have risen from an early time. They continued to be built into the fourteenth and fifteenth centuries; a view from the Aventine done by the Escurial draughtsman shortly before 1500 shows them rising high: isolated towers, towered compounds, and large houses with stepped, crenelated gables, as one usually sees them in the Low Countries or Germany rather than in Rome, but late medieval in any event (fig. 210). Indeed, in the eleventh and twelfth centuries some of the greatest Roman families lived in or came to prominence from Trastevere: the Pierleoni, Papareschi, Stefaneschi, Tebaldi. Their towers, we shall see, rose all through the quarter, remaining in their hands through the Middle Ages, long after the families, the Pierleoni for instance, had established their main residences on the east bank in the town proper. At the same time, Trastevere was at least in the eleventh century a businessmen's quarter; time and again merchants, *negotiatores*, presumably living there, appear as witnesses to deeds made out for the convent of SS. Cosma e Damiano in Mica Aurea on the outskirts of Trastevere, along with local artisans, potters, cobblers, wheelwrights. Some of the *negotiatores* may well have been small traders, possibly with stands in the Borgo not far away, or with shops in Trastevere. But others, like the "*vir magnificus negoticus*," mentioned in 1041, would have been big merchants or possibly financiers. The Pierleoni, in the eleventh century, certainly were. Whether or not there is any link between the noble families and the merchants or financiers, or for that matter the Jews living in Trastevere, must remain an open question. The Pierleoni, the leading Trastevere clan, constitute just such a triple link; but we simply do not know whether any other noble Trasteverini started in, or early went into, business.

As the core of the abitato grew more coherent and more densely settled, and moved into the Tiber bend, it also expanded along its edges (fig. 211). To the north in the Campo Marzio, housing had grown dense by the twelfth century. In 1194 the nunnery of S. Maria in Campo Marzio owned more than 150 houses in the area, half of them close to its own buildings; others spread north almost as far as Piazza Nicosia and Piazza Borghese, where in 1139 the oratory of S. Cecilia de Posterula had been built; replaced in the eighteenth century by the small church of the Madonna del Divino Amore, it still retains its Romanesque campanile. Eastward, the houses owned by the convent extended as far as the neighborhood of S. Silvestro in Capite. The houses around the convent cannot have been other than row houses, built close together. One or two houses of uncertain medieval date survive in Piazza Campo Marzio—their colonnades with Ionic capitals and a straight architrave are still embedded in the walls of a later palazzo. Nonetheless, large spaces must have remained empty in the very heart of the medieval town: as late as about 1280 the Dominicans could build their huge new church, S. Maria sopra Minerva, and the adjoining convent over or near the ruins of the ancient sanctuary of Minerva. Located just east of the Pantheon and no more than

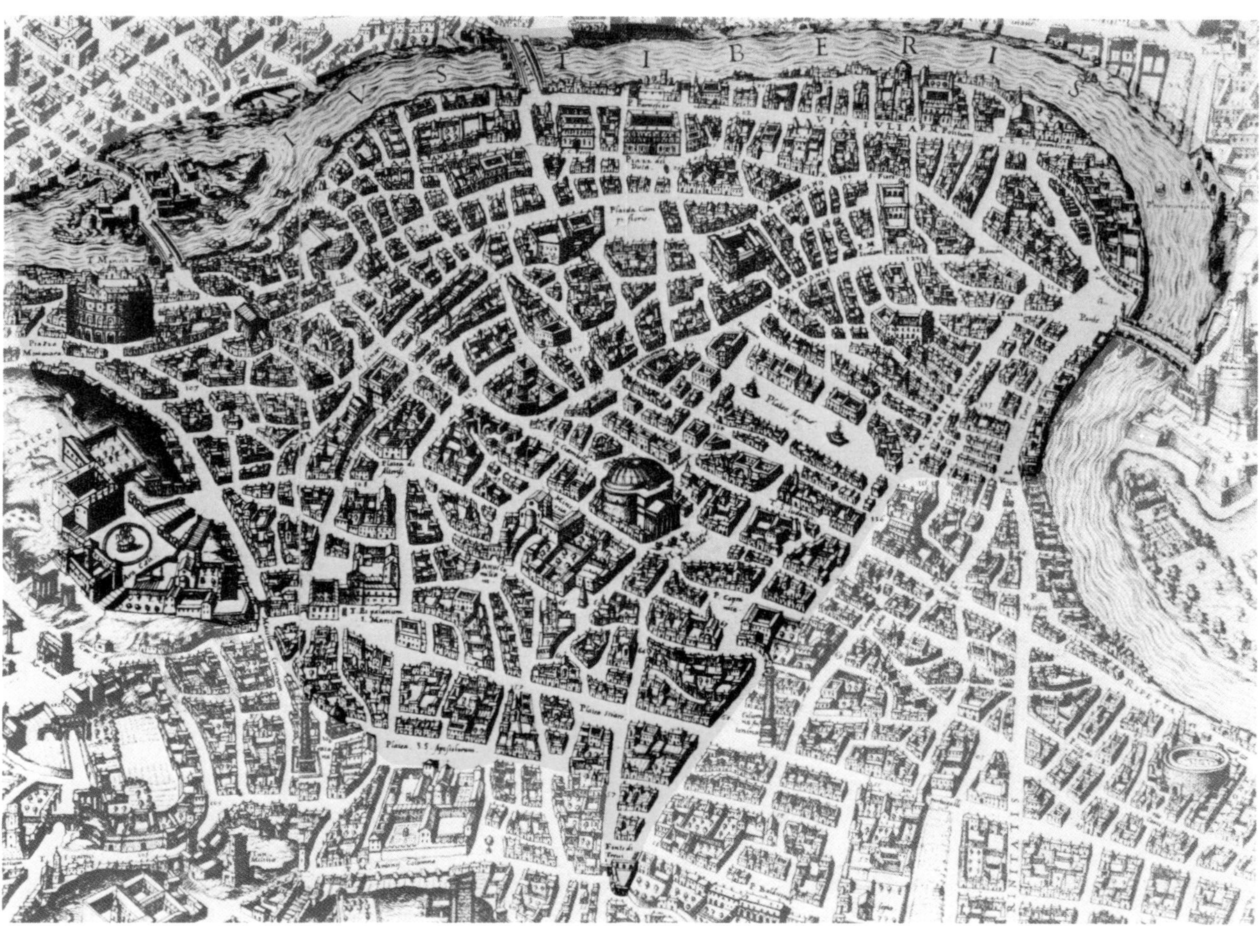

211. Map of Rome, 1577, Du Pérac-Lafréry, detail showing the abitato (post-medieval parts shaded)

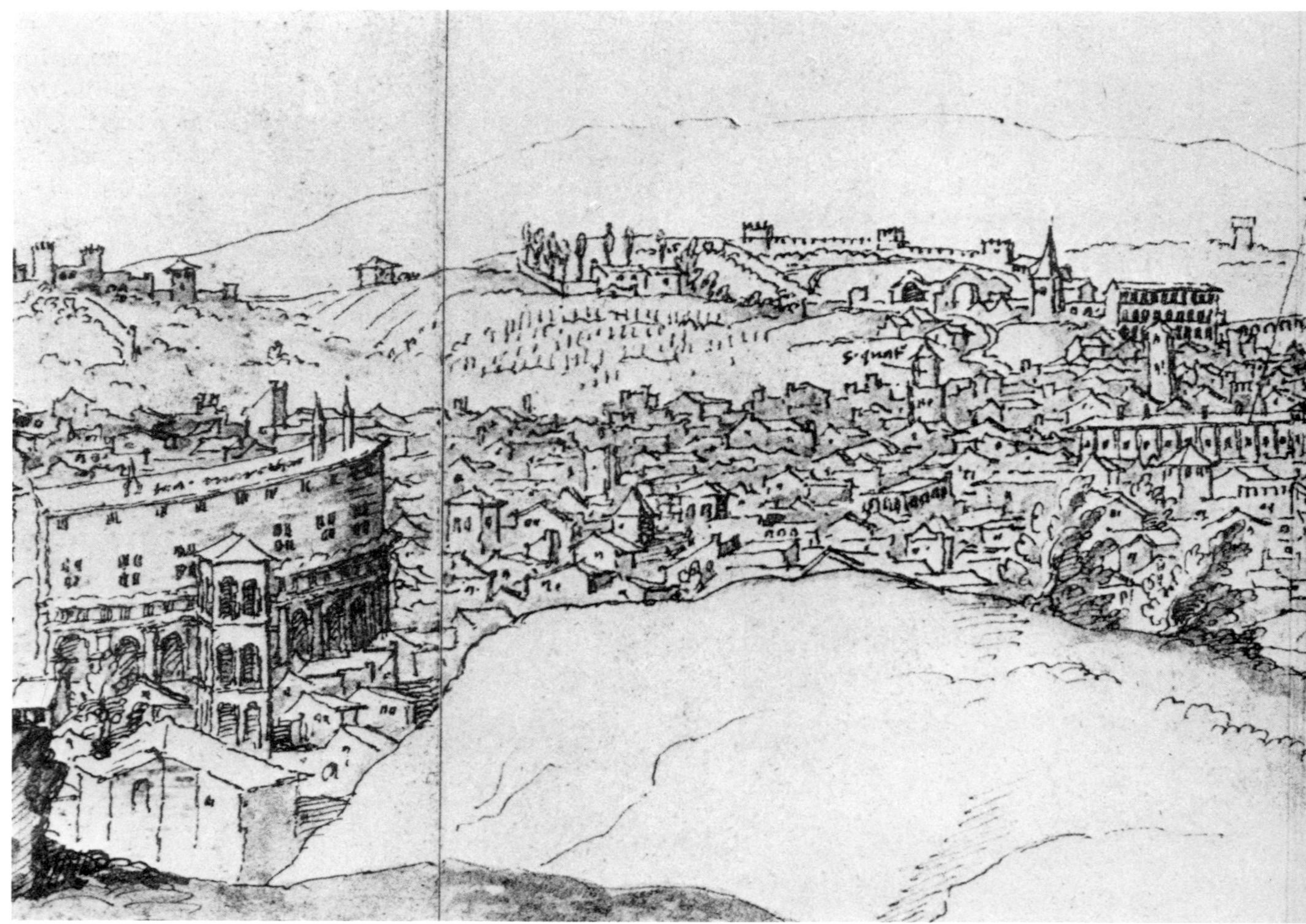

212, 213. View of abitato from Monte Caprino, as of 1534-1536, details, drawing, Marten van Heemskerck, Berlin,

a few hundred steps west of the Corso, the neighborhood would seem still at that time to have retained a suburban note. The Dominicans, as behooved a mendicant order, would seek out just such a site on the rim of town. But then, the core of the abitato by the late thirteenth century would have been all built over and would no longer offer space (figs. 212, 213). Nor were new churches needed anymore in the overcrowded center; and, indeed, none were built until the fifteenth and sixteenth centuries.

As the abitato was built up more densely, the water supply would become a problem. The Acqua Vergine never reached further than the Pantheon, if indeed it still serviced that quarter; its major outlet remained east of the Corso—Fontana Trevi. Elsewhere, wells and water from the Tiber would have to provide. Wells, indeed, were apparently scattered all over and far beyond the main inhabited areas: leases and sales contracts mention them below the cliff of the Aventine, south of S. Maria in Cosmedin, and near S. Maria Nova. Others are recorded in street names: Vicolo dei Pozzi; Via del Pozzo; Piazza or Via del Pozzetto. They appear from the neighborhood of Tor de' Conti to S. Maria in Via and in Trastevere; and in the Tiber bend near S. Maria in Vallicella.

Eastward, too, the core of the abitato expanded. A short distance across the Corso from what is now Piazza Colonna, a settlement had started to form quite early around the Trevi Fountain. By the middle of the tenth century a few small churches had been established in that neighborhood at the foot of the Quirinal, as outposts in the fields of S. Silvestro in Capite.

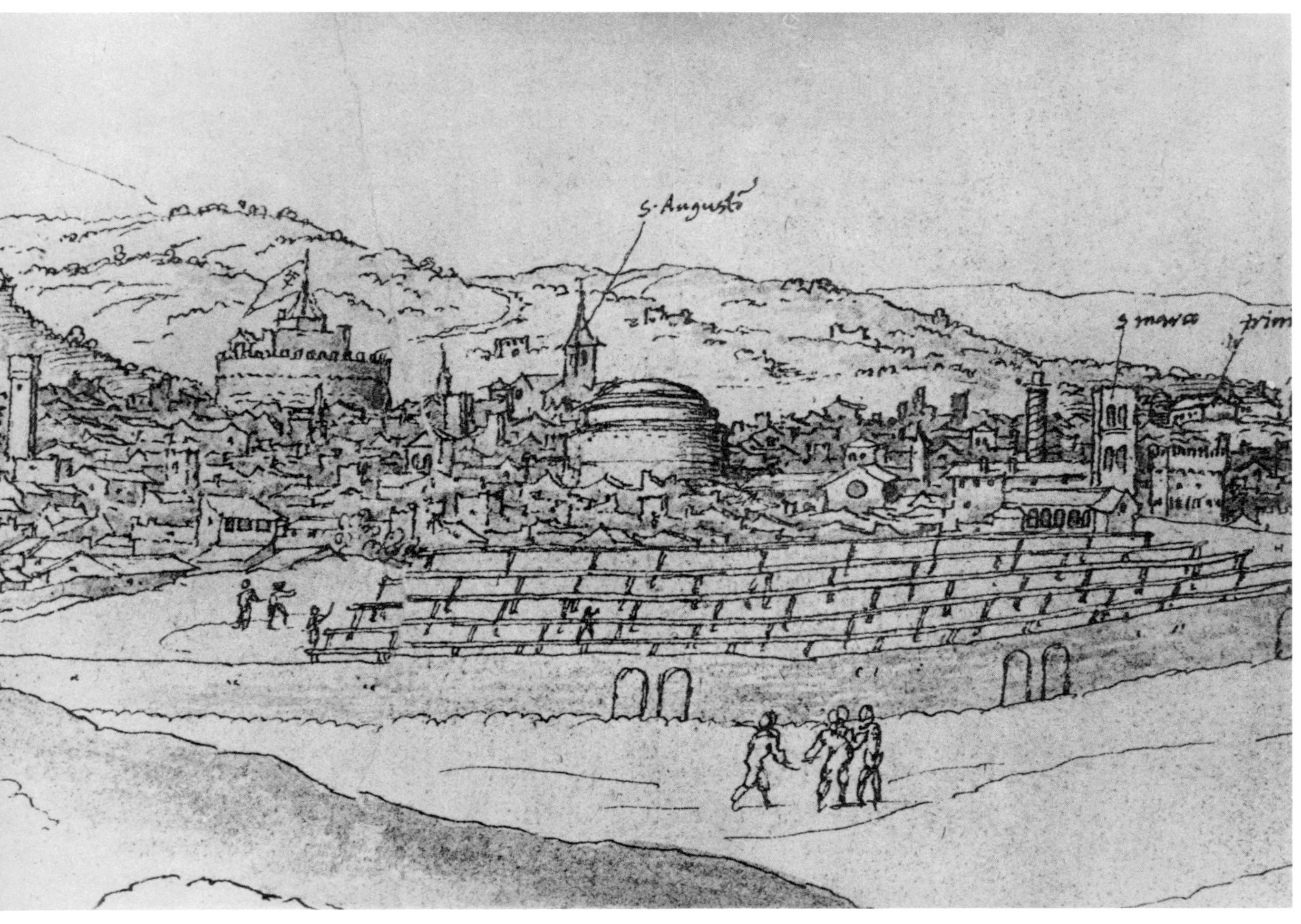

Kupferstichkabinett, 79 D2A, fols. 91^{v}, 92^{r}

The old hostel founded by Belisarius, though probably no longer functioning, and its oratory by the fountain, S. Maria in Xenodochio, may have been a focal point. By 1042 the church of S. Maria in Via is documented for the first time; apparently a small chapel then, it was replaced in the sixteenth century by the large if not very exciting church behind the Galleria. Throughout the eleventh century a policy of settling the area was apparently pursued, no longer by S. Silvestro in Capite alone, but by S. Maria in Via Lata and the adjoining nunnery of S. Ciriaco, by then apparently the owner of large tracts of land in that neighborhood. In 1019 the convent of S. Ciriaco sold four small lots "to build houses adjoining S. Maria in Xenodochio," tiny houses obviously. In 1042 a house was sold, "recently built . . . as a dwelling . . . with apple trees . . . not far from the church of S. Maria in Via." By 1065 real estate and cottages, called *casarine*, were being sold further up the Quirinal Hill near the marble horses. The area apparently remained semirural for a long time. Houses near the Trevi Fountain belonging to S. Silvestro in Capite far into the thirteenth century were one-storied with gardens, some having an extra cottage in the garden; or they were simple cottages with gardens; or else, as in the case of a lot at the north foot of the Quirinal as late as 1217, located between two gardens and containing vaults, perhaps ancient ones, there were several cottages and a garden. Two row houses now opposite the Trevi Fountain would seem to date from a time when the rural note of this Trevi suburb was disappearing; their Ionic capitals and clumsy columns supporting trabeated continuous ground-floor porticoes suggest a thirteenth- or possibly fourteenth-century date. By and large, though, the rim of the abitato retained its rustic character far into the High Middle Ages. The property of S. Silvestro in Capite, extending north of Piazza Colonna to S. Lorenzo in Lucina, was given over to gardens with small cottages: one had a tent in place of a roof in 1207 and still in 1229. It was all suburban and practically open country.

The ceremonials of papal processions indicate with some precision the main streets through the core of town. The earliest ceremonial preserved; the order of Benedictus Canonicus, was compiled around 1140-1143, but it is based on older traditions. The pope on his way to his coronation descended from the Lateran by way of the Via Maior, now Via S. Giovanni in Laterano, to S. Clemente and to the Colosseum; veering northwest, he passed through the arch in the rear of the Forum of Nerva and continued along the huge rear wall of the Forum of Augustus and up the Salita del Grillo to Torre delle Milizie and along the southwest slope of the Quirinal to SS. Apostoli. Crossing the Corso near Via dell'Umiltà, called *Via Quirinalis* in the Middle Ages, he passed S. Maria in Aquiro, traversed Via di Campo Marzio, and along Via delle Stellette, Via dell'Orso, and Tor di Nona he reached Ponte S. Angelo to proceed toward St. Peter's. Conversely, on his return, he took a route through the southern sector of town. From Ponte S. Angelo he passed slightly west of the Arch of Theodosius, Arcadius, and Honorius—it stood near what is now the end of Via Giulia but was then confused with the Arch of Valentinian and Gratian further downstream—and by Via dei Banchi Vecchi reached the "Palace of Cromatius," an ancient ruin covered with mosaic, we are told, where a delegation of Jews made obeisance. He then proceeded through Via del Pellegrino, turned north to the Parione quarter and street—now Via del Governo Vecchio and its eastward continuation, which has been swallowed up by a stretch of Corso Vittorio Emanuele—and finally passed between the Theatre of Pompey to the south and the Arch of Alexander to the north, the latter unidentified but possibly part of his Thermae. Through the Thermae of Agrippa, the *porticus Agrippinus*, behind the Pantheon, the papal procession continued a short way north, only to return south and reach S. Marco by way of Via delle Botteghe Oscure. From there across the Forum along the Via Sacra, it arrived at the Colosseum and ascended to the Lateran.

Fifty years later, the ceremonial of Cencius Camerarius traced what appears to be roughly the same route. But the picture is more lively. On the piazza below the steps of St. Peter's, the pope passed the stands of the straw vendors—bedding for pilgrims and feed for horses—the money changers, the candle and torch sellers. Through the main street of the Borgo he reached Castel S. Angelo and crossed the bridge. From there the route of the procession and the places where money was distributed are marked in the ceremonial by houses and streets rather than by churches and ancient monuments: "the arch"—possibly that of Theodosius—"where there is the house of Johannes Pauli"; the house of Stefano Nizo; the marble house; "the tower of Stephanus Serpetri, which is at the start of Parione . . . and where the Jews make obeisance" on Piazza del Campo, now dell'Orologio—the site for the Jews' audience had apparently changed; the house of Massimo—perhaps one of the Massimi; the palace of Cencio Musca Inpunga "in Via de Papa"; the tower of Odo Bonfigli—the family was minor nobility; "the house of John with the Clogs and the adjoining cottage of Nicholas, son of Hugo"; Via dei Calcararii; the almond tree—a street intersection; and so on to S. Marco and further east. At the coronation procession, arches, presumably festooned, spanned the streets and house owners responsible were remunerated. The buildings, one gets the impression, stood higgledy-piggledy, cottages, mansions, ordinary dwellings, and towers; and since the ceremonial lists only a selection of houses along the route, and those presumably chosen among the more important, it seems likely that the buildings stood close together, in rows or only short distances apart. One can see the procession winding its way through the streets, under the festoons of the arches, stopping here and there, the house owners receiving their money presents and the

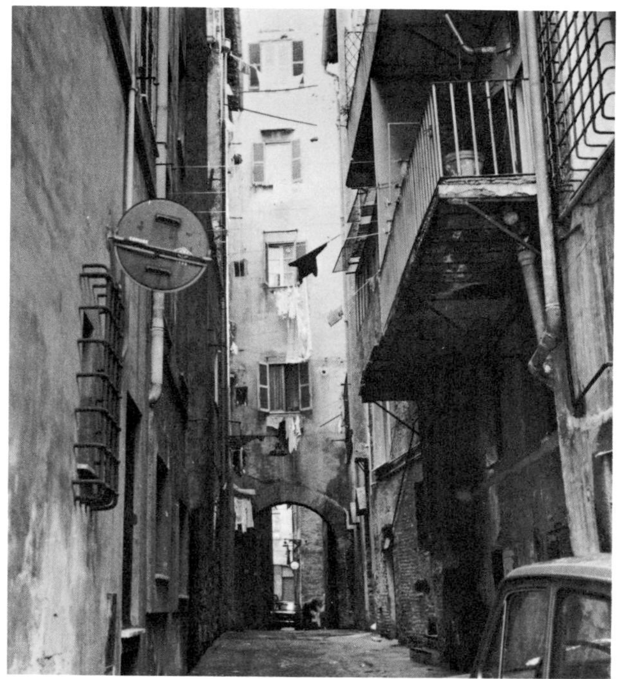

214. Vicolo dei Tre Archi

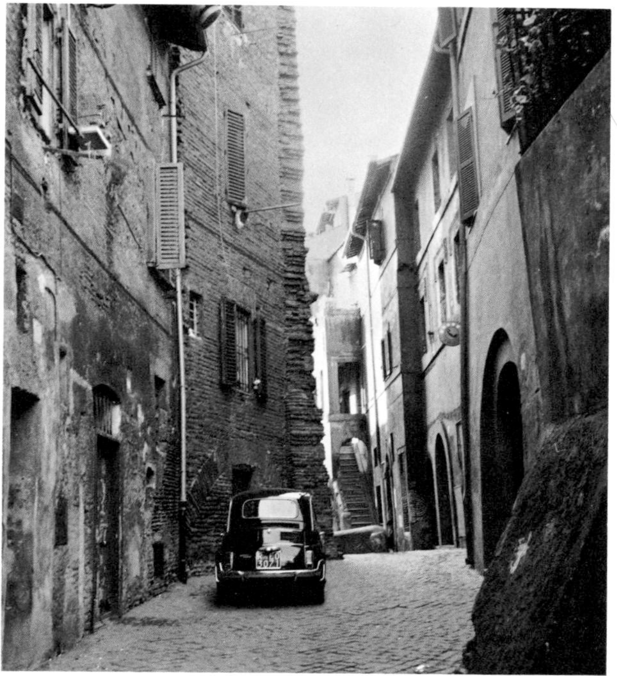

215. Vicolo dell'Atleta, outside stairs of medieval house in background

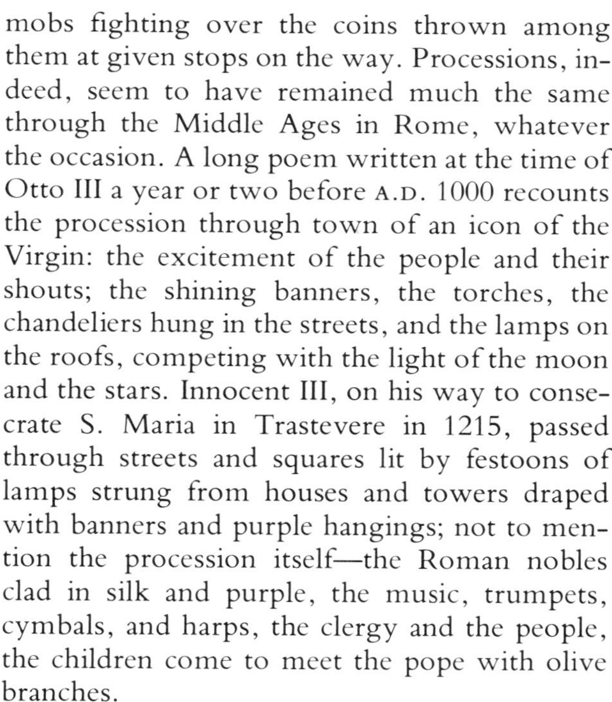

mobs fighting over the coins thrown among them at given stops on the way. Processions, indeed, seem to have remained much the same through the Middle Ages in Rome, whatever the occasion. A long poem written at the time of Otto III a year or two before A.D. 1000 recounts the procession through town of an icon of the Virgin: the excitement of the people and their shouts; the shining banners, the torches, the chandeliers hung in the streets, and the lamps on the roofs, competing with the light of the moon and the stars. Innocent III, on his way to consecrate S. Maria in Trastevere in 1215, passed through streets and squares lit by festoons of lamps strung from houses and towers draped with banners and purple hangings; not to mention the procession itself—the Roman nobles clad in silk and purple, the music, trumpets, cymbals, and harps, the clergy and the people, the children come to meet the pope with olive branches.

Everyday reality showed the streets in a different light. The houses lining the streets of medieval Rome, to be sure, have been remodeled time and again over the past six hundred or seven hundred years. But the streets themselves survive. Street systems are conservative and the majority of old thoroughfares and alleys in the core of town from the Corso to the Tiber bend and south to the island still retain the direction and often the width of their medieval predecessors. They are crooked and winding, and where they ran straight for a stretch it was so noticeable as to invite the name *via recta*, "straight street." Narrow alleys had been a feature already of ancient Rome—the one running between the two Roman houses in the excavations under S. Clemente gives an idea; there is just enough room for one pedestrian to pass comfortably between the two buildings. Whether ancient or medieval, though, it seems that streets were narrow and dark—Via del Pellegrino, a major thoroughfare in the Middle Ages, is just 5 meters wide; Via dei Coronari, 4.70 meters; others are narrower still—Vicolo della Cuccagna, 2.80 meters wide; Vicolo del Divino Amore, 2.40 meters; Vicolo Savello, 2.30 meters; Vicolo dei Tre Archi, 2.35 meters (fig. 214); while in Trastevere in 1250 two streets measured only 1.30 meters and 1.80 meters respectively and Vicolo S.

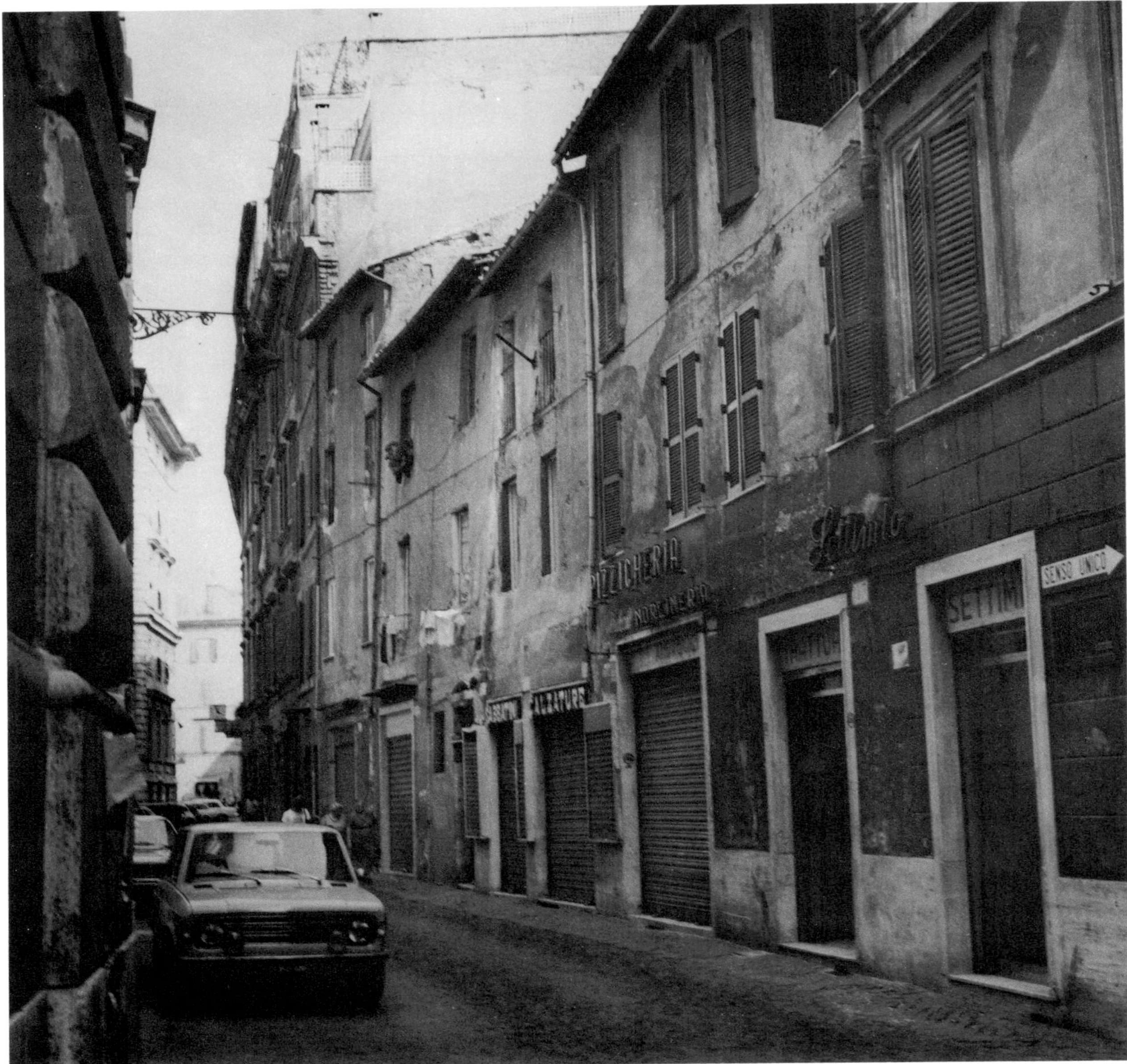

216. Via del Pellegrino, houses rebuilt

Trifone off Via dei Coronari is to this day but 1.38 meters wide. As the medieval abitato was filling up more densely in the core of town, around the Pantheon, on either side of Via dei Coronari and Via della Scrofa, around Campo dei Fiori, in the Campo Marzio, and in Trastevere, need for more housing caused every nook and cranny to be exploited. Houses packed closely wall to wall, narrow and two, three, or even four floors high, lined the streets. Vicolo dell'Atleta to the present day preserves its medieval aspect, notwithstanding the rebuilding of most houses in later centuries (fig. 215), as does Via del Pellegrino (fig. 216), or for that matter a side street in Trastevere, Via della Fonte d'Olio (fig. 217). As the abitato filled up, gardens and empty lots disappeared, though never completely; a few plots with trees crammed in between the houses or even a goodly sized garden are seen in the very center of town, near the

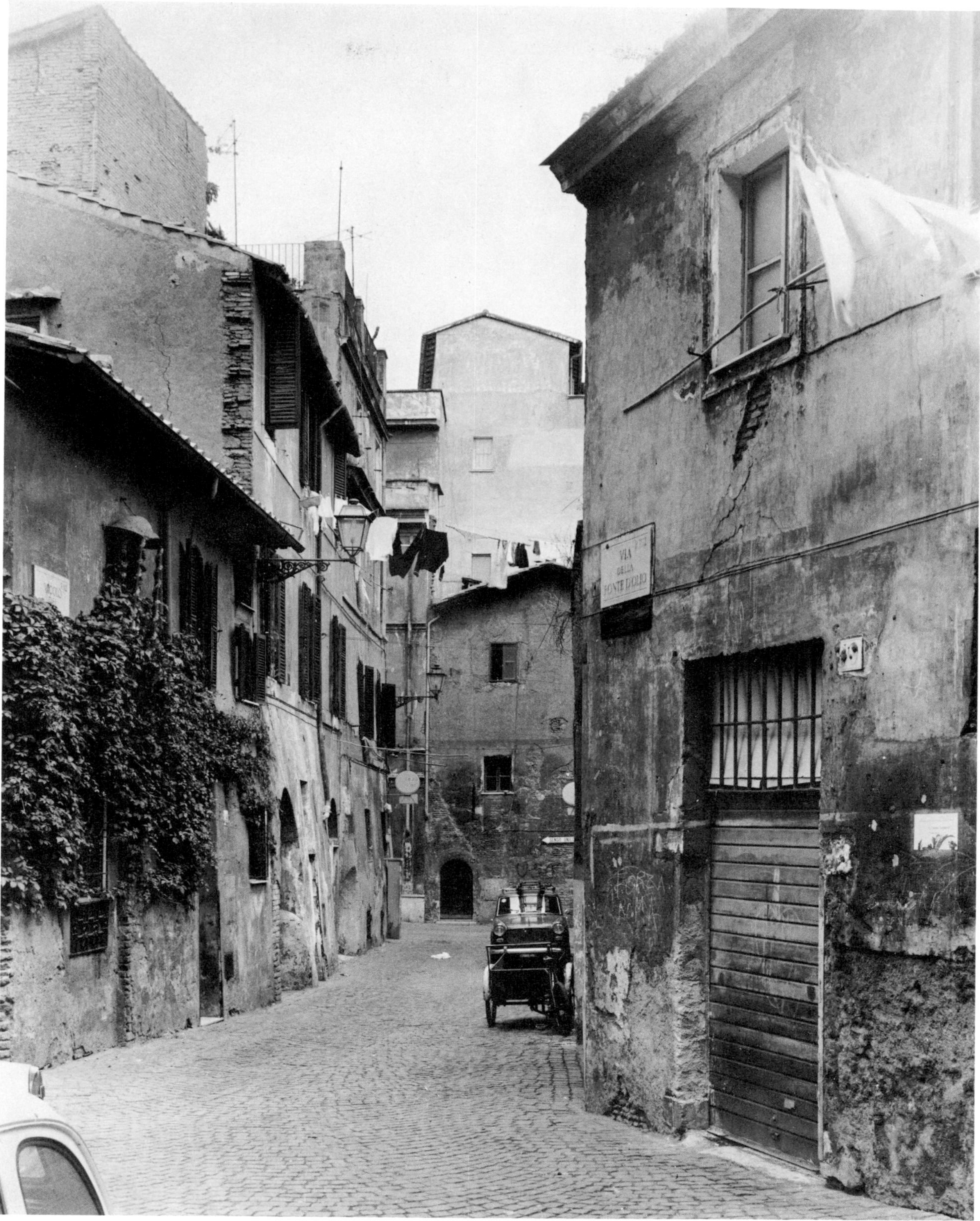

217. Via della Fonte d'Olio, Trastevere, medieval street, houses later rebuilt

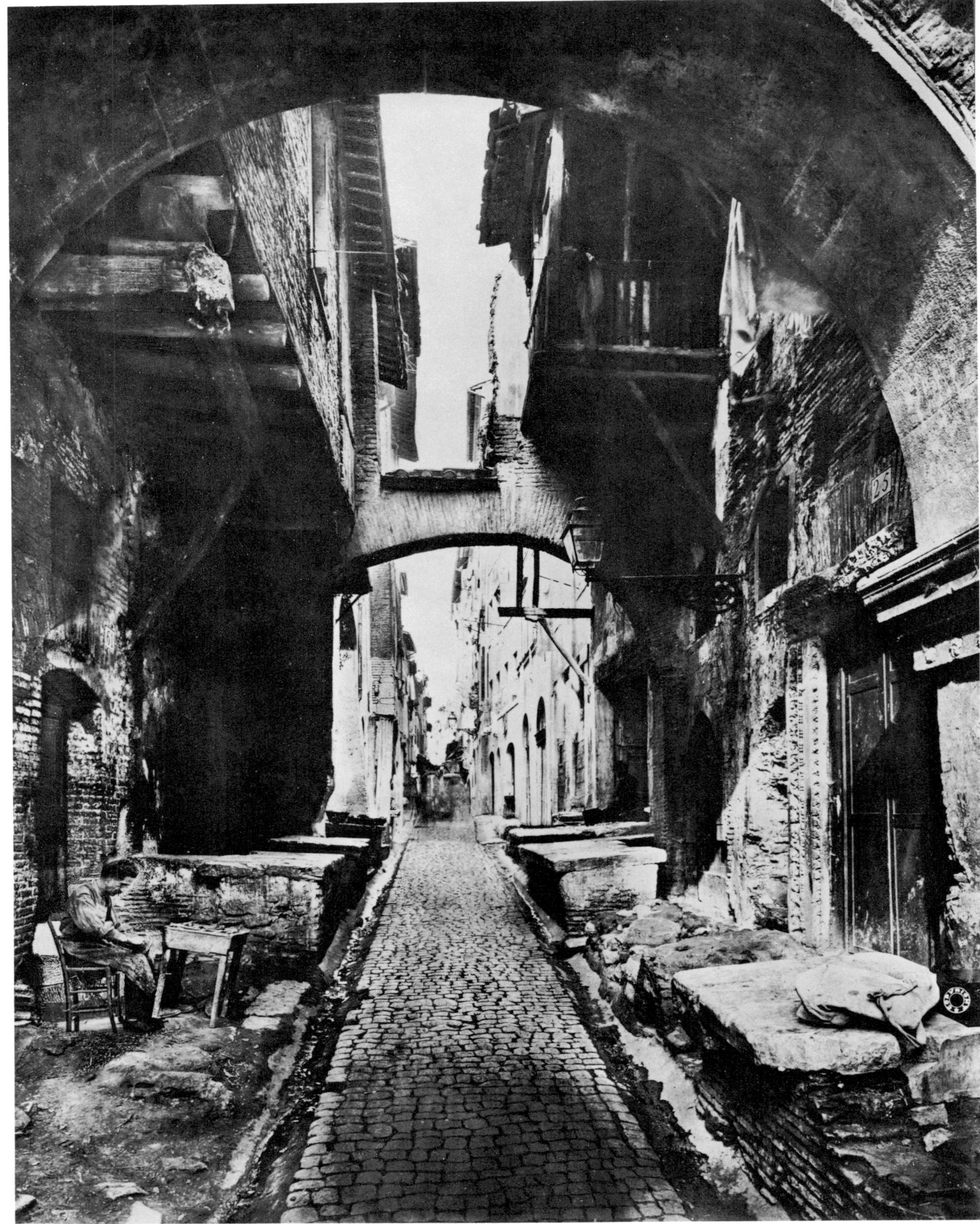

218. Street in Ghetto from S. Angelo in Pescheria, with fishmongers' slabs in foreground, ca. 1850

Pantheon or near Campo dei Fiori, behind Palazzo Spada, still in views and maps of the sixteenth century. But by and large through the Middle Ages the abitato became the labyrinth of houses large and small, tiny piazze, open or enclosed, courtyards with or without wells, narrow and dark passages still to be seen in Via degli Osti, Vicolo dei Tre Archi, or between Via di Monte Brianzo and Via della Scrofa near the Albergo dei Due Torri. Streets were spanned by deep arches to secure opposite structures or to support a connecting wing. Dozens have been lost in the cleaning up of Rome in the late nineteenth century (fig. 218); but the Arco dei Tolomei survives in Trastevere off Via dei Salumi, as do the Arco dei Sinibaldi linking Via Monterone and Via Torre Argentina, and still others in Piazza dei Cenci and, as the name implies, in the Vicolo dei Tre Archi off Via dei Coronari (fig. 219). Arches, in the thirteenth century anyway, had to be high enough, as stipulated for an alley in Trastevere in 1250, "for a woman carrying on her head a large and on top of that a smaller container to pass underneath." Crowding in the abitato would have increased in times of prosperity in the twelfth and thirteenth centuries. Deeds of lease and sale and inheritance settlements convey some idea of the cramming of buildings, large and small, onto and into one another. Maps and views still of the eighteenth and nineteenth centuries depict the density of such overbuilding. The alleys and courtyards of the Ghetto as they survived until eighty years ago only reflect a situation that prevailed all through the medieval abitato (fig. 220). The older quarters of Florence, or better still of Venice, with their narrow alleys, *sottoporteghi* and pitlike *corti* show what Rome, too, must have looked like in the thirteenth and fourteenth centuries. They also convey an idea, as do the settlements or inheritances so vividly presented and explained by Robert Brentano, of how the rich and the poor lived side by side in the same building complex: the owner in a colonnaded palazzo and house; a scribe, a saddler, a barber's widow, a goldsmith in the same buildings; shops, supposedly with living quarters in the palazzo, in all likelihood under its colonnade. Or else, such *popolo minuto* lived in houses built against the

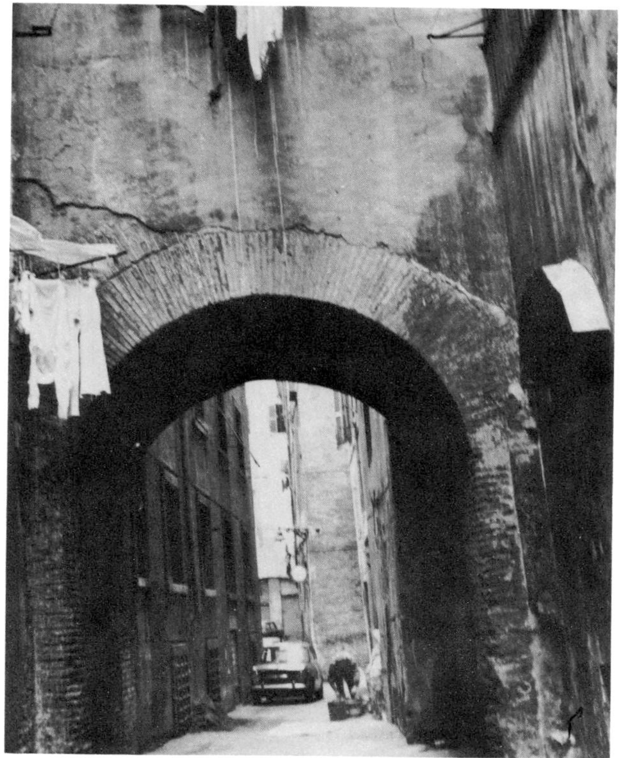

219. Arch in Vicolo dei Tre Archi

walls of a noble mansion: next to a crenelated palace are the modest dwellings of a shoemaker, a smith, a scribe, a spice dealer. The Savelli, in the fortified Theatre of Marcellus, leased the vaults on the ground floor to butchers and craftsmen; and the canons of S. Angelo in Pescheria leased the stone benches in the portico to fishmongers (fig. 218). Income from ground rent was welcome and needed; and, as Professor Lewine pointed out to me, "so were the people themselves, henchmen in times of internal warfare."

Narrow streets, hard to negotiate and overcrowded, were further cramped by projecting buildings and porches and littered with offal from butchers' and cobblers' shops; households threw garbage on the streets, dirty water from dyers and tanners spilled over them. Maintaining and keeping them free from such encumbrances was the concern of the municipal au-

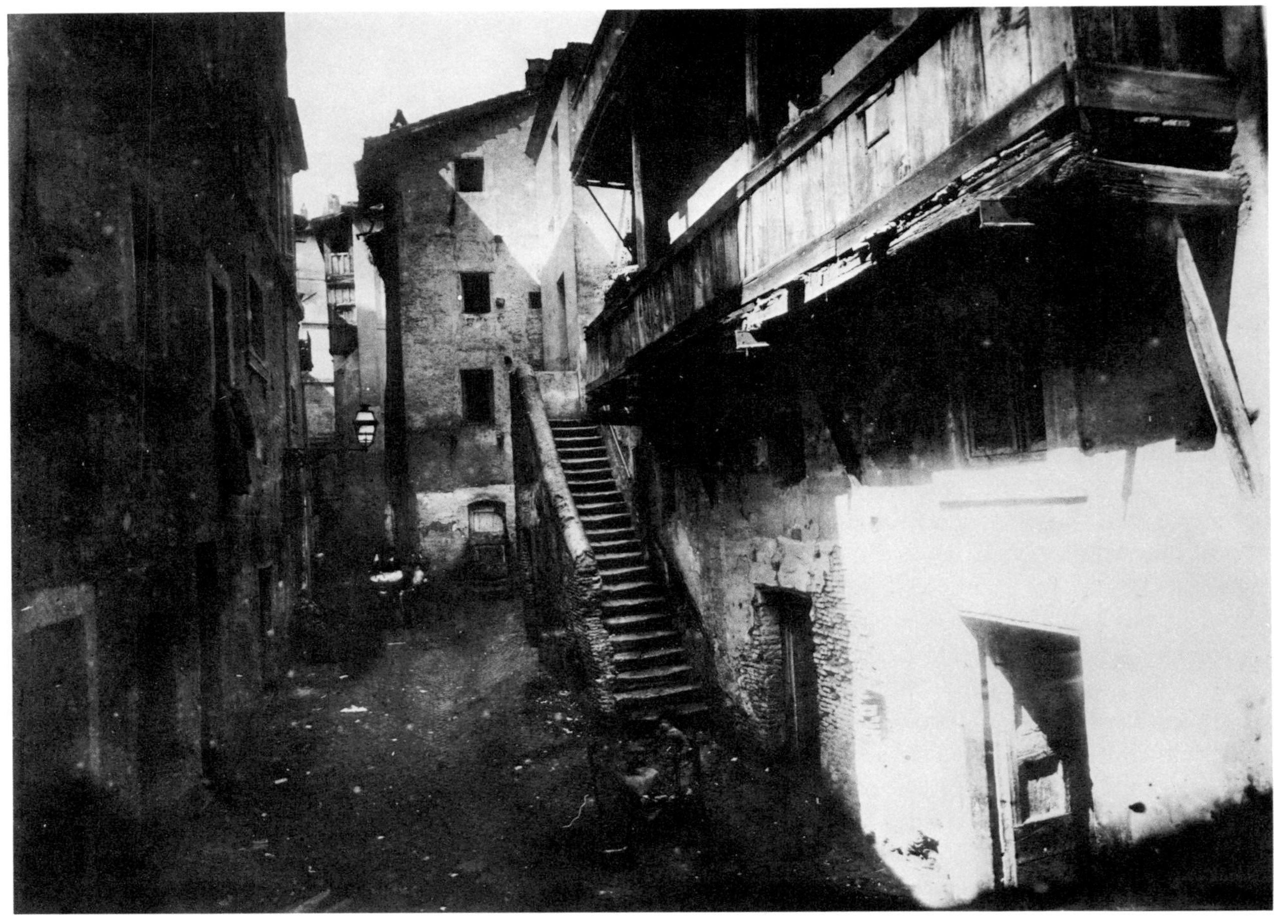

220. Via delle Azimelle, Ghetto, prior to 1890, Museo di Roma

thority in charge, the *magistri stratarum, maestri di strada*. Documented without interruption from 1233 through the eighteenth century, they were originally elected by the Senate, rather than being appointed by the pope as was the case from 1425 on. However, they may have been set up earlier in the thirteenth century or indeed after the middle of the twelfth, when their parent body, the Senate, was reconstituted. Their duties and powers, while constantly enlarged and clarified, remained fundamentally those stipulated in 1233: "to decide on all questions concerning walls, houses, streets, public squares and their parts within the city and beyond, and all structures in general." That meant in particular preventing stands and porticoes from projecting beyond a set limit into streets and squares: up to 1.50 meters on St. Peter's Square and on the street approaching the square from the north, the ruga Francigena, clearly of considerable width; less on narrower streets. It meant watching building lines and boundaries of building lots; having refuse removed from an empty lot; forcing a firm of dyers—Jews incidentally—to have a gutter dug to drain the dirty water from the street in front of their shop. In the fourteenth century, they had further to prevent private parties from occupying parts of a street; to forbid water spouts shedding water or dirt on the street; to have fences or temporary structures removed; to maintain aqueducts; to have the street cleaned weekly, the refuse to be thrown in the river; and, lastly, to regain control of public property occupied by private parties, such as "vineyards, gardens, triumphal arches and bridges, structures [presumably ancient], and walls." All this conveys a picture of conditions on the streets of medieval Rome: covered with dirt, unpaved, impassable in rain and bad weather; flooded time and again by the Tiber; congested by beasts of burden and by porters carrying their loads; filled with obstacles, from porches and stands to fences; and taken over all along by craftsmen at work in front of their shops or by housewives and maids doing their washing and cooking on the street. All this continued through the Middle Ages and after, notwithstanding decrees to the contrary, ever repeated and hence clearly in vain. The street, after all, was in the Middle Ages an extension of the house rather than a self-contained entity, as it more or less still is in the inner cities of Naples, Jerusalem, and Damascus, and as it was in Rome a hundred years ago.

At the eastern edge of the abitato, the Capitoline Hill, the very center of ancient Rome, remained neglected through the early Middle Ages, part of the disabitato rather than of town. Radical transformation came in the middle of the twelfth century, in the wake of the rebellion in which the people of Rome, first against the papacy then in a compromise with it, claimed their part in deciding and running the city's affairs.

It is hard today to envisage the Capitol in any but the final design of Michelangelo: the trapezoid *area Capitolina*, facing west and carrying on its oval center the statue of Marcus Aurelius; the three framing palaces, the Museo Capitolino and the Palazzo dei Conservatori flanking the Palazzo del Senatore; S. Maria in Aracoeli higher up to the left, likewise facing west; the ramp, the *cordonata*, ascending from Piazza Aracoeli to the area Capitolina. One keeps forgetting that in Roman times the principal buildings of the Capitol faced east overlooking the Forum: the towering arcaded front of the Tabularium, rising from the east cliff of the rock and now carrying the Palazzo del Senatore; the Temple of Jupiter on the southward extension of the hill, Monte Caprino as it was called still in the sixteenth century, terminated by the Tarpeian Rock; the Temple of Juno Moneta, on the northern excrescence, where the church of S. Maria in Aracoeli now stands; and, between the two humps, north and south, a patrician house and several minor shrines. The main approaches, too, were from the east; the paved road, which, after restoration, winds up Monte Caprino again today; and a narrow, steep staircase, ascending north of the Tabularium. A third ascent, climbing the west slope of the hill, was apparently of only secondary importance; it led to the dell between the two excrescences of the hill and perhaps to the market that in late antiquity was held on the Capitol. The exact site of that market is unknown, but wherever it was located, it seems merely to have extended uphill the market area of the Forum. A large apartment house leaned against the western foot of the hill—its ruin remains (fig. 14). In contrast to the east cliff, then, the west slope was commonplace rather than monumental.

By the Middle Ages, the situation had radically changed. The temples were gone; the bottom floors of the Tabularium had been transformed by the Corsi clan into a fortress facing east, with upper floors and towers presumably added, to command the road leading beyond the abitato to the Lateran. On the crest of the hill, to the west and north of the fortified Tabularium, debris and earth had accumulated, roughly six meters above the ancient level. The surface of the hill remained full of hillocks and holes and uneven up to the time Michelangelo laid out his area Capitolina (fig. 222). To the north, perhaps using the ruins of the Temple of Juno, the monastery and church of S. Maria in Capitolio had been set up by the eighth century or earlier. The church, like its twelfth-century rebuilding, was located probably on the site of the transept of the present S. Maria in Aracoeli, facing south, and parts of the twelfth-century campanile are still visible adjoining the south transept of the present church. On Monte Caprino, perhaps in or near the Temple of Jupiter, a portico had by the twelfth century been taken over by rope makers, who were plying their trade still in the sixteenth century. Most important, though, in the context of mapping medieval Rome is the market, likely going back a long time, held in front of S. Maria in Capitolio on the uneven expanse of the hill; a Bull of Anaclete II (1130-1138) refers to it. Moreover, this market extended down the west slope of the hill to Piazza Aracoeli, where two churches drew their names from it, one inserted into the remains of the Roman apartment house, whence its tiny campanile still rises. Thus, while the stairs ascending the Capitol from the Forum remained in use, as expressly stated in the Bull of Anaclete, the main approach to the hill was then, and presumably had been for some time, from the west, that is from the abitato.

A decisive change in direction had thus taken place. But neither the new approach nor indeed the layout and character of the buildings on the Capitol had anything monumental about them yet. The Bull of Anaclete lists houses, vaults, courtyards, gardens and trees, stones and columns, loosely scattered it would seem. By 1061, indeed, there must have been housing for an imperial emissary, possibly in an ancient ruin, the "palatium Octaviani." There was also the "porticus Camellariae"—perhaps, it has been surmised, the Tabularium, by the time of Anaclete II no longer a Corsi fortress but property of the monastery like the entire hill and anything but grand.

Still, the Capitol had never lost its old fame as *caput mundi*. A legend of the seventh century or even earlier, the *Salvatio Romae*, depicting statues of all the provinces subject to Rome standing on the Capitol, kept alive the memory of its ancient grandeur. The emperor's envoy in 1061, an antiquity buff anyhow, was highly conscious of it. Hence, it was but natural for the Roman republic of 1143/44 to establish its Senate on the Capitol: "to rebuild the Capitol, to renew the dignity of the Senate, to reform the order of knights" were the aims attributed to the revolutionaries. Rebuilding the Capitol, or what medieval men would have considered such, must have started forthwith. However, the layout of the Capitoline still retained more than a trace of ambiguity. The new assembly hall of the Commune, installed perhaps in the old Corsi mansion, need not have faced west. It may have looked east toward the Forum or north, where S. Maria in Capitolio, rebuilt at roughly that time, had its façade and campanile, facing the building of the Commune. Between the palace and the church façade, sometime in the twelfth or possibly the thirteenth century, an ancient obelisk was set up on the raised medieval surface of the hill. By 1200, then, the Palazzo del Senatore, the fronting area, and the market site probably faced west (fig. 221). The church and obelisk, on the other hand, still took into account a lane crossing the hill east to west from the stairs ascending from the Forum.

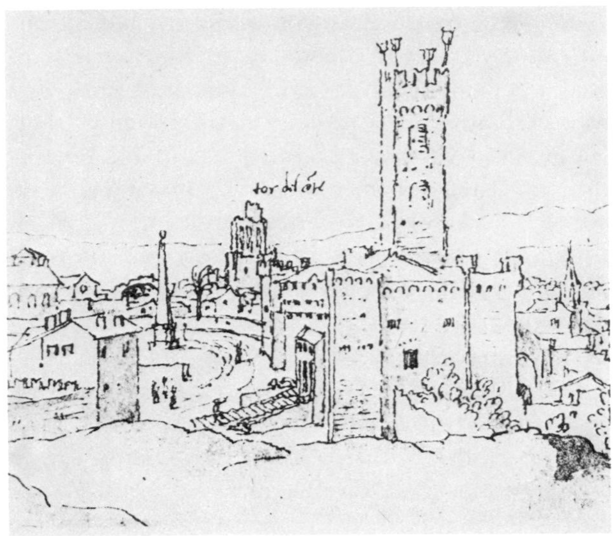

221. Palazzo del Senatore and area Capitolina from Monte Caprino looking north, as of 1534–1536, Marten van Heemskerck, detail from panorama of Rome, Berlin, Kupferstichkabinett, 79 D2A, fols. 91ᵛ, 92ʳ

The map of the medieval Capitol took its final shape in the thirteenth century, and this determined Michelangelo's design three hundred years later. On the remains of the Tabularium, the Palazzo del Senatore—the twelfth-century Senate, one recalls, gradually gave way to a single senatore as chief executive of the city—was thoroughly rebuilt, as mentioned before. At present it is enough to stress that the imposing new palace dominated the hill and beyond, the eastward part of the abitato; and that it did so together with the new church and convent of S. Maria in Aracoeli, as it was then named, which in the thirteenth century took the place of the church and convent of S. Maria in Capitolio (fig. 222). The old buildings were ceded to the Franciscans in 1250, and construction seems to have been completed in ten years, beginning in the late 1250s; only small parts of the old structure were incorporated in the large new church, a timber-roofed basilica of the pattern all too traditional in Roman church planning, and updated by just a few Gothic elements: pointed windows, rose windows in the façade, chapels along the aisles. That the Franciscans would seek to establish themselves on the Capitol is perhaps explained by the close ties which, from its beginning in the second decade of the thirteenth century, linked the order to the communes and developing urban settings. Still, there is a difference: in France, England, the Rhineland, North Italy, and Tuscany, where cities and communes had evolved early and placed their civic buildings in the center of town, the order had settled on the periphery in the slums; in Rome, the late rise of a civic movement as well as the emotional values and traditions of the Capitoline Hill had forced the civic center to the edge of town and thus impelled the Franciscans to settle close by. Indeed, as early as 1242 if not before, the old church of S. Maria in Capitolio and its convent functioned collaterally as civic buildings: edicts were publicized in front of the church and the city council, which assisted the senatore, met at the convent, possibly in one of the cloisters.

In the context of medieval Rome, S. Maria in Aracoeli loomed large. Facing the abitato at the foot of the hill, the new church stood high up to the left of the Palazzo del Senatore, on a more forward and thus more prominent site. Its towering position was further underscored when in 1348 the steep stairs were built ascending from Piazza Aracoeli. Jointly, the group of the Palazzo del Senatore as it stood by 1300 and S. Maria in Aracoeli became a symbol of the medieval Commune, as they appear time and again on fourteenth- and fifteenth-century maps and views of Rome (fig. 223). One should remember, after all, that the gilded marble pile of the Monumento Nazionale, ever since its completion in 1911, has dwarfed the Capitol, hiding it and usurping its prominence in the townscape. Before that gigantic monstrosity was set up, the

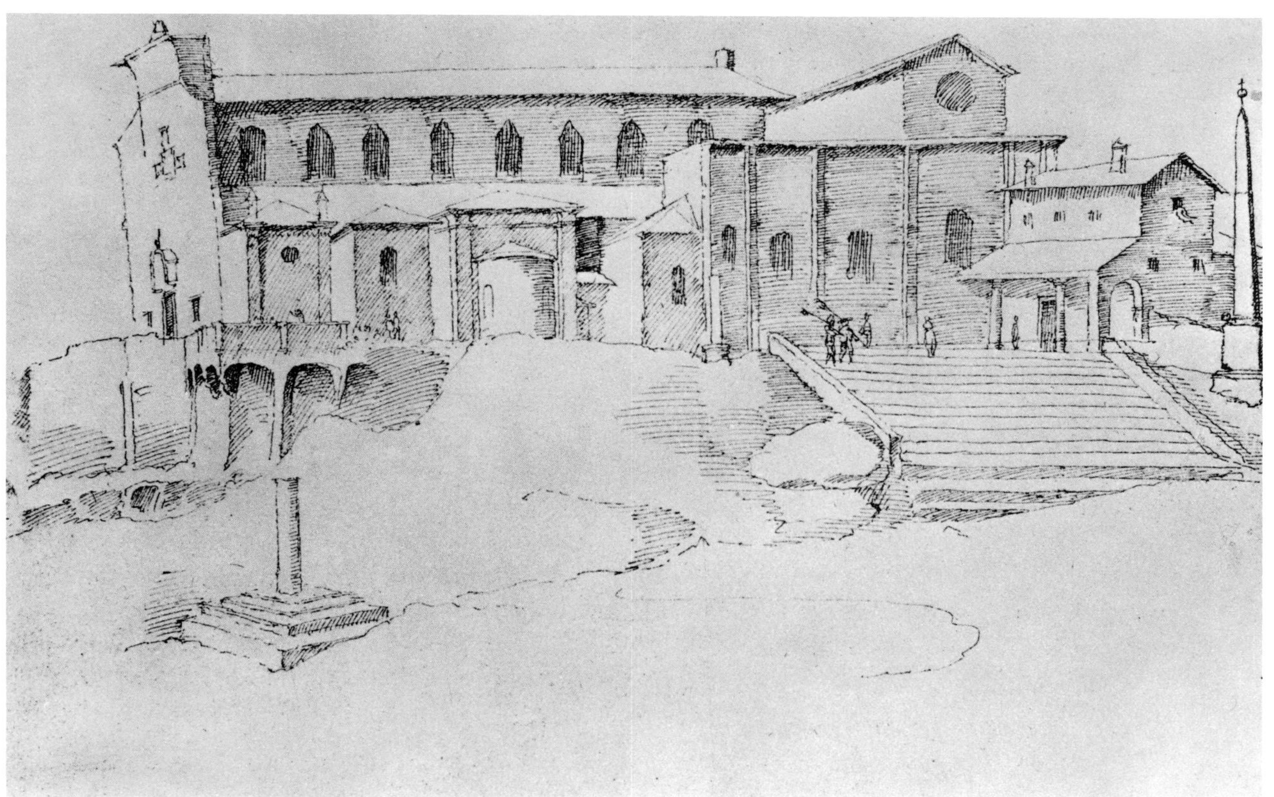

222. S. Maria in Aracoeli from south, as of 1534-1536, Marten van Heemskerck, Berlin, Kupferstichkabinett, 79 D2A, fol. 164

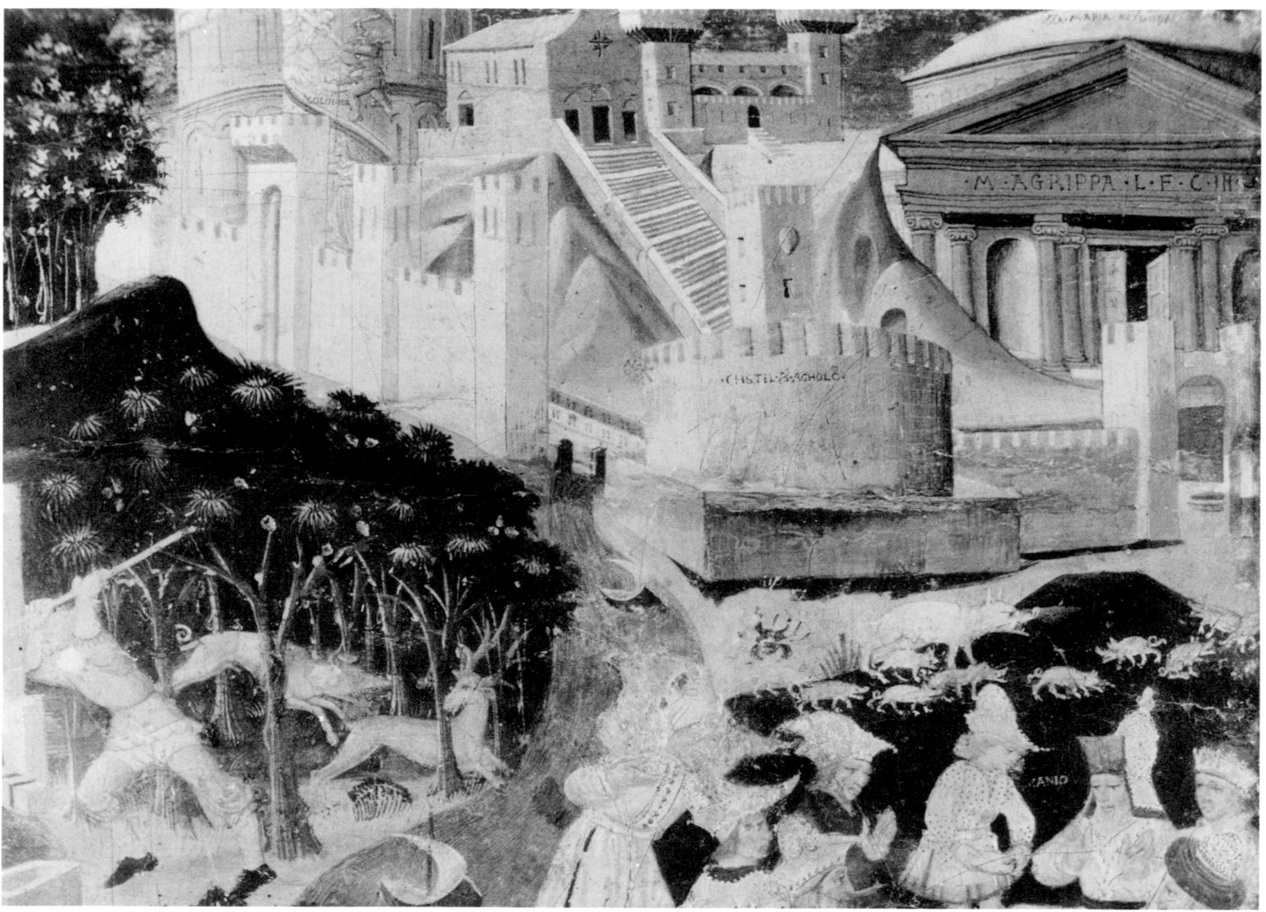

223. View of Castel S. Angelo, Pantheon, Colosseum and Capitol, with S. Maria in Aracoeli and Palazzo del Senatore, ca. 1450, idealized, Apollonio di Giovanni, *Incidents from the History of Dido and Aeneas*, detail, cassone, Yale University Art Gallery, James Jackson Jarves collection

buildings on the Capitol and S. Maria in Aracoeli jointly and visibly towered over both the disabitato, from the Lateran and the Gianicolo to Porta del Popolo and Monte Mario, and the abitato, which from the foot of the hill extended to Ponte S. Angelo, St. Peter's, and the thirteenth-century Vatican Palace. The opposition of papacy and Commune, while politically ironed out by 1280, remained alive in their visible foci at the outer edges of town. The Capitol, however, notwithstanding its great traditions and its renewed importance as a political focus in medieval Rome, topographically remained on the outskirts of town, a last outpost on the rim of the disabitato. It exerted no influence on the growth of the abitato; nor did it change its map. The town was forever attracted westward toward the quarters of the Tiber bend, Ponte S. Angelo and the Borgo, the living center of medieval Rome.

CHAPTER THIRTEEN

Houses, Towers, and Mansions

What houses looked like in medieval Rome is not always easy to visualize. Archaeological evidence for secular building is scarce and the few surviving houses do not always give the clearest picture: they are over-restored; they are of late date, hardly a one prior to the thirteenth century; they are solidly built and represent upper-class housing; and they stand in the abitato, often as row houses and deprived of the garden plots that formed an integral part of many of them far into the sixteenth century. If any early and more modest housing survives in altered shape or has been excavated, its remains have not been thought worth recording. Clearly, houses, like streets in the medieval part of Rome, regardless of their later dates of construction, are apt to rest on or incorporate the substructure or some wall of their medieval predecessors. But archaeologists have paid no attention to the type and character of secular building, nor to the distribution and density of settlement in medieval Rome. As things stand, it seems best, before discussing the few structures surviving, to turn to *vedute* of late-fifteenth- and sixteenth-century date and to deeds of sale and lease of medieval times. They provide a far truer and far livelier picture of the housing in and beyond the abitato through the Middle Ages.

The view of Trastevere done by the Escurial draughtsman (fig. 210) and his other *vedute*, or indeed a view done by Heemskerck around 1535, all convey the same overall impression. The few buildings of fifteenth- and sixteenth-century date, as they appear in such *vedute*, can easily be discounted in the context of the medieval town, as it remained essentially untouched. Houses were closely packed, with their gables or the sloping sides of their roofs facing the street. Already, Fra Paolino's map of 1323 (or its thirteenth-century archetype) shows, along with nonattached houses, row houses lining the streets, particularly in the Borgo and on the east bank near Monte Brianzo; but the draughtsman used both as mere symbols, and row houses are likely to have been common through the core of town (fig. 182). Correspondingly, gardens in the core of town shrank, it seems, both in number and size as time went on. On the river bank, the Escurial draughtsman shows both modest and more pretentious houses and towers sloping down to the river. The Roman City Wall from Ponte Sisto to at least Ponte S. Angelo carried houses from medieval times on, as they still rose, though rebuilt and raised ever higher, a hundred years ago along Via di Monte Brianzo (fig. 224). Further downstream opposite the Tiber Island as well, where no old fortifications lent support, houses precariously sloped down both river banks: higgledy-piggledy, of different heights and varied types, close together in rows or at short distances from each other. Granted, the houses seen by the Escurial draughtsman or by Heemskerck need not antedate the fifteenth century. However, secular building, particularly of the lower classes, is conservative in the extreme, and many a fifteenth- or indeed seventeenth-century small house preserves all the hallmarks of an earlier time. There is no reason to think that a modest house in the eleventh or twelfth century would have looked so very different from those shown by the Escurial draughtsman on the east bank opposite the Tiber Island or below Castel S. Angelo: tiny, with a porch on the ground floor, arched in front and sideways, and with only a loft above, or indeed no upper floor; or else, two-storied houses with loop holes rather than windows on the upper floor (fig. 225).

If archaeological remains and evidence from *vedute* are scarce, deeds and sales contracts give a vivid picture. Lots were small, often only 36 by

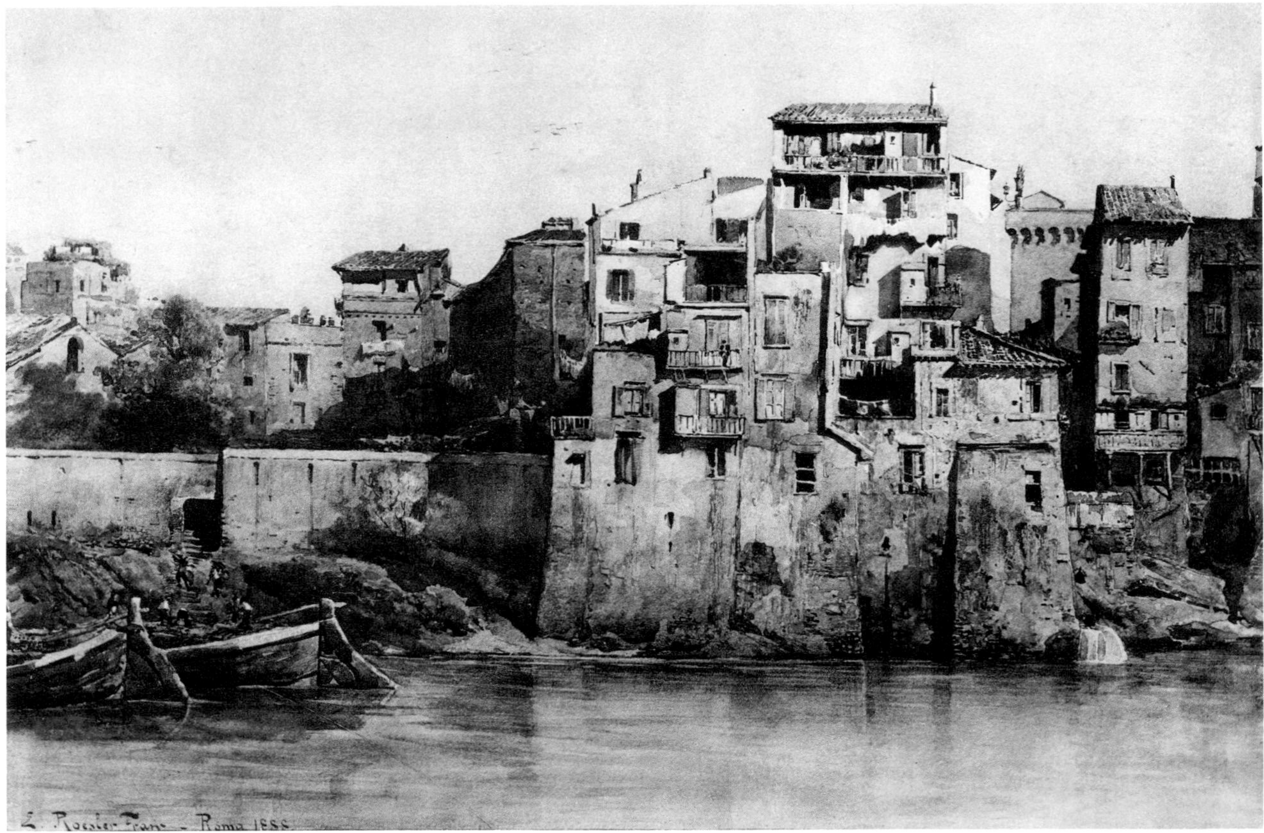

224. Houses along Via di Monte Brianzo, placed on ancient city wall, as of 1886, watercolor, E. Roesler Franz, Museo di Roma

36 feet (10.60 meters square); rarely did a lot measure as much as 110 by 44 feet (32.50 by 13 meters). Rights of access were always carefully defined—a path from the public road "for a cart or an ass or a man on horseback." Most houses had gardens in front or at the back, with apple and olive trees and sometimes a fig tree or a vine—always carefully listed in the deed of lease or sale. Often there was also a small courtyard in front or a porch. Building material was sometimes brick, *tegulicia*, most likely pilfered from Roman ruins. At other times, houses are described as *scandalicia*, meaning roofed, or possibly revetted, with shingles. But more often than not, roofs were thatched; and sometimes both types of roofing may have been combined. Houses were frequently one-storied, *terrinea*; sometimes they were two-storied, *solarata*; the upper floor would be reached by an outside staircase, sometimes of marble, like those that survive in the small medieval towns of Latium, or in Trastevere in the Vicolo dei Moroni extending toward the Aurelian Walls near Porta Settimiana—the row of houses may well be of sixteenth-century date, but the type is medieval (fig. 226). Both one- and two-storied houses are described over and over again in sales deeds near S. Maria Nova, from the tenth century on: "a house with an upper floor built of brick and shingles . . . with its little courtyard and a marble staircase in front, with its garden behind, in which there are olive and apple trees" in 982; in 1127, an elegant residence, "with a room with a fireplace [*camminatam*] above and below, of brick, with a staircase in front and a porch and its stones and a garden likewise with its stones," possibly a flagstone terrace; or a "one-storied house, with shingles and thatched, with a little garden at the back . . . near the Arch of the Seven-Armed Candlestick," the Arch of Titus. To find such a cottage in the rural surroundings of S. Maria Nova is not surprising. But a similar

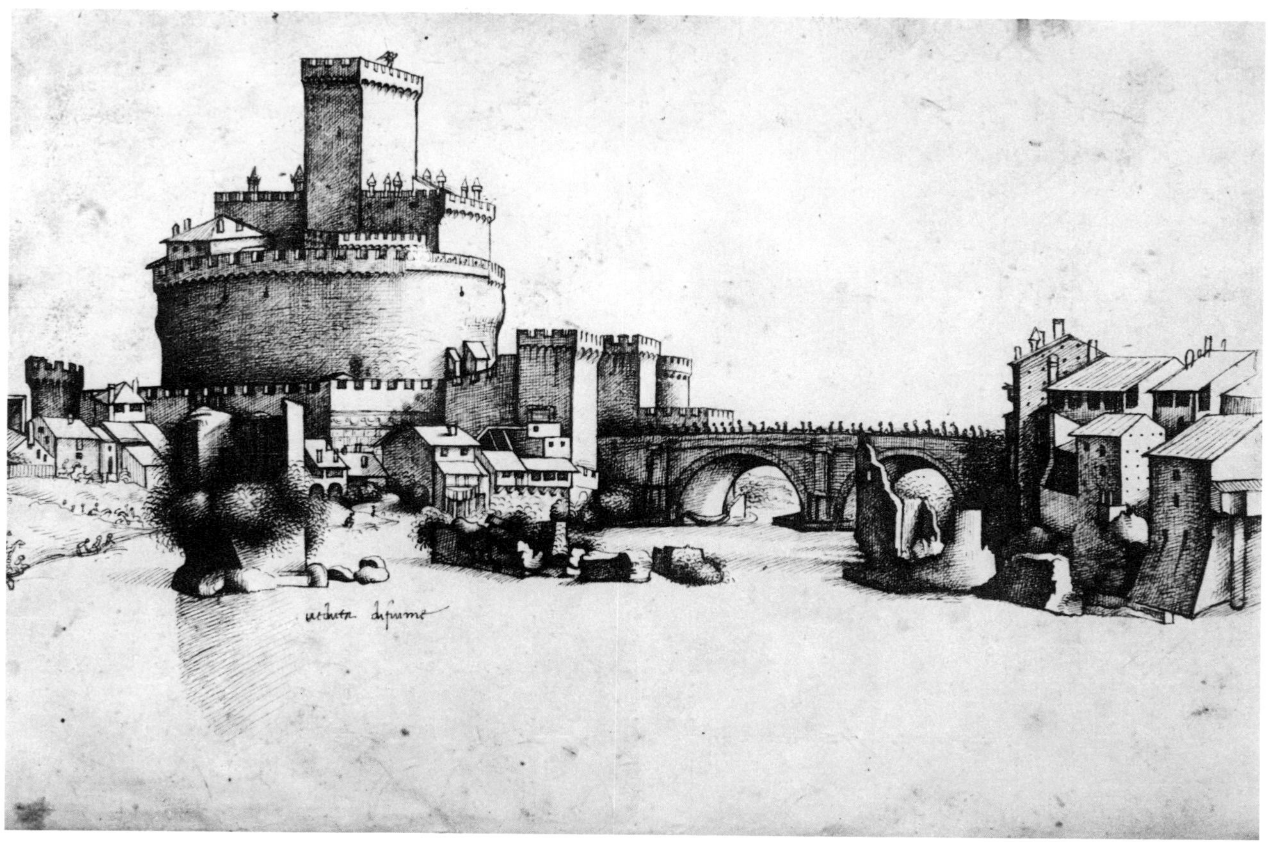

225. View of Castel S. Angelo with medieval houses, as of ca. 1495, drawing, *Escurialensis*, fol. 26v

cottage stood in 1008 just off the Corso by S. Maria in Via Lata, in the best neighborhood of eleventh-century Rome: "a house of shingles, with a thatched roof and with its little garden in front, in which stand a vine pergola and apple trees . . . situated in Rome in the fourth region near the marble arch," the Arch of Diocletian spanning the Corso. In the suburb of S. Maria Maggiore near S. Prassede, in 1091 a house is described, "all of brick, having two rooms and above them some sheds [perhaps an attic?] . . . covered with planks . . . and an olive grove," the planks having been provided by the lessee. Similarly, on the northern rim of the abitato in the Campo Marzio, as late as 1154 a cottage has a straw hut next to it. Each house, one- or two-storied, thatched or roofed with shingles, has its courtyard in front, its own garden, and, more often than not, empty lots nearby. Near the Ripetta port, where up-river traffic docked, storerooms were for lease to boatsmen. Only gradually in the core of the abitato did the build-up grow into the maze of houses, and empty lots or gardens disappeared, though never completely. In their majority, though, they gave way to the maze of alleys and arched passageways so typical of urban nonplanning in the High Middle Ages. Such entangled over-building and substantial house types seem to appear quite early. By 1092, near S. Apollinare in the Scorticlaria, stood a house with shingles and a porch in front and a *preforulum* in which "to do business," apparently adjacent to each other; the front porch was perhaps a single-bay ground-floor arcade like those on the drawings of the Escurialensis master, while the *preforulum* was presumably either an overhang to protect a shop window or stand, or a collapsible shutter. Half a century before, indeed, row houses built against each other may have lined a street near S. Maria in Trastevere: "half a house with an upper floor and a shingle roof" was

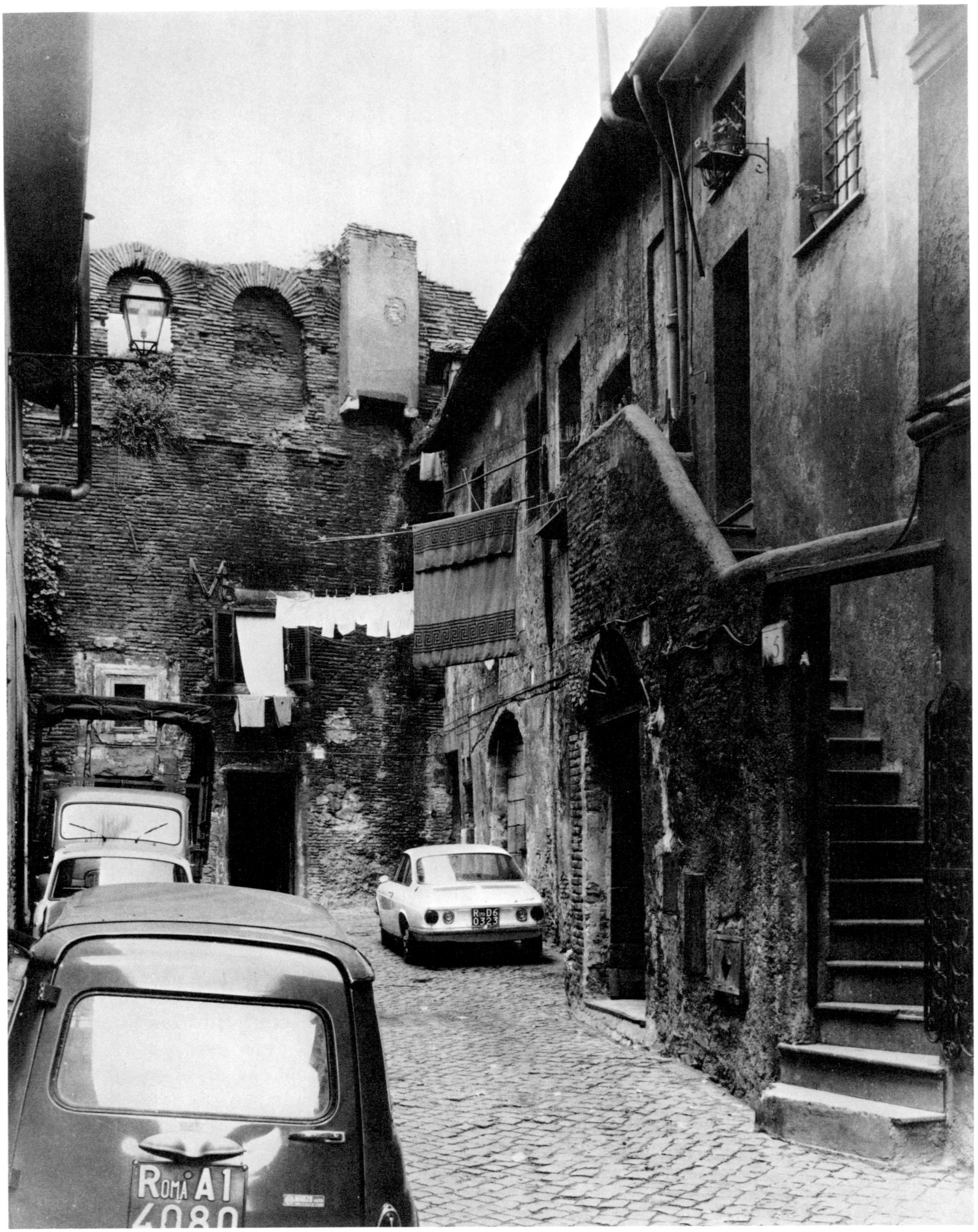

226. Vicolo dei Moroni

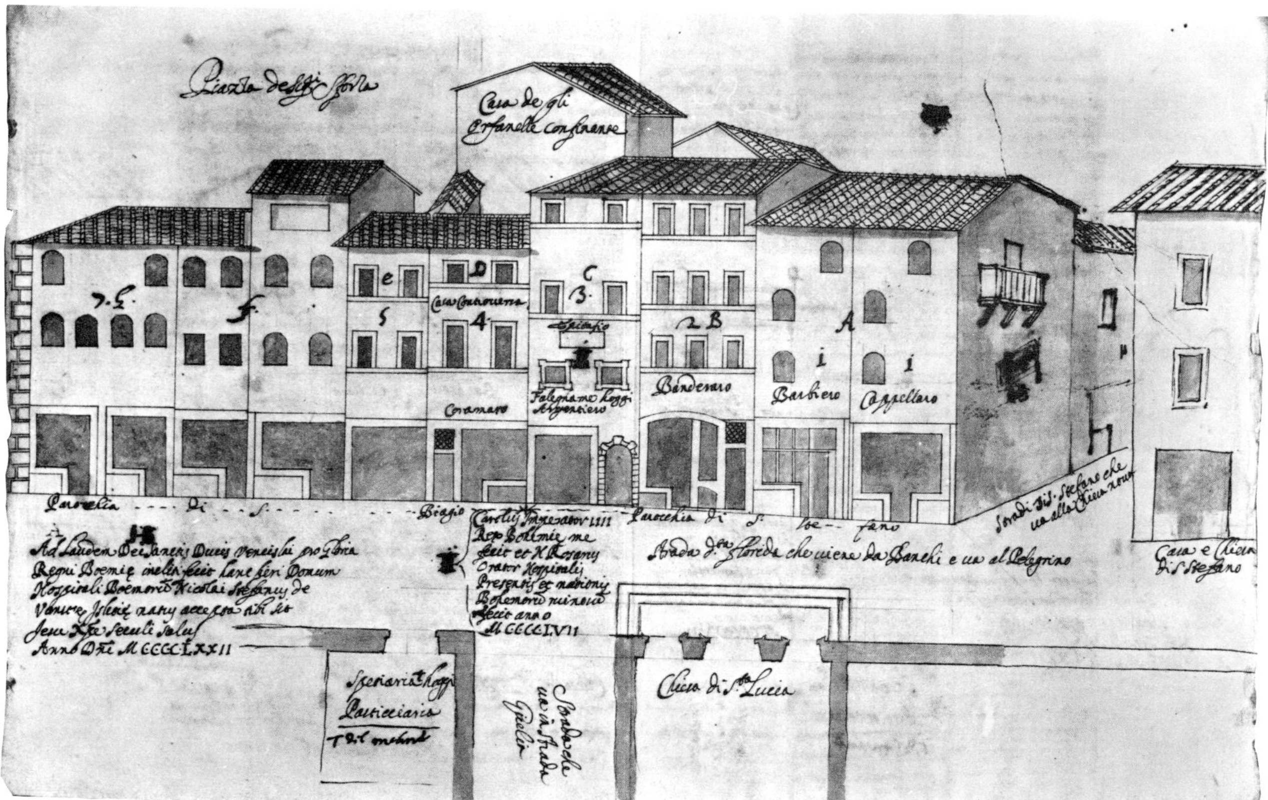

227. Houses in Via del Pellegrino, as of ca. 1600, Archivio di Stato, Roma

given in 1038 to the church, "bordering on one side my own [the donor's] house, on the other the house of Urso, on the third an empty lot, on the fourth the street." Such row houses, more often than not, would open on the ground floor in two or more arcades and thus provide continuous porticoes, if of different height, along the street. A house on Via dell'Arco della Pace (fig. 229), though probably of thirteenth-century date given its construction in small tufa blocks, *opus saracinescum*, seems to preserve what appears to have been a traditional type; a porticoed house by 1041 stood in the Borgo: "two-storied . . . of brick, with its garden at the back and two booths to be set up in its porch . . . bordered by . . . the monument [probably an ancient ruin] . . . and the portico leading to St. Peter's."

In the business section of town, by the High Middle Ages row houses would presumably have been the rule. Via dei Banchi would hardly have changed in appearance from the twelfth century to 1600 when the Ospizio della SS. Trinità dei Pellegrini had a survey prepared of its real-estate property (fig. 227). The houses—three at the left and two at the right end may be medieval or fifteenth century, with only the shop entrances reframed—are narrow, two or at the most four windows wide; they are tall, consisting of a ground floor and two or three upper floors; and in each a shop takes up the entire width of the ground floor, a stone table or even two filling the opening three-quarters or more—the arrangement one knows from Pompeii and even from the sixteenth-century row of shops at Farfa. A hatter, a barber, a draper, a silversmith—his shop formerly a carpenter's—a rosary-maker, a confectioner, have their shops cheek by jowl.

A few medieval houses survive to confirm the picture. Those remaining are narrow, low, and comparatively deep; their street front is rarely wider than 5 meters, their height at the most two or three low stories, 8 meters or so, all told. Low and tall houses, wider and narrower dwellings, stood side by side. Their façades might be

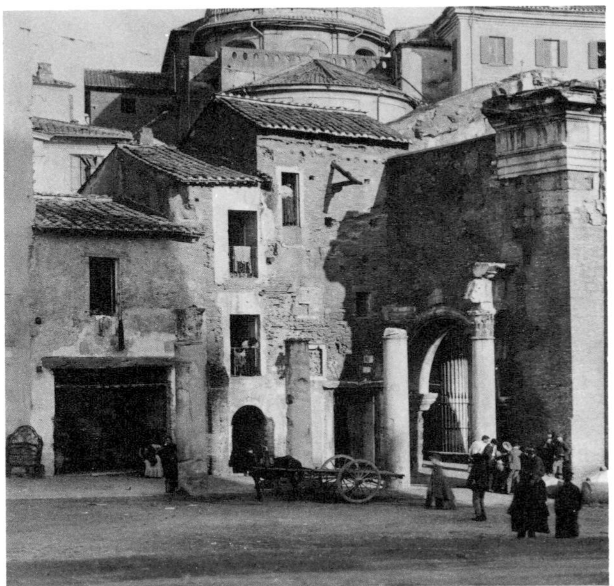

228. Medieval houses near Portico di Ottavia, detail

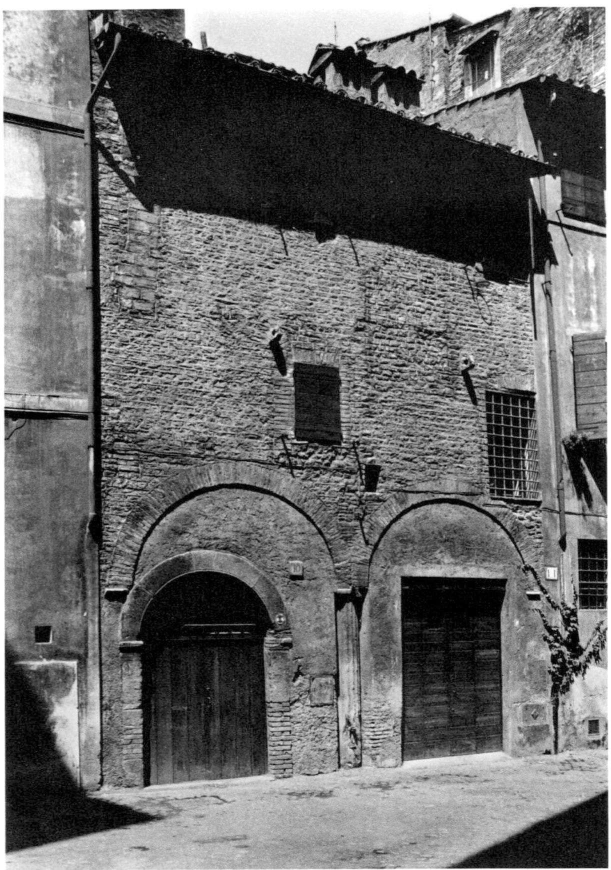

229. Medieval house, Via dell'Arco della Pace 10/11

nondescript with but a door on the ground floor, witness the three houses adjoining the Portico di Ottavia on the left (fig. 228). But often a porch or portico carried by columns—spoils were plentiful, after all—took up as much as half the depth of the ground floor. Sometimes it opened at the sides in a narrow arch, with a wider arch in front, like the houses seen by the Escurial draughtsman; two such small houses survive, one in Vicolo della Luce in Trastevere, the other raised and incorporated in a large building complex on Piazza in Piscinula. Or else the house opened onto the street front in two arches, witness Via dell'Arco della Pace 10 (fig. 229). Or again, there were outside staircases either along the façade or against one of the side walls, as in the medieval houses in Vicolo dei Moroni and at the corner of Vicolo della Luce (fig. 230). Often the stairs were protected by a roof and ascended to a small porch or an open loggia on the upper floor. However, whether the individual house was plain or elegant, provided with a porch or opened in a portico, the variety of a row of houses in height, width, distance, materials, fenestration, and roofing enlivened and enriched the street and altered the profile both of the receding and projecting groundline and of the discontinuous roofline.

As time went on, adjoining houses bought up by a wealthy owner were fused into a single complex, linked by connecting doorways and stairs, notwithstanding the differences in height and floor level. One such mansion stands opposite S. Cecilia in Trastevere, its corner raised towerlike (fig. 231). An L-shaped portico extends along the façade and flank of the building, supported by columns with Ionic capitals and a corner pier. Arches likewise open on the ground floors of four or five tall and narrow houses, one a tower, the Case di S. Paolo. Built against each other at different dates, some apparently in the fourteenth century, and fused, they are located off Via Arenula on Via S. Maria in Monticello. But both this building complex and the one opposite S. Cecilia have been cleaned up and restored so heavily as to make one prefer to look at an old photograph rather than at recent ones (fig. 232). Colonnaded porticoes, arcaded or trabeated and with Ionic capitals, whether spoils

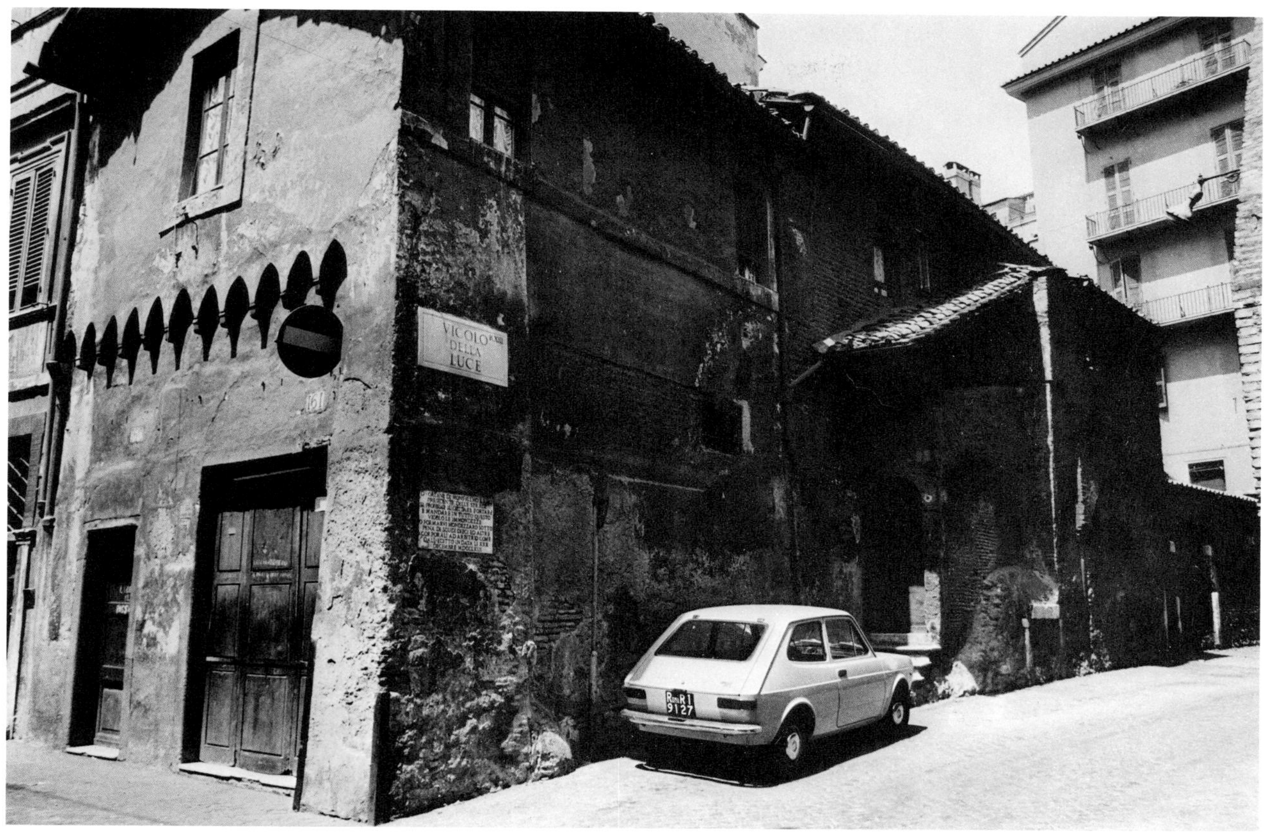

230. Medieval house, Via dei Salumi 161, corner Vicolo della Luce

or of medieval workmanship, seem to have become a hallmark of the more lavish types of housing in high medieval Rome: some as much as five bays long, like a house at Via S. Bartolomeo degli Strengari 29, long demolished but known from photographs; another, Piazza di Campo Marzio 6, its six fat column shafts spaced roughly 3 meters apart. Others were only three bays wide in front, about 9 meters, as at the corner of Via Capo di Ferro 31 and Via Arco del Monte, or in Piazza di Trevi 93 and 93A. Columns without exception seem to have been spoils, slender or stout as best they could be procured; architraves, too, as a rule were spoils, sometimes splendidly rich, as in Via Capo di Ferro, and in one of the houses on Piazza di Trevi, or at a house just opposite Ponte S. Angelo on the east bank (fig. 233). Where such houses were built in rows, such as those facing the Trevi Fountain or the Case di S. Paolo, the colonnades formed a continuous portico along the street. Notwithstanding the disparate heights and designs of columns, architraves, or arches, such porticoes would provide shade in summer, protection from rain, and, perhaps as they were meant to in North Italian cities and probably in Rome as well, facilitate pedestrian traffic. But it is doubtful whether they actually fulfilled this function in Rome. For their main purpose was to provide space for vendors; and their stands or collapsible shutters were bound to block the traffic, just as streets were blocked by vendors' booths or even fenced off, despite all regulations of the *maestri di strada*.

Inside, to be sure, such medieval houses, whether modest or more lavish, have all been rebuilt. But simple house plans at least are conservative, and sixteenth-century surveys, of which there are plenty in the archives of Confraternities, still provide a reasonably good idea of medieval housing, regardless of the actual date of the structure, fifteenth-century or earlier:

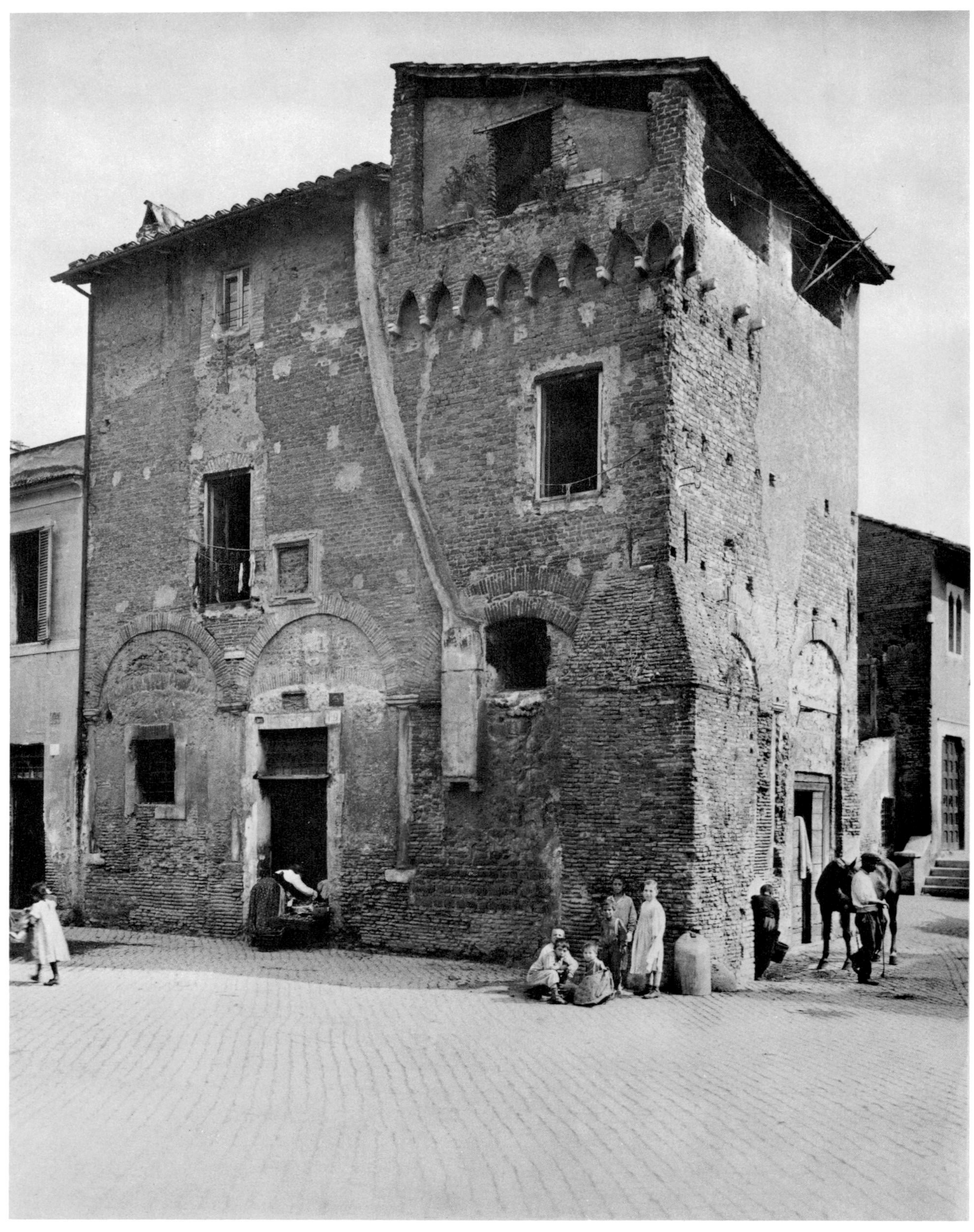

231. Mansion opposite S. Cecilia, before restoration

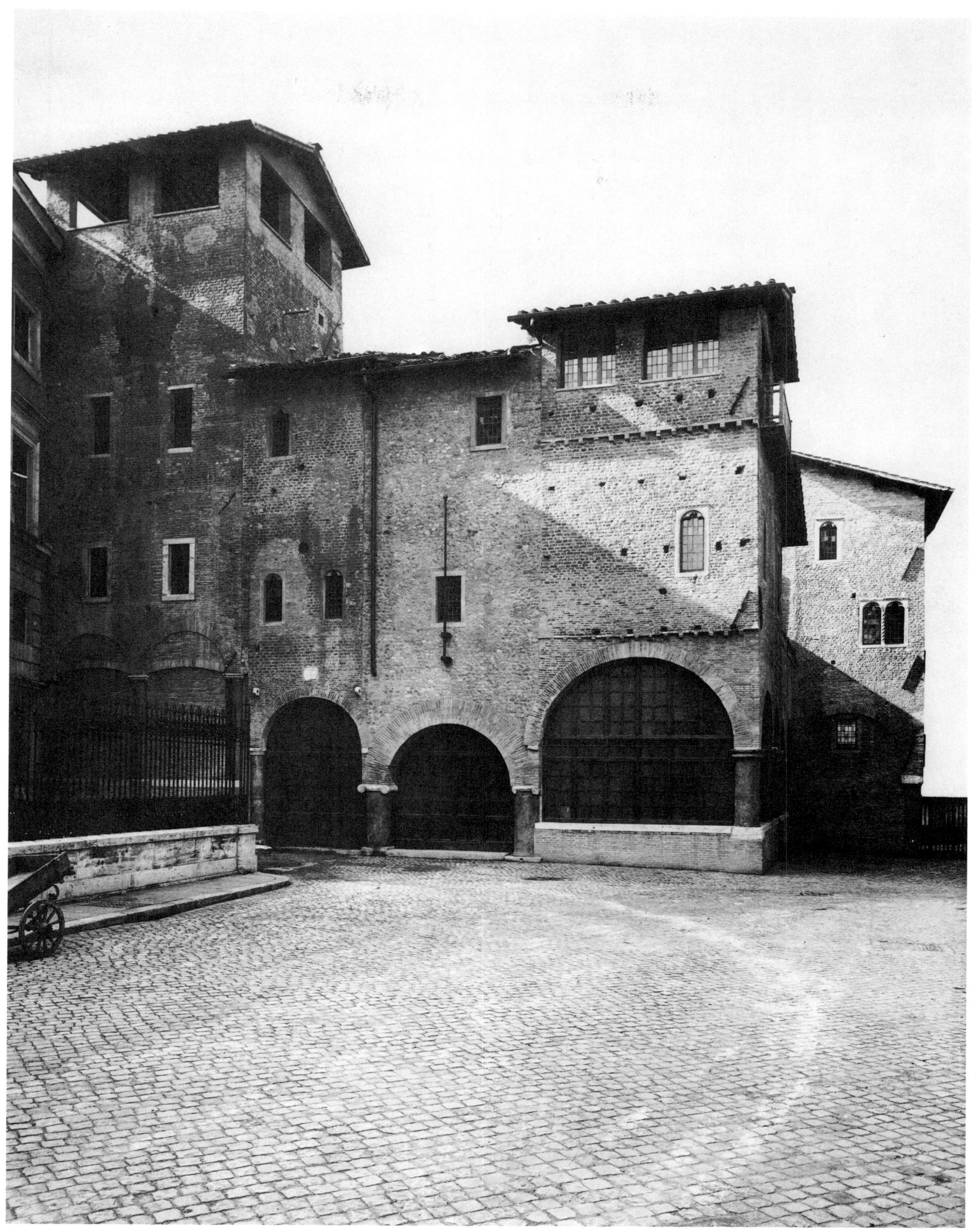

232. Case di S. Paolo, from the north, restored

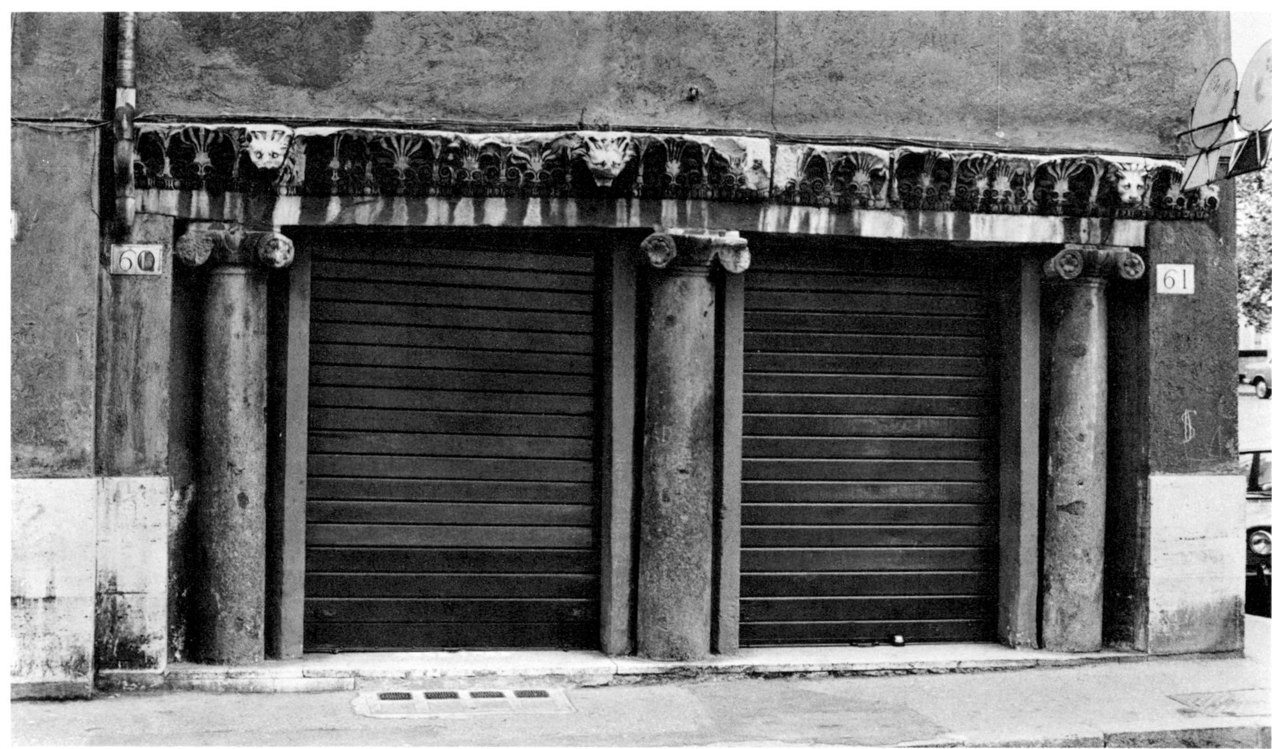

233. Medieval house with colonnaded portico, Via S. Celso 60/61, corner Piazza del Ponte

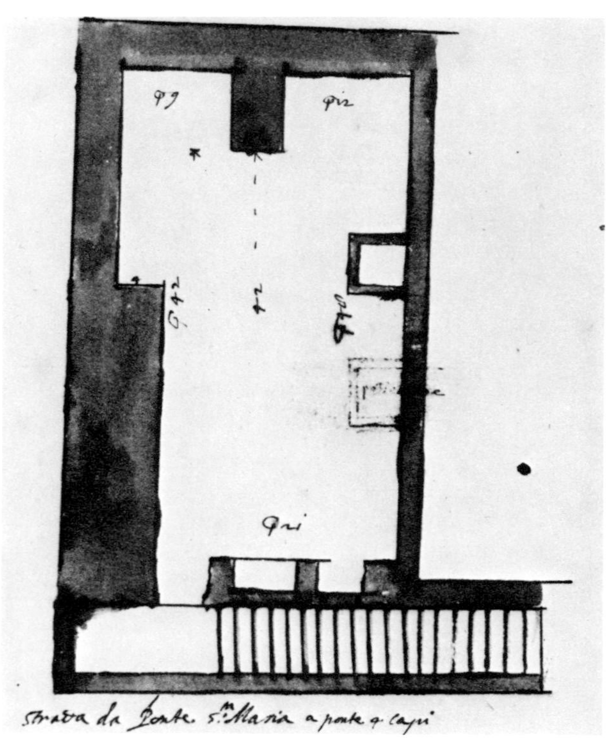

234. Plan of row houses, Archivio di Stato, Arch. SS. Annunziata

one or two rooms in depth on both the ground floor and the upper floor; or, in a more pretentious house, a large *sala* on the upper floor (fig. 234). In an elegant yet small house—one thinks of a bachelor, a clerk perhaps—Vicolo dell'Atleta 14, the stairs are moved inside, parallel to the brick façade, and the upper landing opens in a double-arcaded loggia on columns and piers, surmounted by a corbel table frieze with pointed arches on marble brackets, built of small tufa blocks and possibly added later (fig. 235). Where a large family lived together, possibly needing storerooms and the like for business, a larger house type would be developed, apparently over a long time. The mansion of Saint Francesca Romana's husband in Trastevere, where she lived about 1400, has been described in lively terms by Esch: on the ground floor was the staircase, next to it storerooms and most likely stables—the family were cattle breeders and dealers; on the main floor, grouped around a big *sala* with a fireplace, were bedrooms for the family and servants, the kitchen, a toilet, a loggia toward the courtyard, and a corridor toward

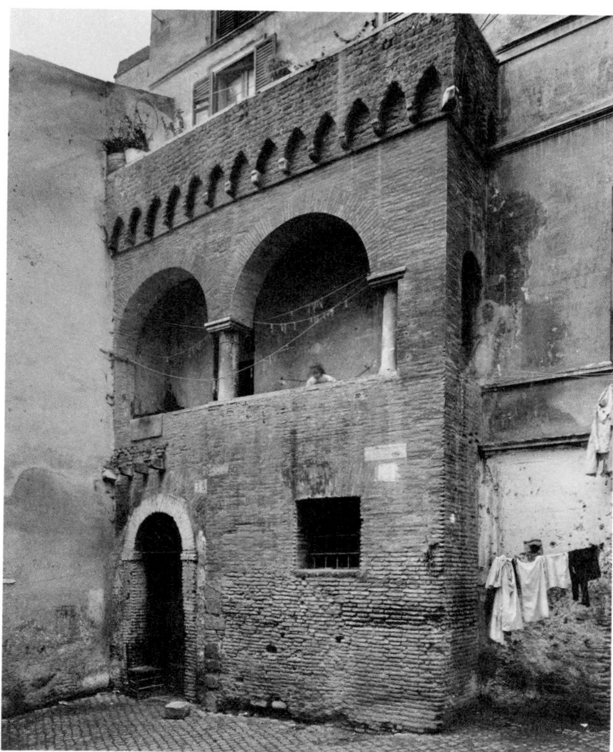

235. Medieval house, Vicolo dell'Atleta 14

the street; finally, there was a roof terrace. Presumably, though, the building would have incorporated older structures as was common practice. In 1433, Francesca bought for the congregation she had founded a high-class bourgeois house of fourteenth-century or earlier date. Located at the foot of the Capitoline (better, the Tarpeian) Hill, it survives to this day, remodeled and enlarged by the purchase of adjoining houses in the course of the fifteenth century; a seventeenth-century enlargement and remodeling changed the complex still further. The fifteenth-century part forms the maze typical of a late-medieval mansion: rooms of varying size—one a huge *sala*, others small cubicles—and on different levels; an inner courtyard, narrow, tall, and dark; an outside staircase, pulled inside in the remodeling; doors broken through walls of adjoining houses; and connecting steps. Whether or not a mansion of that size and type would have existed as early as the twelfth and thirteenth centuries can be neither proved nor disproved. I think it would have suited the needs of the business community developing in Rome in the course of the twelfth and thirteenth centuries. A house in Rome owned around 1130 by Ptolemy of Tusculum—big grain dealer, shipper, and lord in the Campagna that he was—cannot have looked very different.

Ancient buildings were exploited wherever possible throughout the Middle Ages for housing. The Roman tenement house at the foot of the Capitoline Hill was invaded not only by the church of S. Biagio in Mercato, but also by squatters. So were (and are to this day) a row of Roman houses lining Via S. Martino ai Monti, the old Suburra, fronting the atrium of S. Prassede. In Via della Lungarina, until 1877 a tall house apparently of late-antique date was still inhabited, after having served as a medieval tower. The huge monuments of antiquity, theatres, porticoes, thermae, offered convenient shelter. At times a new building was placed atop the Roman ruin. The Palazzo Orsini rising from the top floor of the Theatre of Marcellus is one example. The wing of the palace of the Knights of Malta, the Palazzo dei Cavalieri di Rodii overlooking the Forum of Augustus, though remodeled in the fifteenth century, still shows in its medieval curved wall on its top floor a row of Romanesque windows and a bracketed cornice; nearby, the Markets of Trajan were in part reused for and complemented by medieval towers and housing (fig. 236). To this day in the Theatre of Pompey housing, wine shops, *trattorie*, and other stores fill the vaults of the old structure, their openings blocked, with only a door or a window. The Theatre of Marcellus, too, till the 1920s had its vaults occupied by junk and old-clothes dealers, charcoal sellers (*carbonari*), tavern-keepers (fig. 237). When they moved in is unknown, but it is reasonable to think that it was sometime in the very early Middle Ages. The colonnades of the Porticus of Octavia are similarly filled with housing, as they have been since the early Middle Ages. In Via dei Calderari an ancient arch, framed by a trabeated Doric order, was until the nineteenth century blocked to shelter the ground floor of a tiny house; the upper floor rose from the Roman entablature (fig. 238). All over town throughout the Middle Ages ancient vaults were rented or sold: "an an-

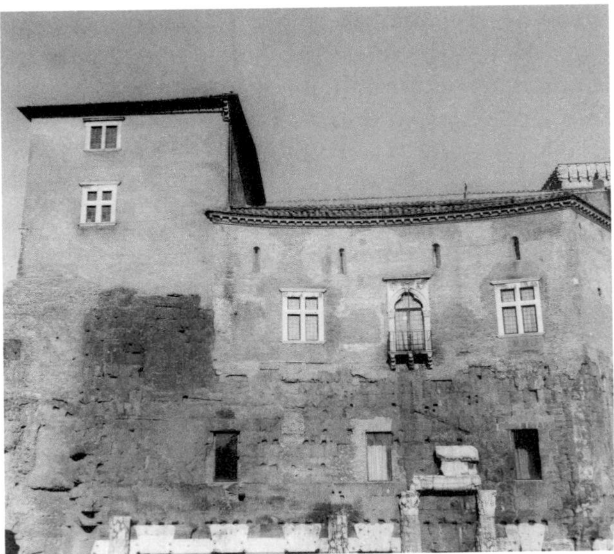

236. Palazzo dei Cavalieri di Rodi, overlooking Forum of Augustus

cient crypt with a small house in front in the quarter of S. Lorenzo in Lucina"; on the Quirinal, "a single-storied house of shingles with apses behind it near the marble horse bordering on . . . the first side two apses, on the second an ancient wall, on the third the entrance to the Thermae [of Constantine], on the fourth the public road"; and a lot with "a vault on it and walls where there used to be other vaults . . . behind the apse of S. Maria in Xenodochio," that is near Fontana di Trevi. Such vaults might be used as workshops independently or might be combined with living quarters, or they formed part of a somewhat larger property, "an ancient crypt waterproofed, with two ancient piers with that entire building which my father has built above said crypt and the tower," near S. Lorenzo in Lucina.

Around S. Maria Nova, in the three great ruins nearby, the Temple of Venus and Roma, the Golden House of Nero, and the Colosseum, vaults—*cryptae* in the documents—and apses were leased, the lessees being drawn from all walks of life: a blacksmith, a butcher, lime burners, a clerk of the Church; all solid citizens, *viri honesti*. Within the Colosseum, by the mid-eleventh century, all or nearly all the vaulted spaces were rented: "a crypt in its entirety, all vaulted, with half of the Travertine piers on either side, in the Amphitheatre which is called the Colosseum, bordering on one side on the crypt and lot of Guido de Berta, on the other the crypt of Doda, on the third the crypt and lot of Singiorectus and on the fourth the public road"—hence it was located on the outer rim of the Colosseum. Or else, "half of a single-storied vault [hence possibly facing the arena] with half of the courtyard in front with its common entrance and exit . . . in the . . . Colosseum, bordering on one side on the other half of the same vault and on the whole vault which belongs to one John, on the second side the vault of Peter Beccli, on the third the vault of Sposa and on the fourth the common entrance." Likewise, the arena of the Colosseum was evidently invaded by housing. A deed of 1060 describes "a two-storied vault and half a two-storied house of brick and shingles, with marble stairs in front . . . that is, the half adjoining the church of the Savior, with its little garden next to it and half an apple orchard behind," the church of the Savior presumably being S. Salvatore de Rota in the arena or adjoining it in one of its vaults. At times, such a vault, even halved, was closed in front by a rough façade, approached over outside stairs, with a little courtyard in front, the measurements given in the deed of sale corresponding to one of the entrance vaults in the Colosseum. At other times, the vaults apparently served as storerooms, workshops, or limekilns: "half of an ancient apse, inside a limekiln [and] at the end of that limekiln, as it divides the apse in half . . . all vaulted . . . with its entrances and exits through those limekilns." The vaults of the Circus Maximus, too, from the thirteenth century on but possibly long before, were given over to housing by the owner, the monastic congregation of S. Gregorio Magno.

Likewise, the ruins around S. Maria Nova and the housing therein were the property of the church and, indeed, churches and monasteries were the big landlords in Rome from the tenth century into the High Middle Ages. Only from the fourteenth century on, it seems, did the rising Confraternities stand alongside and eventually take over from them, the Confraternity of the Sancta Sanctorum and the hospital of S.

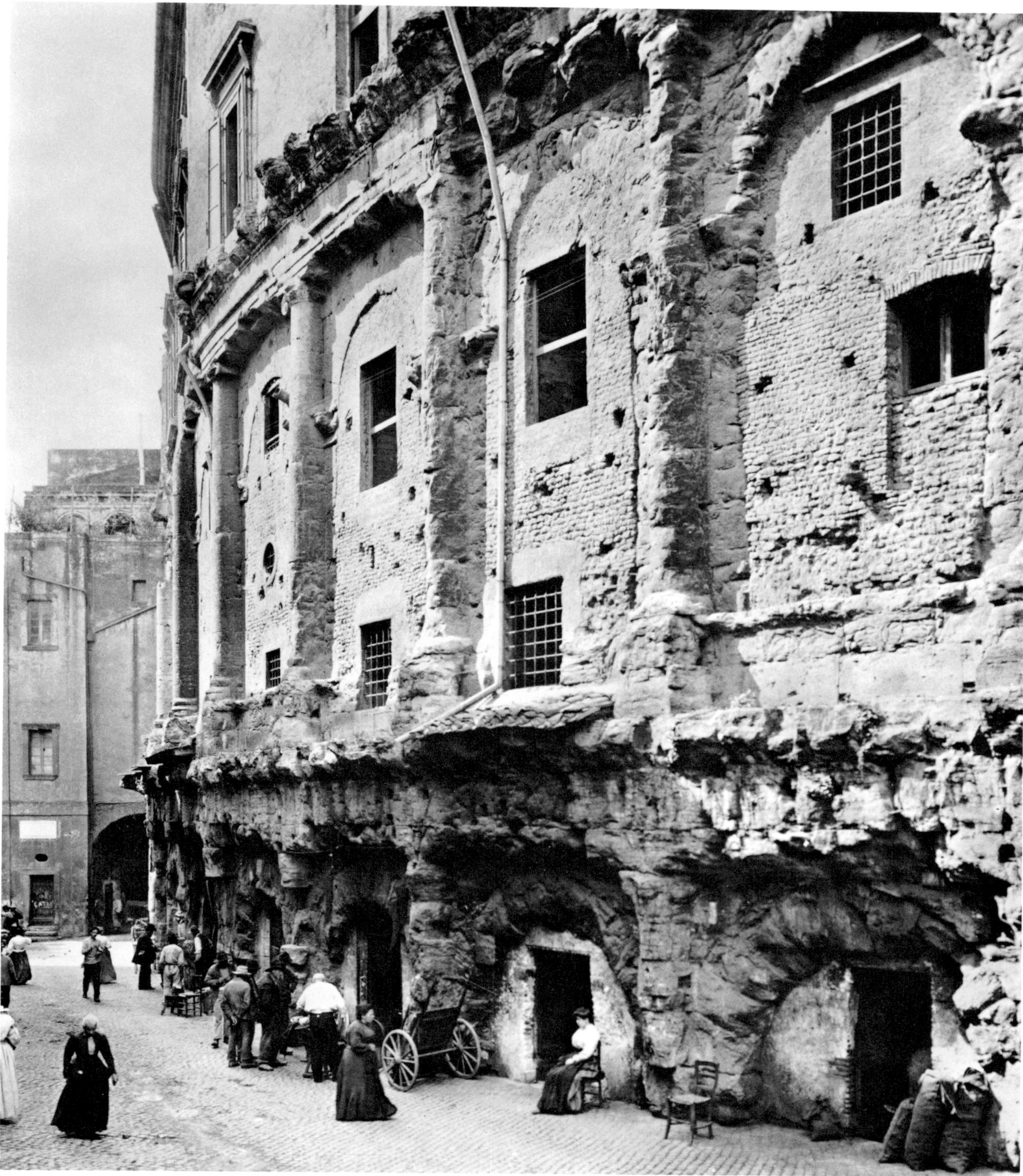

237. Theatre of Marcellus, as of ca. 1880

Giovanni in Laterano foremost. Private landlords from the outset are likely to have owned considerable holdings of real estate both in the abitato and the disabitato. Given the scarcity of documentation of nonecclesiastical property, their importance is hard to evaluate. The large donations made to churches and convents by pious laymen and families on one hand, the in-

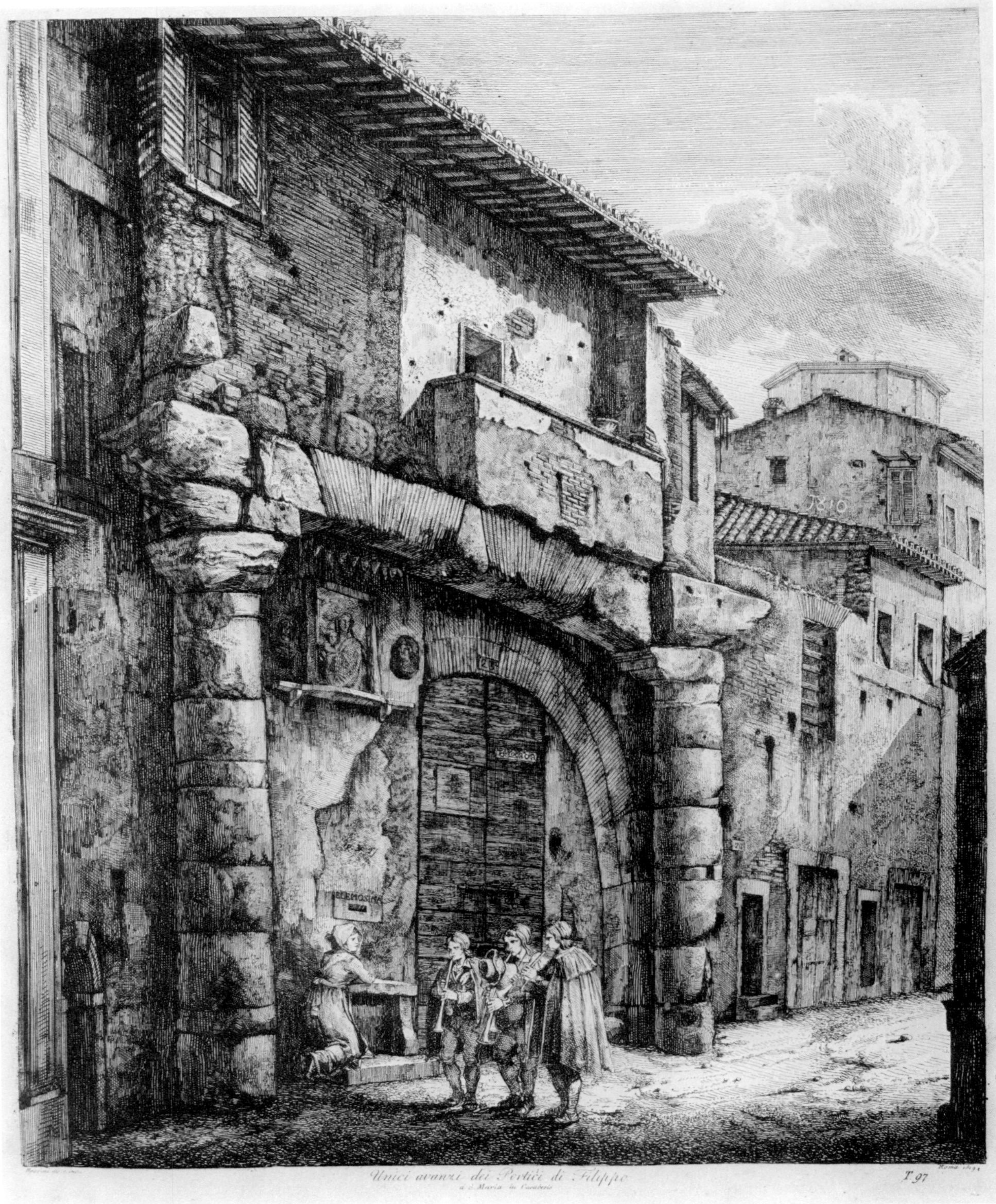

238. House inserted in Roman structure, Via dei Calderari, as of 1819, etching Rossini

termittent alienation of church property on the other, give merely an approximate hint at the extent of real estate in private hands. However, as Professor Lewine points out to me, it is likely that from earliest times old families and rising businessmen would invest in rent-producing real estate as well as in agricultural holdings. From the thirteenth century on, anyhow, private ownership of housing within the abitato can be documented to have loomed large when the great families for both economic and strategic reasons assembled large parcels of real estate within and beyond the abitato. But certainly from early times churches and convents seem to have controlled if not the majority at least a large proportion of the housing in the abitato and the outlying suburbs, along with farms, fields, salt ponds, and other agricultural property in the disabitato and beyond the walls all through Latium. The deeds of lease, sale, and donations speak clearly: St. Peter's, the Lateran Basilica, S. Maria Maggiore, S. Maria Nova, S. Silvestro in Capite, and others were all big landlords, owning sometimes a few dozen, at other times hundreds of houses, large and small. Such property, as a rule, was located near the church; naturally so, since the donors would have been parishioners living nearby. But some churches or convents apparently owned houses in other city quarters as well; this was especially true of St. Peter's.

As the town expanded and settlement grew denser, the skyline, too, changed radically. Hundreds of towers were built from the eleventh century or before and into the fifteenth century. Dozens of them rise from among the densely huddled houses in Masolino's panorama of Rome, painted in 1435 (fig. 239), and still in the *vedute* of Heemskerck (figs. 212-213) and Naldini (fig. 187). Their construction and their

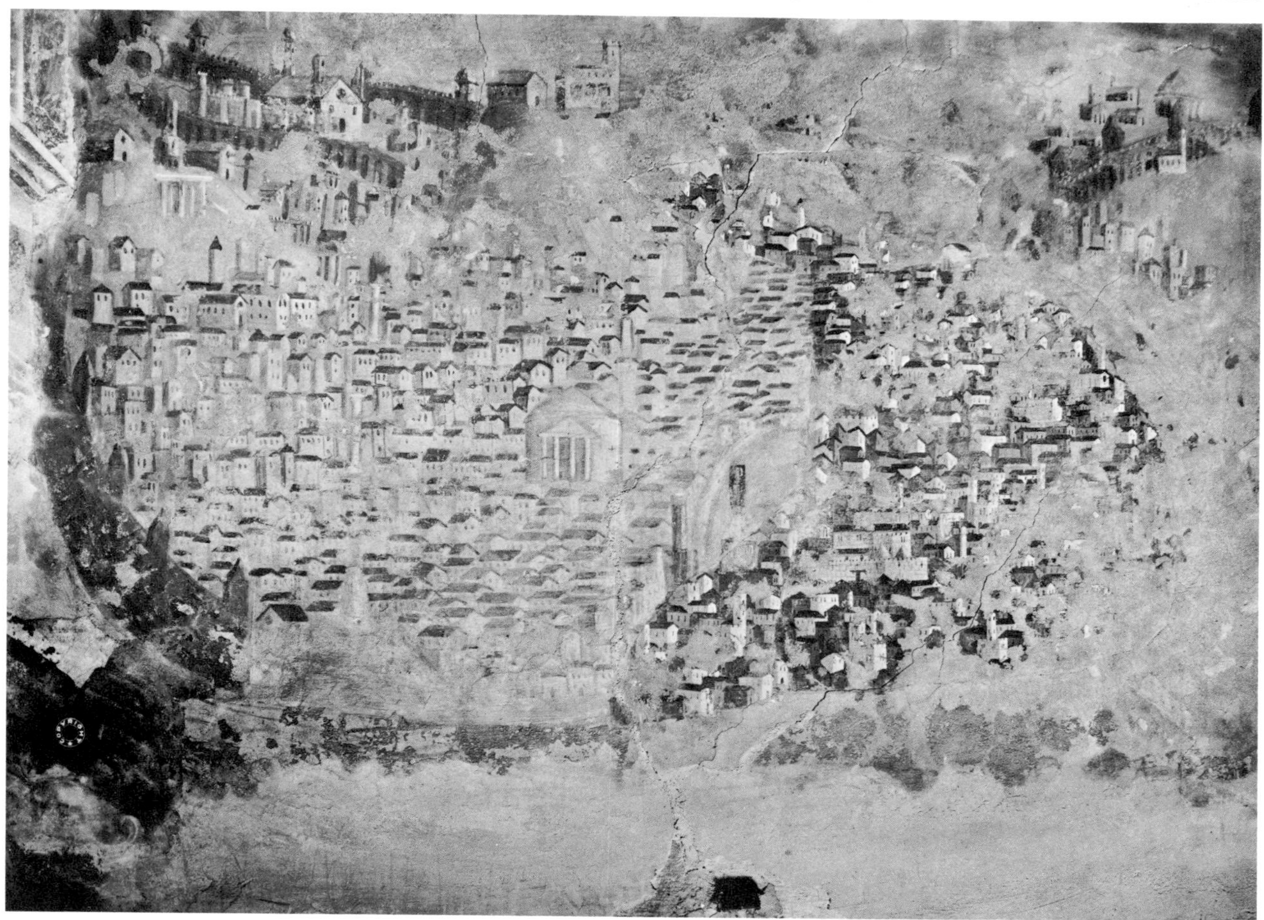

239. Panorama of Rome, as of 1435, fresco, Masolino, Castiglione d'Olona, Baptistery

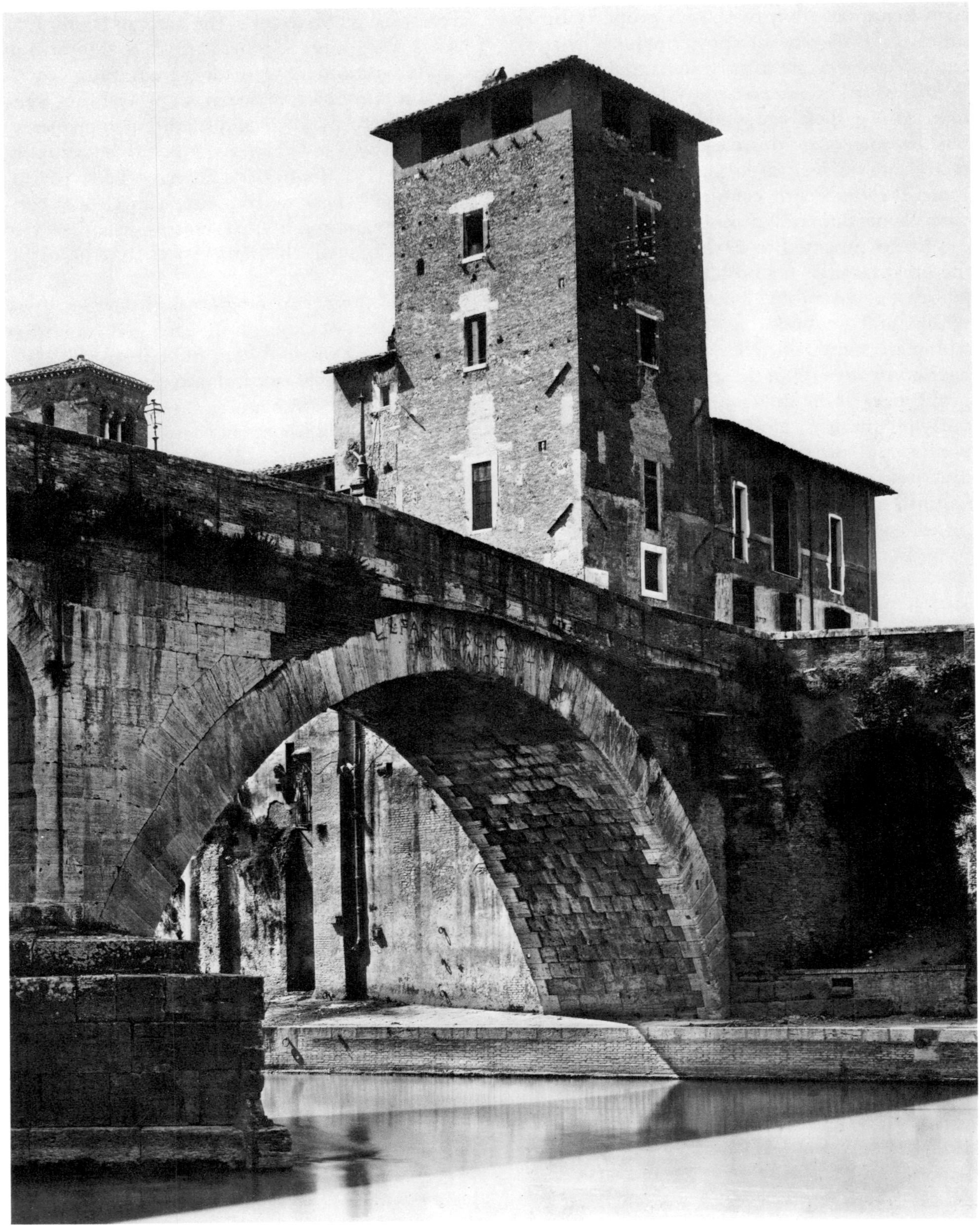

240. Tiber Island, tower guarding Ponte Fabrizio

continuous increase in number until the mid-thirteenth century, wholesale demolitions aside, were linked, of course, to the rise of the new town-based nobility. Many of the new families were settled in Trastevere and across the Tiber in the Ripa, from the river bank to the foot of the Capitoline Hill. The Papareschi had their towered mansion near S. Maria in Trastevere. A huge tower, its name and ownership unknown, commanded the west-bank bridgehead of Ponte Santa Maria, the Ponte Rotto. Two more still stood in the eighteenth century opposite the atrium of S. Cecilia, on Piazza de' Mercanti; in the late fifteenth century they were seen by the Escurial draughtsman (fig. 210), seventy years later by Naldini (fig. 187); but a dense cluster of towers in that general neighborhood was noted already by Masolino. The Tebaldi, Romani, and Bracucci families, too, were Trasteverini. So were the Pierleoni. The location of their original mansion is unknown; possibly it was close to the bridgehead opposite the Tiber Island, for by the end of the eleventh century they were ensconced on the island. A tower, presumably theirs, even today commands the bridgehead of Ponte Quattro Capi—Pons Judeorum—crossing from the Ripa to the island (fig. 240). By 1100, too, the Pierleoni had built a fortified mansion below the south cliff of the Capitoline Hill, the Tarpeian Rock; barbarously cleaned up and overrestored twenty years ago, part of the mansion, of later medieval date it seems, still rises opposite S. Nicola in Carcere (fig. 241). More Pierleoni towers appear to have stood further north, near S. Marco on the site of Palazzo Venezia. To the south near the east-bank bridgehead of Ponte Rotto, a branch of the Normanni family, a member of the Corsi clan, ominously called Petrus Latrone, and one Bulgamini, all allied with the Pierleoni in 1119, occupied a cluster of fortified mansions. The Theatre of Marcellus, the anchor point of the Ripa, by the twelfth century was apparently in the hands of another noble family, the Faffi or Fabii. In the thirteenth century it fell to the Savelli, later to the Orsini. There is no proof that the Pierleoni ever held the monument; but, since around 1100 they dominated the neighborhood, it is hard to believe they left the most powerful stronghold in other hands.

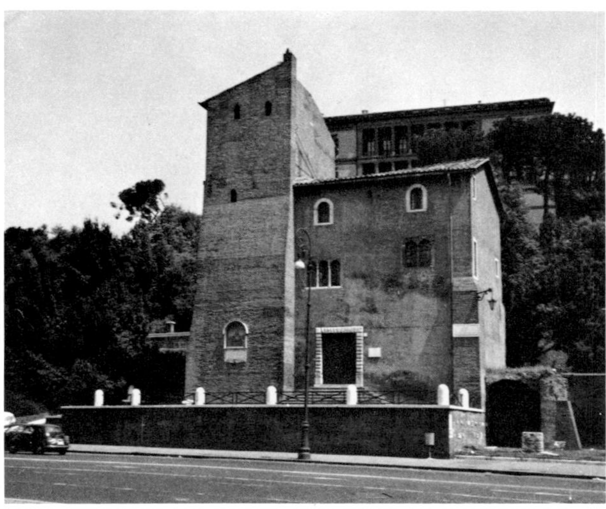

241. Pierleoni Mansion (?)

As the Pierleoni dominated the Ripa, the Cenci seem to have held sway over the Tiber bend. On Piazza dell'Orologio, then called the *Campo*, "where the Parione starts," stood till 1536 the "Tower of Stephanus Serpetri," around 1050 the head of the Cenci clan; it was perhaps in this tower that Gregory VII, kidnapped at Christmas Mass in 1075 at S. Maria Maggiore, was held prisoner. The tower—rather, a many-towered mansion, it seems—covered the approach to Monte Giordano, and perhaps that hillock too was occupied by the Cenci; Orsini property in the thirteenth century, its many interlocking buildings, though remodeled time and again, nonetheless provide a splendid example of a medieval fortified mansion growing and mushrooming over the centuries (fig. 242). Another Cenci tower, built in 1074 to block Ponte S. Angelo, was torn down the following year by Gregory VII, archenemy of the Cenci. More towers of theirs stood at the borderline of the Ripa, either on Monte Cenci or in Piazza Paganica, or even in both places. The towers of "those of S. Eustachio," also called Statii, obviously stood close to that church and thus near the Pantheon. By the early thirteenth century, the Orsini also had a stronghold in the ruins of the Circus Flaminius. Nearer the edge of the abitato prior to 1100, two towers, one built atop a Roman arch, rose close to the nunnery attached to S. Maria in Via Lata. On the

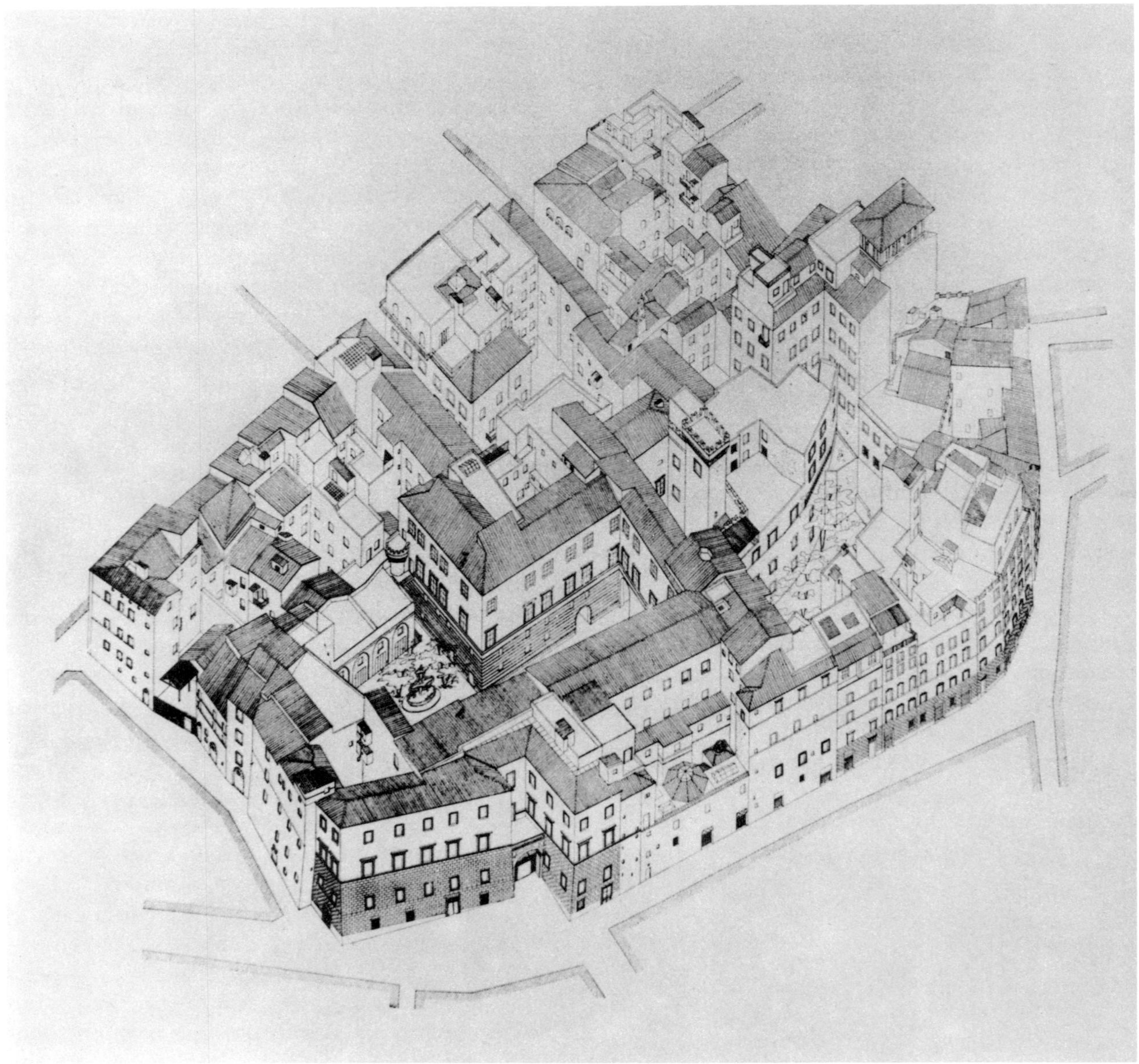

242. Monte Giordano, as of 1950, isometric view, drawing, M.P.F. Asso

Capitoline Hill, the Corsi clan until 1118 had its fortified mansion, presumably where the Palazzo del Senatore now looms over the remains of the ancient Tabularium.

Few if any of the towers thus documented inside the abitato seem to have survived and those remaining are ill-documented and few: Torre del Papito on Largo Argentina; Torre Sanguigna north of Piazza Navona; Torre della Scimmia off Via della Scrofa; Torre dei Margani on the Piazza of that name (fig. 243); a huge unnamed tower in the courtyard of Palazzo Mattei di Paganica; another of the Boveschi family in Via della Tribuna di Tor dei Specchi; Tor Millina on Via dell'Anima, remodeled with the adjoining mansion around 1490 from earlier structures; in Trastevere the tower of the Anguillara family. Many more appear on sixteenth-century maps and *vedute*: the Torre del Merangolo, incorporated in Palazzo Patrizi near S. Caterina dei Funari; on Campo dei Fiori, Torre dell'Arpacata, to mention only these.

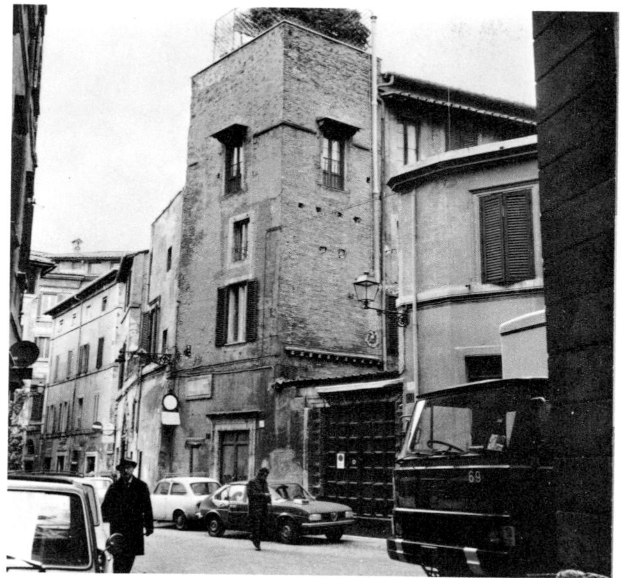

243. Torre dei Margani

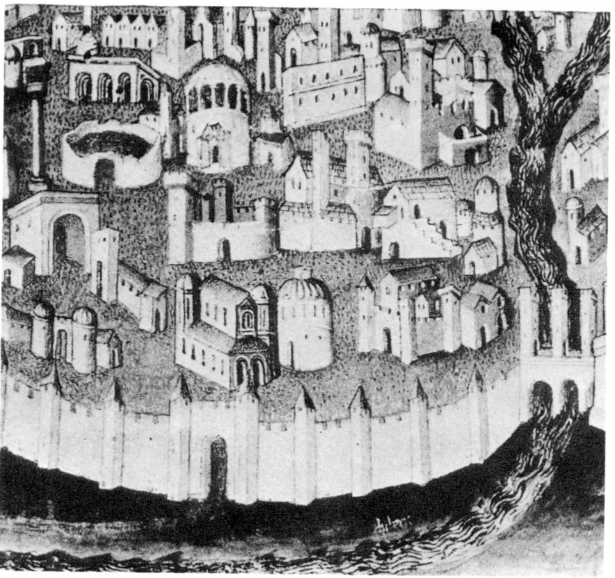

244. Towered mansions in Tiber bend, Map first quarter of fifteenth century

Hardly any towers, though, stood in isolation as they are seen today. Presenting them as monuments lonely and forlorn on an empty square was the unfortunate ninteenth-century conceit of twentieth-century city planners: Torre del Papito on Largo Argentina is a sad example. Rather, in the Middle Ages, towers formed part of larger building complexes. Over and over again contemporaries refer to the tower and mansion of a family, *turris* and *domus* jointly and interchangeably. Clusters of towers, too, were frequent, like those seen near S. Cecilia by the Escurial draughtsman, whether belonging to allied or hostile families—and obviously, alliances were apt to break down quickly. In 1238, the Arcioni family leased part of the Thermae of Constantine on the Quirinal on condition that the lessee from the top of the ruins, obviously fortified, "may make war and peace on anybody except the Arcioni" and vice versa. Maps and views, even from the sixteenth century, and a few precious remains picture such tower clusters and towered mansions (fig. 244). Some were defended by an outer circular crenelated wall and outside towers, protecting a tall, commanding keep inside. Others formed rectangular compounds, their walls crenelated; stables and dwellings, at times including a tall manor house, were built against their inside faces and one corner was fortified by a tower. The mansion of the Anguillara family, in Trastevere beyond Ponte Garibaldi and opposite S. Crisogono (fig. 245), while of thirteenth-century and later date, represented the type to perfection before it was scrubbed and cleaned inside and out; a watercolor by Roesler Franz shows the courtyard prior to that face lifting (fig. 246). The mansion of the Margani, first built before 1305 but in its present state of fourteenth- and fifteenth-century date, albeit restored and overcleaned, consists of a tower facing the piazza and a porticoed wing extending back along a walled courtyard, its entrance framed by the fragments of a Roman cornice. The earliest such compound surviving seems to be the cardinal's palace at S. Maria in Cosmedin, where building blocks of different size, plan, height, and date are joined, the obligatory tower's place being taken by the campanile of the church. Whether or not the palace incorporates eighth- and ninth-century elements, the majority of its sections appear to have been built and altered from the early twelfth to the fifteenth centuries. Indeed, most of the towered mansions known from old views appear to have been built in successive campaigns. A compound, fortified by a low tower,

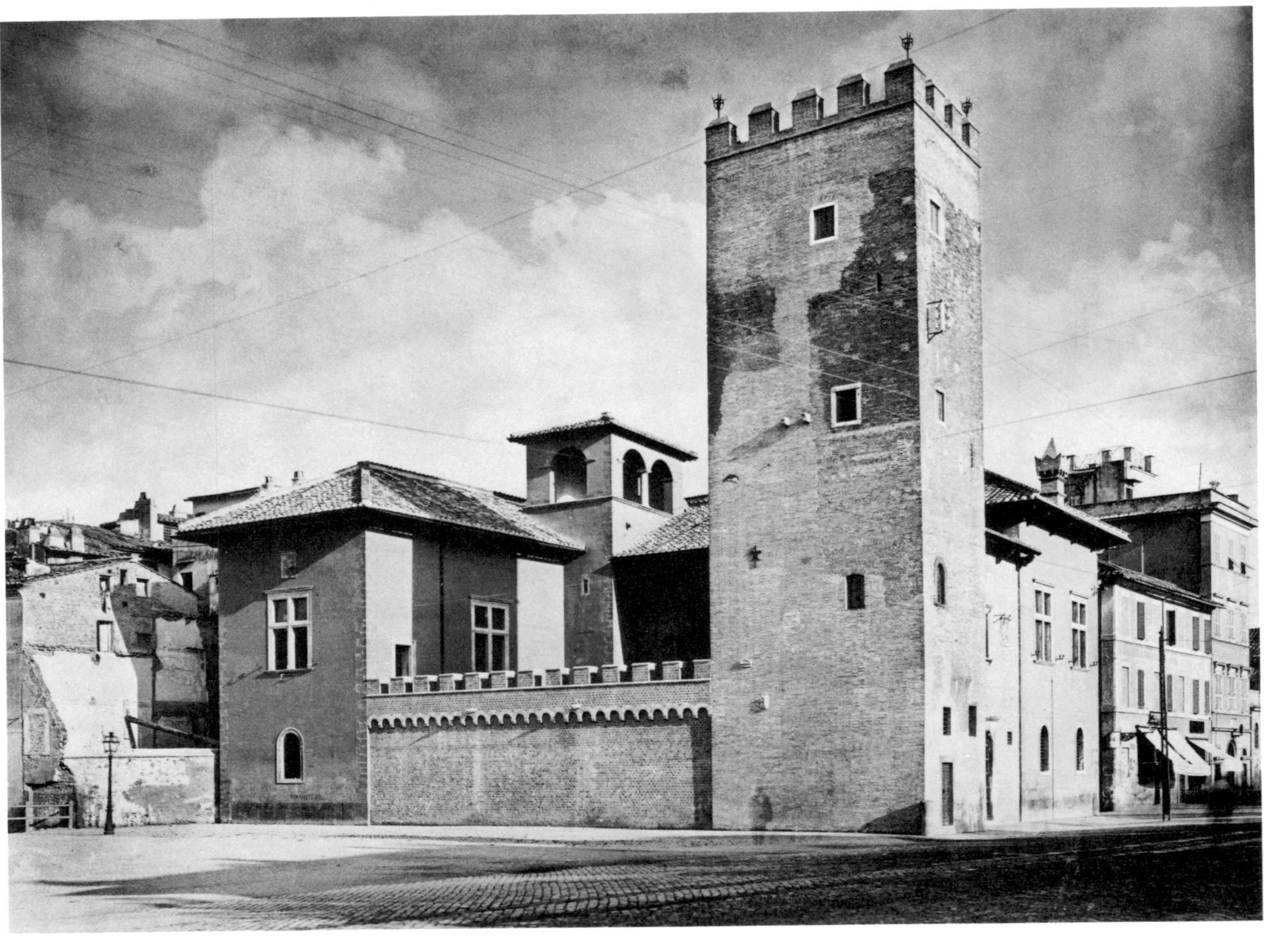

245. Anguillara mansion, exterior, as restored

was attached to the Tor de' Conti still when the Escurial draughtsman sketched it; but it may have been built at the same time as or later or even earlier than the surviving huge tower (fig. 255). Sometimes a tall mansion, large or small, though not fortified—possibly a late medieval type—was linked to a tower: the residence of the Millini on Via dell'Anima consists of two wings, built in the late fifteenth century against the older family tower, which was restored at the time of the new additions; Torre della Scimmia, too, on Via dei Portoghesi shows traces of such a mansion-*cum*-tower.

Early maps convey an idea of this link between tower and mansion customary in medieval Rome. However, they also distort the overall picture of the abitato by showing mansions and churches, their points of reference, in isolation. The reality was very different. Mansions were engulfed on all sides by houses, as were church buildings, large and small. Masolino's *veduta* in the early fifteenth century (fig. 239), as well as the views of the Escurial draughtsman and of Heemskerck, the first seventy, the other one hundred years later, give a truer picture. So do the few examples that survive, if altered and remodeled over the centuries. The church and convent of S. Prassede are still enveloped on all sides—in front of the atrium, along the flanks of the church, and behind its apse and transept—by housing, all containing a medieval or indeed an earlier core. Similarly, S. Cecilia, by the early fifteenth century, was surrounded by dwellings, among them, in the Jews' Court, a small double-storied house built against the wall of a chapel of the church. The structures on Monte

Giordano, too, while remodeled over the last five hundred years, still show to perfection how the mansions of a family cluster, each branch housed in a wing of its own (for privacy and safety), were entangled with each other and how they engulf the twelfth-century apse of the small church of S. Simeone. They also show how on all sides smaller houses lean against the walls of the Orsini mansions (fig. 242). Or else, a document of 1279, brought to life by Brentano, reflects the intertwining of the family mansion of the S. Eustachio clan, near the Pantheon, with dozens of houses owned by them and by others: the mansion proper with a small tower and an arched entrance, bordering on one side a wall of the Pantheon and on the other the dwelling of another family; a fortification adjoining the Pantheon, part-owned by the S. Eustachio family—we do not know what it looked like; the shop of an apothecary; a "palace" occupied by a blacksmith and next to it a one-storied house; another house inhabited by a member of the family with a dome and an arch—could it be the Arco della Ciambella in the Thermae of Agrippa and a hundred meters south of the Pantheon? And, then, there are more houses interspersed with sheds, all built close together with narrow streets in between and occupied by all sorts of people: lawyers, clerks, craftsmen. There is no topographical class distinction: nobles, notaries, and cobblers live side by side and in the same building, as was the rule still a hundred years ago and is still the case in many of the old palaces; shops and craftsmen occupy the ground floor and invade the courtyard of the palace, while the Costaguti or some other noble family live on the *piano nobile*. There were no separate rich and poor neighborhoods in medieval Rome.

Many of the towers and mansions, whether surviving or known only from old *vedute*, were of late medieval date. Already in the twelfth and

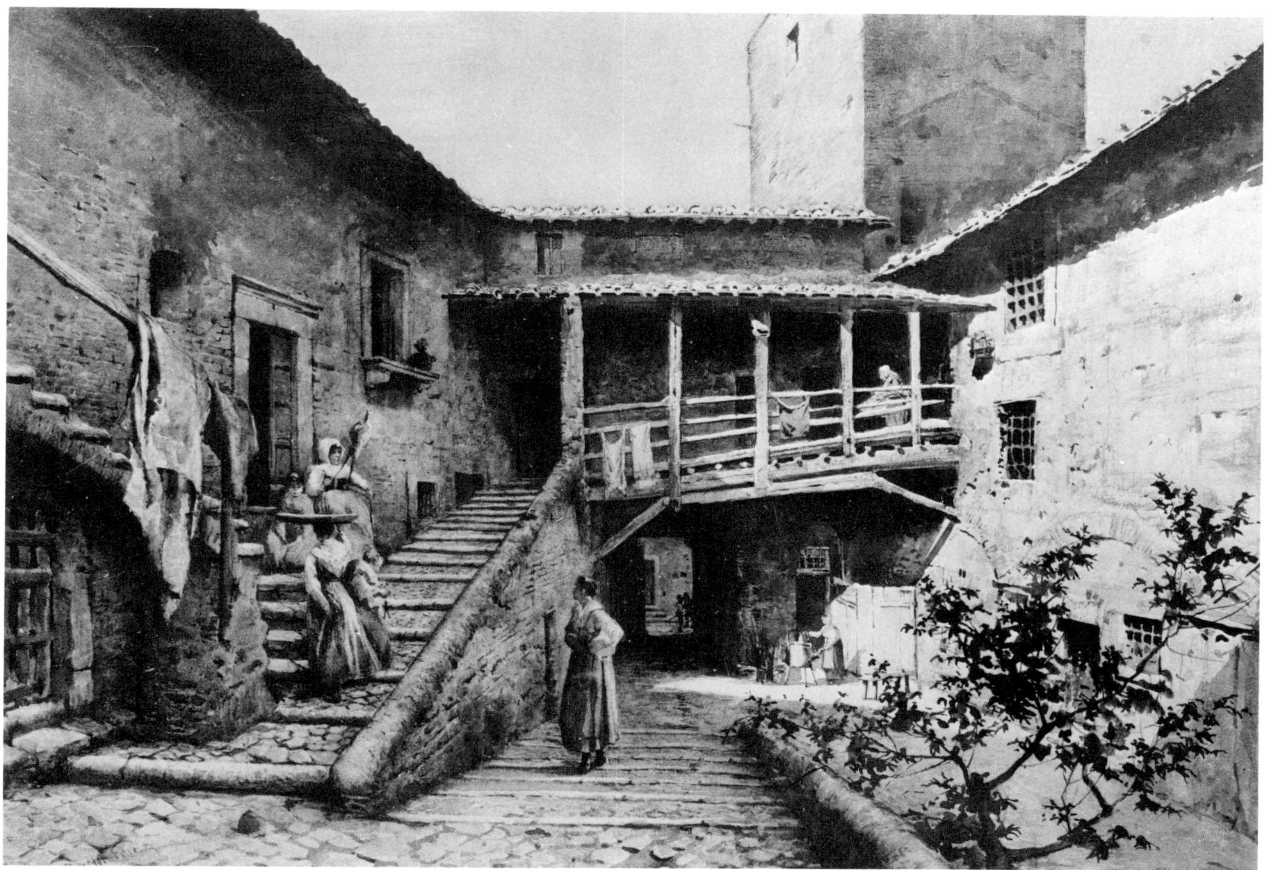

246. Anguillara mansion, interior, before restoration, as of ca. 1880 (?), watercolor, E. Roesler Franz, Museo di Roma

early thirteenth centuries, however, their number was large: one hundred and forty were demolished in 1257 by Brancaleone di Andalò; a century before, the short-lived republican Commune had torn down those of families supporting the papacy; and earlier still in the Investiture Wars, other family towers had been destroyed. But towers were quickly rebuilt or replaced by newer and stronger ones or built from scratch as late as the fifteenth century.

Towers through the Middle Ages dominated the skyline of Rome, both abitato and disabitato. From the narrow crooked streets and the mass of houses closely crowded, or indeed from the encircling wasteland extending to the city walls, the towers of the great families soared skyward; so did the numberless *campanili*, an integral part of church planning in Rome from the second half of the eleventh century on: tiny ones, like those of S. Benedetto in Piscinula—as early as 1069—and S. Rufina, both in Trastevere, and the one at S. Biagio in Mercato, rising from the ruin of a Roman house at the foot of the Capitol and visible since the 1930s, when the eighteenth-century church of S. Rita da Cascia was moved stone by stone almost half a mile away to near the Theatre of Marcellus; or, tall structures, such as the bell towers of SS. Giovanni e Paolo, S. Maria Nova, S. Crisogono, S. Maria in Trastevere, and S. Maria in Cosmedin. For the better part of the Middle Ages, Rome must have had the hedgehog look that S. Gimignano retains to this day, and which Bologna still had in the eighteenth century. Still, there is a difference: despite family towers and *campanili*, it was the ruins and buildings of antiquity that overpowered the skyline of medieval Rome. They were, we think, the "palaces" that jointly with "the seed of towers" impressed the Englishman, Magister Gregory, looking down from Monte Mario—any ancient ruin, and especially thermae, was termed a *palace* in medieval Rome. Emerging from the abitato, Gozzoli, the Escurial draughtsman, Heemskerck, and Naldini saw the Pantheon, Castel S. Angelo, the Theatre of Marcellus, its crenelated wall forbiddingly turned riverwards (figs. 187, 208, 210, 212, 213). Even at present the view from SS. Trinità dei Monti toward the dome of the Pantheon, if one blots out the nineteenth- and twentieth-century constructions intervening, conveys an idea of the overwhelming dominance of the ancient buildings and ruins over the medieval abitato; so did the Theatre of Marcellus fifty-odd years ago, when it was still crowded in on all sides by housing. And at least the Thermae of Caracalla and the Colosseum make one aware of the overpowering impression these ruins made standing forlorn in the surrounding wasteland. Masolino's panorama of around 1435, though unreliable in topographical detail, splendidly brings out the crowded housing in the core of town, the towers, three- or four-stories high, and a few ancient ruins emerging from the mass and seeming taller than they were in reality, the whole set off against the sparsely settled disabitato.

CHAPTER FOURTEEN

The Disabitato and the Lateran

To the east right behind the Capitol, to the south starting at the Theatre of Marcellus or at S. Maria in Cosmedin, to the north from S. Lorenzo in Lucina and the Campo Marzio, started the disabitato, encircling the town proper and extending to the Aurelian Walls. Written sources aside, Heemskerck's panorama, regardless of its late date, conveys the best idea of what that zone looked like. Just below the eastern cliff of the Capitol, cottages and a few houses with gardens stood among the columns of the Temple of Concord; others opened into the vaults of the substructures of that or another building; two others leaned against the base of the "columna perfectissima," possibly the Column of Phocas, with an olive grove in between (fig. 247). Things had changed very little three and four hundred years later, and the houses that then had invaded the Basilica of Maxentius may well have been among those listed already by Cencius Camerarius in 1192 (fig. 248). The ruins of the Forum and the crest and slope of the Palatine were covered with trees, fields, and vineyards; further on, the Celian and the Little Aventine—where S. Saba stands—were likewise overgrown; and along the crest of the Celian, from the Lateran to SS. Giovanni e Paolo and down to the valley below

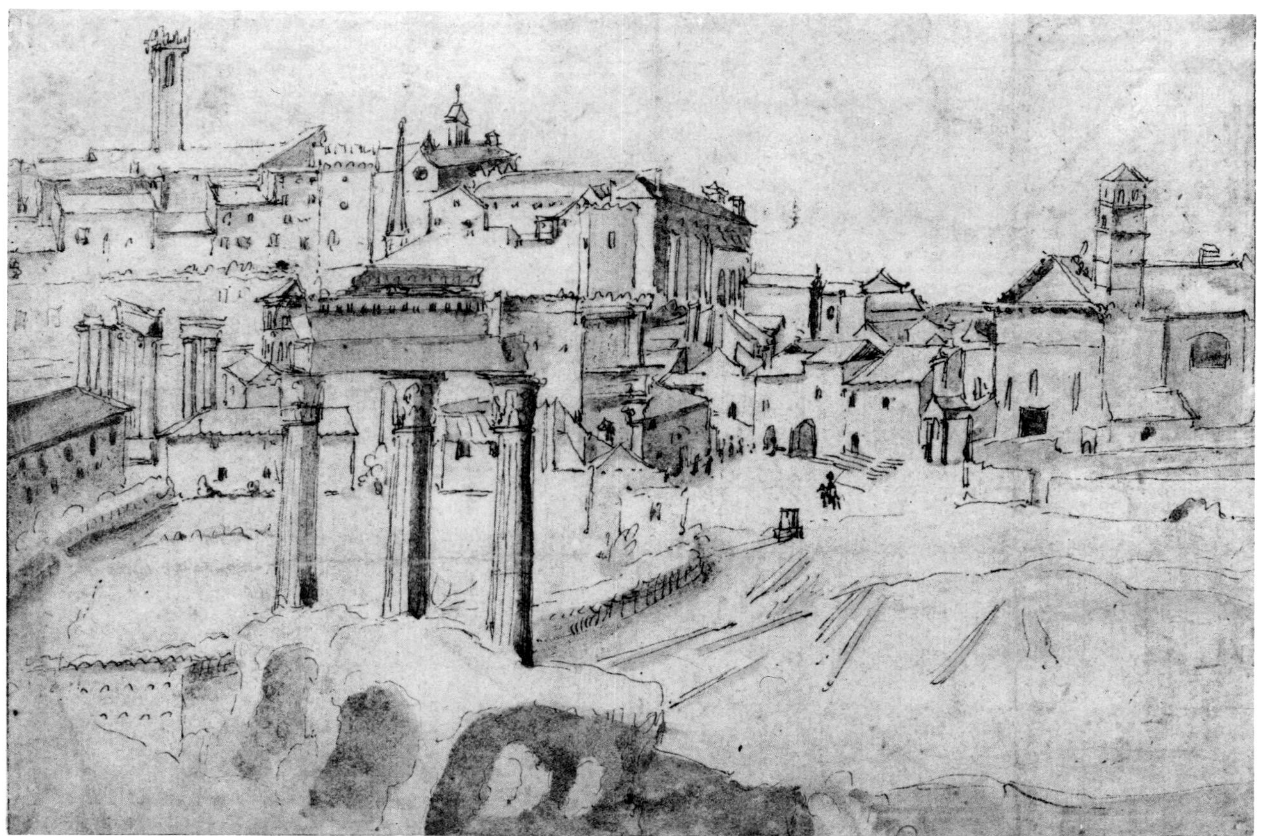

247. Forum invaded by houses, looking toward Capitoline Hill, as of 1534-1536 drawing, circle of Marten van Heemskerck, Berlin, Kupferstichkabinett, 79 D2A, fol. 12r

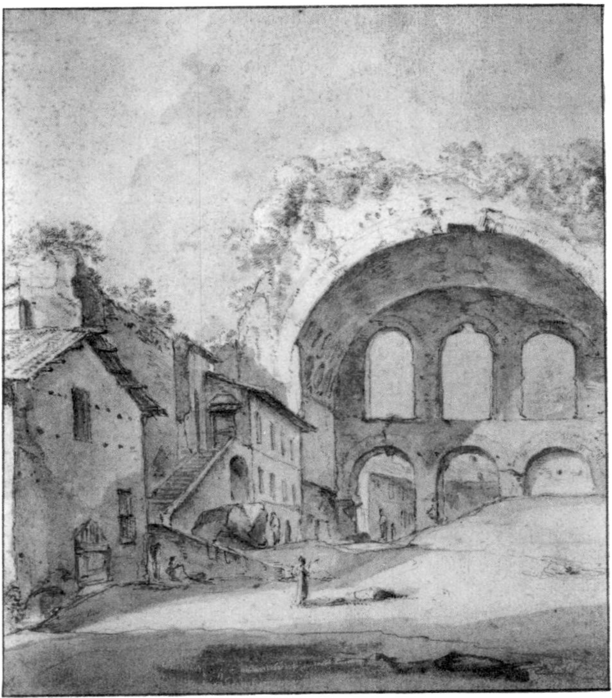

248. Housing near S. Maria Nova in Basilica of Maxentius, as of ca. 1625, drawing B. Breenbergh, Amsterdam, Rijksmuseum

S. Gregorio Magno, and eastward as far as Porta Maggiore, dozens of documents list through the Middle Ages fields, vineyards, pastures, and a few farmhouses. Near Sto. Stefano Rotondo, for example, the convent of S. Erasmo by 938 was deserted, "with its buildings and gardens or fields with olive and apple trees all around, . . . adjoining on one side the farm of [one] George . . . and the cottage of Peter and those of several others . . . and vaults and the field of Ursus . . . and on the second side the field of the presbyter Leo and on the third side the field of the heirs of Hadrian from Magnanapoli [*de banneo neapolim*] and the vineyard of the noble lady Sergia and on the fourth a cottage"; at the end of the century the convent, meanwhile ceded to Subiaco, was still a big farmstead with "houses, a wine cellar, barn and gardens and vineyards, olive groves and apple trees all around." Also, near Porta Maggiore, a group of farms around a garden and a chapel of Saint Theodore, donated in 924 to the priest (later bishop) Florus; by 958 there were cottages with courtyards and gardens and a larger farm "with its courtyard and pergola and garden and closed-in vineyard and an apple orchard and vaults along the road leading to [S. Croce in] Jerusalem."

On the real Aventine around the Savelli fortress, built as late as 1285-1287 near S. Sabina, Heemskerck saw a few houses and some more crowded around S. Maria in Cosmedin at the foot of the hill; nearby, the Arch of Janus and the church of S. Anastasia were in ruins (fig. 249). Naturally, some earlier buildings had disappeared and new structures had been built by Heemskerck's time. Yet, except for the late-medieval Savelli castle on the Aventine and except for two buildings from the fifteenth century at the foot of the Palatine, the rotunda of S. Teodoro and the hospital and church of S. Maria della Consolazione, the picture Heemskerck drew hardly differed from the appearance of the disabitato of three and four hundred years before. Likewise the entire territory around the north of S. Silvestro, from the Tiber to the foot of the Pincio and from the sites of Piazza Colonna and Fontana Trevi to Porta del Popolo, was agricultural terrain into the first years of the sixteenth century. By the ninth and tenth centuries it had belonged to the convent of S. Silvestro in Capite; outside the walls, the property continued along the Via Flaminia to the crumbling church of S. Valentino and to Ponte Milvio. Amidst the fields rose the monuments of the northern Campus Martius—the Mausoleum of Augustus, the obelisk of his colossal sundial, the column of Marcus Aurelius, as well as the fifth-century basilica of S. Lorenzo in Lucina. S. Silvestro had been given this huge property, wholly or in part, at its foundation in 761; a century later, it reached its full extent, monuments and all, including specifically the Column of Marcus Aurelius, Porta del Popolo, and the Milvian Bridge. It is only reasonable to assume that prior to 761, large parts had belonged to the family of the founders, Popes Stephen II and Paul I. Only toward the end of the tenth century does the property seem to have been partially broken up. By the High and late Middle Ages the Mausoleum of Augustus, fortified for a short while around A.D. 1000, was apparently decaying and gradually fell into ruin; further north on the Tiber bank rose the tower "whence the shade of Nero used to spook," possibly a

Roman ruin rebuilt. Montecitorio may or may not have been a stronghold before the Colonna occupied it in the late thirteenth century. Strategically, it seems, the upper stretch of the Corso, Porta del Popolo and Via Flaminia beyond, had no importance. Still in the twelfth and thirteenth centuries, though, the possessions of S. Silvestro in Capite reached from S. Lorenzo in Lucina and Campo Marzio to Piazza Colonna, where the column of Marcus Aurelius was a prized piece of property, to the neighborhood of Fontana Trevi and the west slope of the Quirinal, and east to Porta Pinciana; all markedly rural, set with small houses, sheds, and straw huts, tiny churches, gardens, fields, and ancient ruins, such as the Baths of Constantine and the Temple of Serapis on the west spur of the Quirinal. Further east the crest of the Quirinal and the Pincio were entirely rural until in the sixteenth and seventeenth centuries they became a suburb of elegant villas.

Nonetheless, in the vast expanse of agricultural property and wasteland that made up the disabitato a few suburbs had formed at an early time: one at the Lateran; another clustered around S. Maria Maggiore; a third at the northeastern foot of the Palatine, around S. Maria Nova (S. Francesca Romana) and the Colosseum. At S. Maria Maggiore a successful effort seems to have been made at an early time, and was sustained through the centuries, to keep open the links to the abitato, to rescue and enlarge the extant ecclesiastical property, and to keep alive and strengthen a populated center. Hadrian I in 786 rebuilt and richly endowed a monastery near the basilica, to have it serviced. In the ninth century, the community centers of S. Prassede and S. Martino ai Monti were replaced by splendid new churches—the former

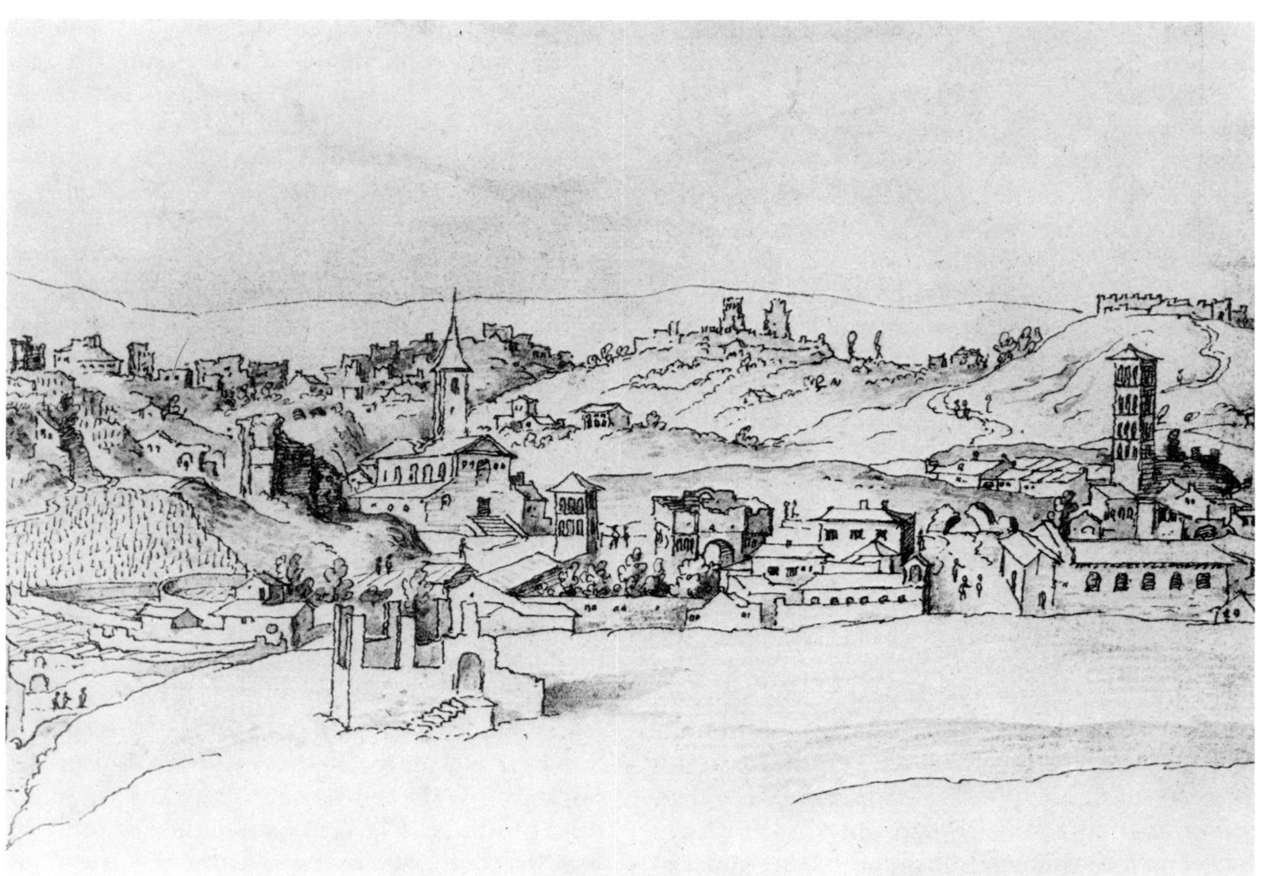

249. View of disabitato, as of 1534-1536, detail showing S. Anastasia and S. Maria in Cosmedin, Berlin, Kupferstichkabinett, 79 D2A, fols. 91^{v}, 92^{r}

provided with relics to attract pilgrims—and handed over to newly established and well-provided monasteries. Prior to the tenth century (and possibly long before) two monasteries dedicated to Saint Andrew had been installed close to S. Maria Maggiore. Further away, but still relatively close by, the diaconia of S. Vito in Macello was, it seems, likewise attached to a monastery from the ninth century. Further east still, S. Bibiana had been founded as early as the fifth century. Insignificant by 806/7, in light of the small gift it received from Leo III, it was renewed shortly after by linking it to a wealthy nunnery, one of the wealthiest in Rome by the tenth century. Rebuilt, it seems, in the thirteenth century as a tiny basilica, perhaps with trabeated colonnades, it stands to this day as remodeled in 1624 by Bernini. Around these churches and convents a populated center was bound to form, a satellite village on the Esquiline, extending toward the Oppian and with marked rural features. It would have grown over the centuries, and by 1192 over forty houses, with sheds, huts, and gardens, were listed adjoining S. Maria Maggiore and S. Andrea in Catabarbara, all owned by the basilica or one of the nearby monasteries. More such housing was attached to the monastery servicing S. Prassede, extending as far as S. Martino ai Monti some 150 meters to the southeast. As early as the mid-eleventh century a pipeline, perhaps dating from Roman times, carried water to the neighborhood, and a market was held nearby, possibly on the site of the old Macellum Liviae near S. Vito in Macello, more or less where the big market on Piazza Vittorio Emmanuele is held now. Still other housing was built around S. Pudenziana northwest and downhill from S. Maria Maggiore, where Wijngaerde noted it around 1550 (fig. 250). The streets toward the abitato were kept open from early times. To the west toward SS. Apostoli and the south end of the Corso, communications were secured by setting up monasteries near the churches of S. Eufemia and S. Lorenzo in Panisperna. From Roman times on, the area was linked to the neighborhood of the Imperial Fora by two streets kept open through the Middle Ages. Both issued from the Forum of Nerva, the *Forum Transitorium* or "Throughway Forum," as it was called of old, through a huge arch; medieval etymology changed its name, *Arcus Nervae*, "the Arch of Nerva," to *Arca Noe*, "Noah's Ark." Behind it, buildings crowded the site occupied since 1198 by Tor de' Conti, built by Innocent III for his family. By the fourteenth century, but presumably long before, a shopping center had formed there: butcher stalls lined one or two alleys near the tower; and, already around 1200, the Temple on the Forum housed the "Granary of the Cardinals"; perhaps the grain store was sheltered in the towerlike structure, often drawn till the seventeenth century, which nestled in the porch of the temple (fig. 251). Three stories high, divided on each floor into four groin-vaulted bays, and supported by a column on the ground floor, a pier on the second floor and possibly the third, the structure may well have dated from the twelfth century. The neighborhood, then, must have been well settled—the list of Cencius Camerarius confirms it—a half-way settlement between the abitato and S. Maria Maggiore. From the Arch of Nerva in the rear of the Forum, the street toward S. Maria Maggiore ascended in two parallel branches toward the Esquiline and Oppian Hills. One, in ancient times called *Vicus Patricius*, coincided with what are now Via Madonna dei Monti and Via Urbana, passing by S. Pudenziana and ending some short distance behind S. Maria Maggiore; the other, the Roman *Vicus Suburranus*, running more or less along Via Cavour and S. Lucia in Selcis where the ancient flagstones survive, split behind the apse of S. Martino ai Monti. One branch continued by way of S. Prassede to S. Vito in Macello and beyond to Porta S. Lorenzo; the other turned southwest to Porta Maggiore and both connected with the highways across the Campagna, to Tivoli and Palestrina respectively.

Far closer to the abitato than the "village" of S. Maria Maggiore, another suburb had grown since at least the tenth century at the east end of the Forum. S. Maria Nova, built around 855, was its core. Documented from the late tenth century on in numerous leases and continuing through the High Middle Ages, housing ex-

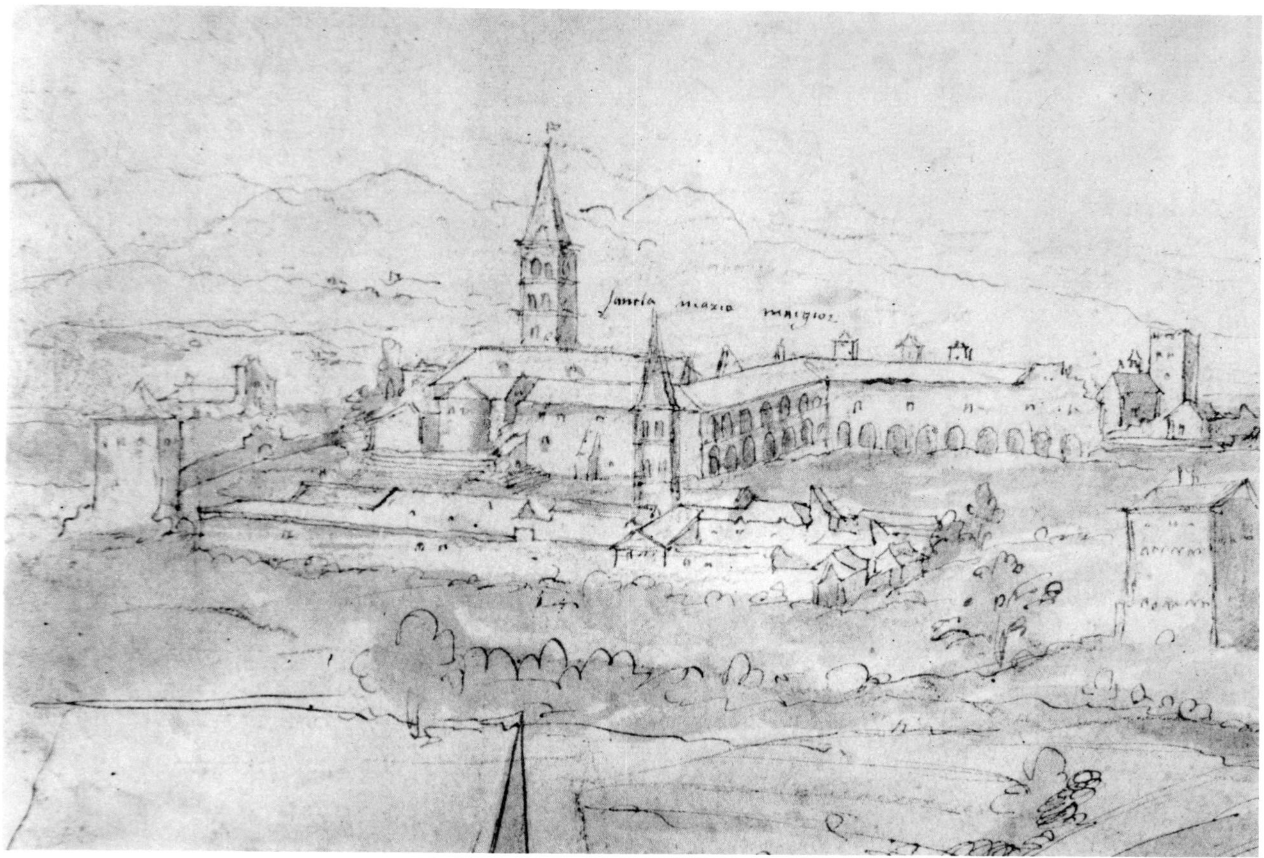

250. Settlement around S. Maria Maggiore, adjoining palace and S. Pudenziana, as of ca. 1550, drawing, A. van den Wijngaerde, detail, Oxford, Ashmolean Museum

tended into the Temple of Venus and Roma, the Colosseum, the House of Nero, and gradually up the slope of the Palatine. The lessees and their witnesses, apparently neighbors, seem to have been mostly craftsmen: coppersmiths and blacksmiths, wheelwrights, a cobbler, a mason, and many lime burners—the abundance of marble from the ruins would attract them so much that the neighborhood, like other similar ones, was known as *calcarium*. Along with such humble folk, though, appear at an early time a *scrinarius*—an employee of the papal chancellery—clerics, a lawyer, a noble; the latter two were perhaps absentee landlords. Also, even before the mid-eleventh century, a banker had his place nearby, at "Banker's crossroads"; and by 1180, a *contrada cambiatorum*, "Bankers' Street," existed near the Colosseum, perhaps serving pilgrims on their way to the Lateran. By the twelfth century, anyway, the suburb was sizable, private ownership had increased, and the social level seems to have risen. Cencius Camerarius, compiling his *Liber Censuum* in 1192, listed over forty houses; one group near some public baths formed the mansion of the Frangipani family; others were owned by clerics, butchers, and other respectable burghers able to afford festooning their houses and the adjoining stretch of street for papal processions. But then, the housing of those unable to pay for such a luxury—cottages, sheds, and huts—would not likely have been listed. The growth and importance of the suburb at that time was probably tied to the Frangipani's occupation of the Colosseum, the slope of the Palatine, and part of the way to town since the late eleventh century. Around the church of S. Maria Nova the cluster of housing swelled and extended both in front of the church and southwards up the slope of the Palatine along a path ascending to

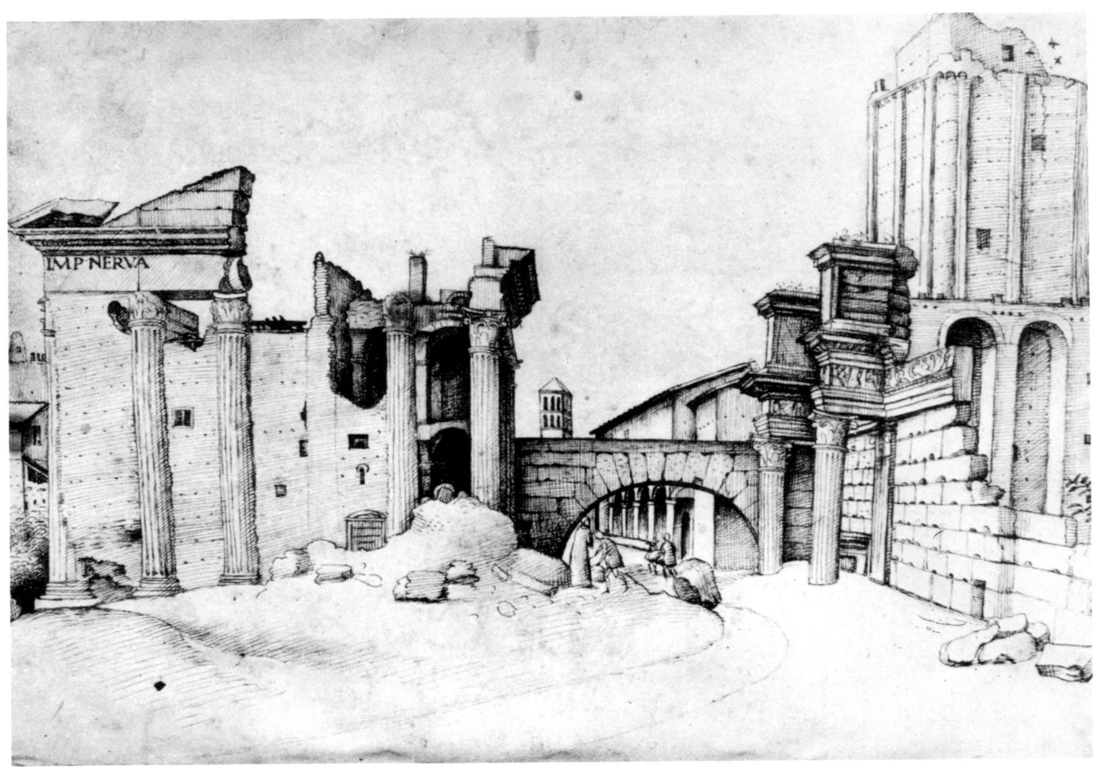

251. Forum of Nerva with "Granary of the Cardinals" inside the Temple of Minerva, as of ca. 1495; center, "Arca Noe" and porticoed house beyond; and, right, Tor de' Conti, drawing, *Escurialensis*, fol. 57v

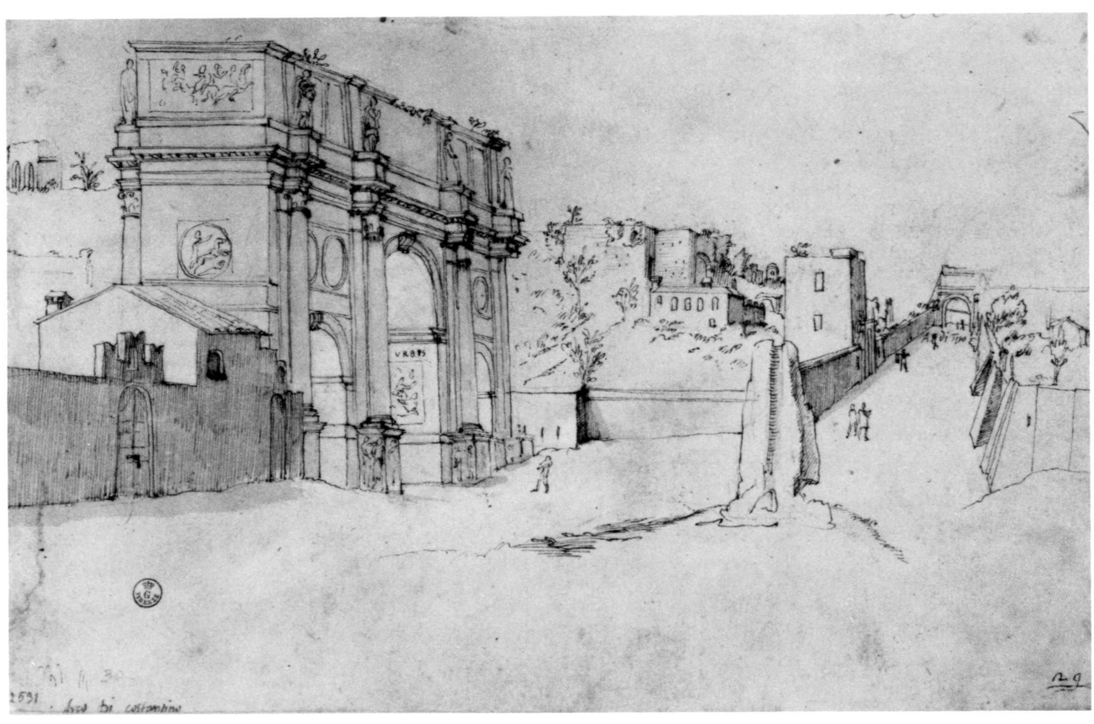

252. Settlement around S. Maria Nova, as of ca. 1560, in foreground Arch of Constantine, drawing G. A. Dosio, Florence, Uffizi

the church of S. Maria in Pallara, now S. Sebastiano alla Polveriera (fig. 252). Two streets, one across the Roman Forum and another passing by the Imperial Fora, linked the area to the edge of the abitato along the north cliff of the Capitoline Hill and on the south stretch of the Corso; a few houses, listed by Cencius Camerarius and strung out along these streets and on the slope of the Palatine near S. Maria Nova and the Arch of Titus, are still seen, though they were presumably rebuilt, in sixteenth-century views.

The village around S. Maria Maggiore on the crest of the Esquiline continued to grow, but the one around S. Maria Nova seems to have dwindled, except for the houses on the slope of the Palatine. No wonder that: the hills were comparatively healthy; the low parts of the disabitato were not to be trusted. The Colosseum and its neighborhood, except for its higher parts, was still unsafe in the late nineteenth century, witness Henry James's *Daisy Miller*, and though the carrier of the sickness, the anopheles mosquito, was identified less than a hundred years ago, people knew only too well by the twelfth century its breeding grounds whence malaria spread: from swamps and stagnating ponds, it was thought, rose dark mists laden with the fever. From the disabitato it invaded the town and forced the inhabitants to take to the hills every year during the heat, leaving the city abandoned; abandoned, that is, by those who could afford to go away—the others obviously remained. But the area beyond the abitato was scary anyhow: mostly wasteland, set with ruins, where green snakes, black toads, and winged dragons hid, whose breath poisoned the air as did the stench of rotting dead bodies—all this the description of an eyewitness to the epidemic that in July 1155 killed half of Barbarossa's army.

Nonetheless, a bold visitor to the disabitato in the mid-twelfth century would have found it very different from the way it might have appeared to his grandfather. The latter would have encountered only a few churches in bad repair and some lonely huts and farms; his grandson would have seen more cultivation, both inside the city walls and beyond. By the twelfth and thirteenth centuries, craftsmen or clerks owning

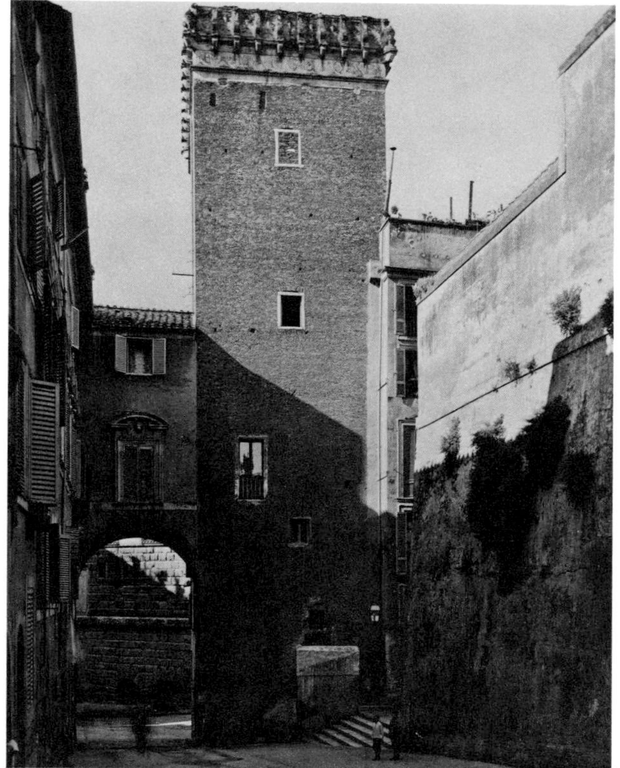

253. Torre del Grillo, prior to 1900

fields or vineyards beyond the gates were quite common. Whether or not the owner of a vineyard and his family went there to disport themselves on a warm day, as they did in the fifteenth century, remains debatable. But the disabitato was opening up, if within limits.

The twelfth- and thirteenth-century visitor, though, would have seen more ominous features as well: fortified mansions and towers by the dozen had been and were being built, and ancient monuments were fortified by the great families of the disabitato—on the Forum, around the Colosseum, on the slope of the Oppian and on the Quirinal, on the Esquiline, and around the Palatine. They commanded the streets that linked the core of town to the suburbs on the Esquiline and the one around the Colosseum and to the Lateran; the streets that led to the roads beyond the city gates and ultimately to family seats in the country. Several towers still stand on the southwest slope of the Quirinal: Tor de' Conti, built apparently from 1198 on by Pope Innocent III, at the lower end of Via

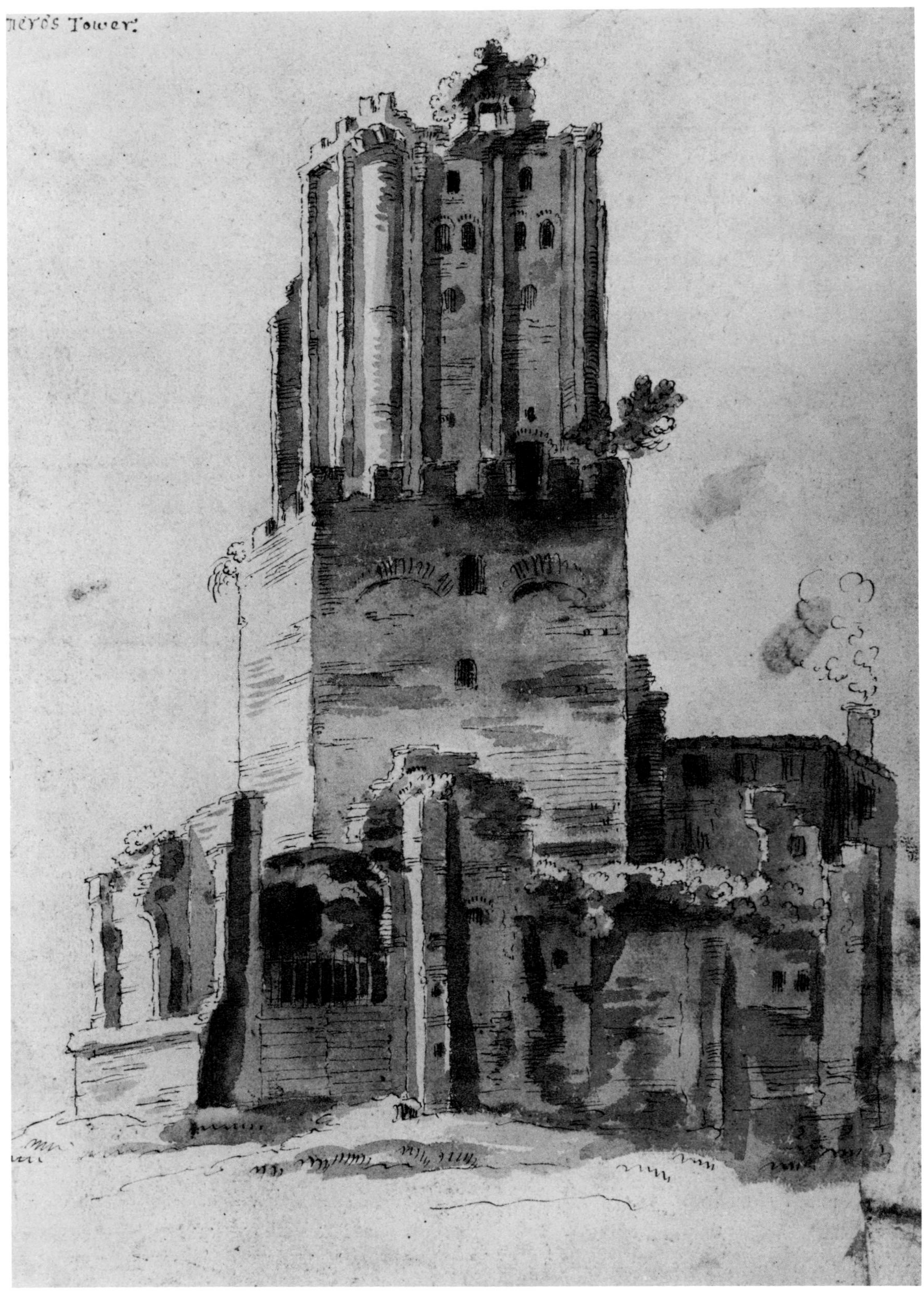

254. Torre delle Milizie, as of ca. 1625, drawing, B. Breenbergh, British Museum

Cavour behind the Forum of Nerva (fig. 162); Torre del Grillo, behind the Forum of Trajan (fig. 253); slightly higher up on Via Quattro Novembre, a tower of unknown ownership and date; on the height of Magnanapoli, near the Market of Trajan, Torre delle Milizie, commanding the view as far as the Pincio and the Gianicolo. Today over 51 meters tall and originally one story higher still, Torre delle Milizie seems to have been built in one campaign over the remains of a much older, possibly Byzantine, fortification; in 1179 it was held by the Frangipani, but it fell to the Annibaldi in 1250, and to the Caetani in 1301 (fig. 254). From its building technique and buttressing, the present tower appears to be a thirteenth- or fourteenth-century construction. Jointly with the Market of Trajan—from the twelfth century on it carried a palace, later of the Cavalieri di Rodi—the three towers rising behind the Roman ruin formed a formidable defense system, provided the clans holding them were not fighting each other. In any event, they make an impressive picture. On the Oppian, two or possibly three towers emerge near S. Pietro in Vincoli. One facing north close to the vaulted stairs ascending from Via Cavour rises from a base built, like that of Tor de' Conti, in bands of black and white stone; a second now serves as the bell tower of S. Francesco di Paolo; a third on the west slope, at one time Annibaldi property, overlooks Via Annibaldi descending to the Colosseum. Behind S. Martino ai Monti rise two more towers, formerly owned by the Arcioni and Cerroni families, later by the Capocci clan. Until the sixteenth and seventeenth centuries, though, there were more towers in that part of the disabitato.

The Frangipani, with the Pierleoni the most powerful family around 1100, had built mansions all over the Forum, the Palatine, and the Colosseum, so that the neighborhood became known as the *Campo Torrechiato* (fig. 255). By 1130, if not before, they had fortified the Colosseum; nonetheless, the vaults at ground level remained the property of S. Maria Nova and continued to be leased as dwellings and workshops for another fifty years or so. The Frangipani also sat on the north slope of the Palatine, around S. Maria in Pallara, now S. Sebastiano alla Polveriera; access was defended by a tower built against the Arch of Titus and known as the *turris cartularia* (fig. 252). Half a dozen towers stood further west: one, Frangipani property, near the Temple of Antoninus and Faustina; two in 1199, probably built long before, stood atop the Arch of Septimius Severus (fig. 256); the southern one, surviving still in 1600, owned by the nearby church of SS. Sergio e Bacco; yet another, the Torre del Campanaro, stood near the Column of Phocas. In 1145 the Frangipani acquired a tower at the eastern end of the Circus Maximus and leased the nearby ruin of the Septizonium, long fortified, at the southwest corner of the Palatine. Other fortifications of theirs stood on the Esquiline close to S. Prassede. In short, the roads to the Lateran from the west and north by 1150 were controlled by the Frangipani, to defend or besiege the popes, depending on circumstances. When in the thirteenth and fourteenth centuries the clan weakened, their towers and fortifications, rebuilt as necessary, went to younger families. By 1240 the Annibaldi had taken over from the Frangipani one half of the Colosseum and a generation later the entire fortified amphitheatre; by 1250 they had also acquired from the same family Torre delle Milizie, most likely a forerunner of the present tower. Indeed, as early as the beginning of the thirteenth century they owned or had built towers all over the neighborhood, from S. Pietro in Vincoli to opposite the Colosseum, and as far as the Lateran, where they placed a tower atop the aqueduct, dominating the approach to the papal palace; they had to remove it again upon the command of Innocent III. Alongside the Annibaldi, the Capocci, like the Frangipani before them, dominated the roads to S. Maria Maggiore on the Esquiline, as their towers still rising behind S. Martino ai Monti attest. The Arcioni in the thirteenth century controlled the west spur of the Quirinal, either from the Thermae of Constantine or the Market of Trajan. The Savelli by the early thirteenth century sat on the Aventine near S. Sabina, whence Honorius III dated some decrees; by 1279 Honorius IV, another Savelli, apparently built the fortified precinct behind the basilica. As early as 1279 when he was still cardinal, he listed in his will

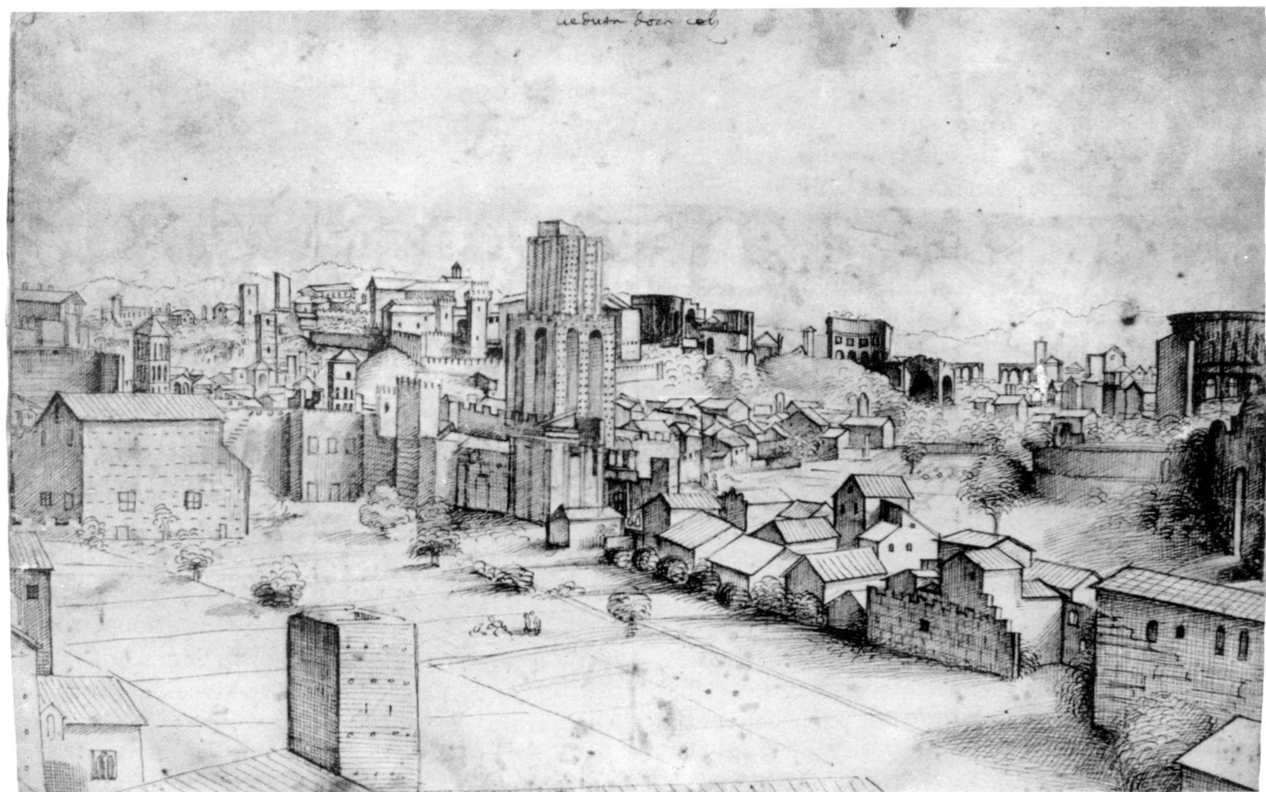

255. View from Aracoeli toward Tor de' Conti; Oppian and Esquiline Hills dominated by towers, as of ca. 1495, drawing, *Escurialensis*, fol. 40v

among his property "all mansions, towers, or ruins of towers that we own from the church of S. Maria ad Gradellis [the temple of Fortuna Virilis] along the Marmorata and the fortification above the Marmorata . . . and other houses and towers which we own from that church toward the Ripa and in the Rione Ripa and the fortification of the *mons Fabiorum* [that is, the Theatre of Marcellus]." Similarly, the Colonna by that time dominated the northern and eastern rim of the abitato, where they sat on Montecitorio and on the west slope of the Quirinal, and where ever since 900 or before they had been ensconced in the ruins of the temple of Serapis. Around 1300 the Caetani became prominent: from the owners of the Tiber Island, supposedly no longer the Pierleoni, they acquired the tower commanding Ponte Quattro Capi, and from the Annibaldi large parts of their fortifications.

The towers obviously played a decisive part in the fights between clans and between papal and antipapal factions. One of these tower-wars in 1203 is vividly described in the *Gesta Innocentii*. The Capocci, the villains of the piece, rebuilt a tower against the command of the chief senatore and attacked the latter's tower near Magnanapoli with wooden siege-towers, walls and moats, fortifying thermae and churches round about, and setting siege machines atop "an ancient monument"—perhaps the Market of Trajan. Against the Capocci the sons of Petrus Alexius built a very tall tower and a Gildo Carbone built three others, while the Annibaldi erected a tower near the Colosseum. It all sounds worse than it was. Fighting was restricted to a tiny section, from Magnanapoli to the church of SS. Quirico and Giulitta and to the Colosseum, fights of street gangs rather than a real war. But the towers were important, if not for serious warfare, then as status symbols.

Under the circumstances and given its isolation, the Lateran wanted protection. To provide it, as early as the ninth century the old titulus of the Quattro Coronati was replaced by a huge church; its entrance tower strategically commanded the Via Maior climbing the hill. In the Wars of Investiture in the early twelfth century, fortification activity along the perimeter of the Lateran was intensified. In 1084 the Normans under Robert Guiscard, in their attempt to relieve Gregory VII, "burned with fire and sword the region of the Lateran [down] to the Colosseum" and the neighborhood from S. Lorenzo in Lucina to S. Silvestro in Capite—evidently moving along the eastern and northern rim of the abitato. The fourth-century basilica of S. Clemente, patched up perhaps only fifteen years later and redecorated, was abandoned around 1115. Instead, a new church was built, 5 meters higher up; and linked to it, houses for the canons, newly built with high, strong walls. When the church of the Quattro Coronati, further up on the way to the Lateran, was rebuilt in 1116, a congregation of monks was transferred from a nearby small monastery; "for," says the papal bull, "the site has been turned into a wasteland because the inhabitants all around have perished . . . through the everlasting wars," thus implicitly stating the intention to create a new focus for repopulating the quarter. The huge convent buildings erected at that time and later additions to them turned the complex of the Quattro Coronati into a real fortress, to protect its monastic community, to secure the approach to the papal palace, and to provide safety for the new settlers. High up on the cliff it still dominates its surroundings (fig. 257). Similarly, the road to the Lateran along the crest of the Celian Hill was secured as part of the twelfth-century defense program. The monastery buildings set up at SS. Giovanni e Paolo sometime between 1099 and 1118 made use of the massive remains of a Roman water reservoir built of solid blocks, the Claudianum, a formidable defense position; it was further strengthened when around the middle of the twelfth century the buildings were enlarged and the low, strong tower built fifty years earlier was raised to its present imposing height (fig. 128). The rebuilding of S. Gregorio Magno across the road from SS. Giovanni e Paolo, probably in 1106, further protected the access to the Celian and thus to the papal palace from the valley road coming from Porta S. Paolo: the colonnaded southeastern corner of the

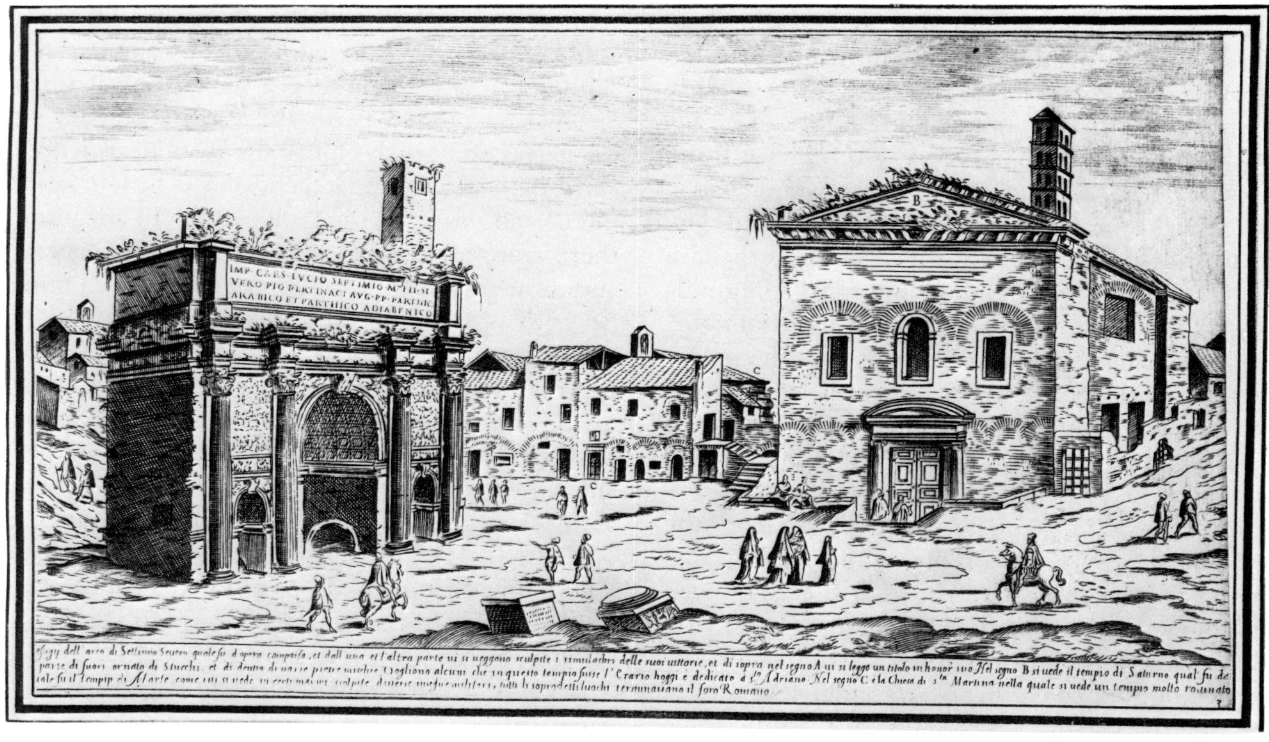

256. Arch of Septimius Severus surmounted by medieval tower, as of 1575, engraving, E. Du Pérac

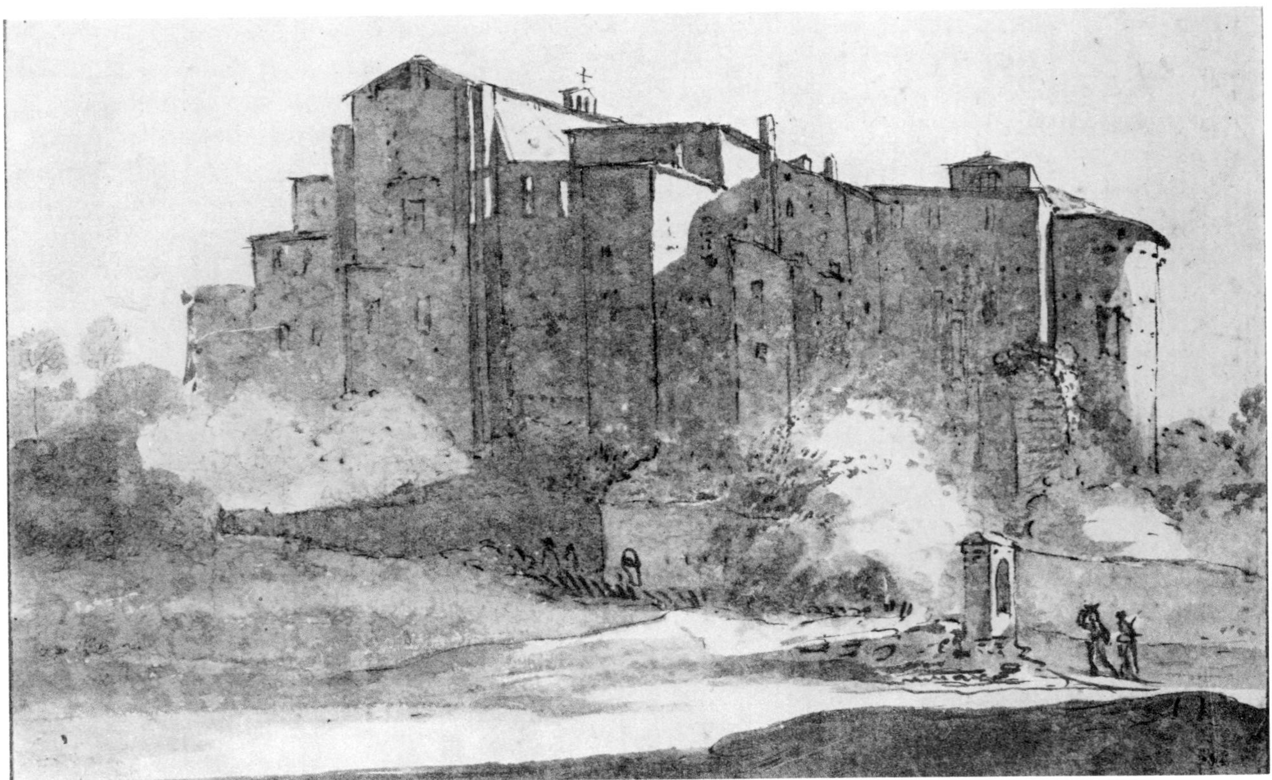

257. SS. Quattro Coronati, church and fortified convent, as of ca. 1625, drawing, B. Breenbergh, Paris, Louvre

Palatine, the Septizonium, across the valley was held as a fortification by the monks of S. Gregorio as early as 975; defended in 1084 against Henry IV—a few columns were knocked down at the time—it again served as a refuge for Pope Paschal II in 1117 (fig. 258).

Creating a defense perimeter around the Lateran Palace and its cathedral was, then, a major aim of papal building and remapping policy in the southeastern sector of the disabitato. By the eleventh and twelfth centuries the palace had become the manor house of a large farmstead, with "vaulted ruins, buildings, vineyards and gardens, with olive trees and apple trees," provided in the twelfth century with mills, a cistern, and a large horse pond, all fed from the aqueduct newly repaired around 1120. The monasteries, and whatever housing had been built or installed in older structures, were by that time seemingly occupied by the canons or rented out to papal officials, servants, and retainers, or to those having business or wanting to be close to the papal court. By the mid-thirteenth century the settlement had grown into a sizable suburb: nearly 250 houses leased by the Lateran canons, some to members of the leading Roman families, extended from the Aurelian Walls to the palace and north of it to the Roman aqueduct and finally along the descent of Via S. Giovanni in Laterano toward the Colosseum. In addition, there were 57 booths, of artisans, shopkeepers, and money changers, a butcher shop, and a public bath. Many of these structures obviously dated from long before. Likewise, hostels for visitors with business at the palace or for pilgrims eager to venerate the relics sheltered in the basilica must have existed by the twelfth century and before. One, whose remains may be those along Via Merulana, housed Saint Francis in 1209-1210. The better known Hospital of S. Giovanni, formerly of S. Angelo, along the street leading to the Quattro Coronati was built only from 1333 to 1348.

All this wanted defending and especially the papal palace. However, building activity at and near the Lateran in the twelfth and thirteenth

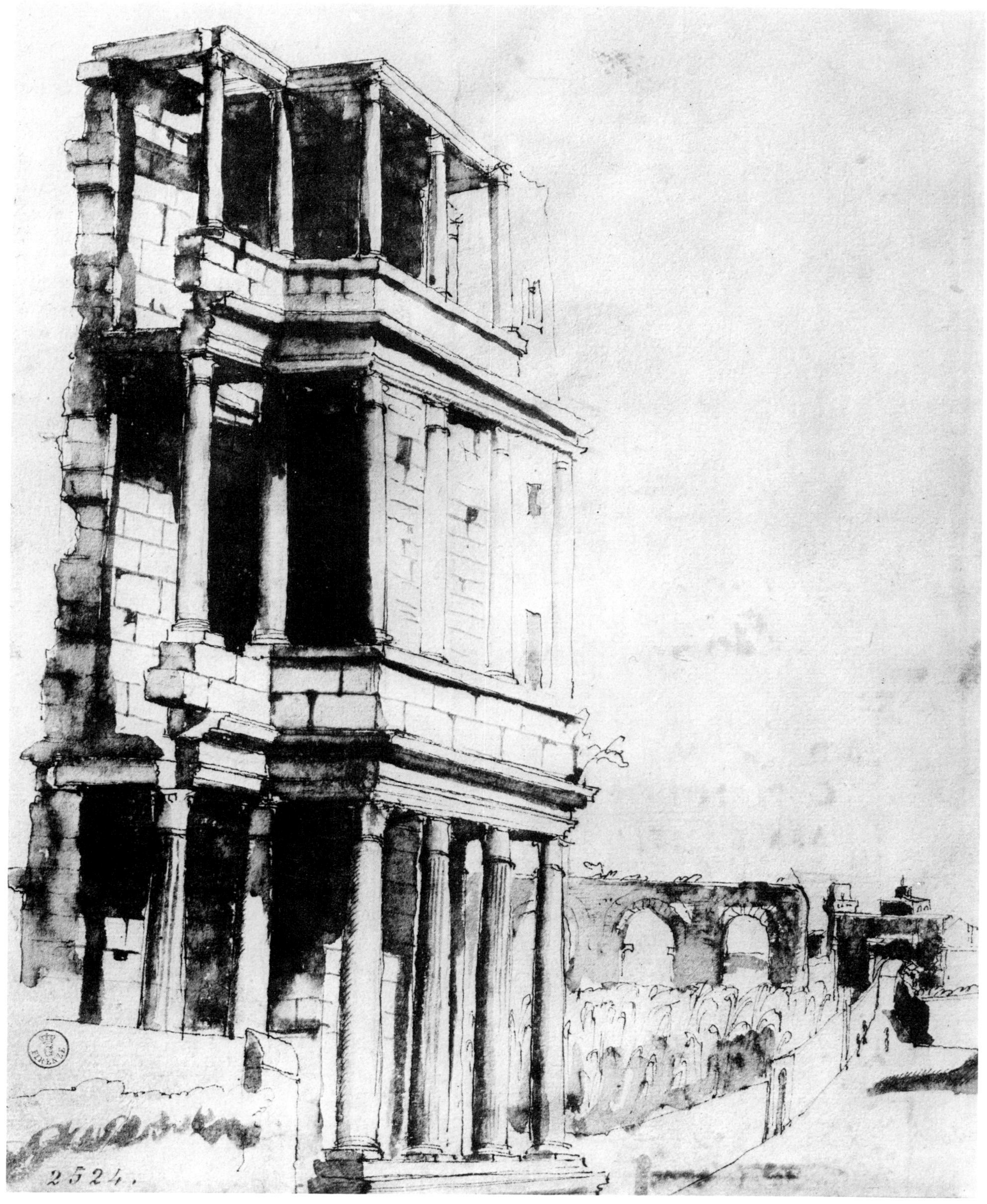

258. Septizonium fortified, as of ca. 1560, drawing, G. A. Dosio, Florence, Uffizi

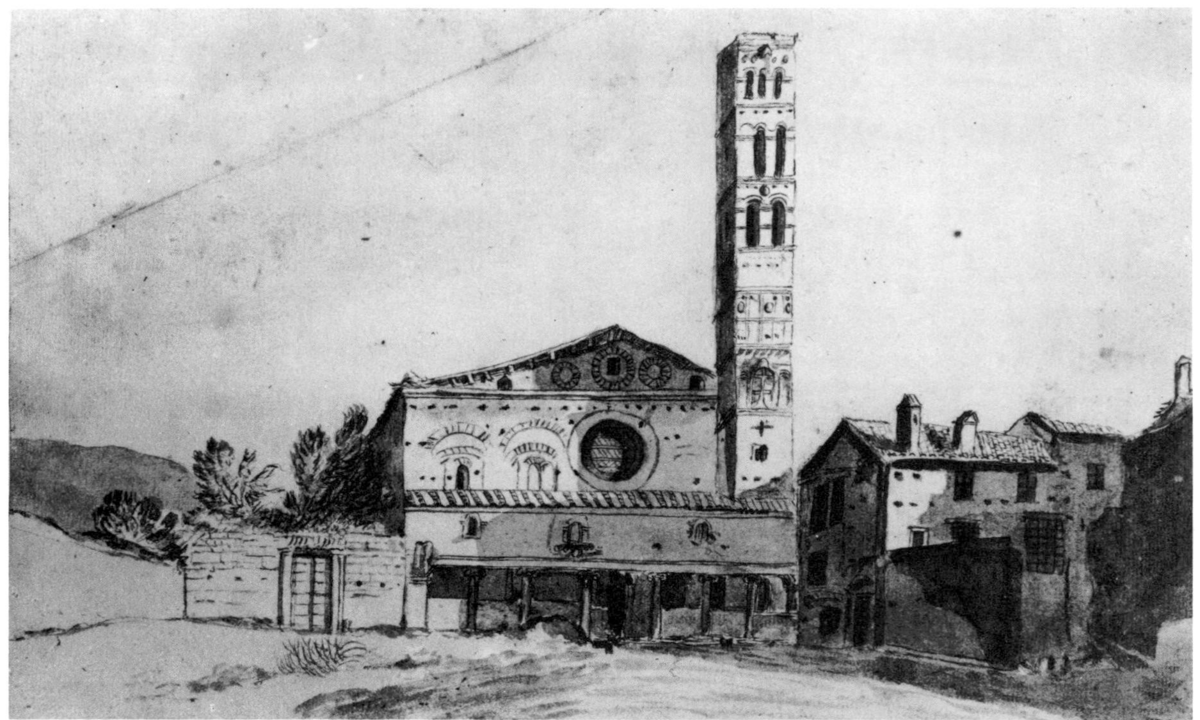

259. View of S. Croce in Gerusalemme, before 1743, drawing, anonymous, Stockholm, National Museum

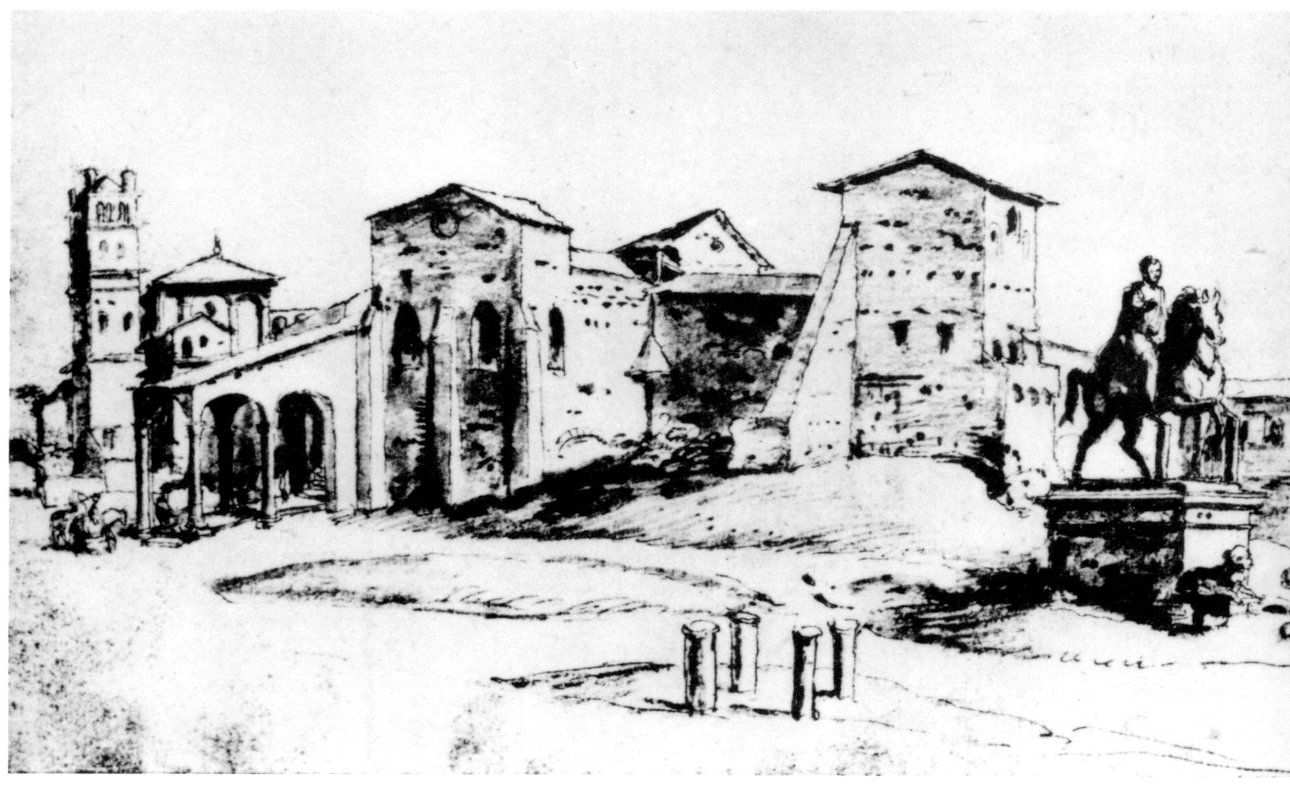

260. Lateran Palace, Basilica, Baptistery and corner of hospital (?) as of ca. 1535, drawing, Marten van Heemskerck, Berlin, Kupferstichkabinett, 79 D2, fols. 12r and 71r

centuries must not be seen in military terms alone; the palace, the cathedral, and the churches in the entire sector underwent extensive rebuilding and refurbishing. To be sure, building new churches or rebuilding and refurbishing old ones formed part of the building and renovating activity that took place all over Rome in the two hundred and fifty years following the middle of the eleventh century; all aimed at a Rome rejuvenated, filled with new or rebuilt churches, a city with a new face. Within this overall renewal, however, special effort was directed at the Lateran and its surroundings. Along the defense perimeter the fortified churches were rebuilt and redecorated. Inside the area, a comparable effort was directed at renovating the old churches closely linked to the Lateran and to the liturgical functions of the cathedral. At Sto. Stefano Rotondo between 1130 and 1143, the arcades leading into the ruined chapels and courtyards of the outer ring were blocked; crossing the center room, a huge triple diaphragm arch was inserted to support the roof, since beams of full length were apparently no longer available. S. Croce in Gerusalemme in 1144-1145 was rebuilt by a similar device: two walls supported by arcades and lightened by the openings of sham galleries—there were no intermediate floors—divided the old hall into a nave, two aisles, and a transept in front of the apse, and these walls were covered with a rich fresco decoration. Adjoining the nave a tall tower was built (fig. 259). To ensure future maintenance and servicing, a community of regular canons was installed in newly erected buildings. Within the same program of renovating and improving the looks of the Lateran and its neighborhood, nartheces were added to the façades of S. Croce, S. Maria Maggiore, SS. Giovanni e Paolo, Sto. Stefano Rotondo, and the Lateran Basilica itself, all shortly after the middle of the twelfth century. A few decades later, shortly before 1190, a palace stood alongside S. Maria Maggiore; it could have been built at that time or earlier.

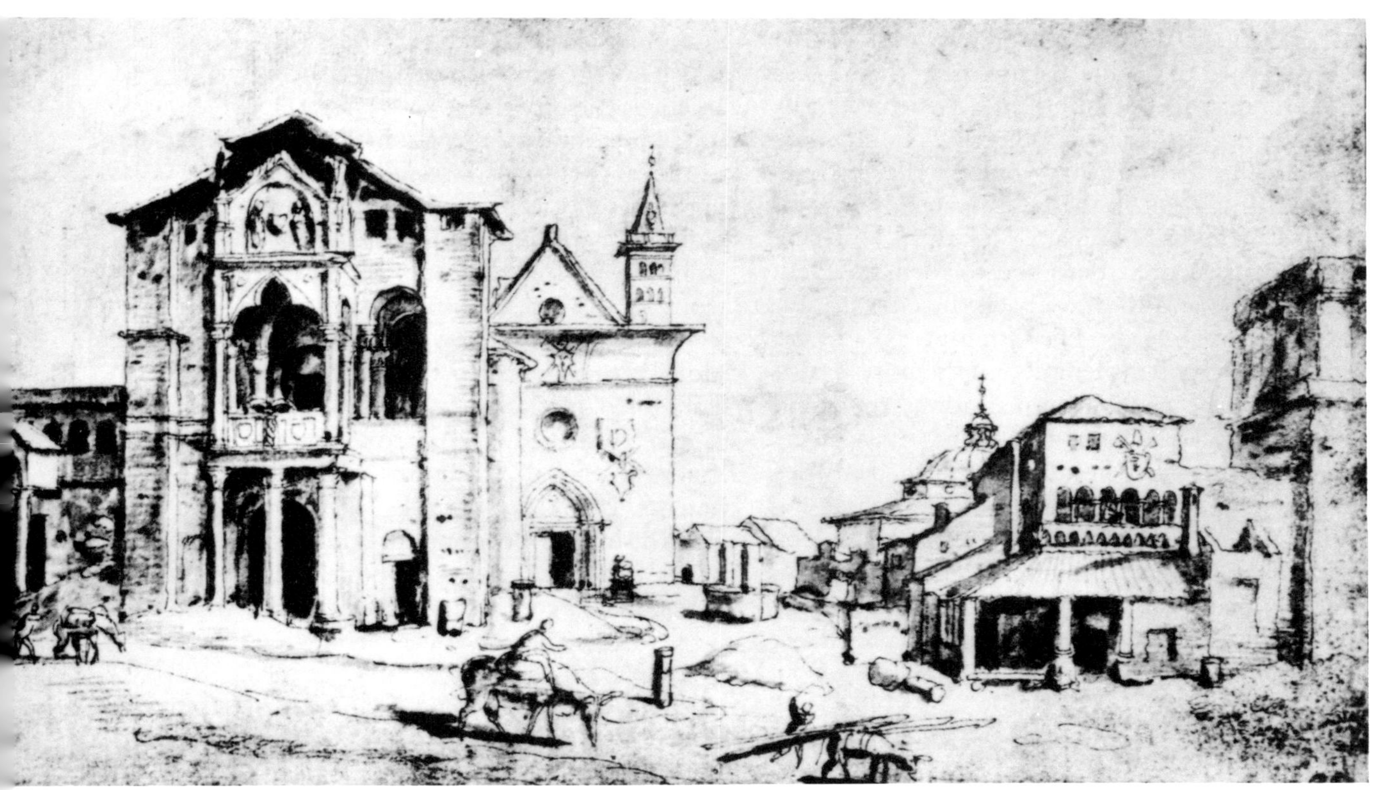

Sixteenth-century draughtsmen still saw it (fig. 250). Within the mid-twelfth-century program, too, the Lateran Palace and its chapels were repaired and decorated with frescoes; we discussed them before. Likewise, the inscription placed on the narthex of the Lateran Basilica and the almost exclusive choice of that church for papal burials from 1063 to 1198—except for popes who died far from Rome, like Gregory VII and two others who were buried for special reasons at St. Peter's—must be seen within the same program. All this refocusing on the Lateran had best be viewed within the framework of the papacy's renewed power won under the reform popes and strengthened by their and their successors' victories, first in the Investiture Struggle and afterwards over the Roman Commune and its republic.

More than a hundred years later, in the last two decades of the thirteenth century, the popes returned to the effort of embellishing the Lateran, both basilica and palace; and of further developing the suburb round about. Extensive though all this building activity was, it was limited in scope. Within the framework of the urban texture of medieval and later Rome and the Lateran's place within it, the thirteenth-century program marks a terminal point. The popes of the fifth century, one recalls, had attempted to lay out in the southeastern sector of the city an expanded papal quarter, with the Lateran at its center, designed to form the new hub of Rome and to draw back the city already retreating westward. The attempt failed; the Lateran, the city's cathedral, and the pope's residence with the papal administration, remained ever more isolated. Papal building activity at the Lateran during the eighth and ninth centuries was extensive, but limited. It was aimed at enlarging the palace, making it ever more splendid, and at keeping the church in repair. The Lateran's place within the urban fabric and its links to the abitato were of no concern. S. Maria Maggiore, rather than being viewed as an extension of the Lateran quarter, became an independent area with its own subsidiary convents, such as S. Prassede and S. Martino ai Monti, rebuilt and surrounded by houses and gardens. The twelfth century at first glance seemed to have taken up anew a project recalling that of the fifth century to create a large "Lateran Borgo" extending east, west, and north as far as SS. Giovanni e Paolo, the Quattro Coronati, S. Clemente, and S. Maria Maggiore. However, whereas the fifth-century program was directed at reaching out toward the retreating city by expanding the papal quarter, the twelfth-century planners strove to build up a defense perimeter around the renovated papal residence. Rather than reaching out toward the abitato, the twelfth-century "Lateran Borgo" closed itself off against the threatening town, separated from it by a wide no man's land. This isolation is preserved in the thirteenth-century campaign. The renovated church and palace, the goal of papal processions and pilgrims, face north and west toward Piazza S. Giovanni in Laterano, where now the obelisk of Sixtus V rises (fig. 260). This was where the main approach from town ended, ascending from the Colosseum. Hence, in remodeling the Lateran Basilica the north façade of the transept was stressed by twin towers rising behind a cavetto gable. Hence, too, in renovating the adjoining wing of the Lateran Palace, Boniface VIII in 1299 remodeled the balcony in front of the ninth-century banqueting hall as a *loggia di benedizione*, whence in the impending Holy Year he was to bless crowds of pilgrims assembled in the square. The square itself, irregular, unpaved, and narrowed in to the east by other medieval structures, was part of the Lateran complex, but like the palace and the church, it did not represent a link to town. The papal residence and the pope's cathedral remained isolated. Their link to the city that they were to rule and serve was broken.

APPENDIX

Chronological List of Popes

(From *LP*, I, p. cclx, and Partner, *Lands*. Antipopes in brackets)

Miltiades	311-314
Sylvester	314-335
Mark	336
Julius I	337-352
Liberius	352-366
[Felix	355-365]
Damasus I	366-384
[Ursinus	366-367]
Siricius	384-399
Anastasius I	399-401
Innocentius I	401-417
Zosimus	417-418
Boniface I	418-422
[Eulalius	418-419]
Caelestinus I	422-432
Sixtus III	432-440
Leo I	440-461
Hilarus	461-468
Simplicius	468-483
Felix III	483-492
Gelasius I	492-496
Anastasius II	496-498
Symmachus	498-514
[Lawrence	498-505]
Hormisdas	514-523
John I	523-526
Felix IV	526-530
Boniface II	530-532
[Dioscurus	530]
John II	533-535
Agapitus I	535-536
Silverius	536-537
Vigilius	537-555
Pelagius I	556-561
John III	561-574
Benedict I	575-579
Pelagius II	579-590
Gregory I	590-604
Sabinianus	604-606
Boniface III	607
Boniface IV	608-615
Deusdedit I	615-618
Boniface V	619-625
Honorius I	625-638
Severinus	640
John IV	640-642
Theodore I	642-649
Martin I	649-655
Eugenius I	654-657
Vitalian	657-672
Deusdedit II	672-676
Donus	676-678
Agatho	678-681
Leo II	682-683
Benedict II	684-685
John V	685-686
Conon	686-687
[Theodore	687]
[Paschal	687]
Sergius I	687-701
John VI	701-705
John VII	705-707
Sisinnius	708
Constantine	708-715
Gregory II	715-731
Gregory III	731-741
Zacharias	741-752
Stephen II (III)	752-757
Paul I	757-767
[Constantine	767-769]
[Philip	768]
Stephen III (IV)	768-772
Hadrian I	772-795
Leo III	795-816
Stephen IV (V)	816-817
Paschal I	817-824
Eugenius II	824-827
Valentine	827
Gregory IV	827-844
[John	844]
Sergius II	844-847
Leo IV	847-855
Benedict III	855-858
[Anastasius	855]
Nicholas I	858-867
Hadrian II	867-872
John VIII	872-882
Marinus I	882-884

Hadrian III	884-885
Stephen V (VI)	885-891
Formosus	891-896
Boniface VI	896
Stephen VI (VII)	896-897
Romanus	897
Theodore II	897
John IX	898-900
Benedict IV	900-903
Leo V	903
[Christopher	903-904]
Sergius III	904-911
Anastasius III	911-913
Lando	913-914
John X	914-928
Leo VI	928
Stephen VII (VIII)	928-931
John XI	931-935
Leo VII	936-939
Stephen VIII (IX)	939-942
Marinus II	942-946
Agapitus II	946-955
John XII	955-964
Leo VIII	963-965
Benedict V	964
John XIII	965-972
Benedict VI	973-974
[Boniface VII	974; 984-985]
Benedict VII	974-983
John XIV	983-984
John XV	985-996
Gregory V	996-999
[John XVI	997-998]
Sylvester II	999-1003
John XVII	1003
John XVIII	1004-1009
Sergius IV	1009-1012
[Gregory	1012]
Benedict VIII	1012-1024
John XIX	1024-1032
Benedict IX	1032-1044
Sylvester III	1044-1045
Benedict IX	1045; 1047-1048
Gregory VI	1045-1046
Clement II	1046-1047
Damasus II	1048
Leo IX	1049-1054
Victor II	1054-1057
Stephen IX (X)	1057-1058
[Benedict X	1058-1059]
Nicholas II	1059-1061
Alexander II	1061-1073

[Honorius II	1061-1072]
Gregory VII	1073-1085
[Clement III	1080-1100]
Victor III	1086-1087
Urban II	1088-1099
Paschal II	1099-1118
[Theodoric	1100]
[Albert	1102]
[Silvester IV	1105-1111]
Gelasius II	1118-1119
[Gregory VIII	1118-1121]
Calixtus II	1119-1124
Honorius II	1124-1130
[Celestine II	1124]
Innocent II	1130-1143
[Anaclete II	1130-1138]
[Victor IV	1138]
Celestine II	1143-1144
Lucius II	1144-1145
Eugenius III	1145-1153
Anastasius IV	1153-1154
Hadrian IV	1154-1159
Alexander III	1159-1181
[Victor IV	1159-1164]
[Paschal III	1164-1168]
[Calixtus III	1168-1178]
[Innocent III	1179-1180]
Lucius III	1181-1185
Urban III	1185-1187
Gregory VIII	1187
Clement III	1187-1191
Celestine III	1191-1198
Innocent III	1198-1216
Honorius III	1216-1227
Gregory IX	1227-1241
Celestine IV	1241
Innocent IV	1243-1254
Alexander IV	1254-1261
Urban IV	1261-1264
Clement IV	1265-1268
Gregory X	1271-1276
Innocent V	1276
Hadrian V	1276
John XXI	1276-1277
Nicholas III	1277-1280
Martin IV	1281-1285
Honorius IV	1285-1287
Nicholas IV	1288-1292
Celestine V	1292-1294
Boniface VIII	1294-1303
Benedict XI	1303-1304
Clement V	1305-1314

Bibliographical Note

I list here the works that have been used, whether I refer to them specifically or not, throughout this volume, setting apart sources from fundamental literature.

The sources first. Foremost in importance is *Le Liber Pontificalis*, ed. L. Duchesne, 2 vols., Paris, 1886-92, reprinted 1955-57, vol. III, ed. C. Vogel, Paris, 1957; hereafter it will be referred to as *LP*, I, II or III. The *Monumenta Germaniae Historica* (*MGH*), published since 1826 and divided into its sections, *Scriptores* (*SS*), *Scriptores Rerum Germanicarum* (*SS RG*), *Auctores Antiquissimi* (*AA*), *Epistolae* (*Epp*), and others, provides an excellent edition of many important works and documents relevant to our theme, which will be quoted with the abbreviations given above in parentheses as occasion arises. The same holds of J. P. Migne, *Patrologiae Cursus Completus, Series Latina*, Paris, 1844-90, suppl. 1958-74; of its 221 volumes, including four of indices, vols. 218ff., the most useful part of this most useful collection, we shall identify parts used as *PL* followed by the relevant volume number. Likewise, the volumes of L. A. Muratori, *Rerum Italicarum Scriptores*, Milan, 1723-54, and its continuation, nova series, Città di Castello (later Bologna 1900-), will be referred to as *RIS* and *RIS*, n.s. when needed. *Italia Pontificia*, I, *Roma*, ed. P. F. Kehr, Berlin, 1906, is an excellent and critical index to papal documents dealing with the clergy, the churches, and the great families in Rome, with references to original sources; it will be quoted as Kehr, *It. Pont.*

So far, historical sources. Topographical data with specific reference to medieval Rome appear in documents from the archives of Roman churches regarding their property; these were published by various scholars around the turn of this century, for the most part in the *Archivio della Società Romana di Storia Patria*, henceforth quoted as *ASRStP*. R. Valentini and G. Zucchetti, *Codice topografico della città di Roma*, Rome, 1940-53, henceforth Valentini-Zucchetti, have excerpted from various sources, though not without errors, references to the urban fabric and its monuments. Long before, C. L. Urlichs, *Codex Topographicus Urbis Romae*, Würzburg, 1870, had published more completely a number of sources of topographical interest; I shall quote him simply as Urlichs, *Codex*. The three volumes of A. P. Frutaz, *Le Piante di Roma*, Rome, 1962, contain a nearly complete collection of maps of Rome, mainly from the thirteenth century almost to the present, also a few samples of the third-century *Forma Urbis*, and maps attempting reconstructions of the ancient and early medieval city.

At this point I want to put in a caution. Many books have been written about the history of Early Christian and medieval Rome, but only some of them will be listed. I am not a historian and this book was never intended as another history of Rome, the papacy, or the Church in the Middle Ages. Hence, my treatment of historical questions will not be as thorough as that of a specialist in these fields.

F. Gregorovius, *Geschichte der Stadt Rom im Mittelalter*, Stuttgart, 1859-70, is in my opinion still the best history of the medieval city. Notwithstanding the accumulation of scholarship ever since and sometimes excellent later books on individual aspects and personalities, Gregorovius remains unsurpassed, and despite his nineteenth-century style and outlook, one is filled with admiration for his knowledge of the documents contained in his footnotes and his presentation. His work has been republished many times and translated into different languages. While I used the German edition cited above, I refer the reader to the English translation by Mrs. G. W. Hamilton, as noted in my List of Abbreviations of Frequently Cited Works. F. Schneider, *Rom und Romgedanke im Mittelalter*, Munich, 1926, though not always accurate, is an imaginative first attempt at presenting the history of the idea of Rome. Of the many books on the papacy, I have used primarily E. Caspar, *Geschichte des Papsttums*, I-II, Tübingen, 1930-33, which, however, terminates at the end of the eighth century. I have also used, though less frequently, W. Ullmann, *A Short History of the Papacy in the Middle Ages*, Rome, 1972. G. Falco's study, in English *The Holy Roman Republic*, London, 1964, despite its title has proved an excellent presentation of the political ideas and events and the economic conditions concerning the papacy. P. Partner, *The Lands of St. Peter*, Berkeley and Los Angeles, 1972, gives a splendid account of the history of the Papal State from its beginnings to the end of the Middle Ages. The little Penguin by R. W. Southern, *Western Society and the Church in the Middle Ages*, Harmondsworth, 1970, reaching from the eighth through the fifteenth centuries, presents a superb summary of the administrative, economic, and juridical problems affecting Rome as the seat of the papacy. R. Morghen's essays, republished as *Medioevo Cristiano*, Bari, 1972, have proved to be among the most stimulating reading.

Leaving aside the standard introductory chapter of the spate of urbanistic studies on Rome published in recent years, for an account of the city's topography the first two sections of F. Castagnoli, C. Cecchelli, G. Giovannoni, and M. Zocca, *Topografia e urbanistica di Roma* (Istituto di Studi Romani), Bologna, 1958, deserve first place. R. Vielliard, *Recherches sur les origines de la Rome Chrétienne*, Mâcon, 1942, was a first valiant attempt at clarifying the formation of Rome from Christian antiquity through the ninth century. Lanciani's numerous books, *New Tales of Old Rome, Christian and Pagan Rome, The Ruins and Excavation of Rome, The Destruction of Ancient Rome*, are a mine of sometimes useful information. U. Gnoli, *Topografia e toponomastica di Roma medioevale e moderna*, Rome, 1939, and P. Romano, *Roma nelle sue strade e nelle sue piazze*, Rome, 1950 (and frequently reprinted) are standard works. Old guide books on Rome have obviously been used time and again. They are listed in L. Schudt, *Le guide di Roma* (Quellenschriften zur Geschichte der Barockkunst in Rom), Vienna and Augsburg, 1930, despite the title of the series not confined to that later period. A modern guide to Roman topography, the *Guide Rionali di Roma*, ed. C. Pietrangeli, is of the greatest possible help; the series is gradually being completed; so is S. Pressouyre, *Rome au fil du temps*, Boulogne, 1973, which presents the urbanistic history of the city in a series of superbly clear, though inevitably at times hypothetical, maps.

For the buildings of Rome, I must refer without undue modesty to the *Corpus Basilicarum Christianarum Romae*, vols. I-V, Vatican City, Rome, New York, 1937-77, hereafter cited as *Corpus*, written by myself and various collaborators. Despite its shortcomings, it gives the basic facts and bibliography on churches built in Rome from the fourth through the ninth centuries and sometimes beyond. More topographical in character yet indispensable is C. Huelsen, *Le Chiese di Roma nel Medio Evo*, Florence, 1927—I shall refer to it as Huelsen, *Chiese*. M. Armellini, *Le Chiese di Roma dal Secolo IV al XIX*, ed. C. Cecchelli, Rome, 1942—hereafter Armellini-Cecchelli, *Chiese*—is at times obsolete; but both Armellini's text and Cecchelli's notes contain a lot of useful information, the latter also regarding out-of-the-way bibliographical and archival references. W. Buchowiecki, *Handbuch der Kirchen Roms*, Vienna, 1967-, is extremely handy and, where I have checked it, highly precise. For individual churches, the series of the *Chiese illustrate di Roma*, like the curate's egg, is good in parts, but each little book has some useful information. G. Ferrari, *Early Roman Monasteries*, Vatican City, 1957, is the basic work on monastic foundations and monuments in Rome from the fifth through the tenth centuries.

Abbreviations of Frequently Cited Works

Armellini-Cecchelli, *Chiese*	M. Armellini, *Le chiese di Roma*, ed. C. Cecchelli, Rome, 1942
Art Bull	*Art Bulletin*
ASRStP	*Archivio della Societa Romana di Storia Patria*
Bartoloni, *Senato*	*Codice diplomatico del Senato Romano*, ed. F. Bartoloni, Rome, 1948
Bertolini, *Roma di fronte*	O. Bertolini, *Roma di fronte . . . a Bisanzio e ai Langobardi*, Bologna, 1941
BISI	*Bulletino dell Istituto Storico Italiano*
Brentano, *Rome before Avignon*	R. Brentano, *Rome before Avignon*, New York, 1974
Bull Comm	*Bullettino della Commissione Archeologica Comunale di Roma*
Burl Mag	*Burlington Magazine*
CahArch	*Cahiers Archéologiques*
Caspar, *Papsttum*	E. Caspar, *Geschichte des Papsttums*, I-II, Tübingen, 1930-33
Corpus	R. Krautheimer and others, *Corpus Basilicarum Christianarum Romae*, I-V, Vatican City, Rome, New York, 1937-77
CSEL	*Corpus Scriptorum Ecclesiasticorum Latinorum*
DissPontAcc	*Atti della Pontificia Accademia Romana di Archeologia, Dissertazioni*
DOP	*Dumbarton Oaks Papers*
Egger, *Veduten*	H. Egger, *Römische Veduten . . .* , Vienna-Leipzig, 1911-31 (vol. I, 2nd ed., Vienna, 1932)
Escurialensis	*Codex Escurialensis*, ed. H. Egger, Österreichisches Archäologisches Institut, Sonderschriften 4, Vienna, 1905-6
Esplorazioni	B. M. Apollonj Ghetti and others, *Esplorazioni sotto la confessione di San Pietro in Vaticano*, Vatican City, 1951
Ferrari, *Monasteries*	G. Ferrari, *Early Roman Monasteries*, Vatican City, 1957
Forcella, *Iscrizioni*	V. Forcella, *Iscrizioni delle chiese . . . di Roma*, Rome, 1869-93
Frutaz, *Piante*	A. P. Frutaz, *Le piante di Roma*, Rome, 1962
GBA	*Gazette des Beaux Arts*
Gnoli, *Topografia*	U. Gnoli, *Topografia e toponomastica di Roma medioevale e moderna*, Rome, 1939
Gregorovius	F. Gregorovius, *History of the City of Rome in the Middle Ages*, trans. Mrs. G. W. Hamilton, London, 1906 (reprinted New York, 1967)
Gregory, *Epp.*	*Gregorii Magni Epistolae*, in *MGH AA*, I and II
Guide Rionali	*Guide Rionali di Roma*, ed. C. Pietrangeli and others, 1967-
Hartmann, *Scae Mariae in Via Lata*	L. M. Hartmann, *Ecclesiae Scae Mariae in Via Lata Tabularium*, Vienna, 1905
Heemskerck	C. Huelsen and H. Egger, *Die Römischen Skizzenbücher von Marten van Heemskerck*, Berlin, 1913-16
Huelsen, *Chiese*	C. Huelsen, *Le chiese di Roma nel medio evo*, Florence, 1927
JDAI	*Jahrbuch des Deutschen Archäologischen Instituts*
JWC	*Journal of the Warburg and Courtauld Institutes*
Kehr, *It. Pont.*	P. Kehr, *Italia Pontificia*, Rome, 1906-
Kitzinger, *Malerei*	E. Kitzinger, *Römische Malerei vom Beginn des 7. bis zur Mitte des 8. Jahrhunderts*, Munich, 1935
Kitzinger, *Byzantium*	E. Kitzinger, *The Art of Byzantium and the Medieval West; Selected Studies*, Bloomington, Indiana, 1976

Krautheimer, *Pelican*	R. Krautheimer, *Early Christian and Byzantine Architecture*, Pelican History of Art, 2nd ed., Harmondsworth, 1975
Ladner, *Papstbildnisse*	G. Ladner, *Die Papstbildnisse des Altertums und des Mittelalters*, I, II, Vatican City, 1941, 1970
Lanciani, *Destruction*	R. Lanciani, *The Destruction of Ancient Rome*, New York, 1899
Lanciani, *Scavi*	R. Lanciani, *Storia degli Scavi di Roma*, I-IV, Rome, 1902-1912
LCL	*Loeb Classical Library*
Llewellyn	P. Llewellyn, *Rome in the Dark Ages*, New York, 1971
LP	*Le Liber Pontificalis*, ed. L. Duchesne, Paris, 1886-92, repr. 1955-57; 3rd vol., ed. Cyrille Vogel, Paris, 1957
Lugli, *Monumenti*	G. Lugli, *I monumenti antichi di Roma e suburbio*, Rome, 1934-40
Matthiae, *Mosaici*	G. Matthiae, *Mosaici medioevali delle chiese di Roma*, Rome, 1967
Matthiae, *Pittura*	G. Matthiae, *Pittura romana del medioevo*, Rome, 1965
MEFR	*Mélanges d'Archéologie et d'Histoire de l'Ecole Française de Rome*
MemPontAcc	*Atti della Pontificia Accademia Romana di Archeologia, Memorie*
MGH AA	*Monumenta Germaniae Historica, Auctores Antiquissimi*
MGH Epp	*Monumenta Germaniae Historica, Epistolae*
MGH LL	*Monumenta Germaniae Historica, Leges*
MGH SS	*Monumenta Germaniae Historica, Scriptores*
MGH SS RG	*Monumenta Germaniae Historica, Scriptores Rerum Germanicarum*
MGH SS RM	*Monumenta Germaniae Historica, Scriptores Rerum Merovingicarum*
Mon. antichi	*Monumenti antichi Accademia dei Lincei*
Nash, *Dictionary*	E. Nash, *A Pictorial Dictionary of Rome*, London, 1961
Panofsky, *Renaissance and Renascences*	E. Panofsky, *Renaissance and Renascences in Western Art*, The Gottesman Lectures, Uppsala University, Stockholm, 1960
Partner, *Lands*	P. Partner, *The Lands of Saint Peter*, London, 1972
PBSR	*Papers of the British School at Rome*
Pietri, *Roma Christiana*	C. Pietri, *Roma Christiana. Recherches sur l'Eglise de Rome . . . 311-440* (Bibliothèque des Ecoles Françaises d'Athènes et de Rome, 224), Rome, 1976
PL	J. P. Migne, *Patrologiae Cursus Completus, Series Latina*, Paris, 1844-90, suppl. 1958-74
Quaderni	Università di Roma, Istituto di Storia dell' Architettura, *Quaderni dell'Istituto di Storia dell'Architettura*
Quellen und Forschungen	*Quellen und Forschungen aus Italienischen Archiven*
RAC	*Rivista di Archeologia Cristiana*
Reg Farf	*Il Regesto di Farfa*, ed. I. Giorgi and U. Balzani, Rome, 1887-1914
Reg Sub	*Il Regesto Sublacense . . .*, ed. L. Allodi and G. Levi, Rome, 1885
RendPontAcc	*Atti della Pontificia Accademia Romana di Archeologia, Rendiconti*
RIS	*Rerum Italicarum Scriptores*, ed. L. A. Muratori, Milan,1723-54
RM	*Mitteilungen des deutschen Archäologischen Instituts, Römische Abteilung*
Röm Jbch	*Römisches Jahrbuch für Kunstgeschichte*
Roma e l'età Carolingia	*Roma e l'età Carolingia*, ed. Istituto di Storia dell Arte del Università di Roma, Rome, 1976
Romano, *Strade*	P. Romano, *Roma nelle sue strade e nelle sue piazze*, Rome, 1947-49 and later editions
RQSCHR	*Römische Quartalschrift*
Schramm, *Renovatio*	P. Schramm, *Kaiser, Rom und Renovatio*, I-II (*Studien der Bibliothek Warburg*, 17) Leipzig, 1929
Schramm, *Kaiser, Könige und Päpste*	P. Schramm, *Kaiser, Könige und Päpste*, I-IV, Stuttgart, 1968-70
Studi Gregoriani	*Studi Gregoriani*, ed. G. B. Boreno, vols. I-VII, Rome, 1947-
Studies	R. Krautheimer, *Studies in Early Christian, Medieval and Renaissance Art*, New York, 1969

Tierney, *Crisis*	B. Tierney, *The Crisis of Church and State, 1050-1300*, Englewood Cliffs, N.J., 1964
Urlichs, *Codex*	L. C. Urlichs, *Codex Urbis Romae Topographicus*, Würzburg, 1870
Valentini-Zucchetti	R. Valentini and G. Zucchetti, *Codice topografico della città di Roma*, 1940-53, vols. I-IV (Fonti per la Storia d'Italia)
Vielliard, *Origines*	René Vielliard, *Recherches sur les origines de la Rome Chrétienne*, Mâcon, 1942 (repr. Rome, 1959)
Waley, *Papal State*	D. Waley, *The Papal State in the Thirteenth Century*, London, 1969
Wilpert, *Mosaiken und Malereien*	J. Wilpert, *Die Römischen Mosaiken und Malereien*, Freiburg, 1916
ZKG	*Zeitschrift für Kunstgeschichte*
ZSRG	*Zeitschrift der Savigny Stiftung für Rechtsgeschichte, Kanonische Abteilung*

Notes

Chapter One

pp. 3ff.

To understand the complex figure of Constantine and his policies regarding Rome, paganism, and the Church, I have reread Eusebius, *Life of Constantine* and his panegyric, both in *Eusebius' Werke I*, ed. I. Heikel, Die griechischen christlichen Schriftsteller 7, Leipzig, 1902, and the material conveniently compiled in H. Dörries, *Das Selbstzeugnis Kaiser Konstantins*, Göttingen, 1964. Among interpretative studies, I refer the reader to H. Dörries, *Konstantin der Grosse*, Stuttgart, 1958; R. Macmullen, *Constantine*, London, 1970; and in particular to A. Alföldi, *The Conversion of Constantine and Pagan Rome*, Oxford, 1948.

The summary description on the following pages of ancient Rome around A.D. 312 and the individual monuments rests mainly on the following: L. Homo, *Rome Impériale et l'Urbanisme*, Paris, 1951; G. Lugli, *Monumenti*; Nash, *Dictionary*; and A. Boethius and J. B. Ward-Perkins, *Etruscan and Roman Architecture* (Pelican History of Art) Harmondsworth, 1970, particularly the last parts by Ward-Perkins. For the overall picture of the city, I refer to the still indispensable *Forma Urbis Romae* published by R. Lanciani, Milan, 1896, and to the publication of the marble plan by G. Carrettoni, A. M. Colini, L. Cozza, and G. Gatti, *La pianta marmorea di Roma antica*, Rome, 1960.

Frequent discussions with Alfred Frazer and suggestions from him have greatly helped in clarifying and enriching my ideas as presented in this chapter.

p. 4

The population figures for ancient Rome and in particular for the beginning of the fourth century are highly controversial. Estimates range from 172,000 to 1½ million. The former figure, computed by J. C. Russell, "Late Ancient and Medieval Population of Rome," *Transactions of the American Philosophical Society* 48, 3 (1958) 64ff., is presumably far too low, while the latter figure (G. Lugli, *Monumenti*, IV, 2, 71ff.) is probably much too high. A figure somewhere between 600,000 and 700,000 (A. von Gerkan, "Die Einwohnerzahl in der Kaiserzeit," *RM* 55 [1940] 149ff.; also F. Castagnoli, "L'*insula* nei cataloghi regionari . . . ," *Rivista di Filologia* 104 [1976] 45ff. who suggests about 600,000) and one slightly under 1 million (J. E. Packer, "The Insulae of Imperial Ostia," *Memoirs of the American Academy in Rome* 31 [1971] esp. 74ff.) appears reasonable to me.

pp. 6f.

Along with the monograph by I. Richmond, *The City Wall of Imperial Rome*, Oxford, 1930, the reader should consult G. Lugli, *Monumenti*, II, 139ff. and the notes and illustrations in Nash, *Dictionary*, II, 86ff. and 198ff., this latter for the gates.

pp. 7f.

The physical renewal of Rome under Diocletian and Maxentius has been dealt with by A. Frazer, "The Iconography of the Emperor Maxentius' Buildings on Via Appia," *Art Bull* 48 (1966) 385ff., and I am shamelessly looting his ideas. For the individual buildings the reader may turn to E. Nash, *Dictionary* and A. Boethius and J. B. Ward-Perkins, as quoted in first note above. For the structure housing SS. Cosma e Damiano, see below, chapter three, note to pp. 71f.

p. 8

For the Sessorium, A. M. Colini, "Horti Spei Veteris," *MemPontAcc* vol. 8, no. 3 (1955) 137ff.; for the excavations west of the Lateran church, *idem*, *Storia e topografia del celio nell'Antichità*, *MemPontAcc* 7, 1944 and the preliminary reports on further explorations undertaken by V. Santa Maria Scrinari, *Egregiae Lateranorum Aedes*, Rome, 1967, and *idem*, "Scavi sotto la sala Manzoni all'ospedale di S. Giovanni in Roma," *RendPontAcc* 41 (1968-69) 167ff.

pp. 9ff.

The street system is still best presented in R. Lanciani's *Forma Urbis Romae*, mentioned above. For the monumental center, the reader is referred to Lugli's and Nash's publications, as above, and to G. Lugli, *Roma antica, il centro monumentale*, Rome, 1946.

pp. 13ff.

The *Regionaria* are conveniently published in Urlichs, *Codex*, 1ff.; in H. Jordan, *Topographie der Stadt Rom im Alterthum,* II, Berlin, 1871; in Valentini-Zucchetti, I, 63ff.; and in A. Nordh, *Libellus de Regionibus Urbis Romae* (*Skrifter . . . Svenska Institutet i Rom*, III, 8°),

Lund, 1949. Regarding the relationship of the two versions, *Curiosum* and *Notitia*, and their date, pre-Constantinian, Constantinian, or slightly later, see Valentini-Zucchetti, *loc. cit.*, and Nordh, *op. cit.*, pp. 60ff.

While the meaning of *insula* is controversial, as witness the works quoted in note to p. 4, the appearance of multiple dwellings is clear enough from remains preserved in Ostia, where they were first studied by G. Calza, "La preminenza dell'insula nell'edilizia romana," *Mon. Antichi* 28 (1914) 541ff.; and A. Boethius and J. B. Ward-Perkins, *op. cit.*, *passim*. Their plans, crowding in on narrow streets, and their penetration into monumental and garden areas are best demonstrated by the remains of the marble plan, referred to in note to p. 3.

pp. 17f.

Further information on Roman mausolea, columbaria and aediculae (there is much) is found conveniently in A. Boethius and J. B. Ward-Perkins, *op. cit.*, *passim*, and J. C. Toynbee and J. B. Ward-Perkins, *The Shrine of Saint Peter*, London, New York, and Toronto, 1956, in particular the sections from pp. 24-124.

Social conditions in ancient Rome seem, to my nonspecialist's mind, described well and in a lively manner by J. Carcopino, *Daily Life in Ancient Rome*, New Haven and Rome, paperback edition 1960. The quote from Virgil is, of course, *Aeneid*, VI, 851ff.

pp. 18ff.

For Christian building in Rome prior to and under Constantine, I can only refer to Vielliard, *Origines*, pp. 13ff.; to the pertinent sections of my *Corpus*; to my *Pelican*, pp. 29ff.; and most recently to Pietri, *Roma Christiana*, pp. 3ff., 90ff.

The *tituli* or *domus ecclesiae* of Rome present a complex problem. J. P. Kirsch, *Die römischen Titelkirchen im Altertum*, Paderborn, 1918, was the first to interpret as evidence of former *tituli* the remains of apartment houses, mansions, or other secular buildings dating from the second or third centuries A.D. that were below or incorporated into major city churches. In Rome, however, which has been a building site these past two thousand years and more, remains of older structures are ever reused and turn up wherever construction goes on. On the other hand, *tituli* are not mentioned in Rome prior to the fourth century A.D., and except perhaps at SS. Giovanni e Paolo, clear archaeological evidence of the remains beneath these churches being used as *domus ecclesiae* is lacking. Pietri, *Roma Christiana*, pp. 83ff., consequently doubts the physical survival in Rome of remains of any pre-Constantinian *titulus*. As things stand, the only known house definitely transformed into a *domus ecclesiae* is the one at Dura, far out in the provinces and in a small town. My present stand on the question of *tituli* in Rome is given in my *Pelican*, pp. 26ff. I may in future modify it along lines of greater skepticism.

pp. 18f.

Martyr shrines and catacombs prior to Constantine have generated an enormous literature. For convenience' sake, I refer the reader again to my *Pelican*, pp. 31ff.; for S. Sebastiano to *Corpus*, IV, pp. 99ff.; for Saint Peter's shrine, to *Corpus*, V, pp. 165ff., based on the official excavation report, B. M. Apollonj Ghetti, A. Ferrua, E. Josi, and E. Kirschbaum, *Esplorazioni sotto la confessione di S. Pietro in Vaticano . . .*, Vatican City, 1951; and J. C. Toynbee and J. B. Ward-Perkins, *The Shrine of Saint Peter*, London, New York, and Toronto, 1956; and E. Kirschbaum, *The Tombs of the Apostles*, New York, 1959.

pp. 20ff.

The donations of Constantine to his foundations in Rome are listed apparently from original documents in *LP*, I, 172ff. See recently Pietri, *Roma Christiana*, pp. 4ff. In a broader framework, Constantine's church foundations throughout the empire and their variations in plan, function, and design have been treated by me in "The Constantinian Basilica," *DOP* 21 (1967) 114ff., and more succinctly in my *Pelican*, pp. 39ff.

pp. 21ff.

For the Lateran, see *Corpus*, V, 1ff.; but regarding the *domus Faustae*, often supposed to have been given to the bishop of Rome by Constantine, E. Nash, "Convenerunt in Domum Faustae in Laterano. S. Optati Milevitani, I, 23," *RQSCHR* 71 (1976) 1ff.; for S. Croce in Gerusalemme, *Corpus*, I, 165ff., supplementing this my now old analysis and reconstruction with A. M. Colini, "Horti Spei Veteris," note to p. 8, particularly pp. 154ff., and (I regret having to quote myself again) with my *Pelican*, p. 51 and n.28. Colini envisages the original third-century structure as unroofed (*Il grande atrio*), presumably because of its wide span. If so, why the windows?

pp. 24ff.

The covered cemeteries of S. Lorenzo, SS. Marcellino e Pietro and S. Sebastiano are described in *Corpus*, II, 1ff., esp. 116ff., III, 190ff., and IV, 99ff., respectively, with further bibliographical references; the one at S. Agnese by F. W. Deichmann, "Die Lage der . . . Hl. Agnes," *RAC* 22 (1946) 213ff. and R. Perrotti, "Recenti ritrovamenti presso S. Costanza," *Palladio*, n.s. 6 (1956) 80ff. On St. Peter's, a covered cemetery, though including the grave of the martyr, see *Corpus*, v, 165ff. My views on the overall problem of these cemeteries are outlined in "Mensa-Coemeterium-Martyrium," *CahArch* 11 (1960) 15ff. and in my *Pelican*, pp. 52ff.

pp. 29ff.
I am afraid I must refer to another publication of mine, in which I first tried to bring out in preliminary form the ambiguity of the siting and splendor of the Lateran Basilica in the framework of Constantine's contrasting policies in Rome, "Il Laterano e Roma . . . ," *Accademia Nazionale dei Lincei Adunanze straordinarie . . . Feltrinelli*, vol. 1, no. 2 (1975) 231ff. H. Grisar, I have meanwhile found out, in a few lines in his *Roma alla fine del Mondo Antico*, I, Rome, 1908, 169f., had already pointed to the avoidance of the Forum by ecclesiastical foundations, attributing it to the prudence of the Church.

Chapter Two

pp. 33ff.
Throughout this chapter, I refer for the churches mentioned to *Corpus*, I-V, *passim*. New discoveries or changes in my point of view, as far as relevant in the present context, will be referred to in the notes. For the overall penetration of Rome by new churches in the course of the late fourth and fifth centuries, see Vielliard, *Origines*, *passim*, and S. Pressouyre, *Rome au fil du temps*, Boulogne, 1973, pls. XII and XIII; the quotation regarding a moral obligation of the newly elected pope to build a church was made by D. Kinney, "S. Maria in Trastevere from Its Founding to 1215", Ph.D. thesis, N.Y.U., 1975, p. 29.

p. 34
The arcaded opening of church façades, possibly local custom in Rome through the first quarter of the fifth century, has been pointed out by G. Matthiae, "Basiliche paleocristiane con ingresso a polifora," *Bollettino d'Arte*, 42 (1957) 107ff.; see also my *Pelican*, pp. 181 and 502, n.8.

pp. 35f.
The continuing repair and embellishment of public buildings and squares through the fourth century has been sketched by R. Lanciani, *The Destruction of Ancient Rome*, London, 1903, pp. 28ff., 47ff.; on the statues along the Via Sacra, *ibid.*, p. 36. For the *macellum Liviae*, founded by Augustus' wife Livia, across the north corner of the present Piazza Vittorio Emanuele, and restored in 367, see G. Lugli, *Monumenti*, III, Rome, 1938, pp. 418f.; the identification of the building found below S. Maria Maggiore with that macellum, as proposed by F. Magi, *Il calendario dipinto sotto S. Maria Maggiore* (*MemPontAcc*, XI, 1) Rome, 1972, pp. 59ff. wants further proof. For the *porticus deorum consentium*, Nash, *Dictionary*, II, 241; for the Basilica of Junius Bassus, Nash, *ibid.*, I, 190, and at greater length, R. Enking, *S. Andrea Cata Barbara e S. Antonio Abbate* (*Chiese illustrate*, p. 83), Rome, 1964, and G. Becatti, *Scavi di Ostia*, VI, Rome, 1969, 181ff. Finally, for the visit of Constantius II in 357, Ammianus Marcellinus, *Rerum . . . gestarum historia*, XVI, X, 13 (*LCL*, 300, 1, London, 1958, 248ff.) and R. Lanciani, *Destruction*, p. 47f.

pp. 36ff.
Outstanding among the rich bibliography on the struggle of paganism and Christianity, the coterminal political contest between the court and the senatorial aristocracy in Rome, the latter's cultural aspirations and its aim both before and after its conversion to save the heritage of antiquity, seem to me: A. Alföldi, *A Conflict of Ideas in the Late Roman Empire*, Oxford, 1952; *The Conflict between Paganism and Christianity in the Fourth Century*, ed. A. Momigliano, Oxford, 1963; P. Brown, *Augustine of Hippo*, Berkeley and Los Angeles, 1967; a number of papers by the same, reprinted *idem*, *Religion and Society in the Age of Saint Augustine*, New York, 1972; J. Matthews, *Western Aristocracies and Imperial Court, 364-425*, Oxford, 1975; and Pietri, *Roma Christiana*, pp. 405ff. The conversion by Christianity of pagan sanctuaries has been dealt with by F. W. Deichmann, "Frühchristliche Kirchen in antiken Heiligtümern," *JDAI* 54 (1939) 105ff., also with reference to the imperial decrees. Cassiodorus' letters are found in *MGH AA*, XII, 1ff., (*Variarum libri duodecem*); *The Letters of Cassiodorus*, ed. Thos. Hodgkins, London, 1886, renders them in Victorian English. Our references are to I, 39 (*Roma comunis patria*); III, 29 (granaries); III, 30 (sewers); IV, 51 (Theatre of Pompey); VII, 13 (crowd of statues and theft of bronze statues); and X, 30 (elephants). Procopius' listing of treasures surviving in Rome is found in his *Gothic Wars*, VII, xxi, 12-14 (*LCL*, 217, 1962) and his reference to the Aeneas canoe, *ibid.*, VIII, xxii, 6.

pp. 39f.
The luxury art of the late fourth century and its classical overtones and pagan vocabulary are brilliantly summed up in R. Bianchi Bandinelli, *Rome, the Late Empire*, New York, 1971, pp. 96ff. Among separate

studies, R. Delbrück, *Die Consular-Diptychen . . .*, Berlin, 1929; S. Poglayen-Neuwall, "Über die ursprünglichen Besitzer des Silberfundes vom Esquilin . . . ," *RM* 44 (1930) 124ff.; F. Gerke, *Der Sarkophag des Junius Bassus*, Berlin, 1936; and, using beautiful photographs, L. von Matt and E. Josi, *Early Christian Art in Rome*, New York, 1961, deal with the Nicomachi-Symmachi ivory, the Projecta casket, and the sarcophagus of Junius Bassus, in that sequence.

p. 40

The conflict of classical education and Christianity, often discussed, is still best summed up in Jerome's Letter XXII, 29 and 30 (Jerome, *Selected Letters*, *LCL*, 262, 1954, 124ff.) whence the quotation. Damasus' attitude clearly reveals itself in his poetry; see A. Ferrua, *Epigrammata Damasiana*, Vatican City, 1942. On the calendar of Philocalus, see H. Stern, *Le calendrier de 354*, Paris, 1953.

pp. 40ff.

The Romanization of Christianity and the leading role of Damasus was brought out some years ago by C. Pietri, " 'Concordia Apostolorum' et renovatio urbis (Culte des martyrs et propagande pontificale)," *MEFR* 73 (1961) 275ff., and again recently, *idem*, *Roma Christiana*, pp. 1571ff. Our Prudentius quotation is taken from his *Peristephanon* II, verses 433ff. (Prudence, IV, *Sources Chrétiennes*, Paris, 1951, p. 44). On S. Paolo fuori le mura, both the fourth-century structure and Leo I's rebuilding, now *Corpus*, v, 93ff., esp. 149ff. and 161ff. (the letter of the three emperors in *Epistolae imperatorum . . .*, ed. O. Guenther [*CSEL*, XXXV], Vienna, 1895, p. 46f.); on the mosaics of S. Pudenziana, conveniently G. Matthiae, *Mosaici medioevali di Roma*, I, Rome, 1967, 55ff.

pp. 43ff.

For the fifth century revival of classical antiquity, I refer to my paper, "The Architecture of Sixtus III. A Fifth Century Renascence?" *Essays in Honor of Erwin Panofsky*, New York, 1961, pp. 291ff., reprinted with a postscript in my *Studies,* pp. 181ff. Of course, I have used a good deal of that material in these pages, though with some modifications indicated already in my postscript in 1969, and supported by Pietri's paper, *MEFR* 73 (1961), his *Roma Christiana*, and the publications of P. Brown and others as quoted above. Rather than focusing the renascence on Sixtus III, I see it shaping up after A.D. 350 among Christian aristocrats and highbrow Church leaders.

Since literary sources making up this concept of a Christian renascence are abundantly quoted in that paper of mine and by Pietri, I can limit myself to quoting again a few among the most striking: on the Sack of Rome in 410 and the shock it caused, Augustine, *The City of God*, I, 1 (*LCL*, 411, 1957, pp. 10ff.) and Jerome, *Selected Letters*, Letter CXXVII, 12 (*LCL*, 262, 1954, pp. 462ff.), whence the quotation used; on the position of Leo I summed up by my quotation from his Sermon 82 (*PL*, 54, col. 423), Caspar, *Papsttum*, I, 427ff. and 489f.; on S. Maria Maggiore, for the building and its date, *Corpus*, III, 1ff.; and for the mosaics most recently, B. Brenk, *Die frühchristlichen Mosaiken in S. Maria Maggiore zu Rom*, Wiesbaden, 1975, and J. G. Decker, *Der alttestamentliche Zyklus von S. Maria Maggiore in Rom*, Ph.D. thesis, Bonn, 1976, supplemented by the plate volume, H. Karpp, *Die frühchristlichen und mittelalterlichen Mosaiken in S. Maria Maggiore zu Rom*, Baden-Baden, 1966, and C. Cecchelli, *I musaici della basilica di S. Maria Maggiore*, Turin, 1956.

pp. 49ff.

The most recent study to deal with the structure of the Lateran Baptistery, G. Pellicioni, *Le nuove scoperte sulle origini del battistero lateranense* (*MemPontAcc* XII, iii) Vatican City, 1973, while thoroughly investigating the archaeological evidence arrives at results which need further clarification. Likewise the chapel of S. Croce nearby requires further study, both of the preserved drawings and the remains still buried.

pp. 52ff.

The reconstruction of Sto. Stefano Rotondo with courtyards between the chapels proposed by S. Corbett, *Corpus*, IV, 232ff., fig. 195, has been splendidly confirmed by an observation of the late Carlo Ceschi, not yet published; his paper on the subject is briefly summarized in the *Verbale* of the *Adunanza pubblica* of the Pontificia Accademia Romana di Archeologia of 22 June 1972, in *RendPontAcc* 44 (1972) xxivf. I obviously withdraw the doubts I expressed, in *Corpus*, IV. On the building and renovation of the martyrs' churches outside the walls, including Old St. Peter's, by Leo I and his successors, see *Corpus, passim*, and L. Reekmans, "L'Implantation monumentale chrétienne dans la zone suburbaine de Rome . . . ," *RAC* 44 (1968) 173ff.

pp. 54ff.

For a preliminary summary of the hypothesis presented on the focal role assigned to the Lateran in the papal building program of the fifth century see my "Il Laterano e Roma . . . ," as cited above, in notes to chapter one. Regarding the new baptisteries established at S. Lorenzo fuori le mura, *LP*, I, 244; S. Marcello al Corso, *Corpus*, II, 205ff.; S. Sabina, *LP*, I, 235 and S. Maria Maggiore, *LP*, I, 233. On the establishment of the Station Services further research is needed.

p. 58

On S. Andrea in Catabarbara, the old basilica of Junius Bassus, R. Enking, *S. Andrea Cata Barbara e S. Antonio Abbate*, as above.

Chapter Three

pp. 59ff.

F. H. Dudden, *Gregory the Great*, London, 1905, is by now out of date. The best presentation of Gregory's personality and policies seems to me still given by Caspar, *Papsttum*, II, 306ff., and I stick pretty close to it. More recent treatments are found in Bertolini, *Roma di fronte*, pp. 231ff. with rich bibliography; and in Llewellyn, pp. 78ff. While obsolete as to details, J. Burckhardt, *Rom unter Gregor dem Grossen*, written in 1857, in *idem, Kulturgeschichtliche Vorträge*, Leipzig, 1930, pp. 20ff., is still a superb summary.

The sources for all recent treatments are the obvious ones: Gregory's correspondence (*MGH Epp*, I, II, quoted henceforth by book and letter), and his biographies, primarily that written by John the Deacon (Johannes Diaconus, Johannes Immonides; see C. Leonardi, "La 'Vita Gregorii' di Giovanni Diacono" in *Roma e l'età Carolingia*, pp. 381ff.) in retrospect almost three centuries later.

Corpus, I, 320ff., on the three chapels on the Clivus Scauri near S. Gregorio Magno, must be supplemented by new findings briefly discussed by I. Toesca, "Antichi affreschi a Sant'Andrea al Celio," *Paragone* 23 (1972) 263ff. A new full investigation of their building history as well as of the Library of Agapitus is badly wanted; at this point, see H. J. Marrou, "Autour de la bibliothèque du Pape Agapite," *MEFR* 48 (1931) 124ff.

pp. 59ff.

On the financial administration and the landholdings of the Church, Partner, *Lands*, pp. 4ff.; A.H.M. Jones, "Church Finances in the Fifth and Sixth Centuries," *Journal of Theological Studies* 11 (1960) 84ff.; and Llewellyn, pp. 138ff. On the papal bureaucracy under Gregory, Llewellyn, pp. 109ff., esp. pp. 114ff., and 141ff. on the Byzantine administration. On the latter, C. Diehl, *Études sur l'administration de l'exarchat* . . . (Bibliothèque des Ecoles Françaises d'Athènes et de Rome, 53), Paris, 1888, is still valuable. See also Caspar, *Papsttum*, II, 306ff.

p. 61

Caspar, *Papsttum*, *passim*, esp. 394ff.; Erich Auerbach, *Mimesis*, Bern, 1946, pp. 53ff., 81ff., and "Sermo humilis" in his *Literary Language and the Public* . . . , New York, 1965, pp. 25ff. (translated from *Romanische Forschungen* 64 [1952] 304ff.) was the first to bring out—superbly—the spirit of the new times through an analysis of language from the fourth century through the pontificate of Gregory the Great.

pp. 61f.

On Benedict and his order, Caspar, *Papsttum*, pp. 320ff.; Bertolini, *Roma di fronte*, pp. 210ff.; L. Salvatorelli in *Dizionario biografico degli italiani*, VIII, Rome, 1968, 249ff. On the mission to England, Bede, *Ecclesiastical History of the English People*, book I, 23ff.; book II, 2ff. and *passim* (*Bedae opera historica*, *LCL*, 246, 1962, 100ff., 204ff. and *passim*).

p. 62

John the Deacon, *Vita Gregorii*, I, 36 and 42 (*PL* 75, col. 78, 80f.) bases himself apparently on the pope's *Homiliae in Ezechielem*, I, ix, 9 and II, vi, 22 (*PL* 76, cols. 873f., 1009f.) and on Gregory of Tours, *Historia Francorum*, x, 1 (*MGH SS RM* I, 406ff.).

pp. 62ff.

On the sieges of Rome, Procopius, *The Gothic Wars*, V, xiv, and VI, x (537-538, first siege); VII, xiii-xx (544, second siege); VII, xxiii-xxxvi (547, third siege); VIII, xxxiii (552, fourth siege) (*LCL*, 217, 1961-62, books III-V, *passim*). Robert Graves, *Count Belisarius*, London, 1962 (first published 1938), esp. pp. 291ff.

For the repairs of the bridges leading to Rome, A. M. Colini, "Ponte Salario attraverso la storia," *Capitolium* 7 (1931) 390ff., and G. M. de Rossi, *Torri e castelli . . . della Campagna Romana*, Rome, 1969, pp. 111f.; *ibid.*, 117f. on Ponte Nomentana. The inscription on Ponte Salario, E. Diehl, *Inscriptiones Latinae Christianae Veteres*, Berlin, 1925, nos. 77 a, b.

On the devastation of the countryside and the repeated threats to Rome by the Longobards, Gregory, *Epp.*, I, 1ff. and *passim*; also, Llewellyn, pp. 93ff., and Bertolini, *Roma di fronte, passim*; on the need to feed the rural population, including monastic congregations, driven into the city by the Longobard invasions, Gregory, *Epp.*, VI, 26.

pp. 64f.

Tiber floods are described in *LP*, I, 317f., 513; II, 145, 153f., 154. For earlier and later ones see, Lugli, *Monumenti*, II, 278ff. The population figures are those given in *Enciclopedia italiana*, XXIX, 767; but they are guesswork.

pp. 65f.
Cassiodorus, *Letters* (as above, note to pp. 36ff.) with reference to the same and additional passages.

For the reuse of spoils in churches, see F. W. Deichmann, "Säule und Ordnung in der frühchristlichen Architektur," *RM* 55 (1940), 114, and quite recently, *idem.*, *Spolien in der spätantiken Architektur* (*Abhandlungen, Bayerische Akademie der Wissenschaften, Philosophisch-Historische Klasse, Sitzungsberichte*, 1975, Heft 6), Munich, 1975.

pp. 67f.
For the Column of Phocas, see E. Nash, *Dictionary*, I; for aqueducts functioning in 536, Procopius, *The Gothic Wars*, V, xix, 13 (*LCL*, 217, 1962, pp. 188f.), and still functioning in 602, Gregory, *Epp.*, XII, 6. River mills were set up by Belisarius, Procopius, *op. cit.*, V, XIX, 20 (*LCL*, 217, 1962, pp. 190ff). For the Forum and baths in use at Gregory's time, see his *Homilae in Ev.*, I, vi, 6 (*PL*, 76, col. 1098), as referred to in Caspar, *Papsttum*, II, 390, n.2; on Constans' sightseeing tour, Lanciani, *Destruction*, pp. 124ff.; on the *curator palatii, LP*, I, 386, n.1.

On the churches listed at this point: SS. Quirico e Giulitta, *Corpus*, IV, 37ff.; SS. Apostoli, *ibid.*, I, 67ff.—but I am no longer sure of the triconch plan's being sixth century; S. Giovanni a Porta Latina, *ibid.*, I, 404ff.—the date 550 being proposed by N. and R. Schumacher, "Die Kirche San Giovanni a Porta Latina," *Kölner Domblatt* 12/13 (1957) 22ff.; SS. Nereo ed Achilleo in the Domitilla Catacomb, *Corpus*, III, 124ff.; and S. Lorenzo fuori le mura, *Corpus*, II, 1ff., esp. 44ff. and 123f.

pp. 69ff.
On the financial position of the Church and her landholdings, above, note to pp. 59ff.

pp. 71f.
Regarding public buildings Christianized, see: B. M. Apollonj Ghetti, "Nuove considerazioni . . . (su) . . . SS. Cosma e Damiano," *RAC*, 50 (1974) 7ff., supplementing and in part revising *Corpus*, I, 144ff., except that I find untenable his contention of a Constantinian Christianization of the hall; C. Bertelli, *La Madonna di Trastevere*, Rome, 1961, 52ff. for the original function as a guardroom of S. Maria Antiqua; for S. Martina, E. Nash, "Secretarium Senatus" in *Essays . . . in memoriam Otto Brendel*, Mainz, 1976, 191ff.; for S. Adriano, converted from the *Curia*, A. Mancini, "La chiesa medioevale di S. Adriano," *RendPontAcc* 40 (1967-68) 191ff.; for S. Lucia in Selcis, *Corpus*, II, 185ff.; for the Quattro Coronati, *Corpus*, IV, 1ff.

pp. 72ff.
On the Christianization of the Pantheon, *LP*, I, 317; Gregory, *Epp.*, XI, 56, on the advice to the mission in England; C. D'Onofrio, *Castel S. Angelo*, Rome, 1971, 56ff., 105f., and C. Cecchelli, "Documenti per . . . Castel S. Angelo," *ASRStP* 74 (1951) 27ff.

pp. 75f.
For Eastern saints with churches in the center of Rome, see H. Delehaye, *Les Origines du culte des Martyrs*, Brussels, 1933, *passim*. The existence of a Byzantine fortification on the site of Torre delle Milizie, the link of the Militiae Tiberianae to Emperor Mauricius Tiberius, and the explanation of Magnanapoli as *bannum Neapolis* are suggested by C. Cecchelli in F. Castagnoli and others, *Topografia ed urbanistica di Roma*, Bologna, 1958, 259f.

pp. 76ff.
Gregory in his correspondence again and again discusses provisioning and feeding of the population, see *MGH Epp*, I, II as above, also Johannes Diaconus, *Vita, passim*, esp. II, 22ff. On the granaries of the Church, Gregory, *Epp., passim*, for instance I, 42; IX, 115; see also *LP*, I, 315 and Llewellyn, pp. 95ff.

The Eastern origin of the diaconiae, their function and administration in Rome as developed into the eighth century have been clarified by H.-I. Marrou, "L'Origine orientale des diaconies romaines," *MEFR* 57 (1940) 95; by O. Bertolini, "Per la storia delle diaconie romane," *ASRStP* 70 (1947) 1ff. and in summary form by G. Ferrari, *Monasteries*, pp. 255 ff. But their first appearance in Rome remains under discussion. Since there they are first referred to (*LP*, I, 364) in 682/83, their establishment in Rome has been assigned to the second half of the seventh century. However, I incline toward dating the first Roman diaconiae in the second half of the sixth century and the first years of the seventh century. Granted (Bertolini, *op. cit.*) that the existence of a church or for that matter a mural or mosaic with religious subject matter, dated by documentary, archaeological, or stylistic evidence prior to or around 600, and linked by later documentary evidence to a diaconia, does not by itself prove the latter's early foundation. On the other hand, at least two reasons make plausible to me the early link of such structures or murals and mosaics to the diaconiae, notwithstanding the late documentation of these latter: their installation in former government granaries or food administration centers—S. Teodoro, S. Maria in Cosmedin, S. Maria in Via Lata (the Seven Sleeper mural preserved only in a photograph, C. Bertelli, "The Seven Sleepers . . . ," *Paragone* 291 [1974]

233ff.); and the appearance of these same buildings as diaconiae in later parts of the *Liber Pontificalis* without reference to their foundation date, which, on the contrary, is nearly always given for diaconiae established after 700. See S. Maria in Cosmedin, *Corpus*, II, 277ff., esp. 300ff.; S. Giorgio in Velabro, *Corpus*, I, 244, esp. 260; S. Maria in Via Lata, *Corpus*, III, 72ff.; S. Teodoro, *Corpus*, IV, 279ff., supplemented by E. Monaco, "Ricerche sotto . . . S. Teodoro," *RendPontAcc* 45 (1974) 223ff.—but I interpret the apsed building excavated below the sixth-century apse as an administrative hall and part of the Roman granary rather than as a church. S. Maria Antiqua, too, may have been linked to a diaconia as early as the late sixth century; see C. Bertelli, *La Madonna di Trastevere*, Rome, 1961, p. 53.

pp. 78f.
Ferrari, *Monasteries*, is the standard work on the subject.

p. 80
The quotations are from Gregory, *Epp.*, IV, 30: see also Caspar, *Papsttum*, II, 397, n.1. Filings from the Apostle's chains are requested by the papal legate as early as 519 for the church of St. Peter's and Paul's, being built by the heir apparent Justinian (*Epistulae Imperatorum* . . . , ed. O. Guenther, *CSEL*, XXXV, Vienna, 1895, esp. 680); also Caspar, *Papsttum*, pp. 291ff., n.4.

pp. 80f.
On "houses for the poor" in Rome, *LP*, I, 261f.; on pilgrims and pilgrimages in general, Llewellyn, pp. 173ff. and *passim*; J. Zettinger, *Rompilger aus dem Frankenreich* (*RQSCHR* Suppl. 11), Rome, 1900; W. J. Moore, *The Saxon Pilgrims to Rome* . . . , Fribourg, 1937; in particular: on Irish and Eastern pilgrims meeting, *Vita S. Cummiani* (*PL*, 87, col. 977; quoted in Llewellyn, p. 181); on hostels on the roads to Rome, Gregory, *Epp.*, II, 382, IX, 197 and *passim*, Muratori, *Antiquitates Italicae* . . . , II, Milan, 1751, 465ff., and Zettinger, *op. cit.*, p. 18f.; on Benedict Biscop, Bede, *Lives of the Abbots* . . . (*LCL*, 248, 1954, II, 400); on Theodo, *LP*, I, 398, and Zettinger, *op. cit.*, pp. 18f. and 44f.; on Hunald, *LP*, I, 441; on the Swiss lady, Zettinger, *op. cit.*, p. 68, and *ibid.* on disreputable pilgrims, quoting a letter by Saint Boniface, *MGH Epp*, III, 301. The letter of recommendation from Marculf's collection of forms, *MGH Epp*, II, 49 (*PL*, 87, col. 755) and Zettinger, *op. cit.*, p. 40; the tasks of Sto. Stefano degli Abissini, *LP*, II, 52; those of a hospital, *Liber Diurnus*, ed. Th. v. Sickel, Vienna, 1889, form 66, p. 62 (quoted in Llewellyn, p. 116 as form 46).

pp. 81f.
On S. Pellegrino, *Corpus*, III, 175ff.; on Sto. Stefano degli Abissini, *ibid.*, IV, 178ff.; on S. Eustachio and S. Maria in Aquiro, *LP*, I, 419f., 440, and Kehr, *It. Pont.*, I, 97; on S. Angelo in Pescheria, *Corpus*, I, 64ff. (the date 755, of which I was not sure forty years ago, is the correct one); on the installation of diaconiae at SS. Cosma e Damiano and S. Adriano, *LP*, I, 509f.; on SS. Sergius and Bacchus, M. Bonfioli, "La diaconia dei SS. Sergio e Bacco," *RAC* 50 (1974) 55ff.

p. 82
The quotation regarding Boniface is from his *Vita*, c. V (*PL*, 89, col. 613). Bede, *Ecclesiastical History*, V, 7 on Cadwalla and Ina; V, 19 on Coinred and Offa (*LCL*, 246, 1962, II, 224, 229); also Moore, *op. cit.*, *passim*. On Benedict Biscop's visits and acquisitions, Bede, *Lives of the Abbots* (*LCL*, 248, 1954, II, 404ff., 412ff.) including the arch chanter, *Ecclesiastical History*, IV, 18 (*LCL*, 246, 1962, II, 96ff.).

On the formation of the scholae, *LP*, II, 36, n.27; F. Ehrle, "Ricerche in alcune chiese nel Borgo," *DissPontAcc*, ser. II, 10 (1910) 1ff.; L. Reekmans, "Le dévelopment topographique de la region du Vatican," *Mélanges . . . Lavalleye*, Louvain, 1970, 197ff.; and on their churches, Huelsen, *Chiese*, pp. 279, 363, 388, 454 (for S. Michele in Borgo, also *Corpus*, III, 125ff.).

pp. 83ff.
The quotations are from *De locis sanctis martyrum* (*Epitome Salisburgense*) and *Notitia ecclesiarum* (*Itinerarium Salisburgense*), G. B. de Rossi, *Roma sotterranea*, I, Rome, 1864, pp. 141 and 139 resp. On S. Lorenzo fuori le mura and on SS. Nereo ed Achilleo in Domitilla, notes to pp. 24ff., 67f.; on S. Agnese, *Corpus*, I, 14ff. On the annular crypt at St. Peter's, and its date, *Corpus*, V, 277f.; on that at S. Crisogono, *Corpus*, I, 156ff. and, revising some points, B. M. Apollonj Ghetti, *S. Crisogono* (*Chiese illustrate*, 92), Rome, 1966, pp. 39ff.; on that at S. Pancrazio, *Corpus*, III, 163, 174; and on the spread of the type in Rome and Latium, B. M. Apollonj Ghetti, "La chiesa di S. Maria in Vescovio," *RAC* 23-24 (1947-48) 253ff.

Chapter Four

p. 89
The coexistence of papal and imperial authority in the temporal affairs of Rome, first brought out by Charles Diehl (above, chap. three, note to pp. 59ff.) nearly a hundred years ago, and taken up by Berto-

lini, *Roma di fronte*, *passim*, is well summed up by Llewellyn, pp. 141ff.; some passages from the *Liber Pontificalis* supply evidence: formation of a Roman duchy, and growing independence, *LP*, I, 392f., 403 and 426ff. and further; papal attendance or representation at Constantinopolitan synods, *ibid.*, pp. 350, 371ff.; visit of Constans II, *ibid.*, p. 343; taxation, *ibid.*, pp. 366, 368f. and *passim*; interference by the exarch and the arrest of Pope Martin, *ibid.*, pp. 328f., 356ff., 369, 390, also *PL*, 88, pp. 113ff., 200.

pp. 90f.

Gay, "Quelques remarques sur les papes grecs . . . ," *Mélanges Schlumberger*, Paris, 1924, pp. 40ff., clarifies the reasons for electing Eastern popes. On the establishment of Eastern congregations in Rome, see: on S. Saba and its church and graveyard, Ferrari, *Monasteries*, pp. 281ff., and *Corpus*, IV, 51ff.; on Tre Fontane, Ferrari, *Monasteries*, pp. 33ff., and C. Bertelli, "Caput Sancti Anastasii," *Paragone* 247 (1970) 12ff., 18ff. For other Eastern congregations in Rome, Ferrari, *Monasteries*, pp. 75, 117, 119, 276; and for the Easterners sent to England, Bede, *Ecclesiastical History*, IV, 1 (*LCL*, 246, 1962).

Eastern relics in Rome are documented, *LP*, I, 310, 331, 334; Eastern feasts and liturgical customs, *ibid.*, 376, all providing *termini ante quos*; see also Gay, *op. cit.* Transfer of relics *ex ossibus* by "Eastern" popes, *LP*, I, 330, 332, 360. For the cross at Sto. Stefano Rotondo and its link to Jerusalem, see E. Mâle, "La Mosaique de Sto. Stefano Rotondo . . . ," in *Scritti in onore di Bartolomeo Nogara*, Vatican City, 1937, pp. 257ff., and A. Grabar, *Les Ampoules de Terre Sainte*, Paris, 1958 (also Matthiae, *Mosaici*, pp. 181ff.).

p. 91

On changes in liturgical furnishings as linked to changing liturgical custom in Rome, Th. F. Mathews, "An Early Roman Chancel Arrangement . . . ," *RAC* 38 (1962) 73ff.; on the trabeated chancel colonnade at St. Peter's, *Corpus*, V, 198, 261, and *LP*, I, 417; on the use of icons (*imagines*), in relief or panel paintings, see *LP*, I, 374, 404 and *passim*. The surviving icons listed will be discussed later.

pp. 91f.

On the dearth of Greek-speaking theologians in Rome in 680, see *LP*, I, 350, and Mansi, *Sacrorum Conciliorum Nova et Amplissima Collectio*, Florence and Venice, 1758-, XI, 230ff.—the envoys sent to the Council of Trullo in Constantinople all being either from Eastern monasteries in Rome, from Ravenna, capital of the exarchate, from South Italy, or from Eastern families; on the improved situation in the eighth century, *LP*, I, 415, 426—both Popes Gregory III and Zacharias active in translations from Latin to Greek and vice versa. On Roman monasteries taken over by Eastern congregations, Ferrari, *Monasteries*, pp. 302ff. and *passim*.

pp. 92ff.

Unsurpassed among writings on seventh- and eighth-century painting and mosaic in Rome and its links both to Byzantium and the Roman late-antique past, remains Kitzinger, *Malerei*, supplemented by some of his later papers, for instance "On Some Icons of the Seventh Century," in *Late Classical and Medieval Studies . . . Albert Mathias Friend*, Princeton, 1955, pp. 132ff., and "Byzantine Art in the Period between Justinian and Iconoclasm," *Berichte . . . XI Internationalen Byzantinisten-Kongress*, Munich, 1958, IV, 1, 1ff. (both reprinted in his *Byzantium*, pp. 157 ff., 233ff.); and lastly, his *Byzantine Art in the Making*, London, 1977, esp. 113ff. The complexity of the problems has been thrown into sharp light by this his new contribution to the lively discussion of recent years: C. Bertelli, *La Madonna di Trastevere*, Rome 1961 (henceforth Bertelli, *Trastevere*); a series of studies by or in collaboration with P. J. Nordhagen, such as P. Romanelli and P. J. Nordhagen, *S. Maria Antiqua*, Rome, 1960; P. J. Nordhagen, "The Earliest Decorations in S. Maria Antiqua," *Acta ad archaeologiam et artium historiam pertinentia*, ed. Institutum Romanum Norvegiae 1 (1962), 53ff. (henceforth *Acta* 1, 2, 3); *idem*, "The Mosaics of John VII," *Acta* 2 (1965) 121ff.; *idem*, "The Frescoes of John VII," *Acta* 3 (1968) 1ff., esp. 101ff.; finally, the surveys and splendid illustrations provided by Matthiae, *Mosaici*, and *Pittura*, *passim*.

pp. 93ff.

On the mosaic of SS. Cosma e Damiano: Kitzinger, *Malerei*, 5f.; G. Matthiae, *SS. Cosma e Damiano e S. Teodoro*, Rome, 1948, though erroneously dating the mosaics on the front wall of the apse to the late seventh century; and, *idem, Mosaici*, pp. 135ff., 203ff. On S. Teodoro, *idem, SS. Cosma e Damiano e S. Teodoro*, and *Mosaici*, 143ff. On S. Lorenzo fuori le mura and S. Agnese: Kitzinger, *Malerei*, p. 6f. and *idem, Byzantium*, p. 172f. and *passim*; G. Matthiae, "Tradizione e reazione nei mosaici romani del sec. VI-VII," *Proporzioni* 3 (1950) 10ff.; and *idem, Mosaici*, 149ff., explaining differences in style in the S. Lorenzo mosaic by the contemporaneous activity of three sixth-century masters, while N. Baldass, "The Mosaic on the Triumphal Arch of S. Lorenzo . . . ," *GBA* 49 (1947) 1ff., sees a twelfth-century hand in the figures of Saints Paul, Stephen, and Hippolytus.

Nordhagen, *Acta* 2, 121ff., considers the prevalent use of glass cubes for the fleshtones in mosaics as a mark of late-antique practice and its survival in Rome. This he contrasts with the use of a large proportion of marble tesserae, an Eastern workshop habit in his opinion. The thesis seems to me in need of further differentiation and proof.

p. 97
General consensus appears to agree on a date in the first half of the sixth century for the *Madonna Regina* at S. Maria Antiqua (Kitzinger, *Malerei*, p. 5; Bertelli, *Trastevere*, pp. 52ff.). On the icon of the Pantheon, C. Bertelli, "La Madonna del Pantheon," *Bollettino d'arte* 46 (1961) 24ff.

pp. 98f.
Kitzinger, *Malerei*, pp. 10ff. and at greater depth *Byzantium, passim*, has established the links between Constantinopolitan and Roman "Hellenism," a phenomenon previously noted, but never explained. His date for the *Fair Angel* and the related "Hellenistic" frescoes ca. 630-640 (*Byzantium*, p. 158; also *Byzantine Art in the Making*, p. 151f.) is being contested by Nordhagen, *Acta* 3, 110f., who proposes a date of 570-580 thus moving back previously suggested dates (early seventh century, Romanelli-Nordhagen, as above; and more vaguely *Acta* 1, 57, "after 576-578"—does he mean "567-578"?). The date 570-580 is apparently meant to coincide with the building's conversion into a church, provided three coins supposedly dating 567-578 were actually found under a column base set up during that conversion, as the excavator Boni reported in 1900. The coins are gone and the report regarding the site of the find has been doubted by Kitzinger, *Byzantine Art in the Making*, pp. 151f. I, for one, am less skeptical. An experienced excavator like Boni still years later recalls the exact circumstances of so extraordinary a find and I feel that the *Madonna Regina*, mutilated in converting the guard room into a church, would have quickly been painted over, presumably prior to 600. But I shall be glad to defer to expert opinion, once the dust has settled.

pp. 99f.
On the murals of the Church Fathers at S. Maria Antiqua, Kitzinger, *Malerei*, p. 8f., and Nordhagen, *Acta* 1, 55; on the mosaics of S. Venanzio and Sto. Stefano Rotondo, Kitzinger, *Malerei*, pp. 12f., 14, and Matthiae, *Mosaici*, pp. 191ff.; on the Saint Sebastian mosaic at S. Pietro in Vincoli, Kitzinger, *Malerei*, p. 21, and Matthiae, *Mosaici*, pp. 199ff. The icon at S. Francesca Romana has been placed by Kitzinger, *Byzantium*, pp. 233ff., in the series of paintings descended from his first Hellenistic wave and dated around 700; Bertelli, *Trastevere*, p. 88, seems to incline toward a slightly earlier date.

pp. 100ff.
LP, I, 385f., on John VII's activities including his project of building a palace above S. Maria Antiqua (*ibid.*, p. 386, n.1, the funeral inscription of his father, Plato) as against the scarce gifts made by his predecessors, e.g. *LP*, I, 375; on the mosaics from his chapel at St. Peter's, Nordhagen, *Acta* 2, 121ff. On the donations of Popes Gregory III and Zacharias, *LP*, I, 417ff., 431f.; on the *diaconiae* newly established by Gregory II and Gregory III, *LP*, I, 397f., 419; on the monasteries, Ferrari, *Monasteries*, pp. 365ff. and *passim*; finally, *LP*, I, 432, on Zacharias' embellishing the Lateran Palace.

pp. 103f.
The frescoes of John VII at S. Maria Antiqua and their characteristics, first brought out by Kitzinger, *Malerei*, pp. 15ff., have been extensively discussed as to their iconography and style and beautifully illustrated in a monograph by Nordhagen, *Acta* 3. Rather than two successive waves of around 630 or earlier and again 705-707 carrying to Rome the "perennial Hellenism" of Byzantium (Kitzinger, *Byzantium*, pp. 193ff.), Nordhagen (*op. cit.*, pp. 110ff.) sees the renascence of Hellenism as penetrating around 570 from secular court art in Constantinople into religious painting carried to Rome and continuing without a break in both Byzantium and Rome until the eighth century when it peters out. All this wants further exploration.

On the icon from S. Maria in Trastevere, Bertelli, *Trastevere*; his attribution to John VII, convincing to me, has been questioned by D. Kinney, "S. Maria in Trastevere," Ph.D. thesis, N.Y.U., 1975, who proposes a ninth-century date, and by M. Andaloro, "La datazione della tavola di S. Maria in Trastevere," *Rivista Istituto Nazionale di Archeologia e Storia dell'Arte* 19-20 (1972-73) 139ff., who proposes a sixth-century date. On the mosaics of John VII, Nordhagen, *Acta* 2, 121ff.

The distinction of the use for different subject matters of different "modes," generally accepted by now as one of the most fertile tools in analyzing the style of Early Christian, Byzantine, and early medieval figural arts, goes back to Ernst Kitzinger (see for instance *Byzantium*, p. 193 and *passim*, and recently, *Byzantine Art in the Making*, pp. 123ff.).

pp. 104ff.
On eighth-century painting in Rome after John VII in general, Kitzinger, *Malerei*, pp. 26ff. and 31f.; also

Matthiae, *Pittura* and *Mosaici, passim*. In particular: on S. Saba, P. Styger, "Die Malereien in der Basilika des hl. Sabas . . . ," *RQSCHR* 28 (1914) 49ff., esp. 60ff., and on their style and its survival in the ninth century, C. Davis-Weyer, "Die Mosaiken Leos III . . . ," *ZKG* 29 (1966) 111ff.; on the murals of Theodotus and Popes Paul I and Hadrian at S. Maria Antiqua, Kitzinger, *Malerei, loc. cit.*; *ibid.*, 43ff., on the portraits of Popes Gregory III and Zacharias and the resulting date of the Theodotus murals; see also, *idem*, *Byzantium*, pp. 256ff.; and on S. Crisogono, *idem*, *Malerei*, p. 32, and B. M. Apollonj Ghetti, *S. Crisogono* (*Chiese illustrate* 92), Rome, 1966, p. 59f.

pp. 104f.
On Byzantine influence in late-eighth- and ninth-century Rome possibly by way of Greek centers in the West: P. Battifol, "Inscriptions grecques à St.-Georges au Velabre," *MEFR* 7 (1887) 419f.; C. Davis-Weyer, "Die ältesten Darstellungen der Hadesfahrt Christi," in *Roma e l'età Carolingia*, Rome, 1976, pp. 183ff.; and on church architecture, *Corpus*, I, 46ff., S. Angelo in Pescheria; *Corpus*, II, 277ff., S. Maria in Cosmedin, and 308ff., S. Maria in Domnica; *Corpus*, III, 128ff., SS. Nereo ed Achilleo.

p. 106
On Benedict Biscop, above, chapter three notes to pp. 80f. and 82.

pp. 106f.
On the position held and claimed by the papacy in Western Europe, for instance, R. W. Southern, *Western Society and the Church*, Harmondsworth, 1970, pp. 58ff., where the quote from the letter of Gregory II, *PL* 89, 520ff. On the popes' being forced through the second third of the seventh century by Longobard and Byzantine pressures to turn to the Franks, *ibid.*, *loc. cit.*, and Llewellyn, pp. 202ff. On the part of the great families in a Roman quasi-independence movement, as represented by militiae and populus from the mid-seventh century on, *LP*, I, 337f., 371ff., 383, 386f.; and correspondingly on the growing alienation from Byzantium, Llewellyn, pp. 165ff. and *LP*, I, 392, 403ff., 430 (Pope Zacharias greeted as shepherd of his people).

pp. 107f.
On Pope Stephen's journey to Pepin (and the preceding appeal of his predecessors to Charles Martel), *LP*, I, 444ff. and Llewellyn, pp. 208ff., referring to Stephen's letters, *Libri Carolini*, nos. 4, 5, 6 (*MGH Epp*, III, 487ff.); on the term *patricius*, Llewellyn, p. 212; on the ambiguous position of Byzantium, Partner, *Lands*, pp. 17ff. and *LP*, I, 442ff.; on the place gained for Rome by Stephen II, Llewellyn, p. 215f. On the identification of Rome and the papacy with Saint Peter, for instance, Gregory III's letters to Charles Martel, *Libri Carolini*, nos. 1, 6 (*MGH Epp*, III, 476f. and 488ff.; Saint Peter's *peculiaris populus*, and *res publica Romanorum*, respectively); see also F. Kampers, "Roma aeterna et sancta Dei ecclesia rei publicae Romanorum," *Hist. Jbch. Görresgesellschaft* 44 (1924) 240ff. On the *patrimonium Petri* in the later eighth century, Partner, *Lands*, pp. 15ff. Finally, on papal elections, *LP*, I, 371 and 471, demonstrate the participation of the lay leaders from the late seventh century on; see also Llewellyn, pp. 130, 159, 217, 225. On the use of old Roman and Byzantine titles including *senatus nobilium*, *LP*, I, 486, 506, and *ibid.*, II, 6 and *passim*, and Llewellyn, *passim*, for instance 217; for *Senatus Populusque Romanus* see *LP*, II, 91.

Chapter Five

pp. 109ff.
I am greatly indebted to Professor Robert Brentano for reading this chapter and suggesting major and minor revisions.

pp. 109f.
On Hadrian's background and character, *LP*, I, 486, whence the quotations; on the eighth-century Longobard invasions and subsequent devastations prior to Hadrian's pontificate, the biographers of Gregory II, *ibid.*, pp. 396ff., Gregory III, *ibid.*, pp. 415ff., and Stephen II, *ibid.*, pp. 441ff., and *Libri Carolini, MGH Epp*, III, 494ff., this latter on the devastations in 755; the conflict in his early reign, *LP*, I, 494ff., *Libri Carolini, loc. cit.*, and summing up, Llewellyn, pp. 199ff.

pp. 110f.
On the *domus cultae*, prior to Hadrian, *LP*, I, 434f., and *MGH Epp*, III, 494ff., concerning the devastation wrought in 755; on their revival through him, *LP*, I, 501f., 505f., 508f. Also Partner, *Lands*, pp. 36ff., and on their end, pp. 50 and 93ff.; in greater detail, *idem*, "Notes on the Lands of the . . . Church," *PBSR* 34 (1966), 68ff., and O. Bertolini, "La ricomparsa . . . di 'Tres Tabernae' . . . ," *ASRStP* 75 (1952), 102ff.; and, on the structures excavated at Capracorum near Veii, the brief report in A. Kahane, L. Murray Threipland, and J. Ward-Perkins, "The Ager Veientanus . . . ," *PBSR* 36 (1968), 1ff., esp. 161ff. On the food distribution in the Lateran portico, *LP*, I, 502.

pp. 111f.
Concerning diaconiae newly established under Hadrian I and Leo III, *LP*, I, 508f., 512; II, 12, 21; and Vielliard, *Origines*, pp. 115ff. On the repairs of

aqueducts, *LP*, I, 503ff., 510ff., 520; II, 77, 154, and the Einsiedeln Itinerary in Valentini-Zucchetti, II, 173; see also note to pp. 113f. On repairs of the city walls prior to Hadrian, *LP*, I, 388, and under him, *LP*, I, 493, 501, 503; on the Tiber embankment, *LP*, I, 507; and on the organization of the labor force, *LP*, I, 504.

pp. 112ff.

On the building, repair, and refurbishing of churches: in general, *LP*, I, 499, 501 (whence the quote), and *passim*, 499ff.; on S. Maria in Cosmedin, *LP*, I, 507f., and *Corpus*, II, 277ff., esp. 306; on major roof repairs, *LP*, I, 500, 503, 505f., 508, and *Libri Carolini*, nos. 65, 78 (*MGH Epp*, III, 592, 609ff.); on curtains and silver furnishings, *LP*, I, 499f., 504, and *passim*.

pp. 112f.

Abortive attempts at repairing the catacombs and the switch in 761 to transferring the relics into the city are illustrated by *LP*, I, 420, and 464f., and by the foundation document of S. Silvestro in Capite as ratified in 762, V. Federici, "Regesto del monastero di S. Silvestro in Capite . . . ," *ASRStP* 22 (1899) 213ff. Hadrian's policy, indecisive in that respect, tends on one hand to restore catacomb chapels (*LP*, I, 509), on the other hand to transfer relics to city churches, as witness the hall crypt at S. Maria in Cosmedin (*Corpus*, II, 298f., 306f.). The policy of transfer, general through the first half of the ninth century, is documented by the annular crypts becoming a regular feature (*Corpus, passim*; B. M. Apollonj Ghetti, "La chiesa di S. Maria in Vescovio . . . ," *RAC* 23-24 [1947-48] 253ff.; see also above for annular crypt installed at St. Peter's, chapter three note to pp. 83ff.), and by the long if restored list of relics at S. Prassede (U. Nilgen, "Die grosse Reliquieninschrift von Santa Prassede . . . ," *RQSCHR* 69 [illegible] 7ff.).

pp. 113-42

The Carolingian Renascence, as reflected in church building, was outlined many years ago in my article "The Carolingian Revival of Early Christian Architecture," *Art Bull* 24 (1942) 1ff. (repr. *Studies*, 203ff. with postscript). In recent years, Caecilia Davis-Weyer, "Die Mosaiken Leos III . . . ," *ZKG* 29 (1966) 111ff., likewise sees the return to late-antique features as beginning in the first years of Leo III, though in the lost mosaic at S. Susanna rather than in the triclinium mosaic. The full-fledged revival of Early Christian models she would prefer to place in the pontificate of Paschal I. H. Belting, "I mosaici dell'aula Leonina," in *Roma e l'età Carolingia*, pp. 167ff., on the contrary, reverts to the thesis of the start of the movement in the mosaics of the Triclinium of Leo III and thus, so it seems to me, links it implicitly to the alliance of the papacy with Charlemagne and the consequent new concepts of its mission held by the papacy.

As I see it in the present chapter, the phenomenon needs to be viewed both on different levels and as slowly unfolding. The physical renewal of Rome and the idea of her revival as the hub of the Christian world shape up locally under Hadrian I. Meanwhile, north of the Alps a rebirth of learning was being prepared in the monasteries of England and on the continent, and this cultural revival in the last decades prior to 800 came to full flowering at the Frankish court. But it reached Rome only late, around the middle of the ninth century. Finally, the political concept of a renascence, focused on Constantine and on Rome as the seat of a papacy which viewed itself as successor to the Roman emperors, was adumbrated at the papal court through the later part of the eighth century. Under Leo III it was conceived, both in Rome and at the Frankish court, though never clearly, as being embodied by both the pope and the newly "invented" Carolingian emperor; Rome was viewed ideally as the capital of both. Shortly after Leo's and Charlemagne's deaths, a split occurred: the papacy, beginning with Paschal and culminating under Nicholas I, viewed itself as the head and Rome as the seat of a universal monarchy, while the empire far more vaguely pursued the dream of rule over the world and of Rome as its capital.

pp. 113f.

On S. Petronilla, *LP*, I, 455, 464; also A. Angenendt, "Mensa Pippini Regis . . . ," *RQSCHR*, Suppl. 35, 1977, 52ff. On the revival of a Constantinian terminology in the *Liber Pontificalis, LP*, I, 503; II, 20f., 54, 79, and C. Huelsen, "Zu den römischen Ehrenbögen," *Festschrift . . . Otto Hirschfeld . . .* , Berlin, 1903, pp. 423ff. H. Geertman, *More veterum*, Groningen, 1975, pp. 143ff., explains the reappearance of the term *titulus* as due to the use of old lists by the compilers of the *Liber Pontificalis*; but this does not alter the argument. On the date and significance of the Itinerary of Einsiedeln, Valentini-Zucchetti, II, 154ff., and previously R. Lanciani, "L'itinerario di Einsiedeln . . . ," *Mon. antichi* I (1891) 473ff., opposed by C. Huelsen, "La Pianta di Roma dell'Anonimo Einsidlense," *DissPontAcc*, ser. II, 9 (1907) 379ff.

pp. 114f.

For the vexing questions of the Constantinian Donation, its date, origin, and meaning, and of Charlemagne's coronation in the context of Frankish and papal policies, I supplement the sources and discussion given in the notes to my paper of 1942 and the 1969 postscript by referring to a few selected recent publications: H. Fichtenau, *L'Impero Carolingio*, Bari, 1974 (transl. from *Das Karolingische Imperium*, Zürich, 1949), 59ff.; P. Classen, "Karl der Grosse, des Papsttum und Byzanz," in *Karl der Grosse . . .*, I, ed. H. Beumann, Düsseldorf, 1965, 537ff.; H. Fuhrmann, *Das Constitutum Constantini . . .*, in *MGH, Fontes Iuris Germanici*, X, 1968, text and dating; W. Gericke, "Wann entstand die Konstantinische Schenkung?" *ZSRG, Kanon*. 43 (1957) 1ff., and *idem*, "Das Constitutum Constantini und die Sylvesterlegende," *ZSRG, Kanon*. 44 (1958) 343ff. On the coronation, on the vague and divergent views held by contemporaries of the emperor's position vis-à-vis the papacy and ancient and contemporary Rome, and the *imitatio Constantini*, the sources: *LP*, II, 6, as against *LP*, I, 496f.; *LP*, II, 7; *MGH SS*, I, 38, 189, 305f.; *Einhardi Vita Karoli . . .*, *MGH SS RG*, ed. G. M. Pertz and G. Waitz, 1911, p. 32; *MGH, Poetae Lat.*, I, 226, and II, 36f., 65—to name just a few.

pp. 115f.

Professor Davis-Weyer has thoroughly studied the triclinium mosaic of Leo III. She has convincingly established its date, 798-799, in her paper "Die Mosaiken Leos III," as above, esp. p. 114f.; she has raised doubts regarding the restoration in 1625 of the left-hand group on the apse arch with Constantine ("Eine patristische Apologie des Imperium Romanum . . . ," in *Munuscula Discipulorum . . . Studien Hans Kauffmann . . .*, Berlin, 1968, pp. 71ff., esp. 73f.)—but who else would typologically correspond to Charlemagne in late-eighth-century thought?—(see also Belting, "I mosaici dell'aula Leonina," as above) and has distinguished among the surviving fragments an original piece and one of seventeenth-century date ("Karolingisches und nicht-Karolingisches," *ZKG* 31 [1974] 31ff.).

pp. 116f.

Regarding the imperial terminology used, see the sources quoted above in my note before last. For the new situation arising under Charlemagne's and Leo III's successors, O. Bertolini, "Osservazioni sulla 'Constitutio Romana' . . . dell'824" in *Studi . . . in onore di A. de Stefano*, Palermo, 1956, pp. 43ff.; also *MGH LL, Capitularia*, I, 323; *MGH SS*, I, 216 (*Einhardi Annales* ad an. 827); *LP*, II, 87ff., 97f. and *passim*; and Llewellyn, pp. 259ff.

pp. 117ff.

The main sources for the Leonine Wall and the formation of the Leonine City are *LP*, II, 123, and a *capitulare* of the emperor Lothar II, quoted by Duchesne, *LP*, II, 137, n.46, where the construction of the wall is decided on in 846 on the initiative of the emperor. For the structure, repairs, inscriptions, and course of the wall, see I. Richmond, *The City Wall of Ancient Rome*, London, 1930, p. 43; A. Prandi, "Precisazioni . . . sulla Civitas Leonina," *Miscellanea . . . Nozze Jacovelli . . . Castano*, Massafra, 1969, pp. 109ff.; *idem*, "L'Antiquarium del Passetto di Borgo," *Strenna dei Romanisti* 34 (1973) 356ff.; C. Belli Barsali, ". . . La civitas Leonina . . . ," in *Roma e l'età Carolingia* (as above), pp. 201ff.

p. 120

Leo III's gifts to churches, *LP*, II, 3ff., *passim*. The list of donations made to all churches, diaconiae, and monasteries has been closely studied by Geertman, *More Veterum*, analyzed as to the principles of distribution and dated 807 rather than 806.

pp. 120ff.

Notwithstanding the monumental publications of C. Rohault de Fleury, *Le Latran au Moyen-Age*, Paris, 1877, and P. Lauer, *Le Palais de Latran*, Paris, 1911, layout and building history of the medieval Lateran palace remain to be clarified. The scarce surviving data are: scattered remarks in the *Liber Pontificalis* and in medieval documents; vague descriptions antedating its destruction by a few years; a plan dating about 1560 in the Lateran Archive (Lauer, *op. cit.*, p. 311, fig. 116 in a tracing); views, by Heemskerck done in 1534-1536, in Sixtus V's library hall in the Vatican, around 1586, and on maps of the 1570s; and, as the only archaeological element remaining, the chapel of the Sancta Sanctorum, 1278-1281, and its much older substructures, both located behind the Scala Santa. We are slightly better informed only on the two structures built by Leo III: on the triconch triclinium through a sketch of Ugonio's in a Vatican codex (Barb. lat. 2160, fol. 5^r), through the engravings in N. Alemanni, *De parietibus Lateranensibus*, Rome, 1625, through their descriptions, and through the hints given in *LP*, II, 3f.; on the *accubita*, again through a sketch and descriptions of Ugonio's in Barb. lat. 2160, fol. 157^v, 158, through a passage in *LP*, II, 11, and through two exterior views, one done by Heemskerck, the other a fresco in the Vatican Library of Sixtus V. I have dealt with the *accubita* and the presumable dependence of the hall and the adjoining parts of the palace on the corresponding sections of the Imperial Palace in Constantinople ("The Enneadeka-cubita . . ." in: *Tortulae, RQSCHR*, Suppl. 30, Freiburg, 1966, pp. 195ff.) and can supplement my remarks by pointing to further examples of niched banqueting halls in Constantinople (Alemanni, *op. cit.*, p. 18) and Ravenna (A. Weis, "Der römische Schöpfungszyklus im Triklinium Neons zu Ravenna," *Tortulae*, 300). On the *macrona, LP*, II, 28f.; on the additions of Gregory IV and Nicholas I, *LP*, II, 76, 81, 166. See also E. David, "Ueberreste des vatikanischen Trikliniums Leos III. im Campo Santo," *RQSCHR* 31 (1923) 139ff.

pp. 123ff.

On S. Prassede, *Corpus*, III, 232ff., for the building and its history; on the mosaics, along with plates 115ff. in Wilpert, *Mosaiken und Malereien*, see Matthiae, *Mosaici*, I, 233. Nordhagen, "Un problema . . . a S. Prassede," in *Roma e l'età Carolingia*, pp. 159ff., points to resemblances between S. Prassede and SS. Cosma e Damiano both in technique and in the placing of the mosaics in the transept, and concludes that S. Prassede draws directly on SS. Cosma e Damiano. I still prefer to think that both derive from a common prototype.

p. 127

I accept the dates as proposed by Geertman, *op. cit., passim* for SS. Nereo ed Achilleo, S. Prassede, S. Cecilia, S. Maria in Domnica, and S. Marco. For S. Susanna I prefer, as in *Corpus*, IV, 254ff., esp. 276, for the entire building campaign the date 799 suggested for the apse decoration by C. Davis-Weyer, "Das Apsismosaik Leos III . . . ," *ZKG* 28 (1965), 177ff.

p. 128

Byzantine elements in Roman ninth-century iconography have been stressed, perhaps overmuch, frequently in recent years: for S. Maria Egiziaca, the Temple of Fortuna Virilis, see F. Lafontaine-Dosogne, *Peintures médiévales dans le Temple . . . de la Fortune Virile*, Brussels and Rome, 1959; for the *Harrowing of Hell* mosaic, C. Davis-Weyer, "Die ältesten Darstellungen der Hadesfahrt Christi . . . ," in *Roma e l'età Carolingia*, 183ff.; for the Tempio della Tosse, B. Brenk, "Die Wandmalereien im Tempio della Tosse," *Frühmittelalterliche Studien* 5 (1971) 401ff.; and, outstandingly important, on the program of the Zeno chapel, *idem*, "Zum Bildprogramm der Zenokapelle . . . ," *Archivio Español de Arqueologia*, 45-47 (1972-74) 213ff.

Professor Davis-Weyer's forthcoming study on the mosaics of ninth-century Rome is going to present fully the material and the problems of technique, style, iconography, sources, development and links to Byzantium, the North, and the near and far Roman past; problems of style and technique are adumbrated in her previous work such as her papers on the triclinium mosaic of Leo III, *ZKG* 29 (1966), and *ibid*. 34 (1974), as above. Undoubtedly her findings will lead to revisions in the picture as I try to present it and will place our knowledge of the period on a sounder basis.

pp. 130ff.

For the Zeno chapel, *Corpus*, III, 252ff.—the identification of the sixteenth-century drawing, shown therein, fig. 222, as a plan of that chapel is a mistake for which I apologize; it represents a late-antique mausoleum, perhaps that of Tiburtius. For the mosaics, Brenk, "Zum Bildprogramm der Zenokapelle . . . ," as above, on the program; for a brilliant analysis of the style of figures and drapery and its sources, C. Davis-Weyer, *ZKG* 29 (1966), pp. 121ff.; and for the antecedents in ancient art of the "peopled scroll" as it appears in the Zeno chapel over the altar-niche, J. B. Ward-Perkins and J. Toynbee, "Peopled Scrolls . . . ," *PBSR* 18 (1950) 23ff. For the fifth-century decoration of the S. Croce chapel, A. M. Colini, *Storia e Topografia del Celio* (*MemPontAcc* VII), Vatican City, 1944, p. 309; for the presumed presence of an etimasia at the Lateran, T. Buddensieg, "Le coffret d'ivoire de Pola," *CahArch* 10 (1959) 157ff., esp. 178 and fig. 130.

pp. 134ff.

Corpus, IV, 178ff. for Sto. Stefano degli Abissini; *ibid.*, 1ff. for the Quattro Coronati; for S. Maria Nova (S. Francesca Romana), *ibid.*, I, 220; for S. Martino ai Monti, *ibid.*, III, 87 and following; for S. Giorgio in Velabro, S. Marco, S. Maria in Domnica, *ibid.*, I, 244ff., II, 216, esp. 243, and 308ff.; *Corpus*, I, 94ff., on S. Cecilia is to be supplemented by E. Bentivoglio, "I progetti del xix secolo per S. Cecilia . . . ," *Quaderni* 97-114 (1975) 133ff. For the Carolingian rebuilding of the SS. Quattro Coronati, *Corpus*, IV, 1ff., esp. 29f.

Neither in the original 1942 version of the *Carolingian Revival* nor in the 1969 postscript did I realize the likelihood of S. Giovanni in Laterano's being the model for the Carolingian churches without transept or that of arcades having been preferred simply because of the scarcity of long trabeated pieces. The natural explanation always hits one last.

pp. 138f.

It was Professor Milton Lewine who pointed out to me the likelihood of the Church's economic power in Rome having been strengthened by the new monasteries' being established in the disabitato—one of many suggestions for which I am happy to thank him.

Corpus, IV, 144ff., for S. Silvestro in Capite. Blocks from the "Servian" Wall as early as 755 were used for the foundations of S. Angelo in Pescheria, *Corpus*, I, 64ff.; *ibid.*, 42ff., for S. Anastasia.

p. 139
The present state of our knowledge on Carolingian churches north of the Alps is conveniently laid down in *Vorromanische Kirchenbauten*, I-III, ed. F. Oswald, L. Schaefer, R. Sennhauser, München, 1966-71; on Fulda, *ibid.*, I, 84ff., to be reconstructed possibly with arcades rather than trabeated; on the wooden tower over St. Peter's, *LP*, I, 454; on the activity of Wilcharius, *Libri Carolini, MGH Epp*, III, no. 60, pp. 592, 605; on the tower of the Quattro Coronati, *Corpus*, IV, 36.

pp. 140f.
The northern origins of the Carolingian Renascence have been underscored by E. Panofsky, *Renaissance and Renascences*, esp. 43ff., and are generally accepted, e.g. Llewellyn, *passim*, and Fichtenau, *op. cit., passim*. For the rare if significant imports to Rome of works of art and artists from the North, see: J. Ramackers, "Die Werkstattheimat der Grabplatte Papst Hadrians I," *RQSCHR* 59 (1964) 36ff.—it comes from Aix-la-Chapelle or nearby, this rather than Aquitaine as formerly believed; *La cattedra lignea di S. Pietro in Vaticano*, ed. M. Maccarone and others (*MemPontAcc* 10), Vatican City, 1971, and *Nuove ricerche sulla cattedra*, ed. *idem* (*MemPontAcc* in 8°), Vatican City, 1975; on the Assumption in S. Clemente, G. Ladner, "Die italienische Malerei im 11. Jahrhundert," *Jahrbuch der kunsthistorischen Sammlungen in Wien*, n.s. 5 (1931) 33ff., esp. 90ff.

p. 141
Professor Robert Brentano kindly pointed out to me the importance of political concepts and the Gregorian roots already in Bede's thinking.

Chapter Six

p. 143
Nobody has any business trespassing onto fields beyond his ken. But life is too short to become expert in more than one field, if that; and the foolhardy who try to cover a thousand years of Rome find it impossible. On the other hand, in a book dealing with the history of the city as reflected in her monuments, the reader has a right to ask for at least a few pages summing up the most important facts, factors, and ideologies underlying that history. The only way out of the dilemma for the poor outsider is to purloin shamelessly the findings of those who have thoroughly dealt with the field, and to admit it.

Hence I have drawn what I needed for this chapter unabashedly from a small number of works written with an eye not so much on scholars as on the educated public, among which I count myself: inevitable and basic is Gregorovius, superb I think, if outdated in detail and colored by his mid-nineteenth-century liberal, nationalistic, and romantic bias; and, among more recent classics, Schramm, *Renovatio*; Falco, *The Holy Roman Republic*, New York, 1964, translated from the Italian second edition, *La Santa Romana Repubblica*, Milan, 1954; Raffaele Morghen's volume of collected essays, *Medioevo Cristiano*, Bari, 1972; R. W. Southern, *Western Society and the Church in the Middle Ages*, Harmondsworth, 1970; Partner, *Lands*; the last chapters in Llewellyn; P. Toubert, *Les structures du Latium mediévale . . . du IXe á la fin du XIIe siècle*, Rome, 1973; Waley, *Papal State*; and R. Brentano, *Rome before Avignon*. These led me to key papers in *ASRStP, Studi Gregoriani, BISI, Traditio, Dizionario biografico degli Italiani*, and other places too numerous to list. I have no more than dipped into published sources, in the first place the *MGH* and the *RIS*, and not touched those unpublished. Bartolini's *Codice del Senato* and the *Liber Pontificalis* I have used more thoroughly. But I have not undertaken any archival research of my own in matters beyond my competence. I have attempted simply to present as clearly as I could facts and ideas as gathered and interpreted by my betters.

Even so, I remember with trepidation the critical notes and question marks I scribbled in the margins of publications by colleagues, in other fields, trespassing into the history of art. Inevitably the outsider lacks a solid foundation; inevitably he oversimplifies; and inevitably he lags behind the more recent discoveries and interpretations. I have tried to remedy the worst shortcomings by requesting two friends of mine, professional historians, Professors R. Brentano and G. E. Caspary, to read over this chapter and to eliminate the most blatant blunders. Those that remain, I am guilty of. The buck stops right here.

p. 143
We have dealt previously with the *domus cultae* and the pertinent bibliography; see above chapter five and note to pp. 110f.

pp. 143f.
For the tenth century in general I have been drawing on Llewellyn, pp. 286ff., and Partner, *Lands*, pp. 77ff., and for the ideological background of the

period, on Schramm, *Renovatio*, I, 44ff. and 68ff. Alberic's family background, personality, and policies are splendidly summed up in the short monograph contributed by G. Arnaldi for the *Dizionario biografico degli Italiani*, I, 647ff. The best source, notwithstanding his pro-imperial and anti-Roman bias, is still Liutprand of Cremona (*Liutprandi opera omnia*, ed. J. Becker, *MGH SS RG*, 1915), both in the *Antapodosis*, bk. III, xlv, and *passim*, and in the *Historia Ottonis*, I, viii ff. (*MGH SS RG*, 1915, 97f., 164f.). To sketch extent and impact of the Cluniac reform in Rome, I have used B. Hamilton, "Monastic Revival in Tenth-Century Rome," *Studia monastica* 4 (1962) 19ff., and P. Fedele, "Le carte del monastero di SS. Cosma e Damiano in Mica Aurea," *ASRStP* 21 (1898) 471ff., esp. 474ff.

p. 144

The concept of Rome as *caput mundi, Roma Aurea*, and so forth, stands at the center of Schramm's *Renovatio*; the use of the expressions and their variations from late antiquity to Otto III are listed *op. cit.*, I, 37f. For Nicholas I, *ibid.*, I, 24ff., based on the sources: the biography, *LP*, II, 151ff.; the letters *MGH Epp*, VI, *passim*; and contemporary opinion, such as Regino of Prüm, *MGH SS RG*, ed. F. Kunze, Hannover, 1890, 94.

pp. 144f.

For the revolts against Otto I and their repression, see *LP*, II, 252, and the summaries in Gregorovius, III, 360ff., 367ff., and Partner, *Lands*, p. 90. The lament of Benedict of Soracte in *Chronicon di Benedetto . . . di S. Andrea*, ed. G. Zucchetti (*Fonti della Storia d'Italia* 55) Rome, 1920, p. 186.

p. 145

The few lines on Otto III, his concept of Rome as capital of his universal monarchy and see of the Apostles, and of his own role as *isapostolos*, are but a summary of Schramm, *Renovatio, passim*, whence I have also purloined the quotations (I, 108f., 132, n. 5; II, 62ff.—"Gaude papa, gaude Caesar . . ."); but see also Morghen, *Medioevo Cristiano*, 71ff. The state portrait in the Munich Gospels (Cod. Monac. lat. 4453, cml. 58, fol. 23ᵛ, 24ʳ) has been interpreted as to its political meaning by Schramm, *Renovatio*, I, 118f. and *idem, Die deutschen Kaiser und Könige in Bildern ihrer Zeit*, I, Leipzig-Berlin, 1928, 93f. For Otto's addressing the "consuls of the Senate," Schramm, *Renovatio*, I, 128f.

pp. 148f.

The bibliography on the Reform of the Church in the eleventh century, on the Reform Papacy, the culminating figure of Gregory VII, and the Investiture Struggle, is endless. I have sought information in A. Fliche, *La réforme Grégorienne*, I and II (*Spicilegium Sacrum Lovaniense* 6, 9), Louvain-Paris, 1924-25; in Morghen, *Medioevo Cristiano*, 91ff., 189ff.; in his *Gregorio VII e la riforma della Chiesa . . .*, Palermo, 1974, and in other papers of his published in *ASRStP* and in *Studi Gregoriani*. I have also drawn for these pages on some basic sources: *LP*, II, 331ff., 351ff. for the period antedating Gregory's pontificate; for the latter, *ibid.*, II, 282 ff. and the biography by Paul of Bernried, *PL*, 148, 39ff.; and I have dipped into Gregory's letters, *Gregorii VII Registrum*, ed. E. Caspar (*MGH Epp Selectae* II) Berlin, 1920, 1923. Some of the material has been selected, translated, and commented on by Tierney, *Crisis*, esp. 40ff., 49f. (the *Dictatus Papae*), and 57ff. For a summary, also Partner, *Lands*, 107ff. and 117ff.

pp. 149f.

Gregorovius, IV, 127ff., in my opinion still provides the best picture of the fight between Hildebrand-Gregory's party and the antipope in the sixties; *ibid.*, 175ff., of the struggle of Gregory VII; and *ibid.*, 213ff., of the fighting for and in Rome, 1081-1084. Benzo's memorandum on his mission in 1061 and on the sieges of Rome by Henry IV in 1081-1083, are found in *MGH SS*, XI, 591ff., esp. 612ff. and 658ff.; the street fighting in Rome in 1062 is described in *LP*, II, 336f.; the kidnapping of Gregory on Christmas Eve, 1075, in *ibid.*, p. 282, and Paul of Bernried, chap. V, *PL*, 148, 56ff.; the fighting in the Leonine City in 1082 and 1083 and the relief expedition of the Normans in 1084, in Benzo's work and in *LP*, II, 290.

p. 150

The restless pontificates of Urban II, Paschal II, and Gelasius II, the continued fighting in the city and the invasions by Henry V in 1111 and 1117 are depicted at length and documented in their biographies: *LP*, II, 293f. (Urban and the Pierleoni); *ibid.*, pp. 296ff. (Paschal and the restiveness of the town, p. 298f.; the invasion of 1111, the pope's compromise and abduction, pp. 300ff., 338ff.; the one of 1117, *ibid.*, p. 303f.); and, *ibid.*, p. 311ff. (Gelasius' kidnapping, liberation, and flight, *ibid.*, p. 313f.). For the continuing war of propaganda, the abortive Paschal compromise, and the final conclusion through the Concordat of Worms, Tierney, *Crisis*, pp. 74ff., 89f., and 91f.

pp. 150f.

For the contest between Anaclete and Innocent II, I have relied on P. F. Palumbo, *Lo schisma del MCXXX* (*Miscellanea Dep. Romana di Storia Patria*),

Rome, 1942; on Innocent's biography in *LP*, II, 379ff.; and on a perusal, all too random perhaps, of the letters of the two pretenders in the *Bibliotheca Rerum Germanicarum*, V, *Monumenta Bambergensia*, ed. P. Jaffé, Leipzig, 1869.

pp. 151f.
The Lateran murals are illustrated and have been thoroughly discussed by Ladner, *Papstbildnisse*, I, 195ff. (Paschal II, Calixtus II, Anaclete II), and II, 17ff. (Innocent II); see also E. Kitzinger, in the forthcoming volume in honor of Charles Haskins; the manuscript was kindly made available to me by Mr. Kitzinger. The arguments ensuing in 1157 and 1158 are followed best in the excerpts, Ladner, *op. cit.*, II, 21f.; see also Tierney, *Crisis*, pp. 106ff. To present halfway thoroughly the thesis of papal supremacy in both its spiritual and temporal implications would require reading and quoting whole libraries, written and yet unwritten. To an outsider like myself, the questions seem well summed up by Tierney, *op. cit.*, pp. 97ff., 110f., 116ff., and 127ff. Schramm, *Kaiser, Könige und Päpste*, IV, 1, deals, 186ff., with the imperial insignia claimed by the papacy; with the corresponding terminology applied to Calixtus II and Innocent II, 183f., n.26; and with the history of the papal tiara, 107ff., supplementing Ladner's basic paper, "Die Statue Bonifaz VIII . . . und die Entstehung der dreifachen Tiara," *RQSCHR* 42 (1934) 35. The presumably apocryphal anecdote about Boniface VIII goes back to Franciscus Pipinus, *Chronicon*, chap. 47, in *RIS*, IX, 745; his authenticated statements regarding papal supremacy are collected and commented on by Finke, *Aus den Tagen Bonifaz VIII*, Münster, 1902, pp. 151ff. For the inscription on imperial bulls, Schramm, *Die Bilder der Deutschen Kaiser und Könige,* I, Leipzig, 1928, p. 122, and W. Erbes, *Rombilder auf kaiserlichen Siegeln*, Graz-Vienna-Leipzig, 1931, p. 40.

p. 152
The role of the popes as territorial overlords in Latium and the gradual formation of a papal state forms the backbone of Partner's *Lands*, pp. 154ff., 200ff.

p. 152
The revival of a political terminology *all'antica* has been traced, for the period from Charlemagne to Otto III and with special attention to Pope Nicholas I and his immediate successors, by Schramm, *Renovatio*, I, 44ff.; for its renewal under Henry IV, *ibid.*, pp. 257ff. and Benzo's memorandum, *MGH SS*, XI, esp. 614 and 657f., the "New Rome of tents." The letter of the Roman nobles to King Lothar in C. Baronius, *Annales* . . . , XII, Rome, 1607, 195.

pp. 152f.
I have not come across any recent comprehensive history of the Roman republic from the revolt in 1143 to the pontificate of Innocent III. Events are best followed: for the early years in Otto of Freising, *Chronica*, VII, 27ff. (*MGH SS RG*, ed. Hofmeister, 352ff.) and in *LP*, II, 385ff.; for the events in 1155, in Otto of Freising's *Gesta Frederici imperatoris*, I, 29, and II, 20ff. (*MGH SS*, XX, 404ff.; the address of the Roman delegation and Frederick's rebuke, also Tierney, *Crisis*, p. 103f.); in the verse rendering by the poet Gunther, *Ligurinus sive de rebus gestis Frederici*, IV, vv. 15ff. (*PL*, 212, 378ff.), in particular the lively accounts on the fight in the Borgo and the malaria epidemic (*ibid.*, vv., 73ff., 185ff.), and in *LP*, II, 391ff. For the battle at Monte Porzio in 1167 and the following street battle around St. Peter's, see *LP*, II, 415f., together with the recounting in Gregorovius, IV, 581ff., where the pertinent passages are excerpted in the footnotes. The ideas underlying the establishment of the republic and the gradual shifts in emphasis are reflected in the senate documents of the *Codice del Senato*, I, *passim*.

pp. 153f.
Partner, *Lands*, p. 201, discusses the break between Frederick Barbarossa and Alexander III. The compromise of 1188 between city and papacy is found in Bartoloni, *Senato*, pp. 69ff. For Benedictus Carushomo, the changes in the Senate, and the increasing territorial aspirations of the Roman citizenry, see Waley, *Papal State*, pp. 23ff.

p. 154
The best sources for Innocent III are still the *Gesta Innocenti, PL*, 214, xviii ff., and his letters, *ibid.*, 214, 1ff.; 215, 9ff.; and 216, 9ff. The broad outlines of his Church policies have been sketched by Morghen, *Medioevo Cristiano*, pp. 149ff. For his temporal policy specifically regarding Rome and her expansion in Latium, I have relied on Waley, *Papal State, passim*, whence the two quotes (his pp. 39, 80); on Partner, *Lands*, pp. 229ff.; and on Brentano, *Rome Before Avignon*, pp. 101ff. The clash in 1203/04 between papal and "Roman" factions is recorded in the *Gesta*, pp. c, cxxx ff. (*PL*, 214, clxxxii ff.); we shall come back to it when discussing the map of Rome in the Middle Ages.

p. 155
The increasing feudalization of the big landholding families under the papacy and their impact on it, as

well as their role in city politics, outlined already by Partner, *Lands*, pp. 159ff. and 229ff., have been thoroughly investigated by P. Toubert, *Les structures* . . . , esp. pp. 493ff. and in a summary, pp. 1355ff. The penetration by foreigners of the papal administration is pointed out by Partner, *Lands*, p. 159. Toubert, *op. cit.*, pp. 635f., 673ff., based on the documentation in the archives of Roman churches and of the abbey of Farfa (see below), sums up and broadens the older studies on the guilds of Rome; but Hartmann, *Zur Wirtschaftsgeschichte Italiens* . . . , Gotha, 1904, pp. 16ff., is still basic.

pp. 155f.

Duchesne, "Les regions de Rome au Moyen-Age," *MEFR* 10 (1890) 126ff. (repr. *Scripta Minora*, Rome, 1973, pp. 90ff.) remains basic and supersedes E. Re, "Le regioni di Roma nel medioevo," *Studi di Storia e Diritto*, 10 (1889), 349ff. The quotes are from *LP*, I, 497f., and II, 252, 313, and—the one of twelfth-century date—from the *Ordo* of Benedictus Canonicus in the *Liber Censuum*, ed. P. Fabre and L. Duchesne, II, Paris, 1905, 141.

pp. 156f.

The documentation regarding merchandizing and banking in Rome prior to the thirteenth century, scarce as it is, has been collected and interpreted by Toubert, *Structures*, pp. 669ff. Of the two business ventures of the Ptolemies of Tusculum, father and son, the first in 1105 (*Codex diplomaticus Caietanus*, II, Monte Cassino, 1891, p. 169, no. 278) illustrates their "international" dealings with a ship owner at Gaeta, the second in 1127 (*ibid.*, no. 312) their partnership with the monks of Monte Cassino and the cooperation with the ruling families in Rome. See also Partner, *Lands*, p. 142. The flow of funds to Rome and the ensuing need for banking facilities is brought out by Falco, *The Roman Republic*, p. 248, while its cause, the accumulation of business at the Curia, is splendidly discussed by Southern, *Western Society and the Church*, pp. 111ff. For the rôle of Tuscan (and Roman) bankers at the Curia in the thirteenth and fourteenth centuries, see Jordan, *De Mercatoribus Camerae Apostolicae*, Rennes, 1909.

p. 157

The domination in various parts of Rome of the great families has been pointed out first by Tomassetti, *La Campagna Romana*, I, Rome, 1910, 137ff. and repeated, illustrated by a map, in L. Casanelli, G. Delfini, D. Fonti, *Le mura di Roma*, Rome, 1974, p. 84, n.38, fig. 87. Brentano, *Rome before Avignon, passim*, esp. pp. 34ff., 182ff., gives independently a lively picture of the preponderances, economic and political, of these families in their quarters and their symbiosis with the *populo minuto*. For the beginnings of the Pierleoni, see D. B. Zema, "The Houses of Tuscany and of Pierleoni," *Traditio* 2 (1944) 155ff.; for the other great families, see papers scattered through *ASRStP* and the concise and lively remarks in Brentano, *op. cit.*, pp. 173ff.

p. 158

Rome as a power center in politics, law, and administration is brought out by Southern, *op. cit.*, pp. 105ff.; her role in European financing and banking by Falco, *op. cit.*, p. 248, whence our quote.

pp. 158f.

For Brancaleone di Andalò, see *Dizionario biografico*, III, 45ff., Waley, *Papal State*, pp. 157ff. and Partner, *Lands*, pp. 258f.; for Charles of Anjou, Waley, *Papal State*, pp. 172ff.; and for Nicholas III, *ibid.*, pp. 189ff., and Partner, *Lands*, pp. 269ff.

p. 159

The deterioration of the papal bureaucracy is stressed by Southern, *Western Society and the Church*, pp. 121ff., 131f. The figure regarding the tithes' deposits is quoted from K. Kaser, *Das Späte Mittelalter*, Stuttgart and Gotha, 1925, pp. 60ff., the one regarding pilgrims' offerings from Gregorovius, V, 552. The papal policy of building up family fortunes is discussed by Partner, *Lands, passim*, esp. pp. 275ff. with regard to Nicholas III and pp. 287ff. with regard to Boniface VIII.

pp. 159f.

Publications on the Holy Year in general and that of 1300 in particular are numerous. I am relying on Morghen's paper in *Medioevo Cristiano*, pp. 265ff., and on rereading the most important sources: Ventura, *Chronica Astense*, *RIS*, XI, 191f. and G. Villani, *Cronica*, bk. VIII, ch. 36, Florence, 1587, 311.

Chapter Seven

pp. 161-75

No comprehensive study has been undertaken so far of twelfth-century church building—not to mention secular building—in Rome. Even good monographs are rare. Outstanding among the latter are G. B. Giovenale, *La basilica di S. Maria in Cosmedin*, Rome, 1927, and D. Kinney, "S. Maria in Trastevere from Its Founding to 1215." Ph.D. thesis, N.Y.U., 1975; some of the small monographs in the series of the *Chiese illustrate di Roma* contain useful if necessarily abbreviated accounts of the building or remodeling of individual churches in the Middle Ages. And, though unreliable, Armellini-Cecchelli, *Chiese*, remains indispensable also for this period. As it is, the twelfth-century church of S. Clemente still awaits a full study; regarding its date and consecration—no longer fixed to the year 1128—and that of the shoring-up of the lower church, see L. Boyle, O.P., "The Date of the Consecration of the Basilica of San Clemente, Rome," *Archivum Fratrum Praedicatorum* 30 (1960) pp. 418ff., and H. Toubert, "Le renouveau paléochrétien à Rome au debut du XIIe siècle," *CahArch* 20 (1970) 100, note 4. For the two successive remodelings of the church of the SS. Quattro Coronati at that time, *Corpus*, IV, 1ff. attempts to sum up the evidence; the monograph on S. Maria in Trastevere I have quoted above. R. Malmstrom, "The Colonnades of High Medieval Churches in Rome," *Gesta* 14 (1975) 37ff. has made an important contribution by pointing out the function of the piers frequently inserted into nave colonnades to mark the liturgical division of clergy and lay sections.

Mosaics and paintings, illustrated in Wilpert's *Mosaiken und Malereien*, are discussed by G. Matthiae, *Mosaici*, and *idem, Pittura*, in terms of style, schools and development. I have relied to some degree on Matthiae's results. But my mainstay throughout this chapter has been Toubert's brilliant paper just quoted, supplemented by some papers by Ernst Kitzinger and Otto Demus, which will be quoted as I go along.

pp. 163f.
The plan of S. Maria in Trastevere, Gabinetto Nazionale delle Stampe, Rome, Inv. 2826, fol. 2510, F.N. 32746 (35), is considered a remodeling proposal by Kinney, *op. cit.*, pp. 225ff. For the time being I suspend judgment. Likewise the suggestion of a thirteenth-century rather than a twelfth-century date for the *opus sectile* pavement is Kinney's. Ernst Kitzinger, in a paper shortly to be published, has suggested as a source for the composition of the apse mosaic an "antiquarian" reflection of the processional encounter, long customary in Rome, of two famous icons of Christ and the Virgin respectively.

pp. 166ff.
On the small tenth- and eleventh-century churches: see *Corpus*, I, 39, for S. Agnese in Piazza Navona; G. di Geso, "Un caso lamentevole: la chiesa di S. Barbara dei Librai," *Bollettino dei Curatores dell'Alma Città di Roma* 16 (1976) 4ff., for S. Barbara dei Librai; L. Paterna-Baldizzi, *La chiesa di S. Maria Egiziaca . . .*, Naples, 1928; P. Fedele, "Una chiesa del Palatino—S. Maria 'in Pallara,' " *ASRStP* 26 (1903) 343ff. Professor U. Nilgen is preparing a study on the latter church. On those of twelfth-century date mentioned: L. Huetter, *S. Salvatore in Onda* (*Chiese illustrate*, 51); P. Styger, "La decorazione . . . del secolo XII . . . di S. Giovanni ante Portam Latinam," *Studi Romani* 2 (1914) 261ff.; Sister Margaret Manion, I.B.V.M., of the University of Melbourne is preparing a more up-to-date study of the twelfth-century frescoes, based on her Ph.D. thesis, "The Frescoes of S. Giovanni a Porta Latina in Rome," Bryn Mawr, 1972; for the church of S. Stefano del Cacco, Armellini-Cecchelli, *Chiese*, I, 572ff.—the donor portrait extant from prior to 1607 in the apse being presumably that of Paschal II rather than Paschal I. Regarding major twelfth-century churches, and rebuildings, see B. M. Apollonj Ghetti, *S. Crisogono* (*Chiese illustrate*, 92), p. 68ff.; *Corpus*, I, 40f. and 165ff. for SS. Bonifacio ed Alessio and S. Croce in Gerusalemme, respectively, both based on eighteenth-century accounts of their medieval layout. On S. Bartolomeo in Isola, P. Casimiro, *Memorie istoriche delle Chiese . . . dei Frati Minori*, second edition, Rome, 1845, pp. 370ff. and *idem, Dissertazioni . . . di S. Bartolomeo in Isola*, Rome, 1742, still seem to be the last word on the subject.

pp. 173ff.
For the campanili, one has to fall back on the monumental publication of A. Serafini, *Torri campanarie di Roma e del Lazio nel medioevo*, Rome, 1927; unreliable though it is and biased by preconceived ideas about workshops and development of the type, it does at least have good illustrations. Regarding twelfth- and thirteenth-century church furniture and the successive workshops active in that field, one still has to turn to G. Giovannoni, "Note sui marmorari romani," *ASRStP* 27 (1904) 5ff. and his "Opere dei Vassalletti," *L'Arte* 11 (1908) 262ff., both excerpted by A. M. Bessone Aurelj, *I marmorari Romani*, Rome, 1935, and to E. Hutton, *The Cosmati. The Roman Marble Workers of the Twelfth and Thirteenth Centuries*, London, 1950. Professor Malmstrom's paper dealing with the liturgical division effected by the furnishing has been quoted above. The *opus sectile* pavements have been investigated by D. Glass, "Studies on Cosmatesque Pavements," Ph.D. thesis, Johns Hopkins University, Baltimore, 1968; Professor Glass' study known to me in manuscript is about to be published in extended and revised form. Professor Malmstrom is working on a major study of cloisters in Rome; I am eagerly looking forward to it. Joan Barclay Lloyd's Ph.D. thesis, in preparation, on the canons' buildings attached to S. Clemente, promises to be a major contribution to the study of monastic

building and of construction technique in medieval Rome.

pp. 176ff.

The retention (or revival?) of Early Christian types in medieval church planning in Rome has been discussed along the same lines by Kinney, *op. cit.*, pp. 306ff.

pp. 178f.

The architecture, decoration, and furnishings of Desiderius' church at Montecassino can be envisaged in broad lines from the description given by Leo of Ostia, *Chronicon Cassinense*, Bk. III, chs. 26ff., from the remains excavated after World War II, and from its filiations. See A. Pantoni, *Le Vicende della basilica di Montecassino attraverso la documentazione archeologica*, Monte Cassino, 1973; *idem*, "La basilica di Montecassino e quella di Salerno," *Benedictina* 10 (1956) 23ff.; the best edition of Leo's text is found in O. Lehmann-Brockhaus, *Schriftquellen zur Kunstgeschichte des 11. und 12. Jahrhunderts* . . . , Berlin, 1938, pp. 476ff.; a convincing reconstruction drawing by K. J. Conant and H. M. Willard appears in the latter's "A project for the graphic reconstruction of . . . Monte Cassino," *Speculum* 10 (1935) 144ff. For the abbreviated filiations of Monte Cassino referred to, I fall back on J. Wettstein, *Les fresques de S. Angelo in Formis*, Geneva, 1960 (the dating of the several parts of the cycle, again under discussion, see W. Paeseler, "Bauwerk und Bildkunst von Sant'Angelo in Formis . . . ," *Actes . . . XXe Congrès International . . . Histoire de l'Art . . . Budapest 1969*, Budapest, 1972, pp. 259ff., is of little concern in this context); on Castel S. Elia at Nepi, see most recently, O. Hjort, "The Frescoes of Castel Sant'Elia. A Problem of Stylistic Attribution," *Hafnia* (1970) 7ff., and P. Hoegger, *Die Fresken von S. Elia bei Nepi*, Frauenfeld and Stuttgart, 1975.

On the abbey's history and its leadership in the eleventh and twelfth centuries, H. Bloch's masterly study, "Montecassino, Byzantium and the West . . . ," *DOP* 3 (1946) 166ff., is still the most important. It is to be followed presently by his *magnum opus* on the subject.

pp. 179f.

The fragments of the Salerno mosaic have been identified as reflecting the corresponding Monte Cassino mosaic as their archetype and related to the mosaics on the apse arch at S. Clemente in Rome and to their historical context by E. Kitzinger, "The Gregorian Reform and the Visual Arts: A Problem of Method," *Transactions of the Royal Historical Society*, 5th ser., 22 (1972) 87ff. (repr. *idem, Byzantium*, pp. 271ff.). O. Demus, *The Mosaics of Norman Sicily*, London, 1949, pp. 206ff. has suggested the participation in the work at Monte Cassino of Sicilian or South Italian Byzantine trained artists.

For the bronze doors ordered for S. Paolo, Monte Cassino, and sundry South Italian towns from Constantinople, see G. Matthiae, *Le Porte bronzee bizantine in Italia*, Rome, 1971, and E. Josi, *La Porta Bizantina di S. Paolo*, Rome, 1967.

pp. 180ff.

G. Ladner, "Die italienische Malerei im 11. Jahrhundert," *Jahrbuch der Wiener Kunsthistorischen Sammlungen*, n.s. 5 (1931) 33ff., still seems basic to the understanding of Roman painting in the eleventh and early twelfth centuries and of the decisive role played by Monte Cassino. Recent research has supplemented his findings by pointing out the strong impact of Byzantine, perhaps South Italian, elements at Monte Cassino and the consequently greater independence of Rome from that center; see O. Demus, *Byzantium and the West*, New York, 1970, pp. 103ff. The phenomenon of the Early Christian renascence as reflected in style, technique, ornament, and iconography in Roman painting from the frescoes in the lower church of S. Clemente to those from S. Nicola in Carcere and to the mosaics of S. Clemente and S. Maria in Trastevere, their dates, and the intellectual background, have been brilliantly brought out by Hélène Toubert in her paper *CahArch* 20 (1970) 99ff.

Hardly noticed before, the frescoes from S. Nicola in Carcere are now in the storerooms of the Vatican Museums; my warm thanks to Dr. F. Mancinelli for giving me access to them. O. Demus, *op. cit.*, pp. 205ff., had already pointed to the role played by the Benedictines, in particular those of S. Paolo fuori le mura, within this renascence movement and the impact on it of Early Christian mosaics at St. Peter's and S. Paolo fuori le mura.

p. 187

E. Panofsky, *Renaissance and Renascences, passim*, was the first to view jointly the two facets, visual and literary, and the successive renascences of antiquity through the Middle Ages.

pp. 187ff.

The different, often diametrically opposed, attitudes toward antique decorative or figural sculpture and the use of spoils have been discussed with care and brilliancy by A. Esch, "Spolien," *Archiv für Kulturgeschichte* 51 (1969) 1ff. See also R. Lanciani, *Scavi*, I, 8ff. and 22ff., where reference is made to the *calcararii* quarters; for the latter, see also Gnoli, *Topografia*, p. 44f. The role of the *marmorarii*, as antique dealers, is discussed by R. Lanciani, *op. cit.*, pp. 9ff.;

P. Fedele, "Sul commercio delle antichità in Roma nel XII secolo," *ASRStP* 32 (1909) 465ff.; Panofsky, *Renaissance and Renascences*, I, 73, n.1, warning against overestimating the extent of such commerce; and A. Esch, *op. cit., passim*. See also J. B. Ross' lively and useful "A Study of Twelfth Century Interest in the Antiquities of Rome," *Medieval and Historiographical Essays in Honor of J. Westfall Thompson*, Chicago, 1938, pp. 302ff. Suger's project to bring to Saint-Denis columns from the Thermae of Diocletian, in E. Panofsky, *Abbot Suger*, Princeton, 1946, p. 90f. The quotation in my text p. 189 is from a letter of Giovanni Dondi written in 1375, see R. Krautheimer, *Lorenzo Ghiberti*, Princeton, 1956 (repr. 1970), p. 296.

pp. 189f.
The often quoted passage on Henry of Winchester is from John of Salisbury, *Historiae pontificalis quae supersunt*, ed. R. L. Poole, Oxford, 1927, p. 81f. (chap. 40), and I knew it first through J. B. Ross' reference, *op. cit.*, p. 308f. Magister Gregory's account—his personality and the date of his visit still undetermined to my knowledge—has been edited several times, most recently by R. B. Huygens, *Magister Gregorius . . . Narracio* (*Textus Minores*, 42) Leiden, 1970; but see also the older editions by G. McN. Rushforth, "Magister Gregorius de Mirabilibus Urbis Romae," *Journal of Roman Studies* 9 (1919) 14ff., and Valentini-Zucchetti, III, 137ff.; see also J. B. Ross, *op. cit.*, pp. 316ff.

pp. 190f.
On the Lateran frescoes and the narthex mosaic, Ladner, *Papstbildnisse* . . . , I, Vatican City, 1941, 195ff. and II, Vatican City, 1970, 17ff.; C. Walter, "Political Imagery in the Medieval Lateran Palace," *CahArch* 20 (1970) 155ff., esp. pp. 162ff. and *ibid.*, 21 (1971) 109ff. (On the fresco cycle in the Cappella di S. Silvestro in the Quattro Coronati, *ibid.*, pp. 124ff.) Also, G. Matthiae, *Pittura politica del medioevo Romano*, Rome, 1964.

p. 191
The raising of the originally low transept of St. Peter's in 1154 was first pointed out by J. Christern, "Der Aufriss von Alt-St. Peter," *RQSCHR* 62 (1967) 133ff.; see also *Corpus*, V, 176 and 278.

pp. 191f.
For the reuse of antiques in the context of the twelfth century political and cultural renascences, pagan and Christian, in Rome: K. Noehles, "Die Kunst der Cosmaten und die Idee der Renovatio Romae," *Festschrift Werner Hager* . . . , Recklinghausen, 1966, 17ff.; H. Toubert, *op. cit.*; and F. Gandolfo, "Riimpiego di sculture antiche nei troni papali del XII secolo," *RendPontAcc* 47 (1976) 203ff.

pp. 192ff.
The collection of antiques at the Lateran has been investigated and brilliantly, if at times speculatively, interpreted by W. S. Heckscher, *Sixtus IIII Aeneas insignes statuas Romano populo restituendas censuit*, The Hague, 1955; information on the dates when the statues are first documented at the Lateran is given in his footnotes. For the juridical significance from at least the ninth century on of some of the monuments, A. Erler, *Lupa, Lex und Reiterstandbild* . . . , Wiesbaden, 1971. The shifting interpretation of the equestrian Marcus Aurelius as representing Constantine or a folk hero has been sketched by J. S. Ackerman, "Marcus Aurelius on the Capitoline Hill," *Renaissance News* 10 (1957) 69ff.; the twelfth-century date of the lions that carried the statue at the time Heemskerck saw it (fig. 153), has been suggested by Noehles, *op. cit.*

pp. 197f.
Professor Bernhard Bischoff in consultation with Dr. Rudolf M. Kloos kindly suggested for the inscriptions on the Casa di Crescenzio a date between the end of the eleventh century and the middle of the twelfth with strong preference for an early date within the period (letter from Professor Bischoff, July 22, 1976). If this is correct (and there is no reason to go against the considered judgment of the best epigraphers), the building of which the inscriptions form an integral part must be viewed as anticipating *ante litteram* around 1100 the spirit whence sprung the Roman republic forty years later.

The documents regarding the Columns of Marcus Aurelius and Trajan respectively appear in P. L. Galletti, *Del Primicerio* . . . , Rome, 1767, p. 323f., doc. 16, and Nibby, *Roma nel MDCCCXXXVIII*, I, 2, Rome, 1839, 642. On the twelfth-century church of S. Maria in Capitolio, predecessor of S. Maria in Aracoeli, see now R. E. Malmstrom, "The Twelfth Century Church of S. Maria in Capitolio and the Capitoline Obelisk," *Röm Jbch* 16 (1976) 1ff. For the erection of the obelisk on the Capitol and the supporting lions, all now at Villa Mattei, Malmstrom suggests a date about 1200, as against K. Noehles, "Die Kunst der Cosmati und die Idee der Renovatio," *Festschrift W. Hager*, Recklinghausen, 1966, pp. 17ff., who proposes a mid-thirteenth-century date, linked to the regime of Brancaleone, or a mid-fourteenth-century date linked to Cola di Rienzo's rule, this being suggested by C. D'Onofrio, *Gli obelischi di Roma*, Rome, 1967, pp. 214ff.

pp. 198f.

The latest edition of the *Mirabilia* is the one by Valentini-Zucchetti, III, 1ff., with a good introduction and explanatory notes, the latter not always convincing. Among older editions, I list Duchesne's in the *Liber Censuum*, ed. P. Fabre and L. Duchesne, Paris, 1905, I, 262ff., and Urlichs' in his *Codex*, pp. 91ff. The authorship of Benedictus Canonicus and the *terminus ante* 1143 have been convincingly proposed by L. Duchesne, "L'auteur des Mirabilia," *MEFR* 24 (1904) 479ff. The sources known fifty years ago have been discussed by P. Schramm, *Renovatio*, II, 45ff., 105ff.; recent additions have been made, e.g. by M. Demus-Quatember, "Zur Weltwunderliste des Pseudo-Beda," *Römische Historische Mitteilungen* 12 (1970) 67ff.

pp. 199f.

The love-hate approach of the Middle Ages to antiquity has been stressed recently by T. Buddensieg, "Gregory the Great: The Destroyer of Pagan Idols," *JWC* 28 (1965) 4ff., whence p. 47, n.9, I have used the quotation from Martin of Oppau.

pp. 200f.

The Latin text is as reprinted in Schramm, *Renovatio*, I, 300ff. Father Christopher Dillon, O.S.B., kindly translated the crucial lines.

Chapter Eight

p. 203

From among the rich bibliography on the thirteenth century in Rome, I refer again to the principal works mentioned in notes to chapter six, p. 143: Waley, *Papal State*; Morghen, *Medioevo Cristiano*; Southern, *Western Society and the Church*; Partner, *Lands*, and Brentano, *Rome before Avignon*; the biography of Innocent III, *Gesta Innocentii Papae III* in *PL*, 214, col. XVII ff., his correspondence, *ibid.*, pp. 1ff., and *PL*, 215 and 216. For Brancaleone di Andalò I rely on the article by E. Cristiani in: *Dizionario biografico degli Italiani* 3 (1961), 45ff.; on the series of Roman popes both initiating and terminating the century, Brentano, 116ff.

pp. 203f.

On papal building activity, ecclesiastical and secular, and church decoration, see the useful compilation by H. Schröder, *Die kunstfördernde Tätigkeit der Päpste im 13. Jahrhundert*, Ph.D. thesis, Leipzig, 1931. The list of donations made by Innocent III in *Gesta*, chaps. CXLV-CL (*PL*, 214, cols. CCIII-CCXXIII); also A. Mai, *Spicilegium, Additamentum*, pp. 300ff. On SS. Sergius and Bacchus, *Gesta*, chaps. IV and CXLV (*PL*, 214, cols. XVIII, CCVII) and M. Bonfioli, "La diaconia dei SS. Sergio e Bacco . . . ," *RAC* 50 (1974) 55ff., esp. 62f. with further references; on repairing the Lateran palace and setting up an infirmary (*cameram egestivam*), *Gesta*, chap. CXLVI (*PL*, 214, col. CCXI); on the hospital of Sto. Spirito, *ibid.*, chap. CXLIV (*PL*, 214, col. CC f.) and vividly, Brentano, *op. cit.*, pp. 19ff., with notes on the older bibliography, in particular the Statute of the hospital; on Tor de' Conti and the link between building the tower and founding the hospital, Ptolemy of Lucca, *Historia Ecclesiastica*, XXI, p. 16 (*RIS*, XI, 1127), and *idem, Annales* (*ibid.*, 1276); better, *idem, Die Annalen des Tholomeus von Lucca*, ed. B. Schmeidler, *MGH SS*, n.s. 8 (1930) 90; likewise Riccobaldo of Ferrara, *Historia Pontificum Romanorum* (*RIS*, IX, 179), and for the foundation of Sto. Spirito, Franciscus Pipinus, *Chronicon* (*RIS*, IX, 632). Finally, on the Vatican Palace built by Innocent, "honorabile et utile," *Gesta*, chap. CCXI (*PL*, 214, col. CCXI; also F. Ehrle and H. Egger, *Der Vaticanische Palast . . .*, [*Studi e documenti per la storia del Palazzo Apostolico Vaticano*, 2] Vatican City, 1935, p. 33f.) and, in our context more important, D. Redig de Campos, *I Palazzi Vaticani* (*Roma Cristiana*, 18) Bologna, 1967, where on p. 22f., the extant parts of the palace of Innocent are identified, accompanied by convincing graphic reconstructions.

On Honorius III and Gregory IX as patrons of art, Schröder, *op. cit.*, pp. 22ff., 33ff. In particular: on the rebuilding of S. Lorenzo fuori le mura, *Corpus*, III, 1ff., esp. 35ff., 139f.; on the possible partial funding of the building by a layman, Ladner, *Papstbildnisse*, II, 92f.; on Honorius' work at S. Paolo, see the following note; on Gregory IX's hostel at the Lateran, Cardinal of Aragon (Nicola Roselli), *Vita Gregorii Papae IX*, *RIS*, III, 1, 577.

pp. 205f.

For the mosaic of Old St. Peter's, Ladner, *Papstbildnisse*, II, 56ff.; it is best known from the copy done for Jacopo Grimaldi (*Descrizione della Basilica Vaticana*, ed. R. Niggl, Vatican City, 1972, p. 196f.; henceforth Grimaldi, *Descrizione*), whence J. Ciampini, *De sacris aedificiis . . .*, Rome, 1693, pl. XIII; see also J. Ruysschaert, "Le tableau Mariotte . . . ," *RendPontAcc* 40 (1967-68) 295ff., for a slightly different copy. Two surviving fragments, the heads of the Ecclesia Romana and of Innocent III (Ladner, *Papstbildnisse*, II, 64f.) are at the Museo di Roma; see Matthiae, *Mosaici*, pp. 327ff. Ladner, *op. cit.*, p. 66, convincingly interprets the pairing of Pope and

Church as representing the latter, embodied in the former, as leader of Christianity. Regarding the Early Christian composition preceding the Innocent mosaic, C. Davis-Weyer, "Das Traditio-Legis Bild und seine Nachfolge," *Münchner Jahrbuch* 12 (1961) 7ff.

On the S. Paolo mosaic, Ladner, *Papstbildnisse*, II, 80ff., referring also to Franciscus Pipinus, *Chronicon*, II, 42 (*RIS*, IX, 664), and *LP*, II, 453, n.6.

pp. 206f.

On building the *Palazzo del Senatore*, C. Pietrangeli, "Il palazzo Senatorio nel Medioevo," *Capitolium* 35 (1960) 3ff., with reference also to the sources, such as F. Bartoloni, *Senato*—pp. 216ff. have the document of 1257—provides the first clear report on the medieval parts surviving inside Michelangelo's structure and their presumable dates; for Michelangelo's rebuilding and the views showing it under construction, J. Ackerman, *The Architecture of Michelangelo*, London, 1961, *Catalogue*, pp. 49ff. and *Plates*, 30a ff.

pp. 207f.

Patronage in late-thirteenth-century Rome, especially under Nicholas III and Nicholas IV, is the subject of a superb study (unpublished but known to me through the author's kindness) on which I largely base my work—Julian Gardner, "The Influence of Popes' and Cardinals' Patronage on the Introduction of the Gothic Style into Rome, 1254-1305," Ph.D. thesis, Courtauld Institute, London University, 1969. I am most grateful to Professor Gardner for acquainting me with his early work and subsequent studies, and for many an instructive and pleasurable talk.

Outstanding among inventories surviving are: L. Mortari, *Il tesoro della Cattedrale di Anagni*, Rome, 1963, and E. Muentz and A. L. Frothingham, "Il tesoro della Basilica di S. Pietro," *ASRStP* 6 (1883) 1ff.; the dates of the (late) inventories of 1361 and 1436 represent only *termini ante quos*, while that of 1303, taken from the *Liber anniversariorum* of the Basilica Vaticana, *Necrologi della Provincia Romana*, I (*Fonti per la storia d'Italia* 44), ed. P. Egidi, Rome, 1908, 260ff., comprises only donations of Boniface VIII. For gifts by Nicholas III, see *ibid.*, p. 288. See also *Mostra tesori d'arte sacra di Roma e del Lazio*, Rome, 1975, pp. 53ff., for the objects from Casamari, now at Veroli. The sums spent by Cardinal Stefaneschi on work for St. Peter's are listed in the *Liber anniversariorum* of the Basilica Vaticana, *op. cit.*, p. 222f.

pp. 208f.

On the Vatican Palace as enlarged by Nicholas III and after him until 1300, D. Redig de Campos, *I Palazzi Vaticani*, pp. 25ff., and *grafici* 3-5, identifying, illustrating, and graphically reconstructing the parts surviving, with reference also to the documentation in Ehrle and Egger, *Der Vatikanische Palast . . .*, pp. 37ff.; on the murals uncovered, D. Redig de Campos, "Di alcune traccie del palazzo di Niccolo III . . . ," *RendPontAcc* 18 (1941/42) 71ff.

p. 209

When important in the context of the profile—and hence far too superficially as I well know—the work of the great artists active in Rome in the last third of the thirteenth century will be presented below. However, it may be just as well to list here the major publications on which I have relied, aside from Matthiae, *Pittura*, II, 175ff., and *Mosaici*, pp. 343ff.: J. Gardner's thesis as quoted in the previous note to pp. 207f.; J. White, *Art in Italy, 1250-1400* (Pelican History of Art), Harmondsworth, 1966; A. M. Romanini, *Arnolfo di Cambio*, Milan, 1969; J. Gardner, "Arnolfo di Cambio and Roman Tomb Design," *Burl Mag* 115 (1973) 422ff.; *idem*, "The Tomb of Cardinal Annibaldi by Arnolfo di Cambio," *Burl Mag* 114 (1972) 136ff.; and still H. Keller, "Der Bildhauer Arnolfo di Cambio und sein Werkstatt," *Jahrbuch der Preussischen Kunstsammlungen* 55 (1934) 205ff. and 56 (1935) 22ff.; G. Matthiae, *Pietro Cavallini*, Rome, 1972, and previously S. Lothrop, "Pietro Cavallini," *Memoirs of the American Academy in Rome* 2 (1918) 77ff.; J. White, "Cavallini and the Lost Frescoes in S. Paolo," *JWC* 19 (1956) 84ff.; J. Gardner, "S. Paolo Fuori le Mura, Nicholas III and Pietro Cavallini," *ZKG* (1971) 240ff.; P. Hetherington, "The Mosaics of Pietro Cavallini in S. Maria in Trastevere," *JWC* 33 (1970) 84ff.; and, close to Gardner's thesis, Hetherington, "Pietro Cavallini, Artistic Style and Patronage . . . ," *Burl Mag* 114 (1972) 4ff.; R. Bertos, *Jacopo Torriti*, Ph.D. thesis, Munich, 1963; and J. Gardner, "Pope Nicholas IV and the Decoration of S. Maria Maggiore," *ZKG* (1973) 1ff., where also the frescoes on the outer façade wall are dealt with; finally, on Giotto's work in Rome, W. Paeseler, "Giottos Navicella und ihr spätantikes Vorbild," *Röm Jbch* 5 (1941) 49ff. (hereafter "Giottos Navicella"), W. Kemp, "Zum Programm von Stefaneschi—Altar und Navicella," *ZKG* 30 (1967) 309ff., M. Gosebruch, "Giottos Stefaneschi Altarwerk . . . ," *Miscellanea Bibliothecae Hertzianae*, Munich, 1961, 104ff., and recently J. Gardner, "The Stefaneschi Altarpiece . . . ," *JWC* 37

(1974) 57ff., where an early date prior to 1300 is proposed rather than the frequently accepted date of 1314 or later. Writings listed in this note henceforth will be quoted only by the author's name, year, and, if needed, abbreviated title of publication.

Cimabue appears in Rome as witness to a document, 1272 (see E. Battisti, *Cimabue*, Milan, 1963, p. 93).

pp. 209f.

See for the watercolor copies done 1630-1640 of the S. Paolo murals (Barb. lat. 4406, Vatican Library) St. Waetzold, *Die Kopien des 17. Jahrhunderts nach Mosaiken und Wandmalereien in Rom* (*Römische Forschungen der Bibliotheca Hertziana*, 18), Munich-Vienna, 1962, pp. 55ff. J. Garber, *Wirkungen der frühchristlichen Gemäldezyklen* . . . , Vienna-Berlin, 1918, based on these seventeenth-century renderings, attempted to distinguish among the lost originals scenes newly invented by Cavallini, others copied by him after fifth-century compositions, and fifth-century originals preserved until 1823—a hazardous undertaking at best. Indeed, I am told the separation suggested by Garber is again under discussion. The hand of another thirteenth-century master earlier than Cavallini has been observed by Gardner, *ZKG* (1971). Cavallini's activity in the *Sancta Sanctorum* chapel has been frequently doubted (Matthiae, *Pittura*, p. 195); the question is being investigated by J. Wollesen, who has presented his preliminary thoughts in a number of lectures in 1976-77. A 1291 *terminus ante* for the mosaics at S. Maria in Trastevere (White, *op. cit.*, 1966, p. 97) rather than *terminus post* (Hetherington, *JWC* [1970]) seems to me much more plausible. The date for the S. Cecilia frescoes, 1291-1293 or slightly later, and the evident link to both the Early Christian and Cavallini's murals at S. Paolo, are likewise White's and more or less generally accepted. (The series of papal portraits, once at S. Cecilia, is mentioned by G. Marangoni, *Delle cose gentilesche . . . delle Chiese*, Rome, 1744, p. 311—a passage so far unobserved.) For the lost works at St. Peter's, *Lorenzo Ghibertis Denkwürdigkeiten*, ed. J. von Schlosser, Berlin, 1912, I, 39, and J. Grimaldi, *Descrizione*, fol. 120ᵛ, 121ʳ, p. 156f.; for S. Crisogono and the façade mosaic at S. Paolo, Ghiberti, *loc. cit.*, for the latter also N. M. Nicolai, *Della basilica di S. Paolo*, Rome, 1815, pl. VI, and J. Gardner, "Copies of Roman Mosaics in Edinburgh," *Burl Mag* 115 (1973) 583ff., esp. 589f. with older bibliography, who inclines towards seeing resemblances to Cavallini's style.

p. 210

On Torriti: Bertos, 1963; Gardner, *ZKG* (1973); and Ladner, *Papstbildnisse*, II, 235ff. (the mosaic at S. Giovanni in Laterano with the 1292 inscription) and 241ff. (the apse vault at S. Maria Maggiore; the inscription in the sixteenth century read 1296, but I accept Gardner, *op. cit.*, pp. 2, 8, 12, *et passim*, giving 1290 and 1295). On Rusuti, Gardner, *op. cit.*, pp. 21ff.; *ibid.*, pp. 18f., on the nameless master of the transept murals, "closely connected with the Isaac Master . . . at Assisi." On the Tre Fontane cycle, C. Bertelli, "L'enciclopedia delle Tre Fontane," *Paragone* 235 (1969) 24ff.

pp. 211f.

J. Gardner, "Nicholas III's Oratory of the Sancta Sanctorum," *Burl Mag* 115 (1973) 283ff., presents the history and analyzes the style of the chapel, linking it to the transept of S. Francesco at Assisi transposed into the "ponderous classicizing manner of contemporary Roman architecture." R. E. Malmstrom, "S. Maria in Aracoeli at Rome," Ph.D. thesis, N.Y.U., 1973, analyzes the present church and its building phases as well as the extant parts of its twelfth-century predecessor, while G. Urban, "Die Kirchenbaukunst des Quattrocento in Rom," *Röm Jbch* 9-10 (1961-62) 73ff., esp. 119ff., presents the case for S. Maria sopra Minerva. On the remodeling of S. Maria Maggiore and S. Giovanni in Laterano, all too briefly, *Corpus*, III, 1ff., and *ibid.*, V, 1ff.; a study of the medieval rebuilding of the Lateran Basilica has been begun by Professors Malmstrom and V. Hoffmann. On the conservative attitude of Roman medieval church planners, D. Kinney, "S. Maria in Trastevere," Ph.D. thesis, N.Y.U., 1975, p. 306f.

pp. 212ff.

Burial in ancient sarcophagi: F. Gregorovius, *Die Grabmäler der römischen Päpste*, Leipzig, 1857, *passim*, esp. 33 (Otto II); J. Déer, *The Dynastic Porphyry Tombs of the Norman Period* . . . (Dumbarton Oaks Studies V), Cambridge, Mass., 1959, pp. 146ff. (Innocent II), p. 150f. (Anastasius IV), p. 152 (Hadrian IV); also G. Marangoni, *Delle cose gentilesche*, Rome, 1744, *passim*. For the penetration into Rome and into temporary papal residences of the Gothic tomb type and for Arnolfo's part in that movement, I rely heavily on Gardner's papers, *Burl Mag* (1972 and 1973), and likewise on Ladner, *Papstbildnisse*, II: 209ff., on the tomb of Nicholas III—only the *gisant* survives in the Grotte Vaticane; 229ff., tomb of Honorius IV, the fragments at S. Maria in Aracoeli; and 302ff., that of Boniface VIII, originally under a clumsy, old-fashioned and all too emphatically Gothic baldacchino, the sarcophagus and *gisant* now in the Grotte Vaticane, the half-size portrait, blessing, formerly on a side wall of the canopy, now in the papal apartments, the mosaic on the rear wall, signed by Torriti, as well as Arnolfo's signature, lost (Ladner, *op. cit.*, II, 310ff., with reference also to Grimaldi, *Descrizione*, p. 44f.), the whole completed prior to January 1301 (Ladner, *op. cit.*, p. 310). On the canopies at S. Paolo and S. Cecilia, Romanini, *op. cit.*, pp. 57ff., 75ff., and *passim*.

p. 215

M. Salmi and B. Bearzi, "Il problema della statua bronzea di S. Pietro" and "Esame tecnologico e metallurgico della statua di S. Pietro," *Commentari* 11 (1960) 22ff., 30ff., have by now definitely assigned to the last years of the thirteenth century, possibly the years 1296-1298, the bronze statue of Saint Peter. Both H. Keller, "Der Bildhauer Arnolfo di Cambio . . . ," *Jahrbuch der Preussichen Kunstsammlungen* 55 (1934) 223, and Romanini, *op. cit.*, p. 181, believe the statue to have been done by the workshop. With Salmi, I incline to consider it as by his hand, though in a material unfamiliar to him.

pp. 217ff.

Again, I must plead incompetence and leave aside fundamental questions such as the links between Roman and Florentine art of the ending dugento or the role of Assisi in shaping the new art of Rome. Even limiting myself to surveying briefly the oeuvre of the Roman masters, I can refer only to, and have freely drawn on, the most important publications as quoted in the note to p. 209. On the murals in the Silvestro chapel, Matthiae, *Pittura*, pp. 146ff., and *idem, Pittura politica del medioevo romano*, Rome, 1964, pp. 86ff. (a new study is being undertaken by Professor John Mitchell); on Anagni, *Pittura*, pp. 132ff.—but might not 1231, the date of the crypt pavement, constitute as well a *terminus ante quem* as one *post quem*, this latter being Matthiae's view?

pp. 220f.

The impact of Byzantine art on the Roman masters and on Torriti in particular has been brought out in the frame of a comprehensive study by E. Kitzinger, "The Byzantine Contribution to Western Art of the Twelfth and Thirteenth Centuries," *DOP* 20 (1966) 27ff., reprinted in *idem, Byzantium*, pp. 357ff., whence I liberally paraphrase. Independently, yet along similar lines, the topic has been pursued by O. Demus, *Byzantium and the West*, New York, 1970, pp. 121ff., in particular pp. 226ff.

On Torriti at S. Maria Maggiore, I base myself primarily on Gardner, *ZKG* (1973), and for both this and the Lateran mosaic on Ladner, *Papstbildnisse*, II, 241ff. and 234ff.; see also the summary paragraphs in Matthiae, *Mosaici*, p. 355. The activity of Sicilian mosaic workers on the St. Peter's mosaic has been suggested by O. Demus, *The Mosaics of Norman Sicily*, London, 1950, pp. 453ff.; the letter of Honorius III regarding S. Paolo fuori le mura is found in *Regesta Honorii III Papae*, ed. P. Pressuti, Paris, 1888, p. 173, and quoted Ladner, *Papstbildnisse*, II, 80ff. On Sopoćani, Kitzinger, *Byzantium*, pp. 373ff.; Demus, *Byzantium and the West*, pp. 226ff.; V. J. Djurić, *Sopoćani*, Belgrade, 1963.

pp. 221ff.

Links between Torriti's *Coronation* and the apse mosaics at S. Clemente and S. Maria in Trastevere have been suggested by Gardner, *ZKG* (1973). In broad lines the revival of antique models in thirteenth-century Rome has been sketched by W. Paeseler, "Der Rückgriff der römischen Dugentomalerei auf die christliche Spätantike," in: *Beiträge zur Kunst des Mittelalters, Vorträge der ersten Deutschen Kunsthistorikertagung . . . 1948*, Berlin, 1950, pp. 157ff. (hereafter "Der Rückgriff"). I agree with Paeseler on the thirteenth-century revival's producing new creations rather than mere copies; but his definition of late-antique painting as "Alexandrian" is by now obsolete and his range of models drawn on by the thirteenth century seems to me overly broad.

p. 223

The differences in character between medieval renascences north and south of the Alps were first brought out brilliantly by Erwin Panofsky in his *Renaissance and Renascences*. Likewise the thirteenth-century renascences have been discussed by Panofsky in this work, *passim*, esp. 62ff. (Rheims), 65ff. (Frederick II), 67f. and *passim* (Nicola Pisano); on Frederick II also E. Kantorowicz, *Kaiser Friedrich II*, Berlin, 1927, pp. 483ff.; and on Nicola Pisano and antiquity, recently M. Seidel, "Studien zur Antikenrezeption Niccolò Pisanos," *Mitteilungen des Kunsthistorischen Instituts Florenz* 19 (1975) 307ff.

pp. 223f.

French impact on Torriti, presumably by way of Assisi, has been pointed out by Gardner, *ZKG* (1973). For the links suggested between Cavallini and France, I have to take full responsibility. On Giotto and antiquity, Paeseler, "Giottos Navicella" and "Der Rückgriff," as above. Regarding the controversial dates assigned to Giotto's Roman activity, I can list only a few examples: P. Murray, "Notes on Some Early Giotto Sources," *JWC* 16 (1953) 58ff. (Navicella ca. 1300); Paeseler, "Giottos Navicella"

(Navicella 1306/7-1311); M. Gosebruch, "Giottos Stefaneschi Altarwerk . . . ," *Miscellanea Bibliothecae Hertzianae*, München, 1961, pp. 104ff. (altar after 1313); W. Kemp, "Zum Programm von Stefaneschi-Altar und Navicella," *ZKG* 30 (1967) 309ff. (both after 1309); J. Gardner, "The Stefaneschi Altarpiece . . . ," *JWC* 37 (1974) 57ff. (both altar and Navicella around 1300, linked to Holy Year).

p. 227

On honorary statues, Ladner, *Papstbildnisse*, II, 215, in general, referring also to Frederick II; *ibid.*, p. 226, on that of Nicholas III; p. 253f. on the one in Palazzo Venezia, perhaps Nicholas IV; on those of Boniface VIII, pp. 296ff. for the one at Bologna, p. 301 for that at Amiens, pp. 322ff. for the one at Florence, pp. 332ff. for those at Orvieto, pp. 337ff. for those at Anagni, and p. 339 for the one planned for Padua. See also U. Sommer, *Die Anklage der Idolatrie gegen Bonifaz VIII*, Freiburg, 1920, and H. Keller, "Die Entstehung des Bildnisses am Ende des Hochmittelalters," *Röm Jbch* 3 (1939) 227ff.

p. 228

On the marble stairs ascending to S. Maria in Aracoeli, the inscription giving the name of the master mason and the date 1348, Forcella, *Inscrizioni*, I, 127, no. 453. On the altar canopy at S. Giovanni in Laterano, A. Monferini, "Il ciborio Lateranense e Giovanni di Stefano," *Commentari* 13 (1962) 182ff.

Chapter Nine

pp. 231f.

Population figures for Rome from the sixth century on and through the Middle Ages are notoriously difficult to come by. For the figure given by Procopius of but five hundred men surviving—men rather than people—see *The Gothic Wars*, VII, XX, 19 (*LCL* IV, 328f.). Regarding the Middle Ages some light has been thrown in recent years on the demographic history of the countryside and the small towns of Latium, particularly in the fourteenth and fifteenth centuries, based on tax lists; but the interpretation of the figures varies at times widely and the estimates remain rough at best. See Partner, *Lands, passim* and in particular pp. 354f., 389f., 420ff.; A. Esch, *Bonifaz IX und der Kirchenstaat*, Tübingen, 1969, pp. 209ff., regarding the time around 1400; and, though not so recently, K. J. Beloch, *Bevölkerungsgeschichte Italiens*, Berlin-Leipzig, 1937-39 (but written before 1929), in particular, II, pp. 36ff. For the controversial interpretation of the figures based on lists of house and salt taxes, as levied 1420-1422 from the district of Rome alone and excluding the city, see G. Tomassetti, "Del sale e focatico del comune di Roma . . . ," *ASRStP* 20 (1897) 313ff., arriving at a population figure of roughly 460,000; and G. Pardi, "La populazione del distretto di Roma sui primordi del Quattrocento," *ASRStP* 49 (1926) 331f., whose figure of only 176,000 seems to agree with the low estimate proposed by Beloch, *op. cit.*, II, 37f. Likewise, J. C. Russell, *Medieval Regions and their Cities*, Bloomington, Ind., 1972, 51ff., as previously in his *Late Ancient and Medieval Population* (*Transactions of the American Philosophical Society* 43, 3), 1958, insists on low estimates: 17,000-20,000 for the late thirteenth century—based on a questionable proportion, 1:3 or 1:4, clergy as against general population—the figure of roughly 5,000 clergy being incidentally early fourteenth rather than thirteenth century. However, returning to Pardi's figures, the population by 1420, in the countryside ravaged by a century of warfare, plague, and desertion of farms and villages, as suggested by Partner, would have been much lower than it was a hundred and fifty to two hundred years before, when Latium was flourishing (Partner, *Lands*, pp. 189ff.).

For the twelfth and thirteenth centuries, the only available figure appears to be the size of the Roman levy in 1167 at the battle of Monte Porzio: 30,000 men, as reported by the *Annales Colonienses Maximi, MGH SS*, XVII, 766, and more reliably by Acerbo Morena (*Das Geschichtswerk des Otto Morena und seiner Fortsetzer*, ed. F. Güterbeck, *MGH SS RG*, n.s. 7, 1930, 197ff.), where the levy is given as 30,000, the number of those slain as 2,000.

Beloch, *op. cit.*, II, 1, considers the figures of such levies—the 22,000 men cited for 1362—as totally unreliable. I am not so sure; for Rome and the district, rather than Rome alone as he seems mistakenly to assume, the figure of 22,000 seems quite likely in 1362. Held together with the population figure of roughly 180,000 for the district, as in 1420, perhaps a few thousand less in 1362, plus 17,000 or thereabouts for the city, it provides a convincing proportion of 1:8 or 1:9, levy against total population. Admittedly this proportion differs much from that of 1:3.5 accepted by D. Herlihy, *Medieval and Renaissance Pistoia*, New Haven and London, 1967, pp. 72ff. However, if I understand his argument correctly, 1:3.5 is the proposed proportion of only male citizens, age seventeen to sixty or more, taking an oath of loyalty (*ibid.*, p. 73; also *idem, Pisa in the Early Renaissance*, Port Washington, N.Y., and London, 1973, reprint, p. 36). But surely, not much more than one third of the male population over seventeen would be able or willing to bear arms, an eighth or ninth of the total population. Hence, a levy of 30,000 for Rome and her district suggests to me a total population of 240,000 to 270,000.

For the population of the city of Rome alone not counting the district, even such rough estimates are hard to obtain. The number of 20,000 dead in the malaria epidemic of 1167 in Rome itself, as given by the *Annales Cameracenses, MGH SS*, XVI, 540, is unreliable; if accepted, it probably comprises both Romans and those from the district. Brentano, *op. cit.*, p. 13, with some hesitation accepts for the twelfth and thirteenth centuries the figure of 35,000 inhabitants in the city, as proposed by F. Cancellieri, *Lettera sopra il tarantismo*, Rome, 1817, p. 19, for the time of Innocent III and as adopted as possibly correct by Beloch, *op. cit.,* II, 1; Beloch's estimate of 25,000 for the end of the fourteenth century, *ibid.*, II, 2 seems unconvincingly high; and though the population figure of 17,000 was misread by Cancellieri, *op. cit.*, p. 26, and corrected by Beloch, *loc. cit.*, it need not have been much higher. In any event, the figure was much lower than between 1150 and 1300, when Rome was an important European bureaucratic and legal center. Its rise as such with visitors on business and pilgrims coming from all over the West is brought out, for the early Middle Ages, by Llewellyn, pp. 109ff., and *passim*, for the High Middle Ages by R. W. Southern, *Western Society and the Church in the Middle Ages*, Harmondsworth, 1970, pp. 105ff.

The census of 1527 has been published by D. Gnoli, "*Descriptio Urbis* o censimento . . . di Roma avanti il sacco Borbonico," *ASRStP* 17 (1894) 375ff.

pp. 232f.

For streets, see R. Lanciani, *Forma Urbis Romae*, Rome, 1893-, where ancient and modern streets are marked. Likewise and notwithstanding their late dates, maps of sixteenth- through nineteenth-century origin as conveniently compiled in Frutaz, *Piante*, remain useful: Rome for a long time retained nearly unchanged the medieval network of streets. See also the facsimile reproductions of some of these maps (F. Ehrle, *Roma al tempo di Guilio III*, Rome, 1911; *idem, Roma prima di Sisto V. La pianta di Roma Du Pérac-Lafréry del 1577*, Rome, 1908; *idem, Roma al tempo di Clemente VIII. La pianta di Roma di Antonio Tempesta del 1593* . . . , Vatican City, 1932; *idem, Roma al tempo di Urbano VIII. La pianta di Roma Maggi-Maupin-Losi del 1625*, Rome, 1915; *idem, Roma al tempo di Clemente X. La pianta di Roma di Giambattista Falda del 1676* . . . , Rome, 1931; *idem, Roma al tempo di Benedetto XIV. La pianta di Roma di Giambattista Nolli del 1748*, Vatican City, 1932), and the two maps appended to Huelsen, *Chiese*. For street and place names, see Gnoli, *Topografia*, and P. Romano, *Roma nelle sue strade* . . . , Rome, 1950. For municipal control and cleaning of streets, see E. Re, "Maestri di strada," *ASRStP* 43 (1920) 5ff.; *idem*, "Maestri delle strade del 1452," *ASRStP* 46 (1923) 407ff.; C. Scaccia-Scarafoni, "L'antico studio dei 'magistri stratarum,' " *ASRStP* 50 (1927) 239ff.; and E. Rossi, "L'albergo dell'Orso," *ASRStP* 50 (1927) 51ff. For the routes of processionals in the twelfth century, see *Liber Censuum*, ed. Fabre and Duchesne, Paris, 1905, II, 139ff. (Benedictus Canonicus) and I, 290ff. (Cencius Camerarius).

For bridges kept in use in the Middle Ages, see Nash, *Dictionary, passim*, and Gnoli, *Topografia*, pp. 219, 222ff.

S. Pressouyre, *Rome au fil du temps*, Boulogne, 1973, gives a bird's-eye view of the location of built-up areas through the centuries. Much important information is given in the *Guide Rionali*, as listed among frequently quoted works, with the name of rione, and number of volume.

For churches, see: *Corpus, passim*; Huelsen, *Chiese*; Armellini-Cecchelli, *Chiese*; and the volumes in the series *Chiese di Roma Illustrate*. New foundations are referred to in a variety of sources—inscriptions, the biographies of the popes, for instance—which will be quoted as the need arises. For convents and monasteries, in the early Middle Ages, Ferrari, *Monasteries*, is the standard work. A list of monasteries as of 806-807 is given in *LP*, II, 22ff.; of abbeys in the twelfth century, P. Mallius, *Historia basilicae Antiquae S. Petri* . . . , *Acta Sanctorum*, June VII, appendix 51*, Paris and Rome, 1867, and in the *Liber Censuum*, I, 309.

Churches and monasteries, newly founded in the Middle Ages, are best traced through Huelsen, *Chiese, passim*, and his Plan II. For diaconiae and aqueducts functioning or repaired, see above, chapters four and five.

Natural disasters, recounted in the *LP, passim*, and in contemporary chronicles or other documents, will be referred to in the appropriate places.

For housing, the richest sources are legal documents about property owned by Roman churches and monasteries. Many have been published in the volumes of the *ASRStP*. I list them here according to church or monastery in alphabetical order and cite the full title of each publication; henceforth, I shall cite only the relevant volume of the *ASRStP* and the document number and its date; the page number will be added only where more than one *cartularium* are published in one volume:

- *SS. Alessio e Bonifazio*: A. Monaci, "Regesto dell'abbazia di Sant'Alessio all'Aventino," *ASRStP* 27 (1904) 351ff.; continued *ASRStP* 28 (1905) 395ff.
- *S. Bibiana*: see below, *S. Maria Maggiore*
- *S. Cecilia*: E. Loevinson, "Documenti di S. Cecilia in Trastevere," *ASRStP* 49 (1926) 355ff.
- *SS. Cosma e Damiano in Mica Aurea*: P. Fedele, "Carte del monastero dei SS. Cosma e Damiano in Mica Aurea," *ASRStP* 21 (1898) 459ff.; continued *ASRStP* 22 (1899) 25ff. and 383ff.;
- *S. Maria Maggiore*: G. Ferri, "Le carte dell'archivio Liberiano dal secolo X al XV," *ASRStP* 28 (1905) 23ff.; and *ASRStP* 30 (1907) 119ff.
- *S. Maria Nova*: P. Fedele, "Tabularium S. Mariae Novae ab an. 982 ad an. 1200," *ASRStP* 23 (1900) 171ff.; continued, *ASRStP* 24 (1901) 159ff., *ASRStP* 25 (1902) 169ff., and *ASRStP* 26 (1903) 21ff.
- *St. Peter's*: L. Schiaparelli, "Le carte antiche dell'archivio Capitolare di S. Pietro in Vaticano," *ASRStP* 24 (1901) 393ff.; and *ASRStP* 25 (1902) 273ff.
- *S. Prassede*: P. Fedele, "Tabularium S. Praxedis," *ASRStP* 27 (1904) 27ff. and *ASRStP* 28 (1905) 41ff.
- *S. Silvestro in Capite*: V. Federici, "Regesto del monastero di S. Silvestro in Capite," *ASRStP* 22 (1899) 213ff. and 489ff.; continued *ASRStP* 23 (1900) 67ff. and 411ff.

Similar documents published elsewhere refer to property owned in Rome by the abbeys of Farfa and Subiaco and by churches and monasteries in Rome, other than those just listed. Roman property of the great abbeys is referred to time and again in *Reg Farf* and *Reg Sub* as listed among frequently quoted works, and occasionally in *Chronicon Farfense*, ed. U. Balzani, Rome, 1903. For *cartularia* of churches and monasteries other than those listed above, see:

- *S. Agnese and S. Costanza*: P. F. Kehr, "Papsturkunden in Rom," *Göttinger Nachrichten* (*Nachrichten der K. Gesellschaft der Wissenschaften zu Göttingen*), 1900, pp. 140ff.
- *S. Lorenzo in Damaso*: J. Ciampini, *De Sanctae Romanae ecclesiae vicecancellario*, Rome, 1697, pp. 140ff.
- *S. Maria in Campo Marzio*: E. Carusi, *Cartario di S. Maria in Campo Marzo (986-1199)* (*Miscellanea della Società Romana di Storia Patria*, 17) 1948, henceforth quoted as Carusi, *Cartario*; and F. Martinelli, *Roma ex ethnica sacra*, Rome, 1653, p. 201f.
- *S. Maria in Trastevere*: P. A. Galletti, *Chartularium S. Mariae Transtiberim*, Vat. lat. 8051 (unpublished).
- *S. Maria in Via Lata*: Hartmann, *S. Maria in Via Lata*, and L. Cavazzi, *La diaconia di S. Maria in Via Lata*, Rome, 1908. The property and the church belonged to the wealthy convent of SS. Ciriaco e Nicola.

More information is contained in P. F. Kehr, *It. Pont.*, I, *Roma*, Berlin, 1906 (repr. 1961), and II, *Latium*, Berlin, 1907 (repr. 1961), *passim*, where further indications about the whereabouts of church and monastic archives are given.

Brentano, *Rome before Avignon*, *passim*, provides superbly vivid descriptions of medieval housing and householders in Rome, drawn mainly from the sources indicated above and further unpublished documents.

For the *catasti* of confraternities in Rome in the sixteenth and seventeenth centuries, see R. Fregna and S. Politi, "Fonti di archivio per una storia edilizia di Roma," *Controspazio* 3 (1971) fasc. 9, 2ff., and *ibid.*, 4 (1972) fasc. 7, 2ff.

pp. 233ff.

For views of Rome from the fifteenth into the nineteenth century, see primarily: the *Codex Escurialensis* from the last years of the fifteenth or the very first years of the sixteenth century; the Heemskerck sketchbooks in Berlin, mainly from the 1530s; Egger, *Veduten*; and Frutaz, *Piante*. Likewise, catalogues of exhibitions of drawings and engravings come in handy and will be referred to in the appropriate place.

The standard work on early maps of Rome is Frutaz, *Piante*. For the map of Fra Paolino da Venezia, see most recently B. Degenhart and A. Schmitt, "Marino Sanudo und Paolino Veneto," *Röm Jbch* 14 (1973) 1ff., especially regarding the date 1323; more fully, W. Holzmann, "Der älteste mittelalterliche Stadtplan von Rom," *JDAI* 41 (1926) 56ff.

For the Golden Bull of Louis the Bavarian, Frutaz, *Piante*, and W. Erben, *Rombilder auf kaiserlichen und päpstlichen Siegeln . . .*, Graz, Vienna and Leipzig, 1931, 55ff. and *passim*. Finally, see Millard Meiss, *French Painting in the Time of Jean de Berry*, III, *The Limbourg Brothers and Their Contemporaries*, London and New York, 1974, 209ff., for the map of Rome in the *Très Riches Heures*, that of Taddeo di Bartolo, and a third one heretofore unknown (Meiss, fig. 4), all reproducing with different fidelity the same lost original.

Chapter Ten

pp. 237ff.

On the Tiber and its role in the life of Rome in general, C. D'Onofrio, *Il Tevere a Roma*, Rome, 1970. The ever-recurring floods are briefly listed: for the first through third centuries, Lugli, *Monumenti*, II, 278ff.; for the early Middle Ages, chapter three above; for the one in 1231, Cardinal of Aragon (Niccolò Rosselli), *Vita Gregorii Papae IX, RIS*, III, 1, 578, whence our quotation. A list of floods recorded by markers from 1180 to 1870 is found in P. Frosini, "Una inondazione di Roma . . . 1557," *Strenna dei Romanisti* 27 (1966) 183ff. Descriptions of 1495 and 1530 respectively provide a good idea of the flooding mainly of the rioni Trastevere, Ponte, and the Borgo: G. Dati, *Del diluvio di Roma di MCCCCLXXXXV* . . . Rome, 1495; E. Amadei, "Il diluvio di Roma del 1530," *Strenna dei Romanisti* 13 (1952) 263ff., quoting D. M. Novara, *Del diluvio di Roma*, Bologna, 1531. On the repeated collapse and rebuilding of Ponte Rotto, Nash, *Dictionary*, II, 182; Gnoli, *Topografia*, 223f., and both, *passim*, on the other bridges.

pp. 239ff.

On navigation and harbors: Ripa Grande (Ripa Romea), C. D'Onofrio, *op. cit.*, pp. 242ff., first mentioned 1074, *ASRStP* 22 (1899) n.76; see also Gnoli, *Topografia*, p. 267, and *LP*, II, 115 on Leo IV's harbor defenses, and Huelsen, *Chiese*, p. 372 on S. Maria in Turri trans Tiberim; on S. Maria in Gradellis (S. Maria Egiziaca) Huelsen, *Chiese*, p. 336; on the nearby dock (if that it was) *Ripa Graeca*, Gnoli, *Topografia*, p. 266; on the medieval antecedents of the Ripetta, Carusi, *Cartario*, no. 3, dated 1010; on the sandbanks, in particular the *isoletta*, and the sloping river banks, aside from any old photograph or drawing, V. Campajola, "Il ghetto di Roma . . . ," *Quaderni* 67-70 (1965) 67ff. Finally, a few examples out of many on floating mills and fishing rights: Kehr, *It. Pont.*, I, 82, 931-936, floating mill "with its ropes and access" near the Cloaca Maxima; *ibid.*, p. 89, no. 10, based on Bull of 1194 (Carusi, *Cartario*, pp. 115ff., no. 62); F. Martinelli, *Roma ex ethnica sacra*, Rome, 1653, pp. 201ff., another mill off the Marmorata; Kehr, *It. Pont.*, I, 129, no. 4, based on Bull dated 1123 (G. B. Crescimbeni, *L'istoria di . . . S. Giovanni avanti Portam Latinam*, Rome, 1716, 243ff.); three, owned by S. Maria in Trastevere at the "*pons Aventinus*" (possibly misread for *Antoninus*, unless Ponte Rotto is meant), and a fishing jetty or pool (*piscaria*) at the "*pons fracta*," this being the pons Antoninus, near Ponte Sisto, see Gnoli, *Topografia*, p. 224; more mills on the Tiber Island, *ASRStP* 21 (1898) no. 1, in A.D. 948/949; in Trastevere, *ASRStP* 22 (1899) no. 38, in 1033, pp. 64ff., and P. A. Galletti, *Chartularium S. Mariae Transtiberim*, Vat. lat. 8051 (unpublished) fols. 13ff., 20, dated 1073 and 1082 respectively, this one near Porta Settimiana, and *ibid.*, fol. 9f., a *piscaria* in the same neighborhood, mentioned 1062-1063.

On the ancient monuments inside the abitato, abandoned or reused: the palace of Cromatius, *Liber Censuum*, ed. Fabre and Duchesne, Paris, 1905, I, 272 (*Mirabilia*, chap. XLI), also Valentini-Zucchetti, III, 212, 219; Piazza Navona, Nash, *Dictionary*, II, 387, Gnoli, *Topografia*, 186ff. referring to *Reg Farf*, nos. 474, 690, 804 (dated 999, 1012, 1044 respectively), also Huelsen, *Chiese*, p. 168 and *Corpus*, I, p. 39 for S. Agnese in Piazza Navona; the Theatre of Pompey in the Middle Ages is poorly documented, see, however, Huelsen, *Chiese*, p. 204 on S. Barbara dei Librai; for the Theatre of Marcellus, see C. Huelsen, "Sulle vicende del Teatro di Marcello . . . ," *RendPontAcc* 1 (1921-23) 169ff. with reference also to the will of Cardinal Jacopo Savelli, 1279 (Honorius IV), in *Les régistres d'Honorius IV*, ed. M. Prou, Paris, 1888, pp. 579ff. (where it is "*Mons Saffo*" [*Faffo*]), and G. Marchetti-Longhi, "Theatrum Marcelli et Mons Fabiorum," *RendPontAcc* 20 (1943/44) 14ff.; also *Guide Rionali, S. Angelo*, I, 6ff. and on its aspect prior to the over-cleaning of the 1930s, P. Fidenzoni, *Il teatro di Marcello*, Rome, 1970; on the nearby market referred to in 998 "*sub templo Marcelli*," *Reg Farf*, no. 459.

pp. 244ff.

The ancient street system is still best seen in Lanciani's *Forma Urbis*, supplemented by *La pianta marmorea di Roma*, both quoted above in the note to p. 3. The main lines of the medieval street system are reflected in the routes of the papal processions, as given by Benedictus Canonicus (*Liber Censuum, op. cit.*, I, 292ff., 298ff.) and other *ordines*; and through its being largely preserved still in the fifteenth through eighteenth centuries, see maps such as Strozzi's of 1474 based on an original ca. 1447 (Frutaz, *Piante*, pl. 159; G. Scaglia, "The Origins of an Architectural Plan of Rome," *JWC* 27 [1964] 137ff.), Bufalini's of 1551 (Frutaz, *Piante*, pls. 189ff.), and still Nolli's of 1748 (*ibid.*, pls. 396ff.). See also T. Magnuson, *Studies in Roman Quattrocento Architecture* (*Figura*, 9), Stockholm, 1958, 21ff. and pl. II, and S. Pressouyre, *Rome au fil du temps*, Boulogne, 1973, pls. XIV-XVII. Regarding Via del Papa, del Parione, del Pellegrino, dei Banchi Vecchi, and so forth, Gnoli, *Topografia*, *passim*.

pp. 249ff.
S. Pressouyre, *op. cit.*, pl. XIV, sees as we do the early core of medieval Rome extending north and west from the Ripa (Theatre of Marcellus) with the difference that she marks its westward expansion as far as the present Ponte Mazzini. Likewise, our ideas coincide in our viewing the early town as being formed in clusters rather than as a coherent mass.

pp. 252f.
On housing near the Pantheon, apparently a mansion, *Reg Farf*, no. 428, dated 998; on the *calcararium*, G. Marchetti-Longhi, "Le contrade medioevali della zona in Circo Flaminio. Il calcarario," *ASRStP* 42 (1919) 401ff.; on the Campo Marzio, Carusi, *Cartario, passim*; on the oratories in the Thermae Alexandrinae, *Reg Farf*, nos. 458f., dated 998, also Huelsen, *Chiese*, pp. 212, 378, 455; on Piazza Navona and some oratories its vaults sheltered, *Reg Farf*, no. 474, dated 999, and Huelsen, *Chiese*, p. 168. On the *Scorticlaria, Reg Farf*, nos. 458, 539, 557, the latter two dated 1017 and 1019, and Gnoli, *Topografia*, 294ff.; *ASRStP* 24 (1901) nos. 23, 24, dated 1066, pp. 485ff., "terra vacante"; *ibid.*, no. 25, dated 1073, pp. 488ff., a thatched cottage. On Monte Giordano, M.P.F. Asso, "Monte Giordano," *Quaderni* 1 (1953) 12ff. and *Guide Rionali, Ponte*, II, 30ff., also Gnoli, *Topografia*, p. 179f. (s.v. Monte Roncione), and P. Pecchiai, *Palazzo Taverna a Monte Giordano*, Rome, 1963; on the mansion *in Parione* of Cencio di Stefano prefetto, *LP*, II, 282; also Gnoli, *Topografia*, p. 197, Valentini-Zucchetti, III, 332 and Nash, *Dictionary*, II, 414, regarding the controversial location, Piazza Paganica or Piazza Cenci.

pp. 253f.
On the Tiber Island, still deserted in 987 and 996, it seems, *ASRStP* 27 (1904) no. 2, pp. 365ff., no. 5, pp. 371ff.; and, after the building of a bishop's mansion (near S. Bartolomeo or near S. Giovanni Calabita?), Kehr, *It. Pont.*, II, 20, dated 1018. On housing in Trastevere, *ASRStP* 21 (1898) 459ff., and *ASRStP* 22 (1899) 25ff. and 383ff., and, better, P. A. Galletti, *Chartularium S. Mariae Transtiberim*, Vat. lat. 8051, fols. 7ff., 16ff., 18ff., 21, all near S. Maria in Trastevere and Porta Settimiana, dated 1038, 1075/76, and 1089.

pp. 254f.
On the mansions of noble families outside the abitato, in general, *Reg Sub*, no. 155, dated 942 (also Gregorovius, III, 326); in particular, Paul I (S. Silvestro), *LP*, I, 464; Hadrian I's family, *LP*, I, 486; Stephen V, John XII, son of Alberic (see anon), *LP*, II, 247, both "*de regione Via Lata*"; Leo VIII, *LP*, II, 250, "*de clivo argentario*"; Benedict VI, *LP*, II, 255, "*de regione VIII sub Capitolio*"; John XV, *LP*, II, 260, "*de regione Gallinae albae*" (Quirinal?); John XVII, *LP*, II, 265, "*de regione Biberatica*"; John XVIII, *LP*, II, 266 "*de regione secus partam Metrovi*"; Crescentius "*de Caballo marmoreo*," "*dux Gregorio de Canapara*," and Petrus Canaparius, all three named in 963 in Liutprand, *Historia Ottonis*, chap. 9 (*MGH SS RG*, 166, *Liutprandi Opera omnia*, ed. J. Becker, 1915); also Johannes Canaparius, around 1000, abbot of SS. Bonifacio ed Alessio (F. Nerini, *De templo . . . Bonifacii et Alexii . . .* , Rome, 1752, pp. 134ff.); Alberic's family mansion, *Il chronicon di Benedetto . . . di Soracte*, ed. G. Zucchetti (Fonti per la Storia d'Italia, 55) Rome, 1920, p. 163; also *Reg Sub*, no. 155, dated 942 (as quoted above) and *Reg Farf*, no. 637, dated 1013 "*. . . domus domni Alberici eminentissimi consulis et ducis iuxta sanctos apostolos . . .* "; for the Mausoleum of Augustus, *ASRStP* 22 (1899) 268, nos. 3, 4, dated 955 and 962 respectively, when still property of S. Silvestro in Capite and *ibid.*, p. 532, no. 19, dated 1002, when in the hands of "Stephanus Prefect of Rome" (signed in Greek lettering).

C. D'Onofrio, *Castel S. Angelo*, Rome, 1971, pp. 73ff., on its history in the Middle Ages; also C. Cecchelli, "Documenti per la storia antica e medioevale di Castel S. Angelo," *ASRStP* (1951) 27ff. and *idem*, "Castel S. Angelo al tempo di Gregorio VII," *Studi Gregoriani*, II, Rome, 1947, 103ff.

pp. 255f.
On the Aventine: Georgius de Abentino, ca. 890, *LP*, II, 225; a synonymous Gregorius, 963, Liutprand (as previous note); Palace of Euphimianus, *ASRStP* 27 (1904) no. 1, pp. 364ff., spurious, confirmed *ibid.*, no. 5, pp. 372ff. in 996; Alberic's family mansion, restored by his grandmother Theodora (A. Muñoz, *La basilica di Santa Sabina*, Milan, 1925, p. 40) and donated 936/37 by him, "the house where he was born on the Aventine," to the newly founded monastery of S. Maria in Aventino (Ferrari, *Monasteries*, p. 205). The healthy location of the hill, *Vita S. Odilonis* (*Acta S. Benedicti*, VIII, 1, Venice, 1733, 698).

On the site of the palace of Otto III on the Palatine, rather than the Aventine, C. Brühl, "Die Kaiserpfalz bei St. Peter und die Pfalz Otto III auf dem Palatin," *Quellen und Forschungen aus italienischen Archiven* 34 (1954) 1ff.

p. 257
On the Lateran Palace and the attached outbuildings, Kehr, *It. Pont.*, II, 25, dated 1037, confirmed 1050 (*loc. cit.*) and 1154 (*ibid.*, p. 28) where the term *suburbium* seems to imply the existence of housing near the

palace. On convents on the Celian Hill, in particular S. Erasmo, Ferrari, *Monasteries*, pp. 119ff.; on farmhouses, *Reg Sub*, nos. 82, 91, both dated 1003. On a farm settlement near Porta Maggiore, traceable through the tenth century, *Reg Sub*, nos. 27, 59, 79; on other farmland near S. Bibiana, *ASRStP* 27 (1904) p. 441ff., nos. 172f., 181f., 195ff., 442, traceable to 981-1148.

Chapter Eleven

p. 261

The veneration of Saint Peter and his basilica has been a key point through many of the preceding chapters. For the accumulation around this church of minor churches, convents, hostels, diaconiae, foreigners' compounds, and hostels, I refer again to L. Reekmans, "Le dévelopment topographique . . . du Vatican," *Mélanges . . . Jacques Lavalleye*, Louvain, 1970, pp. 197ff. For the papal quarters near St. Peter's built by Leo III, *LP*, II, 8, 27f. and *ibid.*, I, 420 for older ones extant by 731-741; on their continued use till at least 983, *Reg Sub*, no. 185, and Kehr, *It. Pont.*, II, 90, no. 22. In fact, a papal building near the obelisk, "*domus Aguglie*," is still referred to in ca. 1143 by Benedictus Canonicus, *Liber Censuum*, ed. Fabre and Duchesne, Paris, 1905, II, 143. For the "palace" of Charlemagne and its continued use beyond the ninth century, *De imperatoria potestate libellus*, ed. G. Zucchetti (Fonti per la storia d'Italia, 55), Rome, 1920, pp. 197f., 203, and *Reg Farf*, nos. 325, 537, dated 872 and 1017 respectively; also C. Brühl, "Die Kaiserpfalz bei St. Peter und die Pfalz Otto III auf dem Palatin," *Quellen und Forschungen aus italienischen Archiven* 34 (1954) 1ff.

p. 264

I have discussed the foundation of the Leonine City, in chapter five. Its place, separate from Rome both in popular opinion and in law, is reflected: in the inscriptions on the wall ("*civitas leonina vocatur*"; A. Prandi, "Un'iscrizione frammentaria di Leone IV . . . ," *ASRStP* 74 [1951] 149ff.); in Benedict of Soracte's lament (*Il chronicon di Benedetto . . . del Soratte*, ed. G. Zucchetti [Fonti per la Storia d'Italia, 55], Rome, 1920, p. 186); or in a reference in 998 to Castel S. Angelo as "the tower which is outside the city [meaning Rome] beyond the Tiber" (Rodulphus Glaber, *Historiarum libri IV*, I, 4, *MGH SS*, VII, 56); and in legal documents, starting with the privilege issued in 854 in favor of the convent of S. Martino by Leo IV, *ASRStP* 24 (1901) no. 2, dated 854, pp. 432ff. ("in this our new Leonine City"), and continuing as *ibid.*, no. 16, dated 1053, pp. 467ff., "all the people of the Leonine City," or Hartmann, *Scae. Mariae in Via Lata*, XXXVI, dated 1014, "inside this new city called Leonine."

pp. 264ff.

Housing, gardens and building lots in the Leonine City are listed repeatedly, starting in 854, *ASRStP* 24 (1901) no. 2, pp. 432ff., "the church of S. Michael of the Frisians [S. Michele e Magno] . . . with houses, vaults, wells, trees . . . (and) a garden . . . at the beginning [head] of the porticus," this latter the porticoed street leading to St. Peter's; *ibid.*, no. 10, in 1030, p. 456f., the two-storied house with its stable at the *cortina*, as quoted in the text; *ibid.*, no. 29, in 1088, p. 495, a building lot in the Frisian compound next to an extant house; *ibid.*, 25 (1902) no. 54, in 1166, pp. 309ff., an empty lot, apparently agricultural, near the wall; *ibid.*, no. 69, in 1185, pp. 329ff., a lot and a vineyard; and so forth. For the density of the build-up by the thirteenth century, see also the *Liber anniversariorum della Basilica Vaticana* in: *Necrologi della Provincia Romana*, I, ed. P. Egidi, Rome, 1920, 174ff., *passim*.

Business properties are frequent, too. For those quoted in the text, *ASRStP* 24 (1901) no. 12, dated 1041, p. 460f.; *ibid.*, no. 13, dated 1043, pp. 461ff.; and *ibid.* 25 (1902) no. 35, dated 1127, p. 277f.; see also, *ibid.*, no. 40, dated 1144, pp. 284ff., "a single storied house of brick with a *ponteca* [*apotheca*, 'storeroom'?] inside and shops in front in its large portico . . . near the Meta," that is the so-called *Meta Romuli* just west of Castel S. Angelo.

In addition to shops in houses, tradespeople are listed by the *Liber Censuum*, I, 299 (also Valentini-Zucchetti, III, 224) on the route of the Pope coming from St. Peter's; presumably they set up stands or booths, in this sequence: vendors of straw (*paliarii*), money-changers, vendors of phials (*fiolarii*); there was also a fish market, probably near S. Lorenzo in piscibus, a church till 1938 on the Borgo Sto. Spirito. A long list of tradespeople stationed in the fourteenth century in the Borgo is given in P. Pecchiai, "Banchi e botteghe dinanzi alla basilica Vaticana . . . ," *Archivi d'Italia*, ser. II, 18 (1951) 81ff. For tradespeople near St. Peter's in the twelfth century, see also I. Guidi, "La descrizione di Roma nei geografi arabi," *ASRStP* 1 (1878) 173ff., quoting the Arab traveler Idrisi's somewhat fantastic description.

Inns and lodging houses in the Borgo appear as early as 1053; *ASRStP* (1901), no. 16, pp. 467ff., lists among residents of the Leonine City along with house owners and tenants on long leases, *tabernarii*, presumably innkeepers, and *servientes*, probably waiters, as against nonresidents, namely pilgrims and other strangers (*advenae*), and refers to lodging *oratores* and selling the necessaries of life. For Brancaleone's breaking the Borgo monopoly, see Bartoloni, *Senato,* no. 86, in 1235; on the invasion of the basilica by tradespeople, *ibid*., no. 108, in May 1244.

p. 267
On the diaconiae and their functions, above chapter three; on the hospital of Sto. Spirito, chapter eight, and on its functions, P. De Angelis, *Regula . . . hospitalis Sancti Spiritus*, Rome, 1954, and R. Brentano, *Rome before Avignon*, pp. 19ff. The claims of precedence for St. Peter's over the Lateran are reflected in P. Mallius, *Historia Basilicae Antiquae S. Petri*, in *Acta Sanctorium*, June VII (repr. Paris, 1867) 37*ff.; as to the inscription of Innocent III, see above, chapter eight, and note.

pp. 267f.
On the medieval Vatican Palace and its predecessors, above, chapter eight, with references to F. Ehrle and H. Egger, *Studi e documenti per la storia del Palazzo Apostolico*, Vatican City, 1935, 11ff., and D. Redig de Campos, *I Palazzi Vaticani*, Bologna, 1967, 19ff.

pp. 268f.
On Castel S. Angelo, C. D'Onofrio, *Castel S. Angelo*, Rome, 1971, *passim*, and the older bibliography, as quoted above, chapter eight.

Chapter Twelve

p. 271
For the overall picture, I refer again to the *Guide Rionali* as mentioned in my bibliographical note and the list of abbreviations. For S. Lorenzo in Damaso, A. Fonseca, *De Basilica S. Laurentii in Damaso . . .*, Fano, 1745, where the bull of Urban III is given in extenso, pp. 250ff.; see also Kehr, *It. Pont.*, I, 94, Huelsen, *Chiese*, p. 284, and Armellini-Cecchelli, *Chiese*, pp. 457, 1326f. For the minor churches in the area listed by us in the text, dated in the early twelfth century and surviving or known from old illustrations, see: L. Huetter, *S. Salvatore in Onda* (*Chiese illustrate*, 41); G. Segni, C. Thoenes, L. Mortari, *SS. Celso e Giuliano* (*Chiese illustrate*, 88) esp. pp. 29ff.; G. Marchetti-Longhi, "Le trasformazioni medioevali dell'area Sacra Argentina," *ASRStP* ser. 3, 26 (1972) 5ff.; and, of course, under their respective names, Huelsen, *Chiese*, Armellini-Cecchelli, *Chiese*, and Forcella, *Iscrizioni*.

pp. 272f.
On the Rione Ponte in general, *Guide Rionali*, Ponte I-IV. On Via dei Banchi Vecchi: Romano, *Strade*, p. 70; Gnoli, *Topografia*, pp. 31, 106ff. (s.v. Via Florida), p. 165 (s.v. Via Mercatoria). On the residents of Rione Ponte, many still simple folk in the late fourteenth century, who were replaced gradually by Florentine banking houses, A. Esch, "Vom Mittelalter zur Renaissance: Menschen in Rom 1350-1400," *Jahrbuch der Akademie . . . Göttingen* (1970), 26ff. esp. 29ff., and *idem*, "Florentiner in Rom um 1400," *Quellen und Forschungen* 52 (1972) 476ff. On inns, U. Gnoli, *Alberghi ed osterie di Roma nella Rinascenza*, Spoleto, 1935; on the claim of the Borgo, Bartoloni, *Senato*, no. 86.

On the Ripa, *Guide Rionali*, S. Angelo I. On its churches and on those on the island, see Huelsen, *Chiese*, Armellini-Cecchelli, *Chiese*, and: G. Matraca, *Historia (di) . . . S. Maria in Portico*, Rome, 1627; C. A. Erra, *Storia . . . di Santa Maria in Portico . . .*, Rome, 1750; and L. Pasquali, *Santa Maria in Portico*, Rome, 1902; G. B. Proia, *S. Nicola in Carcere* (*Chiese illustrate*, 112), also Th. Mommsen, "Petrarch and the *Sala Virorum Illustrium* in Padua," *Art Bull* 34 (1952) 95ff. (fourteenth-century drawings of church, p. 110), and H. Toubert, "Le rénouveau paleochrétien . . . ," *Cah Arch* 20 (1970) 100 n.4. See also my chapter seven. On S. Bartolomeo in Isola, practically unexplored, like the medieval predecessor of the neighboring S. Giovanni Calibita, still P. Casimiro, *Memorie istoriche . . .*, Rome, 1845, pp. 370ff., and *idem, Dissertazioni*, Rome, 1742; documentation for S. Bartolomeo, Kehr, *It. Pont.*, I, 112, and II, 17ff., where the *curtis*, the manse, of the bishop of Porto are referred to. For the tower at the Ponte Quattro Capi, *Liber Censuum*, II, 109, and Kehr, *It. Pont.*, I, 189.

pp. 273ff.
On Trastevere, see Galletti, Vat. lat. 8051, *passim*; on the business people, *negotiatores*, living there, *ASRStP* 21 (1898) nos. 16, 17, both dated A.D. 1000, and *ASRStP* 22 (1899) nos. 20, 45, 46, 56 (Leo "vir magnificus et laudabilis negotiator"), dated 1003, 1041, 1041, and 1051 respectively, pp. 25ff., 79ff., 81ff., and 97ff.

pp. 275ff.
The northward expansion of the abitato through the eleventh and twelfth centuries is easily traced through Carusi, *Cartario, passim*; for the dense build-up by the end of the twelfth century, Kehr, *It. Pont.*, I, 89, no. 10, dated 1194, based on F. Martinelli, *Roma ex ethnica sacra*, Rome, 1653, p. 201, where the document appears in Italian translation; for

S. Cecilia in Posterula (Madonna del Divino Amore), Huelsen, *Chiese*, p. 228; for S. Maria sopra Minerva, *ibid.*, p. 346f., and J. J. Berthier, *L'eglise de la Minerva*, Rome, 1910, and G. Urban, "Die Kirchenbaukunst des Quattrocento in Rom," *Röm Jbch* 9/10 (1961-62) 73ff., esp. 119f. On the eastward expansion of the abitato, around Trevi Fountain, Hartmann, *Scae. Mariae in Via Lata*, XLI-XLIV, all dated 1019, LXXXI, 1051—all near S. Maria in Xenodochio; *ibid.*, LXXIV, 1042, LXXXX, 1063 and others near S. Maria in Via; and LXXXXIII, 1065, "near the marble horse" and the Thermae of Constantine on the Quirinal.

pp. 278f.
The routes of the papal processions are found in *Liber Censuum*, II, 139ff. (Benedictus Canonicus), and I, 290ff. (Cencius Camerarius); see also Valentini-Zucchetti, III, 210ff., 213ff., in excerpts. The poem describing the procession under Otto III, first in W. Giesebrecht, *Geschichte der deutschen Kaiserzeit*, I, Leipzig, 1881, 898ff.; the procession of Innocent III to S. Maria in Trastevere, S. Kuttner and A. Garcia y Garcia, "A New Eyewitness Account of the Fourth Lateran Council," *Traditio* 20 (1964) 115ff.

pp. 280ff.
Gardens or fields near Palazzo Spada on Tempesta map, 1593, Frutaz, *Piante*, pl. 272, and in Wyngaerde's panorama (New York Metropolitan Museum) ca. 1550, detail C. L. Frommel, *Der römische Palastbau der Hochrenaissance* (*Römische Forschungen der Bibliotheca Hertziana* 21) III, Tübingen, 1973, pl. 30f. The ordinance regarding the minimum height of the arch in Trastevere, in Galletti, Vat. lat. 8051, I, fol. 41, dated 1250. The passages on rich and poor housing intermingled, in R. Brentano, *Rome before Avignon*, pp. 37, 39f., 41ff., the latter referring to the Theatre of Marcellus. On housing in the Ghetto, A. Milani, *Il Ghetto di Roma*, Rome, 1964, pp. 201ff., and V. Campajola, "Il Ghetto di Roma . . . ," *Quaderni* 67-70 (1965) 67ff.

pp. 283ff.
On the *magistri stratarum* and their ordinances, L. Schiaparelli, "Alcuni documenti sui 'Magistri aedificiorum urbis.' " *ASRStP* 25 (1902) 5ff., and E. Re, "Maestri di Strada," *ASRStP* 43 (1920) 5ff.; and C. Scaccia-Scarafoni, "L'antico statuto dei 'Magistri Stratarum,' " *ASRStP* 50 (1927) 239ff. The examples quoted from L. Schiaparelli, *op. cit.*, 6f., doc. I, the statute of 1233 and the limitations of porches and porticoes at and near St. Peter's, the latter repeated in doc. V, in 1279; doc. III, in 1238, the dyers' establishment; doc. X, in 1306, garbage on the lots opposite Sto. Spirito; the later ordinances and tasks outlined from E. Re, *op. cit.*, *passim*, based on bull of Martin V, March 29, 1425, codifying older precedent. The quotation regarding the street being an extension of the house, *ibid.*, p. 7; Professor Frank E. Brown tells me that even by law in ancient Rome the width of the sidewalk belonged to the house plot. To this day, after all, in the United States the home-owner is responsible for the stretch of sidewalk in front.

pp. 285f.
On the Capitol in general, *Guide Rionali,* Campitelli, II, *passim*; in antiquity, G. Lugli, *Roma antica. Il centro monumentale*, Rome, 1946, pp. 3ff., also E. Rodocanachi, *Le Capitole Romain*, Paris, 1905, pp. 1ff., and C. D'Onofrio, *Renovatio Romae*, Rome, 1972, pp. 12ff. On the situation in the Middle Ages: E. Rodocanachi, *op. cit.*, pp. 51ff., where p. 62, n. 1, refers to the bull of 1130 issued by Anaclete II (also C. L. Urlichs, *Codex*, p. 147, and Kehr, *It. Pont.*, I, 101); C. D'Onofrio, *op. cit.*, p. 72, suggests, wrongly in my opinion, that the bull repeats one issued by Gregory III (731-741); C. Cecchelli, "Il Campidoglio nel medioevo," *ASRStP* 67 (1944) 209ff.; C. D'Onofrio, *op. cit.*, pp. 72ff.; on the Corsi fortifications, *LP*, II, 290, 298, and C. D'Onofrio, *loc. cit.*; on the ropers' area on Monte Caprino, E. Rodocanachi, *op. cit.*, pp. 106ff., with reference to the *Mirabilia*; on the market down the west slope and at the foot of the hill, C. Cecchelli, *op. cit.*, Huelsen, *Chiese*, 218, 273, and the bull of Anaclete; finally, on the twelfth-century church of S. Maria in Capitolio, in part incorporated in the fabric of S. Maria in Aracoeli, R. E. Malmstrom, "S. Maria in Aracoeli," Ph.D. thesis, N.Y.U., 1973, *passim*, and *idem*, "The Twelfth Century Church of S. Maria in Capitolio . . . ," *Röm Jbch* 16 (1976) 1ff.

pp. 286f.
The reference made in 1061 to the *palatium Octaviani* in Benzo's memorandum to Henry IV, *MGH SS*, XI, 612f. and above, chapter six. On the *porticus Camellariae*, mentioned in Anaclete's bull, and its presumable identification with the *Tabularium*, C. D'Onofrio, *op. cit.*, p. 73. On the legends linked to the Capitol, above, chapter seven, and A. Graf, *Roma nella memoria . . .*, 2nd edition, Turin, 1923, *passim*.

On the historical and political significance of the Capitol in medieval eyes, Benzo's memorandum, *loc. cit.* Duchesne, *Liber Censuum*, I, 106, and "L'auteur des *Mirabilia*," *MEFR* 24 (1904) 479ff., based on *LP*, II, 313, has suggested its use as a place for popular assemblies and the seat of the prefect of Rome as early as 1118. On its official reoccupation by the Roman republic, Otto of Freising, *Chronica*, VII, c. 27 (*MGH SS RG*, n.s., ed. A. Hofmeister, 1912, 352ff.; also *MGH SS*, 20, 263); *idem, Gesta Friderici Imperatoris*, I, 28 (*MGH SS RG*, 44, ed. G. Waitz, 1912). On the Palazzo del Senatore, above, chapter eight, and note to pp. 206f. with reference to C. Pietrangeli, "Il palazzo Senatorio nel Medioevo," *Capitolium* 35 (1960) 3ff.; on the twelfth-century church of S. Maria in Capitolio and the Capitoline obelisk, see above, chapter seven; on the stairs leading to Aracoeli and the date of construction 1348, given by an inscription on the façade of the church, Forcella, *Iscrizioni*, I, 127, no. 453, and above, chapter eight.

Chapter Thirteen

p. 289

It may seem incredible, but no inventory exists of the medieval or later houses surviving in Rome. The attempt to compile a list, in the *Inventario dei monumenti di Roma*, ed. Associazione artistica dei cultori di architettura, Rome, 1908–, I, 369f., has long been obsolete; nor is A. Prova and P. Romano, *Roma nel Cinquecento*, Rome, 1935 (compiled according to *rioni*), of any great help. One had best go through the *Guide Rionali* picking out those mentioned there. Old photographs, such as J. W. Parker's and A. Moscioni's, give a fair impression of what survived in comparatively large numbers in the second half of the nineteenth century. For Fra Paolino's map of 1323, for maps and *vedute* of fifteenth century and later date, and for housing in general, see chapter nine, notes to pp. 232f.

Plans of houses antedating the late sixteenth century survive by the hundreds in the *catasti* of Roman confraternities and churches, in the *Archivio di Stato*, a source still practically unexplored. For selections, see P. M. Lugli, *Storia e cultura della città italiana*, Bari, 1967, p. 146f., and R. Fregna and S. Polito, "Fonti di archivio per una storia edilizia di Roma," *Controspazios* 3 (1971) fasc. 9, 2ff., and *ibid*. 4 (1972) fasc. 7, 2ff.

pp. 289ff.

Regarding the size of lots leased for building houses, see Hartmann, *Scae. Mariae in Via Lata*, nos. XLII, XLIII, XLIV, all dated 1019 and all measuring 36 x 36 Roman feet; and XXVIII, dated 1017, measuring 110 x 44 Roman feet. It is of interest that lots in ancient Rome and smaller ancient Roman towns, such as Cosa, as Professor Frank E. Brown tells me, had similar measurements, 30 x 30 Roman feet.

Descriptions of houses and their paths of access abound in legal documents about housing—as listed above in chapter nine, notes; the quotation regarding access comes from *ASRStP* 23 (1900) no. 13, dated 1042, p. 206f.; see also *ibid*., no. 15, dated 1052, pp. 211ff. Building materials and the overall aspect of houses are given in any document as listed above, chapter nine. The terminology is clear and Du Cange's explanation of the term *scandalicia* as "covered with shingles" seems unassailable. The question is whether it refers to outside revetting of the wall or to roofing only; the texts leave this in doubt.

The examples I list near S. Maria Nova are from *ASRStP* 23 (1900) no. 1, dated 982, pp. 182ff.; from *ASRStP* 24 (1901) no. 45, dated 1127, pp. 180ff.; and *ASRStP* 23 (1900) no. 19, dated 1062, p. 218f. (For the Arch of Diocletian spanning the Corso until 1491, Nash, *Dictionary*, I, 120, s.v. *Arcus Novus*.) The thatched house on the Corso, in Hartmann, *Scae. Mariae in Via Lata*, XXIX, dated 1008; the house near S. Prassede, *ASRStP* 27 (1904) no. 10, dated 1091, pp. 62ff.; the cottage in the Campo Marzio, Carusi, *Cartario*, no. 49, dated 1154; *ibid*., no. 3, dated 1010, the storerooms near the Ripetta.

The aspect of the city in the late fifteenth and the sixteenth centuries comes out best in the *vedute* of the Escurial draughtsman, of Heemskerck, and of Wijngaerde and on Tempesta's map (Frutaz, *Piante*, pl. 262ff.) as late as 1593.

For the *Scorticlaria*, above, chapter ten, p. 253 and note; the house, described here, Gnoli, *Topografia*, p. 295, cited from Schede Marini, Vat. lat. 9113, c. 8 (but the indication of the *carta* is erroneous).

pp. 291ff.

The house near S. Maria in Trastevere is described in Galletti, Vat. lat. 8051, I, fols. 7ff., dated 1038; for the house in Via dell'Arco della Pace, 10-11, see *Guide Rionali*, Ponte, II, 50; the house in the Borgo, Hartmann, *Scae. Mariae in Via Lata*, XXXVI, dated 1014. For row houses, owned by the Ospizio della SS. Trinità, see the documents in the Archivio di Stato, Rome (ASR), Buste patrimoniali, n. 192, and R. Fregna and S. Polito, *op. cit., Controspazio* III (1971) fasc. 9, 2ff., esp. p. 19, and *ibid*. (1972) fasc. 7, 2ff. For the Case di S. Paolo, see *Guide Rionali, Regola*, III, 44, some old photographs, Museo di Roma and a watercolor by Roesler Franz, in that museum; for the house in Via S. Bartolomeo degli Strengari, H. Bergner, *Rom im Mittelalter*, Leipzig, 1913, p. 89, fig. 105.

pp. 295ff.

The interior layout of a medieval house, as reflected still in that of S. Francesca Romana's family, in A.

Esch, "Die Zeugenaussagen im Heiligsprechungsverfahren für S. Francesca Romana," *Quellen und Forschungen aus italienischen Archiven* 53 (1973) 93ff., esp. 121f.

Milton Lewine pointed out to me the existence in the convent of Tor de' Specchi of the medieval house purchased by Saint Francesca Romana. I feel ashamed that I did not know it, notwithstanding its being described in *Guide Rionali*, Campitelli, I, 46ff.

pp. 299ff.

The Roman houses along Via S. Martino ai Monti, in B. M. Apollonj Ghetti, *Santa Prassede* (*Chiese illustrate*, 66), 12ff. with numerous survey drawings; the house in Via della Lungarina, Lanciani, *Destruction*, p. 202, fig. 35. Housing, workshops and storerooms ensconced in ancient monuments are mentioned time and again in legal documents, see above, chapter nine, notes on housing. The house in Via dei Calderari, *Guide Rionali*, Regola, I, 50f. and L. Rossini, *Antichità Romane*, pl. 97 (1819); for the Theatre of Pompey, *Guide Rionali*, Parione, II, 147ff. The texts quoted are from *ASRStP* 22 (1899) no. 22, dated 1158, p. 497f.; Hartmann, *Scae. Mariae in Via Lata*, LXXXX, dated 1065, and LXXXI, dated 1051; and, the one incorporated into a larger property, Carusi, *Cartario*, no. 17, dated 1076.

For housing in the ancient ruins near S. Maria Nova, see sources quoted above, in chapter nine notes on housing. Passages quoted in the text are taken from *ASRStP* 23 (1900) no. 10, dated 1038, p. 204f.; no. 8, dated 1061, pp. 216ff.; no. 17, dated 1060, pp. 214ff.; and no 3, dated 1011, pp. 187ff. For the Colosseum in the Middle Ages, see also M. Di Macco, *Il Colosseo*, Rome, 1971; for S. Salvatore de Rota, Huelsen, *Chiese*, p. 452; for the vaults of the Circus Maximus, Lanciani, *Scavi*, I, Rome, 1902, 31ff.

The property of the Confraternity of the Sancta Sanctorum and the hospital of S. Giovanni in Laterano as of 1326 is listed in *Necrologi della Provincia Romana*, I, ed. P. Egidi, Rome, 1920, 317ff.; for property owned in the 1330s by the local priorate of the Order of Saint John of Jerusalem, R. Brentano, *Rome before Avignon*, p. 41. On privately owned housing in the later Middle Ages, *ibid*., pp. 27ff.

pp. 303ff.

No satisfactory publication exists so far on the medieval towers of Rome. The only scholar to have recently made a thorough study of the subject appears to be Milton Lewine. Much of what is contained in these pages regarding both towers extant or lost and the broader aspects involved, goes back to conversations I have had with him over the years and to the many pages of suggestions he turned over to me after reading my manuscript. By no means, though, did I make use of all his suggestions. It would not have been fair. His knowledge of the monuments and their documentation and his insight into the general conditions underlying the construction of towers in medieval Rome is so extensive and deep that I must leave untouched the better part of the matieral he generously passed on to me. I cannot thank him warmly enough.

In the following, *faute de mieux*, I refer to the publications available so far. For the towers still standing, see the *Guide Rionali, passim*; others are known from *vedute* and maps, as above, chapter nine, notes. Documentary evidence is scattered over a wide variety of sources, such as the *Liber Pontificalis*, the *Mirabilia*, the *Liber Censuum*, contemporary accounts of street warfare among Roman clans (such as *MGH, De Lite*, I, 606; and *Gesta Innocentii Papae III*, *PL*, 214, chap. CXXXVII), and in documents relating to real estate owned in Rome, see the chapter nine notes. Some information, though not always reliable, is given in F. Sabatini, *Monumenti e reliquie medioevali della città di Roma*, Rome, 1907. General studies of towers include G. Tomasetti, "Torri di Roma," *Capitolium* 1 (1925) 266ff.; and the one book on the subject, E. Amadei, *Le torri di Roma*, Rome, 1969 (first published 1932).

We briefly list towers of great families known only from documentary or graphic sources. For those located in Trastevere, see Galletti, Vat. lat. 8051, I, fol. 13f., dated 1073, the bridge of Antoninus "not very far from the tower of the heirs of Giovanni Brazuti"; on those of the Papareschi near S. Maria in Trastevere, Gregorovius, IV, 401, n.2. On the tower on the Tiber Island, possibly Pierleone property, see Kehr, *It. Pont.*, I, 189; on the Pierleoni's hold on the island by 1118, *LP*, II, 311; on their mansion below the *rupe Tarpeia* near S. Nicola in Carcere, *LP*, II, 294 and 303, dating 1099 and 1116 respectively; on their towers near S. Marco, *ibid*., p. 380, n.1. For the mansions of Stephanus Normannus, Petrus Latro of the Corsi clan, and the Bulgamini, all clustering on the river bank near the Temple of Fortuna Virilis, *LP*, II, 314ff. For the Theatre of Marcellus, I refer to the will of Jacopo Savelli (Honorius IV), 1279; see *Les registres d' Honorius IV*, ed. M. Prou, Paris, 1886, p. 576. For the Cenci tower below Monte Giordano, the Torre del Campo, see M. T. Russo, "La Torre del Campo a Monte Giordano," *Strenna dei Romanisti* 26 (1965)

374ff. On Monte Giordano and its fortifications, M.P.F. Asso, "Monte Giordano," *Quaderni* 1 (1953) 23ff.; on the Cenci tower blocking Ponte S. Angelo, see Benizo *ad amicum* (*MGH, De Lite*, I, 603, 605). For the towers of the Statii near S. Eustachio, see Brentano, *Rome before Avignon*, p. 199; those in the Circus Flaminius, *Gesta Innocentii Papae III, PL*, 214, chap. CXXXVII. Again, for the towers near S. Maria in Via Lata, belonging to the Adelmari family, Hartmann, *Scae. Mariae in Via Lata*, CXV, 1086 and CXXI, 1094—two different towers. For the Corsi fortifications on the Capitol, *LP*, II, 290, 298f. For at least one of the Frangipani family towers, E. Tea, "La Rocca dei Frangipani alla Velia," *ASRStP* 44 (1921) 235ff. Some towers, no longer surviving, are clearly marked, though not always with the name of their owners, on early maps, such as the Tempesta map of 1593 (Frutaz, *Piante*, pls. 262ff.) and in *vedute*, such as Heemskerck's *Panorama* (*ibid.*, pl. 176).

Towers surviving in the abitato, aside from those mentioned in E. Amadei, *op. cit., passim*, and in G. Tomassetti, *op. cit.*, as well as in Gnoli, *Topografia*, pp. 319ff., are dealt with in some, if frequently insufficient, detail in the following studies, which we list with the towers in alphabetical order: for the Anguillara tower, D. Camillo Massimo, *Cenni storici sulla Torre Anguillara*, Rome, 1847 (2nd ed. 1869), and U. Gnoli, "La famiglia ed il palazzo dell'Anguillara in Roma," *Cosmos Catholicus* 3 (1907) 670ff.; for the tower in Largo Argentina, sometimes referred to as Torre Argentina, see below under "Torre del Papito"; for Torre dell'Arpacata, Gnoli, *Topografia*, p. 320, and *Guide Rionali,* Parione, II, 150f.; for Tor de' Conti, F. Mora, "Di Tor de' Conti," *Atti del Collegio degli Ingegneri ed Architetti in Roma* 9 (1885) 37ff., C. Cecchelli, "Tor de' Conti," *Pan* 3 (1934) 540ff., and A. M. Colini, "Forum Pacis," *Bull Comm* 65 (1937) 7ff.; for Torre Margana, *Guide Rionali*, S. Angelo, I, 82f.; for Torre del Merangolo (Melangolo), *Guide Rionali,* S. Angelo, I, 71f., and in detail, Gnoli, *Topografia*, p. 326f.; for Tor Millina, G. B. Giovenale, "Tor Millina," *Annuario Accademia di San Luca* 1 (1909/11) 127ff., and *Guide Rionali,* Ponte, I, 34f.; for Torre del Papito, D. Gnoli, "La Torre Argentina in Roma," *Nuova Antologia* (1908) 3ff., and G. Marchetti-Longhi, "La turris Papiti . . . ," *Capitolium* 8 (1932) 245ff., and *Guide Rionali,* Pigna, I, 24ff.; and for Tor Sanguigna, F. Sabatini, *op. cit.*, p. 31, and P. Adinolfi, *La Torre dei Sanguigni*, Rome, 1863.

Towers in the disabitato are discussed in chapter fourteen.

p. 307

On clusters of towers and towered mansions: the ruins leased by the Arcioni family, *ASRStP* 23 (1900) no. 94, dated 1238, p. 74; typical compounds with towers are shown in Frutaz, *Piante, passim*, in particular, pls. 148 (Limbourg Brothers), 150 (anonymous, first quarter fifteenth century), 159 (Strozzi map); the Anguillara compound in the previous note as is the Margana mansion; the compound of S. Maria in Cosmedin, G. B. Giovenale, *La Basilica di S. Maria in Cosmedin*, Rome, 1927, pp. 48, 278ff., and for its reconstruction, 406ff.

pp. 308f.

Crowding of houses: around S. Cecilia, *ASRStP* 49 (1926) no. 8, dated 1404; around the Pantheon, R. Brentano, *Rome before Avignon*, p. 199.

p. 310

The number of towers once in Rome is uncertain. F. Sabatini, *Monumenti e reliquie medievali . . .* , Rome, 1899, gives a figure of more than 900 for the thirteenth century, 360 for the sixteenth century, and still 30 for the eighteenth century, but he gives no source; for the demolition of towers by Brancaleone, see E. Amadei, *Le torri di Roma*, Rome, 1969, p. 11, wherein further demolitions are said to have taken place in 1313; on the destruction of towers by the Roman people in 1144, see Otto of Freising, *Chronica*, VII, 31 (*MGH SS RG*, 12, ed. A. Hofmeister, 1912, p. 360), but how much was destroyed?

p. 310

For medieval campanili in Rome, I refer again to A. Serafini, *Torri campanarie di Roma e del Lazio nel medioevo*, Rome, 1927, with a repeated caution, and to my brief remarks in chapter seven. Magister Gregory's *Narracio* I have discussed in that same chapter and the various editions cited in note to pp. 189f. Masolino's panorama is described and illustrated in Frutaz, *Piante*, I, 128f., and II, pl. 152.

Chapter Fourteen

pp. 311ff.

Housing at the foot of the Capitol and the "columna perfectissima" are mentioned in a privilege of Innocent III, *PL*, 214, cols. 651ff.; see also Cencius Camerarius' list, *Liber Censuum*, ed. Fabre and Duchesne, Paris, 1905, I, 300.

For the Forum and the Palatine in the Middle Ages, see G. F. Carettoni, "Il Palatino nel medioevo," *Studi Romani* 9 (1961) 508ff. and *idem*, "Il foro romano nel medioevo e nel rinascimento," *Studi Romani* 11 (1963) 406ff.

On the rustic character of the Celian and its eastward extension, see *Reg Sub*, no. 24, dated 938 (also Ferrari, *Monasteries*, p. 121) regarding the convent of S. Erasmo, whence our first quotation; and *ibid.*, doc. 13, dated 997; and on the farms near Porta Maggiore, *ibid.*, doc. 27, dated 924; doc. 3, dated 967; doc. 12, dated 958; and doc. 15, dated 1015. On the Aventine, a Savelli residence would seem to have existed perhaps in the monastery of S. Sabina by 1216 (*Regesta Honorii Papae III*, ed. P. Pressutti, Rome, 1888, docs. 89, 153, 196, 553, and 878, all dated 1216-1217). A fortification on the hill is listed in 1279 in the will of Cardinal Jacopo Savelli (Honorius IV), *Les registres d'Honorius IV*, ed. M. Prou, Paris, 1886, p. 576, and the building of "a palace and many other constructions" during his pontificate recounted by Ptolemy of Lucca (*Die Annalen des Tholomeus von Lucca*, ed. B. Schmeidler, Berlin, 1930, *MGH SS*, n.s. 8, 204; also *Historia Ecclesiastica,* xxiv, 19, *RIS*, xi, 1194). Whether or not farms still continued at the foot of the hill along the *Marmorata*, as they had existed in the tenth century (*Reg Sub*, doc. 19, dated 926) remains unknown. On the northern sector of town up to Porta del Popolo, see *ASRStP* 22 (1899) no. 1, dated 761, pp. 254ff.; no. 2, dated 844, p. 263f.; nos. 3 and 4, dated 955 and 962, pp. 265ff., and so forth. For the "tower whence the shade of Nero used to spook," Frutaz, *Piante*, pl. 158.

pp. 313f.

On the suburb formed around S. Maria Maggiore, see *LP*, i, 511 (Hadrian's monastery); *LP*, ii, 54f. (S. Prassede) and 96 (S. Martino ai Monti); Ferrari, *Monasteries*, pp. 51ff. (S. Andrea in Massa Juliana or in Catabarbara and S. Andrea in Assaio), 68ff. (S. Bibiana), and 345ff. (S. Vito). Documentation from the eleventh century on: *ASRStP* 27 (1904) 147ff.; *ASRStP* 28 (1905) 23ff., and *ASRStP* 30 (1907) 119ff.; where *ASRStP* 27 (1904) no. 22, dated 1192, pp. 451ff. gives the long list of houses, gardens, and fields close to the basilica. For the housing around S. Prassede, see *ASRStP* 27 (1904) 27ff., for instance, no. 10, dated 1091, no. 37, dated 1143, and no. 49, dated 1209, all concerning houses adjoining the church and monastery. The pipeline, in a street running along the convent of S. Lorenzo *ad gradatas*, and because of these steps presumably behind the apse of S. Maria Maggiore, is mentioned in *ASRStP* 27 (1904) no. 9, dated 1056, p. 190 ("fistula domnica qui dicitur centinaria"), where reference is also made to a paved street ("silice publica") and to a street leading to the market.

On the Forum of Nerva, its name and the neighborhood in the Middle Ages: Gnoli, *Topografia*, 8 ("Arca Noë"); see also *Polistoria Johannis Caballini de Cerronibus*, as quoted by Urlichs, *Codex*, p. 140; Magister Gregory (the "Granary of the Cardinals"), as quoted above, in the last note of chapter thirteen. Valentini-Zucchetti, iii, 156, n.1, refers the designation to the residence of three Conti cardinals in the nearby family tower.

pp. 314ff.

For the suburb of S. Maria Nova, *ASRStP* 23 (1900), *ASRStP* 24 (1901), *ASRStP* 25 (1902), and *ASRStP* 26 (1903); for the *calcararium*, Lanciani, *Scavi*, i, 25 and *passim*, and *ASRStP* 23 (1900) no. 13, dated 1042, pp. 206ff.; for the people living there, *ibid.*, no. 1, dated 982, pp. 182ff.; no. 3, dated 1011, pp. 187ff.; no. 4, dated 1017, pp. 190ff., and *passim; Liber Censuum*, i, 300, for the list of Cencius Camerarius; Gnoli, *Topografia*, p. 46, and *ASRStP* 23 (1900) no. 15, dated 1052, pp. 211ff. (banker's crossway, *trivium cambiatoris*); finally, *ASRStP* 23 (1900) no. 29, dated 1092, p. 233f., and *ASRStP* 24 (1901) no. 61, dated 1147(?), p. 176f., and frequently from there on, the expansion along the slope of the Palatine.

pp. 317ff.

For malaria in the disabitato and beyond the walls, see the Ligurinus poem, bk. iv, vv. 185ff. (*PL*, 212, col. 382). For fields beyond the gates, see Brentano, *Rome before Avignon*, pp. 27, 51, and *passim*; for the fifteenth century, see A. Esch, "Die Zeugenaussagen im Heiligsprechungsverfahren für S. Francesca Romana . . . ," *Quellen und Forschungen* 53 (1973) 93ff., esp. 133ff.

On towers in the disabitato, see E. Amadei, *Le torri di Roma*, Rome, 1969, and in particular: on Torre delle Milizie, Kehr, *It. Pont.*, 193 (owned in 1179 by the Frangipani), but no architectural study seems to have been undertaken; on the Frangipani fortifications, the Torre Cartularia and their other towers all over the *Campo torrecchiano* see Gnoli, *Topografia*, p. 323 (the name); E. Tea, "La rocca dei Frangipani," *ASRStP* 44 (1921) 235ff., 244ff.; Gnoli, *Topografia*, 322 (Torre Cartularia); Urlichs, *Codex*, p. 110 (Frangipani tower at the temple of Antoninus and Faustina); letter of Innocent III (*PL*, 214, 631ff.; towers atop the Arch of Septimius Severus); J. B Mittarelli, *Annales Camaldulenses*, iii, Venice, 1758, app., col. 417, doc. 271 (tower in Circus Maximus; the document is dated March 18, not to be confused with

Kehr, *It. Pont.*, I, 191, January 31, 1145); on the towers near S. Prassede, *LP*, II, 316. Finally, on the Colosseum as a Frangipani fortification in 1133, Ptolemy of Lucca, *Annales (Die Annalen des Tholomeus von Lucca*, ed. B. Schmeidler, 1930, *MGH SS RG*, n.s. 8, 47f.; also *RIS*, XI, 1263), and Cardinal of Aragon (Nicola Roselli), *Vitae Pontificum Romanorum (RIS*, III.1, 434), both referred to in P. Colagrossi, *L'anfiteatro Flavio . . .*, Florence, 1913, p. 150f., and M. Di Macco, *Il Colosseo*, Rome, 1971, p. 113f. The occupation of the Colosseum by the Roman Republic (Colagrossi, *op. cit.*, p. 151f.) cannot be documented (Di Macco, *op. cit.*, p. 114, n.24). In any case, it is Frangipani property through the second half of the twelfth century and into the thirteenth, when they have to share it with the Annibaldi (Di Macco, *op. cit.*, pp. 31f. and 113f., notes 20, 26).

Other towers in the disabitato, such as the so-called Capocci towers behind S. Martino ai Monti and Torre del Grillo, do not seem to have been studied in any great detail, although they are discussed in E. Amadei, *op. cit, passim*.

pp. 319f.

Concerning the great families' hold on various sectors of Rome, see G. Tomassetti, *La Campagna Romana*, I, Rome, 1910, 137ff., and correspondingly L. Casanelli, G. Delfini, D. Fonti, *Le Mura di Roma*, Rome, 1974, p. 84, n. 38 and fig. 87. In particular, on the Arcioni, *ASRStP* 23 (1900) no. 94, dated 1238, p. 74f., and C. Corvisieri, "Il trionfo romano di Eleanora d'Aragona," *ASRStP* 10 (1887) 629ff., esp. 685ff., doc. V, the latter suggesting a location perhaps in the Market of Trajan; on the Savelli, the will of Cardinal Jacopo Savelli as quoted in the first note to this chapter; on the Colonna, descendants of Alberic's family it appears, P. Colonna, *I. Colonna dalle origini al secolo XIX*, Rome 1927.

The tower war of 1203 in *Gesta Innocentii Papae III*, chaps. CXXXVII and following (*PL*, 214, cols. CLXXXV and following).

pp. 320ff.

Regarding fortified churches and convents on the perimeter of the Lateran, see: on the destruction wrought by Robert Guiscard, *LP*, II, 290; on S. Clemente, my remarks and the bibliography in chapter seven; on the Quattro Coronati, see the same and P. F. Kehr, "Papsturkunden in Umbrien," *Göttinger Nachrichten (Nachrichten der K. Gessellschaft der Wissenschaften zu Göttingen*), 1889, pp. 379f., also Kehr, *It. Pont.*, I, 41f.; on SS. Giovanni e Paolo, A. Prandi, *Il complesso monumentale della Basilica . . . dei SS. Giovanni e Paolo*, Rome, 1953, esp. pp. 249ff., 355ff.; on S. Gregorio Magno, *Corpus*, I, 320ff., and on the Septizonium as a defense position and refuge, J. B. Mittarelli, *Annales Camaldulensium*, I, Venice, 1955, 117f., dated 975, and *LP*, II, 290 referring to 1084, and 344 referring to 1117.

p. 322

The extension of the Lateran Palace and of the surrounding suburb is documented through a number of bulls: 1037 (F. Ughelli, *Italia Sacra*, I, Venice, 1717, cols. 100ff., esp. 104); also Urlichs, *Codex*, p. 205, and Kehr, *It. Pont.*, II, 26); 1050 (C. Rasponi, *De Basilica et Patriarchio Lateranensi*, Rome, 1656, p. 110; Kehr, *It. Pont.*, I, 25); 1061-1073 (Kehr, *ibid.*) where "houses around the basilica" are mentioned; 1153 (Kehr, *ibid.*, p. 28, from *Bullarium Romanum*, II, Rome, 1739, 345); and 1154 (G. B. Crescimbeni, *Istoria della Chiesa di S. Giovanni avanti Porta Latina*, Rome, 1716, pp. 248ff.; also Kehr, *ibid.*) where the "suburb . . . around the Basilica" is mentioned, "with houses there and at the aqueduct and houses *in cancello* [?] and houses along the via maior . . . and gardens and a pond . . . and the mill at the end of the pond outside the Gate of S. Giovanni." When confirmed in 1216 and 1228 (*Regesta Honorii Papae III*, ed. P. Pressuti, Rome, 1888, appendix, pp. lvii, lxi, employing the term *suburbium*; Crescimbeni, *op. cit.*, pp. 251ff.), more houses and vendors' stalls are listed. See also *LP*, II, 379 on the water supply "brought from the old aqueducts," and "the pond to water the horses," the several mills built there, and "many vineyards and orchards" around the pond.

The big suburb existing in the later thirteenth century is outlined as of 1242 and 1247 in two lists of rents paid to the canons (Ph. Lauer, *Le Palais de Latran*, Paris, 1911, p. 236f.).

pp. 325f.

For the renovation of churches near the Lateran, see: for Sto. Stefano Rotondo, *Corpus*, IV, 199ff.; S. Croce in Gerusalemme, *Corpus*, I, 165ff., and for the frescoes, G. Biasiotti and S. Pesarini, "Pitture del secolo XII . . . in S. Croce . . . ," *Studi Romani* 1 (1913) 245ff., G. Matthiae, *Gli affreschi medioevali di S. Croce in Gerusalemme*, Rome, 1968, *idem, Pittura*, pp. 93, 252 and C. Bertelli "Un problema medioevale 'romano,' " *Paragone* 231 (1969) 3ff. and for installing the Regular Canons, *LP*, II, 385; for the palace at S. Maria Maggiore, Kehr, *It. Pont.*, I, 36, and G. Biasiotti, "Una descrizione . . . di S. Maria Maggiore nel secolo XII," *Atti III Congresso*

Nazionale di Studi Romani . . ., II, 1935, 5ff.). For the murals in the Lateran Palace, Ladner, *Papstbildnisse*, I, 198ff. and II, 17ff., also above chapter seven; for papal burials, in the basilica, see Johannes Diaconus, *Liber de Lateranensi Ecclesia*, and O. Panvinio, *De septem praecipuis basilicis Urbis Romae*, both in Ph. Lauer, *op. cit.*, pp. 392ff., esp. 400f. and 439f.; finally, for the transept and palace façades being turned toward the piazza and the approach from the abitato, *Corpus*, V, pp. 15, 61f., and figs. 2, 70, 71, 72.

Index I

Places and Subjects

(All entries refer to Rome unless marked with an asterisk.)

Index II

People

Library of Congress Cataloging in Publication Data

Krautheimer, Richard, 1897-
Rome, profile of a city, 312-1308.

Bibliography: p.
Includes index.
1. Rome (City)—History—476-1420. 2. Rome (City)—History—To 476. 3. Church history—Primitive and early church, ca. 30-600. 4. Church history—Middle Ages, 600-1500. 5. Rome (City)—Buildings. I. Title.
DG811.K7 945'.632 78-70304
ISBN 0-691-03947-X
ISBN 0-691-00319-X pbk.